Conceptualizing the Evaluation of Clinical Counseling

Updated Edition

William D. Eldridge

University Press of America, Inc.
Lanham • New York • Oxford

Copyright © 1997 by
University Press of America,® Inc.
4720 Boston Way
Lanham, Maryland 20706

12 Hid's Copse Rd.
Cummor Hill, Oxford OX2 9JJ

Library of Congress Cataloging-in-Publication

Eldridge, William D.
Conceptualizing the evaluation of clinical counseling / William D.
Eldridge. --Updated ed..
p.   cm.
Includes bibliographical references.
1. Counseling. 2. Psychotherapy. 3. Counselor and client. I. Title.
(DNLM: 1. Psychology, Applied. 2. Mental Health Services. 3.
Outcome Assessment (Health Care). 4. Professional-Patient Relations.
BF637.C6 E37c 1997)
BF637.C6E47   1997   158'.3--dc21   96-50978 CIP
DNLM/DLC for Library of Congress

ISBN 0-7618-0679-2 (pbk: alk. ppr.)

⊖™The paper used in this publication meets the minimum
requirements of American National Standard for information
Sciences—Permanence of Paper for Printed Library Materials,
ANSI Z39.48—1984

Dedication

There is no measure of the love,
patience and devotion of my friend Fran
Angiulo, and daughter, Carrie Eldridge, for
putting up with the trials and tribulations
of this book for the duration of its
extensive preparation—thanks and I love you.

Acknowledgement

To: **Helene Bache**
College of Social Work
The Ohio State University

. . . Staff Person Extraordinaire
. . . Word Processor of Perfection
. . . Tenacious Task Master
. . . Woman of Indefatigable Patience
. . . Mother to Confused Faculty Members
. . . Supporter
. . . Friend
. . . Person no Longer Stuck on
this 🌟 🌟 🌟 Book Project

It is impossible to articulate my appreciation for your work on the total preparation of this manuscript and book, along with your responsibility for my other four attempts at scholarship in book form.

Because this current project was produced so poorly by another publisher, your patience and guidance through the scanning, initial text reconstruction, chart preparation, and four or five editorial excursions—was unimaginably dedicated, energetic (when you had *no* energy left at times), precise and accurate, and always kind and supportive, even though much unnecessary work was caused by the personality of the author.

Additionally, you did all of this work over **years** of time, in the evenings and on weekends (never during prohibited work hours), which certainly diminished the quality of your recreational life . . . but contributed profoundly to the quality of this book and the growth of its writer.

I thank you from the deepest dimension of my being—and will never forget what you have accomplished here.

Bill
September 1996
The Ohio State University
Columbus, Ohio

Table of Contents

Foreword vii

Chapter One

Problems Related to the Evaluation of Clinical Counseling 1

    Domains of Accountability 2
    Development of Professional Accountability 2
    Evaluation Processes Within Groups and Systems 7
    Evaluative Methodology and Scientific Technology 9

Chapter Two

Evaluation of Characteristics of Clients 23

    Defining Clients and Their Problems 25
    Individual Clients as Deviant Symptom-Carriers 31
    Client Reference Groups and Culture 39
    Client Motivation 51
    Neurosis 62
    Personality or Character Disorders 88
    Children as Clients 125
    Psychosis 130

Chapter Three

Intrapsychic and Sociopsychic Perceptions
of Clinical Counselors and Clients 153

    Personality Development and Self-Actualization
        as Part of Evaluation 155
    Personal and Cultural Philosophy and Values 198
    Spirituality 226
    Individual Perspectives on Learning 240

Chapter Four

Clinical Inputs 271

    Nominal Categories of Inputs 272
    Specific Types of Inputs 282
    Process and Inputs 350
    Intensity, Power, and Strength of Inputs 472
    Termination of Counseling 474

Chapter Five

Clinical Outcomes 505

    Empirical Definitions 507
    Developmental Nature of Outcomes 532
    Personality/Social System Structure for Defining Outcomes 545
    Generic vs. Specific (Differentiated) Nature of Outcomes 591
    Primary, Secondary, Tertiary Levels of Thoughts,
        Feelings, and Behaviors 595
    Outcome Stability, Transiency, and Responsiveness to Inputs 600

Chapter Six

Implications of Clinical Evaluation 617

    Education 618
    Certification and Licensing 624
    Policy and Administration 625
    Clinical Practitioners 629
    Researchers 631

Foreword

Twenty-five years ago the subject of clinical evaluation was depressing. Those who labored in the human service professions of social work, psychology, pastoral counseling and psychiatric nursing for example, were able to adduce very little evidence to support contentions that their efforts were useful and helpful to persons in need. In fact, there were a small but emerging number of studies which seemed to demonstrate that the efforts of these helping professions, made in behalf of individuals seeking counseling and clinical assistance, made "no significant difference" when compared with control and contrast groups of people who did not seek the services of these professionals. In addition, there was the general difficulty of determining what it was that counselors did or did not do that made any difference, on those rare occasions when significant differences were discerned. Thus, not only were helping professionals unable to claim positive results for their efforts, but also they were unable to assert with any degree of certainty, what it was that made a difference when modest differences were found.

These negative and confusing results tended to disturb academics, students and serious minded practitioners who sought, through the newly developing methodologies of program evaluation, to provide better information which would bear upon questions of practice effectiveness and the sources of client system change. This dismal picture has been well documented by such chroniclers as Mullen and Dumpson, Fisher, and Wood. In fact, the results of the one field experiment conducted by William Reid and Ann Shyne in the late 60s and published under the title of *Brief versus Extended Casework*, led a prestigious social agency to alter its approach to serving clients, and to temporarily suspend direct clinical practice as a mode of helping persons in need.

More recently, a body of literature has emerged which suggests that clinical interventions can be shown to be effective with certain kinds of problems and certain types of clients or client-systems. If the results of twenty-five years ago were depressing, the new findings have had an opposite impact upon the helping professions. Moreover, the new studies on clinical effectiveness suggest that practitioners have learned from the earlier research, to modify their interventions and their approaches in ways which heighten the probability of success. For example, the informed contemporary clinician would proceed in a counseling situation first by defining outcome goals, and then by agreement on a working contract which would probably contain time and contact frequency parameters. These developments suggest that contemporary clinicians have learned from the results of the earlier evaluation research, and if this is so, then this too is a heartening development.

vii

In *Conceptualizing the Evaluation of Clinical Counseling,* Dr. Eldridge provides us with an excellent road map for delineating the size and shape of the prodigious number of complicated questions and issues which face the clinical practitioner today in relation to the subject of evaluation of practice. It is significant that this book is more about "conceptualizing" than it is a book about evaluation or clinical practice. What Dr. Eldridge seeks to do in this book, is to bring his considerable clinical experience and academic acumen to bear on the problem of identifying and defining the issues which confront clinical practitioners who seek to evaluate the effectiveness of their practice. This work, therefore, represents an attempt to help the field of clinical counseling, as it is broadly conceived, to gather itself, consolidate progress, and examine the new questions, issues and problems which have emerged during the past two and one-half decades of study and examination of this subject. Dr. Eldridge examines five categories of issues related to evaluation, namely: 1) outcomes for clients, 2) technical and methodological inputs of counselors, 3) intrapsychic factors which affect evaluative decision-making, 4) special evaluative issues for particular client categories, and 5) major organizational dynamics which influence counselor evaluative competency. Students of the human service professions will find the book highly applicable to cognitive and empirical issues encountered in the context of evaluating interventions, and current practitioners in human service organizations will find the book useful as a reference source for clinical staff.

This work makes a highly significant and utilitarian contribution to the conceptual needs and requirements necessary to strengthen our ability to evaluate clinical practice. This in turn should lead, as has been demonstrated, to an improved clinical practice which will benefit the clients of a wide range of helping professions.

Dr. Richard E. Boettcher, Professor
College of Social Work
The Ohio State University

Chapter One

Problems Related to the Evaluation

of Clinical Counseling

Introduction

To appreciate the rationale for evaluation, and stimulate further thinking and study, the reader must understand the importance of *accounting* for professional competence and service delivery. This includes understanding types of individual and organizational validation of input, process, and outcome of clinical counseling, therapeutic services, or casework; and various demands from staff, clients, administrators, boards, and funders, to *prove* service effectiveness. In addition, the reader might examine his/her own level of confidence concerning the state of clinical evaluation today, and reflect on possible changes, to personally develop more competent self-evaluative philosophy and practice.

The goals of this text are: (1) to challenge counselors to think critically about their decisions, concerning professional adequacy and clients' growth or change, and (2) to push them to ask the right questions, search for meaningful data, discover and systematically use competent techniques, and recognize/control as many judgmental biases as possible. The discussions that follow, outline major focal points of clinical evaluation, and raise critical and often unanswered/

poorly-answered questions, relating to decisions about how well a client has been helped by the counseling professional.

The first step, then, in approaching study and analysis of self-valuation, is to learn where *self*-assessment or monitoring fit into a comprehensive domain of overall accountability; and to explore problems and complexities of self-evaluation within each context.

Domains of Accountability

Processes of accounting for adequacy, effectiveness, efficiency, success, timeliness, and relevance of all types of social services (including clinical counseling or casework practice), are easy to understand, if accountability is subdivided into categories. These reflect *where* accountability occurs, and *who* is responsible within social institutions to plan, conduct, and assess various approaches to evaluation. Accountability can also be traced from its abstract origins within societal norms and institutions, to specific operational manifestations with the individual clinical practitioner. Because clinical professionals are validated in their social service responsibilities by society, and occupy specific roles and positions within social service agencies; the values, attitudes, and practices of self-evaluation, partly derive their nature and significance from social contexts within which they occur.

Also, theories and methods of individual professional accountability cannot be reviewed separately, from interdependent domains of the counselor's more private assessment of *personal* self-esteem and adequacy. The host organization's evaluation of broad-based program operation and impact, also reciprocally interacts with the activities of each counselor. Additional linkages in this ecological system of accountability, are professional groups to which each clinician belongs, and the interorganizational/governmental arena, which help determine norms for service delivery and client need identification. The continuum of accountability for the clinical practitioner, therefore, begins with broad societal expectations concerning attitudes, values, and practices of those invested with the title "professional"; and extends vertically and horizontally to include numerous domains which play a part in the definition, implementation, and interpretation of evaluative data.

Development of Professional Accountability

Although many textbooks on practice, conclude with a section on ethical responsibility for accountability as a subcomponent of professionalism, humanism (as this implies interpersonal social responsibility),[1] and self-actualization, responsibility for personal growth through self-assessment[2] must be the initial focal point and rationale for clinical practice, rather than assuming less-significant status, as simply a methodology for some form of standardized decision-making.

One significant world change in the late 20th century, is rapidly-increasing knowledge, assertiveness, and legal sensitivity of consuming publics, who help define empirical proof of service effectiveness, as a necessary dimension of *human need fulfillment.* Public funding and educational programs certainly support institutions for advanced training of highly skilled "experts and role models, to understand the human condition, and use proven interpersonal process to improve life-satisfaction."[3] At the same time, cultural norms place increasing pressure on social programs to produce sound measures of social responsibility, and a "clearer measurement of the value of programs that hard-earned and inflation-burned money goes into."[4] This pressure has evolved for professionals because of growing concern among a more sophisticated general public, that practitioners have not been effective in delivering needed human services. Nor have we met social obligations which are promised,[5] as evidenced in increasingly successful litigation against ineffective clinicians.[6] Commitment to professionalism, therefore, not only reflects ethical practice standards, but shows responsiveness to a cost/benefit consuming public,[7] whose principles of defining life and interpersonal responsibility, suggest that assessment is part of humanity's response to humanity.[8] Also, the adversary position sometimes assumed by various forms of public media in exposés of public incompetence, places more pressure on clinicians to perform competent therapeutic practice, and empirically justify competence within a media-sensitive environment.

In reviewing the development of *professionalization* within social services, the notion of "scientific" philanthropy, which grew from survival needs to organize and systematize private charities and public welfare institutions in the early 1900's, emerged with establishment of practice values and guidelines. These were based on developing standardization of democratic and humanistic theory. These areas of practice development included: (1) appreciation of empirically-tested knowledge and skills, through scientific research methodology; (2) development of variable ranges of social science educational competence, and concomitant emphasis on certification through continuing education, licensure, and supervision; and (3) delineation of autonomous social service disciplines and organizations (AMA, APA, NASW, ANA, NEA, etc.),[9] with increased responsibility for developing and monitoring competency standards.[10]

Additionally, professionalization of social services has increasingly produced efforts toward value clarification[11] emphasizing legal rights[12] of "client systems,"[13] and specific improvement of interventive theories and methodologies.[14] Although studying processes and developing models of interventive input, as a result of professional maturation is certainly significant;[15] many professionals have not sufficiently focused on the *value* and *functionality* of evaluation, as the *foundation* upon which professional knowledge, skills, and values about clients are built: "How long will it take for the concept of accountability to visibly influence our thoughts, our attitudes, and our behavior?"[16]

In the author's opinion, many clinical professionals have been neither evaluatively socialized into their roles, nor philosophically and empirically taught to assume self-evaluative attitudes and behaviors, as a necessary condition of professional status and responsibility.[17] They emerge from professional training programs with cognitive information about evaluation, as one professional skill or technique, but lack internalized self-evaluative norms to guide sustained and empirically proficient assessment in professional careers. Also, many clinicians do not fully appreciate the overall picture of evaluative ecology and systemic holism, which includes: (a) evaluation of group and organizational systems, (b) assessment of specific client characteristics, and (c) development of comprehensive systems of evaluative theory and technology. All of these transform an otherwise external methodology, into a living and dynamic integrating focal point, to enhance the overall meaning and value of clinical counseling and social program delivery.[18]

Additionally, attainment of professional status implies some very real detriments regarding accountability, since pressures for *proof* of service effectiveness, threaten elimination of professional positions. This occurs where role occupants cannot measure up to effectiveness or efficiency demands,[19] through demonstration of cause-effect knowledge and highly-specialized skills.[20] In this regard, simply caring about people with social problems, may not be enough to survive in counseling or clinical fields, or "therapeutic psychological environments"[21] of the future. An example of consumer protection, is Michigan's Office of Recipient Rights and Code of Rights,[22] insuring clients they will be kept knowledgeable about their clinical condition and treatment goals/progress, and guaranteeing their right to specifically authorize any recommended treatment process.

In considering accountability as a key component of norms by which professions maintain standards of philosophy, knowledge, and practice skill, there is a serious question of the degree to which evaluation is defined, implemented, disseminated, and reinforced as a normative mandate. This occurs within organizational policy, agency administration, or professional job requirements, to delineate "predetermined patterns and levels" of standardized performance.[23]

Although general mention of accountability occurs within each profession's codification of standards or ethics,[24] it is typically abstract, nonspecific, and unclear, in guiding particular evaluative behaviors. Some excerpts are exemplified as follows:

1.   "evaluating needs and resources, generating alternatives for meeting needs, and making decisions between alternatives";[25]
2.   "collecting information, analyzing and interpreting information, preparing an assessment statement";[26]
3.   "evaluate the extent to which the objectives of the intervention plan were achieved";[27]
4.   "compiling information, processing numerical and statistical information, making listings, carrying out studies, etc."[28]

In these cases, the *verbs* (which represent evaluative action) are almost never defined or operationalized as clearly-understood professional standards of accountable practices; and lack systematic delineation of traditional research methodology,[29] or less formalized qualitative approaches.[30] This is a particularly perplexing dilemma for individual clinicians, because they each hold a separate concept of self-evaluation, involving highly-individualized attitudes about their growth and learning. This includes unique and idiosyncratic thoughts and behaviors, in making personal decisions about their effectiveness on the job. Although each agency may have specific methods of program evaluation, the particular ways individuals within that organization evaluate how well they do their jobs, are often separate and unique processes for each staff member. Although practitioners frequently confuse the concepts of accountability and self-evaluation, the profession has continually emphasized that the most basic level of responsibility for performance evaluation, rests with the individual practitioner.

In considering different ways practitioners approach their self-evaluative responsibilities, counselors should ask several basic questions designed to understand this process, from each individual's perspective:

1.   What are the processes by which individual clinicians make decisions about competence on the job?
2.   What types and sources of information are used for self-evaluation, and how are they assessed and employed, in reaching self-evaluative conclusions?

3.   What areas of personal and professional performance are evaluated, and what are their relative importance in overall assessment of performance effectiveness?

4.   What traditional research methods are used for self-evaluation, or do practitioners employ other systematic procedures to assess performance?

Since many professionals conceive of themselves as service personnel, rather than scientists or theoreticians, there are also problems related to integration of practice-related theories of accountability; along with theories of client functioning, treatment, or service intervention. Despite these differences, accountability is seen either as a generic component of counseling theory, not requiring its own theory; or as a part of research methodology, often seen as separate from, or antithetical to, practice.[31]

Absence of models, theories, or specific guidelines for accountability, also contributes to lack of clarity about who is responsible to evaluate:

"A key and as yet unanswered question in evaluating the effects of psychosocial intervention relates to who should decide if a particular process is helpful or not. Should it be the therapist, other therapists, significant others in the client's life, the client himself or herself, or all of these? There is an agreement that all these persons have a stake in the therapeutic process, although the criteria by which decisions about it are made, are disputed."[32]

The development of an approach to evaluate professional capability involves several steps, including selection of professional activities to be evaluated, defining a system to categorize and assign various competency statuses, and insuring that assessment theories and procedures are valid and reliable in their respective usages over time.

As could be expected, evaluation of counseling involves common, as well as idiosyncratic interpretations of its nature; understanding of specific dimensions of each interventive technique; and client problems and change potentials, indexed for each area of performance. This should include broad goals of clinical counseling within a service agency network, theories of personal and social change, roles, professional standards of ethics and competence, research findings about evaluation per se, plans for professional learning and growth, processes of personal self-assessment decision-making, and availability and proper use of evaluative methodology.

Evaluation Processes Within Groups and Systems

Another problem for the evaluating clinician, is that she or he must adapt and survive within organizational and peer group social systems, whose influential power is sometimes not conducive to sound theories or skills of evaluation. Although professionalism, as noted previously, can be a reflection of cultural expectation for accountability and organizational codes of ethics, and may be assumed to result in competent evaluation; norms and dynamic processes of organizational work or peer groups, may detract from the objectives of accountability. There is little question of the ability of social group norms, pressures, interactive opportunities, or rewards/punishments to influence the behavior of constituent members.[33] This occurs in terms of how the individual internally establishes identity and valued behavior patterns within the group,[34] and performs professional tasks of self-evaluation, with or without the group's or organization's normative sanction.[35] Evaluative theory and methodology, as seen in the literature and the author's experience, unfortunately have not been standardized or clearly delineated as subcomponents of the operation of the social system, which is its host environment.[36]

As the reader can surmise, there are numerous problems inherent in processes of group/organizational dynamics, by which practitioners deal with interpersonal accountability, while striving to maintain interpersonal relationship stability and organizational homeostasis, for personal and group survival. This thesis and antithesis balancing process, has philosophical implications and conflicts in terms of (1) psychological needs of staff, supervisors, and administrators, to reduce anxiety and pressure, by maintaining the status quo; (2) critical assessment demands of accountability,[37] which suggest high probability of exposing inadequacies of those upon whom the clinician depends to some degree, for emotional and physical survival; (3) cultural taboos against judging others from a superior social position; and (4) the Protestant Ethic viewpoint, that hard work in and of itself, brings its own reward, irrespective of particular measures of competence.[38]

At the psychological level, the need to evaluate performance can arouse inner conflict in questioning one's capability—suggesting social isolation as one assumes judgmental roles. Not only is assessment complex and abstract, but sometimes appraisal in supervisory or group process situations, has been conducted to evaluate personality traits. This becomes personally threatening, and often lacks objective criteria, to truly address issues of skill performance. Some reasons why evaluation within systems is difficult and often conflictual, are these:

1.   Defining competence/incompetence is often a unilateral, politically-motivated, or defensive action.
2.   Evaluative judgment is often static, with little developmental perspective on how performance can be improved.
3.   Evaluative results within complex systems (intrapsychic, interpersonal, organization), lack multivariate comprehensive foci.
4.   Assessment of work associates may create anxiety, due to infusion of personal feelings into the evaluative gestalt.
5.   There is a built-in adversary relationship between clientele and professional helpers, where differential power and diagnostic license, can create social inequality and self-protective defensiveness.[39]
6.   Systems survive by maintaining homeostatic balance, which is contradictory to the development and change orientation of evaluative confrontation, of discovering unsuccessful inputs, process, or outcomes.[40]

With this organizational survival atmosphere, the specific nature of outcomes or evaluative results, can mean the difference between receiving or losing funding for clinical or other direct service programs. This can occur where evaluation receives organizational justification, based on providing desired data to special interest groups, which influence policy and funding contingencies.[41] Since organizations survive by pleasing funders and avoiding public criticism which may result from honest evaluative findings, the individual clinician finds him or herself in a volatile, stressful,[42] and presumably defensive posture within the system. The convergence of various role expectations and responsibilities with multiple sources of reward and punishment, makes evaluation a confusing and complex phenomenon,[43] related to behavioral and perceptual congruence.

The main problem, therefore, for individual clinician evaluation, is to develop and maintain a clear focus on the *self*-in-social context, so evaluative relevance and competence are not abrogated to meet needs of the powerful system; while at the same time, realizing individual assessment must fit meaningfully into the agency's or group's evaluative paradigm. It must enhance the system's ability to solve its survival problems, and move toward competent delivery of services. Each counselor must understand the dimensions of individual assessment, to clearly differentiate its unique nature from confounding organizational process. They develop strategy to counteract, wherever possible, the powerful system's influences, which may not enhance the quality of either the individual or social organizational accountability process.

Evaluative Methodology and Scientific Technology

A final general problem, is development of an increasingly sophisticated and accurate set of tools, techniques, and theories/philosophies for evaluation. This places pressure on clinicians to think and behave with more specific, empirical, and systematic evaluative process, in order to be on board with a maturing social "science" community: "We do not view the field of evaluation as having any methodology different from the scientific method; evaluative research is, first and foremost, research, and as such must adhere as closely as possible to currently accepted standards of research methodology."[44]

The connection between practice and science is also evident in the history of individual and organizational performance evaluation, where individual evaluation is ". . . intimately entwined with the concept of science itself."[45] This coincides with the previous discussion of consumerism and professional demands for accountability, as philosophical and political phenomena; but also represents an entirely different social, cultural, and economic context wherein precision computerization, complex management of data and information, and exactness of all forms of service delivery—are an integral part of a world racing into the space age: "The technology available to produce a certain product, may define appropriate tasks in the division of labor within any organization (or profession)."[46]

In the early 20th century, the dominant approach to social problem resolution was the "legalistic-moralistic"[47] literary orientation, where answers to human problems were known through intuition or cultural definitional mores. Scientific method is relatively recent as an epistemology, with accompanying social demands for immediacy, simplicity, and empirical proof of effectiveness[48] (experimentation, systematic observation, and computer data collection and tabulation): "Events are increasingly considered to have 'factual meaning' only when confirmed by empirical evidence"[49] in the merging roles of clinician, evaluator, and researcher.[50]

Orthodox science is only one philosophy of knowledge among others,[51] but reflects a demand for precision and empirical pragmatic truth.[52] Humanistic values and assumptions are no longer taken for granted, but must be reduced to computerized correlations and analysis of variance, wherein mathematical outcomes are the increasingly acceptable index of phenomena.[53]

There has been decreasing patience for artistic, generic, holistic, existential, phenomenologic, or clinical processes. The institutionalization of scientific thought and practice, means that clinicians may be forced to redefine their roles as clinical evaluators/researchers, and arm themselves with measurement instruments and empirical behavioral philosophies, to the exclusion of intuitive practice wisdom, which sufficed in the past.

As Braithwaite[54] notes, science is composed of two parts within the inductive/deductive learning paradigm: theory and model. The scientific perspective requires comprehensive hypothetical thinking about reality, based on propositions in the theory, and testing of these assumptions. It uses precision dimensions of the model to rigorously challenge the theoretical constructs and relationship assumptions, to validate or invalidate their existence in reality.[55] The scientist-technologist must be increasingly concerned with proof of existence or nonexistence,[56] where assumption of the efficacy of humanistic benevolence and good intents, are no longer valid practice foundations.[57]

Increasingly, counseling and clinical services may move in the direction of physical science, where behaviors, rather than abstract feelings and ideas, predominate as a reflection of techno-methodology and bio-medical research.[58] This could also be forthcoming, where only small numbers of clinical practitioners, use or consult scientific or research-oriented methodology, in conjunction with clinical practice activities.[59] An increased focus on behavioral therapies and behaviorally-oriented learning theory, may clarify this trend toward technological practice,[60] with more concentration on specific task-oriented counseling (as opposed to analytic efforts, of total personality restructuring).

As Fischer from *Social Work* noted,[61] various fields of clinical counseling and social service are in a state of scientific revolution. Kuhn[62] observes that professions are governed by superordinate models that guide and structure scientific processes within the profession. These models guide evaluative inquiry, focus practitioners' perceptions, contribute to validation of outcome truths, and insure that evaluative findings will not undermine the paradigm which authorized the investigations in the first place. As professions develop, however, evaluative models may reflect complacent utilization or intellectual skepticism, and crises can occur to usher in a new, but necessarily better, scientific model.[63]

As any profession departs from its previously espoused evaluative models,[64] the clinician must work harder to integrate evaluative theory and practice philosophy, through standardization of inputs or intervention techniques. These must be applied *across* cases, with resultant measurement of specific outcomes of human functioning[65] in the social environment.[66]

As noted by Briar,[67] the new "scientific" clinician does the following:

"(1) systematically monitors and evaluates the progress he or she makes with each case, (2) grounds his or her practice, to the extent possible, in empirically-based knowledge, particularly with numerous interventive techniques already available that have evidence of effectiveness; and uses those without such evidence, only with due caution, and (3) has the skills and attitudes—the commitment—to keep learning and to keep searching for new and more effective approaches to intervention."

Scott Briar, in fact, has labeled this "age of accountability" as requiring individual practitioners to perform systematic self-evaluation of all direct service interventions. The counselor can no longer *assume* that clients change or grow as a result of counseling or therapy:

"No longer can the human service professions make grandiose claims about ability to effect change. Expressive social action . . . and social services, must emphasize results. Our new critics . . . and the growing army of cost benefit analysts, are hostile not because they dislike the effects of what we do, but because they say we simply have had no effect on the problems we claim to be able to solve. Now we have to prove once again that what we do is worth supporting. It is an age when little or nothing will be taken for granted."[68]

Kirk, Osmalov, and Fischer, in writing about social workers' use of research for evaluation of practice, label professional accountability as the central issue confronting social workers. They charge the individual practitioner with the following responsibility: ". . . show that your efforts on behalf of clients are beneficial, that your interventions are effective, that your clients are helped, and that your work makes a difference."[69]

In talking about the meaning of empiricism in scientific method, Briar and Miller[70] suggest that "scientific" social work requires "attitudinal and methodological allegiance" to empiricism, with results of service evaluated through observable evidence.[71]

In looking at empiricism within social science accountability, the concept appears to be translated with increasing frequency, to mean demonstration of service effectiveness through the systematic observation of clients' behaviors, as indicators of change. This is illustrated by Strupp and Bergin as follows:

"Another stimulating and important trend in the current literature is represented by an emphasis on empiricism, innovation, and evaluation. New techniques of therapy and research are mushrooming, but there is a keen insistence on evaluating the therapeutic utility (for clients) of these innovations. The roles of clinician and experimenter are merging, and the clinician proposing a new technique (or using an old one), is becoming aware of the necessity to demonstrate its utility to the scientific community by means of hard core data. The field is accepting—and indeed embracing—empiricism."

Strupp and Bergin go on to point out that the literature stresses the study of "change criteria" for each individual client, which is also part of the empirical approach to accountability: "The notion strongly supports the development of a general trend toward specific, rather than global, improvement indices."[72]

The relationship between professional accountability and proof of effectiveness, is classically illustrated by the following quote from Thoreau: "No ways of doing or thinking, however ancient, can be trusted without proof. What everyone echoes or in silence passes by as true today may turn out to be falsehood tomorrow, mere smoke of opinion."[73] The scientific argument incorporates a belief in the reality of empirical observation, as the only legitimate method of examination. This is best expressed in Hudson's Axiom, which observes that "if a client's problem cannot be measured it does not exist, and if it does not exist, it cannot be treated."[74]

For clinical counselors who disagree with the validity, pressing nature, or change orientation implied in the discussion of a scientific revolutionary movement, some authors suggest that science's emphasis on empiricism and standardization, neglects consideration of social and personal values undergirding relationships and adaptation.[75] Many critics suggest that scientific methods and philosophies contradict the principles of counseling theory and method, and may rob counselors of their creative input and comprehensive assessment, of the personality gestalt[76] and synergy between interactive beings.[77]

The typical connotation of scientific methodology, suggests that the observer or researcher may be external and alien to the phenomenon (client or group system) being evaluated; which raises questions of validity within the unique therapeutic milieu, and concerns about counter-therapeutic contamination of growth-producing relationships.[78] This observer-interference question, partly derives from *power*[79] inherent in the role of scientific technician or evaluator, who can alter responsibility by assumption of objective observer roles; but who, through the nature of their evaluative design and method, has interpretive option[80] to define adaptation or pathology. This can occur within predetermined "defensive" or "reactive" evaluative categories, which may not be subject to validation outside the evaluative paradigm.[81]

In the clinician's quest for knowledge, he or she is confronted with moral responsibility to seek truth,[82] without participating simultaneously in a process which violates human rights,[83] reduces their client-advocacy commitment,[84] or condemns them to be emotionally neutral and ineffective, as energetic therapeutic agents of personal and social change.[85] Saleeby argues, that the experimental model causes an operationalized position, oriented toward the non-compassionate manipulation of clientele: "Practice articulated from the experimental paradigm . . . (assumes) . . . that any degree of manipulation, deception, and control is fair, if done in the service of socially-acceptable or human ends, but the problem is that the method itself . . . may have within . . . (it) the seeds of dehumanization."[86]

The scientific processes of "dissection and reductive analysis,"[87] may define the client to complement the framework and philosophy of the methodology, rather than accurately reflect the client's idiographic nature and personality. This methodology can then become self-protective,[88] to justify its own existence, and become functionally autonomous from the subject of its inquiry.[89] From an epistemological point of view, many practitioners feel that science cannot capture the complexity of the psychologic or interpersonal processes which are critical in therapy;[90] and it neglects a full range of experiences, relevant to the goals of behavior and attitude change. The topographic model[91] of formal scientific inquiry, observes and classifies behaviors at face value, and neglects ability to give comprehensive meaning to the subject (especially symbolic and motivational contingencies, which define its phenomenologic nature). At the same time, the methodologic "activity"[92] serves as a separate form of intervention which causes client change, as opposed to a Taoistic[93] method, for example, which is non-intrusive, passive, and comprehensive.

According to Vigilante,[94] proof in the logical positivist scientific tradition, is impossible when considering interpersonal or deeply intrapsychic phenomena, given the multitude of variables and the other symbolic and developmental components of human nature, in constant state of progression, regression, etc.[95] In the literature, adversaries of strict scientism criticize the limited scope of scientific perspective, in its interest in abstract and global causal relationships,[96] rather than pragmatic problem-solving, outcome, input, or process orientations. Part of this problem, of course, may be that clinicians have been too circumspect in their socialization and learning, so research and evaluative phenomena seem alien to their conceptualization.[97]   There is need for a fuller integration of researcher and practitioner roles, for more creative approaches to each domain.[98]

The scientific perspective may preclude real understanding (not simply categorization and statistical tabulation of frequencies) of interactional dynamics, as well as deeper psychological symbolization and representation. Its inductive-deductive and reductionistic patterns not only obscure what is, but reduce the creativity of the counselor using the methodology, and prevent discovery of other variables and relationships which may existentially be operative:[99] "The current crisis in accountability has illuminated the failure of traditional research to provide sufficiently relevant, effective, and efficient modes of inquiry into social services . . . [and] . . . the classical, academic model of research, may be typified according to its critics, as restrictive and unrealistic for examining and evaluating the issues, roles, functions, and products of actual programs."[100]

If the above interpretation about science is correct, the message for the clinician may strongly resound, for a comprehensive and rigorous qualitative approach to accountability. The absence of a systematic and standardized extreme model, demands the development of precise and accurate internal models of evaluation developed *in vitro,* along with the assumption of greater responsiveness to client-counselor interactional needs and dynamics. Understanding the important evaluative question, and developing an inquiring attitude and soundly-investigative approach to counseling, seem necessary, regardless of the screening paradigm which explains the phenomenon. The clinician's ethical and humanistic interests in the client, can always be enhanced with genuine concern, in the relentless pursuit of information and understanding, which is the foundation for professionalism and therapeutic competence.

References

1.   Mary McCormick, *Enduring Values in a Changing Society* (New York: Family Service Association of America, 1975), p. 3.

2.   Abraham Maslow, *Toward a Psychology of Being* (2nd ed.; New York: Van Nostrand, Reinhold, 1968), pp. 71-102.

3.   Barbara Okun, *Working with Families: An Introduction to Family Therapy* (North Scituale, MA: Dixberry Press, 1980), pp. 94-95.

4.   Roger Kaufman and Susan Thomas, *Evaluation Without Fear* (New York: New Viewpoints, 1980), p. 2.

5.   Edward Mullen, et al., *Evaluation of Social Intervention* (Washington, DC: Jossey-Bass, 1972).

6.   Mary Gottesfeld and Florence Lieberman, "The Pathological Therapist," *Social Casework,* 60:7:387-393, July, 1979.

7.   Robert Washington, *Program Evaluation in the Human Services* (Lanham, MD: University Press of America, 1980), p. xiii.

8.   Roy Lubove, *The Professional Altruist: The Emergence of Social Work as a Career* (New York: Harper & Row, 1975), pp. 140-143; See also, Irwin Sanders, "Public Health in the Community," in *Handbook of Medical Sociology,* eds., H. Freeman, S. Levine, and L. Reeder (Englewood Cliffs: Prentice-Hall, 1963), pp. 369-396.

9.   June Axinn and Herman Levin, *Social Welfare: A History of the American Response to Need* (New York: Harper & Row, 1975), pp. 140-143.

10.   Dorothy Bird Daly, "Introduction Social Work in the 1980's: Part is Prologue," in *Social Work in the 1980's,* eds. R. Washington and B. Toomey (Davis, CA: International Dialogue Press, 1982), pp. 13-20.

11.   Mildred Mailick and Ardythe Ashley, "Politics of Interprofessional Collaboration: Challenge to Advocacy," *Social Casework,* 35:3:133,135, March, 1981.

12.   Frank Baker and John Northman, *Helping: Human Services for the 80's* (St. Louis: C. V. Mosbya, 1981), pp. 18-37.

13.   Allen Pincus and Anne Minahan, *Social Work Practice: Model and Method* (Itasca, IL: F. E. Peacock, 1973), pp. 42-47, 56.

14.   Joel Fischer, "Isn't Casework Effective Yet?" *Social Work,* 24:3: 245-247, May, 1979.

15.   Lawrence Shulman, "A Study of Practice Skills," *Social Work,* 23:4: 274-280, July, 1978.

16.   Martin Bloom and Joel Fischer, *Evaluating Practice: Guidelines for the Accountable Professional* (Englewood Cliffs, NJ: Prentice-Hall, 1982), p. ix.

17.   Pamela Landon "A Correlational Study of Diffusion Theory in Social Work Practice," (Doctoral dissertation, University of Denver, 1975).

18.   Tony Tripodi, *Evaluative Research for Social Workers* (Englewood Cliffs: Prentice-Hall, 1983), pp. 10-11.

19.   Ernest Greenwood, "Attributes of a Profession," *Social Work,* 2:3:55, July, 1957.

20.   James Thompson, *Organizations in Action* (New York: McGraw-Hill, 1967), pp. 85-87.

21.   Oliver Fowlkes, "What are Rights?" *Proceedings of the Symposium on Safeguarding the Rights of Recipients of Mental Health Services,* East Lansing, Michigan (Rockville, MD: National Institute of Mental Health, 1977), p. 2.

22.   Janet Coye, "Michigan's System for Protecting Patients' Rights," *Hospital and Community Psychiatry,* 28:4:375-379, May, 1977.

23.   Irwin Epstein and Tony Tripodi, *Research Techniques for Program Planning Monitoring and Evaluation* (New York: Columbia University Press, 1977), p. 61.

24.   Charles Zastrow, *The Practice of Social Work* (Homewood, IL: Dorsey Press, 1981), pp. 547-555.

25.   Ronald Federico, *The Social Welfare Institution* (Lexington, MA: D. C. Heath, 1973), pp. 146-147.

26.   Frank Loewenberg, *Fundamentals of Social Intervention* (New York: Columbia University Press, 1977), pp. 103-104.

27.   Betty Baer, "Developing a New Curriculum for Social Work Education," in *The Pursuit of Competence in Social Work,* eds., F. Clark and M. Arkava (San Francisco: Jossey-Bass, 1979), p. 106.

28.   Robert Teare, "A Task Analysis for Public Welfare Practice and Educational Implications," in *The Pursuit of Competence in Social Work,* eds. F. Clark and M. Arkava (San Francisco: Jossey-Bass, 1979).

29.   Charles Atherton and David Klemmach, *Research Methods in Social Work* (Lexington, MA: D. C. Heath, 1982), p. 308.

30.   William Eldridge, "Conceptualizing Self-evaluation of Clinical Practice," *Social Work,* 28:1:57-61, January-February, 1983.

31.   Francis Turner, ed., *Social Work Treatment: Interlocking Theoretical Approaches* (2nd ed.; New York: Free Press, 1979), pp. 5-7.

32.   Francis Turner, *Psychosocial Therapy* (New York: Free Press, 1978), p. 205.

33.   George Homons, *The Human Group* (New York: Harcourt, Brace, and World, 1950), pp. 281-312.

34.   Robert Boyd, "Conformity Reduction in Adolescence," *Adolescence,* 10:6:297-300, April, 1975.

35.   Elizabeth Douvan and Joseph Adelson, *The Adolescent Experience* (New York: John Wiley & Sons, 1966).

36.   William Eldridge, "Clinical Peer Group Evaluation: A Descriptive Analysis," (Unpublished manuscript, The Ohio State University, 1982).

37.   Howard Smith and Paul Brouwer, *Performance Appraisal and Human Development* (Reading, MA: Addison-Wesley, 1977), p. 135.
38.   Max Weber, *The Protestant Ethic and the Spirit of Capitalism* (New York: Charles Scribner, 1958).
39.   Mary Gottesfeld and Florence Lieberman, "The Pathological Therapist," *Social Casework,* 60:7:387-393, July, 1979.
40.   Dean Hepworth and Jo Ann Larsen, *Direct Social Work Practice* (Homewood, IL: Dorsey Press, 1982), p. 420; See also, Roslyn Chemesly, "Attitudes of Social Workers Toward Peer Review," *Health and Social Work,* 6:2:67-73, May, 1981.
41.   Eliot Freidson, *Doctoring Together: A Study of Professional Social Control* (New York: Elsevier, 1975); See also, Edward Suchman, *Evaluation Research: Principles and Practice in Public Service and Social Action Programs* (New York: Russell Sage Foundation, 1967), pp. 2-8; and Martin Rein, "Social Planning: The Search for Legitimacy," in *Planning Social Welfare: Issues Models Tasks,* eds., N. Gilbert and H. Specht (Englewood Cliffs: Prentice-Hall, 1977), pp. 50-69.
42.   Robert Hogan and Joyce Hogan, "Subjective Correlates of Stress and Human Performance," in *Human Performance and Productivity,* eds., E. Alluisi and E. Fleishman (Hillsdale, NJ: Lawrence Erlbaum, 1982), pp. 141-163.
43.   Gordon Lowe, "Phenomenological Congruence in the Clinical Milieu," *Canadian Psychiatric Association Journal,* 20:5:367-372, August, 1975.
44.   Edward Suchman, *Evaluative Research Principles and Practice in Public Service and Social Action Programs* (New York: Russell Safe Foundation, 1967), p. 12.
45.   John Ivancevich, Andrew Szilagyi, Jr., and Marc Wallace, *Organizational Behavior and Performance* (Santa Monica: Goodyear, 1977), p. 22.
46.   Frank Baker and John Northman, *Helping: Human Services for the 80's* (St. Louis: C. V. Mosby, 1981), p. 99.
47.   George Lundberg, *Can Science Save Us?* (New York: David McKay, 1947), p. 5.
48.   Carlo Lastrucci, *The Scientific Approach: Basic Principles of Scientific Method* (Cambridge, MA: Schenkman, 1963), pp. 29-34.
49.   Scott Briar and Henry Miller, *Problems and Issues in Social Casework* (New York: Columbia University Press, 1971), p. 2.
50.   Allen Bergen and Hans Strupp, *Changing Frontiers in the Science of Psychotherapy* (Chicago: Aldine-Atherton, 1972), pp. 10 11, 54.
51.   Abraham Maslow, *The Psychology of Science* (New York: Harper & Row, 1966).
52.   Floyd Matson, *The Broken Image* (New York: Braziller, 1964).

53.   Abraham Maslow, *Eupsychian Management A Journal* (Homewood, IL: Irwin-Dorsey, 1965).

54.   Richard Braithwaite, *Scientific Explanation: A Study of the Function of Theory Probability and Law in Science* (Cambridge, MA: Harvard University Press, 1953).

55.   Jum Nunnally, *Psychometric Theory* (New York: McGraw-Hill, 1967).

56.   John Neale and Robert Liebert, *Science and Behavior: An Introduction to Methods of Research* (Englewood Cliffs: Prentice-Hall, 1973).

57.   Martin Bloom, *The Paradox of Helping: Introduction to the Philosophy of Scientific Practice* (New York: John Wiley & Sons, 1975).

58.   Harold Demone, *Stimulating Human Service Reform* (Washington, DC: Human Services Monograph Series, Project SHARE, No. 8, June, 1978).

59.   Walter Hudson, "Social Problems in the Assessment of Growth and Deterioration," in *The Effectiveness of Social Casework,* ed., J. Fischer (Springfield: Charles C. Thomas, 1976), pp. 197-224; and Aaron Rosenblatt, "The Practitioner's Use and Evaluation of Research," Social Work, 13:1:53-59, January, 1968.

60.   Allen Bergen and Hans Strupp, *Changing Frontiers in the Science of Psychotherapy* (Chicago: Aldine-Atherton, 1972); See also, Leonard Ullmann and Leonard Krasner, eds., *Case Studies in Behavior Modification* (New York: Holt, Rinehart and Winston, 1965).

61.   Joel Fischer, "The Social Work Revolution," *Social Work,* 26:3:199-207, May, 1981.

62.   Thomas Kuhn, *The Structure of Scientific Revolutions* (Chicago: University of Chicago Press, 1962).

63.   Edwin Thomas, "Beyond Knowledge Utilization in Generating Human Service Technology," in *Future of Social Work Research,* ed., D. Fanshel (Washington, DC: National Association of Social Workers, 1980), pp. 91-103; See also, Edwin Thomas, "Generating Innovation in Social Work: The Paradigm of Developmental Research," *Journal of Social Service Research,* 2:1:95-116, Fall, 1978.

64.   Jack Rothman, *Planning and Organizing for Social Change: Action Principles from Social Science Research* (New York: Columbia University Press, 1974; See also, Jack Rothman, *Promoting Innovation and Change in Organizations and Communities* (New York: John Wiley & Sons, 1976).

65.   Arnold Lazarus, *Multimodal Behavior Therapy* (New York: Springer, 1976.)

66.   Robert Nay, *Multimethod Clinical Assessment* (New York: Gardner Press, 1979); See also, Carel Germain, "The Ecological Perspective in Casework Practice," *Social Casework,* 54:6:323-330, June, 1973; an Alex Gitterman and

Carel Germain, *The Life Model of Social Work Practice* (New York: Columbia University Press, 1980).

67.   Scott Briar, "Clinical Scientists in Social Work: Where Are They?" (Paper presented at the University of Chicago School of Social Service Administration Alumni Conference, Chicago, Illinois, May, 1974).

68.   Scott Briar, "The Age of Accountability," *Social Work,* 18:1:2, January, 1973.

69.   Stuart Kirk, Michael Osmalov, and Joel Fischer, "Social Workers' Involvement in Research," *Social Work,* 21:2:121-124, March, 1976.

70.   Scott Briar and Henry Miller, *Problems and Issues in Social Casework* (New York: Columbia University Press, 1971), p. 2.

71.   Carlo Lastrucci, *The Scientific Approach: Basic Principles of the Scientific Method* (Cambridge, MA: Schenkman, 1963), pp. 29-34.

72.   Allen Bergen and Hans Strupp, *Changing Frontiers in the Science of Psychotherapy* (Chicago: Aldine-Atherton, 1972), pp. 10-11, 54.

73.   See, Henry David Thoreau in Aaron Rosenblatt, "The Practitioner's Use and Evaluation of Research," *Social Work,* 13:1:53-59, January, 1968.

74.   Walter Hudson, "First Axioms of Treatment," *Social Work,* 23:1:65, January, 1978.

75.   William Gorham, "Testing and Public Policy," (Paper presented at the Invitational Conference of the Educational Testing Service (New York, October 28, 1967).

76.   William Berkman, "Practitioners and Research: First Questions," *Social Casework,* 50:8:461-466, October, 1969.

77.   Charles Windle and William Neigher, "Ethical Problems in Program Evaluation: Advice for Trapped Evaluators," *Evaluation and Program Planning: An International Journal* (1:2:97-108, 1978).

78.   Norman Herstein, "The Latent Dimension of Social Work Research," *Social Casework,* 50:5:275, May, 1969.

79.   Sherri Seinfeld, "The Evaluation Profession in Pursuit of Value," *Evaluation and Program Planning: An International Journal,* 1,2,113-115, January, 1978.

80.   Ernest Nagel, *Logic Without Metaphysics* (Glencoe, IL: Free Press, 1956), p. 35.

81.   Henry Riecken and Robert Boruch, eds., *Social Experimentation: A Method for Planning and Evaluating Social Intervention* (New York: Academic Press, 1974), p. 31.

82.   R. Firth, "Ethical Absolutism and the Ideal Observer," *Philosophy and Phenomenological Research,* 124:317-345, 1952.

83.   John Rawls, *A Theory of Justice* (Cambridge, MA: Belknap Press, 1971).

84.   Alan Keith-Lucas, "Ethics in Social Work," *Encyclopedia of Social Work,* ed., R. Morris (Vol. 1; New York: National Association of Social Workers, 1971), pp. 324-328.

85.   Henry Riecken and Robert Boruch, eds., *Social Experimentation: A Method for Planning and Evaluating Social Intervention* (New York: Academic Press, 1974), p. 246; and George Lundberg, *Can Science Save Us?* (New York, David McKay, 1947), p. 52.

86.   Dennis Saleeby, "The Tention Between Research and Practice: Assumptions for the Experimental Paradigm," *Clinical Social Work Journal,* 7:4:276, Winter, 1979.

87.   Abraham Maslow, *The Psychology of Science* (New York: Harper & Row, 1966), p. 11.

88.   Abraham Maslow, *Religions Values and Peak-experiences* (Columbus, OH: The Ohio State University Press, 1964); See also, Abraham Maslow, *Toward a Psychology of Being* (New York: Van Nostrand, 1962).

89.   Robert Merton, *Social Theory and Social Structure* (Glencoe, IL: Free Press, 1949), pp. 39, 84.

90.   See, David Austin, "Research and Social Work: Educational Paradoxes and Possibilities," *Journal of Social Service Research,* 2:1:173, Winter, 1976; and Aaron Beckerman, "Differentiating Between Social Research and Social Work Research: Implications for Teaching," *Journal of Education for Social Work,* 14:2, Spring, 1978; and Mary Gyarfas, "Social Science, Technology, and Social Work: A Caseworker's View," *Social Service Review,* 43:3:259, September, 1969.

91.   Israel Goldiamond, John Dryud, and Henry Miller, "Practice and Research in Professional Psychology," *The Canadian Psychologist,* 6:1:110-128, January, 1975.

92.   Steven Schinke, "Evaluating Social Work Practice: A Conceptual Model and Example," *Social Casework,* 60:4:195-200, April, 1979.

93.   Abraham Maslow, "Comments on Skinner's Attitude to Science," *Daedalus,* XC:572-573, 1961.

94.   Joseph Vigilante, "Between Values and Science: Education for the Profession During a Moral Crisis or Is Proof Truth?" *Journal of Education for Social Work,* 10:7:112, Fall, 1974.

95.   William Brennan, "The Practitioner as Theoretician," *Journal of Education for Social Work,* 9:2:7, Spring, 1973.

96.   Mark Van de Vall and Cheryl Bolas, "Policy Research as an Agent of Planned Social Intervention: An Evaluation of Methods, Standards, and Data, and Analytic Techniques," (Paper presented at the Annual Meeting of The American Sociological Association, Chicago, September, 1977).

97.   Charles Levy, "Inputs Versus Outcomes as Criteria of Competence," *Social Casework,* 55:6:375, May, 1974.

98.   Henry Murray, "Vicissitudes of Creativity," in *Creativity and Its Cultivation,* ed., H. Anderson (New York: Harper & Row, 1959).

99.   Thomas Kuhn, *The Structure of Scientific Revolutions* (2nd ed.; Chicago: University of Chicago Press, 1971).

100. Melvin Brenner, "The Quest for Viable Research in Social Services; Development of the Mini-study," *Social Service Review,* 50:3:426-444, September, 1976.

Chapter Two

Evaluation of Characteristics

of Clients

Introduction

Significant dimensions of the clinical evaluative gestalt are the nature, etiology, potency, and range of client thoughts and behaviors (which represent outcomes of therapeutic work), as their dynamics affirm, deny, or alter the validity and reliability of assessment. Although characteristics of clients such as resistance, pathological fixation, manipulation, or anxiety are sometimes used as clinicians' excuses for unsuccessful treatment outcomes, these psychosocial-behavioral dynamics are factors which impair or even defeat otherwise sound theories and techniques of evaluation. In some cases, the existential subjectivity and changeability of particular client characteristics or diagnostic syndromes, may present a sufficiently complex conglomeration of individual symbolization and interpretation, to render measurement and evaluation nearly impossible.

All too often the counselor, caseworker, or therapist may ignore the unique and idiosyncratic nature of clients, either as individual repositories of a functional (for them) reality symbolization, or when commonalities of particular diagnostic syndromes, suggest circumscribed evaluative foci and associated questions about effectiveness. The counselor must keep in mind generalized frameworks for evaluation, based on professional methodological requirements or theoretical tenets; but also additional, supplemental, alternate, or even contradicting evaluative issues that only emerge as the client's character, style, and life focus authorize them as relevant concerns.

In all cases, evaluative goals, treatment inputs, and empirical outcome referents should be planned, coordinated, and flexibly altered to match the constant, changing, or illusive contour of clients' efforts—to defend themselves against anxiety and personality disintegration, and functionally adapt to demands of life. Although specific client dynamics and therapeutic procedures will be discussed, general principles for conceptualizing therapeutic approaches to this dilemma, are also listed as a beginning framework for the reader:

1.   The clinician should identity the client's level of growth and development (including capabilities as well as deficits), as this provides clues to (a) transference symbolization, (b) types of defensive distortions, (c) fantasized problems and solutions, and (d) general perspectives about reality, and the nature of interpersonal relationships.

2.   The clinician should scrutinize content of verbal and behavioral communications from clients, and be prepared to place these ideas and feelings into a predetermined conversion formula, to correctly interpret distorted, hidden, or symbolic messages.[1]

3.   The clinician should understand the range of progressive regressions for each pathologic syndrome (including problems defined in terms of family systems, interactions, or community social paradigms), because defensive behaviors (attempts at adaptation) can be used as indices of growth or deterioration; when defined, operationalized, and measured as separate phenomena from idealized success goals.

4.   The clinician should meticulously learn the cognitive processes the client undertakes, from the point of reception or awareness of an idea or message, to the concluding decision about each cognitive piece of information. This demands the clinician's knowledge of clients' a priori, interim, and finalizing interpretive value decisions which give ideas or feelings their healthy or maladaptive character, and upon which subsequent behavioral decisions are predicated. Each decision juncture in the client's array of cognitions, is a point at which evaluative measurements can be applied, to (a) define the types and nature of decisions themselves; (b) measure degrees and directions of decision-making changes as a result of therapeutic inputs;

(c) measure behaviors which are directly or inversely correlated with antecedent cognitive decisions—and assess the type of cognitive-behavioral association; or document the need to activate alternate measurement foci or scales, to monitor symbolic rather than actual meanings of client activities. Herein, reality is switched to new conceptual avenues which must be measured independently, and then interpolated back into previous explanatory patterns, via, the clinician's exchange formula.

Defining Clients and Their Problems

The first issue related to client characteristics which impacts evaluation is, very simply, who the clinician defines as the client. Dynamics of growth, principles of thinking and behaving, alternatives for adaptation (positive outcomes) or irresponsibility (negative outcomes), response patterns to therapeutic inputs, and potential of learning and reinforcing contingencies which influence clients—all vary according to individual, dyadic, marital, family, community, and societal definitions of clientele.

This problem is complicated where clinicians define multiple sources of causality for psychosocial problems, when they are not armed with corresponding theories of interactive causality (i.e., individual ego, plus development of previous family dynamics, plus current reference groups, etc.), to explain interconnections between influences, or guide eclectic approaches to treatment.[2] As suggested by Etzione,[3] the following factors take on highly significant meaning, depending on specific definition of the client:

1. present vs. past influences on behavior;
2. significance of overt behavior vs. subjective experience;
3. social vs. psychological determinants of health or illness;
4. corresponding idiographic vs. nomothetic approaches to analyze behavior.

To develop these conceptual dichotomies and subsequently operationalize interventive and evaluative plans, the practitioner should focus on a single unit of treatment (not necessarily a single individual), and not allow unplanned interpretations of problem variations without rationale for measuring this linkage. They should also reduce (as systematically as possible) intervening conditions from adjacent categories of client definitions, to linearly pair specific treatment inputs, to corresponding dynamics of change within constantly defined client units.

Measurement of any single variable is related to multivariate factors, which may only be explainable or measurable by dividing theories into discrete constructs with increased unidimensional focus, or eliminating theories which exclude some areas of explanation, or which do not allow categorization of new and different relationships between factors in clients' lives. An example, is when the therapist believes the client's cognitive patterns are the primary cause of presenting problems, yet directs therapeutic inputs to the marital dyad of which the client is a member. In this case, changes in cognition can be influenced by dyadic norms, altered spouse inputs with undefined client dependence on these inputs, interactive cognitive patterns, or other relationship dynamics—which may not have been conceptualized in the clinician's theory, or be casually linked (except through possible sequential chain reactions) to specific input techniques.

A reverse example, is the clinician using systems theory to define a family as the client, while attempting to measure only individual changes in members, which may reveal nothing about collective attitudes or behaviors of the unit of focus. This may obscure a more pronounced dimension of pathology or conflict, which continues in existence (or even becomes worse) when any individual in the system makes a change.

In this regard, clients also maintain their own views of who is to *blame* for their problem, or who is appropriately capable of fixing it. They often sabotage attempts to diagnose, treat, or evaluate their situation, if there is discrepancy between their own definition, and that of the clinician. In many cases, the client's judgment about client definition may be superior to the clinician; but in all cases, evaluation, as it reinforces therapeutic plans or communicates supportive structure and security to anxious clients, may have to focus (even as a placebo) on client definitions which are ego-syntonic (at least initially).

Even if clients defensively blame others for their problems, and abdicate responsibility for solutions, they can learn about their defensive and psychodynamic processes, by defining interactive variables as they see them. Therapists then use this process to uncover real causal or correlational linkages, which do not seem ostensibly obvious with preliminary definitions of who the client is, and how the client system operates. Clients may have a 3, 4, or multidimensional perspective which the therapist cannot hope to achieve, until led through the causal labyrinth by following client definitional preferences, and then continually testing for validity as treatment continues.

Regarding the above issue, there is a critical evaluative question about clients' capabilities to accurately conceptualize antecedent, sustaining, and consequent parameters of their problems (which can be assessed in degrees of capability), and the influence the therapist exercises in determining clients' ranges within this self-assessment scale. From a methodological standpoint, many authors suggest that accurate measurement of any client (however defined), demands categorization of similar groupings of clients (although formal sample and control groups are usually not constituted for N = 1 evaluation), at least informally, in the clinician's caseload. This helps the counselor perceive personality inventories and pre and post behavioral measurements that can be checked for validity and reliability, by comparing individual clients to norms for similar categories of clients, so evaluations can be compared across categories.[4] This is particularly true in using psychological tests, standardized with relatively homogeneous categories of individuals.

Although the clinician may describe the structure of the client's personality (including social systems) and its principles of organization and operation, clinical evaluation has its richest impact when clients can also be located by position (a variable which should be continually monitored), on a continuum in relation to similar or different clients. This is the only way to accurately conceptualize the therapist's treatment input as an independent variable, and subsequently compare its differential effects at different times with similar clients, and in a controlled time frame with different clients. The clinician's best interests are served when variability is a function of treatment input, rather than of other contingencies of client definitions or diagnosis.

It is also important to keep in mind that client definitions may change in the course of treatment, because of reciprocal, but often unpredictable, interactions between individuals and their primary group,[5] as a result of more predictable interactions with the professional counselor.[6] The client may behave in a totally different way (definitional category) when experiencing specific types or amounts of stimulation or influence from family members. This necessitates changes in treatment orientation temporarily or permanently, as new or different perspectives come into view.

Also, particular definitions of clients, produce important variations in the ability of either client or counselor to agree on problem focus, which (a) the therapist could erroneously interpret as a negative treatment condition; (b) could prevent the client from becoming productively involved in the growth process; or (c) hampers accurate problem definition indefinitely. An example of this is definition of individual pathology when, in fact, organizational work environment is the real culprit, causing maladaptation in a healthy individual. This type of situation causes clients considerable emotional conflict, as their appropriate reluctance to accept personal pathological responsibility, sometimes reduces nurturance and positive regard from a counselor, who needs to define individuals as deviant clients. If the real clients (i.e., parents instead of children, bosses instead of employees) are not correctly defined, the surrogate person undergoing the treatment may fail to benefit, or be conditioned to learn dependent or other personally-destructive behaviors, to complement the therapist's expectation of deviancy.

Sometimes this situation is created by professionals' need to narrowly define clients, to validate circumscribed skill and service capabilities, or to label client pathology to reinforce their own failing self-esteem. In addition, therapist idealism about the broad world, coupled with simplistic philosophies about individual conformity based on the client's corrected insight or behavior may, again, mark an incorrect definition of either client or adaptation problem.

In today's world of harsh competition for survival, terrorism and intimi-dation of nuclear war, corruption at all societal levels, discrimination, and domination of individual citizens by self-serving institutions, the traditional foundation of optimistic, health-oriented, and relevant clinical counseling or therapy may be seriously threatened.[7] This social environment is the backdrop against which well-intentioned clinicians might enthusiastically[8] define the individual as the client, since this is the easiest avenue to some level of intervention, in a complex world milieu. An unfair and irresolvable burden however, may befall the individual-defined-as-client orientation. Adaptation to the real world may require attitudes, feelings, and behaviors which are unhealthy and compromise the non-sick identity of the client, or may get society off the hook as the logical focus of rehabilitative attention, no matter how difficult broad social change may be.

Humanistic qualities of honest relationships, trust, clear communications, and absence of defense, may be the least desirable or effective modes of survival for some clients in today's difficult societal milieu. Clients who develop conforming work habits, achieve organizational rewards, protect themselves against exploitation, and aggressively compete for personal and family security, may find components of the clinician's definitions of little practical value, and be increasingly unwilling to accept primary client status.[9]

How clinicians integrate their own real or ideal concepts of the world in their relationships with clients, and categorize clients and client adaptation within the social environment, lays the foundation for the client's learning, skill development, awareness of options, attitude adjustment, and successful utilization of therapeutic experience.

Clinicians are always influenced by society's broad definitions of mental health or illness, conformity or deviance, and client/patient vs. non-client definitional categories. Roger Nooe,[10] while introducing a conceptual model to integrate theoretical and underlying philosophical approaches to deviance, notes that the issue of defining deviance (and therefore defining the client), is traditionally approached from either the psychological or sociological perspective.[11]

The psychological framework used most by clinicians, stresses that the problem resides within the individual and is a function of socially learned or behaviorally-conditioned conflict, whose seeds were planted in critical childhood developmental periods. Problem resolution is available through (1) client insight, and awareness of outdated or irrational assumptions about themselves or others, (2) expression of pent-up feelings, which bind productive energy and hide the content of conflict, (3) support for the client's individuality and basic human nature, (4) working through or cognitive/behavioral reenactment of early parent-child negative relational dynamics, so corrections can be factored in the client's life script formula, and finally (5) supportive rewards from the client's significant social milieu, to sustain positive behaviors within an accepting host environment. These significant conditions under which the client enters a therapeutic alliance, offer contingencies for change which are not entirely related to the client's ongoing thought and behavioral process. They are also predicated on a priori classifications of normal processes of growth, development and change.

Sociocultural theories, on the other hand, stress analysis of social conditions or situations, and corresponding individual psychological dependency and receptability to influence, that create or sustain deviance or conformity. This orientation views deviance as an ascribed social role within an interdependent system of behaviorally learned contingencies, related to normative standards of dominant social groups. In reference to the diagnostic definition of deviant status, Erikson notes that . . .

> "Deviance is not a property inherent in certain forms of behavior; it is a property conferred upon these forms by the audience which directly or indirectly witnesses them. . . . The critical variable is the social audience which eventually decides whether or not any given action or actions will become a visible case of deviation."[12]

Relevant social groups or cultures also determine which members will be assigned deviant labels, since there are differential and changing criteria upon which this role is ascribed or achieved:

". . . social groups create deviance by making the rules whose infraction constitutes deviance, and by applying those rules to particular people and labeling them as outsiders . . . Deviance is . . . a consequence of the application of rules and sanctions to define the 'offender.' The deviant is one to whom that label has successfully been applied; deviant behavior is behavior that people so label."[13]

The decision of who is defined within deviant categories, is also dependent on the power and social status of individuals/families, and their social distance and degree of difference from potential labelers. Age, ethnic, and gender demographics also influence definitional process and outcome.[14]

In the author's view, social definition of the client by others[15] does not necessarily have to be preceded by, or result in, negative self-concept changes, and may even produce improved self-confirmation. In the interactive process between psychological or sociological definitional interactions, clinicians should be concerned evaluatively, with the client's intrapsychic mechanisms for handling movement in and out of roles (both active psychological processes, as well as reactive ones), which make them more or less vulnerable[16] to particular influences of social process. At the same time, evaluation should also consider forces in society which predetermine certain definitional outcomes, applying to special groupings of individuals with unique susceptibilities, as well as social dynamics having generally equal influences on all individuals. Some previously healthy people will become pathological as a reaction, and pathological individuals may appear healthier, when experiencing the same social force or stimulus.

Professionals who represent society's (as well as clients') interests and their associated social agencies, also help create and codify social norms through diagnostic process and content, which superimposes an often firm set of input and outcome categories (discriminative prejudgments). These frequently force clients into more deviant roles in order to compromise, receive emotional rewards from counselors (where expectations have been met), or receive other benefits (e.g., welfare payments), contingent on role performance outcomes evaluated by the professional. This problem is specifically noted where clients are not viewed as competent definers of their problem, or are not invited to help plan counseling activities or evaluation tasks.[17]

Individual Clients as Deviant Symptom-Carriers

The traditional foundation of clinical evaluation, is the observation and categorization of client symptoms, by clinical professionals (and sometimes clients), within theoretical paradigms, to pinpoint (1) growth and developmental pathology, (2) onset of adjustment problems, (3) seriousness and length (antecedent and projected) of disturbance, (4) appropriate treatment goals and techniques, (5) prognoses, and (6) other factors which individual practitioners find helpful for therapeutic decision-making.

Since evaluation of client motivation, degree of pathology, and potential for change, typically follow identification and analysis of symptoms, some therapists neglect consideration of the history and process of symptom manifestation, which can be seen as a separate entity of the disease or pathology dynamic. This perception, therefore, requires modification of evaluative lenses, wherein the client can be comprehensively understood as being involved in some meaningful dynamic life ritual, along a continuum from extremely deviant to extremely conforming.

Since diagnosis and clinical interventions are typically activated in response to negative and salient symptom behaviors, clients may be reinforced for social deviancy because of secondary gain of therapeutic intervention, in addition to the primary gain of anxiety-reduction, through symbolic symptom manifestation. As the therapist is involved in this diagnostic and stimulus-response situation, several variable dimensions of symptom manifestation (as a separate index of evaluative functional outcome) may be obscured, due to a narrow focus on causes and results of symptoms, as symbolic representations of intrapsychic phenomena. Although this end-product orientation is necessary, there is also value in conceptualizing the process of symptom presentation, as a direct reference to client strength, adaptability, or change. By considering a comprehensive spectrum of symptoms and their meanings, the evaluator may discover other indices of client behavior, which provide useful measured values to replace other invalid or unreliable foci of evaluation, also providing effective new data to monitor effects of both client and therapist independent variables. Although a consideration of the conditioned social significance of symptoms is not a new or profound revelation, some important issues concerning relevance, validity, reliability, and utility of evaluation relative to symptoms, are discussed separately.

1. Symptom manifestation to stimulate and actually reinforce therapeutic intervention, may be a positive index of cognitive, emotional, and behavioral creativity. It may signify certain dimensions of strength in the

client, including ability to control symptoms, and other behaviors as well. In many cases, symptom development, including (a) perceived need for escape, (b) assessment of available adaptive/defensive alternatives, and (c) symptom style most compatible with personality; is very logical and rational, given the client's current or past perceptions of reality. Outcomes of symptom manifestation, therefore, are actually ostensibly deviant parts of an otherwise sensible progression of decisions, based usually, on incorrect major premises of a psychodynamic syllogism.

2. Assessment of potency, primitiveness, longitude, or severity of the symptom itself, may obscure a necessary perspective on degree of social adaptability of clients, depending on ability of their social milieu to need, reward, punish, or ignore their behavior, in maintaining the social system's functioning. The clinician may make incorrect assumptions about this dimension, since it is difficult and time-consuming to measure, and often requires collateral data-collecting consultations with key people in the client's social milieu. The presence of symptoms with negative connotations, does not necessarily preclude simultaneous occurrence of a range of positive successes or achievements, in other areas of clients' lives. The ritualistic necessity of deviant symptoms, however, to facilitate access into treatment situations and justify the therapist's expert role, can cause the following:

    a. therapist's skepticism of positive reports from the client, who is judged to produce defense resistance and exaggerated reality distortion (lest the therapist become unnecessary), as a regressive pattern;
    b. client guilt and embarrassment over symptom exhibition (and maybe fabrication to please the healer-in-need of a sick patient), which leads to exacerbated symptom development;
    c. discouragement of identifying client successes, because many theories are deficient in providing taxonomic and interventive guidelines for behaviors, thoughts, or feelings in the positive mode;
    d. heightened social visibility of the client, with accompanying prejudicial stereotypes of the mentally, or emotionally ill.

This is a significant social problem noted by Segal,[18] who announces that the contemporary lay community defines a wider array of "mental illness" behaviors than occurred in previous years, which may also be accompanied by increased evaluative categories and expectations of professionals, to complement the social norms. This possible change in social perspective, when viewed carefully, may represent simply an increase in overt labeling, rather than genuine improvement in understanding of the potential client.[19] Segal also asserts that patterns of symptom manifestation, are the major determinants of the positive or negative character of the public's attitude. Some sociologists, including Sarbin and Mancuso,[20] are not optimistic about current efforts to educate the public concerning the nature of mental illness, pointing to the negative impact of the label itself, on the reaction of the public to individuals so defined:

> "There is a strong 'negative halo' associated with the mentally ill. They are considered, unselectively, as being *all things bad.* . . . The average man (woman) generalizes to the point of considering the mentally ill as dirty, unintelligent, insincere, and worthless. Such unselectively negative attitudes are probably due in part to a lack of information about mental illness and a failure to observe and learn about mental illness phenomena in daily life."[21]

In fact, according to one study,[22] the closer the client draws toward the clinical professional for help, the greater the chances of being given a negative social assessment, with presumably more attention to symptoms of a pathological nature.[23]

An illustration of these symptom-related issues is occurring with AIDS sufferers: increased symptom manifestation is precipitating public fright so that, while some avenues of helping are opened, others which were available but receiving limited use, have closed (e.g., many nursing homes which no longer accept AIDS sufferers). Also, pronounced concern with AIDS symptoms may obscure attention to relationship dynamics which affect all families (traditional or nontraditional), particularly because homosexual men are among the predominant carriers, and society did not accept the value or meaning of their relationships prior to public concern with AIDS.

3. Symptom formation may be prematurely assessed as a form of dependence (with direct correlations hypothesized for severity of symptom and degree of dependence) on regressive conflicts, childhood fantasies, parental control and adolescent rebellion, or nurturance from a parental therapist. Timing, style, volume, and visibility of symptoms, however, may conversely reflect autonomy from pathologically constraining social norms. Hereby, the client is truly asserting independence and existential relationality through a limited avenue of alternatives, feared and ostracized by a more dependency-entrapped society. Those with symptoms may be actively

fighting for healthy awareness and process, whereas non-symptomatic members of the social order, may not be aware of conflicts (possibly a more primitive symptom of denial), or have already given up the fight for greater health. For evaluative validity, however, it is important to carefully consider the range of acceptable cognitive and behavioral structures which are available to clients within particular cultures (especially with minority clients in a dominant controlling culture), to understand the real meaning of specific evaluated outcomes. One component of clinical counseling involves the client's restructuring, clarification, testing out, modification, or relearning of cognitive thoughts or thought patterns—to produce more "rational,"[24] less constricted,[25] conflict or guilt free,[26] more conscious (not repressed), or less transferential[27] ideations, which improve psychosocial adaptation:

> "It is a premise of counseling that the intellectual and emotional understanding that the client works out within the therapeutic process will carry over to current and future life experiences . . . with the assumption that what is learned will have general adaptability outside the counseling situation."[28]

In counselor's efforts to "expose and correct irrational factors (thoughts),"[29] some clients (not severely pathological or psychotic) become frustrated seeking rational or sensible explanations of the world's confusing and often contradictory multicausal and correlated events, as distorted by social institutions or normative socialization processes (e.g., governments' plans to assassinate world leaders in the name of peace). "Others, in adapting to their particular frame of life, may cease to question it but not attach much meaning to it, trying merely to fulfill their obligations."[30] On the other hand, clients might suffer more from awareness of true, but painfully abhorrent reality[31] from which they could possibly escape, through creative delusions, illusions, or conceptual alterations of personal circumstances or awareness, which they may be unable to realistically modify or change anyway.[32]

The client's cognitive restructuring, may remove functionally defensive thought content or processes necessary for survival in environments which are hostile, personally degrading, or otherwise anxiety-provoking. The slum dweller's fabrications of personal affluence, for example, insure "hanging on," when legitimate avenues for success are forever closed;[33] social activists may sustain their productive contributions to society, through heightened idealistic conceptions that the world will appreciate their efforts, and protect their right to differ (e.g., Martin Luther King); or the new employee controls anxiety over realistic inadequacy, through mental exaggerations of performance expertise, in competitive job situations offering little emotional support, and which may quickly eliminate ineffective personnel in the interest of efficiency, cost effectiveness, and profit maintenance.

For the clinician, the ethical dilemma may involve competing personal and professional needs to reduce suffering, on the one hand, and help clients develop less "pathological" perspectives about reality (as one symbol of psychic health), on the other. Creative cognition and honest reality orientations, however, to reduce pain, may be mutually exclusive and illusive phenomena. Symptoms of the client's adequacy or nondeviance can misrepresent the real picture of social adjustment as (a) their unwavering conformity may trap them in non-rewarding organizational dead ends (e.g., the Peter Principle)[34] or (b) non-symptom manifestation becomes a reaction-formation defense, as in milder forms of obsessive-compulsions, passive dependencies, hysteria, etc. True growth among these types of clients, may mean giving up non-symptoms of deviance, and taking on symptoms of deviance to more honestly act out their break with dependency, and the strangle hold of naturally-rising anxiety; to clearly signal a socially perceivable cry for help. The real problem relates more to the protection of the self and others,[35] rather than some notion of psychosocial self-actualization. In either case, the clinical evaluator must remember that symptoms stand as indices of psychosocial process (which may or may not be decreased), but also represent reactions to awareness of the disease or pathology condition, reactions to professional definers of those conditions, or very realistic and highly-functional efforts to survive conditions of social insanity, which others choose to ignore.

4.   The client's perceptions of symptoms may differ radically from the therapist's views, so change relative to quantity or quality of these behaviors, may be subjectively scaled and interpreted, resulting in meaningless or confusing analyses by the professional measurer. Assessing congruence, therefore, between client and therapist conceptions of symptomatic meanings, or degree of effort/success in ability to cross-reference and inversely correlate symptoms with negative environmental responses, may provide more meaningful evaluative data.

Although Bellak states that the projective hypothesis[36] underlying diagnosis and evaluation is that every reaction of a client is a reflection of a private world, clinical evaluation only has relevance when the client's personal scaled assessment of symptoms, undergoes a linear transformation to the therapist's subjective scale, or vice versa. In this process, the client's assessment must not lose its original identity as a proportionate ratio of symptomatic behavior vis-à-vis (a) client's perception of the symptom's degree of deviance, (b) the overall danger with which the ego is faced, (c) number and accessibility of alternatives for adaptation or retreat, and (d) severity of consequences for nondevelopment of symptoms. If each of these dimensions were given a numerical score separately, then combined for a composite score, then transformed into the therapist's scale with its own unique cumulative dimensions, and finally given a transformed and composite value; the evaluator might approach an interpretation of symptoms which is relevant to the theoretical dimensions of clinical pathology or deviance, and existential aspects of the client's self-determined behavioral heritage.

In most diagnostic or psychological testing/evaluation situations, the focus is on existence and dimensions of the deviant symptoms themselves, rather than considering the client's process of perceiving his/her own symptoms and those of significant reference groups which, of course, can represent another set of symptoms in and of themselves. The symbolic nature of symptoms, particularly emphasized in analytic-type therapies, may falsely lead the counselor to assume that a higher percentage of client messages are symbolically coded, than is truly the case. This judgmental error occurs with excessive prima-facie attention to symptoms (which often have a sensationalistic tendency to attract spectator interest), with con-comitant neglect of the client as a direct perceiver and communicator of messages, in the form of content and process.

5.   Symptoms, particularly as measured in standardized psychological tests, are viewed relative to degree of correspondence with pathological character profiles upon which the tests have been standardized, and which may have been hypothesized as diagnostic categories by the therapist, early in the treatment process. Symptoms, however, also have evaluative significance when measured against themselves over time, so the concept of deviation has internal validity or significance. This is true, particularly as symptom patterns (nature, timing, strength) change when measured against baseline flexibility, strength, degree of symbolization, amount of constraint on the personality, and co-variation (positive or negative) with other idiosyncratic psychodynamics. Many intricate changes of a quantitative nature cannot be assessed, when only nominally compared to a stationary norm group;

but assume dynamic fluidity and patterned interactive motion, when measured over time with other concurrent symptoms, and against their own base.[37]

6.   The production and manifestation of pathological symptoms, are suggested by several authors as the gateway into a deviant role set,[38] with norms, boundaries, performance expectations, and some privileges of membership (or punishments for role relinquishment), sustaining continued attitudinal and behavioral consonance with new role requirements.[39] What may occur is a form of "spiral action"[40] or chain. This pushes clients to deeper levels of confirmed deviancy once they are aware they have crossed previously forbidden boundaries, and when they experience symbolic losses with cognitive dissonance, if they do not more fully actualize new deviant character styles (even if only transient). Once operationalized, these role behaviors may be partly maintained by the symptomatic manifestations, as seen and reacted to by self and others (including professionals). Psycho-dynamically, clients can experience so much initial guilt for the normative transgression represented by symptom development, that progressively exacerbated symptoms are necessary to (a) justify the degree of guilt, (b) eventually produce psychological or social punishment, which is severe enough to provide retribution satisfactory to the wounded ego, or (c) provide a pleasurable freeing of the inner controlled child, to enjoy forbidden fruits of ultra-autonomous (socially deviant) behavior. In these cases, each new and deeper level of deviance may become a sufficient and necessary condition for further deviance, which in turn has a self-reinforcing dimension.

If the aforementioned developmental, sequential (nonrandom), and inter-dependent pattern of symptomatology is a correct interpretation, the significant evaluative questions relate to (a) whether there is rationale to measure consequent symptoms, as long as initial predisposing conditions are assessed; (b) whether a cumulative indexing or valence-loading scheme is necessary, to accurately determine accumulating potency and causal strength (for symptoms that follow) of each symptom level; (c) whether different inputs and theoretical rationales are necessary for variable levels of symptom patterning; (d) the degree to which prediction of future symptom manifestations is possible, through measurement of kinetic energy associated with clients' perceptions of their degree of role demand and involvement at each level; (e) ability of evaluators to correlate the nature of clients' perceptions of their own symptoms (and changes in this variable), with changing natures of the empirically demonstrated symptoms themselves; and (f) the efficacy of factor analysis or factor analytic type conceptualizations, to understand the associations and influence of specific client character traits, as they vary independently and in combination, with various symptoms at each cumulative level.

In all cases, the deviant symptom itself becomes an independent variable (rather than perceived as reactive client fixation or ego strength, etc.), with circular and reciprocal effects on the client's psychodynamic system. Herein, relevancy in life may relate to creation of imbalance between conformity and deviance, where growth evolves from the thesis/antithesis tension which necessarily evolves.[41]   Unfortunately, the entire process, however defined and operationalized, is excessively complicated by the multivariate nature of personal feeling, behavior, and societal influence, which provide access or blockage to deviant or conforming options for adaptation.

From the perspective of social learning; actions, intrapsychic processes, and environmental activities collectively function as interrelated determinants,[42] so personal anticipations influence outcome behaviors.   Also, the environment's response may cause confirmations or modifications of the original expectations, and confirm or refute the environmental stereotypical normative categories for defining behaviors.[43]

Clinical evaluation in this regard, requires assessment of symptoms as they represent all interactive influences, and as their behavioral manifestation represents an amalgamation of each variable in a new dynamic state. This occurs only when they interact, and not with any area of influence singularly. These areas of interaction occur at junctions of two variables, or at a vortex where all join together. The evaluation, therefore, of interactively determined symptoms, requires not only behavioral assessment, but also the clinician's analysis of antecedent, as well as consequent, cognitive decisions. These are based on the client's perceptions of the interactive contingency values relative to their personal needs, and their expectations of how current symptoms (behavioral manifestations) affect subsequent outcomes for them.[44]

Supporters of stringent behavioral approaches to evaluation, may tend to downplay concerns with intrapsychic constructs of the interactive self. The author strongly feels that this part of experiential reality and environmental reality must be viewed singularly, as well as interactively. This provides a correct and holistic picture of clients' symptoms, the reasons for those symptoms, and a comprehensive perspective about the interactive personal and social process by which normative and qualitative criteria are applied to any set of behaviors or symptoms, relative to personal and community need fulfillment. An important note for clinicians, is that there may be slight, moderate, or wide disparity between symptoms that clients perceive as significant for evaluative focus, and those addressed in counseling.   This also means that behavior defined as evaluatively significant, may be a defensive maneuver to provide diversion by either counselor or client.   As noted by Prager and Tonalra,[45] clients are more motivated and capable of becoming involved in the evaluation process than professionals give them credit for, and acceptable and desirable standards of behavior are very different between clients and counselors.   In the above-noted study, counselors emphasized indices of role functioning, coping skills, and small group behaviors, whereas clients preferred foci on situational determinants of anxiety, depressive symptoms, and social-emotional self-perception.   These interests included self-esteem and self-reliance, where affect and cognition were valued more highly by clients, than role functions valued by professionals.   However, it is important to note that clients were more intellectual than emotional in processes of defining relevant behaviors in a group context; but also rejected measurement and diagnostic frameworks which restricted them to dichotomous outcome categories, rather than to wider ranges of behavioral manifestations for the assessment process.

As noted by other authors, professionals typically maintain exclusive control of the treatment, diagnostic, and evaluation processes, even though increasing research, documents differences in perceptions between clients and mental health professionals in terms of standards, rehabilitation concepts, outcomes, and success or improvement criteria.[46]

Client Reference Groups and Culture

In considering evaluation which empirically reflects the client's existing and potentially changing nature, adaptive success, and orientation toward reality, the clinician also works indirectly and symbolically with the client's reference group or culture.   This includes real or imaginary groups of individuals (heroine images) or normative values, life principles, or role prescriptions (i.e., "passivity") which guide the client's attitudes and behaviors; and concomitant self-evaluation of conformity and ultimate benefits (psychological, social, physical, spiritual, etc.) of membership or exclusion.   This parallel evaluative process, wherein the client judges his or her own conformity or deviance along varying scales, can occur through support or ostracism of group members, or can be hypothesized/fantasized to exist in the client's imaginative subjective judgment

Evaluatively, each reference the cultural or other social group has developed, represents characteristics which systematically insure its survival; and must be interpreted, integrated, translated, or otherwise consciously dealt with by the therapist, as long as clients actually or symbolically retain, desire, or reject membership in the group. In some cases, clients may not be aware of the relevant norm groups in their lives,[47] which may signify different degrees of independent or dependent behavioral contingencies for them. They additionally provide other evaluative categories related to (a) awareness of cultural foundation; (b) degree of ability to identify and access supports from groups or normative ideals; (c) justification for levels of anxiety in nonsupported and "non-referenced" social milieu; and (d) adequacy of efforts (or reasons for inability) by other reference group members, to provide a useful social and psychological framework to assist clients' self and social actualizations.

Degree of individual pathology is always a factor clinicians should filter through a cultural (self and client) perspective, prior to definitive labeling or decision-making in treatment. They must consider degree to which the client is aware of significant reference groups to which he or she has psychosocial-behavioral allegiance, particular specifications of membership, and degree of control the client allows the group to assume, particularly in the absence of other forms of personal or family evaluative feedback.[48]

One study[49] notes five determinants of comparison by which evaluative decisions are made, relative to reference groups:

1. degree of group attractiveness, influences significance of group norms[50] to the individuals;

2. degree of interpersonal vs. task orientation of the individual, defines adequacy of communication between the individual and the group, and also determines the group's emotional significance in the client's life;[51]

3. degree to which the individual sees the self and group referenced images as similar, strengthens power attributed to the group's norms and guidelines;[52]

4. degree to which an individual views similar[53] performance capabilities between self and group members, and relatively commensurate expectations for performance outcomes;[54] makes the group a more comfortable evaluative source;

5. degree of internal vs. external loci of individual control, determines amount of dependence on the group for socialization and direction,[55] and also

influences group cohesiveness,[56] and reduces members' attention to non-group sources of evaluative data.[57]

The clinician should remember that the ways clients use reference groups cannot be underestimated, and objective evaluative decisions must be carefully viewed through the eyes of the culture-bound client. Reference groups have a strong influence, in general and specific frameworks for clients' orientation and definition of reality, and impact alternatives/characteristics they attribute to self for adaptation or maladjustment. Extrapolating from Cloward and Ohlin's theory of differential opportunity,[58] this means that each client reviews personal and social opportunities or avenues of success or failure relative to cultures; and as available to clients for learning, through cultural heritage, artifacts, language, tradition, and other communicative and symbolic forms of enculturation. This results in a culturally specific social self[59] as an interpersonal construct, learned and perceived in the presence of significant others.

In the clinical evaluative situation, the client's ownership, symbolic representations, and actualization of cultural heritage and impact, reveal significant evaluative concerns, which will be enumerated separately.

1.   The client's inclination to even seek help, and view the culture-bound social agency as a legitimate source of psychological assistance, is influenced by the congruence between client and agency culture, and the counselor's success at bridging gaps which are discovered.

      a.   In one regard, effectiveness of interventive inputs is a function of communication, especially *stimulus-response congruence* and *content relevance*. The meaning of a response is perceived to be relevant to one's cultural definition, with expectations that the content will help in problem resolution. Therapeutic messages whose content does not mesh with the client's, or which are delivered in a culturally deviant style, may reduce motivation and outcome success.[60]

      b.   Measurement emphases, here, relate to degree of client and counselor comfort, congruence of agency and client perceptions, collateral definitions of causality or symptoms, and capability of clients to positively value and utilize therapeutic inputs—without unnecessary interference of the individual's cultural conflict attitude or expectation regarding treatment.[61] Practitioners must be especially cognizant, in their culturally correlated degree of variance from differing client expectation, and their own degrees of freedom dealing with their demands for conformity to professional or cultural norms.

2.   The client's ability to activate social and interpersonal opportunities outside the treatment situation to operationalize treatment goals, is also a major concern, as he or she needs to manifest indices of behavioral growth.

     a.   Evaluation must be sensitive to reduced capabilities of clients to register positive behavioral adaptability, and clinicians must develop indices of success within culturally acceptable alternatives (e.g., expecting assertive behaviors among passive Indian clients, where non-Indian society also punishes non-passivity). Measurement scales should be sensitive enough to denote very minor changes, where clients perform non-stereotyped and atypical behaviors, to comply with treatment goals not culturally comfortable for them.

     b.   No matter how effective a treatment technique is, outcomes are all influenced by a variety of unknown extra-treatment experiences of clients, where such factors are reinforced by social tradition and cultural norms. They are difficult, if not impossible, to control in the regular course of treatment.[62]

3.   Differential significance of any form of adaptation in culturally foreign atmospheres, and implications for client strength and flexibility as evidenced by retention of their own identity, in addition to adaption of identities and relationships in new cultures; are major concerns for evaluators who interpret meanings behind specific behaviors.

     a.   Evaluatively, this suggests seeded weightings of adaptive efforts for clients who approach different cultural situations, as a sign of possibly greater capability than required for clients within their own culture (especially true now for women and men changing some areas of stereotypical role performance).

     b.   Another evaluative dimension, is the degree of integration of two or more culturally-specific traits. This includes evaluation of new ego structures created by this process of behavioral and conceptual alternating movement between cultural perceptions, cognitive patterns, feeling states, or behavioral repertoires. This may require open-ended assessment explanations prior to fixed alternative categories of behavior, which might not include these processes of cultural interfusions.

4.   The counselor must be sensitive to the client's definition of adaptative behaviors, in response to client considerations of culturally discriminating forces. Pathology of the behavior, as dictated by the dominant culture, may obscure the counselor's appreciation of the value of these reactive

defenses (e.g., black paranoia in the face of real white distrust and aggression).

    a.   An important concern, is the normative scale used for behavioral measures, by which conceptual average behaviors are defined by the evaluating clinician. This includes standard deviations of each client from normative expectations, and analysis of how normative perspectives overlap or converge. Some examples of different normative scales for populations (hence the normal curve design), and how clients might be variously positioned at the same time, when viewed from different normative perspectives,[63] are noted in Figure 1.

    b.   The meaning of client behavior strictly depends on which normative scale he or she, and the clinician, use for interpretation. These behaviors can be positive or negative, or exemplify varying amounts of growth or regression, depending on which standard of conformity or deviance is envisioned. Referenced interpretations, of course, influence clinical inputs utilized, and the meanings of all potential outcomes relative to concepts of health, morality, happiness, productivity, adaptability, or responsibility.

The relativity of these normative standards infused into the clinical evaluative milieu, is also significant in decisions about overall rationality and relevancy of various treatment goals, and types of expectations formally or inadvertently communicated by the therapist.

One example is the communication of unrealistic optimism to reassure clients,[64] when there is little reason to assume the environment will yield opportunities for them to achieve fantasized hopes, or unrealistic socially limited behaviors or statuses: "In the psychosocial perspective, people are viewed within an optimistic framework . . . within a social context in which the interests, goals and aspirations of others are acknowledged and accommodated."[65]

Another situation occurs when counselors work with clients to identity, express, understand, accept, or change conflictual, hidden, or unacceptable feelings: "The uncovering, redirection, freeing and refocusing of feelings have of course been among the distinguishing objectives of psychotherapy,"[66] with the "expectation that (this) process of helping the client to work on the problem and achieve some degree of success will strengthen the client's capacity to manage for himself (herself)"[67] outside the therapeutic milieu. "The counselor offers a corrective experience to clients when he (or she) demonstrates that such things as

anger, sexual drive, feelings of inferiority . . . will be understood, not con-
demned or rejected."[68]

Figure 1
Various Normative Scales for Perceiving Client Status

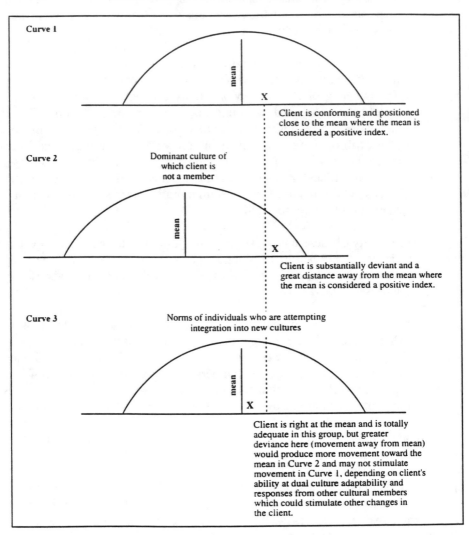

Curve 1

mean

X

Client is conforming and positioned
close to the mean where the mean is
considered a positive index.

Curve 2

Dominant culture of
which client is
not a member

mean

X

Client is substantially deviant and a
great distance away from the mean where
the mean is considered a positive index.

Curve 3

Norms of individuals who are attempting
integration into new cultures

mean

X

Client is right at the mean and is totally
adequate in this group, but greater
deviance here (movement away from mean)
would produce more movement toward the
mean in Curve 2 and may not stimulate
movement in Curve 1, depending on client's
ability at dual culture adaptability and
responses from other cultural members
which could stimulate other changes in
the client.

Although free and healthy expression of feelings may enhance relationships in close-knit primary groups and families, today's impersonal world appears, in many respects, to discourage sensitive human alliances on a broad scale. Many families experience an impersonal "cataclysmic upheaval,"[69] as social forces of change alter culture and lifestyle concerning sensitivity, emotional stability, and security among their members:

> "The disorders of our society, resulting from radical change, invade and infect our daily family and community life. These disorders include the combined impact of technology, a state of continuous war, racial conflict, crowding, violence, and the invasion of personal freedom, the decline of humanistic and spiritual values, and the loss of human connectedness. From these influences emerge the 'mass man,' the orientation to power, manipulation, acquisition, and a trend toward depersonalization. . . . People are being mechanized, dehumanized, brutalized . . . and they no longer seem to care."[70]

The counselor fostering emotional self-expression among clients, without introducing an evaluative orientation to environmental limitations, and teaching guidelines for selective emotional response (survival skills), may provide contradictory and confusing expectations about use of emotional expression, when the environment is not equally supportive.[71] The idealistic or realistic stance which serves as part of the foundation for counseling, simultaneously dictates which independent and dependent variables will be defined for evaluation, the probability which influences degrees of freedom to vary for any particular client, and how positive or negative indices of adequacy are interpreted, for clients and their professional helpers.

Another related concern, with specific behavioral goals for therapy,[72] is the extent of the client's visibility and interconnectedness in social systems, where behavioral change impacts equilibrium of other individuals, consequently influencing the client's opportunity to adapt to his/her environment. Obviously, the degree to which the client occupies more observable public social roles, also affects outcomes, because of increased number of actors who contribute to definitions of reality.

Client change could threaten the security of other individuals in the system who must also survive, and who reciprocally meet emotional needs of the clients in nonthreatening situations. This is especially true where expectations and outcomes are predetermined by formal or informal norms, to the disadvantage of clients who attempt to "grow" beyond the tolerance limits and boundaries of their social environments.

Individuals more isolated from these complex interconnected roles, may have an easier time developing "ideally healthy" feeling-behavior configurations, with less reliance on societal institutions for emotional and survival needs, and without negative repercussions from systems defending their own equilibrium and existence.

Some counselors need to resolve personal inclinations to express utopian or idealistic values,[73] or erroneous cultural ideals, stereotypes, or impressions, as to not impinge on clients' rights to an honest depiction of reality[74] (given the subjectivity of the therapist). Clients should learn useful ways of coping and surviving in a realistically perceived world, with a repertoire of survival skills which take into consideration challenges, demands, norms, and operating procedures of their own (possibly harsh) social environment.

5.   Clients' proclivity to assume different assertive, dependent, active, passive, cooperative, or distrustful postures within treatment, must be viewed not only as an independent psychological process, but also as either positive or negative reflections of their cultural distance, perceived aberration, alienation, acceptance, and integration—relative to dominant cultural conditions. Incorrect definitions of pathological resistance, or ignorance, for example, may require alteration of treatment inputs, to avoid ineffective work with clients who have been culturally misinterpreted, stereotyped, or disenfranchised.

One study,[75] in fact, suggests that the extent of relevant new content introduced by workers in the course of interviews, is significantly related to level of counselors' training and type of client. Whether trained or not, workers introduce appreciably more new topics in interviews with compliant than with aggressive clients, but only with compliant clients do trained workers introduce more relevant content. With the aggressive client, untrained workers introduce more relevant content, and assume a markedly greater content leadership role in interviews with compliant rather than aggressive clients.

The potential reaction of clients to be "institutionalized through structure"[76] of the social service setting, especially affecting minority and disadvantaged clients, may result in the following self-perceptions and approaches to the therapeutic situation:

1. lack of personal confidence or security;
2. ambivalence and inconsistency in thought and behaviors;
3. confused goals and expectations;
4. psychological depression and depreciated self-esteem;
5. adversary orientations to defend against the oppressing enemy.[77]

In these cases, it is important to determine if ethnicity or any form of cultural uniqueness or specificity, are theoretically/philosophically explained in the counselor's mind, as categorical or transactional phenomena.[78] In the categorical sense, clients might be viewed as rigidly locked into cultural trait patterns, which are evaluated as resistant to change or adaptation, through the therapeutic process. For the same reasons, however, they might also be considered as more constant, reliable, and less resistant to varying dynamics of therapists' subjective input, which offers another type of confidence in interpreting behavioral meaning and change.

Within this stereotyped classification process, assessments can take on a nominal and qualitative dimension which proves too general, typically, to monitor specific behavioral/attitudinal indices. It points to prior categories of deviance or average expected behavior, which are often incorrect standards within which specific behaviors are interpreted. Measurement of these behaviors within categories, although potentially providing data on intra-group conformity or deviance, offers little potency for assessing categorically extraneous behaviors, which some clients develop to achieve greater ego-syntonic integration into the multicultural environment. Clients are often at a disadvantage within the categorical model, in developing a workable conceptual integration with professionals, because of the significance of culture in explaining social and psychological problems relative to etiology, symptom formation and symbolization, primary and secondary gain, courses of illness, nosology, roles of the sufferer, nature and expected outcome of treatment, and definitions of acceptable goals and state of resolution.[79] In trait theory,[80] the human condition is viewed as a relatively stable pattern of variables with presumably known dimensions and values, and high probability of predicting stimulus-response reactions with each state manifestation. With high anticipated predictability, the clinical evaluator can easily assume outcomes which don't exist, or explain unsuccessful outcomes as examples of negative traits (client resistance, cultural backwardness), without identifying a full range of relevant variables or stimulus-response relationship patterns. Dispersion of independent variables in the treatment situation (i.e., therapeutic inputs or interventions), may be restricted to coincide with narrow ranges of trait-specific outcomes.

The dilemma implies difficulty categorizing and analyzing differences and changes of client responses (comparing different clients or one client at different observation times), relative to motive, environmental contingencies, known or unknown abilities relative to the client's self-perception, temperament, patterns of self-esteem and mood, group pressure or stimuli, or variable influences of treatment skills. The client is squeezed into a priori trait response categories, which predestines the therapist to also be constricted by client trait definition (e.g., "I can only use these skills or approaches, because they are the only ones the client responds to"). This frees the counselor from responsibility for his/her negative input into therapeutic interchanges. In the transactional mode, the client is seen in a state of dynamic process of communication, role interdependence, conceptual interchange, and other activities, which involve cultural and non-cultural actions, to sustain or change culturally distinctive patterns. Within this focus, the client and therapist must be evaluated and measured relative to their interactive culturally integrating process, which either enhances or retards joint definitions of client adaptation. This happens not only in terms of association of client and therapist inputs to others' outcomes, but also new dimensions of client and therapist degree and type of transactional convergence.[81]

The major conceptual and methodological problem in the transactional model, is to develop an accurate taxonomy of transactional processes (number, strength, nature, onset, duration, change influences, effects, etc.),[82] and understand this phenomenon itself, as an outcome variable for evaluation.[83] It relates also, to change between fluctuating states, in the "integrative milieu"[84] of the transactional movement. Because of the significance of social process, which impacts ability of clients to adapt to society, and simultaneously influences provision or denial of avenues for adaptation, some practitioners may ask evaluative questions concerning their differential roles and ethical responsibilities of treating individuals or social groups/communities, which influences which areas of professional performance will be evaluated and, methodologically, how this is accomplished.

The concern with returning reasonably healthy clients to the milieu which contributed to their "illness," suggests that energy might be more productively expended through intervention with communities, organizations, social policies, and state and federal governments. This is a radical shift in "therapeutic" orientation of specifically defined roles with clients,[85] where clinicians have not been active or effective in macro-level interventions (except some who specifically occupy administrative, policy analysis, or other macro area roles).[86] The inference that "psycho" therapists assume client advocacy roles and develop new attitudes, resources, and skills[87] for "environmental modification,"[88] threatens personal security provided by the therapeutic role, and directly interdicts value premises which support the therapeutic process of healing. In any case, the counselor must consider basic evaluative questions about his or her degree of effectiveness, based on clearly-achieved outcomes with clients (especially long-term), which has to include criteria of client adaptability in the real world of here and now. This question should then be followed by examination of the most effective and efficient ways to produce the greatest impact on clients, and the society in which they live. This relates to basic value premises about causality and responsibility for maladaption, especially when clients manifest reactive symptomatology in their role of victim of pathological family development, social injustice, etc.

Any profession's commitment to broad issues of social welfare and justice, provides a valuable humanistic foundation and guiding principles to shape identity and direction of each practitioner, especially with broadly-defined ambitions for social justice, promoting psychosocial health, and combating ills of society's institutions and survival pattern.[89] Professionally-sanctioned concerns for human rights and dignities, therefore, are a unifying theme and ethical standard for all to share. However, clinical counselors performing face-to-face interventions with clients or their families, may espouse these global professional standards, yet question their personal opportunity or tactical capability to directly influence cultural norms or societal institutions, within a circumscribed, methodological world of therapeutic intervention. This includes concerns with the client's overall social status, role definition, equal opportunity and justice, or discriminatory experiences in culture, outside the therapist's office.[90]

Since it is unreasonable to expect clinical counselors to adopt roles as policy analysts or government planners, there is a critical question in determining how clinicians support social action aspirations of their professions through theory and technique, including evaluation, as a guiding question for input planning.[91] To appreciate the significance of clinical roles and skills in affirmative social action, the power of therapeutic techniques as agents of social change (individual attitudes and behaviors) must be illustrated. As an example, the powerful "expert role model and teacher" as noted by Okun and Rappaport,[92] depicts the counselor's incisive entry into family systems to change rules and stimulate new behaviors,[93] as a result of client submission to authority. This motivation to risk and change, evolves from client pain and disequilibrium, but requires a powerful, authoritative, directive, analytic, and energetic therapeutic posture to animate client or family, to perceive and change destructive process.

On an individual level, the cognitive restructuring of Ellis and Harper,[94] as well as the physical reinforcements of behaviorists,[95] suggest strong confrontation and control in defining and correcting undesirable attitudes or behaviors. In a more subtle source of therapeutic power, the development of intimate, trusting relationships in which clients feel safe and protected, often creates parental transference, wherein the counselor strongly influences feelings and emotions.[96] When the client relaxes defenses and anxiety, clinical access to inner thoughts and vulnerable feelings, provides analytic and interpretive capability as the authority defines needs, translates reality, and "orchestrates" conceptual process.[97]

Through dramatic interventions timed to accent emotions or expose conflicts, the counselor may manipulate client energy, and use communicative style and content to affirmatively illustrate, interdict, or change patterns of discrimination or prejudicial injustice, as they unfold within the client's repertoire of thoughts, feelings, or behaviors. The counselor can start and stop client communication, invalidate roles or attitudes through selective attention, raise anxiety around human rights issues by exposing or defining deviance,[98] and forcefully influence perceptions by analyzing reality, as the client yields to professional status and socially-validated expertise. The clinician can even exercise socially and culturally directed power, through evaluation and measurement of client outcomes and target behaviors, as case evaluation signals important areas in the client's life, and because "behavior might change by the very act of measurement itself."[99]

In the above examples, power is not only a function of the clinician's knowledge and skill, but is intricately connected to dynamics of therapeutic and evaluative process, though society's attribution of "exaggerated power and wisdom"[100] to its professional representatives.[101] Given the presence and importance of this strong influence, the critical question concerns its ethical[102] use or dormancy, in addressing issues of human rights and social justice among clinical clients. This is critical, as power occurs in the following areas of therapy and evaluation process, including processes of teaching and modeling, diagnosis, interpretation, and communication control.

With regard to specific theoretical approaches to situational assessment and treatment, which might facilitate a socially-conscious practice orientation, the term "social situation" is considered by many professions as a basic expression and concept to denote:

> ". . . the social functioning of persons in life situations, viewed with empathy and considerable objectivity, in terms of the meaning of the

situations for the self-realization and growth of individuals, with balanced concern for both inner and outer factors as they affect functioning . . . to see the wholeness of personality and situation, to assess multiple factors within the configuration, and to identify the crucial elements calling for intervention—to do all this with considerable effectiveness . . ."[103]

A renewed interest in situation theory, with its concern for interplay (trans-action) and holism of individual and social system, suggests awareness and analysis of domains of identity actualization, and categories of integrated out-comes, including both individual and milieu as one unit of reality.

In evaluating cultural situations which impact clients, the counselor should consider the following specific components, as factors needing measurement and evaluation:[104]

1.   the structural adequacy in providing resources, role occupants, ecological opportunities, and personal relationship options;
2.   cultural competency and completeness concerning values, symbols, roles, and norms as a guide to behavioral adaptation, and assimilation of a wide range of differentiated constituents, to balance need demands and resources;
3.   efficient and effective operational processes and relationship guidelines, to accomplish group goals, while insuring stability and balance for the system as it necessarily changes in the process;
4.   clear and accepted communicational mechanisms and philosophies for accessing the system, accepting resource allocations providing educative feedback, and negotiating changes in areas of deficiency and rewards for acceptable outcomes;
5.   elucidation and confirmation of definitions of reality domains in which the system offers security, nurturance, and opportunity for personal and col-lective control;
6.   availability of effective and satisfying external relationships, so there are continuities to provide trans-situational role reciprocity and longitudinal stability.

Client Motivation

Another factor impacting clinical evaluative thought and procedure, is the motivation with which the client approaches the therapeutic experience. Most authors agree that some clients are more "open"[105] to therapeutic influences than others, and degree of enthusiasm and dependence on therapy (and the therapeutic power of the healer), directly influence energy invested in eliciting appropriate and desired behaviors (perceived as positive outcome indices), or in distorting (exaggerating or hiding) negative behaviors to increase support or avoid rejection. Although a comprehensive matrix of client motivation postures and commensurate evaluative counter plans is still far from demonstrable, typical scenarios detailed in the literature, and in the author's practice experience, are noted in Figure 2.

As the reader can see in this outline, each varying degree of motivation in the left column (along an imaginary continuum of negative to positive), is accompanied by potential distortions in the client's perspective of the therapeutic situation, therapist reactions to these dependent perspectives, and finally, issues of validity/reliability/planning, necessary to approach the evaluative process comprehensively and competently.   These are only a selected listing of motivation-related problems, intended to alert the reader to general critical evaluative questions that must be asked, as each motivational dilemma material- izes and creates cumulative effects when operationalized in therapy. In casework, counseling, or psychotherapeutic process (including work with families and groups), each counselor must consider a comprehensive framework of client- centered motivational concerns, to ultimately make the best therapeutic and evaluative decisions. This is especially necessary to avoid the trap of simply accepting baseline motivational dispositions as evaluative constants, or viewing only bits and pieces of a complex array of bio-psychosocial factors.

In 1980, the publication of the American Psychiatric Association (APA) *Diagnostic and Statistical Manual of Mental Disorders III (DSM III),*[106] was a major step in more closely associating client characteristics with treatment considerations and processes, through its multiaxial system of diagnostic assessment.   In Axis IV, where treatment is planned relative to severity of stresses which accompany a particular personality category, consideration is given to clients' motivations for seeking help, given current life circumstances, socio- cultural background, and interpretation of their own life's stresses.[107]

Some specific motivational situations which might emerge within this framework of assessment, which have important evaluative impact, are enumer- ated as follows:

1.   There are questions for the clinician about how clients invest psychic, social, and physical energy, as participation will increase or decrease probable occurrence of selected target behavioral outcomes. Energy invest- ment may be related to personal validation and acceptance of particular goals as reasonable and legitimate; amount of attention invested in con- ceptualizing, remembering, and focusing on targets for change; effort

Figure 2
Motivational Scenarios and Associated Evaluation Counter-Measures

Client Motivational Posture	Possible Client Distortions	Possible Therapist Distortions	Validity/Reliability Issues for Measurement	Evaluative Plans
1. Desperation — Perceived need for emergency support, protection, nurturance, rescue with insufficient perceptions of personal capacity to mutually cooperate in change process	1a. Symptom exaggeration 1b. Manipulation for closeness, excessive helplessness and conformity	1a. Exaggerated impressions of pathology 1b. Anger, distance to counteract manipulation 1c. Attempts to rescue, overcontrol over nurturance	1a. Incorrect attention to empirical behaviors rather than intentions or self-perceptions 1b. Incorrect symptom selection — inverse indicator 1c. Prima facie strengths attributed to symptoms rather than symbolic values	1a. Use crisis rather than long term therapy theory 1b. Evaluation of short term objectives
2. Dependency and Security — Perceived need for external control, loss of "self," need to be trapped, retention of childhood roles, positions, "scripts"	2a. Projected internalized or symbolic anger 2b. Attention to helpless behaviors and impulse control 2c. Excessive valuation of closeness 2d. Excessive compliance and conformity to therapy goals and identification with therapist 2e. Excessive guilt and irresponsibility	2a. Viewing decreased anxiety as growth 2b. Incorrect support of client-therapist goal congruence 2c. Failure to support correct amounts of dependence 2d. Viewing independent growth as aggression or resistance 2e. Failure to define groups of clients who are always incapable of handling active participation required of most traditional therapies (i.e., passive culture)	2a. Values of indices of reduced anxiety vs. real goals of independence which will raise anxiety 2b. Accurate measurement of small degrees of dependent-independent continuum 2c. Careful indexing of conformity — deviance as inverse symbols of dependence and independence	2a. Measure "deviant" movement away from therapy controls 2b. Control excessive length of therapy 2c. Measure degree of compliance as inverse index 2d. Anti-"game" treatment techniques

Client Motivational Posture	Possible Client Distortions	Possible Therapist Distortions	Validity/Reliability Issues for Measurement	Evaluative Plans
3. Fluctuating motivation — Variable perceptions of adequacy, failure, gain-loss, safety — vulnerability etc. (clients are cyclical in motivation)	3a. Acceptance of too much responsibility for success — do not see interactive therapeutic dynamics 3b. Blaming others, projection, failure to see core personality conflicts (forest vs. trees), fear of change 3c. Shows only variables they feel comfortable having measured	3a. Narrow view of simple symptoms and obscuring of more complex symptom clusters 3b. Failure to view inadequate treatment techniques as independent variables 3c. Failure to view client termination as potentially positive 3d. Ignoring existentialist client posture or change and freedom to fluctuate 3e. View fluctuations as total pathology vs. periodic efforts to change, positive movement 3f. Confusion of accident and condition (see section on character disorders for more discussion)	3a. Question of accuracy of entire complex spectrum of symptoms as they reflect more abstract concepts of personality 3b. Inaccurate delineation of client behavioral cycles and pinpointing various positions on cycle when therapy begins, ends 3c. Measurement of structured rather than more meaningful unstructured variables 3d. Measurement of accidental variations and correlations of accident with therapeutic inputs	3a. Gearing treatment to correspond to positions on client cycle with variable techniques and evaluative indices 3b. Plan to correlate external symptoms with internal identity changes and fluctuations 3c. Measure total attitude-behavioral gestalt 3d. Treatment of characterological conditions rather than acute accidental or situational factors 3e. Unique nature of clients and their unpredictable place in history may make any fixed, schematic knowledge of them impossible, evaluative methods may need new mobility and changing nature

Client Motivational Posture	Possible Client Distortions	Possible Therapist Distortions	Validity/Reliability Issues for Measurement	Evaluative Plans
4. Positive motivation; client-therapist attractiveness, desire for help, compatible demographics: a. socioeconomic status b. values c. social reference groups d. fluency, sophistication level e. attitude toward hope f. marital status (Note: all the above are noted in various literature sources as conditions for client-counselor compatibility)	4a. Failure to attend to differences with therapist as example of independence and autonomy 4b. Good intentions but desires for unreachable goals as function of motivation to grow 4c. Client may over-analyze, explain, attend, etc., and miss bigger or more simplistic picture of psycho or relationship dynamics	4a. Reluctance to view controlling dynamics and ineffective skills of therapy since some success has already been negotiated via motivation 4b. Too optimistic or unrealistic in supporting some goals 4c. Combining non-close work with caring role with similar client may create confusion — need to sort out this dilemma 4d. Over-assessment of motivation to encourage tasks which are beyond psychologic capability and therefore lead to failure 4e. Inability to control personal biases and view client's goals and awareness as correct and valid - and failure to define negative or "pathologic" expressions as positive because of client's "open" process 4f. Failure to see proper dynamics or excessive amounts of theory because of client attractiveness	4a. Failure to accurately understand correct correlation between client's positive, more structured orientation and non-directive, unstructured therapy orientation (e.g., existentialism) 4b. Motivated client may also be successful in other social roles which mitigate against closeness. This healthy negative factor must be indexed in evaluative interpretations 4c. Correct evaluation of effort vs. accomplishment 4d. Adequacy of therapist's resources when client-therapist conflicts are similar and avoidance of some client conflicts	4a. Realistic ambiguity about closeness in social roles must not become part of pathologic assessment 4b. Designing coordinated plan to reward action toward goal, plus goal attainment scaling 4c. Separate measures of attractiveness from those relating to other relationship dynamics 4d. Consider need to match clients and therapists re: relatability

Client Motivational Posture	Possible Client Distortions	Possible Therapist Distortions	Validity/Reliability Issues for Measurement	Evaluative Plans
5. Total involuntary client, angry, forced, controlled, alienated, etc.	5a. Associate therapeutic agent with forced system 5b. Generalized responses 5c. Exaggerate symptoms to motivate unresponsive system 5d. Substitute distancing symptoms (anger, hostility, craziness) for symptoms of fear and vulnerability	5a. Generalize stereotypes to all clients		5a. Measure degrees of resistance on interval rather than dichotomous nominal scale 5b. Discover behavioral areas which are most independent from systemic control and generalized response 5c. Assess degree of manipulation by therapist to force motivational change 5d. Index generalized response to primitive system to degrees of expected motivation and change 5e. Measure intervention with non-client actors, significant others, society 5f. Measure awareness of deviance, understanding rather than unrealistic change 5g. Work on and measure alternate ways to express deviance with most probability for reduced damage to society/client commensurality. Think here about the role theory 5h. Measure degree of correctness of prediction of non-change by the worker 5i. Degree of effectiveness of social service system to not lose control, avoid manipulation, etc., and control own idealism

expended (in concert with the therapist's effort to produce a synergistic and more powerful effort) in overcoming pathological resistance; and courage clients demonstrate, in attempting new behaviors, especially with (a) personal histories of negative outcomes, (b) fantasies of negative future outcomes predicted on irrational regressive conceptions, and (c) prospects of real negative outcomes in the future, without tested assurance that survival will accompany new behavioral repertoires. The selection of planned outcomes involves tactical use of therapeutic inputs with clients, in a potential power-booster role relative to motivational level, which activates investment or withholding of energy, and contributes to successful outcome measures.

2. The clinician should also develop questions about clients' ranges of life interests and relevant events or goals, to which they attach motivational value.[108] Each unique cultural heritage, life script, vertical and horizontal philosophical focus on events, relationship, and interest, dictates the array of actual and symbolic behaviors and hypothetically-probable outcomes, which should not become dissonant with stable lifestyle habits or patterns. Clients should contribute to therapeutic efforts which plant seeds within their own backyards or those relatively adjacent, as the motivational curve may drop off when outcomes become culturally deviant or asymmetrical, within normal boundaries of existence and normative frames of reference.

As an adjunct to the motivational issue, in research examining self-concepts, vocational attitudes and preferences of black and white urban adolescents, Rosenthal, et al.[109] reiterate Super's[110] theory of vocational maturity. Life occupational themes, interests, and choices are an extension and manifestation of more basic self-concept patterns related to role consistency. This includes orientation toward future work roles, independence in decision-making, and preferences for vocational choices. Holland[111] also states that career interests and life events, are extensions of personality that bring consonance between personal and role orientations. Since self-concept is a function of development life history, experience contributes to this personality foundation, until a stable profile is consolidated, with distinctions emerging for separate cultural categories of clients.[112] Back to motivation, our third point follows:

3. Evaluation must also deal with clients' motivations as symbolic, direct, or indirect relations of satisfaction within the therapeutic relationship. The degree of satisfaction with experience, should logically determine amount of influence they allow their counselor to exercise, and energy invested in change. Unfortunately, each client represents a different agenda for

satisfaction, which must be carefully outlined as early as possible, so the clinician can correctly direct influences (inputs), to corroborate forms of satisfaction which lead to growth, or plan indirect counterinsurgent influences. The agendas will [1] provide temporary or pseudo-satisfaction, while other strategies are slowly introduced (independent variable alternating or combined pairing techniques), [2] confront defensive or unhealthy positions of satisfaction, and offer emotional rewards to the client for behaviors mutually exclusive of less-healthy activities, or [3] confront pseudo-types of satisfaction and regressiveness, to produce anxiety, create awareness of conflict, and force the client to struggle for independence, within peripheral supportive (but not directly reinforcing) parameters of the treatment alliance.

Typical satisfaction postures the client may adapt, which the counselor must quickly define and understand, are as follows:

a. satisfaction with the growth struggle, the anxiety associated with painful self-awareness, and excitement of achieving feared/forbidden behavioral outcomes (this can vary with different rates of growth which are attempted);
b. satisfaction with attention or support provided by the interested counselor (validation of the client's self, adequacy, or significance), irrespective of particular growth outcomes, and often diminishing as confrontation or anxiety result from insight-oriented therapies;
c. satisfaction with the dependency and regressive security of transference (child protected by parent), which may inversely vary with amounts of pressure from the therapist to change to independent decision-making autonomy, and internal superego development;
d. satisfaction with congruence of client-therapist content opinions or similarity of personality style, which may fortify defensive excuses the client uses to avoid anxiety and conflictual situations;
e. satisfaction with the success of acting out defenses, manipulations, false scenarios of growth, active and passive aggressions, and goal failures, which establish therapeutic relationships as a corroborative and reinforcing framework for defense, and set up the counselor as a socially legitimate repository of the client's conflictual feelings.

These types of clients frequently pursue resolution of subsidiary problems to achieve a partial, but safe, gain, so as not to tackle really traumatic problems in their lives. This involves presenting a false (e.g., physical symptom) or moving target to the therapist (symptom generalization and frequent changes, i.e., hysteria, hypochondria, etc.), projecting problems to others (paranoid), or becoming a therapist for the therapist (rescuer). Some clients helplessly need external control, others need to be punished by the counselor to avoid more serious fantasized pain of rejection, and still others reject closeness through emotional manipulation, against being vulnerable and hurt (e.g., psycho-sociopathic personality).

The important message for the clinician/evaluator, is to discuss type, direction, and forcefulness of each client's satisfaction pattern, so therapeutic inputs can be appropriately adjusted to maximize, minimize, or control this facet of the process of client awareness and cooperation.

4. There are also questions concerning clients' psychosocial capabilities to handle anxiety, honestly reveal inner-most fears and conflicts, and make changes in the following areas:

    a. develop new concepts, new definitions of old concepts, or new behaviors, to provide a fuller range of opportunity for adaptation, or reduce number of excessive cognitive concepts or behaviors, which overwhelm their system's capability to respond;

    b. develop new conceptual, philosophical, or normative categories to explain the concepts or behaviors mentioned in (a) above, or to reduce or consolidate them so each thought, feeling, or action can be integrated into an acceptable predetermined framework, so as not to produce conflict;

    c. develop skills and processes of associating or connecting the concepts/behaviors in (a) above, with their conceptual ego-syntonic explanatory categories in (b). Of course, clients' capabilities determine the motivation to accomplish a difficult job with insufficient *tools,* the probability of failure (especially if a failure life script has already been established) if they lack ability to overcome obstacles, or probability of success if they have the right tools, but lack ability to handle new challenges once elementary success is achieved. In this regard, the following should be included in the formula for reaching a conclusion about motivation-related capability:

        (1) degree of previous emotional trauma, as this relates to (1) awareness of conflict, (2) permission the client gives the counselor to enter the protected recesses of the vulnerable and

wounded psyche, (3) basic levels of autonomy, as preliminary and necessary foundation units of capability, and (4) current processes in the client's inner or social life, which continue to produce trauma, weakness, irrationality, etc.;

(2)   relationship capability as an arena to test new manifestations of growth, to allow (1) acceptance of the counselor as a teacher and role model, (2) tolerance of initial therapeutic dependence, to stabilize the regressing or deteriorating ego, for growth within a nurturant milieu, (3) ability to risk and be honest, and (4) ability to handle eventual loss of the therapist, and continue life autonomously;

(3)   insight capability to understand (1) varying ways the self can be explained, and (2) cognitive and social processes by which self-concept develops, and dynamics by which these processes change and are causally linked to antecedent events and desired future outcomes;

(4)   level of personal anxiety (as well as anxiety with the client's primary social groups, as homeostatic equilibrium might be disrupted by client healthy behavior) which is related to (1) strength of defenses and level of regression, (2) length of time defenses have been operating (onset of trauma), (3) social supports or reinforcements for the client's pathology, (4) the client's proclivity for response generalization and symptom substitution, (5) degree of symbolism attached to symptoms, and (6) each client's unique fantasies of catastrophic consequences in his or her life, if defenses fail and emotional nurturance becomes nonexistent (what happens if regression runs its full course).

5.   Finally, the client's motivation may directly influence, and be influenced by, actual selection of target problems (not necessarily behavioral outcome indices), which fall into the following categories, accompanied by built-in levels of motivation due to the nature of the problem itself:

a.   problems of immediate cognitive concern, as primary foci in the client's mind, and to which the client provides immediate self-rewards as resolution is accomplished;

b.   problems as detours in psychosocial growth and development, necessary to gain more permanent growth, and which must be resolved before other issues (which follow temporally or developmentally);

c.   problems which cause the most pain or aversive consequences in the client's mind, and require attention to alleviate anxiety or provide emotional stability, to address other significant, but not necessarily more subjectively-painful, issues;

d.   problems most easily corrected, when the client needs evidence of success, and self-confidence to handle difficult issues at a later time (complexity of problems relates to number of real and fantasized actors involved in the client's life, and variables with which the actors collectively must deal).

A separate but related issue, is the voluntary vs. involuntary nature of the client's referral and participation in counseling (e.g., negative legal consequences attached to noncompliance with planned regimen). One discussion by Murdach,[113] relates to practice situations in which clients are forced by parents, spouses, and police/courts, to seek assistance from social service agencies. Conflict[114] representing a different structure and set of expectations from voluntary treatment situations, requires interventions designed more to redress power imbalance, than relieve individual suffering, with negotiation (bargaining and persuasion) as the critical input factor. In nonvoluntary situations, clients often assume partisan[115] and self-serving antagonistic roles, with variable definitions of the problem, objectives, energy used to achieve outcomes, and attention to influences of professional input. In many situations, inputs to be evaluated may, nontypically, include negotiation, bargaining, contingency management, manipulation, persuasion, or detachment. Furthermore, some studies show these skills as effective and ethical parts of clinical intervention,[116] incorporating a more holistic[117] and relative view of clinical influence[118] and helping.[119]

In evaluation related to the uses of power with involuntary clients, counselors must initially insure they can ethically accept the degrees of control which seem necessary to some mental health, family service, or welfare organizations; and also insure their input behavior is consistent with sound theories of growth and change, upon which they fashion their practices. Outcomes may then be measured as specific observable behaviors; and in terms of counselor projections about motivational longevity of these behaviors, competency in negotiations relative to power differentials, and client awareness of feelings and conflicts about contingency situations which cannot be changed.

Counselors can also measure motivation as a separate phenomenon from mandated behavioral outcomes, especially as inner psychological changes help the client grow in small degrees. These may be antithetical to the dependency required of "good clients," but may be products of qualitative involvement with the counselor. Regarding all aforementioned motivational concerns, the evaluator can define the situation and plan treatment effectively, by following these procedural steps:

1.   Develop a comprehensive and collectively-exhaustive categorization of all variables related to motivation which potentially enhance, delay, or alter the eventual course of therapy.

2.   Conceptualize differing amounts, potencies, and strengths of each of these variables, and rank them in some hierarchy, so clear differences can be seen.

3.   Develop a formula to conceptually add, subtract, multiply, or divide each motivational factor with all other treatment considerations, to give a quantifiable or qualifiable value that articulates the potential for interventive success.

With the above mathematical-type model, each motivational factor can be compared to others, so the worker can more easily predict probability of success, given hypothesized ways each client may systematically help or hinder counseling with his or her motivational input.

Now that broad issues of client definition, deviance as a phenomenon, reference groups and culture, and motivation have been presented as foundation concerns, it may help to understand additional evaluative issues of traditional diagnostic classifications of clients. These areas include neuroses, personality or character disorders, childhood syndromes, and psychotic or borderline conditions.

Neurosis

Neuroses[120] involve developmentally-oriented psychodynamic syndromes, manifested by anxiety through a physiologic disturbance, or symbolically represented through rigid behavioral deviance (defenses). The internal struggles between unconscious and conscious needs are characterized by insufficient resolution, through either internal or external relations. There are, of course, many theories about the significance and processes of symptom manifestation and functionality, and as Rogers[121] points out, there is still uncertainty about whether the counseling goal is eliminating symptoms, reorganizing the psyche, treating disease entities, or dealing with imbalance between individual and societal adjustment.

Symbolic and Developmental Considerations

With a broad view of neurosis in mind, the clinical evaluator must remember that therapeutic intervention and assessment occur at two primary domains of the client's reality. In the first, the current adult struggles to deal with anxiety as a focal point of the illness (which includes ramifications of defensive symptoms, which are attempts to handle anxiety); in the other, are underlying symbolic childhood intrapsychic conflicts whose turmoil, especially as consciousness is approached, actually causes the anxious reaction. In this light, the therapist assesses several levels of actual and symbolic dynamics, often interactive simultaneously.

The most internalized and difficult factor to assess, is the client's emotional need deprivation, specifically concerning childhood ideations and values relative to needs, including (1) the legitimate right to "need," and to have had support for various levels of adequacy from primary caregivers (usually parents); (2) understandable feelings of fear, rejection, anger, and isolation, when this empty cup is perceived relative to manifested current life situations, or recollected when repressive defenses do not retain these awarenesses within unconsciousness; and (3) confusing desire to retain or regain closeness with parental sources of nurturance, while simultaneously realizing that this necessitates dependence, loss of autonomous identity, and return to childhood inadequacy. Specific evaluative problems within this typical neurotic conflictual scenario, are discussed separately in the following paragraphs:

1.   The first, involves accurate measurement of levels of childhood emotional deprivation, as a foundation upon which conflict emerges and anxiety becomes manifest, so that these indices can be compared over time to determine degree, direction, potency, and type of change connected to varying input strategies. Evaluation also necessitates:

   a.   development of current empirical referents for need deprivation/ satisfaction, which have direct linkage to childhood past experiences;
   b.   development of referents which take into account cumulative changes in needs, as goals of each growth stage are accomplished or failed;
   c.   development of measurement strategies and analytic paradigms which differentiate actual from irrationally-perceived deprivations, along with secondary gains and systemic variables, that function to maintain distortions which are inaccurate representations of reality;
   d.   development of valid and reliable classification categories to pinpoint the client's position or degree of advancement at each development

level, so a corresponding category of treatment input can be correlated for appropriate and need-related rehabilitative actions;

e. awareness of dimensions of fear, horror, disintegration, and cata-strophic consequence attached to childhood primary process thoughts/ emotions (representing the child's fantasized anticipations of continued need frustration or feared parental rejection), and how this cognitive and emotional material is transformed as a neurotic compromise (symptom), with loss to the client each time energy is expended for this emotional manipulation;

f. assessment of the client's "relative autonomy,"[122] with delineation of ego functions which survived childhood conflictual struggles, and decisions as to how to use each strength to counteract personality deficits;

g. assessment of how the client perceives the self, as compared to actual behaviors for learning about self-validation, past emotional experiences to assess etiology, and current rationality, (i.e., "blind stops");[123]

h. measurement of irrationality employed by the client, in identifying needs or need deprivations, so that even minute changes in cognitions can be behaviorally reinforced or detected as signs of regression.

2. The counselor should also be concerned with taxonomy relative to the adequacy, need-meeting capability, motivation to change, and relationship closeness of the client's actual parents (or other primary nurturers during key growth stages). This is a road map in helping the client (a) regress in some aspects of relationships with parents, to regain selected nurturant goals, (b) enter therapy together with parents, to discuss previous conflicts and structure new adult relationship, or (c) discontinue relationship efforts with seriously pathological parents, and seek other internal or peer relationship resources.

3. Progressive measurement of stressors and avenues of adaptation within the client's current life circumstances, is a third component of comprehensive psychosocial evaluation. It includes the impact these events have on perceptions of personal adequacy, threat to need fulfillment, and danger to the psychic system (symbolic meaning of anxiety), with continued participa-tion in social relationships, roles, and positions:

a. in neurosis, maladaptive behaviors are responsive primarily to anxiety, and secondarily to the symbolized emotional conflict, so the clinician must assess events which cause symbolic anxiety, in addition to abili-ties of the client to remove, alter, or neutralize these real situational events, to allow time/distance and sufficiently-reduced anxiety for fortification of other personality strength;

b.   development of indicators of the client's system of classification, symbolization, and emergency decision-making vis-à-vis varying types, intensities, and frequencies of stressors is very important, along with understanding formulas to predict how these separate factors are combined to determine varying client reactions,[124] (i.e., stressor 1 x stressor 2 + stressor 3, stressor 4 - deprivation factor 1 - ? + adaptive capability 3 = acute flight reaction, etc., etc.);

c.   assessment of factors in the client's social systems which heighten, neutralize, lessen, or have no effect on potency/significance/range of stressors and supports, is also an evaluative necessity, including family dynamics, peer relationships, characteristics of other social roles, education, socioeconomic status, culture, intelligence, age, gender, etc.;

d.   the clinician must insure measurement of the process (including times, places, and frequencies) by which the client is aware of the symbolic interconnection between current events (stressors), past conflicts, adaptive capability, personality deficits, anxiety, and defenses/symptoms, including changes in client awareness of these psychosocial dynamic relationships;

e.   classification of categories of past attempts to activate environmental support should be measured, along with degree of energy utilization, efficiency, cost effectiveness, specific skills, and cognitions, necessary to activate and utilize new categories of support.

4.   Due to "pathological persistence"[125] of neurotics' childhood needs and emotional conflicts into adulthood, the clinician is hard-pressed to measure these factors in the unconscious. Although insight, self-awareness, hypnosis, gestalt, or other techniques can bring unconscious ideations into preconscious or conscious awareness, there is never assurance these constructs are valid, representative samples, of the unconscious thought population. Measurement schemes require sophisticated probing capabilities and monitoring techniques, to compare individual thought content with previous ideations, for degree of congruency. It is also necessary to identify each pattern of conflict symbolization, so the therapist can make necessary conversions to (a) identify which behaviors represent conflicts in past or present, and (b) hypothesize degree to which unconscious material is converted into empirical indicators, after transformation processes have occurred. These "missing parts of self"[126] are the elusive prey of the insight-oriented counselor, who questions which externalized behaviors

represent internalized conflicts and, which external behaviors represent absence of targeted neurotic conflicts. This is a particular methodological problem, because evaluation must weigh the reliability and validity of the following possible combinations:

a. absence (or progressive decrease) of external behavior representing desired absence (or progressive decrease) of parallel inner conflict;

b. absence of external behavior representing change in symbolism, but continued presence of inner conflict;

c. absence of external behavior representing more serious regression/ conflict development, and incapability of the psychodynamic system to make symbolic transformations;

d. absence of external behavior representing decrease in stimulus or rewards for that behavior in present circumstances (unrelated to symbolic or actual inner conflicts);

e. absence of external behavior representing causal connections in therapy transactions, reflecting the client's conformity to expectations, suggesting either dependence (as one minor conflict), or rational behavioral choice necessary to receive contingent help, unrelated to inner conflict;

f. presence (or progressive increase) of external behavior which is new strength, representing desired absence (or progressive decrease) of parallel inner conflict;

g. presence of external behavior which is new strength, but is still incapable of decreasing targeted inner conflict;

h. presence of external behavior representing change in symbols, with continued presence or worsening of inner conflict;

i. presence of external behavior representing new independent variables in the psychodynamic system or external environment, which may or may not relate to targeted inner conflicts;

j. presence of external behavior which must be combined with other behavioral additions or deletions, prior to probability of change in inner conflicts (positive or negative synergy);

k. presence of behaviors whose outcome effects or antecedent causes are so confusing or multivariate in nature, as to make it unclear whether they are adaptive or defensive;

l. absence or presence of external behaviors which are signs of positive client growth, but are given negative interpretive meaning through biased decision-making paradigms of the therapist, providing useless evaluative input and consequent confusing messages to the client, which may result in consequent negative behavior for her or him;

m. presence or absence of external behaviors not representing inner conflicts, but not perceived by the client as part of his or her reality and, therefore, have limited self-awareness payoff.

Since each client displays unique characteristics for the aforementioned combinations of symbolic indices,[127] diagnosis of individual uniqueness is extremely critical. Classical diagnostic methods may not clearly differentiate individuality, because of overemphasis on common personality traits which have not dealt with idiosyncratic behavior. Closely related to the above issues, is the evaluator's concern with the intricate relationship between inner and outer conflicts, and degree of pathology supported by the psychodynamic and external environments of the client. It is difficult to measure, correlate/factor, and analyze specific variables in these environments that reinforce fixation perceptions, or block alternate avenues of adaptability (negative reinforcements for growth-oriented thoughts, feelings, or behaviors). These variables often act independently, serially in cumulative linear fashion, or concurrently in a systemic, multiple-impact fashion; so identifying independent variables, and differentiating *necessary* from *sufficient* conditions for conflict to be reactivated, are nearly impossible. Then, the client's interpretive screening of independent, dependent, and intervening variables, is also considered. The problem is geometrically compounded because the externally-viewed variable equation is transformed into an internal framework, which adds or subtracts possibly unknown dimensions, and can even add entirely new variables to the dynamic arena of the stimulus-response condition for conflict arousal.

Also, once regression to points of fixation has occurred, the client enters what is, virtually, another world. It is difficult for the therapist to identify benchmarks for support or therapeutic input along the route of regression, or to differentiate normal versus regressed level of anxiety.[128] These fluctuating movements to adapt or defend by moving toward, against, or away from simultaneously feared and needed love objects, can so rapidly interchange in relation to one another, that the therapist needs a stop-action measurement device or a rapidly-mobile scale, to measure any one posture in its predominate or dormant state, or in its movement between states of visibility and unconsciousness.

5. There are also concerns when dealing with transference[129] between the client and a significant other, symbolized in the person (role, position, character, style, or specific comment) of the therapist. Specific information needed for evaluation is as follows:

a.   degree of perceptual distortion characteristic of each client (resulting from significance and duration of childhood emotional trauma), which determines frequency and completeness with which former roles (i.e., parent) are fantasized as belonging to the therapist;

b.   ability of the client to accept responsibility for thoughts and actions, and allow others to do the same, therefore presenting a framework within which appropriate roles and associated behaviors and feelings, can be assumed by their proper role inhabitants;

c.   strength, fearfulness, desirability, or omnipotence of the client's learning (frequently irrational) about the parent position in his or her life, as this determines control, continued reliance engendered by this social status, transferred perceptions of subsequent survivability (how *right* were parents about their definitions of reality), and capability in achieving internal control and psychosocial autonomy, within the deterministic nature of social positions;[130]

d.   actual or countertransferential[131] nature of the counselor's input, which reminds the client of parental images, and the degree to which the counselor is unable to identify this process of mistaken identity, to help the client approach current reality more adaptively;

e.   existential nature of trans-personal regression, and whether the human organism can actually move back in time to previous relationship, or whether conflictual perceptions and expectations are simply part of the client's continuing psychodynamic efforts to adjust, and are therefore only related to present relationships;

f.   degree to which powerful control and expert influences of the therapeutic process, negate necessary aspects of the adult developmental stage of the client (this applies to actual stage appropriate levels of children, and adolescents as well), thereby forcing childhood feelings and behaviors, which the client feels are necessary compromises to receive other forms of therapeutic help or benefits.[132]

Defenses

In the process of symptom formation (as one empirical referent for defense employment), although neurotic symptoms are painful to the client, they also have adaptive purpose, and are typically weak, but relatively effective attempts to resolve conflict. Defensive reorganization of the client's intrapsychic world with ritualized behaviors or symbolic cognitive constructions, requires evaluative analysis for both its positive and negative designs, as well as measurement of the point at which the negative-positive scale is tipped in either direction. The client needs to decrease energy investment for comfortable, but pathological defenses, while increasing attention to minimal levels of anxiety, which symbolize decreased defensiveness and increased opportunity to utilize strength. An example, is delusional thought content, which has negative self-depreciating implications as the client envisions regression to feared conditions of personality destruction; but simultaneously, has positive connotations of contact (through delusions) with a fantasized world of people and things, which provide a primitive form of grounding for the disintegrating ego. Figure 3 depicts needed changes in how clients invest self-appreciative energy, especially as defenses come and go in therapeutic process.

Figure 3
Self-Regard Relative to Defensive Posture

Defensive Presence

	Low Defensiveness as Regression Begins	Moderate Defensiveness as Fixation Approaches	High Defensiveness as Fixation Occurs	Moderate Defensiveness as Strength Increases	Low Defensiveness as Strength Predominates
Low Self-Regard for weakness in using Defenses			X	X	
Decreasing Self-Regard (from High to Moderate or Moderate to Low) for increasing use of Defenses	X	X			X
Increasing Self-Regard (from Low to Moderate or Moderate to High) for increasing ability to defend Self with Defenses	X	X			
High Self-Regard for Adaptation with minimal or no use of Defenses	X				
High Self-Regard for ability to defend Self with Defenses	X	X	X	X	
Increasing Self-Regard for use of Strength to minimize need for Defenses				X	

(Row label on left: **SELF-REGARD RELATIVE TO DEFENSE OR ADAPTATION**)

Although Figure 3 is not a comprehensive analysis of all possible categories of bivariate contingency for self-regard and defensive posture, it does suggest that the client's feelings can change in degree and direction, based on varying perceptions and uses of defense, necessitating categorical classification and measurement of these convergent positions, as each appears and changes. In clinical situations, the counselor may correctly select an evaluative index of defensiveness, but not understand that variables must be viewed together and, therefore, indices of the relationship should represent the systematic nature of an interactive outcome, rather than any singular dimension.

Given selective perception of defensiveness as anxiety increases, the client may make necessary contact (via awareness) with forgotten or repressed feelings. This has a positive therapeutic valence that should be communicated to the client, despite his or her probable inclination to view anxiety negatively. Also, use of defenses can give the client a feeling of self-imposed security and self-protective esteem, which is also positive, and an evaluative focus can bring this posture into the spotlight. Interpretation of rising or falling levels of anxiety and defensiveness can have positive or negative therapeutic value, depending on how the client is invited to be a participant, in documenting and interpreting movement of psychodynamic forces in his or her mental and physiological repertoire of responses. There is also secondary gain (in the form of attention, rescuing, or control) from symptomatic manifestation, which interjects another contingency that must be correlated with the rewards of defensive self-protection, and social and psychological punishments of symptom manifestation resulting in alienation, rejection, and/or isolation.

Examples of association between positive and negative defensive dynamics, in serious cases of neurosis or borderline psychotic personalities, are "ego-splitting"[133] (isolation and division of behavior and conscious awareness, to handle excessive anxiety associated with traumatic life crises), serious developmental fixation,[134] or major problems in separation from parents[135] in narcissism and borderline situations.[136]

In addition to evaluative issues in ego-splitting, specific concerns relate importantly to other defenses as well. Each is discussed in the following paragraphs:

1. Projection: As clients eject unacceptable impulses or conflictual feelings from their fragile self-awareness, and attribute these impulses to others, monitoring requires categorization of fantasy representations of significant others, to directly measure defensive cognitions as they symbolically exist. This is particularly significant if clients are to receive early conditioning for evaluative self-monitoring,[137] while not forcing them to accept full

responsibility for their fearful projections, before a relationship of trust is established with the therapist. Comparative measurements of the ratio between projected and non-projected feelings, concurrently compared to characterizations of feeling strength or weakness, might assist clients in understanding this process of feeling transfer. They also learn how they define self and others as capable of hosting conflicts, rejecting ownership of conflicts, or redefining conflicts to negotiate their resolution. Defensive behavior in paranoid reactions requires measurement of adaptivity in using whatever strength can be identified, since clients who are strongly projecting, do not accept responsibility for their irrationality, but can become partners with the therapist in monitoring their behavior, if its saneness is not challenged initially.[138] It is important for counselors to "respect clients' needs to protect themselves and not arouse more anxiety than they are able to deal with at a given time."[139]

2. Identification: This defense is interesting, since measurement takes into simultaneous account several dynamics, which have different and possibly mutually-exclusive interpretative meaning:

   a. degree of imitation as a reflection of the therapist's domination and control, which may be necessary to deliver insight and model adaptive behavior, yet reflects dependency and transference, which can also be reviewed negatively;
   b. imitation as a reflection of correctly perceived personality deficits, as a positive index to develop goals and objectives for therapy;
   c. strength of identification as an inverse and curvilinear indicator of perceptions of inadequacy, with need for the therapist to discourage imitation as a prelude to individuation and development of autonomy, yet encourage imitated behaviors if they represent examples of adaptive behavior.

   In these cases, measurements qualify various dimensions of behaviors, yet absolute numeric findings must be carefully interpreted (and sometimes inversely correlated), to give insight into symbolic underpinnings of the identifications. This includes accuracy of clients' modeling and degree of closeness in relationships (which are modeled), as a positive sign of relationship building and interpersonal valuation and trust.

3. Compulsive Ritual and Undoing: The obsessive-compulsive pattern of rejecting negative self-condemnations or contradictory ideations, through systematic self-punishment and/or rigid patterning of exclusionary behaviors

(rituals), presents a complicated evaluation problem. First, obsessions are difficult to identify and validate as directly linked to specific measurable behaviors, yet direct assessment is critical because their elimination may be linearly associated with (a) causal determinants in the erroneous interpretation of degree of parental control, (b) unavailable avenues to express legitimate and acceptable autonomy, and (c) magical potential to correct (irrationally perceived) unacceptable behavior, to avoid serious psychic trauma or ego/relationship disintegration. The tendency to exclusively measure obvious compulsive behaviors may obscure necessary attention to cognitive antecedents, which can deceptively be maneuvered to become submerged in a multitude of socially acceptable and rewarded behaviors.

Since many compulsive clients exhibit deviant social behaviors, not by nature (e.g., hard office work), but frequency of acts (7 days and nights per week), differentiation of proportionality is significant, to represent positive dimensions versus negative deviance. Evaluations need to consider patterns of behavioral manifestation, so distance between similarly-caused behaviors, numbers of interpersonal noncompulsive behaviors, or juxtapositions of behavior, can be correctly accounted for and interpreted.

A second consideration is measurement of compulsive behaviors, thoughts, or feelings, which are consequent to the antecedent obsessions, and provide some corrective experience to transform the guilty or fearful party into a forgiven, competent, or safe state of existence. These periods of adequacy are helpful to the self-monitoring client, as one source of positive feedback relative to perceived helplessness, because of the otherwise absent positive reinforcement in childhood and adulthood.

4.   Denial or Repression: The major evaluative problems here, are that empirical referents must be tested for validity as unconscious or quasi-conscious representations of conflictual feelings or unacceptable needs, since the client is typically an unknowing assistant in this discovery process. Measurement must be accompanied by new hypotheses to be tested, and comprehensive accounting for correlations between a range of varying behaviors, which represent hidden thoughts or feelings. As denied and repressed content surface in the client's conscious awareness, behaviors which formerly represented this vigorously protected material, may change in response to increasing anxiety. Therefore, measurement needs to quickly be implemented, as new referents guide introduction of particular therapeutic inputs. Degree of distance between current concept (or object) awareness and hypothesized conflictual material, is a necessary

measurement scheme, but the client should be made aware of how this evaluative process helps them learn about defenses, and how to take control (consequently build self-esteem) of this distancing process.

Although only a few defensive postures have been discussed, they illustrate variations in evaluative strategy and measurement tasks, which must be attuned to unique characteristics of clients' efforts to avoid their painful realities, and protect fragile psychodynamic systems.

Specific Neurotic Formats

In addition to particular nuances of defense, each pattern of neurotic adaptation necessitates specific evaluation designs, to correctly provide data for clinical assessment. A few major assessment issues highlight general perspectives about different neurotic patterns, and encourage counselors to dig comprehensively into each neurotic tendency, to discover necessary questions to impose evaluative theory and method.

1. Basic Anxiety Reaction:
    This condition involves various manifestations of diffuse anxiety, warning that unconscious conflicts are emerging into conscious awareness, as the symbolic image of approaching undifferentiated destruction, and fear of serious undefined loss. The body physically energizes to handle stress, but excessively produces overactions of fatigue, hypertension, aches and pains, or disturbances to other organ systems. Basic evaluative concerns which accompany anxiety reactions or anxiety neurosis in clinical situations, are these:

    a. With absence of an accustomed defensive strategy by the client, the subjective situation is defined as a crisis, with physiology and emotionality perceived as out of control and very frightening. Evaluation is related to the temporary development of defensive fortifications to return the individual to a state of equilibrium, subsequently replaced by more permanent patterns of defining reality, establishing supports, etc., as therapeutic intervention proceeds. It is easy in these situations for the client to assume excessively dependent postures vis-à-vis the rescuing counselor, so evaluative attention must not be focused exclusively on the product of shoring up the crumbling personality, but also on processes attempted, failed, and successfully used by the client, in taking care of him or herself.

b. Proliferation of multiple seemingly-separate symptoms can be confusing and anxiety-producing (secondary anxiety and fear) for the client. Attention must be given to combining specific individual symptoms into categorical clusters or collective symptom manifestations, as an index of level of anxiety and internal self-perception, relative to emergence of conflictual cognitive material into vulnerable consciousness. Also, symptoms are not always directly responsive to efforts to restore intrapsychic and physical equilibrium, and must be understood in their degree of delayed reaction and symbolism, as empirical references of emotional dynamics. Evaluation must focus on many behind-the-scenes phenomena, to gain a complete clinical panorama of each client.

c. Stress perceived by a client in crisis, is highly symbolic and regressive/fixated in nature, even if there are obvious fear or anxiety-inducing external events (i.e., job loss, child-rearing problems, death, etc.). The counselor may be misled into defining independent dynamics of external stresses associated with the dependent reactions of the client to those stresses, rather than infusing other significant independent variable contributions from childhood, more relevant in explaining the high degree of traumatic impact, duration, and illogical fearfulness of the neurotic condition. This error of false causes can sometimes be seemingly resolved externally (client gets new job, meditation causes relaxation), but does not necessarily change internal predisposition of the client (original independent-dependent configurations from childhood remain in-tact). He or she often suffers additional episodes in the future.

d. The fact that the client is controlling, to some extent, the mobilization of symptoms to handle stress, may be positive if developed into a broadened sense of self-control,[140] despite behavioral negative outcomes. Evaluation focus may be a self-awareness facilitator, if sharp decrease in symptoms as a symbol of adaptivity and integrated cognitive health, is not necessary. Therefore, the client can negotiate a more graduated symptom decline, with developmental increase in awareness of self-control—even over negative symptoms.

2. Hysterical Neurotic Manifestations:
In these disorders, conflict (similar in origin to anxiety neurosis) is expressed with physical representations, altered states of dissociated consciousness or depersonalization, and exhibitionistic drama or hyper-

manipulative emotionality and sexuality.   There are several evaluative concerns that must carefully be considered by the clinician:

a.   Heightened emotional turmoil and dramatic sensationalism of this disorder, are very encompassing of the client's energy and attention,[141] and prevent an objective view of the symbolic acting out (can't see the forest because of the vigorously-burning trees). Although the clinician can measure decreasing numbers of hysterical behaviors as an index of growth, client self-centered observational process is exactly parallel to the sensationalistic and dramatic symptom presentation, which represents the pathology itself.   These clients easily become ultra expert measurers, as this empirical accountability procedure helps validate their ostentation, and fuels fires of increased defensiveness.

A behavioral approach, for example, suggests that emotionally charged behavior be reduced, to allow the client to return to a resting or pre-anxiety baseline, for insight to develop. Negative reinforcements of hysterical behaviors might be implemented, to include reduction of attention (ignoring) which rewards the behaviors, and/or addition of other rewards, to condition mutually exclusive and contradictory non-hysterical behavior repertoires.[142] In these cases, the clinician might identify and measure non-hysterical behaviors which demand that the client step back (take time out) from the highly charged emotionality, to be a more objective observer (e.g., systematic desensitization, meditation, relaxation).   Also, the client possibly should not become a collaborator in measuring hysterical manifestations, as this could become another symptom within this psychodynamic defense pattern.

b.   Because of extensive fantasy production, emotional lability, and ambivalence about inner or outer affective states, hysterical clients move rapidly and randomly between confusing symbolic behaviors. They frequently pretend to develop or replicate insights (espoused by the counselor), as a form of approach and then avoidance. An evaluative validity challenge exists, because of repeated emotional smoke screens and distortions.   The therapist initially may not measure specific feelings, but, rather, the client's attempts to examine, study, and question reliability and validity issues around feeling *correctness* and *manifestation*. The client's self as a reliable and valid instrument of awareness, may be the best initial measurement focus; and the assessment of specific nature of feelings, becomes a secondary focus for latter stages of therapy. This scheme is seen graphically as follows:

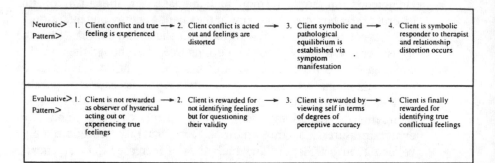

c. Because of highly-observable behavior of the hysterical syndrome, the client's validation of dependency, external control, or self-condemnation; there is frequently a rejection of the significant other or the hated self. As a role model, counselors may measure their own responsiveness to manipulations, share the outcome results with clients to expose them to their own process, and model generalized behavior of nonresponsiveness to dramatic inclinations, as one form of self-control. This does not directly attack client defenses, but begins to create a dichotomy between manipulation and non-manipulation, as indices of adaptation for the client. This interrupts pathological transference, and illustrates to clients, the lack of realistic caring which may be part of many relationships—giving the therapist time to establish a reward contingency between manifestations of their own caring, and non-manipulative stimuli from clients.

d. Because emotional nurturance and clinical interpretation seem contradictory to the client, inputs delivered by the counselor are often seen as withdrawal or rejection, which exacerbates the client's efforts to gain childhood acceptance and unconditional emotional nurturance. The hysterical personality's symbolic, manipulative, and dramatic relationship style with distorted perceptions, may also force the therapist to adapt a client-centered approach, avoid interpretations which are misinterpreted, and work with the client to measure approximations to self-initiated insights—since methods of counting behaviors also become a reward for the client, to replicate attention-getting activity. An example, is the male therapist's nonresponse to a female client's (1) seductive crossing of legs, followed by (2) asking if he liked her, followed by (3) crying. In this case, the therapist might remain totally silent to await the client's possible approach to insight: (1) Why aren't you answering me? (2) Don't you care about me? (3) You're not saying anything. (4) Don't I seem real to you? — at which point the therapist notes this on an interval scale as 1 (one) relatively honest and non-manipulative comment among four, therefore a 25% ratio for the client to think about. This type of evaluation, measurement, and reinforcement strategy can, of course, be carried out with other types of hysterical behaviors which distort interpretations from transferred parents, with whom clients have anger/dependency conflicts.

3. Depressive Neurosis:
In these situations, anxiety about intrapsychic conflict is controlled and redirected into self-deprecation and anger, directed at the self. It has fantasized functions of:
a. punishing the self to the extent that better behavior (parent-pleasing) will develop when one's debt has been paid;
b. re-creating parent-child closeness via the reward/punishment interactive transaction, which represents some level of attention and desired caring;
c. directing anger away from desired love objects, so they are not driven farther from the client, who desperately needs them and cannot affect honest confrontation;
d. providing self-punishment to arouse pity, and attempts, by inflicting guilt on parents or others, to rescue and nurture the suffering victim.

The neurotic-depressive reaction is also present when precipitated by a current loss or deprivation in the adult's sociocultural world. The neurotically depressed individual appears psychosocially isolated, sad, and lonely, with negative and pessimistic perceptions of self and most social situations. There may be associated somatic disturbances and agitation.

Negative reactions to loss exist on a continuum,[143] reflecting varying degrees of potency and secondary impairment of other areas of social functioning. It is, therefore, difficult for the evaluator to factor out level and type of actual loss, versus retroflection or internalization of anger over self-esteem, dependency, and lost parental love during childhood. When the client's neurotic experiences do produce actual significant losses, the clinician may develop two separate measurement philosophies and scales:

one for independent variable effects of actual losses (with consideration that these situations might require collateral social interventions), and a second measurement scheme for independent effects of fantasized losses and self-inflicted anger, secondary to low self-esteem. This may dichotomize the dependent variable, so that truly neurotic components can be treated separately from more normal elements of loss, as they form interactive continua.

Neurosis is more devastating when constitutional (i.e., premorbid states of childhood conflict) factors are combined with situational experiences in a direct correlational configuration, where both increase together on a journey of synergistic pathology. As each vector increases, a geometric progression of weakening capabilities in the alternate area, causes more pathology in the first area considered. For example, if one's constitution predisposes anxiety based on low self-esteem and expectations of actual environmental loss, a real loss can be precipitated by lowering of defensive or adaptive capability. An actual loss, will lower self-esteem to create more anxiety about subsequent probable losses. Measurement involves scaled correctional perspectives, with incremental valence loadings for synergistic or collective effects, requiring separate initial measurements of constitutional and environmental variables, and combined measurements to assess cumulative effects.

An additional symbolic dimension of depression (and other neuroses as well), is the important role of anger at a lost (or feared-lost) love object (whether retroflected, projected, displaced, denied, etc.), to maintain some form of contact with the symbolized nurturant object, via a strongly energized emotional medium. Clients feel it is better to be angry at someone desperately needed, rather than have no feeling at all, and possibly lose the needed person totally. From an evaluative perspective, this inverse index can be positive in its general function or relationship valuation and maintenance, and negative in its reflection of simultaneous destructiveness to the healthy ego, and the secondary dissolution of a relationship which may not tolerate anger.

The operationalized expression of anger at external objects (rather than in self-annihilation) is also an evaluative dilemma, as increasing increments of behavioral manifestations can be positive indices of non-internalizing anger, yet may be symptom substitutions, if continued to excess or used inappropriately. However, externalization can positively represent autonomous separation of self (as children) from valued love objects (usually parents), and should be encouraged to build self-esteem; but then it must be converted to other indices of adaptation (non-expression of anger), as positive self-regard and independence make anger unnecessary. The evaluator monitors this conversion process, to insure that measurement scales for evaluative conceptualizations are compatible, continuous, and closely linked with the correct therapy inputs to insure continued growth, even though they may appear to be contradictory measurements.

Suicidal behavior is also complicated, because external controls imposed to save lives, are responsive to (and reinforcers for) manipulations, which create additional dependence. Adaptive evaluative goals must often be delayed until hospitalization or suicidal crises pass, so evaluation methodology must be flexible to integrate delaying actions. Goals must be assessed for potency, frequency, and duration of occurrence, as other therapeutic gains are expected to begin taking place.

Attention-getting foci of suicidal gestures or manipulations must be shared with clients (despite the fact they continue to act them out until therapy begins to work), so they understand their psychodynamic defensiveness, through the framework provided by evaluation.

4. Obsessive-Compulsive Neurosis:
    Obsessions are fearful and uncontrollable specific or diffuse thoughts which invade conscious awareness, assuming a variety of content forms, including criticisms of self or others, sexual or other forbidden fantasy impulses, or aggressiveness. In most cases, all of these are deviant relative to client or cultural norms. The compulsions, which follow obsessions, prevent original obsessive thoughts from coming true, and insure use of energy in socially acceptable ways (e.g., achievement, hard work, etc.), or in self-indulgent, but nondestructive rituals (checking gas stove, locked doors, etc.). Clients experience self-consciousness about the rigid and cumulative power of obsessions, with accompanying feelings of dependency and entrapment, since the rituals also provide self-centered security and control.

    In dealing with this client problem, there are specific evaluative concerns related to obsessions and compulsions, which the counselor must remember:

    a. The evaluator needs to separate foci on obsessions from associated compulsions, and realize that (1) the obsession is a dependent variable relative to norms, cognitive representations, reward/punishment contingencies, or parent-child relationship dynamics, which reflects cognitive distortions of the adult—remembering real or fantasized childhood experiences; (2) the obsession is an independent variable affecting employment of compulsive rituals to bind energy, act out, or control negative impulses; (3) the compulsion is a dependent variable reactive to the obsession, but also an independent variable affecting self-perceptions, perceptions of others about the client, relationships, achievement, social adequacy, or success, etc.; and (4) the compulsion is an independent variable which may influence the original obsession, or contribute to definition of the original conflictual situation.

b. The symbolic nature of obsessions must be defined and traced to specific origin, and continuing roles in basic conceptual frameworks the client possesses. These cognitive and emotional frameworks should then replace the obsession as the primary focus of insight-oriented change. The degree of direct or indirect representation should be carefully quantified, to guide the counselor toward corresponding high or low frequency conceptualizations of the intentions manifested through (but not directly represented by) the obsessions. Secondarily, measurement of factors antecedent to both obsessions and compulsions, will guide the counselor to basic (baseline) components of psychodynamics which must be changed, for therapy to realize optimal effectiveness.

c. The predominance of obsessional or compulsive symptoms is also significant in diagnosing strength of ego boundaries, degree of regres-siveness of the illness, and adaptiveness of which the client is capable. This differentiation further clarifies the borderline psychotic vs. personality (character) disordered client, and helps achieve correct and meaningful prognostications.

d. Although it is fairly easy to document and quantity frequencies of compulsive rituals, the evaluator should struggle also, with similar operationalization of obsessions, or even cognitive presumptions which precede the obsessions. Decreasing frequencies of compulsive behav-iors may not be indicative of progress, because of: concomitantly increasing compulsive client dependency; projected compulsiveness onto the therapist, who is compulsively trying to help the client; intrapsychic compulsions which are generalized symptoms to substitute for overt physical behaviors; negative consequences from the client's social system, where specific compulsive behaviors are rewarded for maintaining homeostasis in the system (i.e., compulsive rescue attempts of a wife toward an alcoholic husband). In these cases, physical empirical referents must be screened for external validity, and correctly interpreted as referents for intrapsychic processes.[144]

5. Psychophysiological Disorders and Conversions:
    Conversion reactions constitute an unconscious mechanism, whereby intrapsychic conflicts are expressed in symbolic fashion in the safer outside world, through unnatural alteration of physical activity or bodily functioning. Fear-producing ideas are converted into symbolic, yet perceptually more distant physical, and psychological symptoms, which allow clients to focus on their bodies rather than conflictual thoughts.

    There are multiple possibilities for primary or secondary gain from the conversion reaction, where symptoms (1) serve as a defensive barrier to avoid painful intrapsychic phenomena; (2) stimulate sympathy or support from others; (3) help control an anxiety-ridden milieu, both internally and externally; (4) provide status or lessened expectations within socially validated sick roles; (5) provide self-punishment to handle feelings of guilt; or (6) punish others for inferred causes or exacerbations of the illness condition.

    The most significant problem in assessment of symbolic physical expressions of emotional conflict, is to establish correct hypotheses of psychological causality, rather than correlation,[145] and avoid incorrect emphasis on physical etiology. Since the client's primary conflicts are camouflaged, and they experience reduced pressure through discomfort of free floating anxiety, they consequently offer little insight or motivation to discover and deal with origins of symptoms. The clinician may be misled by physical symptoms and, as a result, attend to reactive stress. Hereby, they help clients develop pseudo-resources to handle physical problems (including family support, which often provides the desired secondary gains), rather than viewing psychological conflicts which precede physical conversions.

    Societal acceptance of the legitimacy of physical illness, and general ignorance of physiology among lay people, lend credence to the symptom display. The clinician may become the unwelcome explorer of a puzzle, which clients and their families feel does not require a psychodynamic solution. Without localization, categorization, and measurement of causal independent variables, the clinician can become lost in a vast array of interventive variables associated with the symptom itself, but leading on a wild goose chase for insight into neurotic conflicts.

For clients to assume a responsible and cooperative self-evaluative role, the clinician needs to establish two measurement schemes initially: one to support the client's perceived defensive need for symptom manifestation for symbolic emotional survival, and to assess decreasing degrees of incapacitation relative to the physical impairment; and a second scale to assess intrapsychic conflict, even when correlational changes in the conversion symptom do not keep parallel and direct pace. The first process is difficult, however, because of the "emergency nature"[146] of many conversion onsets, their lack of reliable stability or resistance to rapid change, and difficulty in accurately relating them to otherwise healthy organ systems, to rule out true illness or disease.

Secondary gain which ensues, constitutes a rationale for a third measurement category for the following reasons:

a. many families and primary social groups incorporate the client's sick roles into their pathological interactions, so changes in this area require separate system-related interventions and measurements;
b. secondary gains which clients receive (e.g., sympathy, attention, self-punishment, etc.), become stimuli for other changes in self-attitude and adaptability, which require separate monitoring;
c. secondary gains may serve as more empirically verifiable examples of the problem, so their measurement helps clients accept responsibility, causes changes in secondary gain contingencies, and progressively stimulates change relative to primary conversions, which are more closely associated with the original conflict.

Also, some forms of secondary gain have beneficial effects for the client, so the evaluator may devise a measurement continuum with degrees of gain dichotomized as positive or negative—to build self-esteem, healthy dependence, or communicative competence. The decision about when secondary gain transverses the positive/negative divider is a difficult one, and this assessment process may confuse the client. Therefore, considerable care must be taken to clearly describe the continuum, and illustrate its therapeutic utility. This problem is also complicated because clients generally have no conscious, voluntary control over symptoms. What appears to be an independent variable (the conversion symptom), may be actually another dependent variable, which some clinicians may wish to ignore in their treatment philosophies, except as a measurement of baseline and posttest outcomes. Measurement is also challenging because of multiple symbolizations which are possible in clients' fantasy experiences, so the clinician must do considerable exploratory research,[147] to even identity all the correct variables.

In considering psychophysiologic symptoms separately from conversions, these somatic reactions lack the complicated symbolism of the hysterical conversion, and more closely reflect generalized anxiety manifestations, as the body expresses psychic discomfort physically.

Measurement of the physical symptoms (headache, diarrhea, backache, etc.) can provide a useful index of level of anxiety, especially among clients who have difficulty verbalizing feelings. It can also provide inverse correlational data on increasing ability to talk out, rather than act out, conflicts. Biofeedback machines provide more precise measurements, but clients can improve their somatic awareness by documenting frequency of particular symptoms, and charting their interactive association with psycho-socially stressful events, thoughts, or persons in their lives. This provides a payoff in awareness of physiology, and more importantly, signals critical need to discuss feelings, expectations, and irrational assumptions about specific stressors. The therapist can use body awareness and self-monitoring to teach systematic desensitization and relaxation exercises, to symptomatically control manifestations of conflict and, as a prelude/addendum, to deal with conflict in a more insightful fashion.

One major problem with psychophysiologic reactions, is possible confusion with conversions, so physical indices of presumed symbolic nature can frequently provide invalid data. This consequently produces incorrect hypotheses about the psychological pathology, and diverts therapeutic focus from its correct perspective. The clinician/researcher/evaluator must vigorously question internal validity, and utilize multiple referents within (a) the client's history of growth and development, (b) ego skills and defensive postures, (c) current processes of trying to adapt, (d) quality of relationship, (e) onset, duration, and cost-effective sequence and results (e.g., secondary gain, etc.) of symptoms—before differentiating psychophysiologic and conversion syndromes. In these cases, categorization, description, documentation, operationalization, and explanation are more valid and reliable to monitor outcome.

Another problem in assessing physiology, is that real and serious metabolic and structural changes can occur in the reacting organism, to initiate new physical pathology, intensify existing physical problems, or create additional stresses which activate new cognitive emotional conflicts. This causal nature of psychophysiologic reactions is an independent variable (which at the same time, is a dependent factor as discussed earlier), which requires evaluative assessment and accompanying medical treatment. When medicines are employed, however, symptoms are often relieved or extinguished, which may hamper the therapist's efforts to identify and systematically monitor physical empirical referents of conflict, and fool the medical patient into believing original conflictual problems are improving. In these situations, some clients become resistant to continued psychological interventions, to treat and evaluate relationships between physical and emotional factors.

Degree of client reliance on drugs or medical intervention, may give an inverse index of dependence or strength of defensive somatization. The client must be taught by the therapist that he or she is responding rationally to a deductively-reasoned syllogism which, in itself, is easily seen as correct, but excludes a more complete minor premise (see Figure 4 for an outline of this reasoning process).

Very often symptom substitution occurs, which becomes a learned defensive maneuver used by the client and inadvertently supported by the physician, nurse clinician, medical technician, etc. The secondary gain potential of somatization is similar to that of conversions (with shorter symbolic mileage in some instances), where the client can be protected from irrational feelings of emotional failure or inadequacy, and receive parental nurturance or sick role deference, as a substitute for more mature adaptation. Physical fatigue which is often manifest, may require abatement through mood or metabolic stimulants, to give the client even minimally-sufficient energy to productively take advantage of psychological counseling. This step is not in vain if the client understands the limited and supportive role of drugs; symptom improvement as a necessary, but not sufficient, condition of psychological growth; and implications of defensive dependency and rationalization, which can accompany somatic improvement at the expense of emotionally independent growth and conflict resolution.

In summarizing about psychophysiology, a range of interactive and often contradictory measurement scales come into play, with an equally wide array of scale directionality, both inversely and concomitantly. As

Figure 4
Correct (but incomplete) Medical Model Syllogism
Related to Psychophysiologic Reactions

1. **Major Premise** — Medicine (X) can correct physical symptom (Y)

2. Correct but incomplete **Minor Premise** — I have physical symptom (Y)
   I took medicine (X)

3. Conclusion — I can potentially have the physical symptom corrected.

Correct and Complete Medical and Psychosocial Syllogism

1. **Major Premise** — Medicine X can correct physical symptom Y
   Psychotherapy can help correct psychological symptom A which
   may be related to physical symptom Y

2. **Minor Premise** — I have physical symptom Y
   I also have physical symptom A

3. Conclusion — I can have the physical symptom Y corrected by medication X
   The correction of physical symptom Y may not also correct
   physical symptom A

noted in the following figure (5), as nominally represented scales (High, Medium, Low) of one aspect of personality and/or physical adequacy change direction (from High to Low, for example), other scales of symbolic nature or physical adequacy, might conceivably move in the opposite direction. This means the clinician must be constantly vigilant for (1) different types of variables indicative of therapeutic status, change, etc.; (2) various nominal, ordinal, or interval scales to validly provide data on each variable;[148] and (3) possible differential directions each scale can take, reflecting both individual and collective indicators of various client statuses.

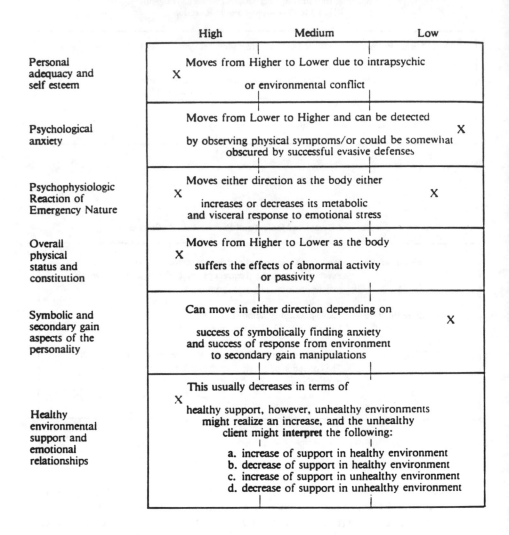

Figure 5
Levels of Scaled Indices for Psychophysiological and Conversion Reactions

	High	Medium	Low
Personal adequacy and self esteem	X Moves from Higher to Lower due to intrapsychic or environmental conflict		
Psychological anxiety	Moves from Lower to Higher and can be detected by observing physical symptoms/or could be somewhat obscured by successful evasive defenses		X
Psychophysiologic Reaction of Emergency Nature	X Moves either direction as the body either increases or decreases its metabolic and visceral response to emotional stress		X
Overall physical status and constitution	X Moves from Higher to Lower as the body suffers the effects of abnormal activity or passivity		
Symbolic and secondary gain aspects of the personality	Can move in either direction depending on success of symbolically finding anxiety and success of response from environment to secondary gain manipulations		X
Healthy environmental support and emotional relationships	X This usually decreases in terms of healthy support, however, unhealthy environments might realize an increase, and the unhealthy client might interpret the following: a. increase of support in healthy environment b. decrease of support in healthy environment c. increase of support in unhealthy environment d. decrease of support in unhealthy environment		

Because most counselors deal with clients holistically in all areas of their functioning, the sexual lives and symptoms of conflicts are also important domains for evaluative investigation. In the case of specific *sexual dysfunctions*[149] as *psychophysiologic* reactions, several concerns must be kept in mind:

a. Many clients experience real and treatable physical problems (e.g., dyspareunia, vaginal infections, penile lesions, colitis, etc.), which impact sexual functioning. In some cases, they fail to seek medical help due to embarrassment or guilt, but passively allow the psycho-therapeutic psychogenic explanatory interpretations, rather than experience more fearful physical exams that would document sexual deficiencies. Although there are certainly psycho-sociocultural problems of self-esteem, guilt, embarrassment, and ignorance operative here, physical symptoms are often linearly associated in a psychologic causal chain, without the symbolism attached to some other mental disorders.

b. Sexuality is an excellent focus for the therapist, as a communication medium into unresolved conflicts or hidden feelings. Many clients have been socialized to view sexuality with heightened significance (investment of psychic, erotic, sensual energy), and as a separate phenomenon from other areas of performance functioning. The author has found it helpful to de-emphasize (de-cathect) sexual separateness in the process of evaluation, because of this skewed socialized energy focus, and in order to measure sexual performance as one index of communication, and as a symbolic referent to more basic concerns about autonomy, self-esteem, superego function, etc. The evaluative focus can be a detriment, if inordinate attention is invested unilaterally in sexual performance indicators, which may alternatively suggest the value of combined indices or more global assessment of personality, to include, but not pay undue attention to, sex. Also, sexuality remains a socially desired, yet prohibited form of self-expression, often not a good direct index of change in other life areas. Its expression is dependent on social mores and is not necessarily linked to all other aspects of the personality. Some clients may achieve personal change, but do not manifest corresponding reactive sexual change, because other norms and systems of societal and religious definition control the expression of sexuality.

c. Finally, sexual behavior is never empirically verifiable to the ethical therapist, so self-report is the only avenue to validate measurement. Manifestation of sexuality to the therapist is also suspect, since it can represent the hysterical and manipulative client, and can be conditioned by a needy counselor and dependent client. Embarrassment means the client will distort reports, so the therapist is continually guessing about the accuracy of this particular behavior index.

In the author's experience, many counselors are reluctant to pursue clients' concerns related to sexuality, due to its socially private and taboo nature, and counselors' discomfort with the topic. This reluctance, of course, limits data available for cross-validating the importance and dynamics of other physical symptoms, and robs counselors of additional behavioral indices, which might trace a clearer pathway to clients' unconscious conflictual reality, upon which any symptoms are predicated.

Personality or Character Disorders

In disorders of personality or character, most authors suggest that early emotional malnutrition among children in destructive family systems, as well as severe contradictory emotional interaction of independence/dependence needs with weak ego-adaptive capacities, necessitate development and lifelong sustenance of defensive patterns, to protect fragile personalities as a component of lifestyle. These syndromes are recognized by rigidity, predictability, minimum presence of observable anxiety (which is controlled in the impregnable behavior patterns), and ego-syntonicity of the abnormality; including roles, positions, and relationships which create minimal anxiety-producing stimuli, conflict, or dissonance.[150]

Environmental Response and Evaluation

When clients successfully find a supportive work or relationship environment to accept their characterological idiosyncracies, they usually do not seek therapeutic intervention. If they do come to the attention of social services, or seek private counseling, they frequently are referred by external sources (spouses, employers), or their behavior has been officially defined as deviant/illegal, and the court has mandated therapeutic intervention. Because of the length, severity, degree of integration of the disorder (client's life adaptation), and lack of client motivation capability for change, counselors may have greater success with assessment of job or relationship needs, within the distorted range of characteristics. This can be accompanied by the pairing of client needs with specific characteristics of work or relationship environments, to arrange a more successful fit. This typically does not necessitate confrontation of client defenses, or long-term insight-oriented therapy; but does require an environmental, social systems perspective, and a dual micro-macro approach to evaluation. Some evaluative foci within this framework, include the following for each component of the system:

1. Client:
   a. categorization and measurement of adaptive capabilities within specific tasks required for employment, relationship maintenance, etc.;
   b. assessment of degree of rigidity in symptom manifestation, as a projection of flexibility for matching personality to social situation;
   c. taxonomy of typical environmental stressors which the individual interprets as threatening, and measurement of tolerance thresholds for each;
   d. delineation of client-perceived supports and rewards, and assessment of degree of rewarding feedback necessary to maintain the behavior pattern, prevent conflict reincarnation with too much support (inverse index), and prevent excessive dependence (in some disorders), through environmental control of both rewards and punishments;
   e. measurement of the range of options available within the awareness of the client, since this facilitates correlation with specific job, residence, schooling, or relationship situations;
   f. systematic calculation of the client's ability to protect the ego, display multiple defenses, rationalize the strength of defensive postures, and ignore outside stimuli which threaten ability to survive.

In each condition, the therapist is considering a baseline measurement predicated on some scale of degree of pathology, and hypothetically determining units of deviation from the mean for each client. Each range of deviation must also be matched with capability of respective social environments to tolerate, reward, punish, or ignore the deviated behavior. Analysis of the environment, therefore, is also an important dimension of comprehensive evaluation of personality disorders:

2. Environment:
   a. analysis of healthy or pathological needs of particular environments (sometimes this necessitates collateral consultation with the client's boss, peers, friends, family, etc.), and requirements of role conformity, as they match (variance in units of deviation) client capabilities;
   b. measurement of each environment's range of flexibility in validating, not punishing or ignoring, specific client behaviors (at various stages of stress level), and the strength of norms, boundaries, and relationship ties which allow client behavioral reciprocity;
   c. description and measurement of stressor potencies for various environments, range of environmental reactions to client stress, and level of

client's awareness of these contingencies, as he or she considers the acceptability of potential life roles;

d. categorization of available environmental rewards, delineation of avenues to attain these rewards, and types and degrees of conformity (specific skills) necessary to maintain sustaining membership in the organization, and not receive too many rewards to create additional stress (e.g., Peter Principle)[151] through promotion or advancement.

In the above situations, the evaluative focus is on the convergent vortex of client style and environmental need, where clinicians systematically consider each pair of match-ups from each category (environment-client), as to degree of complementarity and probability (0-100%) of successful coexistence. This is a more challenging task than simply working with the client out of context, since only half of the picture may be envisioned, in exclusively intrapsychic models of practice.

Individual Therapeutic Response and Evaluation

In cases where the client with a personality disorder becomes voluntarily or involuntarily involved in counseling, with at least minimal intention of personal growth, the evaluative picture is basically different from the environmental response discussed previously, although both may be used in tandem.

The most critical factor, is gaining entry through extremely solid defenses, to encounter the vulnerable, potentially healthy child, who can respond to caring and nurturance, and trust in either the external supportive environment, or his or her own (no matter how limited) ego-adaptive skills. The therapist, in search of some source of psychic anxiety to reveal the whereabouts of the salvageable (if any exists) personality core, will focus therapeutic skills of empathy, reward, insight, support, or interpretation of the protected nucleus of the personality, which was severely traumatized in childhood.

From an evaluative standpoint, the clinician is responsible for identifying secondary defensive fortifications (Figure 6), so proper diagnosis and prognosis can be established; etiology of trauma, fixation, conflict, etc. can be pin-pointed; number of defenses and their strengths can be delineated; and plans can be hypothesized, to use defenses to gain access to inner sanctums of the personality structure. It is important to note that most counselors know the general destructive function of defenses, but may not completely understand their dynamic nature relative to potential for client change. Counselors may also be unsure theoretically, of specifically how to use, avoid, or manipulate defensive thoughts and emotions for greatest therapeutic impact.

Figure 6 also illustrates that defenses are necessary components of the client's adaptation, and must be measured according to degree of counselor support in the artificial therapeutic relationship. This is in addition to the client's perceived early relationships with parents, as each one provides a host environment in which defensive symptoms have a unique functional meaning. Defenses also have developmental growth sequences and reality testing dimensions, as part of a systematic relationship with nondefensive or adaptive behaviors. At this stage of evaluation, defenses are the foundation for a nominal level classification system, which may be converted to an interval level scale later in therapy, to measure decreasing frequencies and potencies of defense, as progressively unnecessary bulwarks for a growing personality. Some therapists, unfortunately, are misled to erroneously presume that defenses themselves are the core personality, rather than simply reactive expressions of behavior to permanently control anxiety and antecedent trauma/conflict. The counselor, therefore, who spends appreciable time concerned with content of compulsive rituals or paranoid ideations, for example, is probably using evaluative perspective too narrowly, and will miss the depth of the forest, for a too-close look at a couple of trees.

Once defenses are identified, it is most helpful to initially accept and support the continued temporary need for self-protection,[152] and use this opportunity to teach the client about basic components of psychodynamic functioning (also called "structuring").[153] Evaluation may include indices of client awareness, acceptance of their human psychodynamic condition, amount of learning taking place, and frequency and accuracy of self-monitoring of defensive postures, etc.; with no necessary or deliberate assessment of defensive change or personality growth per se. As a matter of fact, behavioral changes which do occur, may be a smoke screen to keep the invading therapist at bay, and/or are reflections of increasing pathological dependence, and consequent efforts to please controlling parent substitutes.

In discussing self-monitoring which the client might perform as a prelude to personality growth, Kazdin[154] reports that self-observation is a typical practice, yet rarely accomplished in a goal-directed or purposefully organized way.[155] Clients selectively perceive and recollect their own actions, which can also have a "reactive effect" in subsequently changing the behavior itself (without significant insight). This is because of rewards usually attached to positive behaviors, and the punishing implications of monitoring a negative symptom.

Figure 6
Evaluation and Client Defensive Structure/Strategy

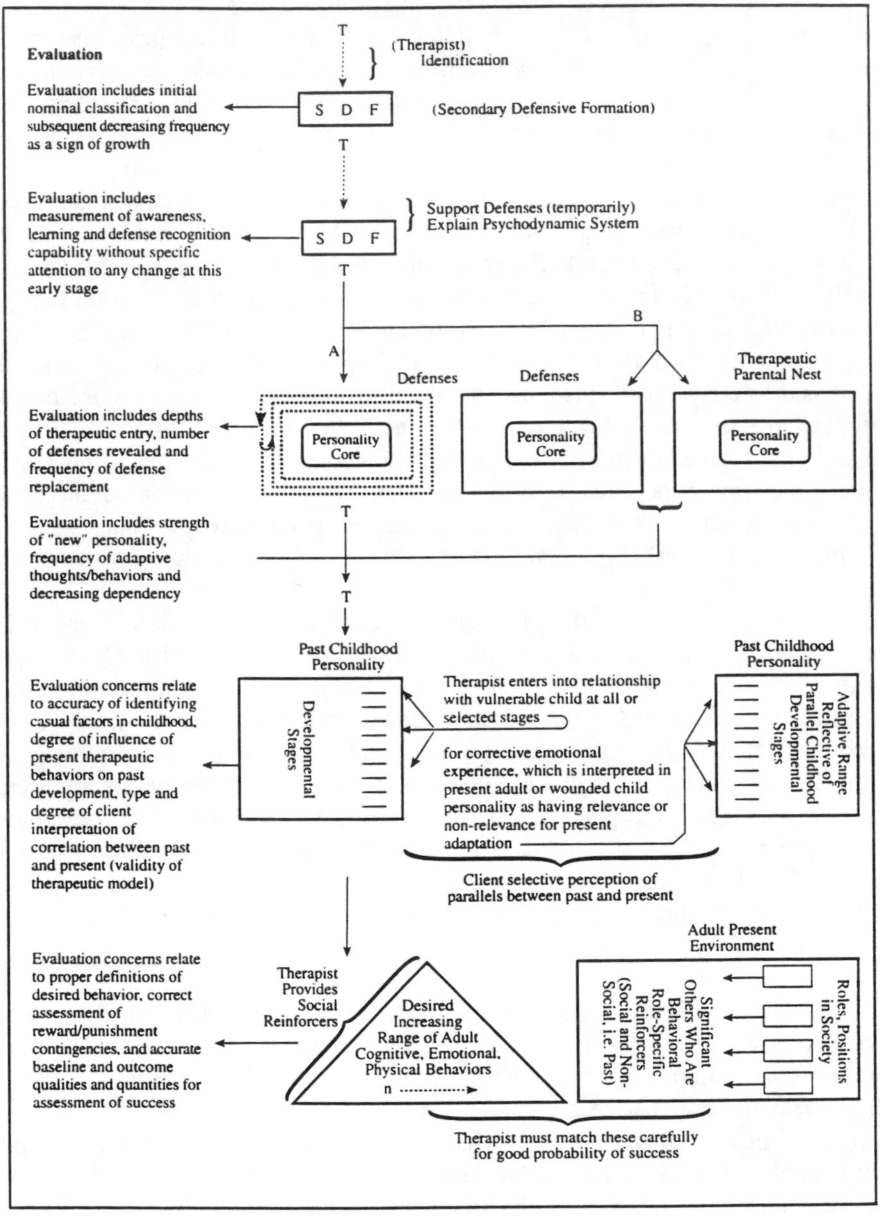

Sometimes, behaviors change only when monitoring occurs in association with other factors in clients' environments,[156] or in the therapeutic relationship. Self-monitoring allows access to behavioral situations not typically observable to the counselor (e.g., home behaviors), and in some cases, clients are taught to modify the external environment,[157] and apply certain stimulus techniques to themselves to provide their own therapeutic inputs.[158]

All this obviously relates to the client's goals for change, self-rewards for specific kinds of behaviors, symbolic meaning of each behavior in the client's functional approach to normative criteria of performance, and degree of client dependence on expression of correct social behavior. This may be viewed as a self-imposed symbolic transference reaction, with the monitoring device or methodology seen as the parent, for any particular client.

In considering Figure 6, again, evaluation of defenses has a two pronged axis which can materialize in direction A or B, depending on pathology of the client, and therapeutic skill of the counselor. One approach, (A), is to work via the content[159] of client-communicated defenses, and accept the validity of successive levels of defense, to ultimately move closer to the primary irrational assumption of the injured child in each client. The therapeutic process keeps defenses in place and develops trust through nonconfrontation, until access to inner recesses of the psychodynamic system is negotiated. At this point, defenses can be gently challenged and tested at inner and outer layers, and replaced by other defensive structures which are increasingly more adaptive, valid as representations of reality, and less rigid. Evaluation examines depth of therapeutic entry into the maze of defensive blockades, number of defenses the client allows the therapist to see and accept, and frequency of defensive replacement, as the therapist develops trust; by first shoring up the decayed foundation with similar fortifications, and then introducing new and less pathological building blocks at incrementally successive stages. This process is necessary in the most rigid, angry, paranoid, and frightened clients, who maintain impregnable defenses which they occasionally allow the interested, but nonaggressive observer, to behold.

In part B, which can substitute for, or serve as an addendum to plan A, the more helpless and dependent client, having successfully resolved some crises with positive trustful experiences in the first two years of life, is the focus of attention. In this approach, the therapist surrounds the helpless child (inner core) with a massive parental surrogate defense, and takes full responsibility to begin renurturing (re-parenting) the traumatized personality, toward growing self-esteem. Obviously, this approach is lengthy, and involves only selected groups of character-disordered clientele. The critical interests are strength of the developing personality, types and frequencies of positive cognitions and behaviors, and inverse allowance by the clients of their dependency, as they grow progressively toward autonomous functioning. In this re-parenting model, the therapist may encounter a curvilinear dependency on the part of clients, requiring a flexible interpretive perspective for effective use of therapeutic power. Clients initially need a relatively-high dependency index to allow therapeutic parenting, with motivation to see the therapist as a valued role model, learning resource, supporter, and guide. As the child grows ideally without crises, conflicts, deficits, or malnurturance of original parenting, dependency gradually decreases. At this time, the therapist should cross-index decreasing dependency with increasing autonomy, as operationalized by an individually relevant range of behaviors, thoughts, and feelings. This should eventually eliminate rejection of the therapist as the client becomes self-sufficient.

The selection of variables, as well as cause-effect relationships to be defined and measured, is a complex process in working with character-disordered clients. Identifying specific causal factors is initially difficult, with the general absence of anxiety as a barometer to show the therapist where probing is in correctly sensitive areas. Causes, during original parenting, may be diffused by layers of rigid defensiveness, and have to be re-traced through inductive logic, beginning with definitions of present pathological behavior, and retroflectively inducing cumulative causes all the way back to childhood. This process requires considerable faith and patience of the client, to intellectually understand and maybe only hypothesize corresponding feelings; or considerable external control by therapists for nonvoluntary clients, to receive other rewards (or avoid punishments) for compliance with therapeutic plans. As a researcher, the clinician repeatedly generates hypotheses about causal factors, to test them immediately through client recollection and corroboration, empirical verification in the history of the client's childhood behavior, or through interpolation by noting present attitudes, feelings, behaviors, and defenses. Without correct identification of childhood causal factors, however, personality reconstruction is unsuccessful, unless behavioral modification approaches are employed to condition the proper external conforming behaviors. Cumulative effects of multiple causes are also difficult to assess, as the therapist, acting in "loco parentis," attempts to substitute a different causal influence, and evaluate the effect: both as the vulnerable child viewed in the past, and also as viewed by the scarred and defended child/adult in the present. Client decision-making is also critical to assess, as it points to ability to translate past experiences (even re-parented positively) through time and successive stages of development, to finally rest in significant here-and-now insights. The therapist must use a highly mobile and sensitive methodological and measurement philosophy, to relay data on the following client decisions and judgments:

1. location of judgment and perception in a wide range of past, present, and future time zones;
2. depth of regression in viewing self as child, and ability to view self progressively through various growth stages;
3. frequency of perception of therapist as actual transferred parent, and as reinforcer and correct interpreter of a new and healthier reality;
4. degree to which adult perceptions alter definitions of past phenomena, and the amount, direction, and nature of variation in these retroflexive decisions;
5. degree to which present or past childhood interpretations, actually altered the true nature and impact of causal factors;
6. number, time of occurrence, client awareness, and influence of intervening variables which the client cannot remember, and presence of similar stimuli in the current environment;
7. length of time client is able to visualize the self at various stages of development, and successfully block out present environmental stimuli and phenomena, to allow incremental regrowth to proceed through necessary stages of unfolding (this might be viewed as a regressive fantasy or even psychotic experience, which some theorists argue is inappropriate and impossible for therapeutic growth—and which could be a defensive escape and, therefore, constitute an index of negative implications).

There are also personality traits or conditions of relative constancy (specifically related to physiology, tension level and threshold, need, motivation, and temperament), which may not be reactive to behavioral stimuli, but have natural unfolding processes. These might occur unilaterally in the personality, become stimuli for other reactive variables, or develop interactively with other traits in a synergistic fashion.

It is difficult to differentiate traits from learned responses, or factor out each variable or constant, to note consequent changes. This is especially true, since there is questionable reliability in assuming close parallels, between original childhood and transferred parent-child relations in therapy. There may, in fact, be no validity to current findings as they retell the past, since complete re-entry into childhood may be impossible, or very subjective, as interpreted uniquely and maybe randomly by each client.

As the therapeutic process continues, the final stage of counseling consists largely of parental (therapist) support for learned behaviors, and eventual relinquishment of control, as these functions are performed by significant others in the environment, or by the client's internal processes of guilt, value decisions, or self-esteem (superego functions). This therapeutic process is similar to an entirely separate behavior modification paradigm, which serves as the third major approach to dealing with clients having character and behavior disorders. The behavior modification approach can stand alone as a separate treatment entity, or be the final stage (with minor modifications) of the long-term therapeutic process.

Behavior Modification Approach

As seen from this approach, the client is typically aware of adjustment problems (job, marriage, etc.), and is experiencing decreasing rewards from others, or insufficient personal need gratification. Clients who are successfully at the final stages of long-term therapy, have typically made some internal changes and now require icing on the cake, with empirical demonstrations of behavioral success. Presence of character disorders in clients can be partly confirmed by noting the location of anxiety and disequilibrium, demonstrated by others who interact with the client and become frustrated with some form of deviance. The professional role is to define empirically verifiable behaviors (including behavioral referents for thoughts or feelings), followed by elucidation of a hierarchy of client-valued rewards, which are nonsocial (money, tokens, food, etc.) and social (smiles, verbal praise, etc.) in nature. The client is taught an operant stimulus-response plan, significant others in the environment (if available) are introduced as reinforcers or controllers/monitors of rewards, and a written contract is developed. This approach cannot promise internal personality change, but purports more ego-syntonic adjustment when the client learns to display externally adaptive behaviors and receive the rewards, which contributes to improvement of internal esteem and self-concept.

Evaluation concerns principles of learning and contingency management, and can be applied to the individual client, as well as her or his immediate social milieu. Major issues are as follows:

1. assessment of client ability to perform the desired behaviors, or incremental approximations of those behaviors;
2. determination of correct reinforcement criteria and contingencies (causal relationships), and development of accurate hypotheses of variable strength of rewards, to produce corresponding quality or quantity of desired behavior;

3. assessment of short- and long-term reinforcing capabilities of the environment, and assurance of the correct match-up of specific client behavior with the accommodating role specific need, and environmental interest/capability in rewarding the behavior;
4. establishment of qualitative and quantitative baselines and outcome goals, to determine type and degree of success in the program;
5. identification of all intervening factors which provide competing and antithetical rewards/punishments, or those contingencies which diminish (by degree) or neutralize the power of reinforcers.

In modifying behavior, the process of monitoring, counting, evaluating, or interpreting the behaviors themselves, is also a significant catalyst for behavioral change in some clients. If monitoring is used as a direct therapeutic strategy itself, the counselor must correctly identify the proper independent variable, because outcome success or failure must relate to the dynamics that produce the actual results, in order for the client to understand how and why they changed, and for the therapist to reproduce the outcomes at other times. Clients who change because they observe their own behaviors, may do so because of cognitive decisions relative to the process of self-monitoring, and it will help them to know how they make certain decisions or judgments when observing the self.

In all cases of character disorder, an important question arises as behavior changes, and clients become aware of the discrepancy between the pathological, but relatively anxiety-free character style, which has become ego-syntonic; and the ostensibly healthier behavior which they might model, although higher levels of accompanying anxiety may seem painful to them. This continuum of character disorders to neurosis to normality, may mean clients get worse before getting better.[160] With two hypothetically-separate continua, the reader may consider whether therapeutic progress and evaluation are best when movement stays within the realm of characterological impairment (see Figure 7), or whether greater progress involves a combination of characterological and neurotic personality dynamics.

The evaluative questions relate to conversions between scaled dimensions of pathology/normality, and degree to which the counselor properly interprets behavioral and symptomatic indicators within or between scales.

Specific Disorders of Character

1. *Antisocial, Passive Aggressive, Paranoid, Compulsive, and Explosive-type Personalities:*

The *antisocial personality* has been reared with serious absences of love, support, training, and structure in generally fearful environments, leaving him/her under-socialized. Behavior styles prevent healthy inter-dependency, and place him/her continually at odds with authorities, social rules, and values. Lacking ability for trusting interactive attachments with others, this person is typically self-centered, emotionally insensitive, irresponsible, impulsive, and does not respond positively to learning experiences.

The *passive-aggressive personality* handles anger at dependence-independence struggles, via passive expression of resentment through moodiness, subtle rigidity, obstructionism, biting humor, and situational mediocrity in life tasks or work roles.

The *paranoid personality* is characterized by defensive fortifications in response to a "persecutory" world, using projection to externalize intrapsychic conflicts related to basic fear and secondary anger. He/she is aggressive, overly sensitive, condemning of others, judgmental, rigid, and self-centered.

The *explosive personality* shows unstable emotional reactions which are easily inflamed. Their styles include irrational outbursts to stress, poor judgments during crisis periods, and sometimes childlike emotional displays to gain recognition. These symptoms are efforts to symbolically reflect fears of external domination, handle dependency frustrations, and implement primitive efforts to achieve personal potency and subsequent forgiveness as a secondary gain.

Finally, the *compulsive personality* seeks systemic regularity; is rigid, perfectionistic, and self-absorbed in life agendas; demands hard work and success beyond normal situational requirements; and has tremendous fear of loss of control and independence.

The author specifically grouped the above characterological syndromes together, to suggest common concerns for clinical evaluation which relate to them collectively. Each disorder, of course, can be considered separately or in other groupings, to analyze factors in etiology, defensiveness, development conflict, and treatment potential; but the possible combinations are numerous and beyond the scope of this discussion.

Figure 7
Change Inside and Outside of Characterological Domain

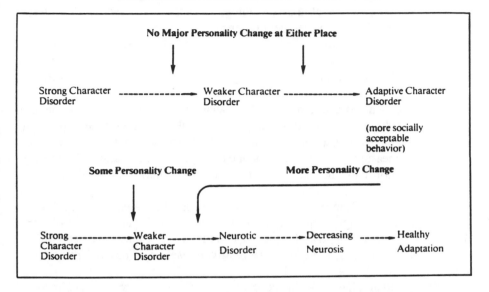

The present grouping reflects the specific and general role of aggression against loved (needed), feared, and potentially (previously) controlling love objects (individuals, transferred parents, society, etc.), within emotionally needy personalities.   These individuals also externalize feelings to displace and/or project anger outside the self, to a hostile and rejected environment, to avoid self-hate and feared inadequacy. These patterns of conflict and defensive selection, suggest shared concerns and questions for clinical evaluation.

a.   One common behavioral characteristic is distance from people, which the clinician must creatively discern within (1) patterns, amounts, types of communication messages; (2) reciprocal responsibilities and conforming behaviors within each client's unique relationship network; (3) degree of mentally conceived or fantasized distance, as separately formed indices of physical distance; (4) degree of distance among differentially-valued love objects, as an index of change in closeness, relative to amount of fear or level of attraction; (5) degree of closeness to the therapist as an index of trust vs. defensive manipulation vs. symbolic expression of anger, through secret devaluation of the helping role; (6) increased closeness for provisional security, wherein conflicts are not dealt with, so homeostasis can be maintained.

All the above carry important questions of validity, and offer challenge in operationalizing definitions and indices, of qualitative and quantitative social and psychological distance and space. A systems, family, or group therapeutic perspective would also measure conflict-ridden needs for receipt of anger, masochism, dependency, guilt, or self-punishment experienced by *others* in personal relationships with explosive, paranoid, passive-aggressive, or antisocial personalities.

The nature, strength of association, degree of coordination, and synchronization of this anger-related role reciprocity, are important evaluative concerns, not only as educative awareness for clients, but as measurement to assess change or stagnation of relationships, in connection with individual or system-oriented therapeutic inputs.

Also, since anger drives significant others away, it is difficult to measure angry expression, since objects (significant people) of anger who could elucidate frequencies and intensities, may have been pushed far away and, therefore, are relatively useless as key informants.

b.   Another diagnostic index is degree of openness vs. concealment of anger, particularly relating to goals of the therapeutic strategy. Clinical theoretical models which emphasize the need to honestly express (and ego-syntonically accept) and correctly deliver anger to appropriate persons, require precise identification of appropriate objects of anger, assessment of degree of angle of deflection in missing the proper and desired mark, and finally, determination of the relative success in the discharge of pent up angry feelings, and quality of the resultant relationship ex post facto. Models which emphasize development of internal autonomy and self-esteem, suggest that expression of anger is sometimes an inverse index of health, therefore making expression of anger unnecessary in the self-actualized personality. An important issue in the development of measurement schemes, is to decide not to differentiate the significance of active versus passive, physical vs. cognitive, actualizing vs. destructive, and other expressions of anger, as they represent graduations on the same scale, or entirely different phenomena which must be separated for evaluative purposes. Some models suggest using separate scales, along with a third integrated perspective, to combine them to look more abstractly at the client's general anger. This is an important decision, either way, for each clinician to make.

c.   A third consideration, given the preponderance of anger in this personality style, is the precision of scaling, to note even minor increases or
decreases in number and intensity of angry verbalizations, expressions,
or overt behaviors; and assessment of angry cognitions which are less
empirically obvious to behavioral monitors.   The social disruption of
explosive or antisocial anger, and the secretive subtlety of passive-
aggression, make scaling a difficult problem, when these displays are
visualized on opposite ends of an empirical continuum.   Accurate
measurement is also a problem because of the bright, intelligent
characteristic often noted among passive-aggressive, paranoid, and
antisocial clients.   This means they frequently assume adversarial and
subversive roles in thwarting clinical evaluative activities.[161]   Numbers
of angry expressions vs. intensity, may give confusing interpretive
data relative to the function of anger (frequency vs. strength), as a
symbol of conflict and depth of pathology, vulnerability of ego
boundaries, and trust in relationships.   Are five expressions of passive
anger, for example, equal in value and meaning to five more overt
expressions, and how is intensity measured and converted to symbolic
developmental meaning, in either the passive or more active conditions?   Also, as some clients express violent anger, they experience
severe guilt at their massive failure, causing more anger of a secondary and reactive nature.   These varying primary or secondary conditions need differentiation by the clinician, since the client may respond
to different conflictual stimuli for various levels of anger, and because
the secondary reactive anger may be less serious as a direct symbol of
conflict.   This is true, even though the anger may possibly appear
more serious, due to its intensity and prolongation.   An example, is
a building which is on fire: the significant causal factors relate to the
initiation and perpetuation of the fire (primary factor), but the most
significant damage to human occupants is usually smoke, which is a
reactive secondary factor.   Prevention and cure for the problem are
focused on the fire, seen as the critical dependent variable responding
to environmental conditions (dryness) or stimuli (electrical spark),
while decisions are also made about allocations of resources to rescue
people from both fire and smoke, and detrimental effects of their
tertiary panic.

d.   Finally, the obsessive-compulsive pattern needs specific analysis as it
represents unique expression of aggression, as well as a process of
controlling a selectively-perceived fearful environment.   Presence of
compulsive rituals or habits in the highly controlled client, may

mislead the evaluator to measure these symbolic external referents, rather than concentrate on obsessions which highlight the original trauma or conflict. Measurement of antecedent cognitions is difficult, because they are charged with more anxiety for the client (who must act out the compulsions, to reduce tension and bind aggression), but also, obsessions represent at least two levels of client functioning: childhood recollections and fantasies, and current adult cognitive structures, wherein compulsions (especially if socially valued, like hard work or neatness) are legitimized or rewarded. Behavioral change in compulsions is not necessarily reflective of change in the foundation personality structure, since symptom generalization is common, and non-compulsion (passive and subversive acting out) can be as resistant as more overt behavioral manifestations. The important evaluative strategy here, focuses on the following:

(1)   degree of client awareness of cumulative irrational cognitions which precede actual obsessions;

(2)   degree of rigidity of conceptual mental categories of description, causality, alternative behavioral options, or past-present time options, and frequencies of attempts to alter the baseline framework which serves as the host environment for the obsessive-compulsive pattern;

(3)   frequency of client utilization of symbolic representations of both anxiety and aggression, frequency of awareness of these occasions, and frequency of efforts at more honest and direct emotional expression.

Since compulsive rituals also structure a childhood reactivated (from unconscious or preconscious domains) disorganized reality, the evaluator may find it helpful to work with the client to see the positive strategy—but the ineffective negative obsessive-compulsive technique-which is involved. This may, in fact, work toward some form of compulsive (at least in early stages) substitution of more positive reality-organizing behaviors, with measurement of empty spaces in the client's conceptual schema (degrees of unorganized reality), as an inverse index. Degree of other—directedness vs. internal superego controls, is also significant, since the client learns that rituals are an example of planning and organization, in addition to last-ditch efforts to save the disintegrating ego. Measurement focus at this point, is an important part of communicating values and healthy models of functioning.

2.   *Schizoid, Aesthenic, Passive-Dependent, and Depressed Personalities:*
       The *schizoid personality* withdraws from close personal relationships, and has limited social attributes and communication skills.   They are isolated and lead private lives, where meaning-of-life philosophies are often known only to them, since they appear reclusive. Schizoid personalities are withdrawn and appear dependent, although their revolution to gain autonomy, is a movement inward, rather than an external manifestation. Detachment prevents further emotional demands and hurt, reduces anxiety relative to rejection fears, and utilizes time and effort in solitary activities.

       The *cyclothymic personality* is friendly, but relationships are strained by intermittent periods of depression, unpredictability, and withdrawal. During depression, the patient is pessimistic and unproductive, feeling that everything will result in failure or absence of need satisfaction. He or she often does not recognize inappropriateness or illogic of alternating periods of unexplained enthusiasm and mood elevation.

       The *asthenic personality* is characterized by lethargy and general low levels of adaptive life energies.   They do not tolerate normal biological, social, and emotional demands of life, and often do not complete tasks for which they are responsible.   They have limited sustained energy to create or maintain meaningful personal relationships.

       Schizoid, asthenic, passive-dependent (part of the passive-aggressive syndrome) and depressed personalities (also manic-depressive personality disorders), are grouped together for evaluative consideration, because of their retroflective[162] and internalizing[163] nature of withdrawal.   In these cases, the client fights the struggle for love and approval (and fear of loss due to perceived emotional depravation) internally, as a silently private and passive phenomenon.   It is characterized by anger at self (depression); denial of need for love, by withdrawal from interactions and emotionality (schizoid phenomena); convincing oneself of energy deficit to avoid conflict (asthenia); or helpless submission to controls of others, to buy love and security (dependence).

       As in previous grouped characteristics, each disorder possesses idiosyncratic characteristics viewed unilaterally, which can be used for different groupings, to consider other evaluative paradigms. The author emphasizes one salient feature that all four diagnostic categories share: indecisive action with external objects, withdrawal, internalization of conflicts, and general passivity.

a. Clients with passive and internalized defensive patterns, viewing them-
    selves as separate entities from past or present external love objects
    (parents, siblings, friends, etc.), cause a serious evaluative problem in
    (1) the clinician's ability to identify critical independent and dependent
    variables (which include significant others), and to hypothesize and
    test the nature of their relationships; and (2) clients' confusing and
    distant recognition and understanding of the role of significant others
    in their lives, as one evaluative index of growth.   Circumscribed
    reasoning of schizoid, depressed, and dependent clients does allow
    recognition of independent and dependent variables, frequently located
    inside the client, where causal and correlational relationships may be
    based on a limited number of variables, which they allow themselves
    to consider. This problem of evaluative scope and dimension, initially
    requires exploratory research techniques[164] to help the client discover
    the full range of variables, followed by descriptive and experimental
    perspectives, once the full arena of causality has been uncovered.
    Clients with a character pattern of noninvolvement and internal seclu-
    sive struggle, need experience in investigating the inner sanctum of the
    self, through unstructured evaluative schemas. These permit pursuit
    of unexpected leads which arise in an interview, and identity issues,
    concepts, and questions within inner and outer space, where the client
    denies or distorts conceptualizations of interpersonal mutuality and
    interactive correlation. A specific example, is when clients do not
    recognize parents as interdependent negative causal stimuli, and refuse
    to recognize themselves (when they were children) as blameless depen-
    dent victims, rather than the evil perpetrators they spend their lifetimes
    punishing. This illustrates an interesting puzzle in determining relative
    value and utility of separate evaluative scopes (clinician's views vs.
    client's view), and deciding how these separate perceptual worlds
    might converge, both as a third dimension to define outcome
    adequacy, and as a test (checks and balances system) of the reliability
    and validity of evaluations in the other purview. This is illustrated
    schematically in Figure 8.

    The degree to which these perspectives merge or remain separate
relative to inclusion of extra-personal variables (significant others), is
a significant determinant of how clients' problems are defined, how
much they share in diagnosis and planning, and how success will be
viewed and measured.

Figure 8
Evaluative Checks and Balances in the Clinical Counseling Milieu

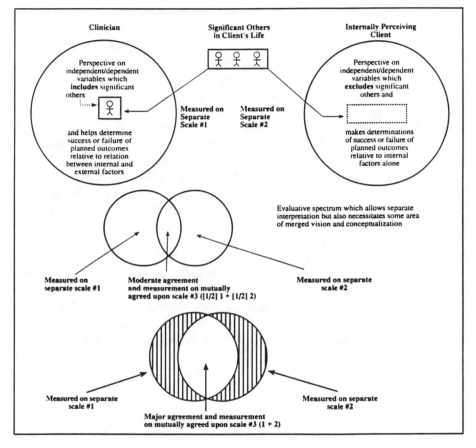

b.   A second issue, is the interpretation and use of client compliance and passivity, decreased hope, masochistic self-denial, and energy depletion (seen with each of the four disorders), as part of treatment planning.[165] The clinician may be initially faced with a massive void of overt, physical, cognitive, and emotional behavior as empirical indicators of change, although degree of inaction can certainly be assessed as a pathological symptom. In this case, there is generalized inactivity among depressed, schizoid, asthenic, and passive-dependent clients. Therefore, the clinician needs a more immediate, specific, and focused scale of smaller increments, to make daily judgments about the effect of therapeutic inputs, to provide the client with evidence of progress, and document even small examples of success related to outcome. Although therapy can aim at internal cognitive and emotional changes in client self-perception, and perceptions of transferred and present significant others, there is passivity and withdrawn resistance among many clients, producing little tangible evidence of change, regression, or growth.

The clinician and client must then incorporate a deferred gratification or intermittent reinforcement philosophy, so both understand substantial time lags (especially in early stages of therapy) between therapist inputs, and client verbal/behavioral positive outcomes. These "repertoire deficits"[166] for thoughts, feelings, or behaviors can sometimes be successfully dealt with using the following evaluative procedures:

(1)   The client helps develop categorical definitions of internal and external behaviors, and a mutually understood list of referents (especially for internal thoughts and feelings), with small increments of measurement that can be seen on a daily basis. The client and therapist use this system to develop positive alternative external responses (mutually exclusive from internal withdrawal), to (a) define a new external reality and (b) measure behaviors or approximations to behaviors (behavioral shaping)[167] which begin to occur.

It is crucial to associate learned external behaviors with changed internal decisions, (extrinsic and intrinsic motivations) feelings, or other personality conditions, so clients perceive power of self-control in eliciting chains of stimuli, and consequent environmental responses yielding positive results of support, interpersonal closeness, and/or social rewards.[168]

(2)   There should be a system of coding[169] to associate internal and external referents of growth and change, and to retroflectively attach initial insights, inputs, or client decisions to current behavioral indices.

(3)   Some form of reinforcement is necessary for the client's time, effort, and pain in waiting for behavioral success outcomes, as a process to teach objective-setting and decision-making, contingent on empirical goal attainment.

(4)   Finally, clients' internal decision responses[170] must be carefully understood and monitored (including baseline, longitudinal manifestations, and desired goal identification), to create awareness of reasons and times they decide to defend themselves, remain isolated, or not manifest behavior as a symbol of their childlike, irrational, inappropriate, and outdated conceptualizations of a negative past reality.

The above client-centered self-analysis and assessment are particularly critical with introverted and isolated clients, since society often provides inadvertent rewards for passivity (which clients can interpret as support or safety), contradicting the internal struggles the client must recognize and master.

In the case of grossly inadequate personalities, the above classification system (including a list of possible positive and negative responses from others, and their weighted degrees of desirability and reward/punishment value for the client) is necessary to give some organization to personality style, characterized by ineffectual and poor judgment responses to social, intellectual, emotional, and behavioral situations.   The client's routine reactive attempts to adapt to demands, are typically inadequate relative to others' expectations.   In this regard, then, high frequency counts in measuring inappropriate behaviors, must be counter-acted with a firm, fixed system to identity types and ranges of positive behavior, and relate them to dynamics of client initiative and goal directedness.

This plan can include global, all inclusive, behavioral categories to increase the probability of clients falling somewhere within a positive behavioral repertoire, with more refined specific behaviors for use with advanced clients.   The clinician, of course, must decide when to change from global assessment scaling to more precise specific behavioral documentation and measurement, and have a rationale to explain these shifts to the client, who may see behavior modification as random, haphazard, and senseless.

Another dimension of dependency, withdrawal, and internalization of the schizoid, depressive, dependent and asthenic disorders, is manipulation and reversed expression of anger, via compliance and passive-dependent allowance of pseudo external control by others (who are also dependent and helpless, due to their need to control and dominate). In these cases, withdrawal has several simultaneous meanings, whose differentiation is a challenge for clinicians doing the evaluative measuring:

a.   expression of negative emotions (which is positive, if incorrect internalizations of personal, exclusive causality are corrected, and the client sees anger as justified);
b.   expression of negative emotion in non-direct and manipulative ways (which is dishonest and destructive to health relationships);
c.   expression of need for significant others (which is positive, if the client learns to see the healthy child hidden inside, and recognizes transference);
d.   expression of misperception of excessive need and illegitimacy of need, with the necessity of concealing this emotion from external love objects;
e.   expression of internal control and power over the self (which is positive), but self-destructive use of power for retroflected blame, punishment, or fear;
f.   non-expression of healthy external manifestations of self, which could improve interpersonal relations and provide empirical success outcomes.

Because of the often-concealed nature of these very active psychodynamics, the clinician must search hard for indicators of the internal process, probably providing more helpful therapy by considering both positive and negative sides of withdrawal and passivity. The richness of dynamic symbolization is certainly present, but the clinician must view inaction, as well as actions, with equal scrutiny, to conceptualize and measure the correct phenomena.

3.   *Drug, Alcohol, and Food Dependencies:*
With clients exhibiting chemical and food-related dependencies and psychological/physical addiction, the clinician faces a difficult and complicated evaluative problem. First, clients possess a neurotic, psychotic, or characterological disorder with the associated measurement, conceptual, and other evaluative problems discussed in this chapter. Secondly, symbolic and physiological dependency is superimposed upon the baseline

personality structure of the client, but the addiction may also be considered a separate disease entity, which many clinicians feel has a distinct etiology, nature, and causal effect on cognitive and behavioral physiology.

Physical alterations related to metabolic, neurologic, muscular, gastro-intestinal, reproductive, and other body/organ systems, can also result in permanent new disease pathologies of physical (i.e., cirrhosis of the liver), neurologic (organic brain syndrome), or psychologic (schizophrenia) nature, with separate degenerative etiology and pathway. These conditions, there-fore, require coordinated diagnosis, treatment, and evaluation related to their ultimate cause, within the client's personality dynamics. In the third instance, public behavioral manifestations of drug or alcohol dependence, violate legal and traditional moral codes, resulting in traumatic societal responses, creating additional anxiety and conflict for clients. This can cause them to conceptualize their problems within multiple (and often mutually-exclusive) theoretical frameworks (e.g., spiritual, social, medical, physiological, psychological, behavioral, or historical), which complicates evaluation. The results (or separate outcomes based on various contin-gencies) also reduce realistic opportunities for multiple relations between therapeutic input and client outcome, particularly when clients are unable to undertake proper treatment due to incarceration; or where social institu-tions with legal power over clients, predetermine many behavioral out-comes, irrespective of related goals of the counselor, or treatment program.

Also, treatment of many drug, alcohol, or food dependencies requires introduction of other tranquilizing, sleep-producing, antipsychotic, stimu-lating, or deconditioning/aversive (for example, anabuse) chemicals to reduce anxiety, stabilize the client, or create negative reactions as an adjunct to psycho- or socio-therapeutic endeavors. This is complicated because one variable can serve as cause, reaction, or adjunctive solution to the problem, and present confusing theoretical and methodological models for clients, in understanding various dimensions of the illness.

Finally, traditional treatment for alcohol, drug, and food dependencies has frequently included both individual and group therapeutic efforts, which add forms of input the clinician must consider, in making evaluative assessments, decisions, and plans.

To further understand complications of evaluation with the above dependencies, each area will be discussed separately, to help the reader apply specific examples from his or her own practice or theoretical perspective, to illustrate the points.

a.   Client's baseline personality organization:
The primary evaluative problem here, is the conceptual and methodological separation (or planned and systematized integration, if possible) of baseline client behaviors, representing any of three major syndromes: (1) primary personality disorder with addictive reactions as defenses; (2) primary personality disorders with the addictive disease as a separate, primary entity with its own dynamics; or (3) primary addictive disease with personality and relationship problems as secondary consequences (see Figure 9).

Figure 9
Patterns of Dependency — Addictive Disease Development

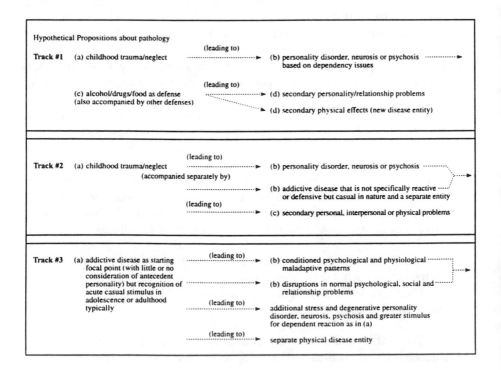

Some clinicians have trouble differentiating the relative significance of personality disease, personality defense to pathological
anxiety, personality defense to normal anxiety, physical disease, or
personality and social effects, of either antecedent personality disease
or addictive disease. This is complicated because there is not necessarily a direct correlation between type, amount, and degree of
compulsiveness of drug or alcohol use, and associated underlying
personality pathologies, which could help the clinician merge or
separate these entities, as appropriate.[171]

Some counselors are uncertain whether they treat a basic personality problem or an addictive disease, and also confuse causes,
effects, primary and secondary anxiety, and defenses, as they explore
which phenomena to measure and why. Since behavioral manifestations of alcohol or drug use are dramatic, pronounced, and crisis-
oriented, it is easy to focus on symptoms rather than basic personality
problems; or to interchange perspectives on each one inadvertently
(particularly since society ostensibly demands attention and correction
of symptoms—not their antecedent causes). Since specific utilization
of drugs or alcohol (and manifested intoxicating effects) occurs outside
the therapeutic session, the counselor can be evaluatively misled
(particularly with minimal cross-validation, through consultation with
significant others in the client's social milieu) by decreased or changed
symptom frequencies, or resistively distorted client reports. Lag time
and possible lack of correlation between therapeutic inputs (skill
utilization, insight of confrontation or support, etc.), symptom
manifestation (intoxication, drug utilization, etc.), and feedback about
symptoms from clients (complicated by drug/alcohol related memory
distortion or defensiveness), confuse the evaluative focus upon either
basic personality dynamics, or chemical disease-related behaviors and
secondary dynamics.

b. Altered states of clients:
A second issue, concerns physically and psychologically-altered states
or existential conditions[172] of chemically-dependent or addicted clients,
as these may represent different *personalities* with which the therapist
must work. One question, involves differential perceptions of the self
which the client encounters during periods of non-usage (or perceived
abstinence/vulnerability/impotency) and usage, intoxication, safety
periods, etc. These awarenesses, states of consciousness, unique
fantasies, and delusional conditions, are related to autonomic and

central nervous system effects of the chemicals;[173] and the client's hopes, expectations, and cognitions/feelings of safety, adequacy, protective dependency, self-punishment, or relaxation when anticipating or utilizing chemical, alcohol, or food substances.[174] Evaluation must understand the client's state of mental adequacy, competency, rationality, and responsibility, as he or she perceives dependency (when using or not using), particularly as the analytic orientation stresses the childlike, indulgent, and narcissistic state of oral need gratification.[175]

Fixation or regression to states of childlike awareness, cause clients to perceive periods of actual existence within childhood arenas of entrapment, and allow dependent clients the fantasy license, to indiscriminately substitute various symptoms of their conflict (or attempts at survival, self-cure, punishment, etc.). The clinician may never be sure when symptom generalization or substitution have occurred, and which direction or confusing pattern has been taken. An associated question, is how physical and psychological effects of usage, serve unilaterally or collectively to (1) regress clients to healthy states of correct childhood need awareness (a self-correction on the delusional life of adulthood), (2) regress them to well-defended states, with sufficiently reduced anxiety to ward off devastating personality disintegration or psychosis, and allow them to work on problems in a state of functional pseudo-protection, (3) regress them to delusional states of personality disorganization and grosser inadequacy, or (4) advance them to states of cognitive and psychic awareness (noted particularly in the psychedelic and transcendental experiences with certain drugs—usually hallucinogenic). Some therapists suggest that clients are more honest, aware, natural, or uninhibited while experiencing the actual crisis of drug or alcohol abuse or withdrawal, so indicators and feedback during these periods might have value to work on anger, guilt, sexual conflict, love, tenderness, or vulnerability, while the wound is actually open. Others, feel chemicals must be totally removed; and with more complete surrender of the defense, the person returns to a more natural and workable state of consciousness and awareness. A concern here, is whether chemical withdrawal creates sufficient trauma to force the client into totally new dimensions of psychopathology, which might be observed in conjunction with pseudo-positivism, created with decreasing chemical frequencies. Clients can elicit dependent symptoms through pleasing the counselor or compulsive social conformity, so the clinician may factor in substitute increase-oriented indicators of health, as chemical frequencies decrease. Here, inverse correlations help monitor pathology or health in the altered drug-free state. An entirely new, more dependent, or more complex individual may be highlighted as part of this process.

Although freedom from reactive or addictive chemical dependency is certainly positive, many clients are terminated from outpatient counseling or discharged from hospitals, without long-term evaluative follow-up to determine if chemical discontinuance is also a stimulus to begin or exacerbate other gradually-unfolding pathological dynamics, not evident at termination. This phenomenon is probable because of collaborative and interdependent pathological roles of others in the identified patients's primary social systems (family, friends, etc,), as they frequently are excluded from direct treatment, and are assumed to be positively affected when the identified client discontinues chemical utilization. What really happens, however, is that some clients are left defenseless and vulnerable with the removal of both personal chemical defenses, and the protection of their deviant social role. The negative scenarios are personal regressions for these significant others; gradual, insidious counterinsurgent sabotage of the growing chemically-free partner or friend; or development of a new social system with different pathological dimensions or manifestations, but little change in degree of health or adequacy.

Also, as clients are psychologically and physiologically moving between various states of chronologic awareness, dependency, ego-capacity, and biologic capability, it is difficult to develop a stable measurement procedure that correctly traces their cognitive whereabouts, interprets their awareness of their status, accounts for cumulative and delayed effects of drugs/alcohol which modulate this conceptual locale, and correctly identifies indices of strength in the correct state, wherein further inputs can yield additional successful results. The cumulative effects of drugs and alcohol on physical tolerance, need, and responsiveness, also produce a constantly moving behavioral (and probably psychological) baseline, as more chemicals are increasingly needed to produce previous effects; but client perceptions also are changing, as physiology is progressively altered. This is, indeed, a difficult moving target for any clinician desirous of stable and meaningful evaluation.

Of course, secondary short- and long-term effects of overloading the physical system with toxic substances (including overdoses of food), alter the organism, and change the data upon which the client predicates decisions related to self-esteem, alternatives for success achievement, relationship potential, identification of feelings, etc. Additions of self-perceptions related to true physical illness (compounding fears of psychological vulnerability); impending death; addiction or emotional dependence; loss of appetite, sleep, or sexual capability; or alterations in physical attractiveness (e.g., obesity), signify personal decision panoramas which are altered in confusing patterns. These may invalidate the nature of fixed operational definitions and scales of personal performance adequacy, so the clinician must flexibly redefine independent, dependent, and intervening variables, to hypothesize new relationships as variables change (especially related to client self-awareness and subjective interpretation of reality), and measure mobile and sometimes erratic baselines.

c. Social deviance and the individual client:
    The illegality of public manifestations of alcohol and drug abuse, presents complications to evaluation. Heightened social awareness and involvement related to chemical abuse, accompanied by myths,[176] cultural mores, moralistic prohibitions, and social stigmatic definitions; provide confusing, limited, antagonistic, and incorrect definitional categories. Clients and counselors use these, consequently, to build judgments about nature of the problem, motivations, causes and effects, and personality of the client. Experimental drug users may be defined as chronic addicts, drug addicts can be labeled as incurable and immoral, and high frequency uses of prescription drugs can be defined as normal, which complicate validity and reliability of evaluative data.

Some combinations of definitions are noted in Figure 10, illustrating a range of possible outcomes, as client and therapist interpret different aspects of the drug or alcohol problem. As the reader can surmise, the client's social position or cultural, racial, and ethnic heritage, are influential factors in predisposing particular outcomes of decision or judgment. The reader will also note, that to each category, are attached qualitative dimensions which are certainly not exhaustive, but suggest directional factors which influence ultimate decisions or perceptions by clients or counselors.

Figure 10
Factors Which Influence the Client's and Therapist's
Perceptions of the Client, the Problem, and Potential Solutions

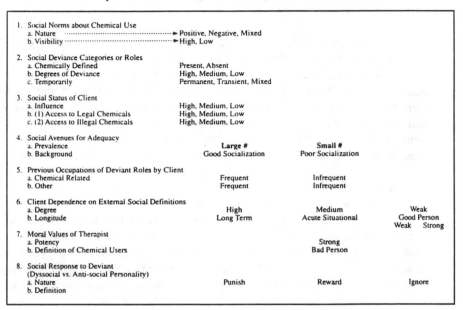

1. Social Norms about Chemical Use
   a. Nature ....➤ Positive, Negative, Mixed
   b. Visibility ....➤ High, Low

2. Social Deviance Categories or Roles
   a. Chemically Defined   Present, Absent
   b. Degrees of Deviance   High, Medium, Low
   c. Temporarily   Permanent, Transient, Mixed

3. Social Status of Client
   a. Influence   High, Medium, Low
   b. (1) Access to Legal Chemicals   High, Medium, Low
   c. (2) Access to Illegal Chemicals High, Medium, Low

4. Social Avenues for Adequacy
   a. Prevalence   Large #   Small #
   b. Background   Good Socialization   Poor Socialization

5. Previous Occupations of Deviant Roles by Client
   a. Chemical Related   Frequent   Infrequent
   b. Other   Frequent   Infrequent

6. Client Dependence on External Social Definitions
   a. Degree   High   Medium   Weak
   b. Longitude   Long Term   Acute Situational Good Person
                                                                            Weak   Strong

7. Moral Values of Therapist
   a. Potency   Strong
   b. Definition of Chemical Users   Bad Person

8. Social Response to Deviant
   (Dyssocial vs. Anti-social Personality)
   a. Nature   Punish   Reward   Ignore
   b. Definition

The large number of factors influencing definitions of roles and behaviors available to the client with drug, alcohol, or eating problems, and complex interaction of social and personal interpretive dynamics in viewing reality, suggest that the therapist (also in a social vs. client advocacy dilemma) has a difficult evaluative problem. This involves selection of client outcome objectives, which are simultaneously (1) of primary interest in the client's motivational hierarchy, based on subjective perceptions of the world, self, and significant others; (2) syntonic with the counselor's values and agency role requirements; (3) conforming to social expectations in the client's milieu, so as to reduce social negative reactions; (4) commensurate with developmental needs of the client, even though of lower immediate priority to the client; (5) realistic in terms of facilitating access to socially available avenues of success, adequacy, nurturance, etc., which are culturally and situationally idiosyncratic (especially considering sick, crazy, or bad social roles); (6) current and timely in terms of the client's changing roles, society's fluctuating role opportunities and definitions of its members, variable reactions of society to deviant and normal citizens, social agency views based on value realignments and funding exigencies, and other intervening variables.

Because meaning of outcomes is strongly influenced by social opportunity, expectations, positions, and self-perceptions, the deviant or conforming client substance abuser, is influenced in a variety of ways, due to his or her unique method of adaptation/defense/acting out. Society's framework within which the client defines adequacy, failure, etc., also provides feedback, socialized data, and reinforcement/punishment for various states of being within which behavioral outcomes are defined by the client, and operationalized by the evaluating therapist.

This is particularly confusing with moralistic, spiritual, or religious norms which can be variously interpreted, yet remain within the realm of spiritual mysticism, with often unavailable direct empirical feedback, except for personal religious experiences (visions, awareness, etc.), or faith alone. Views, expectations, and feedback from God or other supreme spiritual entities, are not always clearly identifiable, so the client interpreting his or her status vis-à-vis spiritual phenomena, requires considerable help in (1) ruling out interventive influence of psychopathology; (2) assuring that he or she gives ample consideration to accuracy of their perceptions (e.g., I have sinned in performing drug-related behavior A); (3) helping to factor in social and psychological influences, so true spiritual phenomena or contingencies remain isolated; (4) helping with correct use of multiple indices of spiritual feedback for the greatest chance of validity, in a complex arena of theological, philosophical, and metaphysical science (e.g., combining voices heard in quiet church, interpretations of personal scripture reading, or consultative outcomes with a rabbi; with emotional feelings at other times, meanings of specific behaviors, feedback from friends, etc.).

The clinician is negligent in dismissing spiritual concerns about outcomes because of presumed deficits of empirical evidence, since many clients' lives are defined within their spirituality, relative to mystical/transcendental/religious contingencies which are *real* in their reality.

In these cases, outcome decisions and observations can be isolated and, although assessed in terms of degree, frequency, potency, or duration, have no other qualitative significance relative to the client's life gestalt.[177]

d. Rehabilitation regimen:
A fourth issue for evaluation, is the use of chemical substances in actual treatment of problems involving pathologic use of drugs or alcohol. One concern is stimulus generalization, where the client has difficulty conceptualizing the difference between drugs as an anxiety-reducing escape from conflict-ridden reality, and chemotherapeutic substances, as antithetical anxiety-reducing approaches to conflict resolution. This generalized view is difficult to ignore with pronounced physical effects of abused or therapeutically-prescribed drugs, and the ease with which physiology can become an exaggerated and inappropriate focus of both problem and solution. The therapist must assess the client's viewpoint about the causal nature and rehabilitative potential of chemicals, noting that clients vary in their (1) faith in effectiveness of drugs, (2) medical and physical orientation to bio-psychosocial problems, (3) need to cathect energy into substantive, rather than less obvious, emotional components of personal and social dynamics of growth or regression, and (4) dependence on therapists, who show varying positive or negative feelings about the value of drug use, or chemotherapeutic treatment (either alone, or as an addendum to psychotherapy). Conflict between clients and counselors may be acted out using drugs or medication, to elucidate struggles for independence and expression of anger. In these cases, medication becomes a symbolic pawn in a deeper and more complicated socio- and psychodynamic gamelike struggle.

Clients who respond both to what is real in life, relative to the value and effect of drugs; and also to what is best for them—may selectively manifest behavior which is ego-syntonic (and therefore safe and positive for them), yet simultaneously alter (increase, decrease, or change) behavioral indices. Counselors may be left with false data, if unaware of the client's personal value baseline, established prior to development of operationalized behavioral symbols.

Another related issue, is the prevalent occurrence of conflictual psychological dependence among drug/alcohol/food abusers, wherein antagonists to the use of drugs, insist that passivity and compliance are increased, and chemical dependence is rewarded with chemotherapy. Clients may experience power, authority, and control of psychiatrists or physicians who prescribe drugs, which some feel is an unnecessarily-imposed transference. Opponents, however, argue that drugs simply neutralize excessive anxiety and heighten optimism, to allow counselors to effectively deal with psychologic origins of dependence, with minimal interference from defensive resistance.[178]

If therapeutically-introduced drugs, in fact, increase dependence, then counselors are challenged to interpret the apparent inverse correlation between therapeutic chemical input, and client independence (as one dependent variable outcome); and to discover the point at which decreased symptoms of drug abuse can be interpreted as growth, given added effects of a second source of dependent artificial control. Some counselors argue that the growth curve begins to increase relative to length of therapy (either drug or psycho), as presenting symptoms decline. Even if pharmacotherapy drugs are eventually withdrawn, the clinician must correctly assess possible substitution of psychologic and social dependence in counseling relationships, and search for indices of independence, which can be measured irrespective of transient dependence-producing phenomena (drugs or counselor influence). Although some research suggests that maintenance dosages of medication, and psychotherapy to a lesser extent, forestall symptom recurrence in psychotics,[179] it is possible that counseling only encourages clients to continue drug dependence (i.e., take their legal medication regularly), and has no independent growth effect to counteract strong dependence-inducing effect of drugs.[180]

The "additive" effect of drugs and psychotherapy is uncertain,[181] as are precise independent effects of therapeutic support vs. drug support, as both may be interchanged at different times to reduce anxiety, or allow anxiety to stimulate awareness, motivation, security, etc.

The counselor should find critical levels of anxiety in each client, which are necessary to allow confidence and stability for therapy to work, but remain of sufficient intensity to assist growth. This critical level is hard to measure when there are multiple physical and psychologic factors which reduce, increase, or stabilize anxiety. Increased dependence, of course, can precipitate increases in secondary emotions or behaviors like anger, manipulativeness, or seduction. This can cause the client, again, to focus on the wrong basic phenomena, yet provide sufficiently-pronounced empirical behavior that the counselor/ evaluator either systematically ignores or measures, since it has conversion symbolization relative to more fundamental foci of treatment and client personality dynamics.

Another problem affecting decisions about independent or interactive use of psycho- vs. pharmaco-therapy, is the underlying personality organization of the client. Some research suggests that either drugs or therapy may be more effective, depending on diagnostic category,[182] each client's baseline level of anxiety, and their proclivity to express anxiety in volatile, dramatic, and excessive ways.[183]

The use of drugs may also obscure the baseline state of anxiety, by not letting it exist as an independent phenomenon, or manipulating it, so that clear foci or independent-dependent relations, are poorly visible. If this is the case, clients are less reliable cohorts in measurement, and may increase anxiety as they experience vulnerability to external control or influence, decreased self-esteem, or changes in self-perceptions of adequacy, stability, or autonomy.

The length of time the client remains in treatment, during which measurements are taken, provides differing frameworks for inputs and outcomes to materialize. Whether there is an independent effect of therapy or medication, a joint synergistic effect, or no effect of either; time influences client receptivity to inputs, in the following ways:[184]

(1) psychotherapy may have latent or delayed effects, for which cumulative inputs are necessary for sufficient insight, and where·
   (a) prior drug use delays this process even further,
   (b) current therapeutic medication delays this effect by creating or sustaining more dependency, or helps this process via anxiety-reduction and symptomatic remission,
   (c) medication reduces anxiety substantially, but the client requires a lengthy anxiety-reduced state, prior to becoming receptive to therapy;

(2) psychotherapy may have no effect until medication has sufficient time to:
   (a) reduce anxiety,

(b) stabilize the client,

(c) create or assist in positive perceptual or physiological change;

(3) therapeutic medication may act independently of psychotherapy when:

(a) the client values the medical model and associated regimen, and feels medicine *heals,*

(b) the therapy relationship is not effective in either the short or long run,

(c) the client has sufficient strength or help from significant others to change, once medication reduces anxiety,

(d) medication creates or extends dependency where the client feels secure, appears healthy, or manifests conforming behavior as an example of pseudo-strength,

(e) therapy is effective for brief crises, and medication has longer power of support, or contributes to client expectancy for change, etc.;

(4) psychotherapy and medication may have interactive effects when:

(a) they supplement each other's deficits, and jointly reduce anxiety,

(b) dependence on medication and therapy, are contingent conditions for gradual reduction in frequencies of both chemical and therapeutic controls, and rewards are concurrently given for autonomous functioning.

Because the literature remains undecided about effects of these independent variables (medication and therapy), there is uncertainty as to measurement focus, time frame, reliability, and validity. The complicated interaction of medication/drug characteristics and similar natures of the psychotherapeutic phenomena, are illustrated in Figure 11. This suggests that varying dynamics of chemical activity are paired with similarly-varying dimensions of psychotherapy, and specific client outcome is affected by strength, influence, and curative dynamics (including selective client perception) of both phenomena.

In situations where medication has high ability to produce compliance via dependency, reduce anxiety, and work quickly; and can function as a reliable defense in the past, viewed as helpful and having minimal side effects—paired with a therapist who (1) powerfully sustains dependency, (2) cannot build trust or reduce anxiety (so

Figure 11
Drug or Medication Characteristics
Interacting with Counseling Contingencies

Psychotherapy and Psycho-Social Counseling	Capability to Produce Dependency	Capability to Reduce Anxiety	Length of Time for intended Action	Length of Past Usage	Length of Present Usage	Flexibility in Usage Regimen	Reputation as Positive Helping Agent	Location of Use in pt. — out pt.	+ or - Side Effects	Capability to change user & capability to Alter Perception/ Behavior
Power of therapist to Produce Dependency	H M L	H M L	Long Med Short	Long Med Short	Long Med Short		Good Med Bad		Min Max	
Strength of Trust Building	H M L									
Capability to produce insight and change										
Capability to Reduce Anxiety	H M L									
Length of Time for intended Action	Long Med Short									
Length of Therapy	Long Med Short									
Flexibility to change the approach										
Subjective value of Therapist and therapy to client										
Transference or side effects or complications of therapeutic Relationship										

medication fills the void), (3) requires extended work before the client sees results (also dependent on the client's degree of pathology), and (4) has only a short time to work with the client—the result may mean a greater value effect from medication, as opposed to psychotherapy. Any one of a host of different combinations can conceivably produce different results.

e.   Group process:
The last evaluative concern involves group therapeutic activities associated with inpatient and outpatient drug or alcohol programs. As noted by Levine,[185] the character and behavioral similarities of addicts in groups, may prevent a range of differential interactions, ideal for the therapeutic process. The challenges to existing behaviors through awareness and confrontation by others, and presentation of alternatives seen in heterogeneous social group living, do not necessarily occur in the group process. Support of defensive patterns may occur through incorrect focus on the addiction itself, and members may comfortably identify with each other, so group norms foster dependence.

The clinical evaluator must study conformity to group norms[186] as growth vs. entrapment, particularly because clients may be influenced by the powerful nature of the group process, with inclination to focus on individual deviance, as negative. Intra- and extra-group behavioral goals should be established, monitored, and compared, as to their unique meaning for each client. Also, control of the group (especially on members' attitudes and behaviors outside the group) should be assessed and held constant (or systematically decreased), particularly as cohesion develops in later stages of group process, when it may be more difficult for groups to allow member autonomy. This process of counter-dependence[187] may interfere with the therapeutic mission, and can be misinterpreted by the counselor-evaluator. Also, the group as a whole, should be measured for independent holistic progress, separate from specific members. This serves as an index of gross therapeutic effectiveness and success with individual members, ultimately manifested through individual rejection of the group during planned termination.

The hard-hitting confrontation seen in some groups of alcohol or drug clients, should be carefully studied within the framework of "therapeutic" methodology, but also as a dynamic process, which may encourage destructive (to self and others) utilization of anger and guilt, under the guise of developmentally-oriented therapy. The evaluator must operationally define all inputs as they theoretically relate to desired outcomes, making sure they are mutually exclusive, in not allowing multiple definitions or interpretations of clients. In cases where excessive group coercion, dominance, or aggression are utilized, the evaluator should assess member avoidance, withdrawal, counter-aggression, and termination, in their positive as well as negative connotations.

Countertransference of the therapist, is sometimes seen in the behaviors and norms or dynamics the leader tolerates or encourages among group members,[188] and should be separated out (not ignored) as a different independent variable for decision-making, relative to treatment focus, orientation, and topics for work.

4.   *Antisocial Personalities:*
     Evaluation with this group is challenging, principally because of difficulty in delivering meaningful and lasting therapeutic service. Indices of therapist-client relationship are scarce, due to socio- and psychopathic inability to form trusting liaisons (or angry manipulations of pseudo relationships, for selfish gain). Operationalizations of any forms of insight are minimal, since this deeper growth is frequently absent.[189] The nature of generalized client anger, distrust, and alienation from humanistic and personal goals, coupled with social distance, selfish manipulations, and self-serving task orientation; are strong determinants of the types of evaluative foci which are rationally valuable for this personality category. Some specific considerations for clinical evaluation, however, are as follows:

a.   One problem with antisocial personalities, is lack of motivation and capability for personal insight, and inability to demonstrate change in relationships, self-awareness, or other forms of intrapsychic development. This, and client distrust of the therapeutic experience, rob the counselor of opportunities to designate, observe, and document small units of growth or change, which frequently do not materialize as clients distort data, in either positive or negative directions. Change which does occur, must be carefully checked to assure its validity, and weighed as to possible short-term functionality or symbolic and superficial meaning, as an example of self-serving manipulation.

     Global long-range social measures may be of greater value, since awareness of major indices of conformity and deviance does not necessarily require small incremental units of personality change; and because their authenticity can be more easily corroborated through policy, court, probation, parole, employment, hospitalization, and other public reports.

b.   Inability of antisocial personalities to work on substantive individual change, means that counselors frequently help them discover and secure social positions (in jobs, relationships, lifestyles, etc.), which complement or tolerate unchangeable or idiosyncratic behavior. Appropriate evaluative foci include: (1) degree of actual fit between personality and role; (2) client ability to do accurate role assessments, and correctly perceive person-situation congruence; (3) ability to negotiate/manipulate to secure necessary life-sustaining positions; and (4) ability to play appropriate social games, to maintain role opportunities and social rewards. This includes evaluation of ability to avoid manifestations of public deviance, even if symptom substitution must be taught by the social service professional.

c.   In some situations, antisocial clients are so overwhelmed with periodic acute anxiety (converted to anger, denial, projection, and other forms of acting out), or are so controlled by their behavioral patterns, that the maladaptivity of their personal style becomes oblivious to them, and they are unable to even selfishly figure out a way to survive. The counselor, in these situations, may desire an evaluative focus which (1) measures increments of ability to perceive external manifestations of self (including measurement of ability to select and monitor external behavioral feedback), and/or (2) assesses the client's need (symptomatic needs assessment) for additional defenses to adapt more successfully, and monitor adaptation of additional defenses which assist in more functional avoidance of public deviance.

Within this overall process, the counselor can help clients evaluate approximations toward their ability to accept the characterological, permanent, and serious nature of their disorder. This includes the concomitant ability to make modifications; to incorporate the non-changing self into a society which has differential avenues for integration, protection/isolation; and, at least, superficial adaptation.

d.   Finally, degree of generalization of defensive response can be a target, as the counselor helps clients focus their acting out, so their symptoms become more localized to specific objects. This evaluative strategy involves variance or degree of dispersion of defensive foci, with positive change representing reduction of targeted objects for the clients, and narrowing width of defensive self-expression. Because of poor ability to discriminate, however, many clients experience failure at this reductionism also, so benefits of changes in symptom range or scope, could be negated. Narrowing of angry feelings, for example, to one or two people in the client's life, might reduce the empirical probability of achieving public recognition, but could affect gains, with the future destruction of personal relationships necessary to support the client's already-precarious balance. The evaluator, however, should consider both reductionist and expansionist perspectives, in helping the client select evaluative goals.

Children as Clients

There are numerous problems evaluating work with children, beginning with development of proper diagnoses, and concluding with difficulties in measuring outcome maturation and development. Significant evaluative concerns will be outlined below, with a reminder to counselors that children must be considered an integral part of the contextual nature of the family environment, within which they are socialized and must grow, adapt, and survive.

Validity of Behavioral Indicators

To identify and measure baseline behavior at most preadolescent stages, are difficult processes. This is partly because children's dependence on parental control and influence, suggests they may be only barometers of parental pathology (reactors in a game they neither fully understand, nor control, to any appreciable degree), and behave in relatively adaptive fashion, within a deterministic and controlled environment. To assess children's behavior in the above surrogate and symbolic framework, the evaluator runs the risk of not treating asymptomatic parents, or treating and measuring children as discrete primary indices of specific targeted problems; but neglecting to concurrently measure changes in the children, which (a) reflect pathology resulting from their roles and behaviors as parental barometers, (b) developed through maturation during the period they were symptom bearers, or (c) resulted from other independent variables, not related directly (maybe related transferentially) to parents. Also, if children are the identified clients, evaluative attention may artificially increase or decrease their behavior (which children may not recognize or report), which leaves the real independent variable (the parents, family system, etc.) untreated. Therefore, this parental force continues to exert influences, or alters its influence, while the counselor is incorrectly seeking causal linkages inside the child (really a dependent variable), or is seeking causal connections in a backwards fashion, i.e., from child as stimulus, to parent as respondent.

Constant Variable Change

The continual and often rapid maturational process (which differs between children), makes standardized comparison or scoring difficult among moving and deceptive targets. Cognitive ability frequently undergoes advancement, retreat, and resting, so insight is an elusive outcome which can have validity and reliability one day, but insignificant meaning as a foundation for consequent behaviors, feelings, or values the next day, week, or month. Pairing insight, as an outcome, with specific behavior, is also confusing, as correlation may be nonexistent, curvilinear, or inverse (depending on maturational dynamics, plus the child's selective interpretation). Possibly, the only meaningful way to assess therapeutic outcome with the constant flux of childhood development, is to utilize long-range assessments of global outcomes. This, however, can be a problem of logistics, parental and societal demands for therapeutic immediacy, and inability to connect inputs at an earlier age, with personal causal outcomes farther down the road. The powerless status of children, of course, suggests that parents or therapists with consistent, powerful reinforcers and behavioral controls, can apparently condition almost any desired behavior. This is only an index of dependence, relative to conformity to externally-imposed rules, not necessarily symbolic of healthy adaptation.

The constant experience of children also, is no assurance that any one child is serious about the significance of any one thought/feeling/behavior, at any one time. Measurement may reflect temporary infatuation or curiosity, and not relate specifically to real personality core. Therapeutic inputs, therefore, may be correctly utilized for the wrong behaviors, with limited relevance for short- or long-term interests of the experimenting child, both in terms of pragmatic, as well as symbolic learning or developing.

Questionable Feedback Reliability

A third evaluative problem working with children, is their frequent inability to fully or correctly perceive and understand their needs and feelings, and verbalize or otherwise communicate accurate and consistent feedback about the value of therapeutic inputs, other phenomena in their lives which influence their development (i.e., pressures from parents), or outcome results of therapy, in terms of feeling, attitude, conceptual, or behavioral change. Although feedback can be obtained from external observers, this data is second-hand, and predicated on presumed behavioral indices or biased perceptions, which may distort true internal characteristics of children.

Work with children requires considerable time and focused attention, to completely draw out feelings and thoughts, separate constant characterological feeling/thought patterns from more transient or experimental ideations, and validate hypothesized findings through multiple observational and testing strategies and consultative feedback reports from significant others, as well as the children themselves.

Additionally, the prevalence of fantasy, juxtaposed on reality throughout early childhood, suggests that practitioners develop a baseline system of categorization[190] (or structured observation).[191] This is necessary to record types of fantasy and reality conceptions; antecedent and consequent behaviors which pinpoint the presence of fantasy vs. reality thoughts; and other factors which designate a baseline pattern, in comparing ideations and associated behaviors in standardized degrees of deviation or conformity, to the norm for each child, or for a typical caseload. The clinician who does not define children's ideations in reference to an a priori framework, may be confused about progress or regression, and have trouble making a correct diagnosis. This is very important, for example, to rule out psychosis, or identify thought patterns which are taught and maintained as necessary to family or cultural roles and norms, as opposed to individual autonomous fantasies, representing serious intrapsychic disturbance.

Peer Influence in Advanced Latency and Adolescence

In working with young people in this age range, the clinical evaluator struggles with individual vs. group normative influence/control of the client. This means, entering therapy with a handicapped vulnerability to external control alternating with internal control (for the counselor, an uncontrolled independent variable), complicated because this state of fluxuation is normal, and should not be totally interdicted by additional powerful influence of the therapist. The client, in fact, might be broadly conceptualized as the youth *culture* or the specific peer *group* which has an agenda of growth, experimentation, and turmoil[192] (alliances, rejections, deviance, conformity, subgroups, rituals, territory, etc.), that may take precedence over any conceptualization of the individual client.

Strong norms of the group, and ability to protect members from external control, suggest high probability of altering planned therapeutic outcomes of individuals. Also, conformity to therapeutically-desirable outcomes, may place the client in a highly-visible and vulnerable position of deviance, and consequent group ostracism. The way to avoid this, is to develop prematurely individual ability for autonomy, or attempt to make changes in the whole group, which is logistically improbable. Evaluation may be more realistic and valid, if measured goals are attainable, irrespective of group acceptability (individual behavior in home situations or with one close friend), or if outcomes are selected which incorporate real exigencies of peer-group existence:

1.   the clients initially identify and record frequencies of times they conform to group behavior (without any personal or group change expected), when this also compromises other personal value, social, or legal standards;
2.   adolescents develop target goals for suggesting changes in group norms or collectively-accepted behaviors, with positive therapeutic outcomes assessed only for efforts to precipitate change, and not verifiable concrete results;
3.   clients document deviant behaviors in the context of their peer group lives, and are assessed on the quality with which they discuss how they handled fear, anxiety, or guilt, so defensive behavior is not threatened, but becomes an acceptable and rewarded behavioral target for assessment.

In some cases, the counselor can schedule occasional appointments with the identified client and selected peers, to operationalize the systemic model for diagnosis and treatment, although this is time-consuming and logistically difficult, and requires exceptional dedication. When this is not possible, the counselor must keep in mind issues of validity and reliability, and develop perceptive plans to double check legitimacy, feasibility, and accurate report of specific designated targets.

Developmental Immaturity and Premature Goals

One dynamic problem in working with children and evaluating them, is that their capability for therapeutic gain, is constrained by developmental behavioral and cognitive ceilings at each state of growth. They are, therefore, frequently unable to use more advanced skills to help the process of change, at their present positions. Tools for change may develop at roughly the same rate as the consequent behavior, so change capabilities must frequently be borrowed or utilized from within the skill reservoirs of parents or others, or used prematurely by the child from his/her own future resources. Therapists should scrutinize their expectations, so internal bio-psychosocial capabilities are seen as potential targets, rather than placing evaluative attention simply on dependent conditioned behavior, on the part of the reflexive or reactive child. Since the child may not presently have skill or capability to assist in his or her own change, the therapist needs to question the rationale for working with him or her at all, or carefully focus on independent variables within the child, which have a reasonable chance of producing relevant change. Otherwise, exclusive work with parents, teachers, or other reinforcing agents, may be the more rational way to proceed and evaluate validly.

This brings into question the nature of corrective experiences[193] with children, and their capability to really participate in this process, or exclusively be evaluated in terms of conformity to externally imposed parental behavioral norms. Work with children directly, can sometimes be a facade, wherein therapeutic inputs have no capability of interacting with undeveloped skills. Measurement may be random, as the child arbitrarily behaves irrespective of isolated inputs, with no channel of reception within the client. Other times, measurement is predicated on parental input, which is external to particular dimensions of the therapeutic process with the child.[194]

Self-Determination Among Children

The last problem, is that most behaviors of children and adolescents are diagnostically assessed vis-à-vis parental and socially-imposed mandates, regarding how they should think, feel, or act, given assigned roles (school learner, church attender, listener to parents, etc.) and parentally-controlled social norms. In the first place, the counselor may approach the clinical situation with a reactively nonauthoritarian framework, which suggests that outcomes representing change internally in the child or conditioned external behavior, may stifle creative potential and cause subsequent conflicts, relative to conformity and constricted autonomy. These are either (1) not measured, because present conformity suggests case closing, or (2) measured subsequently, but not attributed to either therapeutic inputs or conflicts which appeared to occur later, but actually occurred as success was initially judged and incorrectly associated with conformity. The counselor must consider the evaluative meaning of dependent conformity, and degree of ego-syntonic conceptualization the child needs to artificially manufacture, to please society; and the meaning of this reality integration (what the child wants and needs vs. what society/parents want or need), as a process measured as either growth or deterioration. Nonconformity or conformity, therefore, must not only be evaluated as dependent variables, but also independent variables, affecting future conditions of the psyche.

Psychosis

In considering clinical evaluative issues for these serious psychosocial illnesses, the reader might keep in mind functional theories which stress the continuum of mental illness (neurosis, psychosis, character disorder), in terms of development of the syndrome predicated on antecedent conditions of dynamic functioning, as well as severity of manifestation, ranging from normal to grossly deviant.[195]

Evaluative questions about psychoses are partly dealt with, as representing exaggerations (based on combination of increased anxiety/stress, and depressed ego or social support adaptive capacity) of thought, mood, or behavioral patterns. These also serve as stimuli (the symptoms themselves) for reactions of the responding counselor (or social system/community), and the frightened client, who experiences regression and personality deterioration. As one example, Rosen[196] believes in linear development of pathology, from neurosis through manic-depressive disorders, toward schizophrenia. Arieti[197] also believes, that among factors which delay or completely avert psychosis, is ability of the patient to resort to additional neurotic defenses.

On the other hand, psychosis may also represent a totally separate phenomenon from other syndrome categories, and carry an independent set of evaluative questions which reflect the unique and autonomous nature of this mental health problem. The following sections discuss the author's perspectives on major evaluative concerns, which include both the continua interpretation, and the separate phenomenon explanation.

Frequency of Inpatient Collateral Treatment

The frequency with which psychotic clients require permanent or acute hospitalization, adds a unique and potent dimension to the evaluative scenario. The consistency and control capability of the secluded and restrictively isolated inpatient milieu, allows excellent potential for systematic behavioral modification, planning, and evaluation.[198]

It may be an excellent way to define and isolate immediate/short-term independent and dependent variables, and engage the patient in psycho- and socio-dynamic learning processes, as part of an interactive cause and effect network of relationships and activities.[199] However, *connection* between (a) short-term empirical behavioral criteria of performance adequacy for clients (which is fairly easy to measure); and either (b) internal psychologic changes, which truly represent autonomy, rather than operantly conditioned reflexive response (learned dependency), or (c) long-term relational and social survival capability—is still tenuous and hypothetical.[200] The evaluator should certainly assess reinforced behavioral changes of each inpatient, but carefully match evaluation here, with therapeutic need to transfer independent variable reinforcers from the hospital staff, to both client and significant others, in their social milieu outside the hospital. Further, the therapist should measure/evaluate the acquisition process itself, as reinforcement capability and responsibility are transferred relative to the actual outcome effectiveness of reinforcements. Also, evaluation may attend to critical learning of some form of deviance on the part of the client, so they will not only resist powerful dependency control of the hospital setting, but reject controlling power of pathological family systems, to which many will be discharged in the hopes of sustained recovery.[201] Evaluation requires assessment of re-entry capability of each patient's family of origin or nuclear family (or other social situation within which patients will occupy post-discharge roles and positions), as simple classification categories can be developed, to conceptually determine some degree of probability of support from each family or social system under consideration.

Specific conditioned behaviors which patients learn in the hospital, must be converted (in their minds) to equivalent behaviors outside the hospital. The clinician should assess degree to which each patient is able to categorize and use various conversion models, so accurate classification and long-term assessment can be negotiated. This avoids halo effects of safe therapy inside the hospital, and placebo effect of pseudo or fantasized treatment effectiveness—both of which are shattered, with early post-discharge returns to the hospital.[202] In this light, readmission, conformity, or dependency on the presumably healthier environment of the hospital ward (as opposed to the crazy or pathological family, with its ambivalent need/aversion conflict for the client), can also be seen as a positive behavioral repertoire (which the client needs to understand, since it implies some form of strength and search for adequacy). Yet, it must be systematically withdrawn, and replaced with similar supportive structures and processes outside the hospital. Clients should be full participants in understanding the artificiality and pseudo-support of their inpatient states, but they must help design and implement alternative plans to replace this safe haven, with personally and socially reasonable and effective supportive resources, external to their inpatient situation. Programs emphasizing deinstitutionalization, develop graduated procedures to systematically and slowly allow clients to test coping skills in increasing periods of time "off campus"; but measurement is often neglected in documenting frequencies of (a) adaptive behaviors, (b) clients' abilities to draw conceptual parallels (find parallel supportive structures) between hospital and community environments, (c) decreased dependence (maybe increasing alienation, rejection, and deviance) on hospital systems of monitoring and behavioral modification, and (d) awareness (and subsequent modification) of "crazy" acting out, as this helps clients be rescued, and communicate their desire and need for removal from pathologic inner conflicts, or outer environments which threaten survival.

Strength of the Environment as an Uncontrolled Intervening/Independent Variable

Although the social environment, with pressures for performance and inadvertent support of pathologic family systems, is a significant factor in the cause and exacerbation of psychotic illness; the environment is also significant in influencing type, range, and success probabilities of varying outcomes for clients attempting to recover. A typical outcome success measure for the post-hospitalized psychotic client, is some manifestation of social competence[203] (job relationship stability, self-support, schooling, noncriminal activity, etc.). This is not necessarily correlated to criteria for hospital discharge, so there are serious questions of validity, when length of time away from the hospital, is used as an index of treatment success.

In some cases, skills learned in the hospital for survival there, are not directly transferable to extra-hospital settings, so it is difficult to match up clinical input outcomes. Even though some clients survive, it is unclear how and to what degree, they modify adaptive strategies for survival in the "real world." Also, the community and its significant spokespeople (employers, landlords, teachers, etc.), serve as powerful influences on the mentally ill person, through stereotyped discrimination, applying performance pressure, or exhibiting intolerance for graduated patterns of recovery (and progressive manifested adequacy). Community reaction is a variable, causing a variety of reactive outcomes among clients, which (a) influence overall self-perceptions and adaptive capacity and, therefore, may mitigate or alter effectiveness of previous clinical inputs, or (b) cause additional outcomes, which confuse a more desirably clear picture of cause-effect relations (also possibly creating interactive effects between outcomes, which cannot be traced to specific inputs, or are explained due to input-interactivity, which may be impossible to isolate once the client resides in the community at large). All these factors are influenced by the general low status attributed to citizens with serious physical, social, or mental illnesses.

Also, the community provides an arena for manifesting outcomes in which clients can idealistically meet individual needs of life circumstances, yet each avenue for success has a relative probability, which suggests overall relative frequencies of achieving adequacy, given specific environmental conditions (e.g., low inflation), and particular characteristics of individuals. These factors appear generally independent of any one psychotic or mentally ill individual, and may present an array of outcomes, based on broad concepts of social norms and societal expectations. In specific terms, this may mean the discharged patient is rapidly fired from a new job, based on inability to produce timely normative behaviors (their idiosyncratic style may deviate drastically from the employer's perceived mean). This can be interpreted as a negative outcome (not necessarily the full responsibility of the recovering client), and create more anxiety, to ultimately stimulate other negative outcomes. In all cases, evaluation is confusing as these intervening factors become operative, and are particularly hard to understand, if the evaluative plan does not include a flexible mechanism to index client outcomes, based on varying influences of social conditions. A moderately negative outcome (i.e., job loss, but subsequent job-seeking behavior) may be defined as positive, if that particular client is attempting to survive in a social milieu with low survivability probability. Of course, the client must also be taught to employ this selective and variable interpretation, and should be evaluated based on learned ability to correlate his or her own abilities, with environments yielding a high success probability (personal expectations of patients is a third standard to consider, for baseline and goal directed measurement). There is also a logistical problem in measuring long-term social competence, as increasing success or failure make the client inaccessible, invisible, or unmotivated.

Creativity and the Psychotic/Deviant Phenomenon

One characteristic of the psychotic phenomenon, is high degree of symbolism, massive reconstruction of reality as an attempt at self-cure, and nontraditional innovative cognitive representation, which places psychotic clients, truly, in a class by themselves. Autistic individualism of each client ignores and substantially negates normal baseline behavior (except as it symbolized an irresolvable conflict, or other form of anxiety-provoking entrapment). This situation represents infusion of primary process[204] conflictual material, into an ego which interprets weakened defenses due to the strength of repressed material, or inadequacy of the personal/social adaptive gestalt. Additionally, this ego transcends present reality by regression to childhood perceptual states, or futuristic efforts to change painful reality via fantasy expectations, changing role configurations, or social rule alterations. Measurement of this highly idiosyncratic re-created reality is nearly impossible, due to the volume of unconscious cognitive concepts and constructs (and relations between them) which can be used, and the rigid pattern in many psychotics, of not developing a pattern of rules. Measurement of each conceptual paradigm against itself as a baseline, necessitates an excessive number of multiple baselines, which confuses evaluative decision-making, and causes a series of narrow views of a segmented personality. Repeated use of psychotic process as an unsuccessful attempt at adaptation, causes more anxiety and redoubled efforts to make craziness work, so the process becomes more exaggerated, less predictable, and difficult to measure.

Another problem, is that clients may certainly envision a norm, standard, or ideal adaptive community or group to which they aspire to belong, but have difficulty communicating this model to the counselor, who often invalidates its credibility as an acceptable temporary standard for measurement purposes (these clients also see a traditional normative community or group from which they are alienated, and where they have failed). Getting on the same track with each psychotic client, is not only critical for initial trust and relationship building, but mandatory for effective evaluation, in the world which each client re-creates and which, in confusing ways, serves as a behavioral standard reinforcement for thoughts, feelings, and actions.

Therapists can establish criterion normative baselines of traditional thought and behavior for psychotic clients, but need to ask probing questions about the process by which they either (1) enter the psychotic's world and use power/influence to create change, or (2) use power/influence from outside (an external position) this world to create stimulus for change, which clients either (a) filter back through their own world or (b) convert to adaptive perceptions and behaviors in the world from which they are estranged.

Evaluative questions are directly related to goals and therapeutic dynamics of each counselor's theory of intervention, but become even more pointed, as the severity of separation of two or more realities, is manifest in the seriously disturbed individual. It is difficult to discover the etiology of each conceptual and emotional distortion of the psychotic, but even more complicated to select an input (therapeutic word, gesture, affect, behavior, etc.) with high probability of creating a stimulus for change; and then make a consequent self-evaluative decision regarding adequacy of this strategic choice, to globally lump a whole series of inputs together, and look at broader outcomes. There is always the problem of possible random use of independent input therapy variables, and much more difficulty in sorting out true change (based on theory of psycho-socio-dynamics) versus reactive learning of outcomes, based on unknown individual or clustered stimuli. If this occurs, it ultimately relegates the therapeutic thought process (what the counselor thinks or conceptualizes) to nominal level variables, which can be internally random or disconnected, or correlated only by their occurrence simultaneously, during the therapeutic hour—leaving no rationale for counselors learning specific theories or techniques (especially, insight-oriented).

Influence of Physiologic Causality in Psychotic Illness

The increasing appearance of genetic, hormonal, endocrinologic, cerebral, or other physiology-based explanations of psychoses (especially schizophrenia), both helps and hinders evaluative process. Physical indices of empirically tested pathologies, certainly lend themselves to more vigorous control, manipulation, and accountability, especially due to rapid and increasingly predictable responsiveness of the body, to a wide range of safe and effective medications (including potential effectiveness of surgical interventions in cerebral areas). If physiologic outcome indicators can be isolated from the significant influences of psychological self-interpretation and emotional conditioning of small group and social system processes, a fairly clear linear causality explanation can be hypothesized and tested. Hereby, are explored different independent samples, matched pairs, or varying presentations of the independent variable longitudinally, on the same sample.[205] The combined effect of physical and socio/psychological dimensions clouds the picture, and may initially require separate evaluative designs and autonomous treatment planning, since the integrated relationship can only be selectively interpreted by the client, and secondarily hypothesized by the therapist. Further research findings, of course, suggest that gradual conversion of these two parameters, seriously distorts the evaluative picture, if done unsystematically and informally by the individual counselor on a case by case basis. The exact role of physiology as both stimulus and response of psychological dynamics, is unknown as well, given ability of the individual to develop other adaptive skills and orientations, to compensate for physiologic deficit and produce desirable social outcomes (possibly equivalent to those that could have occurred in the absence of a physical deficit). Also, society's proclivity to reward effort, progress, and hard work as part of the work ethic,[206] suggests added incentives and avenues (which should also be part of the accountability and evaluation scenario) for successful outcomes irrespective, and maybe because of, genetic or physiologic dimensions based on client awareness, self-perception, goal orientation, and motivation.

Influences of Heavy Tranquilizers and Other Antipsychotic Medications

Primary concerns here, are the significant effects of these chemicals in reducing number of potential variables for evaluation and treatment, as many clients (especially those hospitalized) require such substantial dosages, as to seriously reduce their interactive response capability with the environment.

Drugs, of course, can be viewed as another defense (see section on alcohol and drug abuse), and the client who is significantly dependent on this therapeutic addendum, should be assessed relative to degree of dependence and substitution of nondrug-related adaptive behaviors, as one index of effective outcome.

The capability of some antipsychotic drugs to free clients of debilitating anxiety or depression, may exonerate otherwise-diminished and inhibited ego capabilities, then evaluated as they contribute cumulatively to unlock associated adaptive abilities, to eventually reduce need for medications. Much adaptability is possible, however, before drug use is decreased, so the counselor must use a finely skeptical perspective to define small units of adaptive change, while the overall individual organism is still generally protected by the umbrella of psychotic-related medication.

Unfortunately, many illnesses and social approaches to treatment, suggest drugs are the only treatment of choice and availability, leaving the psycho-dynamically-oriented clinician hamstrung, to accomplish meaningful therapeutic input or evaluation.

Diagnosis

In conclusion, several points should be made about diagnosis, as this official form of decision-making guides selection and implementation of inputs, and creates categories of expected and predicted outcome (including defensive, manipulative, reactive, and growth-oriented). This is especially important because of the recurrent absence of pure diagnostic types of clients, with frequent admixtures of symptoms to confuse the clinical evaluator.

Inherent in the defining process, are specific problems in differential diagnosis, presented by the confusing manifestations of client syndrome. These include separating neurotic from borderline psychotic conditions, differentiating between psychotic subcategories, and separation of lifetime, character patterns and psychoses, from other reactions to stress created by severe crisis emergencies. This differentiation requires comprehensive explanation and investigation in a series of personal interviews, a complete history (physical, mental, social), use of appropriate psychological tests,[207] physical and neurological assessments, spiritual analysis, etc.

Since each diagnostic group exhibits psychodynamic functioning predicated on continua of self-esteem, superego controls, ego skills and boundaries, impulses and repressed conflicts, tolerance for anxiety, and social supports; there is overlapping and cumulatively-building symptomatology conceptualized and measured in degrees, which in turn help key specific diagnostic hypotheses.

Pursuit of finite diagnostic differentiation based on characteristics of client psychodynamics and symptom presentations, must include the potential influence of social milieu (support and opportunity system), as this creates or negates opportunity for empirical manifestation of various positive outcomes or accomplishments. In fact, removal of some clients from their supportive neighborhood or social system (regardless of how pathological it is), creates stress beyond their tolerance and, therefore, exacerbates both symptoms and regressive seriousness of the particular illness.

In considering a full range of diagnostic criteria, the counselor must take all of the following into consideration: personal traits, psychosocial states of identity and mental status, level of integration, processes of personality disintegration, life management potential, environmental supports, and stress hierarchy.

Wolman[208] and others, propose classification of psychogenic mental disorders based on different social maladjustments, according to aims of individual clients relative to need satisfaction (instrumental), relationship needs (vectorial), or both (mutual acceptance). An adaptive healthy person has homeostatic social relations, is functional in adjusting to life's demands, shows interdependency in relationships, and is competent in meeting needs of those who are dependent or negotiate for reciprocal need-meeting. Those who have psychological conflicts: demonstrate nonequilibrium, are hyperinstrumental, show little independence in overcoming obstacles, are over indulged in self-neglect and anxiety, or show ambivalent dependence-independence as defined by paramutualism.

References

1.   Joel Charon, *Symbolic Interactionism* (Englewood Cliffs: Prentice-Hall, 1979), pp. 35-62.
2.   Scott Briar and Henry Miller, *Problems and Issues in Social Casework* (New York: Columbia University Press, 1971).
3.   Amitai, Etzioni, *A Comparative Analysis of Complex Organizations* (New York: Free Press, 1961).
4.   David Rapaport, Merton Gill, and Roy Schafer, *Diagnostic Psychological Testing* (New York: International Universities Press, 1968), p. 11.
5.   Martin Bloom, ed., *Life Span Development: Bases for Preventative and Interventive Helping* (New York: Macmillan, 1980).
6.   Sonya Rhodes, "A Developmental Approach to the Life Cycle of the Family," in *Life Span Development: Bases for Preventive and Interventive Helping,* ed., M. Bloom (New York: Macmillan, 1980), and Norbert Weiner, Cybernetics (New York: John Wiley & Sons, 1949), and Ludwig Von Bertalanffy, *Problems of Life* (New York: Hayes and Brothers, 1960).
7.   William Eldridge, "The Illusion of Rational and Relevant Clinical Practice," *Corrective and Social Psychiatry,* 20:4:131-136, May, 1978.
8.   Gerald Loeslse and Mary Croouse, "Liberalism—Conservatism in Samples of Social Work Students and Professionals," *Social Service Review;* 55:2:193-205, June, 1981.
9.   Although the author is currently a clinical Associate Professor at The Ohio State University, prior clinical work as an Army Captain and current private practice and consultation in Columbus, Ohio, offer numerous case examples and observations of clinicians to illustrate the major theme of this point about idealistic definitions of client situations.
10.   Roger Nooe, "A Model for Integrating Theoretical Approaches to Deviance," *Social Work,* 25:5:366-370, September, 1980.
11.   Edwin Lemert, *Human Deviance, Social Problems, and Social Control* (Englewood Cliffs, NJ: Prentice-Hall, 1967.
12.   Kai Erikson, "Notes on the Sociology of Deviance," *Social Problems,* 9:4:307, Spring, 1962.
13.   Howard Becker, *Outsiders: Studies in the Sociology of Deviance* (New York: Free Press, 1963).
14.   Roger Nooe, "A Model for Integrating Theoretical Approaches to Deviance," *Social Work,* 25:5:368, September, 1980.
15.   American Psychiatric Association, *Diagnostic and Statistical Manual of Mental Disorders* (3rd. ed.; Washington, DC: American Psychiatric Association, 1980).
16.   Abdul Hague, "The Learning of Nationality Stereotypes during Childhood," *Topics in Culture Learning,* 4:3-5, August, 1976.

17.   Gerald Bateson, et al., "Toward a Theory of Schizophrenia," *Behavioral Science,* 1:4:251-264, October, 1956.

18.   Steven Segalk, "Attitudes Toward the Mentally Ill: A Review," *Social Work,* 23:3:21-217, May, 1978.

19.   Bruce Dohrenwend, et al., "Social Status and Attitudes, Toward Psychological Disorder: The Problem of Tolerance of Deviance," *American Sociological Review,* 32:5:511, June, 1967.

20.   Theodore Sarbine and James Mancuso, "Paradigms and Moral Judgments: Improper Conduct is not a Disease," *Journal of Consulting and Clinical Psychology,* 39:2:161, August, 1972; and
        Samuel Kirk, "The Impact of Labelling on Rejection of the Mentally Ill: An Experimental Study," *Journal of Health and Social Behavior,* 15:2:108-117, June, 1974.

21.   Jum Nunnally, *Popular Conceptions of Mental Health: Their Development and Change* (New York: Holt, Rinehart and Winston, 1962).

22.   Derek Phillips, "Rejection: A Possible Consequence of Seeking Help for Mental Disorders," *American Sociological Review,* 28:4:963-972, December, 1963.

23.   John Clausen and Carol Huffine, "Sociocultural and Sociopsychological Factors Affecting Social Responses to Mental Disorder," *Journal of Health and Social Behavior,* 16:4:405, December, 1975.

24.   Albert Ellis and Robert Harper, *A New Guide to Rational Living* (Hollywood: Wilshire Boulevard, 1975).

25.   Francis Turner, *Psychosocial Therapy* (New York: Free Press, 1978), p. 45.

26.   Golda Edinburg, Norman Zinburg, and Wendy Kelman, *Clinical Interviewing and Counseling* (New York: Appleton-Century-Crofts, 1975), p. 23.

27.   Roger MacKinnon and Robert Michels, *The Psychiatric Interview in Clinical Practice* (Philadelphia: W. W. Saunders, 1971), pp. 11-16.

28.   Theodore Sarbin and James Mancuso, "Paradigms and Moral Judgments: Improper Conduct is not a Disease," *Journal of Consulting and Clinical Psychology,* 39:1:6-8, August, 1972.

29.   Hilde Bruck, *Learning Psychotherapy* (Cambridge, MA: Harvard University Press, 1974), p. 58.

30.   Karen Horney, *Our Inner Conflicts: A Constructive Theory of Neurosis* (New York: W. W. Norton, 1945), p. 191.

31.   Clark Moustakas, "The Experience of Being Lonely," in *Growing Older,* ed., M. Huyck (Englewood Cliffs, NJ: Prentice-Hall, 1974), pp. 143-149.

32.   William Reid and Laura Epstein, *Task-centered Casework* (New York: Columbia University Press, 1972), pp. 101-102.

33. Richard Cloward and Lloyd Ohlin, *Delinquency and Opportunity: A Theory of Delinquent Gangs* (New York: Free Press, 1960), pp. 97-103.

34. Lawrence Peter and Raymond Hull, *The Peter Principle* (New York: William Morrow, 1969).

35. Jules Henry, *Pathways to Madness* (New York: Vintage Books, 1965), p. 107.

36. Leopold Bellnak, "On the Problems of the Concept of Projective Hypothesis," *Projective Psychology,* eds., L. Abt and L. Bellak (New York: Knopf, 1950), pp. 7-32.

37. David Rapaport, Mertin Gill, and Roy Schafer, *Diagnostic Psychological Testing* (New York: International Universities Press, 1968), p. 222.

38. Herbert Strean, "Note Theory," *Social Work Treatment: Interlocking Theoretical Approaches,* ed., F. Turner (New York: Free Press, 1979), pp. 385-407.

39. Lee Robins and Eric Wish, "Childhood Deviance as a Developmental Process: A Study of 223 Urban Black Men from Birth to 18," in *Life Span Development: Bases for Preventive and Interventive Helping,* ed., M. Bloom (New York: Macmillan, 1980), pp. 264-269.

40. Alvin Mahrer, ed., *New Approaches to Personality Classification* (New York, Columbia University Press, 1970), p. 22.

41. Medard Boss, *Psychoanalysis and Daseninalysis* (New York: Basic Books, 1963), p. 37.

42. Albert Bandura, *Social Learning Theory* (Englewood Cliffs, NJ: Prentice-Hall, 1977).

43. John Perceval, *Perceval's Narrative: A Patient's Account of His Psychosis,* ed., G. Bateson (Stanford, CA: Stanford University Press, 1961), pp. 1830-1832.

44. William Estes, "Reinforcement in Human Behavior," *American Scientist,* 60:6:623-729, May, 1972.

45. Edward Prager and Henry Tonalra, "Self-assessment: The Client's Perspective," *Social Work,* 25:1:32-34, January, 1980.

46. Henrietta Williams, et al., "Some Factors Influencing the Treatment Expectations of Neurotic Outpatients," *The Journal of Nervous and Mental Disease,* 14:4:208-220, September, 1967;
     Aaron Lazare, et al., "The Walk-in Client as a 'Customer'. A Key Dimension to Evaluation and Treatment," *American Journal of Orthopsychiatry,* 42:5:872-883, October, 1972.

47. Leon Festinger, "A Theory of Social Comparison Processes," *Human Relations,* 7:2:117-140, May, 1954.

48.   Richard Miller, "Preferences for Social Versus Nonsocial Comparison as a Means of Self-evaluation," *Journal of Personality,* 45:3:343-355, September, 1977.

49.   Irving Janis and David Hoffman, "Facilitating Effects of Daily Contact Between Partners Who Make a Decision to Cut Down on Smoking," *Journal of Personality and Social Psychology,* 17:1:25-35, January, 1971.

50.   Fred Fiedler, *A Theory of Leadership Effectiveness* (New York: McGraw-Hill, 1967).

51.   Robert Merton, "Contributions to Theory of Reference Group Behavior," in *Continuities in Social Research: Studies in the Scope and Method of The American Soldiers,* eds., Robert Merton and Paul Lazarsfield (Glencoe, IL: Free Press, 1950), pp. 40-105.

52.   Ann Weick, "Reframing the Person-in-environment Perspective," *Social Work,* 26:2:140-143, March, 1981.

53.   Rainer Martens and Virginia White, "Influence of Win-Loss Ratio on Performance, Satisfaction, and Preference for Opponents," *Journal of Experimental Social Psychology,* 11:4:343-362, July, 1975.

54.   Julian Rotter, "Generalized Expectations for Internal Versus External Control of Reinforcement," *Psychological Monography,* 80:1:609, January, 1966.

55.   Urving Janis, *Victims of Groupthinking* (Boston: Houghton-Mifflin, 1972).

56.   Ronald M. Friend and Joel Gilbert, "Threat and Fear of Negative Evaluation as Determinants of Locus of Social Comparison," *Journal of Personality,* 41:3:328-339, September, 1973.

57.   Richard Cloward and Lloyd Ohlin, *Delinquency and Opportunity: A Theory of Delinquent Gangs* (New York: Free Press, 1960).

58.   William James, *Principles of Psychology* (New York: Holt, 1890).

59.   Donna Ostraushras, "The Integration of Self and Significant Others," *Psychiatry,* 40:4:352-362, May, 1977.

60.   Julian Rotter, "Generalized Expectations for Internal Versus External Control of Reinforcement," *Psychological Monographs,* 80:1:609, April, 1966.

61.   Eugene Edgington, "Statistical Influence from N=1 experiments," *The Journal of Psychology,* 65:2nd half 195-199, March, 1967.

62.   Aaron Rosen and Dina Lieberman, "The Experimental Evaluation of Interview Performance of Social Workers," *Research Project Report* (Hebrew University of Jerusalem, Paul Baerwald School of Social Work, 1973), p. 396.

63.   Albin Mahrer, ed., *New Approaches to Personality Classification* (New York: Columbia University Press, 1970).

64. Joan Zaro, et al., *A Guide for Beginning Psychotherapists* (Cambridge, England: Cambridge University Press, 1977), pp. 79-80.

65. Francis Turner, *Psychosocial Therapy* (New York: Free Press, 1978).

66. Barbara Collins, "Defining Feminist Social Work," *Social Work,* 31:3:214-219, May-June, 1986.

67. Margaret Schubert, *Interviewing in Social Work Practice* (New York: Counsel on Social Work Education, 1971), p. 57.

68. Herbert Stream, *Clinical Social Work Theory and Practice* (New York: Free Press, 1978), p. 207.

69. Nathan Ackerman, "Family Healing in a Troubled World," in *Social Work With Families,* ed., Carlton Munson (New York: Free Press, 1980, pp. 165-172.

70. Harry Specht, "The Deprofessionalization of Social work," *Social Work,* 17:2:3, March, 1972.

71. Charles Zastrow, *The Practice of Social Work* (Homewood, IL: Dorsey Press, 1981), p. 79.

72. William Reid and Laura Epstei, *Task-Centered Casework* (New York: Columbia University Press, 1972), p. 118.

73. Karen Horney, *Our Inner Conflicts* (New York: W. W. Norton, 1945).

74. All counselors would be well advised to review the major concepts and principles of their respective professional Code of Ethics to assess their relevance, rationality, and attainability in today's difficult and ever-changing world environment.

75. Aaron Rosen, "Social Psychological Factors in Outcomes of Psychotherapy? A conceptualization and Preliminary Findings," *Proceedings of the Third International Congress of Social Psychiatry,* September, 1970 (Zagreb, Yugoslavia, 5:118-129, 1971).

76. Roland Warren, "The Sociology of Knowledge and the Problems of the Inner Cities," (Research Report, Florence Heller Graduate School for Advanced Studies of Social Welfare, Brouders University, Walttion, MA, 1970).

77. Leon Chestang, "Character Development in a Hostile Environment," in *Life Span Development: Bases for Preventative and Interventive Helping,* ed., M. Bloom (New York: Macmillan, 1980), p. 47.

78. James Green, *Cultural Awareness in the Human Services* (Englewood Cliffs, NJ: Prentice-Hall, 1982).

79. Frederick Barth, *Ethnic Groups and Boundaries* (Boston: Little, Brown, 1969).

80. Alvin Mahrer, ed., *New Approaches to Personality Classifications* (New York: Columbia University Press, 1970).

81.   Thomas Williams, "The Personal-Cultural Equation in Social Work and Anthropology," *Social Casework,* 40:2:74-80, February, 1959.

82.   Lynn Hoffman, *Foundations of Family Therapy* (New York: Basic Books, 1981), pp. 37-49.

83.   Aubry Fisher, *Small Group Decision-Making* (New York: McGraw-Hill, 1980).

84.   Ruth Benedict, "Synergy," *American Anthropologist,* 72:14:317, April, 1970.

85.   William Eldridge, "Practitioner Approaches to Self-evaluation," (Doctoral dissertation, University of Denver, 1979).

86.   James Wolk, "Are Social Workers Politically Active?" *Social Work,* 26:4:283-288, July, 1981.

87.   Alfred Kahn, *Theory and Practice of Social Planning* (New York: Russell Sage Foundation, 1969).

88.   John Hasimi, "Environmental Modification: Teaching Social Coping Skills," *Social Work,* 27:3:268-274, May, 1982.

89.   Richard Lodge, "Combating Alienation: The Social Workers as Humanizing Agent," in *Social Work in the 1980's,* eds., R. Washington and B. Toomey (Davis, CA: International Dialogue Press, 1982).

90.   Warren Bennis, Kenneth Berne, and Robert Chin, eds., *The Planning of Change* (New York: Holt, Rinehart and Winston, 1969).

91.   Mildred Sirls, Jack Rubenstein, et al., "Group Work Revisited: A Statement of Position," *Perspectives on Social Work Group Practice,* ed., A Alissi (New York: Free Press, 1980), pp. 194-205.

92.   Barbara Okun, *Working with Families: An Introduction to Family Therapy* (North Scituate, MA: Dusbury Press, 1980), pp. 94-95.

93.   Jay Haley, *Problem-Solving Therapy* (San Francisco: Jossey-Bass, 1976).

94.   Albert Ellis and Robert Harper, *A New Guide to Rational Living* (Englewood Cliffs, NJ: Prentice-Hall, 1975).

95.   Roland Tharp and Ralph Wetzed, *Behavior Modification in the Natural Environment* (New York: Academic Press, 1969).

96.   W. McGuire, "The Nature of Attitudes and Attitude Change," *The Handbook of Social Psychology,* eds., G. Lindzey and E. Aronson (Reading, MA: Addison-Wesley, 1969), pp. 136-314.

97.   James Hansen and Luciano L'Abate, *Approaches to Family Therapy* (New York: Macmillan, 1982), pp. 218-221.

98.   Janet Moore-Kirland, "Mobilizing Motivation: From Theory to Practice," *Promoting Competence in Clients,* ed., A. Maluccio (New York: Free Press, 1981), p. 40.

99. Martin Bloom and Joel Fischer, *Evaluating Practice: Guidelines for the Accountable Professional* (Englewood Cliffs, NJ: Prentice-Hall, 1982), p. 201.

100. Gerald Corey, *Theory and Practice of Group Counseling* (Monterey, CA: Brooks/Cole, 1981), p. 427.

101. Erving Goffman, *Asylums* (Garden City, NY: Doubleday, 1961), pp. 326-328.

102. Alice Sargent, *Beyond Sex Roles* (St. Paul: West, 1977), p. 457.

103. Harriett Bartlett, "Characteristics of Social Work," *Building Social Work Knowledge* (New York: National Association of Social workers, 1964), pp. 1-15.

104. Ruth Benedict, "Synergy," *American Anthropolist,* 72:14:320-333, April, 1970.

105. Allen Bergen and Han Strupp, *Changing Frontiers in the Science of Psychotherapy* (Chicago: Aldine Atherton, 1972), p. 42.

106. American Psychiatric Association, *Diagnostic and Statistical Manual of Mental Disorders* (3rd ed.; Washington, DC: American Psychiatric Association, 1980);
    Robert Spitzer, Janet Williams and Andrew Skodol, "DSM-III: The Major Achievements and an Overview," *American Journal of Psychiatry,* 137:2:151-164, February, 1980;
    Janet Williams, "Classification of Mental Disorders and DSM-III," in *Comprehensive Textbook of Psychiatry,* eds., H. Kaplan, A. Freedman, and B. Sadock (3rd ed.; New York: Williams and Wilkins, 1980).

107. Robert Spitzer, Janet W. Forman and John Nee, "DSM-III Field Trials: I. Initial Interrater Diagnostic Reliability," *American Journal of Psychiatry,* 136:4:815-817, June, 1979.

108. William Reid and Laura Epstein, *Task-Centered Casework* (New York: Columbia University Press, 1972), pp. 20-23.

109. David Rosenthal, Barbara Putnam and James Hansen, "Racially Different Adolescents: Self-concept and Vocational Attitudes," *Urban Education,* 13:4:453-461, January, 1979.

110. Donald Super, et al., *Career Development: Self-concept Theory* (New York: College Entrance Exam Board, 1963).

111. John Holland, *Making Vocational Choices: A Theory of Careers* (Englewood Cliffs, NJ: Prentice-Hall, 1973).

112. Elsie Smith, "Profile of the Black Individual on Vocational Literature," *Journal of Vocational Behavior,* 6:3:41-59, 1975.

113. Allison Murdach, "Bargaining and Persuasion with Nonvoluntary Clients," *Social Work,* 25:6:458-461, November, 1980.

114. Elliot Stundt, "Casework in the Correctional Field," *Federal Probation,* 18:3:19-26, September, 1954;

Lloyd Ohlin, Herman Piven, and Donele Pappenfort, "Major Dilemmas of the Social Worker in Probation and on Parole," *National Probation and Parole Association Journal,* 2:1:211-225, July, 1956.

115. For the "exchange" view of human relations see,

Peter Blau, *Exchange and Power in Social Life* (New York: John Wiley and Sons, 1969.

116. For a discussion espousing the view that the central activity of social workers is persuasion see,

William Richan, "A Common Language for Social Work," *Social Work,* 17:6:17, November, 1972.

For a critical discussion of persuasion in the helping process see,

Thomas Szasz, *The Myth of Psychotherapy* (New York: Anchor Press, 1978).

For perspectives that imply the usefulness of bargaining in helping situations see, for example,

Harry Sullivan, *The Psychiatric Interview* (New York: W. W. Norton, 1954), pp. 16-17;

Karl Menninger, *Theory of Psychoanalytic Techniques* (New York: Harper and Row, 1964); and

Robert Carson, *Interaction Concepts of Personality* (Chicago: Aldine, 1969).

117. Hans Strupp, "Needed: A Reformation of the Psychotherapeutic Influence," *International Journal of Psychiatry,* 10:5:114-120, June, 1972.

For a summary of research on influence in therapy see,

Leonard Kransner and Leonard Ullman, *Behavior Influence and Personality* (New York: Holt, Rinehart and Winston, 1973).

118. Morton Deutsch and Robert Krass, "Studies of Interpersonal Bargaining," in *War and Its Prevention,* eds., A. Etzioni and M. Wenglinsky (New York: Harper and Row, 1970), p. 130.

For an excellent introduction to the sociological and political aspects of the bargaining process see,

William Mitchel, "Bargaining and Public choice," in *Readings in Management Psychology,* eds., H. Levitt and L. Purdy (2nd ed.; Chicago: University of Chicago Press, 1973), pp. 588-590.

119. Charles Lindblom, *The Intelligence of Democracy* (New York: Free Press, 1965).

120. Alfred Freedman, Harold Kaplan and Benjamin Sadok, *Modern Synopsis of Comprehensive Textbook of Psychiatry* (Baltimore: Williams and Wilkins, 1972).

121. Carl Rogers, "The Process Equation of Psychotherapy," *American Journal of Psychotherapy,* 15:1:27-43, January, 1961.
122. Robert Holt, "Recent Developments in Psychoanalytic Ego Psychology and Their Implications for Diagnostic Testing," *Journal of Projective Techniques,* 24:4:254-266, 1960.
123. Karen Horney, *Our Inner Conflicts* (New York: W. W. Norton, 1945), p. 132.
124. Ellen McDaniel, "Anxiety Disorders," in *Clinical Psychopathology,* eds., G. Balis, L. Wurmser, and E. McDaniel (Boston: Butterworth, 1978), p. 208.
125. Norman Cameron, *Personality Development and Psychopathology* (Boston: Houghton-Mifflin, 1963).
126. Medard Boss, *Psychoanalysis and Daseinanalysis* (New York: Basic Books, 1963).
127. Karen Horney, *Our Inner Conflicts* (New York: W. W. Norton, 1945).
128. Erik Erikson, *Childhood and Society* (New York: W. W. Norton, 1950), p. 42.
129. Gertrude Blanck and Rubin Blanck, *Ego Psychology: Theory and Practice* (New York: Columbia University Press, 1974), p. 132.
130. Thomas Harris, *I'm OK—You're OK* (New York: Avon Books, 1967), pp. 70-71.
131. Leland Hinsie and Robert Campbell, *Psychiatric Dictionary* (New York: Oxford University Press, 1970), pp. 167-168.
132. Erik Erikson, *Childhood and Society* (New York: W. W. Norton, 1950), p. 42.
133. J. Horowitz, "Imitative and Interactive Aspects of Splitting," *American Journal of Psychiatry,* 134:5:549-553, May, 1979.
134. Margaret Mahler, Fred Pine, and Anni Bergman, *The Psychological Birth of Human Infants* (New York: Basic Books, 1975).
135. Gertrude Blanck and Rubin Blanck, *Ego Psychology: Theory and Practice* (New York: Columbia University Press, 1974), p. 132.
136. Otto Kernberg, *Borderline Conditions and Pathological Narcissism* (New York: Jason Aaronson, 1975).
137. William Eldridge, "Conceptualizing Self-evaluation of Clinical Practice," *Social Work,* 28:1:57-61, January-February, 1983.
138. Nathan Ackerman, *Treating the Troubled Family* (New York: Basic Books, 1966).
139. Helen Northen, *Clinical Social Work* (New York: Columbia University Press, 1982).
140. Frederick Perls, *Gestalt Therapy Verbatim* (Lafayette, A Real People Press, 1969), pp. 1-72.

141.   Neil Smelser, *Theory of Collective Behavior* (New York: Free Press, 1962), pp. 70-72.

142.   Roland Tharp and Ralph Wetzel, *Behavior Modification in the Natural Environment* (New York: Academic Press, 1969), pp. 49-51.

143.   Les Rangell, "Aggression, Oedipus, and Historical Perspective," *International Journal of Psychoanalysis,* 53:1:4-11, February, 1972.

144.   Paul Adams, *Obsessive Children: A Sociopsychiatric Study* (New York: Brunner/Masel, 1973).

145.   Eleanor Jantz, Virginia Huffer, and Daniel Freedenburg, "Psychophysiological Disorders," *Clinical Psychopathology,* eds. (Boston: Butterworth, 1978), p. 432.

146.   Walter Cannon, *Bodily Changes in Pain, Hunger, Fear, and Rage* (New York: Appleton, 1929), p. 13.

147.   Clair Selltiz, Lawrence Wrightsman, and Stuart Cook, *Research Methodology in Social Relations* (New York: Holt, Rinehart and Winston, 1976), pp. 90-101.

148.   Robert Rosenthal, *Experimenter Effects in Behavioral Research* (New York: Appleton-Century-Crofts, 1966), pp. 250-280.

149.   William Masters and Virginia Johnson, *Human Sexual Response* (Boston: Little Brown, 1966).

150.   John Lion, "Personality Disorders," *Clinical Psychopathology,* eds., G. Balis, L. Wurmser, and E. McDaniel (Boston: Butterworth, 1978).

151.   Laurence Peter and Reymond Hull, *The Peter Principle* (New York: William Morrow, 1969).

152.   Hilde Bruh, *Learning Psychotherapy* (Cambridge, MA: Harvard University Press, 1974), pp. 94-95.

153.   William Reid and Laura Estein, *Task-Centered Casework* (New York: Columbia University Press, 1972), pp. 151-155.

154.   Alan Kazdin, "Methodological and Interpretive Problems of Single-case Experimental Designs," *Journal of Consulting and Clinical Psychology,* 46:4:629-642, July, 1978.

155.   William Eldridge, "Conceptualizing the Evaluation of Clinical Practice," *Social Work,* 28:1:57-61, January-February, 1983.

156.   Bernard Guerney, *Relationship Enhancement: Skill-training Programs for Therapy, Problem Prevention, and Enrichment* (San Francisco: Jossey-Bass, 1969).

157.   Lynnda Dahnquist and Anitra Fayt, "Cultural Issues in Psychotherapy" in *The Handbook of Clinical Psychology,* ed., C. Walker (Homewood, IL: Dow Jones-Irwin, 1983) pp. 1219-1255.

158.   Joel Charon, *Symbolic Interactionism* (Englewood Cliffs: Prentice-Hall, 1979), pp. 70-79.

159. Joan Zaro, et al., *A Guide for Beginning Psychotherapists* (London: Cambridge University Press, 1977), pp. 115-116.

160. Otto Pollack, "Treatment of Character Disorder: A Dilemma in Casework Culture," in *Differential Diagnosis and Treatment in Social Work,* ed., F. Turner (2nd ed.; New York: Free Press, 1976).

161. Gregory Rochlin, *Man's Aggression: The Defense of the Self* (Boston: Gambit, 1973), pp. 219-222.

162. Erving Polster and Miriam Polster, *Gestalt Therapy Integrated* (New York: Brunner/Mazel, 1973), pp. 82-89.

163. Harry Guntrip, *Schizoid Phenomena, Object-relations, and the Self* (New York: International Universities Press, 1969), pp. 24-30.

164. Norman Polansky, *Social Work Research* (Chicago: University of Chicago Press, 1960), p. 51.

165. Arnold Goldberg, "The Evaluation of Psychoanalytic Concepts of Depression," in *Depression and Human Existence,* eds., J. Anthony and T. Benedek (Boston: Little, Brown, 1975), pp. 126-127.

166. Edwin Thomas, *Marital Communication and Decision-Making: Analysis, Assessment, and Change* (New York: Free Press, 1977), p. 126.

167. Albert Bandura, *Social Learning Theory* (Englewood Cliffs, NJ: Prentice-Hall, 1977), pp. 96-117.

168. James Bruining, "Direct and Vicarious Effects of a Shift in Magnitude of Reward on Performance," *Journal of Personality and Social Psychology,* 2:2:278-282, August, 1965.

169. Sidney Bijou, et al., "Methodology for Experimental Studies of Young Children in Natural Settings," *Psychological Record,* 19:2:177-210, 1969.

170. Thomas Zurrilla and Marvin Goldried, "Problem-solving and Behavior Modification," *Journal of Abnormal Psychology,* 78:1:107-126, 1971.

171. Leon Wurmser, "Addictive Disorders: Drug Dependence," *Clinical Psychopathology,* eds., G. Balis, L. Wurmser, E. McDaniel (Boston: Butterworth, 1978).

172. Andre St. Pierre, "Motivating the Drug Addict in Treatment," *Differential Diagnosis and Treatment in Social Work,* ed., F. Turner (2nd ed.; New York: Free Press), 1976.

173. Franz Bergel and David Davies, *All About Drugs* (New York: Barnes and Noble, 1970).

174. Clarence Rowe, *An Outline of Psychiatry* (Dubuque, IA: William C. Brown, 1975), pp. 136-160.

175. William Bosma, "Addictive Disorders: Alcoholism," *Clinical Psychopathology,* eds., G. Balis, L. Wurmser, and E. McDaniel (Boston: Butterworth, 1978), pp. 370-386;

Sigmund Freud, "Mourning and Melancholia," *Collected Papers* (Vol. 4; London: Hogarth Press, 1925), pp. 152-170; and

Otto Fenichel, *The Psychoanalytic Theory of Neurosis* (New York: Norton, 1945).

176. Leon Wurmser, "Addictive Disorders: Drug Dependence," *Clinical Psychopathology,* eds., G. Balis, L. Wurmser, E. McDaniel (Boston: Butterworth, 1978).

177. Francis Turner, ed., *Differential Diagnosis and Treatment in Social Work* (2nd ed.; New York: Free Press, 1976).

178. Edmund Uhlenhut, et al., "Combined Pharmacotherapy and Psychotherapy," *Journal of Nervous and Mental Disease,* 1:4:52-64, 1969.

179. Gerald Hogarty, et al., "Drug and Sociotherapy in the Aftercare of Schizophrenic Patients: Two Year Release Rates," *Archives of General Psychiatry,* 31:5:609-618, November, 1974.

180. Loren Mosher, et al., "Special Report: Schizophrenia, 1972," *Schizophrenia Bulletin,* 7:42:12-52, March, 1973.

181. Gerald Hogarty, et al., "Sociotherapy and the Prevention of Relapse Among Schizophrenic Patients: An Artifact of Drug?" *Evaluation of Psychological Therapies,* eds., R. Spitzer and D. Klein (Baltimore: Johns Hopkins University Press, 1976), pp. 285-293.

182. John Lion, "Personality Disorders," *Clinical Psychopathology,* eds., G. Balis, L. Wurmser, and E. McDaniel (Boston: Butterworth, 1978), pp. 350-351.

183. Donald Klein and John David, *Diagnosis and Drug Treatment of Psychiatric Disorders* (Baltimore: Williams and Williams, 1969).

184. Ronald Lipman and Lino Covi, "Outpatient Treatment of Neurotic Depression: Medication and Group Psychotherapy," *Evaluation of Psychological Therapies,* eds., R. Spitzer and D. Klein (Baltimore: Johns Hopkins University Press, 1976), pp. 178-218.

185. Barush Levine, *Group Psychotherapy: Practice and Development* (Englewood Cliffs: Prentice-Hall, 1979), p. 31.

186. Harold Solms and David de Meuron, "Group Therapy for Alcoholics in the Psychiatric Hospital Environment: Preliminary Results of a Practical Experience Under Difficult Conditions," *Toxicomanies,* 2:2:201-216, 1969.

187. Edwin Bordin, "The Ambivalent Quest for Independence," *Journal of Counseling Psychology,* 12:4:339-345, May, 1965.

188. Gerald Corey and Marianne Corey, *Groups: Process and Practice* (Monterey, CA: Brooks/Cole, 1982), pp. 132-133.

189. Merl Jackel, "Clients with Character Disorders," *Differential Diagnosis and Treatment in Social Work,* ed., F. Turner (2nd ed.; New York: Free Press, 1976, pp. 196-207.

190. Harvey Kushner and Gerald DeMaio, *Understanding Basic Statistics* (San Francisco: Holden-Day, 1980), pp. 10-11.

191. Herman Smith, *Strategies of Social Research: The Methodological Imagination* (Englewood Cliffs, NJ: Prentice-Hall, 1975), pp. 200-228.

192. Harry Shulman, *Juvenile Delinquency in American Society* (New York: Harper, 1961), pp. 409-434.

193. Margaret Frank, "Casework with Children: The Experience of Treatment," in *Differential Diagnosis and Treatment in Social Work,* ed., F. Turner (2nd ed.; New York: Free Press, 1976), p. 8.

194. Margaret Frank, "Casework with Children: The Experience of Treatment," in *Differential Diagnosis and Treatment in Social Work,* ed., F. Turner (2nd ed.; New York: Free Press, 1976), pp. 5-13.

195. Silvano Arieti, ed., *American Handbook of Psychiatry* (Vol. 1; New York Basic Books, 1959);
Leon Saul, *Emotional Maturity: The Development and Dynamics of Personality and its Disorders* (Philadelphia: J. B. Lppincott, 1971).

196. John Rosen, *Direct Analysis* (New York: Crume and Stratten, 1953), p. 78.

197. Silvano Arieti, *Interpretation of Schizophrenia* (New York: Robert Brunner, 1955), p. 70.

198. Harry Wilmer, *Social Psychiatry in Action* (Springfield, IL: Charles C. Thomas, 1958).

199. Richard Sanders, Robert Smith, and Bernard Weinman, *Chronic Psychoses and Recovery* (San Francisco: Jossey-Bass, 1967), pp. 32-58.

200. R. Forsythe and G. Fairweather, "Psychotherapeutic and Other Hospital Treatment Criteria: The Dilemma," *Journal of Abnormal and Social Psychiatry,* 62:598-604, 1961.

201. Theodore Lidy, Stephen Fleck, and Alice Cornelison, *Schizophrenia and the Family* (New York: International Universities Press, 1965).

202. Simon Dinitz, et al., "The Post-hospital Functioning of Former Mental Hospital Patients," *Mental Hygiene,* 45:2:579-588, September, 1961.

203. Edward Zigler and Leslie Phillips, "Social Effectiveness and Symptomatic Behaviors," *Journal of Abnormal and Social Psychology,* 61:231-238, 1960.

204. Anna Freud, *The Writings of Anna Freud, Volume II: The Ego and the Mechanisms of Defense* (New York: International Universities Press, 1966), pp. 58-59.

205. John Roscoe, *Fundamental Research Statistics for the Behavioral Sciences* (New York: Holt, Rinehart and Winston, 1975), pp. 217-229.

206. Max Weber, *The Protestant Ethic and the Spirit of Capitalism* (New York: Scribners, 1958), pp. 74-75; and

Ottis Fenichel, *Psychoanalytic Theory of Neurosis* (New York: W. W. Norton, 1945).

207.   David Rapaport, Merton Gill and Roy Schafer, *Diagnostic Psychological Testing* (New York: International Universities Press, 1968).

208.   Bernard Wolman, "The Continuum Hypothesis in Neurosis and Psychosis and the Classification of Mental Disorders," (Paper presented at the Meeting of the Eastern Psychological Association, 1959).

Chapter Three

Intrapsychic and Sociopsychic Perceptions

of Clinical Counselors and Clients

Introduction

In the processes of self-evaluation and decision-making as critical dimensions of evaluation, it is necessary to theoretically consider individual perceptual domains within which evaluation occurs. This suggests that evaluation does not stand alone as a pure methodological phenomenon, but rather becomes the operationalized manifestation of abstract superordinate dimensions of psychological adaptation, cognitive learning, self-actualization, and psychosocial adjustment. Through evaluation, the practitioner and client, as a part of evaluative gestalt, struggle to feel safe, competent, adequate, and fulfilled within and without the therapeutic relationship, and make evaluative decisions based on their unique psychological frameworks:

> "In general, inquiry has its origin in a conceptual structure. This structure determines what questions we shall ask in our inquiry; the questions determine what data we wish; our wishes in this respect determine what experiments we perform. Further, the data, once assembled are given their meaning and interpretation in light of the conception which initiated the inquiry."[1]

Of course, the precise importance of accountability to personal experiences is hard to understand, because of numerous factors with interactive relationships. These include client and counselor identities, types of problems brought to the clinical milieu, treatment goals and techniques, and agency dynamics. Suchman, for example, states the problem as follows:

"The process of evaluation is highly complex and subjective. Inherently it involves a combination of basic assumptions underlying the activity being evaluated and those who are doing the evaluation. Evaluation is a continuous social process rarely stopping to challenge these assumptions or bring the values into the open."[2]

Without consideration of personal and social values, and other conceptual dimensions of evaluator and evaluatee, it is difficult to truly understand the following:

1. selection of types of data to be considered by the unique client and practitioner, for evaluative decisions;
2. possible causes and reasons for distortion of findings, including subjective misinterpretation or misuse of methodological factors, related to conceptual validity and measurement reliability;
3. cognitive procedures (conceptual formulae) for assessing and acting on decisions relative to personal/professional competence, efficiency, and effectiveness;
4. overall end-product and existential meaning of self-evaluative findings to each practitioner, as this impacts subsequent service delivery.

With these issues in mind, it is important to consider intrapsychic components of self-evaluation, from the following domains of personal and social functioning;

1. personalty development and self-actualization;
2. personal, social, cultural, and philosophical value orientations;
3. knowledge acquisition and personal learning.

As each area is specifically discussed, therapists should note that these domains constitute platforms of thinking, feeling, and behaving, from which the evaluator (client or therapist) views the entire clinical assessment process. Therapists are also a set of lenses, providing unique and determinate values for making decisions; relative to importance, effectiveness, and final outcomes of interpersonal therapeutic process.

Personality Development and Self-Actualization
as Part of Evaluation

One set of insights in viewing individual evaluation, comes from selected dynamics of personality growth and development. Contributions from several disciplines identify significant parts of personality functioning, which influence self-evaluative action, motivation, and feeling. A major benefit of these personality dimensions, is to allow realistic appreciation of evaluative differences between practitioners, as reflected in their unique psychological characteristics. Woody and Woody charge that ". . . we have divorced the (self) assessment process from the person who is doing the assessing . . . and have selected therapists primarily on the basis of grade point averages."[3] Houle[4] adds to this argument, by summarizing that most studies of self-evaluation, neglect valuable information concerning attitudes and motivations:

". . . despite tremendous efforts expended, we still do not have objective criteria on the basis of which we can make clear distinctions between effective and ineffective professional workers. Nevertheless, operating quite without objective criteria, practitioners in the fields of education, counseling, psychiatry, social work, theology, generally know . . . who are the fumblers and the experts among their colleagues. There seems to be no doubt that differences exist despite the general failure of research to pinpoint the distinctions."[5]

In reviewing the literature, several factors representing convergence between self-evaluation and significant aspects of personality development, organization, and functioning; appear to affect process and results of clinical evaluation activities. Findings that emerge in terms of individual or interpersonal psychological dynamics, fall into categories related to self-esteem, self-acceptance, and self-actualization. In this context, evaluative perspectives and value-guided actions emerge as intricately related to the ways practitioners view their selves, and the role evaluation (input, process or outcome results) assumes in clinicians' journeys toward goals and objectives, by which their lives are intended to reach fulfillment.

One pronounced connection in the literature, is between self-evaluation and self-esteem. This association is particularly useful in considering contributions of self-evaluative experiences, to overall development of self-image and identity. With Freud[6] as a prominent example of modern thinking, there was acceptance of the personality as a dynamic phenomenon in which the human ego constitutes a system of functions. These serve as a bridge between environment and psychological (id) and parental-social (superego) expectations and needs, of the personality. The ego incorporates mood and energy (libido), making decisions based on integration of various types of interacting evaluative information.[7]

In considering the self as a significant object of awareness and value to the individual, the literature notes the self-creative component of this process, through individual awareness and interaction with the environment.[8] In this case, the image of self is associated and integrated with objects in the social milieu, on whose nature and unique significance the evaluated self depends.[9] Pre-valued and developmental social outcomes are consequently correlated in parallel fashion, with the value of the self and its esteemed nature-in-action.

Other authors[10] concur with the integration of self and other energetic life processes, suggesting the self is recognized through processes of being aware of reflections from others, followed by identity differentiation as part of developing autonomy.[11]

In considering the self as a knower of reality and itself, through evaluative process, developmental unfolding of one's essence and awareness is critical in identity formation. This happens as present images are continually compared with other selves which existed in the past, exist in others, are symbolized in other dimensions of reality, or might exist in the future.[12]

The nature of ability and performance outcome, therefore, is partly determined by anticipatory sense of self, even before ability-related behaviors occur. This connects them, quite significantly, to the (1) evaluator's needs for self-esteem, (2) range and quality of behaviors predetermined by this needs assessment, and (3) outcomes of these behaviors, in providing sufficient or insufficient data about levels of deprivation or satisfaction, as the evaluation-behavior-evaluation cycle continues its path toward need fulfillment.

Personal Need Fulfillment

Each clinician begins every therapy session with personal feelings of potential, and internal perceptions of adequacy or inadequacy, which represent hierarchical levels of need fulfillment or deprivation. As previously noted by Maslow, any person can be dominated by need constellations which specifically and generally influence (1) baseline perceptions of adequacy and, therefore, deprivation level, wherein indices of therapeutic effectiveness are necessary to boost sagging dimensions of esteem; (2) selection of evaluative criteria, which have greater or lesser degrees of probability to produce needed types and amounts of positive feedback; (3) pressure each clinician selectively perceives to possibly distort data in pursuit of positive strokes; and (4) selective interpretation of units of evaluative data (input and outcome), which results in integration or association between bits of information; and the interrelated assignment of values to each data unit, so end results can be engineered to produce necessary findings.

These needs, closely related to psychological dimensions of evaluation, also include domains of security or safety, familiarity, belongingness, and/or love; which are unfulfilled from childhood, or unsupported via here-and-now relationships which the counselor maintains. The actual nature of need, in fact, is relatively insignificant, since the therapist approaching the evaluative situation subjectively chooses to perceive deprivation in any need area—and can also choose to use clinical indicators (even if unconsciously motivated) as referents for need satisfactions in other life areas. The need area, in fact, which seems most related to a priori evaluative perception, is self-esteem. Here, statements about the self reflect various levels of need deprivation (including symbolic statements the counselor makes to the client, which are displaced or projected from the therapist's self), and also confirm one's status relative to significant need hierarchies.

Since some research finds an inverse correlation between level of self-esteem and negative self-evaluative statements,[13] a logical assumption is that previously-lowered levels of perceived need for esteem, also predestine particular therapist words or behaviors. These are not only of negative symbolic nature, but may serve as stimuli for outcome responses from the client, further skewing evaluative decisions in negative directions (or defensive reaction-formation positive directions).

The entire reality gestalt can be defined presently and in future expectations, according to unmet needs and reactions of the self, to those perceived deprivations. Some authors suggest that meaning[14] (including relevance of self-adequacy, based on need satisfaction) is not a quality inherent in here and now experience (e.g., current counseling situation) of consciousness, but is the result of interpretations of past experiences (need-meeting occasions), viewed from the present. Present behaviors, therefore, may be meaningful only when compared to previously existing conceptual categories of need fulfillment or deprivation. In doing therapy, the counselor anticipates outcomes of interventive inputs (future perfect conceptual time—that which will have been done), then remembers the action in terms of anticipations of success or failure, relative to patterns of emotional goal attainment or defensive strategies to overcome deficits in self-esteem. This process, relegates true evaluative results to predetermined visions, while the practitioner may be trapped within past conceptual mind sets, to prevent correct interpretation of results of input efforts. The evaluator has a split self, in seeing the past, and performing in the present. Each self possesses considerable editorial license, as the symbolic nature of client behaviors can be selectively interpreted within highly individualized therapist-relevant criteria. In this regard, some therapists suggest the individual is unable to exact a perceptual and observing self from the here and now, so the knower is immersed only in that which is known as it occurs: "the thoughts themselves are the thinker."[15] The phenomenologic question, is whether it is possible to step back from the process of need fulfillment, to clearly see the evaluation activity, especially when the observing self[16] may continue to be deprived with unresolved needs.

This "need"[17] for positive self-regard is described by Piaget,[18] as conflict between feelings of inferiority and superiority, wherein positives and negatives of actions,[19] are accounted for as personal value criteria, guiding predispositions and expectations for future thought, feeling, and behavior.[20] Anxieties[21] develop, therefore, from real or imagined failures or perceptions of deficits, and from cognitive comparisons to other status-related standards.[22]

The confusing dilemma for the practitioner, who determines status of the self within a series of counseling inputs, considering also the results of these inputs; is how to separate various aspects of self-status, as a complex integrated multifunctional system of varying components of the personality. This self is developed and manifested throughout numerous life conflicts, and is stimulated in a multitude of ways in therapeutic communication media.

This view suggests that the clinician's process of defining evaluative outcome categories for the client, the counselor's self and a joint client-counselor status, and the collection of data to build cognitive and empirically related frequencies in these categories—are processes not easily separated from complex striving for centeredness or integration, which include multiple arenas of performance and complex systems of data. A singular perspective about the self, relative to a singular perspective about client outcome, may be too simplistic to achieve. Therefore, the collection of any unitary bit of client-related information, may have no specific berthing position to represent interaction of separate client-counsel gestalts at any particular time—although decisions might be made at later times, when cumulative and integrative processes had occurred. One dilemma, is that clients may also have reoriented themselves in a different way by that time, and delayed registry of success or failure outcomes, which has limited utility for deciding past inputs for the client, toward whom evaluative questions are subsequently directed.

The self becomes a mirror of phenomena outside the self (e.g., the client), evaluatively responsive to more specific data inputs about clients. Yet, it may have limited capacity to make holistic decisions about the total self as a broad service delivery goal, or total self as an index of specific success or failure repertoires for particular clients.[23] This perspective says there are stages of development, but allows possibility of progression, regression, and stage specific judgments, without ability to integrate stages for a less segmented framework for identity. The possibility in clinical settings, therefore, for developmental stage congruence or dissonance between client and counselor, is an important consideration in understanding how evaluative decisions are made.

Regarding stages of adult development, the clinician should be aware of all criteria for determining growth status, particularly where self-esteem is determined by degree to which this ideal is achieved. This is difficult because adequacy includes a combination of successes as isolated activities, or more global successes within the entire personality structure. There are, however, serious questions about validating specific evaluative data and decision-making, based on nature and extent of esteem needs in either category. The clinician struggles with the variable importance of both specific and generalized esteem frameworks, and should have equally significant concerns about the way evaluative information is utilized, relative to each separated or integrated dimension of personality.

According to most theories of hierarchical needs (e.g., Erikson, Maslow, etc.), the higher the need level (or need deprivation) experienced by the individual; the more preconditions, complexity, and individual creativity are necessary for need satisfaction—related to achievement, adequacy, mastery, competence, or status. The more idiosyncratic and abstract these needs become, the harder it may be for clinicians to be satisfied with their therapeutic work, and the more confusing the labyrinth of satisfying outcomes for clients.

As clinicians selectively perceive their individual need hierarchies (and those of clients), they become aware of levels of potential deprivation, which is usually a patterned perceptual format begun in childhood, to feel secure with familiar (even though possibly negative) images of the self. Many times these patterns of need identification have no direct symbolic relevance in the present empirical world, but can be creatively associated with any object or evaluative circumstance, so there appears to be consistency and congruence.[24] This is a complicated process of transferring images between states of remembered and anticipated consciousness, and may not even conceptualize entire panoramas of interrelated needs, but only bits and pieces not understood by the perceiver, subsequently.[25]

As the clinician views his or her world, objects or situations are perceived according to assumed ability to manipulate/control[26] them to achieve need satisfaction, or at least defend the self against perceptions of incongruence between needs and current states of being (not O.K., and O.K.). Thus, perception is not necessarily based on the true nature of the evaluative situation, so the array of data may be perceived as more controllable than actually is the case; or incapable of control, based on irrational remembrances of childhood inadequacies, rather than the correct interpretation of a clinical situation, wherein success may be a highly reasonable possibility.

Clinicians also perceive tasks as to their degree of predictability and, in fact, predetermine categories of expected clinical outcome. These may not necessarily be based on characteristics of clients' personalities, or dynamic nature of the therapeutic relationship, but rather the potency of counselors' unfulfilled needs as seen in varying degrees of ability to meet these needs. This also affects the activity or passivity with which specific task accomplishment is approached.

The interpretive ability of practitioners is phenomenal, and includes capability to: perceive and alter mental perceptions of time sequences,[27] delay cognitive responses to a stimulus, withdraw from sequential thought patterns, activate alternative responses from memory, alter anticipations of future events, and infer causality; all of which materialize perception of need deprivation and potential for need fulfillment.

An example relates to clinicians' choices among achievement tasks[28] as decision makers,[29] with vested and subjective interests in heightening anticipated value of performance outcomes.[30] This means the clinical evaluator is not necessarily a pure and linear respondent to the true nature of client success or failure, as indexed on some behavioral or attitudinal outcome scale. Their responses and evaluative decisions, conversely, may be based on internal perception of personal need,[31] not easily discovered or empirically documented (or controlled during clinical therapeutic process).

The clinician should keep in mind that positive or negative outcomes, may vary with possibility of interactivity between them, as both occur in the behavioral repertoires of either client or counselor. They are also related to the client's and counselor's motivation for achievement, and to each counselor's cognitive formula, which may dictate disposition to experience either positive or negative affect/cognition—following, simultaneous with, or preceding various outcomes. These results may also be influenced by degree to which any real or anticipated outcomes are public or prominent in nature, as opposed to internal and private, for each clinician.

The self can also be seen in terms of its capacity vis-à-vis difficulty of the task,[32] wherein level of aspiration may rise with successful performance outcomes, and decline with failure. Actual performance in this regard, could affect level of aspiration through subjective or empirical estimates of the probability of success, and perceptions of degree of task difficulty. It is uncertain whether the clinician's prior assessment of self-esteem and need satisfaction permits accurate assessment of probabilities of outcomes meeting affective needs, and also whether the clinician can derive maximum benefit from highly probable positive outcomes, which he or she may not clearly perceive or anticipate.

Because of the contingencies and other subjective components of evaluatively related self-esteem noted above, there are several decision-making issues which must be faced. Each clinician views capacity of self partly in terms of difficulty in accomplishing previous developmental life tasks, especially related to earning love, support, and reinforcement of parents for various aspects of personality formation (values, ideas, creativity, etc.). If needs have remained unmet and conflict exists, some practitioners may regress to view themselves as deprived children. This distorts their view of actual dimensions of tasks related to clients, and diminishes the probability of success, by viewing the childlike self as incapable.

Level of aspiration about achieving various representations of success, is also conditioned by early childhood experiences, as parents' capability to aspire to high development levels, was modeled and reinforced for their children.[33] Aspiration for future welfare (as a component of comparative status differential), is not only a dimension of the client's change potential, but a categorical dimension of the clinician's mind set. It possesses differential levels of energy (positive cathexis), ranges and boundaries of aspirational states of being (sometimes operationally defined with empirical referents, or as a vague conceptualization of a hopeful state of being), and levels of aspirational attainment—personally, interpersonally, socially, and spiritually. There is also possibility of distortion of clinical goals and relationships, seen in countertransference[34] as "irrational and infantile attribution of characteristics to another person,"[35] with symbolic power to meet needs in the professional's past or present life.[36] This problem relates to difficulties a clinician may experience in the relationship between his/her own stage of life and that of a client, especially as particular vulnerabilities become part of conscious awareness.

If the clinician either randomly or systematically interpolates a personal incapacity-relative-to-previous tasks *self-perception,* this valuation adds or subtracts from outcome values related to each client. It must be controlled at the onset, or factored out, to undo the linear transformation of outcome values which occurs in decision-making. Of course, the ability of self can be defensively upgraded to protect a negative self-concept, or psychodynamically downgraded to negative levels, to take personal control of failure, rather than allow this judgment to develop more empirically from the outside.

One other problem, is that goal-accomplishment adequacy of children, is controlled by parent power and behavioral/emotional reinforcements or punishments. This transferentially impacts the degree of control clinicians attribute to clients to perceive, use, or be fearful of strengths in accomplishing their own tasks. The points at which decisions enter and leave various time dimensions (childhood, future) and personal spaces (client's gestalt, child gestalt), are difficult to ascertain, as to implications for the nature and direction for evaluative decision-making.

The practitioner and client as well, have potentially numerous discrete states of consciousness,[37] with state-specific memory and valuation of competencies and expectations. Clinicians should, at a minimum, possess a nominal level self-evaluative framework, so they place themselves within each of their relevant categories of competency; and also have a second predetermined framework for objective self-observation, that they activate whenever they move into one specific (subjective) conscious state. The separate self-observational paradigm must contain a correction formula, used to counteract bias and subjective judgments inherent in each state of subjective awareness. This multiple framework (state of observation and consciousness) should be developed with the help of external observers, but will probably be used independently, due to constraints of caseload demands. A simple example of this type of framework, is in Figure 1.

Some theories suggest the self-actualized person has the ability to develop these correction categories, and also control distortions,[38] which include the following evaluative capabilities:

1. ability to free oneself from preconditions or presumptions;
2. tendency to develop efficient perceptions, to see concealed or confused realities more quickly and clearly in others;

3.   capability for self-acceptance of one's own nature, without excessive guilt;
4.   ability to be problem (outside the self), rather than ego-centered;
5.   capacity to be solitary without discomfort, take time out to assess situations, and extract the self from interactive contingencies, in order to be more objective;
6.   desire to be autonomous, with motivation for personal growth, independent of the physical world and culture, and the ability to avoid deficient motivation;
7.   maintenance of appreciation of subjective experience;
8.   ability to discriminate between means and ends, and appreciate *doing,* for its own sake;
9.   ability to resist encultured values and norms, which do not meet ethical and meaningful evaluative goals and agendas, through healthy personal autonomy.

Figure 1
Subject States of Awareness of the Clinician

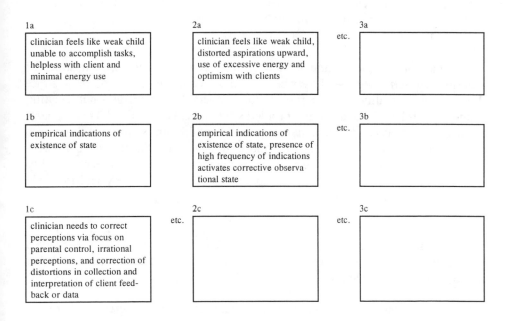

In thinking again about outcomes, one contradictory and confusing phenomenon relative to truth about actual states of client being (growth, regression, fixation, conflict, etc.), is that discovery of specific outcome data, may rob the individual of a more secure position of uncertainty. This provides the capability of entertaining expectations of success, and avoiding clear evidence of presumed failure. Clinicians may seek data which substantiates uncertainty, to avoid pain with actual negative outcomes, that exemplify unmet needs conceived as having low probability of fulfillment in past, present, or future relationships. Clinicians who assume negative or conservative personal aspirational postures, may seek negative data from clients to immunize themselves against feared failures of greater proportion, or keep their fantasies/hopes alive, by allowing awareness of confusing or contradictory outcome data. This keeps them "on the fence," but never responsible or fully committed with their aspirational resources. They may also excessively elevate levels of aspiration, so any failure is smaller than expected, and probably part of a different set of circumstances (phenomena in a different league, so the practitioner can always be idealistically adequate, in an inadequate world). Although this posture is probably necessary in measured portions, to survive the real disappointing experiences of clinical practice, it causes the professional to ignore significant indices of change or regression in the client. The practitioner can idealistically operate at a higher level of abstraction and at a conceptually different locus of dynamic functioning, closely related to childish fantasies of pleasing parents, through *primary process* perspectives and symbolisms of reality.

One form of adaptation related to this, is movement between strata of identity and self-image, and between levels of concrete, inferred, or abstract dimensions of reality used to protect the vulnerable self-image—but creating tremendous reliability and validity problems for clinical evaluation. This suggests the personality may have too many avenues of handling stress, whereas those with fixed character structures, may be more reliable instruments for consistent measurements of some phenomena. The healthier and more flexible personality may have too many loopholes or escape routes, to avoid anxiety and maintain illusions of adequate self-esteem.

Exercising creative control in adapting to an uncertain world, and symbolically representing internal reality, may mean manipulating variables or perceived objects (and their relative value), and manipulating attraction to them, as either independent or dependent phenomena.

This relates to a concept in epistemology concerning degrees of knowing reality,[39] which are altered or varied in response to previous motivational and outcome related concerns, and to observation of oneself in the act of observing

self or other. This is done within a system of categories or categorical definitions, or in assignment of attributes to various phenomena.[40]

Categories are typically defined in qualitative and nominal terms, whereby
attributes more closely assume characteristics of degree and intensity, less summative in nature. Categories and attributes help define each other, although
which one is more controlling of the identity, may be confusing to the clinical
evaluator. These arenas of self, furthermore, also have tenses related to tempo-
rality,[41] or associated with the self the clinician (1) was (completed), or could
have been (reflective); (2) is and continues to be (present continuing), or is and
will remain; or (3) will become (future prospective), or may become (future prob-
abilistic), etc.

These approaches to need fulfillment, however, suggest that practitioners
sometimes do not actively and definitively approach counseling to develop clear
positions for use in evaluative comparisons. They may also lack assertiveness in
their production of relatively-soft foundations of inputs or client outcomes, used
in decision-making.

In this light, the author is concerned that excessive demonstration of nonas-
sertive personality dynamics (regardless of how much professional knowledge or
skill is possessed), prevents counselors from decisively proving their value
through definitive and demanding scientific evaluation. It may offer relatively
mushy perceptions of self or client, in making decisions about motivation, outcome probability, need-meeting, goal directedness, and existing levels of self-
esteem. The self, as a definitive statement of values and directions, may require
clear boundaries and empirically definable characteristics. Thereby, comparisons
with other parts of the need fulfillment/self-esteem hierarchy, can have a solid
backdrop, against which to interact powerfully to determine which variables predominate. A less than definitive personal stance by the counselor, means other
variables have nothing against which to demonstrate dynamic interaction (the
power of other factors may simply overwhelm the counselor status); or counselor
assertiveness may be a decidedly negative phenomenon, causing alienation or
regression in client and counselor alike.

The rising popularity and practicality of developing empirical short-term
outcome objectives[42] within behavioral, task-centered, and crisis-oriented counseling therapies;[43] may invite a concomitant change in the personality style of
some direct service practitioners. They may be required to more assertively
organize their activities, and resolutely structure goals and treatment plans,[44] for

maximum cost-effectiveness and efficiency,[45] and to help clients utilize anxiety[46] for self-awareness[47] and learning.[48]

One author insists, in fact, that practitioners usually do not demand systematic evaluation or measurement for themselves or clients:

> "Skill implies an activity, an ability to perform (which) . . . is clearly distinguishable from knowledge. Skill is the capacity to set in motion and control a process of change . . . (and) is developed only as one turns concepts to convictions. A group (or individual) of workers gets hold of these concepts—has them in his (her) muscles and finds a steady and sure way to . . . make his (her) contributions . . ."[49]

From a research standpoint, every social service professional must become a modern evaluator, who exhibits steadfast resolve to critically examine his/her own competence, and defiantly attack ignorance in all areas of practice. This comes through (1) systematic gathering of facts and information, (2) rigorous hypothesis testing about clients and social problems, (3) challenging peers to prove their skills are effective, and (4) energetically resisting personal defensiveness about research[50] and peer group ideologies,[51] which often encourage false perceptions of adequacy, and discredit empirical scientific knowledge building.[52] In going back to issues of the self, in evaluation and therapeutic pursuits, clinicians also view capacity of the self and probability of desirable task outcomes (including level of aspiration), as functions of social norms and expectations of accomplishment and success.

There will always be concerns, of course, with reliability of assessments or assumed assessments of others relative to the clinician's adequacy, particularly when there are close relations between emotionality, use of clinical skills, and anxiety—associating the relationships between the clinician's self and significant others, to whom evaluative authority is rendered.[53] This is especially true when variability of assessment method or philosophy comes into play, as well as number of times assessments are made. The clinician is in a dilemma, deciding to which socially external evaluative universe, the identity status or categorical adequacy are most correctly applied. This concern has been specifically noted in the literature relative to gender orientation and values of the society normative model;[54] attributed masculinity or femininity of the activity being evaluated, in terms of gender appropriateness;[55] motivation vs. skill attributes as gender-related (e.g., men achieve by skill, women by emotion) for the particular clinician;[56] and previous gender-related self- or other-defined perceptions of the clinician, as success, failure, or some variation within this continuum,[57] as a function of field dependency. An issue here is whether women are socialized to be more aware of the needs and feeling requirements of self or others, and external and internal circumstances affecting the client; as opposed to men, who may be less tuned into this phenomenologic gestalt, for either self or client. Males may be socialized to be more independent of surroundings, and more behaviorally vs. affectively oriented. Of course, degree of other directedness or dependency in each clinician will, to varying degrees, influence extent to which attention is influenced by social or gender-related expectations.

Nevertheless, coping behavior (which includes identifying clinical target goals, establishing professional needs for levels and types of adequacy, providing treatment, and seeking positive evaluations) is learned and often defined, by the source of the reinforcement for the learning. In cases where society defines global expectations for socially conforming and adaptive behavior of clients, clinicians may be pressured to define treatment tasks which are practically unrealistic (or else be, themselves, socially deviant); exacerbate their perceptions of client pathology, so unrealistic goals can never be attempted (but not to the discredit of the therapist, who would attempt the right thing, if only clients were healthier); or define more microscopic and conservative goals for all clients, and ignore global possibilities which might be appropriate for selected categories of clientele.

The problem for the evaluator, is to determine relationship between any individual's behavioral activity (including cognition), and the potent body of knowledge of various socially significant groups; and understand the process by which this relationship dynamic is developed, maintained,[58] and translated into the needs of clients. Social norms define the needs that professional therapists or counselors have, in conjunction with their involvement vis-à-vis client outcomes, which is a function of their idiosyncratic degree of dependency on society, and level of perceived need deprivation or satisfaction.

In the first case, where unrealistic tasks might be defined to conform to socially learned expectations, measurement could incorrectly involve global social goals, yet miss smaller behavioral changes, which may be approximations of the larger goal, or clients' examples of progress in their own direction. Therapists may sometimes distort data about predestined failures, since broader goals can never be achieved. They may also measure success on their own levels of height-ened aspiration, in contrast to diminished client aspiration, as a form of pro-portional differentiation of personal or social realities. They may place excessive pressure on clients to achieve socially-valued goals, at the expense of personal ones.

In cases where increased client pathology must be perceived to defend against socially-unachievable norms, observations may be squeezed into negative categorical measurement models, so there is a perception of change, but incorrect interpretation of its meaning and value as a positive occurrence. Clients can become disheartened with these intrapsychic manipulations of data, and prematurely end treatment, or actually give in and get worse. As clients are routinely defined in adjusted ways to meet the counselor's or society's needs, therapists can experience declines in motivation, become skeptical, question their own integrity, or even burnout with self-perceptions of limited potential; as a defensive reaction against the nature of social definitions of accepted outcomes for helping professionals.

On the other hand, counselors who feel less dependency on socially defined needs, or who are themselves rebelling from social control and dependency, may select inputs which are skewed in this deviant direction and may, in fact, not fully accept the legitimacy of client needs when they are conforming.

This problem with social definitions, extends to even the basic meaning of counseling, where there is lack of consistent agreement and interpretation of qualitative service input vs. outcome[59] (and their relationship), since no empirical clarity or validity of these concepts has yet emerged. In fact, findings about competent practice[60] vary in the above-noted Kegel study, dependent on whether process-versus-outcome, or causes-versus-effect information, were considered by evaluators—especially where good process was paired (in judgments) with bad outcome, and vice versa.[61]

Finally, if more microscopic limited goals are defined for clients (to avoid the pressure of broader social values) as a defense of the counselor, the therapeutic paradigm may lose its value as a psychodynamic and socio-dynamic explanation of reality, and become a sterile behavioral model, which attaches no theoretical or developmental meaning to its empirical referents. Clinicians, unable to inductively and deductively move closer to and farther from their object of study (and who do not have external stimuli to assist them),[62] lose sight of treatment goals, and present a confusing picture to clients. They become ineffective[63] in strategically and tactically presenting a logical set of interrelated inputs, which give appropriate attention to both intrapsychic and social phenomena; where society also plays a part in clarifying cultural expectations, and protecting the integrity and stability of role occupants, with as much logic and reasonableness as possible."[64]

Much confusion can be avoided, when social role prescriptions are related to the needs of society directly, rather than intricately interwoven with the definitional process itself: "The occupancy of the relationship between differentiating criteria and assigned tasks is less important than the social reality created by the system of differentiation—if men (women) define situations as real, they are real in their consequences."[65]

This includes flexibility in conceptualizing awareness of choices, choosing behavior, and exploring avenues, to attain both individual and social goals.

The clinician's personal and social perception of task difficulty, is also related to client defense. This occurs, as nature and difficulty of potential outcomes in the client's life may be falsified, symbolized, or otherwise misrepresented by the clients, as they view themselves dealing with their own socialization, social norms, social opportunities, or blocks to adaptation and survival. This can be related to fear of change, irrational fear of conflict with external social reality, or a correct interpretation of social reality—all of which may be indexed for their perceptions of the counselor, observing them view their own process and outcomes.[66] Clinicians can be co-conspirators in distortions, due to their needs to succeed, fail for self-punishment, be accepted by clients, promote client sickness to feel healthy themselves, conceal their lack of knowledge, or otherwise symbolize internal representations of solutions to psychological conflicts.

In some cases, the counselor may misperceive client, problem, or social situation, and miscalculate aspiration and success probability levels, simply because they do not know enough about the client's history, culture, communicative style, pattern of conceptualizing, or baseline process of converting reality to symbolic referents. Resultant outcomes based on these distortions, may influence the counselor's self-esteem. Predictions of personal adequacy must be based on precise and comprehensive appreciation of client process, especially since this feedback loop becomes a critical source of clinical evaluative data.

In fact, some therapists decide to lower self-esteem levels (in their own perceptions), based on degree to which clients attempt to distort data (as this represents poor trusting relationships), or the counselors have been fooled by client smoke screens. Evaluation, here, does not relate as much to client communication, as to therapist input and dynamics of the therapeutic process and social expectations, about the resistance of clients, paired with the need to be helpful. Possible scenarios of client distortion are these:

1.   Client tendency to distort, may reflect fear of counselor insight and social disapproval, and ability to stimulate change—which is positive relative to counselor self-esteem.

2.   Client distortions may be totally related to transferences, where the counselor is a nonexistent or neutral variable, which is positive as far as not blaming the counselor; but possibly negative, if the therapist has not established a separate and therapy-producing identity in the relationship.

3.   Client cessation of distortions may reflect decreasing anxiety levels due to pseudo-secure dependency, which is negative relative to therapeutic goals of fostering independence.

4.   Clients may distort data as a process of modeling the therapist's distortions (e.g., idealistic distortions of truth in life, etc.), which is positive as the therapist is seen as a social role model; but negative, in that the therapist may represent an incorrect reality for impressionable clients.

5.   Client distortions may represent a typical part of the puzzle of therapeutic relationships, which is positive if the counselor views himself or herself as a puzzle solver relative to increased (not necessarily resolved) knowledge and awareness (which then requires client motivation and humanistic self-determination, for ultimate solution); but negative, if the therapist must change reality as a control process, or dominate individuals, by forcing adaptation regardless of self-determination factors.[67]

6.   Client distortion may be a function of change which has occurred in the client-therapist system, and may be reactive to a new dimension of this system, which cannot be clearly perceived by either participant, and requires an external consultant/therapist to work with the therapeutic alliance. This is neither positive or negative, if the therapist cannot be both participant and evaluator simultaneously, and therefore, is not able to control the system of which she or he is an integral and homeostatic, stabilizing part.

       According to Wagner,[68] consciousness cannot be separated from the object of which it is conscious, so there is concern about whether independent self-evaluation can ever exist—which is more complicated when human systems are part of the evaluative picture. Since relationships also constantly change, evaluative process (according to the structural functionalists) must be mobile, to collect and correctly interpret data, constantly emerging in each new transcendental situation.

7.   Reality distortion may exemplify client creativity, which is positive if the counselor has been an independent variable in stimulating this process, and if this knowledge is shared with clients to help them grow; but negative if the counselor discourages this form of independence, and will ultimately resent client creative attempts to individuate from therapeutic control. The therapist may derive positive self-evaluative benefit from his or her perceptual movement into less traditional social or psychological conceptual territory, if this allows more learning about clients, or allows clients to be adequate vis-à-vis the therapist as a significant other, supporting the client self.

8.   Reality distortion may reflect the client's spirituality or transcendental world, which disagrees with the physical, social, or spiritual world of the therapist. Helping clients transform or explain their distortions may be positive in viewing them holistically, but negative if the counselor does not recognize the existence and relevance of multiple dimensions of awareness, existence, adaptive states of being, or consciousness, etc.:

> "If I recognize only naturalistic values and explain everything in physical terms I shall depreciate, hinder or even destroy the spiritual interpretation, then I shall misunderstand and do violence to the natural man (woman) in his (her) right to existence as a physical being."[69]

Therapists are challenged, to partly base self-esteem and need definition on their ability to build bridges between existential worlds within which humans live, even if this means that clients do not manifest fully healthy adaptation in any of their worlds. The problem may be that clients have not yet discovered the right world for themselves, rather than the subjective fact that they have maladaptive processes, regardless of locus of existence.

9.   Client distortion and symbolism may, in fact, not be distortion within the phenomenologic world, but represent deviance within the therapist's theory-controlled empirical reality. The therapist's ability to reject his or her own theoretical or philosophical presuppositions to move into the client's world (courage to travel in unknown territory), may be positive as an index of personal and professional adequacy; but negative if the counselor is unable

to help clients understand their reality, possible conflicts with alternative realities, and the nature and ramifications of their decision-making, relative to this existential crisis.

From a phenomenological perspective (phenomenon = appearance, logos = mind), the client's world includes intuiting, analyzing, describing, gaining insight into essences, experiencing, and using cognition.

Mistake and Sexton[70] suggest that processes of classical introspection in traditional psychotherapy, reduce impressions to their simplest mental elements (sensations, feelings, images), at which point the counselor may help the client, or even unilaterally assign values of importance, intensity, and duration. This reductionism may be positive for the therapist in helping clients understand the foundations of their ideas, but negative if the symbolic meanings are not retransformed and integrated back into client introspective processes, to assess their full meaning and note any developmental changes.

As the reader can surmise, it is difficult to evaluate intentions[71] of clients, and even if intentions are assessed, it is then a separate challenge to correlate this with outcome probability, input receptivity for the client, and self-esteem rating by the counselor. In thinking of various forms of client behavior (defense, symbolism, communicative input, task awareness/definition), the therapist must systematically use conceptual categories or paradigms[72] which impute meaning to all types of client behavior (cognitive, affective, spiritual, etc.); indexed (for each category and every behavior) to also determine (1) specific meaning of each thought or behavior (constant or variable) relative-to the client's attempts at adaptation; (2) specific meaning of each thought or behavior as it impacts value, relevance, and potential effectiveness of all possible therapeutic inputs; (3) meaning of each behavior, as the counselor symbolically associates that behavior with a particular need—of his or her own—especially given the level of need deprivation, range of alternates for need satisfaction, and capability of client-related phenomena to be effective in need fulfillment.

With this category system, the counselor determines which specific client-related behavior has significance in meeting or causing conflict with the counselor's personal needs; and the counselor either corrects for biases[73] in allocated units of self-esteem, or feels more competent in assigning self-esteem units (rewarding self), where this is justified. This helps clarify confusion when the client displays incongruent responses between two states of being (since transition between behaviors is categorized), and lets the practitioner know the typical response in terms of self-esteem, need definition, etc., when the aforementioned client behavior occurs.   Any incorrect gains or losses to self-esteem can be corrected, or at least confronted, with this concrete plan, so anxiety (as need fulfillment or deprivation conflict emerges) minimally clouds the counselor's judgment.   Where there is incongruence, counselors use their framework to separate conditions of client vs. self-status, and postulate future inputs, outcomes, and evaluative decisions with each condition of interaction.

An example of this process, is the counselor who feels bad when the client changes direction on any issue, with a specified degree of deviance from previous positions, or from some valid and relevant norm.   With an a priori category system, this client behavioral dynamic is classified.   The counselor purposefully corrects the negative behavior, if the category system also specifies that client change of the aforementioned nature is either expected or beneficial, given the dynamics of therapy, or the subsequent inputs of the counselor in terms of confrontation or insight development.

Categories of information, client response, and need (relative to client response), are also essential, because "facts that are known and how (they) are known can affect the knower's actions and can be affected by the knower's actions."[74]   Meanings (including the need satisfaction meaning of each client communication or behavior) are a product of the client's experiential self-definition and behavioral manifestation which, as the therapeutic relationship develops, may have counterpart awareness and action domains, within the counselor's frame of reference.   Needs that are met or deprived relative to interaction with clients, can be empirically documented and standardized enough to be studied and controlled, in cases where erroneous evaluative decisions about counselor self-esteem, impair the therapeutic process.   These need dispositions, as well as obstacles, are solidified and confirmed by counselors' consistent awareness and references to them, their constant employment within the therapeutic process, and counselors' awareness of the consistency and style with which they maintain both personal and professional self-images.

Several ways for counselors to deal with need-meeting obstacles, are noted by one author[75] as follows:

1.   getting rid of, or overcoming (conquering/defeating/changing) obstacles;
2.   getting around or bypassing obstacles (while leaving them essentially unchanged and in their present form, intensity, etc.);
3.   modifying goals, so obstacles are no longer appropriate or necessary. Additions to this list that form the present author's perspective, are:

4. intentional eliciting of obstacles to provide necessary data for analysis, and to confront clients to promote change;
5. neutralizing/diminishing obstacles, to maintain homeostasis in goal definition and input planning, irrespective of probabilities associated with particular empirical outcomes;
6. symbolizing and transforming essences of obstacles to defensively meet substitute needs or avoid conflicts—which usually means pretending that obstacles meet alternate (usually nonadaptive) needs, or exaggerating potency of the obstacle, to provide punishment or justify weakness (e.g., the paranoid's need for symbolic persecutors, and the compulsive's need for exaggerated number of tasks).

The way the client is perceived relative to the practitioner's self-esteem, is certainly a function of mental frameworks about obstacles; and influences the basic definition of client psychological and social dynamics, investment of energy in providing specific types of inputs, assignment of significance to all facets of communicated messages, and level of anxiety (which typically represents a threat, and motivates toward achievement, if it occurs in moderate to small amounts, but paralyzes adaptation in excessive doses) around all processes of relating to clients to build the counselor's self-esteem. Awareness of various models for perceiving obstacles will assist the clinician in comprehensively understanding self in relation to client, and will highlight perceptual seedings which can have a significant impact on self-esteem, potential to earn self-esteem, and need to defend self-esteem.

Self-Image Consistency of the Counselor

In addition to decisions about self-esteem on the basis of needs identified by self or social norms, the counselor also assesses the stability, consistency, flexibility, rigidity, and degree of change of self-image or self-concept, vis-à-vis other potential ways of defining the self and other image positions or statuses.

This area of intrapsychic input is not related to specific nature or content of needs, or types of adequacy-validating mastery over clients or client problems, to achieve need satisfaction (including personal or physical change). It is not even directly correlated with typical indices of adequate personalities, such as achieving more efficient behavior, developing spontaneity/creativity, or acquiring personal autonomy.

It is more closely associated with the stability and consistency of counselor identity images which already exist, particularly as new or old competing images come into conscious awareness. This occurs through relaxation of defenses, emergence of conflictual or transferential cognitive content, or influx of stimuli from the external social system (usually in the form of closing homeostatic and accustomed avenues for need-meeting).

One theoretical perspective[76] suggests that individuals establish interpersonal relationships with persons who are the closest parallels to the self, in hopes of retaining secure images (anchors in reality),[77] and simultaneously bolstering depleted aspects of those images. The degree of defensiveness each counselor possesses, determines the extent to which relations are expected to passively maintain the status quo, or more actively meet needs for personal growth. An important implication for clinical evaluation, includes development and main-tenance of individual "phenomenological congruence,"[78] which is the extent to which a person sees himself or herself as others see him or her, and degree to which one sees others as they see themselves. This does not necessarily imply the self is seen as it really is, or that others are seen as they really are. In studies conducted to test this, assumed congruence did not necessarily exist, even if research subjects reported they agreed to have good rapport. In fact, this congruence is difficult to develop once distortions are discovered, even among experts in interpersonal and psychosocial relationships.

Hildreth,[79] for example, found that phenomenological congruence for both client and therapist, varied throughout therapy in a random fashion, with confusing patterns or no patterns of manifestation discoverable by external observers. It is interesting to note that some expected congruence scenarios did not prove to be true, especially in relationships with (1) a longer history and assumed increasing congruence as therapy progressed, (2) the building of thera-peutic relationships by more experienced clinicians, or (3) greater reported self-consistency, accompanying differences between counselors and specific clients. One set of therapeutic implications emerging from these findings, is that clinical inputs intended to reflect shared perspectives, may not be effective in insuring that counselors and clients are even in the same relationship together; or may be characterized by a reflective randomness, which only parallels image consistencies of the therapeutic partners separately. This may represent a communicational rather than image consistency problem, that can be deceptive in the counseling situation.

Since most counselors would probably agree it is important for counselor and client to see the other party as they view themselves individually, the above considerations suggest that the evaluator needs to be aware of possible discrep-ancies. They should make special efforts to develop inputs, which assist the

collective alliance in examining degrees and types of consistencies and inconsistencies, in perspectives held by each party about the other. From a positive
perspective, although variations of cognitive congruence in psychotherapy may
be fairly normal, it does annotate the complicated nature of the psychotherapy
process, pointing out the need to carefully validate all outcome conclusions based
on cooperative work between counselor and counselee.

If random variation of phenomenological congruence does occur and is
obscured by other processes and conceptions, the unpredictability of therapy is
elucidated, and cautions the counselor to avoid assumptions about types or
degrees of congruence,[80] even if congruence and effectiveness in counseling are
correlated.

As a guide to future action, phenomenological congruences and discrepancies should be identified and measured, since the covariation has significant
impact in the relations between any therapist and a particular client. It may be
good, in fact, to have some degree of incongruence, to continually ensure that
excessive client dependency has not occurred; as well as illustrate to the client,
the necessity of dealing with personal and relationship decisions about image
discrepancies and perceptual conflicts, which routinely develop throughout the
lifelong process of social living.

Some other concerns related to this congruence issue, are as follows:

1.   Counselors seeking to maintain the stability and security of their images (to
      unify and harmonize the system of ideas by which they live),[81] may con-
      sciously or unconsciously reduce their amount of exposure to clients, to
      control stimuli which cause them to perceive image discrepancies, or
      longitudinally compare differences. Selecting out short-term clients, or
      reducing real long-term problems in psychosocial dynamics, to a short-term
      perspective; robs clients of necessary time for growth, or redefines prob-
      lems, so outcome projections cannot become realistic components of the
      therapeutic plan. Although some clients require work for only a short
      period of time, longer relationship development means the client may
      negotiate substantial change and, in turn, expect change in the counselor.
      The therapist with more time to think about degrees and types of dif-
      ferences between client and self, and between present self and other
      potential selves which might be desired, may experience fear because of the
      strain of personal change, and potential loss of need fulfillments if
      homeostasis is interrupted.

2. Some practitioners may seek or maintain longer relationships with passive and less influential clients, or accentuate and attenuate vulnerabilities of clients, so they (the clients) are less likely to disagree with therapist self-images, for fear of retaliation or loss of dependency. Counselors may also extend work with clients to reduce the potency of client need-meeting capability and, therefore, handle therapist fears of dependency and respondent influence. Some repressive relationships over extended time periods prevent honest feeling and action from clients, and become substitute pathological social systems protecting all members from awareness, or changes in consistent images of the self.[82]

3. Therapists who are fearful of deeply knowing the self (and exposing competing images), may symbolically refrain from necessary probing into significant and painful aspects of the client's deeper personality dynamics. Although evaluation can be conducted relative to superficialities, real variables may never be identified. Also, significant relationships between past painful events and conceptualizations about these events, as they pertain to strength and weakness of the self, may never be hypothesized, tested, and worked through.

    Failure to explore, also prevents client awareness of ability to make differentiations in their perceptual fields, to become creatively aware of a wider range of self-concepts, solutions to problems, and adaptation avenues. A client who remains trapped within a narrowly-defined perceptual arena, not only can be more confidently diagnosed and understood (in explaining failures, as a defense for the counselor), but offers less pressure for the therapist to deal with fears of liberality, in defining self in less rigid or less consistent ways.[83]

    The compromise for client and therapist, is that adaptation and need satisfaction associated with adult growth, demand flexibility and dynamic perceptual differentiations, which are antithetical to relationships maintaining identity-threatened systemic homeostasis.

4. Therapists may consciously or unconsciously maneuver the therapeutic process to focus on empirically identifiable concrete and superficial goals (potentially appropriate components of empirical practice), which stabilizes focal points, to direct attention away from awareness of conceptual congruence issues. This may confirm convergence via agreement on external content areas, interpreted as a symbolic representation of self-image consistency. Shared meaning about external objects (ontic perceptions),[84]

can be interpreted incorrectly to signify congruence about identities and self-concepts, as supported by communicative messages concerning topical content, rather than about the selves involved. Excessive attention to external foci and areas of over functional specificity, serves the same function as family scapegoating, which produces inauthentic perceptions of self, others, and relationships. It also prevents the counselor from discovering a fuller range of client needs, possibly more relevant to dynamics of the therapeutic relationship. This is supported by research studies suggesting strong positive correlations between visibility of work, and perceptions of validity of internal, as well as external evaluation.[85]

The same problem also occurs when the therapist centers the focus on single client characteristics, and avoids awareness of multiple systemic interactive characteristics, whose variability from mean identity perspectives, can be unsettling to client or therapist. As Cooley[86] notes, the sense of self is often most conspicuous and available to understanding, when the mind is occupied, undecided, or not specifically focused on a distracting external object. The way to avoid this pitfall, is to seek target foci from many dimensions of the client's gestalt, and allow times in counseling when specific external objects do not move to center stage. They remain in the background, so other identity and relationship issues emerge in the spotlight. However, the counselor with anxiety-ridden fears of image fluctuation, may never allow this much relaxation in external, content-related object identification, and attention.

5.   Another process of maintaining consistent self-image of the counselor, is to accentuate variability, randomness, and fluctuations of client image positions, allowing the practitioner's image variability to appear relatively stable by comparison. This can be accomplished by directing therapeutic comments at the client in various image positions they assume, while failing to develop therapeutic strategies to help consolidated separate images into more encompassing categories, or deal with barriers which prevent acceptance of separate images of the self. Some clients maintain this inconsistency as a way of pleasing the counselor, inadvertently helping him or her maintain the illusion of stability, via comparison. The therapist may assume a legitimate lack of awareness or knowledge of where the client is conceptually, to justify retreating to the safe confines of rigid self-perceptions, which are supported and authorized by some pathology models of clinical practice, which define instability in the client. The therapist may advantageously identify client image loci as rigid within diagnostic categories, which reduces likelihood that the client's more flexible

orientations would disturb the image consonance and constancy of the counselor,[87] or the entire dyadic relationship.[88]

This process binds client energy, dividing and occupying it in diversions, so it never becomes a potent force, to possibly be used against the therapist to challenge the consistency of his or her own images of self.[89]

The above process represents overall reductionism within images, coupled with narrowly conceived descriptive awareness of multiple images. In the analogy of forest and trees, counselor and client perceive each tree instead of the forest, yet are continually aware of the number of trees and existence of the forest, but are not allowed an analytic position of reward and safety from which to perceive forest vis-à-vis trees.

Exaggerated interest in transference by the therapist, may be a subcomponent of the above process. In this case, the client is diagnosed as compulsively responding to a consistent (albeit transferred) image in the therapist (a form of reverse displacement for image consistency), or differential client responses are described as distorted perceptions of love objects, rather than actual changes in the real image of the therapist, which might occur during the course of therapy. The therapist builds in a surrogate identity which can change transferentially along with the client, but may never be seen as real in the here-and-now, or the image is always constant in its transferential stable state.

The overall negative effect, is that clients never get feedback about their own self-perceptions as they really change vis-à-vis the practitioner, since the situational gestalt is encumbered by past baggage which accompanies perceptions, differentiation between self and nonself, and differences between autonomous self-control and influential social (represented by the controlling counselor) expectancy. Clients may also experience decrease in options for rewards of self-discovery, personality variation, and creativity. They may not become aware of their ability to negotiate changes in perceptual field organization, wherein they have mobility to view the self and counselor from different vantage points, to develop awareness of conversion points, consistency, and desired perceptual perspectives and positions.

The evaluative model used by the therapist in regard to the above potential distortions, should ideally encompass assessment of:

- client awareness within each perceptual image field they possess;
- client awareness outside their typical perceptual fields, but within self-evaluative, analytic, or new image scenarios;
- client capability, as analyzer of therapists' perceptual field of awareness;
- client movement in and out of various perceptual positions, to develop awareness of dynamic patterns representing conflictual, childhood, or other fields in and of themselves;
- counselor awareness of distortions within his or her own self-images, through inappropriate, unwanted, unneeded, or excessive efforts to change the client (active countertransference) to be more congruent with the counselor, or to conform to some complementary functional, mythical, or fantasized image.[90] This can existentially become a contrived essence[91] which is inappropriate to both conceiver (therapist) and object (client), and also become an identity toward which the client must launch resistance, which further complicates evaluation, since the practitioner may correctly see the resistance as a personal affront and self-defense.

A second problem, is that each practitioner may possess a theoretical strategy or tactical plan of action, with inputs not directly correlated to the here-and-now counselor/client dynamic relationship. Intervention may relate to incorrect self-images within the client's past life, previous cognitive choice pattern, or earlier developmental states of being, where the past is symbolically, but incorrectly, represented in the present. Evaluation of these inputs relative to client change, may certainly provide data about effectiveness, but negative findings could easily be associated with unnecessary client resistance for change goals they do not desire. Also, positive indicators are suspect in terms of cost/efficiency and cost/benefit effectiveness, depending on whether they are correctly matched up with (a) client problem, (b) therapist need, or (c) client motivational focus. Counselors defining and working with clients relative to their own (therapist's) self-image, may be reluctant to change nature, direction, or potency of inputs to suit changed client dynamics, and may also be rigid in selection of tactics, which are incorrectly assumed to be appropriate. The need and responsibility to change the client, creates added pressure for the counselor in selecting proper amount and duration of input deliveries, which may be increased or decreased, to handle personal anxiety relative to failed efforts to produce symbolic consistency and stability of personal self-image.

As noted by Lecky,[92] when inconsistency arises, personal anxiety causes each individual to personalize the problem, and attempt to alter the situation (in this case, the nature of the client) to produce consistency. The client may also be sensitive to an incongruent image configuration, and confuse his/her own and the therapist's anxiety, further confounding goals and motivations for change.

All of this is further complicated by questions of correlation and reliability of self-respect data, as an accurate reflection of clients' behavior, motivation, or attitudes.[93] This is especially true with confusing functions of linear progression of thoughts relating to behaviors, as well as client decisions relative to broader classification categories that they apply to themselves relative to their own status, or see the counselor using on them,[94] in terms of need to be included, or fear of inclusion or exclusion.

6.   Additionally, the counselor can distort or actually change the image of the client to complement his or her personality, to maintain a consistent image. This typically means (a) selectively attending to only portions of the data (symptoms, thoughts, feelings, history, or relationship dynamics); (b) moving existing facts into unnatural linear configurations, or transposing them with one another;[95] or (c) drastically redefining or altering the meaning of particular facts—all possibly intended to use clients' thoughts/feelings/behaviors to fill missing gaps in an image which is neither complete, nor valued to be adequate. Of course, missing parts of the professional's image are associated with childhood emotional deprivations, developmental deficits, or unexpected life events, and cannot be correctly or successfully met transferentially through clients. Clients synthesized into ontologic[96] life scripts of the counselor, may not productively cooperative with treatment criteria, as viewed by two possible contradictory scales (client's and therapist's). Also, definition of variables and hypothesized relationships may be constantly and irrationally (at least as the client tries to understand the counselor's conversion process) changing, with no stable foundation for validity or reliability decisions, relative to state of existential or social being (status). Clients make some assessments of their behavior as reflected in the counselor's feedback, but would be hard pressed to use the self (client's self) as a standard or normative focal point to assess change, behavioral variations, or deviation.   Resisting the therapist's distortion attempts for the client may, therefore, mean sustenance or development of rigid ego boundaries, since many clients already struggle with confused perceptual boundaries and, therefore, become more anxious when additional and irrelevant alternatives are injected into their already-faulty decision-making apparatus.

Although mental and behavioral flexibility may be the ultimate goal of therapeutic growth as a process of adaptation, internal security through incremental handling of identity-related perceptions, is the first step in giving clients self-assurance, to subsequently juggle multiple perceptual alternatives. Adding the therapist's identity concerns as an extra alternative, grossly confuses the picture, and makes the client even more vulnerable and in need of dependent protection, which can easily come from fitting the therapist's image-building script in life.

The creative ability of the mind[97] to recognize symbolism and analogy, interchange deductive/inductive reasoning, recognize actions and reactions, synthesize and extrapolate, and experience the self (rationally or irrationally); gives counselors considerable editorial capability to rearrange reality to fit self-image contingencies. This pattern is additionally made easier because of the therapeutic process, and socially-validated counselor role of identifying and assessing client motives (conscious or unconscious), rather than simple reliance on observable behavioral outcomes. Diagnostic process allows greater freedom of interpretation and symbolic representation, which is necessary to understand client dynamics, but is subject to selective and incorrect interpretation, where the practitioner needs specific client definitions to complete a picture which is unilaterally important, only to the counselor. When motives, traits, styles, and syndromes are diagnostically articulated, the therapist can assume longitudinal manifestation of client dynamics and, therefore, be more assured of a stable and lengthy defensive system for image maintenance, which cannot easily be refuted by aberrant empirical behavior samples exhibited by clients. The traditional psychiatric and psychodynamic diagnostic model does not, in and of itself, provide easy self-corrective factors, wherein particular client behaviors which deviate from therapist image-related expectations, help both parties discern possible distortions and incorrect interpretations.

The therapist who redefines or distorts client thoughts or behaviors, may also define single behaviors as representative (inadequate and unrepresentative sampling) of more global patterns, thereby substantiating the presence of long-term and relatively-consistent client images, which are inappropriately used for therapist image-building or maintenance.[98]

Handling Guilt

A third major concern in evaluation relative to self-actualization and esteem-building, is the therapist who experiences guilt or self-depreciation. Not every counselor will experience guilt, and each occasion of this inwardly-directed anger may not necessarily symbolically represent the same cause or dynamic life representation. Also, although everyone experiences some guilt, each counselor will vary according to amount of positive image distortion or skewness learned in life tasks and clinical work, used to handle ambivalence about love, separation and personal autonomy, fear of closeness, and symbolic reparation for assumed wrongdoing.

Guilt can be an effective aid, in some ways, to stimulate the therapist to work harder to obtain knowledge and correctly utilize inputs, although there is a tendency to use excessive input energy or clinical power, to perceive more rapid or more pronounced examples of client success. Guilt can be related to previous childhood intrapsychic conflicts, but because etiology of guilt is rooted in resolution of past and no longer existent relationships, counselors may discover there is no direct formula by which specific incidents of success with clients, will ever be converted to viable and believable units of their own childhood adequacy. The harder they work to attain client outcome success, in fact, the more guilty they feel, since each success can be cognitively converted to a failure. Also, increasing energy output to "win," may result in further indications of the futility of one's efforts.

Counselors who experience guilt may be chronically or acutely in personal distress, and have a difficult time being aware of their own process as it occurs. They may also need external assessment and stimulation, to take corrective action to reduce negative effects of their distortion of inputs or outcome indices. Peer review or collegial supervision is the most feasible mechanism to help this problem, yet research shows that, although review processes may be accepted in principle[99] for assumed quality control,[100] actual operationalized practice may not produce qualitative effectiveness, or positive perceptions about evaluation by the participants. This is dependent on the role of administration in the review process, and differences between mandated reviews for accountability, and voluntary reviews for growth, as well as type of data reviewed.

When guilt results in fears of even greater losses to the vulnerable self, the therapist may assume an ultra-conservative approach with clients, so risks are not taken and energy for change is not stimulated. Also, mediocre homeostasis may be supported in the client's intrapsychic or interpersonal system, and rewarded as an index of safety, or interpreted as an index of adequacy to avoid cognitive dissonance.

The therapist sometimes encourages clients to express anger externally, to vicariously act out his or her own internal drama, or focus intently on the client's angry feelings (sometimes even encourage their definition, where they do not exist, or exist to a lesser degree) and, therefore, defocus other areas and dynamics that need attention. This sets up evaluative hypotheses which are invalid, and do not represent true characteristics of an individual client.

The important point about guilt for counselors, is that they need external feedback from a competent peer or supportive supervisor, so times and places where evaluative distortions appear, can be documented and subsequent steps taken to reduce probability of these occurrences, and handle the personality problem via the therapist's own therapy.

Interpersonal System Maintenance

In a final point about personality development and evaluation, counselors must consider the nature and dynamics of interpersonal process and therapeutic relationships relative to *self-actualization,* as this affects the general and specific nature of self and client assessment.

Although stimuli and reinforcing contingencies for self-evaluation can be internal[101] to the practitioner doing the assessing, a bilateral model of evaluation also includes an external perspective. As noted by several authors,[102] approval from others is a significant dimension of self-perception and goal directed activity; and becomes an interactive process which helps define the relationship between client and counselor, and contributes to the relationship's potential to produce growth for the client.

Self-esteem, as a function of external reward, may be linked to development of individual attitudes toward evaluation. This suggests that reward and punishment reciprocity are significant avenues through which client and counselor make comparisons, assessments, and decisions, about their status and adaptability with different approaches to functioning. However, an individual's self-perception, as a function of external evaluation, may be a product of incorrectly perceived opinions from significant others, especially trusted[103] as valuable sources of feedback.

Brisset[104] also stresses the complementary relationship between inner and outer influences on self-evaluation. He divides self-esteem into two social/ psychological processes (self-evaluation and self-worth), which materialize as part of interaction of the individual and social system. Competence, therefore, is not only assessed in terms of goal achievement in the "object world," but also as "symmetry" between one's conception of self, and manifestation of this self-concept through interactive behavioral outcomes. The consideration of only singular behavioral evaluative outcomes within the scientific model, for example, might neglect consideration of this "symmetry," and provide evaluation of only part of relevant dimensions involved, possibly excluding consideration of the types of checks and balances which occur in relationships. Evaluation should include associational dynamics and negotiations in which client change is an integral part of the system's survival, viability, and strength; and interactive evaluative feedback is a necessary component of developing and maintaining this homeostatic balance.

Brisset's research in the area of curricular influence on self-evaluation, also stresses that evaluative experiences have internal as well as external components. He demonstrates that different teaching methods (as socializing experiences which influence internal perceptions) have significant effects on critical assessment abilities of students, in individual approaches to self-evaluation. He concludes that development of critical and analytic attitudes is most pronounced with teaching methods that allow increased student responsibility and participation (investment of self).

Leitner[105] also studied socialization and personality development with respect to individuals' ability for accurate evaluation of themselves and others. In studying "discriminative ability" and "self-assessment," he found that counselors with the most experience and training in self-evaluation, were more accurate in discriminating (evaluating) helpfulness of others and themselves, as compared to counselors with either less training or experience.[106]

Extrapolation of this finding also hypothesizes that relationships which experienced evaluative give and take as part of the foundation, might also be holistically more capable of discriminative assessments of individual and collective characteristics; but might also work more effectively bilaterally, to make decisions about therapeutic or relationship changes, as a result of the process by which this data is a joint learning experience. Fitts[107] seems to concur with these perspectives, noting self-esteem, as a building block for self-concept, is derived from both self and significant other individuals. Esteem is earned as one achieves relevant interactive goals, functions according to certain values, or fulfills standards of internal and external origin. Self-evaluation can be the process of assessing the individual's goal achievement and conformity to specific value standards, which are cornerstones of the therapeutic relationship. Self-esteem may be established, regulated, and applied by the "judging (evaluative) self," by others, or by both, whenever the interactive "behavioral self" is engaged in self-actualizing behavior.[108] Manifestation of self-evaluative behavior, therefore, is fully integrated as a part of esteem and identity of each personality, and can only be understood through consideration of each unique "self," and its relationships with other pertinent "selves."

Marolla[109] is another theorist conceptualizing self-valuation within a network of interchanges between personality and environment, but further noting specific patterns which these associations assume. He suggests that inner self-esteem is a function of congruence between self-defined intents for action and actual behavioral outcomes, as interpreted individually and collectively in relationships. Inability of the individual, however, to define goals for competence, stimulates more personal dependence on evaluation of effectiveness from other sources, within the therapeutic or professional environment. People inclined to self-validation (self-evaluation), are more motivated to achieve inner self-esteem, and have a greater probability of accomplishing this goal. Those who evaluate themselves on criteria other than the reflected appraisals of others, think they are more competent and feel better about how others see them.[110] Inability to develop individually-relevant goals and criteria for performance would, according to Marolla, cause the practitioner to be less responsible for creative and effective self-evaluation, and more dependent on external evaluative sources. Marolla also suggests that criteria for evaluation should be a combination of the practitioner's behavioral outcomes, and self-defined intents based on individual personality needs and characteristics.

A problem with this interpretation, however, is that counselors who feel confident in their inner evaluations and also feel positive about perspectives of others who see them; may obscure negative, but correct, information from the client, and deliver inputs which they (the counselor) feel are valuable. The fact that they feel good about their inner directedness may, in and of itself, be a positive therapeutic influence on clients, actually overshadowing negative impacts of incorrect technique or philosophical strategy.

On the other hand, questioning one's inner directions may be a healthy process to model for clients, but not necessarily result in positive client change, even if therapist changes do result. Clients may resist any input they feel is a reflection of lack of counselor stability, or which clients guiltily feel they have caused, and therefore fear control over the counselor.

It is important to keep in mind that conceptual juxtaposition of self-evaluation and self-esteem, signifies the depth and intricacy of psychological and philosophical processes which underlie individual evaluation. Relevancy of these considerations is sometimes overlooked in the evaluative literature, and can fall outside the conceptual vision of classical evaluative models, especially when reviewing the relationship as a system of significant evaluative impact.

Some specific concerns of evaluative awareness about relationships, are discussed in the numerically listed areas that follow.

1. *Interpersonal Role Clarity:* One central issue for the professional, is degree to which the client is viewed (maybe as a transferred parental judge, or a consumer to whom accountability is expected) as a legitimate, powerful, and accurate judge of the adequacy of professional performance. This is related to the therapist's proficiency in relationship development, expertise in delivering therapeutic inputs (regardless of outcomes), or assessment of congruence between expected and attained outcomes reflecting clinician capability.[111] Although the client's perceptions of the therapist can be real or fantasized, the counselor makes a decision about the degree to which the client is a significant other, perceived personal penalties for varying degrees of negative evaluations, and the use of specific strategies or tactics to win positive interpersonal evaluations.

One question, of course, is the significance of client's feelings about the worker (comfort level, trust, confidence), and whether these feelings help the development of client motivation and capability to change in therapy, and develop a successful working alliance. Another concern, is whether therapists' perceptions of client perceptions and their evaluative role, cause alteration in delivery of therapeutic inputs, which either facilitates or hampers the helping effort. This also depends on the collective (dyadic collective role awareness) reality perceived by both members about the quality, security, and helpfulness of the relationship unit, as this unit is individually and jointly compared to other relationships, seen as more positive, negative, or equal in value to the therapeutic relationship.

As one author interestingly notes,[112] therapists evaluate themselves more positively when there is high variance in the ways others evaluate a trait; and there is a positive relationship between self-esteem and linking for evaluators, when the evaluators are ambiguous, i.e., not clearly accepting or rejecting in their assessment.[113] It seems that origins of self-conceptualizations vary, relative to ambiguity or confusion, related to a personal characteristic which constitutes a subcomponent part:

"Their self-evaluations are unrelated to their self-confidence and if they overrate themselves, it is only to a slight degree. They tend to see themselves as others see them, either because they are influenced by others or because they have observed their performances along with others, and share criteria for making judgments. For the ambiguous attributes, on the other hand, self-concepts are largely idiosyncratic. Self-esteem and the desire to maintain self-esteem shape how persons view themselves on these attributes. In other words, on ambiguous attributes, persons tend to see either what they expect or want to see."[114]

There is great complexity involved, however, in determining:

a. whether therapeutic inputs are more qualitative when the therapist is uncertain how the client feels;
b. whether therapeutic inputs are more qualitative when the therapist feels positive, based on his or her own fabrications (resulting from client ambiguity) vs. positive evaluations (but real fear of also perceiving negative ones), which are more clearly and empirically articulated;
c. whether clients are more prone to effectively use therapeutic inputs when they are (a) ambiguous, or (b) clear in their evaluative perceptions, but perceived to be ambiguous by the therapist;
d. whether liking the client evaluator is, in any way, related to quality of input, or whether being liked as a client evaluator, is related to effective efforts to change;
e. whether varying amounts of positive, or interchanges between positive and negative evaluations, are necessary in determining therapist motivation and energy levels to produce quality inputs;
f. whether maintenance of the relationship or homeostasis is related to specific inputs, and whether these inputs are associated with evaluative perceptions believed by therapist and client, to be connected to relationship solidarity (also how relationship homeostasis vs. stress, impacts the client's motivation and ability to change thoughts, feelings, or behaviors in compliance with therapeutic goals);
g. whether prior self-esteem and need to maintain image constancy relates to inputs, whether these inputs condition ambiguous client responses, and whether these responses are, in fact, necessary to maintain self-esteem; and the extent to which self-esteem in the therapist, is related to client perceptions of their change-agent nature, and the actual delivery of high-change-probability inputs from the counselor.

It is uncertain, however, exactly when diagnostic categories and social roles (therapist vs. client) are interrelated. This includes whether therapists who view clients as pathological, sick, or inferior, would really be comforted by agreements (even positive) in perceptions of evaluated traits, especially when particular theories stress conflicted, transferred, and symbolic natures of client perceptions; or whether clients are more capable of giving correct feedback, when therapist inputs are clear-cut, as opposed to ambiguous.

If there is disagreement on evaluations of specific traits, there are also questions about the positive aspect of this for client independence (is it safe to disagree?), negative aspects of purposeful disagreement to become independent (regardless of the actual correctness of the evaluation), and how the therapist might potentially change inputs, based on assessment of symbolic meaning of the agreement or disagreement. An important aspect of this process is whether the client, as a probable bearer of perceptual problems, is an accurate and qualitative judge of the therapist's performance, and how the therapist makes decisions about whether the judging client is good, fair, or bad at accomplishing these tasks.

Also important, is the influence of inputs on the therapist's perception of the esteem the client holds for her or him, and how these feelings are related to the counselor's efforts to expend energy and time, support, confront/block resistances, offer uncomfortable interpretations, or perform other acts which theoretically have greater or lesser hypothesized probability of success, in dealing with client problems.

"Behavior of people engaged in formal interactions is typically more ambiguous with regard to underlying motives. One of the causes of this ambiguity is that formal interactions are strongly determined by various external factors such as a norm to be pleasant or polite. For example, if a person deviates from his (her) normal route to drive somebody home and is asked to stay for a drink, the offer may be dictated by the wish to continue an interesting conversation over a drink, but it could as well be mere politeness. Even if behavior is not normatively determined, different motives could still underline the same behavior. For example, if at a cocktail party a relative stranger found a conversation rather dull and pretended thirst to get away, was thirst the true reason for his (her) behavior?

Especially if the situation is ambiguous, people may rely heavily on relevant past experiences. Thus, if a person felt (rightly or wrongly) that people had often been bored by his (her) conversation in the past, he (she) would tend to attribute the cocktail party incident to his (her) dullness and the invitation of his (her) passenger to politeness. To a person who feels that he (she) has generally been witty and charming in the past, it might never occur that the party friend left for any reason other than thirst or that the passenger had any motive other than desiring to continue the conversation.

If people do use their past experiences in making inferences about the meaning of others' behaviors and if self-esteem summarizes the evaluative aspects of this past experience, individuals with low self-esteem must, then, differ consistently from high self-esteem individuals in the inferences they draw regarding others' feelings toward them. More specifically, the prediction follows that the lower an individual's self-esteem, the more likely he (she) is to attribute any negative behavior (such as discontinuing a conversation at a party) to disliking rather than other causes and to attribute any positive behavior (such as an invitation for a drink) to causes other than liking (e.g., to politeness). In other words, a person interprets another's behavior toward him (her) as consistent with his (her) self-concept."[115]

2.   *Relationship Continuity:* Another issue of interpersonal process and structure, is assessment by either counselor or client, as this enhances or jeopardizes continued existence and quality of their relationship. Obviously, the relationship must be maintained at some level of observable (often symbolic or fantasized) interaction and empirically verifiable communicative interchange, for the therapist to make even the basic assumptions of her or his significance to the client.

In the case of therapeutic relationships, client and therapist need each other for a host of reasons, and develop individual and collective perspectives on reality[116] and the solidarity of the need-meeting association, which include probability of its continuance, growth, or eventual deterioration.

Each person overtly or tacitly requests the other member to maintain loyalty to the relationship, and avoid premature stimuli which threaten homeostasis or cohesion[117] of the mutuality. This can occur whether the association relates to the necessary motivation of the client to grow, or the manipulative or dependency needs of either counselor or client, for continuance of the association. As norms and processes of dyadic role complementarily develop, both members may control[118] honest and correct evaluative feedback (data input that may be threatening), as a process of submitting, deferring, or mitigating negative influences, to insure personal security while simultaneously maintaining the relationship. In cases where the counselor might be expected to confront client efforts to maintain a safe, but unproductive relationship, Ellis[119] notes the leadership function may involve adaptation and deference of necessary therapeutic or evaluative functions, to specific group (may apply to dyads or families) members who actually control the process:

> "We sometimes believe that the leader assumes the leadership role by structuring the interaction, influencing the flow of ideas and the relationships in the interaction. Ellis' research implies that the leader may indeed attempt to structure the interaction with some members. But in their structure may not attempt to exert any relational authority over them."[120]

In other research, Wood[121] notes that leaders promote a collective identity which provides cohesion and stability to the social system, which ultimately protects members from individual vulnerability and group disintegration. Correct evaluation of the therapeutic or nontherapeutic process may be abdicated, in order to maintain a safe relationship structure.

In these cases, it may be relatively easy for the counselor to interpret homeostasis or relationship stability/continuity as a positive evaluative index when, in fact, the relationship may have therapeutic characteristics that are more important than mere balance, or the relationship requires imbalance in order for it to grow through awareness and problem solving.

If there is real negative data, the counselor may choose to overlook it, as an intervening variable which is to be handled by dynamics within stability-maintaining characteristics of the relationship; or the negative data may be obscured within overall categorical phenomena of the homeostatic balance. Where the counselor's possible imaginative construction or actual awareness of real negative judgments[122] by the client (correlated with degree of countertransference) predominate conscious awareness, the therapist may manipulate process, to the point where more positive judgments are empirically elicited or demanded, (irrespective of actual growth). Also, the counselor may slow down threatening components of intersective process, so mounting negative evaluations do not continue to challenge the relationship.

Although it is important for counselors to have positive concepts of self, when levels of esteem become part of interactive evaluation, there is a confounding effect on the correct interpretation of evaluative data which emerges. For example, when another person's positive or negative behavior could be induced by either internal attitudes or environmental situational stimuli, those with high self-esteem feel that positive evaluation is related more to personal feelings—than do low self-esteem individuals, while negative evaluations are attributed more to external factors. Assumptions that one's judgment about another represents their honest and correct feelings, seem more likely when these feelings (evaluations) match the evaluated person's self-concepts, especially when there is high self-esteem to begin with.[123] This does not necessarily mean a counselor redefines reality: the counselor may simply make judgments with limited clear data, so the evaluative discriminator is *congruence with self,* rather than with associations about real agendas, needs, and impressions of others, who are also subjective interpreters of reality.

Strong negative correlations reported in some studies,[124] relative to high therapist self-concepts and corresponding low client self-concepts in relationships, suggest the importance for self-image complementarity to be assessed early in treatment. This is necessary, to detect situations where clients become more positive and powerful than therapists in some self-image areas, and therefore move beyond the counselor's capability level; or where therapists need to remain in control, to provide security for themselves in the relationship.

The cognitive balance effect may also apply here,[125] which suggests that an individual who evaluates the self negatively, has negative views toward those who hold contradictory views, (i.e., hold positive views toward him or her), and demonstrates more positive views toward those whose opinions match more closely with the self-concept. Other research also suggests that those with higher self-esteem, respond more favorably to external evaluative feedback (positive or negative); while there is a tendency for those with lower self-esteem, to view any type of feedback less favorably.[126] This suggests that persons with positive self-concepts have a stronger assumed perception that others are like them, while those with negative self-images, perceive they are different from others.

The therapist seeking to develop or maintain a positive self-image, may inappropriately engineer the dyadic relationship to provide positive feedback (negatively impacting the client, when they are not pressured to work, or painfully deal with conflicts, etc.), or continue in existence, so positive feedback comes at a later time, while also ignoring negative feedback which already exists. As noted by Robert Bales,[127] goals for clients can be task-directed, identity directed for the client, or identity directed for the therapist. In the latter case, this means alignment or construction of interpersonal roles and functions which are inefficient or ineffective for negotiating therapeutic growth; however, these roles or functions may be effective to enhance counselor self-esteem, or at least avoid manifestation of negative feedback to damage self-esteem. Homeostatic relationships may continue for excessive periods, with the primary function of not providing negative evaluative feedback, and become safe havens for clients and therapists, to collectively conspire (consciously or unconsciously) to escape personal and mutual conflicts. Here are possible complementary role alignments which might prevent therapeutic growth, but maintain a relationship which is safe, predictable, and mutually nondestructive:

Therapist Role	**Client Role**	**Role Interaction**
[1] Passive	Passive	No confrontation
[2] Passive	Active	Client control to insure their own safety and esteem
[3] Active	Passive	Therapist control to provide parental protection
[4] Active	Active	Conflict relationship with each offense preventing feared dependent vulnerability

This simple example suggests the importance of considering strategic role alignments, which insure continuance of a relationship which is non-threatening, and which signifies mutual defensiveness in a dyadic system protected by relationship boundaries, and is perpetuated due to habituation.

Additional important implications of interactive dynamics, relative to relationship continuity and esteem maintenance, are as follows:

a.   Counselors with varying degrees of negative self-perceptions, may value clients who agree with this or view themselves negatively, and perpetuate relationships to maintain this negative balance. They may also evaluate themselves positively for relationship-building, which leads to a superior goal of negative self-concept perpetuation, using input skills to either sabotage client growth, or develop dependency on stronger clients. This may involve use of clinical power to distort the client's perceptions of personal positive attributes, and may dictate use of more aversive techniques to maintain the client's negative images of the therapist. Positive views these counselors hold for persons who view them negatively, may be used evaluatively by clients as an index of growth, or at least relationship success (actually balanced congruence, with a negative foundation), so feedback to the therapist will be distorted correspondingly. Positive views of the therapist for clients who share negative perceptions, may also be validated within theories of pathology and deviance, so the counselor is justified in continuing work to correct the pathological condition of negative perceptions. They evaluate the self positively, in the sense that he or she closely follows theoretical models and "scientific" principles in practice. It is easy for supervisors or peer observers to reward therapists for use of models or theories of pathology, while ignoring the fact that theory can be used as glue to hold negative relationships together, in a state of homeostatic, but destructive balance.

b.   Counselors confronted with clients who view them positively (while therapist self-concept is negative), may be unable to tolerate the relationship and conceptual imbalance, and either invalidate the client's positive perception (and condition negative interpersonal and perceptual processes), perform pseudo positive modeling behavior to complement client perceptions (but not really assume positive identity), or terminate the relationship prematurely to avoid cognitive and relationship dissonance. It may be possible to redefine positive perceptions from clients toward the therapist (who view them negatively, due to need for confirmation of the negative self-concept), with psychopathological models as examples of manipulation, seduction, dependency, control, or submission. Hereby, even sound processes of evaluating defensive changes will be incorrect, since the therapist may define this form of client strength inappropriately. Clients with ambivalence about their ability to relate positively to others, may perpetuate the relationship longer than necessary, in an effort to have their positive overtures rewarded and validated. The therapist may either terminate this game; or insure its perpetuation, so long as the therapist redefines *positives* as *negatives,* or otherwise produces change, so the client's view moves in the negative direction. In some cases, the therapist may eventually accept the inversely-correlated perspectives (imbalance) as one specific form of homeostasis, where balance comes not from corresponding perspectives, but rather from regularity and predictability of relationship dynamics. This means that some therapeutic relationships continue and retain the client's opposing views of the therapist, with degree of stability of the opposition as one positive index of relationship solidarity, and one type of symbolic positive index of effectiveness. As relationships continue, balance theory suggests either the client would change to corroborate views the therapist has of self, or the therapist changes to fit the client's perspective. In some cases that continue, both parties need dissonance to justify personal conflictual agendas, or insure autonomy and self-protection through empirical examples of differences. This latter case may be a more extreme example, where pathology or personality confusion/conflict exist in both parties in the relationship.

c.   In cases where therapists with positive self-concepts believe others are like them, these assumptions of similarity might be useful in communicating new positive norms of client acceptance and support. These assumptions may also be useful in role modeling, but damage evaluative and therapeutic process (especially correct assessment pathology variances, e.g., degrees of stability, longevity, or powerfulness of client defenses), if clients are not seen as unique individuals with the option to differ from authority. The wrong assumption of similarity can result in incorrect diagnosis and usage of input techniques, which are modeled after the self, rather than needs of personality dynamics of clients.

Therapists with lower self-concepts, perceiving greater differences between themselves and clients, can assign excessive measurement values to indices of relationship strength or stability, or view interpersonal convergences as having more variability or dispersion from mean values, than is actually the case. They may also not even view the possibility of working with some clients, who are grossly different from the therapist.

d.   There is another situation where incremental evaluation may be ignored, as the therapist builds a trusting relationship for anticipated therapeutic payoff at a later date (deferred gratification situation). Presumption of future changes (including threats to relationship stability) may cause client and counselor to temporarily ignore, distort, or defer immediate evaluative data, in hope that its negative nature will change subsequently, and it will be positive enough to counteract negative feedback which might appear incrementally. This is dangerous because incremental data, when projected into the future, suggests there is little probability of future payoff, and implies that dynamics occurring in the present, irrespective of the final outcome, are inappropriate guides toward end goals.

One theoretical question is when and how to utilize these differential evaluative foci, when to discontinue one focus and build another, and whether separate foci (for different purposes in the relationship) can coexist simultaneously in integrated fashion. Another issue, when evaluation has produced more immediate learning in the client dyad, is whether this learning (given probable absence of negative evaluative feedback) contributes to significant gains later on. These can occur either through dramatic metamorphosis, or slower developmental process or natural unfolding, which allow the dyad to be safely homeostatic initially, and then incrementally more stable, with effective association for advanced levels of growth. Unfortunately, many theories are unclear on how evaluative foci change, corresponding to presumably parallel and related changes in relationship dynamics and structure.

3.   *Termination Phenomena:*   The last issue in this section of therapeutic relationships, concerns dynamics of terminating relationships with clients. One basic problem, is the interrelationship between immediate objectives within the relationship (experimental personal and interpersonal objectives), and long-range-goals outside the therapeutic boundaries (overall life task achievements and developmental changes). Termination is typically (and idealistically) the point at which goal-achievements have been empirically demonstrated, reliably viewed, measured, and judged in terms of qualitative or quantitative adequacy, by counselor and client. There are, of course, measurement and judgment problems with this process alone (especially regarding validity, need to please the success-seeking therapist, and reliability), which will be discussed specifically in the chapter on outcomes. Intrapsychologically, however, the therapist must, at the point of termination, make highly complicated, symbolic, abstract, and even hypothetical assumptions, by which successes in the present and more immediate past are transferred into a future measurement model—to predict other changes in the client's life. An important intrapsychic concern at the point of

termination, is extent and nature of the counselor's and client's symbolic logic and futuristic conceptualization. This includes degree to which abstract hypothetical thinking is activated, as termination materializes to incorporate evaluative decisions, based on future hypothetical mental formulations of a reality which does not yet exist. The therapist goes through some type of goal achievement transformation process, so goals which are achieved register an index on a "hereafter" scale, which also includes measures or perceptions of past developmental achievements. Therapists who do not have an active fantasy perspective or conceptual scheme for futuristic optimism, may have trouble creating necessary cognitive constructions.[128] These are necessary to boost client motivation, and extrapolate hypothetical outcome findings early in therapy, when critical inputs must be employed to insure success in future time references.

In the author's research,[129] therapists reported making self-valuating decisions about their adequacy, based on hypotheses about future client growth when, in fact, no long-term follow-up assessments were made or planned. Characteristics of terminal events (e.g., end of therapy, death, any critical life incident or existential crisis) which create opportunities for creative thinking and evaluating projectively into the future, require study; especially when multiple goals, subgoals, and tasks from past, present, and future time, become uncharted components of the decision-making formula.

Another termination issue relating to intrapsychic process, concerns real and imagined interpretations of loss of "parental" guidance, support, friendship, etc.; as this trauma may be perceived by the client, to alter other indicators (client states of being) of present or hypothesized future success. Traumatic awarenesses connected to therapeutic termination, may have interactive effects on other dimensions of the personality which, for defensive purposes, may not be consciously manifest to the therapist, or have a developmental effect in the future. Good evaluative process suggests the use of role-play, fantasy thinking, and simulations, to provide tentative exploratory data on possible effects of the actual event in therapy. Also, termination may best occur in gradual stages (e.g., increasing distance between appointments), so changes in past, present, or future anticipated target behaviors can be gradually monitored, to allow corrective clinical inputs, as counteractive and continuing measures to insure growth.

Actual loss of, and real possibility of not ever regaining, a similarly qualitative experience, may suggest a tendency toward induced distortion of reality; so clients can withdraw from a good thing, depreciate the value of the experience over time, or hypothesize similar quality experiences in subsequent relationships. All possible conditions should be measured with a focus on external treatment goals of how to handle non-treatment, and positive indicators must be developed relative to options in dealing with loss.

Another evaluative scheme might focus on the client's ability to incorporate intrapsychic conceptualizations of therapeutic input (similar to parental introjection), with evaluation directed at measurement of the degree of incorporation, synthesis of incorporated concepts with pre-existing concepts of executive function, and ability to activate therapeutic symbolic input symbolizations, correlated with degrees of stress in one's life. This does not necessarily suggest the client has totally rejected the need for his or her therapist, but rather, that he or she has devised a plan to retain some dependence (which some may define as independence) via reincarnated symbolic referents. These referenced images and constructs can be assessed as to their permanency, or can be part of a comprehensive long-range treatment and evaluation program, to remove the artificial implants when other strengths have matured.

In any case, clients must be carefully understood in their individualized subjective interpretations of termination, as early in treatment as possible; and new targets developed, which specifically focus on this special and highly-volatile process.

Personal and Cultural Philosophy and Values

Another area dealing with self-evaluation within the territory of intrapsychic functioning of counselors, concerns cognitive, social and philosophical orientation, in viewing the self and external environment. Particular attitudes which practitioners have about self-evaluation, or specific methods to assess performance, are influenced by their philosophies and characteristic ways of perceiving themselves, the world, and personal interaction.

Kuhn[130] suggests, relative to evolution of knowledge, that individuals are susceptible to distortions in objective reasoning and evaluative analysis, as a result of commitment to specific paradigms of thinking and reasoning. Reality is transformed in cognitive concepts and constructs, to fit pre-existing philosophical perceptual frameworks. Change develops, as Kuhn summarizes, when one's philosophy fails to answer life's questions, but there is no guarantee that reality will be seen differently to match its true nature, because change simply entails development and implementation of new incestual categories, which may represent only alternative evaluative distortions. Change occurs, therefore, not as a result of logical decisions emerging from new knowledge discovery, but from anxiety-producing dissonance, as new information does not fit existing taxonomical frameworks. This may certainly cause needed alteration of philosophical paradigms, but also represents problems when this occurs in a crisis atmosphere, or when the nature of reality is ignored or altered, to keep consonance with the philosophical a priori framework which professionals feel they need to protect.

Hanse, et al.[131] point out differential characteristics of effective and ineffective counselors, in response to need for more comprehensive criteria for admission to counselor education programs. One study (which served as a basis for Jansen's research) involved supervisor ratings of counselor competency, to show differences between high and low rated counselors on the basis of the philosophical perceptual organization (characteristic ways of perceiving) of the rater.[132]

Combs[133] also affirms that persons who are (or perceive themselves to be) effective "instruments" in helping relationships, can be distinguished from ineffective helpers, on the basis of their "characteristic perceptual organizations," along the following dimensions:

1.   general frame of reference
      a.   internal versus external orientation
      b.   growth versus controlling orientation
      c.   conception of perceptual meaning versus primary concern with facts or events
      d.   people versus thing orientation
      e.   orientation toward causation versus orientation toward mechanics of function;
2.   the helper's self
      a.   predominance of feelings of certainty versus preoccupation with self-doubt
      b.   self-revealing versus self-concealing orientation;
3.   the helping task
      a,   helping versus dominating orientation
      b.   self-revealing versus outcome orientation.

Hypotheses supported in his research, that have relevance for the study of self-evaluation as a function of intrapsychic perception, are as follows:

1.   with respect to general perceptual orientation, effective counselors perceive:
      a.   internal frame of reference, rather than external
      b.   people rather than events, as primary areas of focus;
2.   with respect to perceptions of self, effective counselors perceive themselves
      as:
      a.   "enough," rather than wanting
      b.   self-revealing, rather than self-concealing.

The first hypothesis, specifying effective counselors with "internal" frames of reference, has important implications in terms of the subjective and highly personalized components of self-evaluation, concerning utilization of a more objective, external, empirically-oriented model of evaluation, which may appear to some counselors as unresponsive and unrepresentative of their internal assessment needs. An evaluative model for this group includes internal and external frames of reference, to offer a complete evaluative picture.

The second hypothesis, suggesting importance of the perception of self-esteem ("enough"), implies that evaluation is influenced by personal, as well as professional, areas of self-concepts. It may result from nonprofessional relationships and competencies, plus professional performance on the job. A broader perspective on evaluation and actual demonstrated competence, includes both personal and professional areas of the practitioner's life.

Although Combs does not test some other dimensions of his "characteristic perceptual organizations," related ideas are addressed by other authors in reference to evaluative conceptual contexts. Murray[134] discusses "open" and "closed" approaches to experience, as related to diffusion of knowledge (with which self-evaluation was previously related). Murray believes self-evaluative "creative enterprise" involves an incorporation of new information, as well as synthesis of valuable data already part of cognitive/perceptual content. Particular attitudes practitioners have about the experience of self-evaluation, and their ways of perceiving evaluative feedback as part of overall life orientation and its decision-making processes, would be influenced by their degree of openness in approaching all forms of knowledge. Evaluative experience emerges from within creative depths of the individual, and the external environment, as components of philosophical identity and self-expression:

"The greatest contribution to research (and possibly evaluation) will result from the spontaneity of the nation, institution, and individual by which they take up that which grows out of their own unique circumstances as contrasted to a stifling concern for what others are doing. The man [woman] of highest genius respects his [her] work . . . [as] an expression of himself or herself and a means of developing into that which he [she] should become. He [she] is characterized by an open mind and a desire for truth. He [she] is dynamic and challenges existing thought."[135]

Wirsing[136] changes focus slightly, discussing self-evaluation from an educational perspective, in terms of influence of philosophical frame of reference, of the teacher's perception and critique of knowledge (including knowledge of self). She notes the following distinctions between major philosophical approaches to evaluation, and assessment of knowledge:

1.   If the teacher is an experimentalist, the process of "reflective thinking" is equated with scientific method. This process subjects all knowledge to constant critical analysis and empirical verification.

2.   If the teacher is a trans-empiricist, the approach believes that a realm of reality, knowledge, and values exists, beyond that which is conceivable in the empirical world. Rationality, therefore, implies belief in ability of the human mind to transcend sensory experiences, and apprehend self-evident universal truths.

      Trans-empirical philosophy would have vastly different operational manifestations when evaluating performance, while the experimental orientation undoubtedly represents the currently more publicized "scientific" approach to accountability. Theoretical orientations toward professional evaluation, however, are presumptuous to assume that practitioners are "experimental" in philosophical orientation, to the exclusion of other perceptions of the world. This suggests a broader conceptual base for evaluation, to consider relevant aspects of different philosophical orientations, and discover procedures for self-evaluation within each type.

3.   If the teacher is an existentialist, he or she is in opposition to absolute objectivity and "spectator roles" of experimentalism, realism, and idealism; believing that individuals never "get outside their own skin," for truly objective or external assessments of knowledge.

      Wirsing concludes, that a teaching practitioner must develop answers to many practice-related problems involving goals and values. This is accomplished with a "profoundly searching interior self-perspective," combined with an ongoing process of critical examination of all ideas, against a "total philosophic frame of reference."

The previous examples, from different theoretical and practice-oriented disciplines, illustrate the significance of evaluators' philosophies and personal/systemic/world orientations. They serve as functional causal variables in understanding evaluative questions clinicians ask, types of data they seek and open to their awareness, explanations they give for various dimensions of the data, and subsequent decisions based on their findings. Because of numerous subcategories into which these considerations can be divided, several will be discussed separately, to help illustrate some major issues for the evaluating clinician.

Social Determination vs. Ecological Interdependence/ Individual Autonomy Orientation

The degree to which practitioners view personkind as a product and normal integrated component of historical evolution[137] and natural social process (including deviance), as opposed to a more independent and disconnected phenomenon relative to controlling forces of life; may commensurately influence their perceptions of intrapsychic causality, relevance of personal change, personal capability for autonomy, and the value of clients' attempts to alter the natural order of the bio-psychosocial universe.

The perceived relationship between client, counselor, and the world, obviously affects range of behavioral, affective, and attitudinal alternatives which the counselor defines, encourages, or discourages; and degree to which the counselor sees him or herself as a potent influence in altering the course of history for individuals or families. The counselor may directly or inadvertently communicate a view of the dynamics of human nature which is more or less dependent, autonomous, controlled by the system, rebellious, conforming, responsible for system maintenance, etc.; than the client actually believes represents the nature of the world and the self in interaction. Clients may, therefore, alter or confirm perspectives about opportunities, strengths, weaknesses, needs, relationship meanings, personal adequacy, or other clinical outcomes, based on the philosophical views of the counselor, rather than the client's own interpretations of the data—to conform to the real nature of that data, or to philosophical parameters of the client's own life.

The extent of clinical experimentation, autonomous evaluation by clients or counselors, and exploratory manipulation of behavioral or attitudinal options; is predicated on perceived relationship between the client and interconnected social norms, stability of roles and social structures, and between potency which actually exists and is believed to exist, by the counselor and client. This ties them to the dynamics and influential forces of their relationship to one another.

In cases where clients perceive a different range of social options and dynamics of living (degrees of freedom) than the counselor, they both must collectively recognize the differences and share in evaluative experiences, wherein unilateral biases are controlled, and some integration of philosophies occurs. This is essential so client outcomes are not interpreted via a priori conceptual rules; but are based on the client's unique and personal philosophical scale, are evaluated relative to neutral categories of perceived outcome, or integrated into interactive value paradigms of the client and counselor—so client thought, feeling, or behavior are, in fact, relevant components of the client's or the dyad's perception of the world, as it seems to exist in truth.

Individualism

The philosophical difference for evaluation between *individualistic,* internal determinants of human need, adequacy, and control of adaptive change; and more *objective,* externally-caused, and socially-validated outcome indicators— measurably alters types of data perceived by clients and practitioners. Differentiation of phenomena for clinical attention is seen in Wundt's and Titchener's structuralism,[138] which is the analysis of various experiences of states of consciousness, through introspective awareness domains and perceptual images. Within this framework, adaptation or conflict arise as predominate components of internal formulae, by which the individual views and negotiates a relationship with the self. They represent the extent to which images of self, are actualized in the external milieu. This orientation is modified within the functionalism philosophy, where the individual is an integral, and more dynamically interactive component of social adaptation. The evaluative model must take into consideration concepts and relationship dynamics which include various forms of person-environment integration. Within a functional orientation, many authors stress the importance of consciousness, and strongly connect it to environmental adjustment through its association with social learning and psychological need-meeting.

Psychodynamic theories, based more closely on individual autonomy, (except for parent/child development tasks and cultural socialization), give individual personality a central place. As Lowenstein[139] points out, they emphasize inner dimensions of the person, without significant connection to the person's outside life situation. This emphasis also occurs in behavior and cognitive-behavior theories, although there seems to be more appreciation of linkage phenomena, especially with the social learning involved in behavior modification.

Psychoanalytic, object relations, self, and cognitive behavior theories, express an individualistic[140] ethic, that defines the person within a reward and pleasure seeking framework. Although evaluation[141] is directed at the client's personal identity formation, definition, and manifestation; the philosophical orientations may neglect evaluative issues of the individual within the context of group functions, and broader societal membership.[142] More attention may also be needed, evaluatively, to interpersonal morality, spirituality, and other transcendental characteristics of the human interpersonal situation. This will be discussed later in this section.

It will suffice to note now, however, the extent to which philosophical perspectives assume a viewpoint about integration, interaction, dependency, or autonomy between person and environment. This relationship affects the emphasis in evaluation, relevant to (1) degree of direct influence the counselor has in the ongoing social interactive process; (2) potential for natural (environmentally contingent) resolution of problems, with only support needed from the counselor; (3) number of causal variables which must be controlled, for varying probabilities of client change; (4) timing of interventions to coincide with active processes, or resting states within the person-situation interchange pattern; (5) correctness of diagnosis, relative to decisions about pathology, potential for rehabilitation, etc.; (6) types of specific inputs variously designed to control, stimulate, join, enable, block, support, or serve as placebos for other inputs, which are also potent influences (individually or synergistically) on thought, feeling, and behavior.

Within the intrapsychic orientation, which corresponds most closely to structuralism, Western psychological philosophy sees the client with self-determining will and, in some capacities, is free of influence from a controlling external environment. One evaluative challenge in this light, is to understand the function and process of the client's internal self-diagnostic formula, and figure out how to enter this cycle as a therapeutic agent, so the philosophical equilibrium and model are not extrinsically attacked and violated. One aspect of change, in this regard, involves assisting the client to perceive multiple and separate self-diagnostic *selves,* where therapeutic impact comes internally from movement between states of existential being. Clients define their own motivators for behavior and change, and alter the independent variable (or add new independent variables), so a critical mass of stimulus power is created internally, to cause change in the dependent variables. The client within an individualistic orientation, may need to be a very active partner in the diagnosis and measurement process. The therapist can then build a conceptual model of therapy, which takes all intrapsychic dimensions into consideration for evaluative purposes. Therapists must also control their interpersonal influences, which clients may not perceive as relevant (or even existing), so as not to confuse evaluation of inputs as part of external success determinations. This is especially necessary when the client is not able to be rationally perceived in some circumstances, as a responder to these presumed therapeutic conditions.

Another assumption of Western culture and orthodox psychology,[143] relative to the individualistic position, is that the client's ordinary state of consciousness typically represents the most adaptive and rational way the mind can be organized. All altered states of consciousness are defined as pathological (which includes products of social learning, whereby the client changes perception to achieve harmony with the environment). Counselors may have to modify their beliefs about ultra-creative configurations of ideas, traditionally defined as psychotic.

". . . while psychologists are quite familiar with innumerable pieces of evidence supporting the picture of human beings as constantly controlled by implicit assumptions, they practically never apply it to their personal lives or to their scientific work . . ."[144]

One evaluative problem, is deciding what is ordinary or normal for clients separately, and then assisting them to describe and understand variations in existential adaptability within the autonomous conceptual options which they implement. This includes consequences of other individuals in society (with whom they may or may not be related), who also exercise their autonomous options. Pathology or deviance in this context, may derive from clients incorrectly assuming significant human interdependence, rather than evaluating effectiveness of *not* perceiving interpersonal or ecological associations. In this ultimate existential case, the therapist might help develop client insight into the nature of the client's processes of perceiving interconnections, helping clients examine outcomes related to interdependencies, wherein they discover potential for more self-actualization, directly or symbolically, in social relations. Therapists and clients must carefully think about these philosophical stances, since foci for therapeutic endeavors and objects/concepts of attention, have different ramifications. This depends on whether the endeavors are central or peripheral loci of linear or non-linear causal chains, and whether boundaries are placed relative to legitimate mental constructs, for inclusion in self-evaluative formulae which are discovered.

Altered states of consciousness might also be defined differently for function, rationale, and categories of adequacy reasons, as each receives different valuations (especially as compared to past and potential future states of consciousness) concerning internal origin and individualized functionality. This relates to the view that the personality is a relatively unified structure, and capable of self-fulfillment and purposeful homeostasis, irrespective of the nature of intrapsychic structure of others who relate to the client, or the collective influence of the social group or culture:

> "The therapeutic process (within the more individualistic framework) is thus an encounter—a process set up to produce an experience of growth, through which the client can develop an autonomous and creative will, choose self-responsibility, and attain self-realization."[145]

Within individualistic philosophical orientation, evaluation includes variable states of activity and passivity for clients who are predominately centered on the self, and the inner life of clients who more freely use or manipulate the external environment, to enhance inner psychic functions and states of being.

Ecological Perspective

In thinking about evaluation from an ecological[146] rather than intrapsychic/ autonomous personal framework, the relevant boundary within which clients are the dependent variables, and also active operators on their milieu; is extended considerably to include small and large groups, communities, and even whole societies. This systemic environmental philosophy[147] encompasses primary and secondary group systems, where individuals maintain significant interactions, as relationship contingencies define being, status, conflict, and adaptation.

Circumstances within which clients maintain functional associations, are the milieu (what Bronfenbrenner calls a mesosystem)[148] in which social networks operatively link clients to ecological life supports. The clinician is challenged within this philosophy to assume a sufficiently wide-angle perspective, to ask evaluative questions which include all relevant active ingredients of systemic life processes. This includes envisioning the client system as an index of therapeutically-induced outcome which is the product of synergistic and compre- hensive phenomena. Herein, input is conceptualized as potentially directed to the entire system at one time, to one part of the system with developmental sub- influences corresponding to the system's pattern of expected operation, or to other systems which holistically act on the target system and influence only its totality, rather than any singular subunit of its identity.

An example of this becomes clear with individuals viewing themselves as strongly attached to religious, cultural, or family dynamics. These attachments are influential in both redefining the nature of the therapeutic input, and distributing its effect according to normative and operational patterns throughout the system—which then produces a totally different effect, than originally envisioned by the therapist. These influences can partly be explained with philosophies like social learning theory,[149] where causal processes are analyzed relative to reciprocal deterministic frameworks. In this model, client functioning and dysfunctioning involve a longitudinal interactive association between behavior, cognition, and the social environment, viewed holistically to make correct evaluative decisions. A self-system in the social learning model, suggests cognitive image frameworks and perceptual processes for viewing, evaluating, and controlling behavior that are part of the person/environmental configuration, rather than a unitary psychic process.[150]

Unfortunately, with a generalist orientation, the provision of direct inputs is usually subdivided into separate agencies or intra-agency departments and professions. Parallel inputs may be planned, delivered, and correlated, but have not necessarily, ipso facto, represented a unified approach which corresponds to or matches, unit for unit, subcomponents of the holistic system which is the target for change. Even though inputs subsequently produce a change in one of the systems areas, it is speculative to conclude that the input caused changes in the entire target system (even if this is true), unless experimental controls are placed on other interactive elements, whose responses are scientifically compared to hypothesized responses or controlled systems, to show clear patterns of change. This is briefly illustrated in Figure 2.

This diagram suggests there is a normal pattern of change represented by the different geometric symbols, and that this pattern is regular, predictable, and repetitive after the fifth level, where all components are the same (4 stars). An input immediately prior to this time (stage 4), suggests that the star produced for the secondary groups, which were targeted, also produced other stars. It may also suggest (a) the degree of influence of secondary groups was dormant, immediately prior to the 4th stage, (b) the stars were scheduled to come up anyway, as a result of other interactive processes, which excluded the dormant influence of the secondary groups, or (c) these changes are not going to last anyway, since the stages will reverse themselves at stage 5. Any evaluative assumption, therefore, regarding input, cannot be made until the normal pattern is plotted, and influences of other factors are controlled to test independent variable effects.

Ecological philosophies attempt to balance the sometimes limited perspectives of other theories about problem definition and solution, since "cultural and professional myopia,"[151] constitute a serious limitation in understanding the true nature of reality in pluralistic society. The ecological model supports, certainly, the humanitarian philosophy and values of most social services, including need for social integration and conflict resolution, individualism and interdependence, and complementarity and reciprocity in collective need-meeting.

Figure 2
Normal vs. Disconnected Patterns in Systems

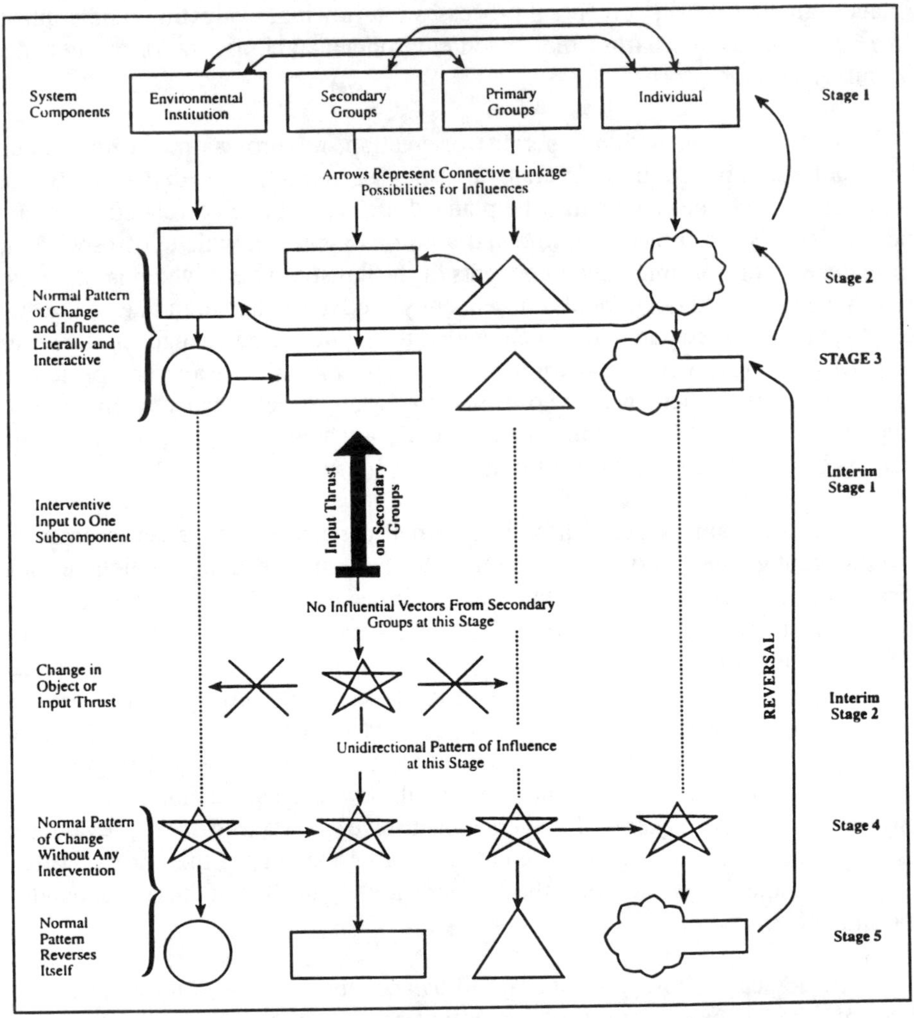

To consider ways ecologically-oriented service inputs should be delivered and evaluated, the counselor needs to determine how the entire array of social system, group phenomena, and institutions, are integrated with the needs of members of society; and diagnosed, as a collective entity relative to established principles of ecological balance, conflict, adequacy, and adaptation.

In considering concepts of ecological systems, it should become apparent that it is difficult to measure any one philosophy or technique of intervention, except with comprehensive social indicators that offer a view of the holistic panorama. Social scientists and practitioners should develop measures that result in a comprehensive analysis of outcomes when *systems* are the events of interest, especially due to difficulty defining varying qualitative statuses of ecological systems, and principles by which the system functions[152] as a self-contained integral phenomenon.[153]

Specific concerns, additionally related to clinical evaluation from an ecological perspective, are as follows:

1. One concern for the clinician, is the degree to which any individual has power to modify or alter the potency of outcome effects, of any interdependent variables within the ecological system. One perspective suggests that individual self-actualization is really the defense of individual (pseudo self-reward) anticipation, idealism, or development of cognitive/emotional fabricated boundaries. This occurs when any client is confronted with social forces of culture which cannot be altered or neutralized, to allow individual growth within the system. If individuals believe they grow and develop autonomously with self-direction, is it simply one aspect of dependent socialization, where status depends on the ability to demonstrate the learned, and socially desired belief, that is conditioned by the system itself? For example, Kohn and Schooler[154] discovered that male research subjects of higher social class, more often than individuals of lower class, place significant qualitative value on self-direction, and maintain that self-direction is desirable and capable of achievement of anticipated personal outcomes. Kohn and Schooler also discovered that social-stratification position is related to values, self-concepts, and social orientations, as a result of effects of specific philosophical ideas, and opportunities for such ideas to be supported and acted out within the social milieu. Because of the power of childhood enculturated forces (accompanied by dependency and vulnerability of the child), and the controlling strength of social roles and positions via adult rewards and punishments; the use of clinical power in the adult therapeutic milieu, might push the client into greater depths of

dependency on perspectives articulated by the social status position, and operationalized within ecologically defined opportunities. Decisions by the client may be pseudo-autonomous manifestations (reinforced by the counselor's possibly false definitions of independence) of continued dependency.

Client and therapist may also be faced with such a complex array of significant environmental influences, that determining linear cause and effect interrelationships between any factors in the ecological system, may be an impossible venture. Evaluatively, the individual and his or her therapist can hypothesize causal factors and respond accordingly. However, potentially confusing outcomes result if the correct cause is defined, but it is impossible for the individual (dependent variable) to extract the self from this influence, without direct modification on the causative variable. Also, evaluation and validity are obscured, if an incorrect cause in the environment is identified, but the individual continues to be influenced by the true cause; while being expected to change the response as a result of the counselor's powerful role which is, in actuality, not powerful enough to supercede the original and correct stimulus.

Since individuals are totally, or in part, a product of their system, the therapist must consider clients' roles within the social system, and determine degrees to which there are separate or similar stimuli to which clients respond; and freedom available to clients, to resist environmental control of a predetermined range of conditioned alternatives.

It should be remembered that power of the counselor as a socialized member of a controlling society, or ecological environment, may render the client subjugated to natural processes, with outcomes and courses predetermined in the counselor's diagnostic schema. Therapeutic attention to symptoms of ostensible client dysfunction may, in this regard, be a natural occurrence of individual ecological settling-in or finding one's nitch; and therapy, although it may speed up this process, may not alter the dynamic outcome. Excessive attention to symptomatic display may, in fact, obscure relevant attention to the overall ecological dynamic pattern, where therapy may be more profitably invested, for higher probabilities of system change. This means that within the ecological network, individuals eventually find their comfortable position, and each position is necessary for supportive sustenance of other complimentary positions, all of which are alterable. This may possibly occur for a select number of individuals, but overall, will not influence the general average adjustment process. The role of therapist may also be socially determined, regardless of individually-oriented outcomes. One illustration by Horner, Reid and Okanes,[155] discusses the manipulative orientation of social service practitioners, as part of authoritarian social control measured on the F and MACH (Machiavellian) Scales,[156] which partly measure one's assumptions about the nature of human beings, and quality of relationships between them. Those with MACH scores show little concern for conventional morality, display affective detachment, respond to others on a cognitive level, initiate and control group structures, and are perceived as persuasive and having leadership capacity. Counseling professions may paradoxically assert the significance of social insight,[157] yet be ecologically incapable of using this technique. This occurs because the quality with which the clinician analyzes and influences relationships[158] between clients and their social systems, helps determine appropriateness of treatment plans, interventive strategies, and follow-up decisions about treatment success.[159]

In thinking about connectedness of individuals and their social milieu, clients in conflict about dependence-independence issues, struggle to gain self-reinforcement capability; but in this case, the relationship to either the dependent or independent resultant ecological outcome, constitutes only predetermined unfolding of previously-learned responses. On the other hand, the neurotic conflict itself may be a conditioned response, which no one can escape. Movement to either independent or dependent sides of the fence, may be a temporary condition which society allows until the struggle re-emerges in the aging or subsequent life processes; or the struggle may actually never end, but only be displaced and resumed within other social roles and positions. In this case, the final answer to the question will never come, since no answer (or question for that matter) has been conditioned at start, middle, and end of the living process.[160] The therapist may choose goals which help the client ignore basic life questions, which disguise non-answers as answers; or substitute a similar form of social ecological determinism with a new question, but unchanged socio-intrapsychic dynamics. Therapists should consider these issues prior to decisions to assist clients in understanding the dynamics of their growth and development, and help clients engage personality resources to alter their status quo within an environment where this may not be possible, or there is little probability of long-term gains.

2.   Another ecologic consideration, concerns the ability of system members to remove themselves from the subjectively-and collectively-perceived system, to envision a fuller picture of the forest and trees, to make more conscious circumstantial choices. This process is of particular interest relative to the

client's ability to envision complexities of past experiences, and the potentials of future options in planning specific target goals, which ideally have more long-range impact. This does not specifically criticize therapy's limitations in ability to foresee the future (although this may be true). It does question, however, the relevance of here-and-now therapeutic plans, tasks, or objectives, without full knowledge of the value and utility of the implementation of these goals (through social behaviors) in the future; where variables may be presently unknown, but where these unknown factors may be of significant ecological impact in the client's future attempts at adaptation. Although the therapist can assist the client in present goal attainment vis-à-vis future hypothetical thinking; present learned behaviors, thoughts, and feelings, may prove of little value or even become detriments. As noted by Goldstein,[161] expectancies are major determiners of human behavior, and anticipated value and relevance of future client behaviors (idealistically seen as improvement), influence selection of targets, interventive strategies, and treatment outcomes. The evaluative danger is to judge effectiveness based on goal-attainment (including cost-efficiency analyses), but ignore cost-effectiveness relative to actual outcomes at a future date, given exigencies of social system dynamics at that time.

One example is the chess game, where the inexperienced player initiates move selections based on current contingencies in the interrelationship network between tokens, not realizing the more skillful opponent may: (a) have a more abstract master plan, with future move alternatives not directly related to the other player's current or future moves (or which are broad enough to encompass long-range strategy changes, based on changing contingencies of the inexperienced player's more circumscribed and narrowly conceived movements); (b) have long-range strategies which demand specific moves of the inexperienced opponent, conditioned through sacrificed token forfeitures or other failed incentives; (c) have current defensive strategies designed to avoid offensive risks, but also block offensive strategies of the nonstrategic (tactical) opponent; so neither player wins or loses, or the smarter player wins by passive, obstructionistic, and wearing down tactics, until the neophyte player defeats him or herself. A final alternative, is that winning and losing are based on probabilities of specific moves and move combinations, often left to random occurrence over repeated trials. In these cases, winning and losing in the long run average out to some undetermined probability based on change (not strategically planned) moves, so outcome prediction of specific games is impossible, but long-term outcomes approach a 50/50 chance of occurrence. Although these probability frequencies may be altered in the short run, given different capabilities of specific players, the overall end result remains relatively predictable.

From a clinical standpoint, this means the selection of specific operant behavioral goals for clients (behaviors conceived as independent and active influencers of their environment), may appear relevant in the here and now, but prove useless given future contingencies. Therapists may have greater long-term impact, with identification of targeted defensive skills for clients to handle a range of unknown environmental stimuli (especially behaviors which encourage withdrawal and isolation from powerful ecological forces), or more conservative, temporally delayed, or spaced target selections, incrementally developed so future contingencies can be more correctly assessed as time goes on. This might suggest, additionally, seeing the client once a month, rather than once or twice a week, to avoid excessive concentration on less relevant immediate personal goals, and more fully appreciate the specific nature of the emerging and often unforeseeable longitudinal ecological environment.

One discussion which supports the minimally controllable relationship between individuals and their systemic environment, is Slomczynski, Miller and Kolins'[162] analysis of social stratification. The major implication of their research, is that significant interaction occurs between self-concept (including evaluative judgment and social/environmental conditions), and actual behavioral performance, which suggests need to carefully select therapeutic goals, with realization that actual outcomes may be largely determined by dynamics of the ecological environment, with minimal options for individual control or circumstantial alteration. Ethical evaluation, in this case, requires that the client fully understand varying possible degrees of effectiveness of behavior learned in therapy, and understand the probability with which extraneous social focus may define, alter, neutralize, or eliminate these desired behaviors, in some future time more removed from the therapeutic milieu.

In the research mentioned above, the authors note that occupational self-direction[163] (a class-connected condition which helps or hinders initiative and autonomous judgment), is one index primarily dependent upon degree of complexity of occupational work, its type and frequency of supervision, and routine vs. dynamic nature. Through response generalization, learning relative to the job is transformed into concepts which describe self-status, as well as views of the social milieu. Being a self-directed worker also means that one values self-direction in personal, as well as professional contexts, and each individual believes personal responsibility and control are possible in life.

The research also shows that occupational self-direction affects perceptual orientation; including moral precepts, interpersonal trust, conceptual conformity, self-depreciation, and anxiety; with these perspectives also influencing work-related performance, autonomy, and initiative. The researchers were not able to determine, however, when relevant influences actually begin and how long they last, nor whether orientations about occupational self-direction occur by fashioning employment roles to correspond to employees' values, or assigning workers into congruently matched roles.

The complex parallel question for the clinical evaluator, is how to develop treatment-oriented models which predict critical points at which clients make decisions about areas of reciprocal influence, and identify conflictual dynamics in personal and ecological spheres, which hinder or block development of inter-active balance. Therefore, it is difficult to decide where along this process of reciprocal interaction, one intervenes therapeutically, given the course of events and influences which precede and follow the input. Another problem stemming from this, is how to trace developmental movement of input awareness, thought, or behavior, to see distinctive influence on clients' orientations about themselves or their milieu, as separate from the normal interactive effects. It may also be valuable to determine degree to which environmental support in the form of behavioral opportunity, is necessary for clients to act out their cognitive impressions, and receive support or nonreinforcement in order for the reciprocal influence process to continue from that point on. Therapeutic input goals may need to be coded or earmarked, for utility in system-specific locations or circumstances. Also, client outcome goal selection, may require scrutiny to shed light on whether goal selection is an autonomous option and directly attributable to therapeutic inputs, which are part of the overall system which defines clients, their options, and possible outcomes.

Cultural Ethnicity Perspective

Another influence with philosophical underpinnings for the evaluating professional, is the culture within which the therapeutic relationship takes place, and cultural interface domain between client and counselor.

Discussions about culture which follow, emphasize that ethnic norms provide security to their dependent members, through development, manifestation, and perpetuation of tradition and stereotypic evaluative questions, and even predetermined answers. Also, dynamics of cultural process and change are played out in intercultural associations between clients and counselors, by dictating normative viewpoints and influencing the relevance and nature of evaluation activities and outcome conclusions. Through ethno-causality and ethno-methodology points of view,[164] counselors may devise interventions for various groups of clientele, without understanding the value and meaning of ethnicity, and factoring it into interventions and evaluations thereof. Ethnicity is an intervening variable, as counselors certainly agree, but also has a role as an independent and dependent variable within the clinical counseling setting.

The first point to be made, is that ethnicity and cultural process function to develop individual identity (through collective identification), and help provide criteria to substantiate personal adequacy and human relevance within multi-cultural interchanges. Ethnic perspectives (whether part of majority or minority subgroups) influence attitudes, preferences, goal priorities, personal character-istics, and actions; and facilitate achievement of self-determination, personal security, and existential relevancy, through group awareness and collective conceptual convergence of knowledge and values throughout time and place.

An additional significant component of ethnicity often excluded in designing evaluation strategies, is its function in formulating the nature of self-determination, including behavioral norms and procedures. Definitions of social success and competence can be suppressed when subordinate cultures are con-trolled by dominant group forces. These behaviors, however, can be symboli-cally used and correctly manifested by clients as a significant force in their life journeys, and adaptive sense of purpose and value, whether part of majority and minority cultural groups.

In viewing ethnicity and cultural diversity as normal social imperatives from a philosophical and practical perspective, the clinician may focus evaluation along three separate dimensions:

1. The counselor may attend to evaluative variation exclusively within cultures, as assessed by those within the culture, where definitions of problems, categories of solutions, degrees of adequacy of solutions, assess-ment of problem solving processes, and degree of personal pathology; are only considered a valid part of reality inside a culture, which is accepted as autonomous within a pluralistic orientation. Intra-cultural norms provide definitions of innate/learned predispositions of humanity; significant time, space, and relationship dimensions for autonomous vs. interactive func-tioning; and varied vs. deviant personality characteristics, which are not related to external society expectations, as the culture chooses to define itself vis-à-vis externalities.[165]

2.   The counselor can also focus on the domain of variations between cultures,
     which includes all cultures which interact or have perceptions of interaction
     (including mystical, spiritual, or illusory/delusional societies). In this case,
     the counselor should attend to thoughts and feelings of individuals influ-
     enced by the culture's definitions of influences by *other* cultures, areas of
     interchange where cultures become involved in stereotyped or contingent
     interactions between separate members, and definitions of feared or desired
     states of acceptance or isolation from alien or nurturant cultures.   This
     phenomenon cannot be fully understood until the natures of all interactive
     cultures are understood, so interchanges between them will reflect the
     identities of each, as well as the new identity of the holistic system.   This
     problem is seen in working with minority clients who desire inclusion into
     "mainstream" society.[166]

     Actual inclusion may mean loss of personal status in the culture of
origin, increase in social opportunity within the majority culture, positive
change in perceptions of dominant cultural representatives for the minority
culture, more resentment by some members of the minority culture for the
dominant culture, or change in a whole range of other possible status,
esteem, or adequacy outcomes that can only be explained on an inter-
cultural basis.

3.   Finally, the professional may stress evaluative variations of the objective
     (probably only pseudo or quasi objective) states of being of those who
     attempt to remain outside cultures, to assess the cultures themselves. This
     possibly separate, and possibly deviant status, may represent a new culture;
     or symbolically represent cultural dimensions plus or minus personal
     dynamics or conceptualizations, which have to be added to or subtracted
     from the evaluative outcome, so both sides of the methodological equation
     are balanced for bias. This perspective includes consideration of universal
     values or ideals traditionally accepted by many cultures, yet not capable of
     operationalization, unless they are done within the socialized confines of a
     specific culture.   The relationship between the standard, as a symbolic
     representation of the viewer of the standard, and the symbol of relation-
     ships between two or more viewers who obscure it, concurrently or sepa-
     rately, and then view each other—must be examined. The role of universal
     symbols can, become part of the self-evaluation of those who define and
     use the symbolic representations for various purposes in their lives.

     Within this extra-cultural framework, or within extreme boundaries of any
one specific culture, is the philosophical position of radicalism—which is a

position vis-à-vis a particular ideological content of the culture, but also a vantage point from which to overcome constraints of biased culture, in order to do effective evaluation:[167]

> ". . . each of us must place himself (herself)—whole and entire—into question, that such questioning must be radical, going to the roots, to the ground presuppositions that shape and guide human life—and that this searching for foundations demands that we bring with us none of the usual operative baggage—the epistemological, methodological, metaphysical concepts we typically use in the course of our daily lives . . ."[168]

Evaluative conclusions, based on the position vis-à-vis traditional culture, therefore, must be interpreted relative to inclusion or exclusion emotionally, physically, and ideologically. The conforming or deviant (radical) status, creates a condition of sound objective judgment or biased ethnocentric congruence.

There may be a need to perform one set of therapeutic processes to move the clients to positions of relative radicalism or cultural nonconformity, to help them evaluate status (former, present, and anticipated) from this radical position. Clients can then move back into more traditional roles for actual change[169] to occur, or decide whether changes in traditional roles can actually be facilitated from either temporary or permanent radical status.

Weinberger comments that the clinician's model of treatment and theoretical understanding, may only publicly advocate cultural pluralistic and personal change perspectives, while actually forcing minority persons to obtain unhealthy integration into dominant cultural standards.[170] In considering the existence of minority cultures within, and relative to, majority cultures; they may be viewed from an ecological perspective, as naturally in a state of conflict over dominance and control. This creates two basic components relative to evaluation:

1. Those in the controlling majority develop positive evaluative outcomes (esteem status, pleasure awareness, etc.) based on (a) membership inclusion criteria, (b) membership exclusion and ethnocentric differentiation, (c) proximity to idealized norms, or (d) other factors within the dominant culture;
2. Those in the ascending, aspiring, or minority cultures develop positive evaluative outcomes based on (a) strivings to attain dominant cultural status, (b) inability to attain dominant cultural status, and acceptance/ enjoyment of the process of struggling (pride of deprivation), or (c) intra-cultural standards irrespective of relations between cultures. This

simplification, of course, does not preclude other explanations of esteem and outcomes of evaluation relevant to clients and counselors alike. The reader might read Erick Fromm,[171] to add to the perspective on the role of culture in mental disease, especially governing issues of social conformity, loss of freedom, neurosis, etc.

The ecological system, as it connotes specific natures of subcultural units, characteristics of outcomes, and dynamics of interaction between subcultural groups, may reduce degrees of freedom with which individual behavior or evaluated outcome are definable and appropriate, as targets of therapeutic input effort. It is unclear how social caste or subcultural status provide opportunities for individuals to feel satisfaction, pain, or other outcome feelings, among either conformers or deviants, vis-à-vis alternate interacting social groups. It is also questionable how awareness of socially stratified, unequal positions, provides direction for evaluative decisions about phenomena the stratified individual is currently experiencing, remembering, or positively or negatively anticipating.

There is an undefined correlation between competitive cultural conditions, individual interpretations of intra-cultural and inter-cultural adequacy and self-evaluative input, constant and variable outcome categories, and self-actualizing roles of deviant individuals within an inter-cultural paradigm, as operationalized or traced to individual self-evaluative decisions.

From the clinical evaluator's viewpoint, culture—as an *intervening* variable that complicates the picture for the dominant culture, or *independent* variable in a diverse ecological milieu—significantly influences the evaluative model, wherein the culture's varying states and types of influences, give different significant dimensions to the evaluative picture:

1. The clinician, who is typically a member or representative of the dominant culture and bureaucracy, can employ individual psychology paradigms to diagnose conformity, deviance, health, pathology, etc., by comparing ideal against observed cognitive (affective/behavioral) functioning, without consideration of specific cultural or inter-cultural dynamics. This, of course, may be extremely biased, but eliminates perceived complications of intervening variables, and may facilitate linear, but not collateral, measurement:

    "In the calculus of feelings, the more one's detached from concern with big things (i.e., major issues of human welfare and inter-cultural dynamics), the more little things enter to fill it, and the little things of life seem to be obsessions . . . Little things can come to fill all life and take on the appearance of bigness . . ."[172]

The closed cultural model has serious questions of validity, and concerns about relevance of goal attainment or failure, vis-à-vis broad principles of social justice avowed by social science professions.

2.   The clinician can maintain two sets of evaluative books. One, measures the client against intra-cultural norms and may contain a full continuum of potential ranges of adequacy, so the client demonstrates self-actualized or pathological identities from a culturally specific standpoint. An important component of this evaluative process, however, is to help the client understand his or her own ethnocentrism, as opposed to inter-cultural normative orientation, so personal motivation and goals can be clearly assessed within and between cultures, and extraneous data appropriately factored out. A second set of books, measures progress toward enculturation, which defines minority culture as a hindrance to goal attainment, or defines norms and boundaries (typically valued as legitimate) of the dominant culture as intervening prohibitive barriers. Clients may be assessed on progress of personal and culture-related change, with attention to degrees of movement away from previous cultural behaviors, and integration into the desired culture.

This philosophical perspective represents an image with political, social, and institutional power as dominant influences, and represents competing cultures as critical elements in determining identity security, and defining incentives and motivation for those in the dominant-submissive continuum. There is some question, in the author's mind, about the efficacy of considering intergroup motivation as a domain of ecological reality, and the role of inclusion/exclusion as a facilitating factor in therapeutic growth and change. The other side of the question, however, is whether there is sufficient motivation (for therapeutic interest and effort) to change, based on dynamics within cultures that are safely boundaried, homeostatic, and secure; or whether need for change is only brought about due to intercultural conflict in a world with diminished resources. Relevant concepts related to this argument, are the worker's output effort required within and between cultures, the failure to meet socialized expectations and desires for success and cultural performance evaluation, difficulty of enculturation tasks, and personal performance satisfaction.

Because some studies show that counseling inputs lack neutrality in ability to be client culture-centered rather than biased,[173] there is concern that social service practitioners maintain multiple standards regarding mental health diagnosis. Treatment interventions may also neglect a correction factor which takes into account clients' culture, and perspectives about their position therein.

A good cultural example concerns viewpoints regarding women,[174] where some professionals limit evaluative flexibility when they traditionally view women only in roles of housewife, mother, male nurturer, etc.; and men predominantly in income provider, leadership, and emotionally strong roles.

Lewis suggests that some counselors limit perceptions of social, behavioral, cognitive, and emotional choices in types of conflicts they validate, and the outcomes they feel are attainable by women—rather than helping women overcome social role stereotypes.[175] In discussing counselor bias, Schlossberg and Pietrofesa[176] pessimistically comment that sexual bias permanently has a significant influence on counselor inputs, while Gardner[177] feels that counselors oriented and skilled in traditional diagnostic and therapeutic models, will be sexist because of sexist perspectives inherent in the models themselves.

Other studies are helpful in assessing sex-role stereotyping (as one form of cultural bias) among students in social work programs. Harris and Lucas[178] studied undergraduate and graduate students who identified characteristics of a competent adult person, woman, and man. No difference was found among the group assessments, until gender of the rater was introduced as an independent variable, wherein male and female students characterized healthy men and women in stereotypically masculine ways. Other studies, however, note that male and female respondents report strength in terms of their own gender, which still retains a biased perspective.[179] Concerns for the evaluator, of course, are whether there is sensitivity to potential bias and if, in fact, practitioners take active steps to proportionately correct bias which exists, as addressed by both client and counselor. In some cases, a bias may exist which the client is unable or afraid to see, but this does not, therefore, justify its unequivocal acceptance within the evaluative or therapeutic paradigm of the professional.

3.   Another issue for ecology-sensitive evaluation, is the counselor's use of process versus content orientation, which can occur from a philosophical perspective within or between cultures.

A philosophical and methodological orientation to process (dynamics and symbolism of interactive behavior and relationship, as indicators of strength or conflict) has been emphasized as a valuable perspective on the adaptive functioning of individuals and groups, and highlights the existential and gestalt nature of personal and interpersonal reality. Process orientation seen by counselors, as an end in and of itself, easily neglects specific diagnostic and evaluative concerns that are specific to individuals and their cultures, within an overarching, intercultural, ecological domain.

This bias unfolds, as clients are compared to norms for either their own baseline interactive behavior, or for ideal behavioral dynamics. These may not fully take into consideration dependency and socialization dynamics which influence past behavioral options, or overarching content areas of personal status, opportunity, or condition specified by culture.

Counselors or clients who are too "process"-oriented, may experience obscured vision of the nature (content) of conflicting needs, values, and interests,[180] with associated tunnel vision of bigger pictures which dictate and control interactive options, and consequent outcomes available to individual clients. Process-oriented counselors may also bias evaluation, by seeking clients deemed appropriate subjects for a "therapeutic process" aimed at "structural" personality change.[181]

The process orientation, on the other hand, provides very significant symbolic indicators of culture-bound personality, but must stand alone as sufficient in and of itself, for decisions about effectiveness; or be incor-porated as interrelated units of change into a comprehensive spectrum to include content, global, and long-term process. In many clinical situations, process is typically, and most easily, assessed (and possibly most validly and reliably measured) in the limited context of the therapeutic interview on a weekly basis. Emphasis on process can communicate a philosophical value to clients, which should be discussed to help them understand how they interpret this emphasis as part of growth efforts, but also to help them understand relative values of the content of their cognitions and judgments about self and others. Immersion into process can be so encompassing as to hinder, or even prevent, periodic objective movements to a content-observational vantage point. Process-oriented movements between conceptual domains may also cause confusion or loss of data, for both client and therapist. Some cultures may be more process than content-oriented, in terms of personal interchange dynamics, time and space dimensions of interaction and existence, and symbolic values concerning social protocol. These unique orientations must be identified and understood by the counselor, and carefully considered as possible off-limit areas to unnecessary change or modification, within possibly indiscriminate powerful dimensions of the therapeutic environment. Client/therapist mismatches, where one is process and the other is content-oriented, provide significant diagnostic data as a part of needs assessment and baseline evaluative theory, but may preclude necessary therapeutic growth, depending on depth and incompatibility of these divergent states of behaviors, consciousness, and philosophy.

In defense of process, Siporin[182] notes that recently, it has been some-what disregarded, and Cooper agrees:

> "Driven by a need to document and account for its results, social work (and many other social service professions) has become obsessed with outcome at the expense of process . . . Outcomes are important, but not at the expense of process and service."[183]

Process implies a "flow of change through phases of time—a sequence of progressive movement from a beginning through a middle and to a definite end."[184] Its evaluation necessitates concern with the sequence and incremental quality of developmental stages, as they have meaning within contexts of philosophical content categories, but are considered more important than the end results themselves. Process may be evaluated in terms of its deviation from or conformity to, its own patterned value, with the client's intrapsychic homeostasis predicated on predictable patterns, rather than abstract symbolic meaning of the process.

Evaluation from a process orientation, therefore, necessitates measurement of this dynamic movement and interplay between changing and counterbalancing forces, as their unfolding has as much meaning as the final resolution, which may actually be no more than another movement in the context of reciprocal interaction.[185] Evaluation may necessitate development of synthesized and collaborative client-counselor resources, to change ways of perceiving and experiencing process as it unfolds. These do not, necessarily, have direct transferability into outcome-oriented behavior, or external empirical manifestations.[186]

A final problem with outcomes which supports the value of process orientation, is that outcome findings which might represent presumed success, can result in premature closure of the evaluative clinical investigation.[187] This happens partly because the counselor may desire, or need, to quit while he or she is ahead/winning, or because of a narrow perspective on short-term outcomes which may, or may not, apply to client phenomena (behavioral change, interpretation, symbolism, etc.) over extended maturational and/or regressive time frames. When these ideas of process vs. outcome are applied to issues of ethnicity and cultural pluralistic dynamic relationships, workers may treat the cultural concerns as extraneous or intervening variables, and ignore inherent value of either process or content,[188] as intrinsic dimensions of each culture-bound personality. One overall approach to developing a systematic framework to conduct and evaluate culture-sensitive and culture affirmative practice, is ethnomethodology.

Ethnomethodology, related to a scientific method used by anthropologists, can help the counselor understand the role played by ethnicity in determining cultural/behavioral performance standards, social needs,[189] and conflicts in multicultural adaptation of predominant and subordinate cultural subgroupings. Ethnomethodological direct case observation and exploratory interviewing, helps the counselor understand the cultural milieu of clients' lives, and operationalized meaning in their overt behaviors.

Factors included in the clinician's ecological evaluation, include economics, power distribution, social stratification, environmental relationships, social opportunity theories, work ethics, and political ideology.[190] Although the author does not suggest that clinicians necessarily become ethnomethodological policy analysts or community organizers (although this option is certainly available), the issue of behavior causality and significant cultural correlations, with various philosophical beliefs about antecedent, associated, and consequent phenomena related to personal thought and action—must undergird any questions of evaluation. There is no disagreement that environment is a complex phenomenon of assessment in defining its principles and formulas of activity; and even more elusive in planning treatment intervention, which does not relegate the client to a reactive powerless position of dependency on clinically assessed facts, psychological dynamics, or skewed and limiting therapeutic inputs.

Counselors must consider extent to which they compromise effective macro level strategies for macro level causes, by using micro level techniques as they think through routes and stages of transformation, to parallel client and therapist behavior, relative to the true model (in their collective awareness) of correct causality. The process, unfortunately, may entail symbolism, illusion, or delusion by clients to achieve consonance with their counselors, in fitting into their intrapsychic treatment modes. It may include pretending that externally-controlled behavior is internal, or requiring special learned skills and strategies on the part of clients, to deal directly with social external causes of their behavior—which may mean therapy provides no direct possibility of change in desired culturally determined outcomes, but only functions to help the client learn new personal inputs to cope with, defend against, or accept macro-level independent variables in their lives.

Some theorists also suggest that therapists assume a combined micro-macro strategy (attempted by some, thorough interprofessional collaboration), to more honestly, realistically, and effectively assault the notion of "omniconvergeance" discussed by Cath,[191] to entail: association of personality structure, physical organism, and socioeconomic/ethical/purposeful environments of the holistic person. This suggests a comprehensive diagnostic system to include individual-within-the-environment (not separated as distinct entities), and coordinated intervention directed by combined environmental and causal phenomena for each client, measured and correlated as both individual and social change,[192] with reciprocal effects which demonstrate progress. Instruments must be developed to assess the smallest changes in the environments. These changes are traced to specific clients, while clients' reciprocal awareness of environmental and personal change-oriented inputs must also be assessed, including quasi-defensive postures to accept temporary social change, or symbolically associate changes with personal adequacy, even if these connections cannot be immediately empirically demonstrated.

Individual therapeutic strategies must be more clearly documented as they are coordinated and integrated with associated macro level inputs, so contradictory goals are not developed which cancel effects of the alternate procedure, both objectively and in the client's subjective viewpoint.

A total macro-level orientation suggests that clients respond only to final dimensions of gross social change, and demonstrate limited substantive attitude or behavioral variability in interim life sequences, prior to the precise moments at which their lives might be affected by broad-based economics, politics, or social changes. If this is truly believed, individual therapeutic efforts prior to these events, are of questionable value unless other evaluation purposes are operative to diagnose or predict client reactions, or measure limited treatment goals which may not be translatable subsequently into global ecologically-related criteria. In either case, the therapist's philosophical beliefs about micro vs. macro vs. combined micro/macro causality, are significant in deciding about motivation for professional help, selection of success-oriented inputs, and measurement of correct and relevant outcomes.

One additional implication for this topic, is related to integration of intrapsychic and sociologic/ecologic factors impacting clinical evaluation. The most common intrapsychic concern in the literature appears to be self-esteem, frequently discussed in terms of black population or subgroups.[193] A common perception about black culture, is the assumption of a collective low self-esteem due to prohibitive racism and social discrimination, coupled with pressure to adapt to lifestyles and orientations of white society. This philosophy suggests psychological ineptness and developmental voids, while neglecting influences of a broad range of interactive psychosocial factors on self-perception.[194]

Numerous theories of self-esteem, including writings of Gurin, Veroff, and Feld,[195] show that perspectives concerning adjustment to life are predicated on numerous social demographic characteristics, and that perceptions of self-esteem do not necessarily suggest a concomitant index of social satisfaction with the milieu. Roseberg also studied economic factors related to self-esteem,[196] noting that social class was minimally related to self-esteem. This was also corroborated in studies by Coopersmith,[197] who suggests a much lesser role of social environment on development and control of self-esteem.

Other writers, however, suggest more closely-linked connections between socialization and esteem, especially considering self-protective boundaries that enable minority groups to survive in a multi-status society, which may include the belief that *blackness* is negative, and dominant white identity is preferential.[198]

Each counselor must remember that such feelings might result from belonging to a particular ethnic or racial group, but also that self-assessment does not necessarily relate to either personal or social factors alone,[199] and may represent a combination of factors, irrespective of overall cultural satisfaction or success.[200]

Spirituality

Another significant, but often overlooked area of the introspective self, relating to the clinician's and client's personal adaptation and overall growth and development, is spirituality and its operationalized manifestations, in personal and organized religious beliefs and practices. As Mead and Piaget suggest,[201] the socially and psychologically developed self has a range of identities and behaviors influenced by religious or spiritual phenomena. These beliefs and values strongly influence need hierarchies, individual identity images, and range of adequate/ good/desirable behaviors (outcomes and inputs) which are available for client or counselor, as part of normal growth and being. Spirituality also helps define quality of life and goals, or expectations for attainment of various levels of preordained or self-selected states of qualitative existence. Spirituality is a domain within which any practitioner or client defines or seeks variable status conditions of awareness, meaning, or understanding; and is also one vortex representing interchange between special micro and macro dimensions of reality. This connection linkage of life forces can occur as the relationship of personhood, organized religious institutions, spiritual values/practices, and actual spiritual deities (God, Buddah, etc.)—materialize in the thoughts, feelings, and behaviors of clients at one level, and may also exist as transcendental life processes in other dimensions of reality in the universe.[202]

The problem in clinical practice situations, is that the professional counselor and client may lose sight of causal, correlational, or consequent nature of spiritual and moral components of both content (norms) and process (dynamics and ways of living) aspects of life. If theological or spiritual phenomena (especially the traditional model of God) are, in reality, significant variables affecting client lives (whether they know/believe it or not), or if clients intrapsychically and/or socially rely on spiritual conceptualizations and behaviors as key components of adaptation, and then ignore the evaluative questions; serious harm or loss of growth opportunities for clients may result.

Counselors are active participants in their own spiritual or religious lives, or have reactive feelings and behaviors, either predetermined to certain destinies as prescribed by theological formulations, or are reactions against the value of a spiritual presence or force in their lives. Any of these conditions influences definition of client, designation of the counselor's spiritual (or non-spiritual) mission with them, and interpretation of outcomes which have empirical relevance in the client's interactive earthly activities, but may also be assigned significance within spiritual or religious realms of meaning.

In addressing these complex issues, the discussion will be subdivided into consideration of personal spiritual dimensions which affect evaluation and, secondly, facets of organized religious process in society. This poses interesting evaluative dilemmas, as well as opportunities for the clinician.

Personal Spirituality

The first evaluative consideration about spirituality of counselors (or clients), is degree to which this dimension of life (including traditional or idiosyncratic religious, moralistic, ethical, divine, transcendental, and emotional components) is a significant factor in explaining past events, personality development, future change options, or life paths. This includes orientations to the hereafter or any form of existence before or after normal mortal life, as these become indices for diagnosis, treatment planning, and evaluative decision-making. The question is important because it provides guidelines to the clinician about the relative proportion of emphasis on different dynamics of living, and enhances awareness of desired and biased (conflictual seeded weightings to the spiritual vs. non-spiritual) answers to evaluative questions.

Many counselors view spirituality of the client vis-à-vis their own positive or negative orientations, so the relative importance of this aspect of life may be informally, inadvertently, or unconsciously given a prefixed priority rating. This conceptual ranking may then move the spiritual domain to relatively corresponding positions in the counselor's hypothetical formula for client development, which may be inaccurate, causing the counselor to focus on incorrect or more/less significant factors to explain conflict (as one example), which may not be equally shared in the client's own view of her or himself.

The author became aware of this problem as a clinical intern in southern Arizona, where work with American Indians was frequently off-base. Factors of life's spiritual union with nature, holistic time dimensions for viewing responsibility and obligations, and predestinations based on natural or spiritual factors which were not empirically verifiable in observing overt behavior—were not recognized as significant variables. Even factors like spiritual or existential view of self as a native American/sensitive human being/holistically-aware Apache/ displaced deviant/defeated victim/ignored citizen/spiritually victorious being— were roles experienced by some clients—but unfathomable by the counselor; yet were extremely significant foundation awareness and life principles, in making assessments and measuring change.

The clinician should also be cognizant of gaps in the client's knowledge of spiritual or theological facts, which may be available for their use as life principles or perspectives. Spirituality may, correspondingly, assist clients in becoming informed and educated, so their thoughts and behaviors can be as self-actualized as possible, within the fullest range of spiritual and human conditions or states of awareness.

An important part of this educational process also involves the clinician, since many spiritual concepts, constructs, propositions, and laws contain inherent definitions of states of being or dynamics of psychosocial functioning. These have important implications for helping clients define goals and objectives, and helping them understand the meaning of various parts of their lives. This includes specific categories of identity options, with differing degrees of availability, qualification, or specification for access by clients (e.g., being predestined, born again, saved, confirmed, ordained, consecrated, etc.). These spiritual domains can place significant boundaries around many areas of thinking, feeling, and behaving which, in non-spiritual paradigms, may be much less structured and less valuable as evaluative benchmarks. Other concepts which readily come to mind as spiritual guidons for specific behavioral outcomes, with quantitative and qualitative value, are: hope, pride, vanity, honesty, goodness, righteousness, truth, justice, honor, love, and others. Although these and similar concepts may be subjectively defined as part of the client's self-actualization or defensive pathology, they also have special definition significance as they traditionally represent religious culture, and have additional value within distinct religious communities or churches, which are social (as well as spiritual) tabernacles of spiritual heritage and meaning.

In thinking specifically about educational processes, and particularly the counselor's assessment of what clients know about their own spiritual nature, and how spiritual learning may be important in their life's development, Arbuthnot notes that:

> ". . . a critical requirement is the ability of the moral educator to assess moral reasoning stages accurately in order to create an appropriate amount of disequilibrium to stimulate advance. Educators, who either over or underestimate their own stage, will not be able to make the appropriate discriminations needed for effective interventions. Given the value-laden nature of Kohlberg's stages, it is likely that educators with minimal training in moral theory will overestimate their own stage."[203]

He concludes that moral educators (clinicians should be added to the list) need extensive training in moral development theory and assessment, including objective feedback as to specific roles of moral dogma, and moralistic thought process in social adjustment.

The clinician, in these circumstances, might work with clients to develop a model of their spirituality, which could be a foundation for decision-making and evaluation through a clinical contract, and help the client utilize a framework for spiritual living after termination of therapeutic work. A significant dilemma occurs when the therapist has a firm spiritual model, especially if it contains rigorously defined principles of spiritual living, and the client does not philosophically subscribe to this orientation, or vice versa. Therapists must then assess their ability to relinquish, redefine, or expand/contract their principles, and deal with changes in perspectives or other costs to the client, as this occurs. Degree of cognitive differentiation must be determined, and areas of conceptual convergence clearly defined, since these bridges to therapeutic influence make a great deal of difference if they facilitate, rather than hinder, clients' journeys into spiritual territories of inner and outer worlds.

One approach therapists have, is to introduce their spiritual framework as another alternative for living, and help the client systematically examine pros and cons of how the client handles the consideration of alternatives, and the exploration of these spiritual dimensions. It must be remembered, however, that this does not necessarily provide definitive answers to the question of specific available outcomes inside the spiritual domain. Violations of self-determinations are, of course possible, with pressure to accept a specific value position. However, counselors may not feel compromised by exerting therapeutic, influential power, to help clients use their generic processes of considering alternatives, or even strongly advocate for client acceptance of specific beliefs. Since assessment of spiritual benefits (or benefits of any alternative lifestyle or thought process) may require investment of energy (prayer, time of learning and exposure, acceptance by a spiritual entity, socialization), the therapist may be evaluatively most sound, by extending therapeutic periods of intervention, to allow clients sufficient and reasonable time to actualize or fully explore the spiritual dimension of their lives. In this case, outcome benefits have a more reasonable probability of materializing, and clients (irrespective of actual spiritual outcomes, i.e., grace, God's love, rebirth, etc.) can potentially understand possible benefits of spiritual inputs, which they might incorporate into a circular self-reward process of behavioral reinforcement of the independent variable ("I feel good when I meditate in church, whether or not God provides specific feedback, benefit, or outcome").

Another dimension, is that rejection of religiosity, its social structures, and moral foundations, can symbolically represent transferential conflict with parent figures (God the Father, Sons of God, The Mother Church, etc). The clinician needs to evaluatively differentiate rejection of authoritative control, from the rejection of the specific content of theological tenets and principles themselves. The clinician should also keep in mind that religiosity and spirituality in many churches and interpretive modes, may demand, ipso facto, a natural dependence on religious norms or spiritual beings (entities), which the clinician must differentiate from psychopathological dependency, so validity and reliability concerning client actions and statuses can be assured.

A second major dimension of personal spirituality, involves the client's or counselor's actual, hypothesized, or anticipated (excluding delusions of relation-ships) relationship with a spiritual being, idea, entity, phenomenon, or proxy representative, in socially sanctioned clergy or even self-proclaimed spiritual leaders. The clinician must be aware of the possible existence of associational certainty or stable image representations in a client's life which cannot be empirically measured, but documented through individual or group behavioral or emotional phenomena (a whole congregation worshiping God is one possible index of the existence of God, and can be emotionally experienced according to many theologians and spiritual leaders, via the mechanism of faith).[204] The tradi-tional Judeo-Christian premise of a personal, influential, and active God- figure, suggests an independent variable phenomenon with powers to evaluate behavior of constituents, and provide inputs of support, punishment, teaching, inspiration, etc. This real stimulus provides, in many ways (within traditional interpretive framework), a unifying force, apex to establish truth, source of norms and outcomes critical in defining individual status,[205] and range of future options (e.g., heaven vs. hell), which contribute to the meaning of life now and in the future.

In working with clients' spiritual realms, the deity or entity must be considered a potentially active and viable member (component) of a system (a finite point of reference for both finite and infinite outcomes). Herein, rules, opinions, statements, and ideas are stimuli to provide feedback to the individual client, to define personal existence (and each segment of it) as part of a possibly larger meaningful whole, and serve as a role model (e.g., Christ and the Bible) for behavior. This means, specifically, that the therapist helps clients discover (sometimes via consultation with clergy) how God or another form of spiritual being would assess their behavior or feelings, and which particular stimulus inputs would be forthcoming to define the nature or quality of past events, or open options for future goals.

Relationship with a spiritual or religious figure, person, God, image, etc., is also important for the counselor whose zeal, enthusiasm, course of therapeutic direction, use of energy, and various value-laden viewpoints—may be predicated, not on information generated by clients, but needs for information or accomplishments to fulfill role reciprocity requirements of a spiritual or religious relationship, which may take precedence over the relationship with the client. Changing certain therapist behaviors, implies that a relationship with a spiritual entity would also systematically have to change, which may not be possible, depending on degree of rigidity of the counselor's need, belief in his or her own spiritual commitments, and actual nature of the relationship as defined by the God figure.

Some examples of Christ's behavior, as models within the Bible, may be used by the clinician to illustrate the framework from which operational definitions might be developed to empirically measure client behaviors, and which serve as therapeutic topics for comparative analysis of the client's approach to adaptation, relative to the Christian (or any other spiritual/religious) model.

The counselor must also place evaluative attention on consequences of spiritual deviance (hell, guilt, sin, etc.)[206] which, from religious or spiritual concepts, are a significant component of living, and a constant around which dynamics of fear, anxiety, conforming behavior, or states of goodness or badness (in reality) revolve. These potential negative outcomes may be assessed in relation to other positive options, so homeostasis is achieved (e.g., the clients remove themselves from a state of sin) in those areas of the spiritual system which are not prone to client reinterpretation, or flexible selective perception or modification. Degree of interpretative, perceptual, or behavioral freedom[207] of clients and counselors is an important dimension, relative to definition and use of qualitative and quantitative criteria to attribute evaluative meaning to client effort-in-fixed circumstance, as opposed to client effort-in-flexible circumstance.[208]

Organized Religious Institutions and Social Morality

Another area of evaluative impact in the therapeutic milieu, concerns type, rationale, and degree of association by counselors and clients, with organized religions of churches/synagogues, and the principles which specifically emanate from social institutional being and activity processes. This is important, since clients seek personal fulfillment through their association and employment of instrumental and relational dynamics which are attached to these institutions, as criteria for opportunities for membership and religious status. A church is not simply a physical or institutional structure, but is used and uses its constituents differentially, and has potential psychosocial-spiritual functionality. Herein, there are significant variables in this reciprocal interdependency to be understood and measured, relative to client growth and change. Some separate and specific issues associated with this interdependency are as follows:

1. *Relative dependencies:* One set of dynamics of organized religious or spiritual collectives, churches, and groups, are the significant effects of shared reality (mutuality), group cohesion, personal interconnectedness, and rewards formally attached to religious principles of group activity, which represent particular relations between the spiritual deity/creator/role model, and the active constituents. The clinician must conduct a thorough client assessment to identify baseline personality characteristics of dependency, guilt, autonomy, initiative, etc., as differential precursive conditions causing clients to view their religious groups in various ways, to meet particular needs. A sound evaluative strategy establishes specific qualitative categories or quantitative indices of positive and negative dependence or independence, along with potential outcome choices reflective of clients' socialization and cultural learning.

    An important part of philosophical and psychological decisions about dependency, is for the clinician to carefully consider independently, and with the client, (1) degree to which some dependency may be a necessary condition of all human life; (2) degree to which some dependency is a necessary condition of the particular client's life, as either a religious or nonreligious person; (3) consequences for the client, if current solutions to their dependency crises were removed or diminished (including religious group participation), as this impacts overall capability for anxiety-free and relatively painless or adaptive existence.

    One example of the connection between the self, as related to social institutions, and one's moral character, appears in the work of McDougall,[209] where he notes:

    ". . . the idea of the self and the self-regarding sentiment are essentially social products . . . the complex conception of self thus attained implies constant reference to others and to society in general, and is, in fact, not merely a conception of self, but always of one's self in relation to other selves. This social genesis of the idea of self lies at the root of morality, and it was largely because this social origin and character of the idea of self was ignored by so many of the older moralists, that they were driven to postulate a special moral faculty, the conscience or moral instinct."

Clients who attain a socially determined sense of self as a partial result of religious or spiritual institution involvement, have an evaluative mirrored arena within which they behave, to assess and confirm the collectively desired and idiosyncratically-accepted self. At the same time, their idiographic behaviors serve as frequencies to support or fashion the group's nomothetic patterns (which the client also personally interprets) that represent the community and its power as a subset of a God's domain, or as a unit of a spiritual/religious social system which has life of its own—including possible need for deviants (sinners), as examples and comparative images to define goodness, conformity, or other group beliefs.[210]

An important evaluative question concerns normal vs. abnormal dependency on the controls, structure, security, companionship, and definitions provided by organized spiritual collectives; and also, the realistic alternatives open to people who, in part, may never attain significant relationships except for those which do exist with the group religious experience. This concern must be offset, however, with attention to real qualitative benefits potentially available to more fully participating community members, which are functions of decreased client input, rather than pathological individual dependency, and fictitious or illusory benefits of the religious institution.

The therapist should help clients evaluate their awareness of personal dependency (the independent act of choosing fulfilling dependency relations) and need-meeting characteristics of spiritual groups, with attention to their ability to conceptualize wider vs. narrower ranges of alternatives, in meeting the needs or accessing the group benefits. Their choosing behaviors within situations, become another index of growth, expanded awareness, and functional capability, even though there may be little change in potency or depths of dependent needs. Also, positive components of dependent status provide a support framework and security to replace nurturing parents, and can be used as a springboard for initiating other levels and types of growth. The clinician might develop an ordered category system to help clients use dependency to hypothesize other areas of growth, and make a decision about their status and, in almost reverse order, utilize the religious group energy (real or fantasized). They consider other life opportunities to invest even more energy in their church or synagogue life. This may involve, for some clients, development of an inverse correlational measurement strategy with behavioral reinforcement, to seek and assess increases in awareness of dependent-safety feelings (with the clinician actively using examples from the group process), as these encourage clients to take greater risks in exploratory and independent conceptualizations. The therapist can utilize the religious group as a transferential parent partner (in tandem with the clinician), to provide a relearning experience of incremental reinforcement of autonomous behaviors by a controlling parent.

In this regard, the clinician must be sensitive to various interpretations of reasons for dependency, and help clients struggle with a variety of interpretations, to counteract traditional religious viewpoints related to badness (guilt), helplessness, or inadequacy. Massive doses of guilt, sometimes associated with religious (and especially cult) groups to insure membership and loyal commitment, often prevent using dependent needs to stimulate other life considerations.[211]

In cults or other powerful institutions of religion, constituents or disciples frequently learn that external social phenomena are evil, and manipulatively lure victims into dimensions of sin or deviancy, to meet their own needs for membership identification and conformity. From an ecological perspective, radical institutions may be necessary antitheses to maintain ecological balance, or to substantiate moralistic values of other religious institutions. The counselor can use both types of institutional systems as comparative normative criteria, to help clients see corresponding dimensions inside their personality frameworks.

Guilt is important as a control mechanism within both radical and conservative religious groups, but also as a rehabilitative procedure to functionally remove a deviant status, as it is associated with penance or ultra-conforming rehabilitative feeling or behavior. Often, there are punishments involved in separation from a cult or controlling institution, so guilt is also connected with anticipatory fear and punishment. In these cases, the counselor must remember that guilt and punishment are real and necessary dimensions of institutional life among many religious organizations, so evaluation requires an assessment of why clients are unable to correctly envision their behavioral outcomes, and accept responsibility for initiating actions to regain a conforming status. Intrapsychically, counselors should decide which parts of their humanistic concerns for client suffering need to be controlled, and if any incorrect philosophical or theoretical propositions about autonomous human choice, cause them to view clients as freer to relinquish some religious institutional memberships, than is the case in reality.

2.   *Functions of social morality:* In considering organized religious institutions
     and societal norms relative to the spiritual character of individuals, practi-
     tioners must think comprehensively about their own and clients' relation-
     ships to moral prescriptions of current culture.   They must especially be
     cognizant of ways these norms contribute to the quality and accuracy of
     their (clients and counselors) views of each other, and how their individual
     or collective reactions to morality or its converse (immorality), help or
     hinder the process and evaluation of clinical intervention.   One function of
     morality (or theological principles and codes of behavior applied to inter-
     acting social groups), provides average or standard normative criteria to
     insure continuation of organized living via socialized rules and the inherit-
     ance of social rituals, which do not threaten successful interactions among
     diverse individuals:

> "The functioning of a social system as a moral order implies a
> capacity for self-objectification, self-identification, and appraisal of
> one's own conduct, as well as that of others, with reference to socially
> recognized and sanctioned standards of behavior.   Without a psycho-
> logical level of organization that permits the exercise of these func-
> tions, moral responsibility for conduct could not exist, nor could any
> social structure function as a moral order."[212]

Within traditional Western Protestant ethics and the Judeo-Christian philosophy generally, early capitalistic-oriented communities seemed organized
and motivated, partly by anxiety over fulfilling God-given potential; or
reconciling for predestined punishment due to original sin, while at the
same time producing economic goods and services to create a new
industrial age.[213]

As a process of interaction between individuals and their moral
normative image, evaluation may be contingent upon empirical examples
of public goal-attainment seen in social outcomes (including delivery of
social service), but also through private examples of spiritual and moral
achievement.   These include factors such as humility, modesty, selfless-
ness, self-sacrifice, and charity, which relate also to psychosocial self-
esteem.   Some perceive concomitant variation in the two principles, so
increases in public aspirations or achievements, can also be accompanied
by self-perceptions of high moral attainment and valued aspirations at a
more internal level.   In either of the above models, an important consideration is not only what the requirements and correlaries of both public
and private morality really are, but also the degree of awareness of each

held by the client or counselor, and their opportunities for free vs. contingent access to either or both.[214]

With individual clients, the clinical evaluator must assess degree of rigidity of these norms and range of options for achievement of both personal and social morality (and determining if this does represent a positive identity image), and range of opportunities for ritualized undoing of moral wrongs. Although some clients can realize they defensively use socially moral rituals or behavioral prescriptions as parent substitutes (for protection or rebellion), many are living within moral guidelines as fully integrated and spiritually validated lifestyles, that cannot always be interpreted by the clinician as defensive or pathological in nature. Evaluation involves assessment of the client's capability for integration or homeostatic syncronicity between moral principles and operational behavioral repertoires. Treatment goals might be designed to help clients more precisely conceptualize associations between morality and behavior, and learn more effective ways of operationalizing moral and philosophic principles. Other measurements may concern clients' resistance to moral or religious norms, as transferred resistance to negatively perceived parental love objects, with attention to developing frameworks to describe defensive decisions, and measure consequent acted-out behaviors which are moral or immoral, as efforts to salvage one's autonomy. This might be coupled with attention to clients' use of their moral framework to define themselves more adequately (especially safe and secure), and develop an extensive repertoire of patterns of utilization of social moral precepts.

In cases where clients perceive themselves to be in deviant status, although pathological guilt and dependency may constitute one set of explanations, the clinician can work within the moral norms to help clients discover ways they prevent themselves from accepting moral boundaries, and learn processes by which they are unable to use existing avenues to regain adequacy status.

The clinician may help clients gain appreciation of their spiritual identity, which theoretically may derive from moral group membership; and help them perceive more clearly empirical, as well as mystical, indicators of various states of adequacy. The public and interpersonal nature of moralism also helps define and create conditions for group collective experiences or awareness, which serve as positive or negative indices of happiness, peace, love, safety, etc., as the client becomes a more perceptive observer of group phenomena.

The measurement challenge is to help the client gain systematic awareness of feelings and conditions of their inner soul, and also correlate
personal and public empirical referents, so they can make judgments about
their own moralistic behavioral processes. Clinicians might dismiss notions
of group awareness or collective mystical perceptions as forms of client
escape or defensive excuse, while ignoring that many theories of group-
oriented spiritualism, clearly specify conditions of existence and states of
awareness which occur through spiritual belief, divine input, and collective
group behavior—as they occur and achieve critical energy mass collectively.

The counselor is, of course, also interactive personally with public
moral principles which have characteristics that can be consistent and
contradictory. Counselors must take a position relative to moralistic values
they feel are substantive and permanent. This is evaluatively necessary, so
some aspects of their therapeutic inputs are communicated honestly to
clients, as constants rather than variables. This helps clients decide if their
spiritual and moral views coincide sufficiently to allow interpersonal connective linkages, and to determine when and where preordained evaluative
questions will be fixed, with a limited range of acceptable alternatives for
positively valued outcomes. An example of this, may be the counselor's
unwavering negative views of extramarital relationships for married persons, wherein therapeutic orientation might be directed at helping the client
perceive the regressiveness, conflict, or dependency interwoven in this
moralistically deviant act; as opposed to another approach which views this
activity as positive, or as neither right or wrong, depending on its amoral
need-meeting functionality.

Counselors will be dependent to varying degrees, on their own conformity to public moral principles, with a philosophic perspective about the
process (and their part therein, as action or reaction participants) of
society's defining principles, and the consequent qualitative nature of
various social outcome behaviors. The challenge for clinicians is to
separate independent and dependent variables associated with the client's
morality, group moralistic goals and processes, and group phenomena,
which can be interpreted by clients as valuable for identity sustenance and
self-definition. As each factor is considered, the therapeutic milieu
becomes an experimental laboratory where clients assume temporary
researcher roles, to examine positive and negative aspects of their moral
environment. They partly accomplish this by objectively separating themselves from potentially controlling process (a possibly deviant role),

hypothetically deciding which empirical factors are most critical for their socialized identity, and noting which ones provide the greatest benefit in short- and long-range effects. They can consider ways in which given characteristics of all of the above conditions, coexist in harmony through their executive function, which in and of itself, may receive its energy and direction from the moralistic milieu of forces which the client believes operate in their lives.

Where clients perceive associations between moral principles and individual behaviors, their guilt or compulsion sometimes causes inefficiency and ineffectiveness in matching correct potencies of their input, and the desired moralistic outcome. Here the clinician can evaluate cost-effectiveness and efficiency in a relatively neutral manner, to help clients achieve desired outcomes with minimal efforts; or successfully plan various moral and other living experiences, to complement one another and prevent conflict in time, energy expenditure, and overlap, etc. Clients can develop abstract or specific conceptual categories to include or exclude specific activities, to maximize the probability of their perceived success hierarchies, and eliminate or consolidate other activities offering less individual or public payoff within their social moralistic framework. For some religious clients, this means helping them realize a wider range of options for charitable accomplishments, or discovering greater possibilities of spiritual reward (both individually and through group involvement) from their existing actions. Hereby, changes in independent or dependent variables provide accelerated moral mileage, with decreasing or more carefully planned energy output. In working with families, the group, based on its own functional (healthy or unhealthy) system of interaction, is an interpreter of moral principles, religious norms, and spirituality. Evaluatively, therefore, the counselor might separate (1) some external norm of morality as a comparative standard, and (2) the family's norms for morality, and (3) the operating principles that obscure awareness of a necessary moral standard, or skew operationalization of an existing norm, which helps the family operate in a way it feels is critical for its survival. Correlations in this process help bring the moral issue into accurate focus, although the other alternative is that a correct focus on the moral issue may produce change in the family process, which is too disturbing to its existing balance.

An example of this dilemma is the parent-adolescent control conflict which is, in the author's opinion, mostly an issue of parental self-esteem which drags moral goodness, honor, sexuality, drugs, etc., (which may not be the moral issues themselves) into the debate, further clouding and complicating the issues. Separating these can be very helpful in therapy, and in evaluating outcomes involved.

Laird[215] discusses this specifically in terms of family rituals, which manifest systems of meaning and values; moral, cultural, and philosophical themes; behavioral norms and attitudes; and patterns of adjustment with hereditary permanency.[216] In processes of socialization and interaction, families develop basic firm beliefs about reality and its environment,[217] which are often invisible to the external behavioral eye. These paradigms are maintained through rituals which solidify concepts and constructs that are collective perceptual cornerstones, helping members negotiate numerous obstacles to the attainment of these various states of being.[218]

Rituals are significant because they communicate in symbolic form, collective images of the world[219] and its moral principles, which then become associated with personal security of family members, who are bound to the group's system of rituals for psychosocial and spiritual survival. The actual moral or philosophical principle, as well as family cultural pattern, may define and formulate social roles and subsequent conforming role behavior, so the behavior may become either a clear or confusing representation of the original moral principle.

Symbols, therefore, may be integrated in ways which enhance or detract from the moral principle itself, but function in other ways to maintain the social system and cultural ethos:

"The implications of ritual theory for understanding and working with families are complex. Family-centered practitioners need to learn how to recognize and understand family rituals, to use the explanatory power of rituals to help understand families to interpret meanings and functions of rituals in preserving family paradigms, and, finally, to learn to employ the ritual form in work with families. Through the medium of ritual, families can be helped to express their traditions and values; to achieve coherence; to adapt to transitions, unsettling life events, and catastrophes; and perhaps to dismantle dysfunctional pat terns of rigid behavior that are perpetuated by certain rituals.

. . . As part of the assessment of a complex family system, the worker needs to discover the rituals and ceremonies that consolidate, communicate, and sometimes mask the family's paradigm, its system of meaning and belief, its values, its rules for relationship and behavior, and its conflicts and paradoxes."[220]

In some situations, the clinician may assist disorganized, confused, or ambivalent families to symbolically represent philosophies, ideas, or morals in more dominant or pronounced ritual form, so they improve family solidarity, connectedness, and boundaries. They also have empirical referents for morals or philosophies which can be viewed by all members, and assessed as to their value and relevance for the family, and then consolidated, modified, or abandoned to better reflect needs for the family unit.[221]

Individual Perspectives on Learning

In further considering intrapsychic factors which influence abilities and styles of self-evaluation, individual approaches to learning must also be discussed. Learning can be described as the "shaping of individuals—their understandings, their attitudes, their values, and aspirations,"[222] as part of individual psychological experiences within particular sociocultural systems. Knowledge may be sought as a response to stimulation from the environment[223] and/or personal need,[224] as the learner becomes a participant (with varying degrees and purposes) in individual growth processes.

As the person interacts with the environment, the self-evaluative process involves comparison of actual and ideal states of knowledge development,[225] as a stimulus for seeking new information or protecting ownership of that which already exists. Development of different approaches to self-evaluation results from interaction of environmental demand, personal need, individual psychological characteristics, and interpersonal relationships; all different for each social service practitioner, client, and practice environment. Landon,[226] for example, confirms differences between practitioners along various dimensions of motivation/capability for seeking information (or learning), which is part of self-evaluative process and has significant impact on therapeutic activity, as well as the counselor's framework for assessing self-efficacy. Knowledge seeking depends upon differential needs of the "professional self," and level of "uncertainty" about practice situations and client personality dynamics.

Integration of learning and self-evaluation within multiple dimensions of life experiences, explains both development and manifestation of different approaches to individual evaluation. Knowles[227] illustrates this within the "androgogic" interpretation of continuity of the learning or assessment process. Education and learning may be viewed as lifelong processes, in which self-evaluation transcends particular stimuli to know or reproduce specific facts or behaviors. From this perspective, the evaluative process is incomprehensible when using unidimensional models (like traditional science alone), and immeasurable by narrowly defined criteria from any one model.

The complexity of this learning process is further illustrated with the androgogic framework, in emphasis on understanding the *how* of knowing and learning. Houle[228] submits that the *what* or end result is only part of the adult learning process, and identifies two additional orientations which extend potential criteria upon which self-evaluation is predicated:

1. *Activity* orientation suggests that circumstances of the learning or evaluative situation have personal meaning to participants, with no necessary connection to overt purposes, content, or results of the activity (this relates to input and process of treatment discussed previously in the chapter).

2. *Learning* orientation indicates that knowledge (and the self-evaluative part of knowledge acquisition) is sought for phenomenologic inherent value, and some self-initiated learning is an integrated part of individual self-conception.

Evaluation of counseling performance involves more complexity, than simple measurement of the final results of treatment would indicate, as concepts of personal learning and knowledge acquisition substantially augment number of potentially relevant explanatory factors. In understanding how learning orientation, as an intrapsychic status, can be an independent variable influencing evaluation, some specific approaches to learning will be discussed in the sections that follow.

Learning For Its Own Sake

The counselor, socialized to understand both personal need and achievement of adequacy, as intrinsically related to processes (not necessarily content) of learning and knowledge seeking, presents a special phenomenon to the therapeutic environment. This type of counselor may approach negative evaluative findings with greater honesty, and pursue collection of valid and reliable data irrespective of the assumed probability of positive or negative outcomes. Approaching data, free of previously interpolated needs for approval or fears of failure, suggests this counselor is more likely to alter interdependent input variables (techniques or methods), to explore multiple effects for their differential quality; and may value nonsuccess (as a form of learned content) as a normal and healthy process of growing through intrinsic value of learning. This learner may also seek a broad range of therapeutic experiences involving personal awareness, with increased psychological freedoms (permission and reward) to seek multiple types of feedback and intense self-analysis, as energy is allocated to growth.[229]

As a clinical role model, personal responsibility for growth for its own sake, provides a foundation for motivating clients to seek similar guilt-free self-awareness, and provides a safe territory within which client and counselor engage and provide energy to seek greater awareness of the psychological learning relationship. This counselor might also establish measurement schemes related to client process, rather than outcome, so therapeutic success is measured relative to: ability to expend energy for growth; degree of knowledge integration and attainment of new conceptual frameworks to define growth process, irrespective of outcome; and attainment of self-awareness, when this is painful or when external behavioral indicators are clearly negative (deviant, failing, etc.) relative to personal or social standards. This learning orientation appears feasible in long-term therapy projects or contracts, and suggests the potential to probe multiple levels of client awareness and personality organization, to identify complex linkages of causality for interrelated stages of bio-psychosocial development and maturation.

Of course, overall orientation of learners does not necessarily mean they will pursue more abstract conceptual learning,[230] as opposed to concrete and less symbolic components of client experiences individually, and in context of relationships. Counselors may avidly pursue learning and growth, but do so on such concrete or simplistic levels, as to prohibit multivariate and multilevel client insights, conceptual learning; and awareness of symbolism, transference, hierarchies of rationally, regression, or other aspects of complex psychodynamic processes.

The general exploratory[231] nature of this learning orientation may be useful in its ability to assume alternating broad, as well as narrow, perspectives about relevant factors in the client's life; and enhance pursuit of a wide variety of leads to explaining psychosocial conflict. It may facilitate formulation of multiple concurrent and sequential hypotheses, and afford flexibility to move back and forth between differing interrelated theoretical formulations, to zero in on the most logical factors which unravel the puzzle of each client's life. The learning orientation provides rewards for the search itself, so the clinician and client may not prematurely push for conclusion (and emotional rewards of reaching a conclusive decision—right or wrong) or experimental closure, to possible exclusion of more relevant or significant factors. In cases where premature conclusions are reached and client change does not occur, it is mutually more acceptable in this type of learning orientation, to value the data and accept the challenge of continued exploration, while having ruled out specific insignificant variable relationships. This, of course, can be offset by the client's definition of self in a crisis mode, where immediate solutions (parental control and childhood escape/ irresponsibility) are seen as a necessity. This occurs when clients develop a defensive strategy where certain preconceived solutions are acceptable, or where they associate process (not outcome) with regression, and cannot tolerate ambiguity of the independent and less-structured learning philosophy. In these situations, the therapist may have to provide artificial structure to temporarily sustain and support client defensiveness, but must also see this process (for the client) as a learning phenomenon, so there is no compromise to therapeutic growth principles in assisting clients.

There are, however, potential problems with the above orientation. One concern, is that learning-oriented therapists become preoccupied with their own agendas, and neglect appropriate consideration of clients' unique needs and capacities for learning, which may not appear enjoyable to counselors. This is professional irresponsibility, which might misdirect the vulnerable and dependent client to perceive significance in nonrelevant components of their history of personal/interpersonal dynamics, which are only of interest to the therapist filling gaps in his or her own knowledge. The client might then predicate actions on erroneous data which, even if new actions produce desirable results in the short run, may not be conceptually understood or subsequently planned, since the client will have not properly understood true cause-effect contingencies in her/his life. As counselors perceive success in their individual learning hierarchy, they may inadvertently reinforce behaviors or perceptions of clients which are of random significance when correlated with the practitioners' actions, and result in ultimate confusion of the client.

Many methodologists criticize the neglect of specific goal-oriented outcomes with a process-of-learning paradigm, since this might interfere with scientific systemization and precision measurement; also possibly accompanied by modeling, which suggests to clients that specific behavioral or attitudinal outcomes should not be a focus of planning or self-assessment. Free floating and sometimes unstructured cognitive impulses[232] associated by some authors with this learning orientation, may not fit the traditional medical model of psycho-pathology, so therapists experience two dissonant frames of reality explanation. In these cases, the process of handling the dissonance of integrating the two models, may have tremendous impact on the client. This represents either a specific cognitive posture on the part of the counselor who has resolved the theoretical dilemmas with an attitudinal choice, or a disruptive therapeutic influence as ambivalence continues. Some even suggest that over concern about the learning process, may be a defense against negative consequences fantasized for specific outcomes. The therapist may, therefore, maintain relative psychic safety with continuous movement through multiple learning options, avoiding negative evaluation if a definitive position, judgment, or outcome is ever reached. Anxiety might be increased when the anchoring effect of specific outcomes is deleted or diminished in importance, and when clients are not encouraged to define their reality as a relatively organized and predictable accumulation of relationships between variables, over which they aspire to gain increasing control via improved use of ego skills, logical reasoning, self-awareness, relationship connections, or planned defenses.

Short-term crisis counseling may be difficult, given length of time required to explore multiple learning avenues. This suggests that learning-oriented counselors may struggle with the rapid framework-building necessary to provide more concrete support[233] in crisis situations, and even the need for immediate answers to anxiety-heightened client questions. Crisis work might seem like artificial control of a delaying process[234] for less structured existential learners. They are unable to place their own learning deficits aside, to deal succinctly and demonstratively with need to structure an individual or family crisis condition within a shortened time frame, which reduces probability of a fully-enriched learning experience. In considering existential[235] adult learning, which involves awareness in the present tense of the essences of phenomena which are in a process of continuous change, a traditional scientific evaluative model of behavioral stimulus-response conditions, might negate the interconnected holism of human nature for the clinical learner.

Learning, for the counselor who represents this dimension of the holistic continuum, conflicts with clients' socialized need to utilize the past as a foundation or active guide to present or future reality; and different time frames for clinical analysis, sometimes result in insurmountable obstacles in achieving counselor-client consensual validation. This might be seen in psychodynamic concepts of the adult's self-perception as a frightened, vulnerable child, and current defenses to protect regressive vulnerability. The therapist who is a learner, must decide whether this vulnerable child can emerge and learn (re-parented growth) in the present; if healthy parts of the adult can regress and help the child of the past learn; how adult learning is even possible in the present, given self-perceptions of past identity still in existence; how to integrate learning with the outcomes theorized for specific stages of bio-psychosocial growth;

whether the learned phenomena actually exist in present, past, or some depersonalized fantasized future. There may be much confusion as client or therapist move between awareness of past, present, and future; and between conceptualization of the holistic vs. partialized human condition. This is particularly true as each may separately assign value and make judgments about the quality of learning, which may not have an operationalized common ground, where the two perspectives meet. In cases where counselor and client are similar learner types, sharing of learning processes and perspectives allows both to assess how they function to stimulate continued or more advanced learning in the other, as part of mutuality.[236] Sharing learning may, in part, be a difficult proposition for the truly independent, autonomous learner, particularly with fewer empirical outcomes to serve as foci for learning adequacy of an interpersonal nature. Formal approaches and structures in education may assume the individual, as learner (or as object of study), is a strictly boundaried and definitive entity, which can be understood via application of past notions, categories of state of the organism, or reaction patterns. An existential learner, however, may find this model constraining and, if required to superimpose traditional mental health and educational frameworks, either apply them incorrectly, or resist their application altogether, causing confusion to the client trying to understand the therapist.

Learning for Specific Outcome Goals

Another distinct approach to learning and self-evaluation, involves pursuit, collection, analysis, and judgment of clinical information, relevant to specific goal orientations of either client or counselor. This type of individual wants to learn a specific fact or element of information within a preset categorical framework. They see value of the assessment process, only relevant to a specific payoff or empirical reward, with the potential to narrowly conceive specific outcome or exaggerate outcome occurrence probabilities, related to particular inputs in the client's life. The clinician, to arrive at learned solutions, may exclude significant concepts of causal linkages between events (possibly interpreting independent variables as interventive variables to be controlled), and even ignore a wider range of other associated or contradictory outcomes, in an effort to hurry or force their reception of cognitive rewards for productivity. A major limitation in explaining reality under these circumstances, is questionable ability[237] to discern and represent complex interactive units simultaneously, which usually necessitates dismantling of more complex units, which have their meaning in the integrated state of synergistic association with other units. The goal-oriented learner may exercise this perceptual option too frequently, to the exclusion of a more beneficial descriptive[238] and integrated explanatory approach, especially dealing with the frequently confusing nature of psychosocial dynamics. Positive and correct linear associations and chain reactions may be postulated and even proven to be correct $(A\text{---}\rightarrow B\text{---}\rightarrow C$ 'outcome'), but other significant conditions may be simultaneously ignored, as the end product receives too much attention:

1.   Other factors besides A which lead to condition $(B\text{---}\rightarrow C)$ can be ignored; or conditions correlated with A might not be seen, which are necessary to give A its apparent causal impact.

$$
\begin{array}{c}
A \\
\uparrow \\
D\text{----}\rightarrow B\text{----}\rightarrow C \\
\downarrow \\
E
\end{array}
$$

2.   The counselor might not see antecedent variables which occur before A and, given possibly neutral effects of A (placebo), are the real causal factors.

$$
Z\text{----}\rightarrow K\text{----}\rightarrow(A)\text{----}\rightarrow B\text{----}\rightarrow C\text{----}\rightarrow
$$

3.   Exaggerating the importance or value of **C** can also occur, which communicates a possibly incorrect perception to clients $(A\text{---}\rightarrow B\text{---}\rightarrow C)$ which might obscure importance of A or B, or an unidentified variable in the client's chain of causal circumstances, producing excessive valuation of outcome goals, to the exclusion of further work or investigation.

In some cases, recognition of outcomes may be envisioned by the counselor, even before therapeutic inputs or investigative data gathering are fully operational. Potential to force clients' behavior or their perceptions into preconceived categories of meaning may, in fact, cause the outcome to occur or be interpreted as artificial, and produce secondary defensive maneuvers, as the client either seeks or avoids this control. It is also possible to interpret data in terms of what is already known (previous outcomes) or partly known,[239] as a way of complementing learning foundations and decreasing anxiety about the unknown.

The counselor may realize artificial or manipulative programming is in process, and harm the quality of theory, as resentment is directed at the self or displaced/transferred to the client, or as other defense is used to justify or ignore the contrived circumstances, to produce desired outcome results for their reward value.

4. Exaggerated devaluation of A or B (a----→ b----→ C) in the client's life, or premature devaluation of therapy inputs associated with outcome C (if C, in fact, turns out to be negative), are also possible occurrences.

In these cases, counselors preoccupied with the high- or low-valued nature and existence of outcomes, are reluctant to examine various qualities of their input, or feel input is insignificant as long as outcome results are not desirable. They may over-interpret failure in skill delivery, and not consider factors in the client's life (motivation, resistance) which interfered with, or necessitated, negative outcomes for overall growth.

Some authors suggest that outcome-oriented learners are overly concerned about significance of end products, which are related to specific traumatic events in their (the therapist's) own anxiety and conflict-laden development. Others suggest that strong behavioral characteristics of outcome orientation (contingent rewards, stimulus-response models, circumscribed behavioral perceptions, etc.), cause this learner to be responsive to the outcome they avidly seek; so a valued specific goal has behavioral reinforcement value, therefore conditioning subsequent behaviors of the therapist. This reasoning implies that therapists could become unresponsive to ongoing dynamics of clients' inputs, and assume a posture detached from the relationship, while conditioned by expected outcomes they feel they need. This signal-type learning[240] inhibits flexibility for effective assessment of needs and problem-solving with clients, and can be seen (1) when answers to questions (outcomes) lead to reluctance to replicate the analysis, by repeating the question; (2) with postulation of other answers, for which different questions were not asked; or (3) in development of other questions which the client wants asked, rather than questions (possibly more pertinent and threatening) which should be asked for effective therapeutic intervention to occur.

Pursuit of the broad concept of therapeutic achievement (operationalized unilaterally and generally, but not exhaustively, in terms of specific outcomes in clients' lives), may also be a characteristic of the goal-oriented learner, which inhibits validation and valuation of small increments of knowledge acquisition or awareness. In this case, the practitioner predicates decisions about energy utilization or learning motivation on only major results, therefore decreasing input energy while waiting for clients to respond in a big way. This may occur when the therapist's energy expenditure or drive may be the necessary factor to produce small achievements which have cumulative, developmental, or maturational affects on larger goals; or produce the greater gains themselves, directly.

This chicken or egg situation is related to concern with evaluative cost-effectiveness. In fact, therapeutic results are often immeasurable for long periods, or are symbolically represented or submerged in maturational processes of child growth in the adult client. Cost-effective, efficient decisions cannot be made relative to present clients, but must be based on mean (normative average) perceptions of their former dynamics, or based on theory alone.

In outcome valuation *per se,* the inclination for counselors to engage in processes of learning to attain specific goals (in their own repertoire, or scripts of clients), suggests the logical necessity to qualitatively or quantitatively place valences on pursued outcomes. This is, of course, essential, but there may be some circumstances in the psychodynamic functioning of clients, when outcomes need to be tentatively accepted with no specific valuation, until their existence has been retested or confirmed; or until the client or other contingencies are given time to allow positive or negative identities and meanings to emerge. Accepting outcomes without immediate assessment of their value (other than for simply existing) may be difficult for the outcome-oriented learner, as they may need to justify these preceding learning efforts by other means, or experience less payoff for themselves if they quickly define outcome quality or quantity.

An example, is where the client develops a physical symptom which might be unrelated to psychodynamics, defined negatively as a mechanism of defense or secondary gain/manipulation, or positively as one form of communication about thoughts or feelings (even though symbolic). A hasty decision by the counselor about what was learned and how valuable it is, causes premature attention or incorrect judgment about a significant, or entirely insignificant and unrelated occurrence. There may be relationship problems as clients and therapists differently define or valuate outcomes, which might also serve as a learned outcome (client-therapist difference in opinion), but then require analysis and negotiation as part of the therapeutic relationship. This problem might be circumvented with less attention to outcome, and more concern with *processes* of dealing with outcomes—which can also confusingly be considered another form of outcome.

The counselor should keep in mind, however, that there are also many advantages of an outcome-oriented intrapsychic process of learning. One advantage, may be the tendency for this type of counselor to provide evaluative structure to the therapeutic process, with pressure to define goals and objectives based on empirically-identified needs assessment, and make judgments of success or failure based on specific degree of goal achievement. This philosophical perspective provides a framework to bring all input and process activity (statements, questions, behavioral posture, insights, confrontations, etc.) into line with a coordinated strategic plan to create intended outcomes, with greater accuracy of evaluative assessment, as inputs have functional meaning as measurable outcomes of client change. Of course, as noted earlier, forcing outcomes may be premature or incorrect for particular clients, but there may be greater danger in not defining outcomes at all, allowing counseling to become a relatively directionless set of unplanned moves and countermoves which, even if positive outcomes are recognized *ex post facto,* provide little definitive data upon which to base scientific evaluative conclusions.

Outcome-oriented learners may also help clients focus on specific types, amounts, and meanings of learned perceptions about themselves, and may be in a position to separate areas of client and counselor learning. This is necessary because some clients are dependent on counsel or power and authority, and accept counselor learning and their (client) learning or focus on counselor learning, as a parental object phenomenon for later passive resistance or more active rejection. The previously-discussed learning-oriented counselor may be so absorbed in process for its own sake, that these finite statuses become obscured, while the outcome orientation brings these factors into more sharply defined focus.

When clients are dependent on behavioral reality perspectives, or remain relatively impressionable children in a relationship with a nurturant and helpful therapeutic parent, the outcome-oriented therapist may be strongly supportive of specific behaviors or levels of client functioning, with clearer provision and association of rewards with specific client attitude or activity. Although this may be inappropriate for some insight, self-awareness, or transference approaches, many clients (e.g., children, low-functioning mentally challenged adults, involuntary clients, highly manipulative or psychopathic individuals) respond best to task and behavior-oriented treatment approaches, and engage therapy only in terms of specific rewards available within their individual or unique situational agendas. The search for specific outcomes enhances clients' learning (operant conditioning),[241] and ability to associate their behavior with rewards as a prelude to internalization, or at least extrapolation of this process, relative to circumstances outside the therapeutic milieu. A more tightly-limited treatment plan and procedure may be possible with this type of client, and outcome-oriented counselor.

Another aspect of outcome orientation revolves around counselors' personal decisions about quality of learning, and degree to which they have or have not advanced, changed, or remained static as professionals. Without some type of outcome, the concept of professionalism or performance adequacy is irrelevant, and leaves agencies and autonomous practitioners in a difficult dilemma, given consumer demands for assurance of performance.[242] Various professionally related states of knowledge acquisition or learning may be more easily discerned within the outcome-oriented learning model, so quantitative discrepancies between real and ideal can, at least, be conceptually assessed to reflect definitive degrees of deviation as an evaluative index. This forces the counselor to make definition decisions, as opposed to alternative approaches, where process is its own reward, but may not provide a sufficiently definite standard for comparative value judgments. The author noted an example of this in a study of peer group evaluation,[243] wherein the basic group process is the presentation of case material by individual members—typically resulting from personal questions—about dynamics of their work with clients. Presentations almost always relate to problematic interactions with clients, either within single interviews, or spanning several therapeutic encounters.

Although presenters articulate specific questions to be answered, ask for information or comments about their work, and receive ideas and suggestions, many do not openly discuss how the group's contributions will actually be used for evaluative judgments. This is not surprising, however, since other research documents clinical practitioners' lack of awareness and inability to specifically describe their personal processes for making evaluative decisions (which may be related to absence of outcomes), and because many practitioners do not make clear distinctions between evaluation, consultation, support, supervision, or other dynamics of group interaction. It appears the group can be most accurate, specific, and focused in offering feedback for evaluative purposes, therefore, if the presenter identifies (1) what decisions about competence need to be made; (2) what types of data are necessary to make these judgments; and (3) how decisions about personal effectiveness will actually transpire.

In observing group interaction, presenters actually make limited conclusive, judgmental, outcome-oriented decisions about their competence. Although there can be strong norms for the presenter to seriously consider the relevance and usefulness of group feedback, there is not necessarily a formal expectation or systematic process for individual decision-making in the group itself. The group also may have little reliable information about the value of its feedback to presenters, and no assurance that individual members actually use group input to help make evaluative judgments.

Considering content of presentations, professionals may discuss concerns about therapeutic process, with less attention to outcome, end products, or client goal-attainment,[244] which are needed for effective evaluation. By not focusing questions on overall successes or failures regarding treatment goals, staff may solicit peer feedback without the benefit of critical outcome data for deciding long-range competency, and neglect real concerns with counselor performance capability.

From a scientific standpoint, changes in therapeutic techniques based on group feedback about process, prevent the counselor from determining the true effect of a consistently administered independent variable (treatment intervention) on the dependent variable (client change), at the outcome of treatment.

Learning as an Interpersonal Relationship Activity

The final learning orientation involves counselors or clients not particularly stimulated by learning for its own inherent rewards, but who enjoy and participate in learning because of secondary (primary for them) gains relative to their relationships with other learners, pleasure in associated activities and communications which lead to learning, or other aspects of the atmosphere of the learning location or personality of the teacher. Some examples, are students who attend college to enjoy parties and community living, people joining community discussion groups to find romantic or spousal relationships, or lonely individuals who escape their entrapment through educational field trips or excursions, etc.

One obvious clinical concern is traditional transference and countertransference, where the counselor enters therapy with unmet personal needs/conflicts, and attempts to resolve these issues or maintain defenses, through various relationship configurations with the client. This presumes inability to perceptually move away from dynamics that produce interpersonal enmeshment, to assume objective and analytic/evaluative learning postures to understand and reflect back client needs and conflicts, without complicating the picture for them by infusing the needy self into the scenario. Because personal need (by the therapist) for the relationship may be symbolic (complicated by client symbolic representations, as well), there is less pressure to reveal honest feelings jointly analyzed, since this tips the counselor's hand and reveals a process or relationship option (rather than learning orientation), not of interest to the client.

In other circumstances, the counselor may simply enjoy normal human contact, the give and take of communication, and the special nature of closeness which develops within a helping atmosphere. This can become evaluatively problematic, if the counselor impulsively supports areas of the client's personality which are positive or similar in nature to parallel areas of the therapist's personality, while possibly neglecting more objectionable, difficult, or unrewarding attributes wherein change should be projected and evaluated. The therapist may perceive positive indicators of relationship building or congruence, where evaluative perceptions reflect complementary experiences supporting the phenomenal self.[245] These may not cause dissonance between information known and desired (about causes of client problems, avenues to solution, or access to higher levels of therapist functioning), which signals a learning deficit, creates psychic anxiety, and increases motivation and behavior of the therapist.

Conversely, closeness attained in a relationship-oriented learning process, may reveal significant information about the client, and provide a solid framework for subsequent growth to occur. An evaluation issue is whether specific facts must be learned about the client by the counselor, and whether planned insight or goal-directed comparison of learned phenomena, are necessary for the client to negotiate changes. The client may possess inherent ability to change as a result only of the caring and congruent relationship. They may be able to discern facts (learned objectives), and put them into new relationships with different outcomes, whether or not the therapist does this for him or her, assists in doing it, or helps remove defenses. This may occur in clients who would have negotiated this dilemma anyway, and are a self-selecting group who change no matter what, but need the therapeutic or social service umbrella, or validation, to put the seal of approval on the process or product.

In other cases, the orientation to learn for the sake of the relationship, may cause greater attention to evaluation at times when the relationship is distant, or the client threatens or insinuates termination. This can have a positive effect of understanding causes for client loss of momentum, and may stimulate assertive and effective behavior to correct factors which impair relationship dynamics. Since healthy relationships are certainly one goal of therapy, this is not necessarily negative. Some therapists allow the relationship with a client to disintegrate, when personal learning objectives decrease for the therapist (irrespective of client needs); or where outcomes do not materialize to justify to the therapist, the cost-effectiveness of continuing their inputs to receive self-rewarded outcomes. Relationships which continue over time for their own sake may, therefore, provide greater longitudinal potential for knowledge building, even if there is a secondary necessity to keep the relationship together, in cases where the client wants more specific results of their input.

Therapists oriented to learning for the sake of the relationship, may also learn more about themselves by not concentrating as much on client-centered outcomes or specific learning agendas, but can grow experientially in an opened-ended fashion, ultimately producing a more sensitive and healthier personality of greater benefit to the client. It is uncertain, however, when there are motivations for the therapist to learn more about the self, in homeostatic relationships which they build within the context of therapeutic learning activities; or how anxiety or disequilibrium stimulate questioning of strength of either personality, and their respective values for personal growth.

Many criticize counselors who conduct sessions, totally oblivious to the theoretical requirements for intervention confrontation and disruption of homeostatic process in treatment. This pressure can be avoided if counselors selectively confront in nonessential areas, or in safe degrees of potency, as not to destroy the relationship. This safety net, however, can serve as a reward-punishment mechanism for pushing clients away or pulling them close, which may be predicated on relationship dynamics exclusively, rather than a theoretically correct perspective on the psychodynamic structure and functioning of a client. The activity-oriented therapist may interpret feelings and help the relationship handle conflict. There may be times when that therapist also needs to be in a less conflictual condition of balance, to perceive a larger picture (principle learning),[246] and help direct operations, based on goals which cannot be established when both persons (client and the therapist) are collectively in turmoil.

Learning may be a process of continually increasing differentiation, and a function of need deprivation, which may not occur when client-therapist relationships, in reality or fantasy, meet sufficient needs to maintain anxiety at a nonthreatening level.

Conclusion

"In general, inquiry originates within a conceptual structure of learning. This structure determines what questions are asked, the questions determine what data is needed, and these needs determine what evaluations are conducted. The data are also given their meaning and interpretation relative to the original conception which initiated the inquiry."[247] Although evaluation of practice (particularly the individual practitioner's self-evaluation) receives increasing attention throughout the profession, the study of its theoretical foundation and the ways evaluative ideals are put into practice, is possibly at an elementary level of development. This chapter suggests additional conceptual frameworks within areas of learning and knowledge acquisition, and psychological development of the individual personality, which expand the conceptual base for evaluation. This illustrates the complexity of this process as part of individual, interpersonal, and cultural dynamics, through awareness of different variables and their relationships, impacting attitudes and behaviors of self-assessment. A complex phenomenon (like self-evaluation) requires a theoretical base or combination of bases, with sufficient comprehensiveness in perspective, to accurately include all relevant aspects and variables, which are part of evaluative experiences.

Woody and Woody,[248] as noted previously, contend there is major neglect of the learner in conceptualizing evaluation, while Houle[249] reiterates the need for research on personal orientations of each learner. The literature describes ". . . what men [and women] do, and not what they think about what they do, or why they do it," which deletes the very essence of the activity.[250]

Fitts'[251] work on self-concept as central to evaluation, both individually and in relationships, along with work of others previously mentioned; ties the evaluative gestalt to the entire global range and domain of personality self-actualization.[252] The manifestation of self-evaluative behavior, therefore, is fully integrated as part of the esteem and identity of each personality, only understood through consideration of each unique "self" and its relationships. Coopersmith addresses the issue as follows:

> "One of man's [woman's] capacities is his (her) ability to be aware of himself (herself). This evaluative tendency of the self is a primary component of self-perception and it provides the material and sustenance for self- esteem."[253]

References

1.   Joseph Schwab, "Problems, Topics, and Issues," in *Education and the Structure of Knowledge,* ed., S. Elam (Chicago: Rand McNally, 1964), p. 9.

2.   Edward Suchman, *Evaluation Research* (New York: Russel Sage Foundation, 1967), p. 11.

3.   Robert Woody and Jane Woody, eds., *Clinical Assessment in Counseling and Psychotherapy* (New York: Appleton-Century-Crofts, 1972), p. 316.

4.   Cyril Houle, *The Inquiring Mind* (Madison: University of Wisconsin Press, 1961).

5.   Arthur Combs and Daniel Soper, "The Perceptual Organization of Effective Counselors," *Journal of Counseling Psychology,* 10:3:222-226, Fall, 1963.

6.   Anna Freud, *The Ego and The Mechanisms of Defense* (New York: International Universities Press, 1966).

7.   Richard Nisbett and Timothy Wilson, "Telling More Than We Can Know: Verbal Reports on Mental Process," *Psychological Review,* 84:3:231-259, May, 1977.

8.   Ellen Dickstein, "Self and Self-esteem: Theoretical Foundations and Their Implications for Research," *Human Development,* 20:3:129-140, August, 1977.

9.   Abraham Maslow, *The Farther Reaches of Human Nature* (New York: Penguin Books, 1971), pp. 40-51.

10.   Abraham Maslow, *Motivation and Personality* (New York: Harper and Brothers, 1954), p. 82.

11.   Ross Vasta and Joel Brockner, "Self-esteem and Self-evaluative Covert Statements," *Journal of Clinical Psychology,* 47:7:776-777, August, 1979.

12.   Ross Vasta, "Covertant Control of Self-evaluations Through Temporal Cuing," *Journal of Behavior Therapy and Experimental Psychiatry,* 7:1:35-37, March, 1976.

13.   Sidney Shrauger and Peter Sorman, "Self-evaluations, Initial Success and Failure and Improvement as Determinants of Persistence," *Journal of Counseling and Clinical Psychology,* 45:5:784-795, October, 1977.

14.   Alfred Schultz, "On Multiple Realities," *The Self in Social Interaction,* eds., C. Gordon and K. Gengens (New York: John Wiley, 1968).

15.   Chad Gordon and Kenneth Gengens, eds., *The Self in Social Interaction* (New York: John Wiley, 1968), p. 31.

16.   Immanual Kant, *Critique of Pure Reason* (London: Macmillan, 1881), p. 347.

17.   N. Braden, *The Psychology of Self-esteem* (Los Angeles: Nash, 1969), p. 211.

18.   Jean Piaget, *Logic and Psychology* (Manchester, England: Manchester University Press, 1965.)

19.   Daniel Fishman and Carl Zimet, "Specialty Choice and Beliefs about Specialties Among Freshman Medical Students," *Journal of Medical Education,* 47:7:524-533, July, 1972.

20.   J. Quadango, "Occupational Sex-typing and Internal Labor-market Distributions: An Assessment of Medical Specialties," *Social Problems,* 23:5:442-445, 1975.

21.   Michael Matteson and Samuel Smith, "Medical Specialty Choice: A Note on Status Rankings," *Social Science Medicine,* 11:6/7:421-423, April, 1977.

22.   Lillian Cartwright, "Conscious Factors Entering Into Decisions of Women to Study Medicine," *Journal of Social Issues,* 28:2:201, 1972.

23.   Thomas Harris, *I'm O.K.-You're O.K.* (New York: Avon, 1967).

24.   Jean Piaget, *The Construction of Reality in The Child* (New York: Ballantine Books, 1954), pp. 87-96.

25.   Chad Gordon and Kenneth Gengens, eds., *The Self in Social Interaction* (New York: John Wiley, 1968).

26.   Ernest Becker, *Revolution in Psychiatry* (New York: Free Press, 1964), p. 25.

27.   Sanford Dornbusch and Wayne Scott, *Evaluation and the Exercise of Authority* (San Francisco: Josey-Bass, 1977).

28.   Ursula Buckert, Wolfe-Uwe Meyer, and H. D. Schmalt, "Effects of Difficulty and Diagnosticity in Relation to Achievement Motivation and Perceived Ability," *Journal of Personality and Social Psychology,* 37:7:1172-1198, July, 1979.

29.   Edward Jones and Steven Berglas, "Control of Attributions about the Self Through Self-handicapping Strategies, The Appeal of Alcohol and the Role of Underachievement," *Personality and Social Psychology Bulletin,* 4:2:200-206, April, 1978.

30.   Julian Kuhl, "Standard-setting and Risk Preference: An Elaboration of the Theory of Achievement Motivation and an Empirical Test," *Psychological Review,* 85:3:239-248, May, 1978.

31.   Alan Kukla, "An Attributional Theory of Choice," *Advances in Experimental Social Psychology,* ed., L. Berkowitz (Vol. II; New York: Academic Press, 1978).

32.   Scott Briar, "The Age of Accountability," *Social Work,* 18:1:2, January, 1973.

33.   B. F. Skinner, *Science and Human Behavior* (New York: Free Press, 1953), p. 180.

34.   Mary Schwartz, "Helping the Worker with Counter Transference," *Social Work,* 23:3:204, May, 1978.

35.   Andrew Curry, "The Negro Worker and the White Client: A Commentary on the Treatment Relationship," *Social Casework,* 45:10:134, March, 1964.

36.   Helen Perlman, *Social Casework: A Problem-solving Process* (Chicago: University of Chicago Press, 1957), p. 78.

37.   Charles Tart, ed., *Transpersonal Psychologies* (New York: Harper and Row, 1969).

38.   Charles Tart, ed., *Transpersonal Psychologies* (New York: Harper and Row, 1969), pp. 203-205.

39.   Charles Tart, ed., *Transpersonal Psychologies* (New York: Harper and Row, 1969), p. 17.

40.   Charles Cooley, *Human Nature and the Social Order* (New York: Scribners, 1902).

41.   Chad Gordon, "Self-conceptions: Configurations of Content," *The Self in Social Interaction,* eds., C. Gordon and K. Gengens (New York: John Wiley, 1968), p. 120.

42.   Srinaka Jayaratne and Rona Levy, *Empirical Clinical Practice* (New York: Columbia University Press, 1979).

43.   Francis Turner, ed., *Social Work Treatment Interlocking Theoretical Approaches* (New York: Free Press, 1979), p. xv.

44.   Helen Northen, *Clinical Social Work* (New York: Columbia University Press, 1982), pp. 241, 248, 255.

45.   William Eldridge, "Streamlining Casework and Counseling," *Public Welfare,* 40:1:23-27, Winter, 1982.

46.   Hilde Bruch, *Learning Psychotherapy* (Cambridge, MA: Harvard University Press, 1974), pp. 83-84, 119.

47.   James Green, *Clinical Awareness in the Human Services* (Englewood Cliffs: Prentice-Hall, 1982), pp. 211-232.

48.   William Eldridge, "Affirmative Social Action and the Use of Power in Clinical Counseling," (Unpublished manuscript, The Ohio State University, Columbus, Ohio, 1982).

49.   Helen Phillips, "What is Group Work Still," in *Perspectives in Social Work Group Practice,* ed., A. Alissi (New York: The Free Press, 1980), pp. 192-193.

50.   Roger Kaufman and Susan Thomas, *Evaluation With Fear* (New York: New Viewpoints, 1980), pp. 4-5.

51.   Daniel Bem, *Beliefs, Attitudes, and Human Affairs* (Monterey, CA: Brooks/Cole, 1970), p. 89.

52.   Claire Selltiz, Lawrence Wrightsman, and Stuart Cook, *Research Methods in Social Relations* (New York: Holt, Rinehart and Winston, 1976), pp. 4-5.

53.   Alvert Farrell, Marco Mariotto, et al., "Self-ratings and Judges' Ratings of Heterosexual Social Anxiety and Shell: A Generalizability Study," *Journal of Consulting and Clinical Psychology,* 47:1:164-175, April, 1979.

54.   Teresa Peck, "When Women Evaluate Women, Nothing Succeeds Like Success: The Differential Effects of Status Upon Evaluations of Male and Female Professional Ability," *Sex Roles,* 4:2:204-213, April, 1978.

55.   N. T. Feather, "Positive and Negative Reactions to Male and Female Success and Failure in Relation to the Perceived Status and Sex-typed Appropriateness at Occupations," *Journal of Personality and Social Psychology,* 31:3:536-548, March, 1975.

56.   Kay Deaux and Tim Emswiler, "Explanations of Successful Performance on Sex-linked Tasks," *Journal of Personality and Social Psychology,* 29:1:80-85, January, 1974.

57.   Gail Pheterson, Sara Kiesler, and P. Goldberg, "Evaluation of the Performance of Women as a Function of Their Sex Achievement and Personal History," *Journal of Personality and Social Psychology,* 19:1:114-118, July, 1971.

58.   Roy Turner, ed., *Ethnomethodology* (Baltimore: Penguin Books, 1974), p. 45.

59.   Jill Kagel, "Evaluating Social Work Practice," *Social Work,* 24:4:292-296, July, 1979.

60.   Jeffrey Bracket, *Education and Supervision in Social Work* (New York: Macmillan, 1904).

61.   Alfred Kadushn, *Supervision in Social Work* (New York: Columbia University Press, 1976); and
    Rosalyn Chernesky and Abrahman Lurie, "Developing a Quality Assurance Program," *Health and Social Work,* 7:1:124, February, 1976.

62.   Alfred Kadushin, *Supervision in Social Work* (New York: Columbia University Press, 1976), p. 317.
    Werner Lutz, *Student Evaluation: Workshop Report* (New York: Council on Social Work Education, 1956).

63.   Ernest Becker, *Revolution in Psychiatry* (New York: Free Press, 1964).

64.   Robert Berger and Ronald Federico, *Human Behavior: A Social Work Perspective* (New York: Longman, 1982), pp. 18-19.

65.   David Mechanic, "Social Structure and Personal Adaptation: Some Neglected Dimensions," in *Coping and Adaptation,* eds., G. Coelho, D. Hamburg, and J. Adams (New York: Basic Books, 1974), p. 38.

66.   Virginia Satir, *Conjoint Family Therapy* (Revised ed., Palo Alto, CA: Science and Behavior Books, 1967), pp. 63-90.

67.   Carl Jung, *Modern Man in Search of a Soul* (New York: Harcourt, Bruce, 1933).

68.   George Psathas, ed., *Phenomenological Sociology: Issues and Applications* (New York: John Wiley and Sons, 1973).

69.   Carl Jung, *Modern Man in Search of a Soul* (New York: Harcourt, Bruce, 1933), p. 218.

70.   Henry Misiak and Virginia Sexton, *Phenomenological Existential and Humanistic Psychologies: An Historical Survey* (New York: Grune and Stratton, 1973).

71.   Janet Coye, "Michigan's System for Protecting Patients' Rights," *Hospital and Community Psychiatry,* 28:5:375-379, May, 1977.

72.   Charles Tart, ed., *Transpersonal Psychologies* (New York: Harper and Row, 1969).

73.   Alfred Schultz, "The Problem of Rationality in the Social World," *Collected Papers* (Vol. II; The Hague Martinus Nyhoff, 1984), p. 85.

74.   Harold Garfinkle, "Aspects of the Problem of Common-sense Knowledge of Social Structure," in *The Self in Social Interaction,* eds., C. Gordon and K. Gengens (New York: John Wiley, 1968), p. 129.

75.   Thomas French, *The Integration of Behavior: Vol. I Basic Postulates* (Chicago: University of Chicago Press, 1952), p. 51.

76.   Clyde Kluckhohn and Henry Murray, eds., *Personality in Nature, Society and Culture* (New York: Alfred A. Knopf, 1953).

77.   Arthur Combs and Donald Snygg, *Individual Behavior: A Perceptual Approach to Behavior* (New York: Harper and Brothers, 1959).

78.   Gordon Lowe, "Phenomenological Congruence in the Clinical Milieu," *Canadian Psychiatric Association Journal,* 20:5:211-215, 1975.

79.   H. Hildreth, "A Battery of Feeling and Attitude Scales in Clinical Use," *Journal of Clinical Psychology,* 2:3:214-221, April, 1946.

80.   Gordon Lowe, "Two Studies of Milieu Effect," (Unpublished manuscript, Psychiatry Department, Kingston General Hospital, Kingston, Ontario, 1974).

81.   Prescott Lecky, "The Theory of Self-consistency," in *The Self in Social Interaction,* eds., C. Gordon and K. Gengens (New York: John Wiley, 1968), p. 297.

82.   John Thibaut and Harold Kelley, *The Social Psychology of Groups* (New York: John Wiley and Sons, 1959).

83.   Arthur Combs and Donald Snygg, *Individual Behavior: A Perceptual Approach to Behavior* (New York: Harper and Brothers, 1959).

84.   Edward Tiryakian, "The Existential Self and The Person," in *The Self in Social Interaction,* eds., C. Gordon and K. Gengens (New York: John Wiley, 1968).

85.   Sanford Dornbusch and W. Scott, *Evaluation and the Exercise of Authority* (San Francisco: Josey-Bass, 1977).

86.   Charles Cooley, "The Social Self: On the Meanings of 'I,'" in *The Self in Social Interaction,* eds., C. Gordon and K. Gengens (New York: John Wiley, 1968), p. 88.

87.   Chad Gordon and Kenneth Gengens, eds., *The Self in Social Interaction* (New York: John Wiley, 1968), p. 303.

88.   John Thibaut and Harold Kelley, *The Social Psychology of Groups* (New York: John Wiley and Sons, 1959).

89.   Charles Cooley, *Human Nature and the Social Order* (New York: Charles Scribner's Sons, 1902).

90.   Carl Jung, *Modern Man in Search of a Soul* (New York: Harcourt, Brace, 1933), p. 218.

91.   Harold Anderson, ed., *Creativity and Its Cultivation* (New York: Harper and Row, 1959).

92.   Prescott Lecky, "The Theory of Self-consistency," in *The Self in Social Interaction,* eds., C. Gordon and K. Gengens (New York: John Wiley, 1968).

93.   K. Pernanen, "Validity of Survey Data on Alcohol Use," in *Research Advances in Alcohol and Drug Problems,* eds., R. Gibbons, et al. (Vol. I; New York: Wiley, 1974).

94.   Ian Cisin, "Community Studies of Drinking Behavior," *Annual,* N. Y. Academy of Science, 107:14:607-642, 1963.

95.   Charles Cooley, *Human Nature and the Social Order* (New York: Charles Scriber's Sons, 1902).

96.   Edward Tiryakian, "The Existential Self and The Person," in *The Self in Social Interaction,* eds., C. Gordon and K. Gengens (New York: John Wiley, 1968).

97.   Harold Anderson, ed., *Creativity and Its Cultivation* (New York: Harper and Row, 1959), p. 45.

98.   Cyde Kluckhohn and Henry Murray, eds., *Personality in Nature Society and Culture* (New York: Alfred A. Knopf, 1953).

99.   Rosalyn Chernesky, "Attitude of Social Workers Toward Peer Review," *Health and Social Work,* 6:2:67-73, May, 1981.

100.   See, for example, P.S.R.O. Basic Information for Social Workers (Washington, DC: National Association of Social Workers, 1976).

101.   Irwin Epstein and Tony Tripodi, *Research Techniques for Program Planning, Monitoring and Evaluation* (New York: Columbia University Press, 1977), p. 61.

102.   Robert Federico, *The Social Welfare Institution* (Lexington, MA: D.C. Health and Co., 1973), pp. 146-147.

103.   William Eldridge, "Conceptualizing Self-evaluation of Clinical Practice," *Social Work,* 28:1:57-61, January-February, 1983.

104.   Dennis Brisset, "Toward a Clarification of Self-esteem," *Psychiatry,* 35:10:255-263, August, 1972.

105. Lewis Leitner, "Discrimination of Counselor Interpersonal Skills in Self and Others," *Journal of Counseling Psychology,* 19:6:509-511, November, 1972.

106. Leitner utilized Carkhuff's 5-point rating scale in assessing discrimination skills of psychology graduate students. He rated the level of function of 4 standard therapist responses on 16 client stimulus expressions and compared the responses to previously validated expert ratings. R. Carkhuff, *Helping and Human Relations* (New York: Holt, Rinehart and Winston, 1969).

107. William Fitts, *The Self-concept and Behavior: Overview and Supplement* (Nashville: Dede Wallace Center, 1972).

108. Ernest Greenwood, "Attributes of a Profession," *Social Work,* 2:2:55, July, 1957.

109. Joseph Marolla, "A Study of Self-esteem as a Two-dimensional Construct," (Doctoral dissertation, University of Denver, 1974).

110. Several authors discuss the relationship between ego-defensiveness and self-evaluation, particularly in terms of stability of the personality. Oliver Bowman, *A Longitudinal Study of Selected Facets of Children's Self-concepts as Related to Achievement and Intelligence* (Charleston: The Citadel, 1974); Arthur Combs and Donald Snygg, Individual Behavior: A New Frame of Reference for Psychology (New York: Harper and Row, 1949).

111. Edna Goldstein, *Ego Psychology and Social Work Practice* (New York: Free Press, 1984).

112. Robert Boyd, "Conformity Reduction in Adolescence," *Adolescence,* 10:38:297-300, Summer, 1975.

113. Martin Lasseigne, "A Study of Peer and Adult Influence on Moral Beliefs of Adolescents," *Adolescence,* 10:38:227-230, Summer, 1975.

114. Elizabeth Douvan and Joseph Anderson, *The Adolescent Experience* (New York: Wiley, 1966), p. 187.

115. Betty Baer, "Developing A New Curriculum for Social Work Education," *The Pursuit of Competence in Social Work,* eds., F. Clarke and M. Arkava (San Francisco: Josey-Bass, 1979), p. 106.

116. Harold Garfinkel, "Aspects of the Problem of Common-Sense Knowledge of Social Structure," in *The Self in Social Interactions,* eds., C. Gordon and K. Gengens (New York: John Wiley, 1968).

117. David Julenson and Frank Julenson, *Joining Together: Group Therapy and Group Skills* (Englewood Cliffs: Prentice-Hall, 1984), pp. 233-253.

118. Gregory Bateson, *Steps to an Ecology of Mind* (San Francisco: Chandler, 1972), pp. 217-222.

119. Donald Ellis, "An Analysis of Relational Communication on Ongoing Group Systems," (Doctoral dissertation, University of Utah, 1976).

120. Aubrey Fisher, *Small Group Decision Making: Communication and the Group Process* (2nd ed.; New York: McGraw-Hill, 1980).

121. Julia Wood, "Leading in Purposive Discussions: A Study of Adaptive Behavior," *Communication Monographs,* 44:2:152-163, August, 1977.

122. Charles Cooley, *Human Nature and the Social Order* (New York: Charles Scribner's Sons, 1902), p. 156.

123. Robert Teare, "A Task Analysis for Public Welfare Practice and Educational Implications," in *The Pursuit of Competence in Social Work,* eds., F. Clarke and M. Arkava (San Francisco: Josey-Bass, 1979).

124. William Fitts, *The Self-concept and Behavior: Overview and Supplement* (Nashville: Dede Wallace Center, 1972).
    William Fitts, et al., *Three Studies of Self-concepts Change* (Nashville Mental Research Bulletin #6, 1969).

125. Morton Deutsch and Leonard Solomon, "Reactions to Evaluations by Others as Influenced by Self-evaluations," *Sociometry,* 22:93-112, 1959.

126. William Fitts, et al., *Three Studies of Self-concepts Change* (Nashville Mental Research Bulletin #6, 1969).

127. Robert Bales, *Interaction Process Analysis: A Method for the Study of Small Groups* (Cambridge, MA: Harvard University Press, 1951.)

128. Helen Prelman, *Social Casework: A Problem-Solving Process* (Chicago: University of Chicago Press, 1957), pp. 186-187.

129. William Eldridge, "Practitioner Approaches to Self-evaluation," (Doctoral dissertation, University of Denver, 1979).

130. Deanna Kuhn, *Intellectual Development Beyond Childhood* (Josey-Bass, 1979), pp. 35-42.

131. Donald Hansen, et al., "Peer Ratings and Self Ratings on Twelve Bi-Polar Items of Practical Counselors Ranked High and Low in Competence by Their Peers," *Journal of Counseling Psychology,* 20:5:419-424, September, 1973.

132. Arthur Combs and Donald Soper, "The Perceptual Organization of Effective Counselors," *Journal of Counseling Psychology,* 10:3:222-226, September, 1963.

133. Arthur Combs, *Florida Studies in the Helping Professions* (Gainsville, University of Florida Press, 1969), pp. 10-18.

134. Henry Murray, "Vicissitudes of Creativity," in *Creativity and Its Cultivation,* ed., H. Anderson (New York: Harper and Row, 1959), pp. 96-118.

135. Robert Carmichael, "Individuality in Research," *Scientific Monthly,* 49:1:514-525, May, 1919.

136. Marie Wirsing, *Teaching Philosophy: A Synthesis* (Boston: Houghton-Miffin, 1972), pp. 42-65.

137. Will Durant, *The Story of Philosophy* (New York: Washington Square Press, 1961), p. 100.

138. E. B. Titchener and Wilhelm Wundt, "Evaluation," *Science,* 52, 1920, pp. 500-502.

139. Sophia Lowenstein, "Inner and Outer Space," *Social Casework,* 60:1:19-29, January, 1979.

140. Max Siporin, "The Therapeutic Process in Clinical Social Work," *Social Work,* 28:3:193-198, May-June, 1983.

141. On identity as a core aspect of personality see, Erik Erikson, *Identity, Youth and Crisis* (New York: W. W. Norton, 1968), and Erving Goffman, *Stigma* (Englewood Cliffs: Prentice-Hall, 1963).

On the cosmic and transcendental selves see, Mihaly Csikszentimihaly Eugene Rochberg-Halton, *The Meaning of Things: Symbols in the Development of Self* (New York: Cambridge University Press, 1981), pp. 189-196; and Edward Sampson, *Ego at the Threshold* (New York: Delta Books, 1975).

142. On the inter-relationship of identity and social role functioning as the focus of clinical social work see, Helen Perlman, *PERSONA* (Chicago: University of Chicago Press, 1968), pp. 177-192; and Elliott Studt, "Deviant Roles and Social Recollection," *Leadership Training in Mental Health,* eds., G. Magner and T. Briggs (New York: National Association of Social Workers, 1970), pp. 72-92.

143. Charles Tart, ed., *Transpersonal Psychologies* (New York: Harper and Row, 1969), p. 62.

144. Charles Tart, ed., *Transpersonal Psychologies* (New York: Harper and Row, 1969), p. 62.

145. Anita Faatz, "Reflections on the Meaning of Process," *Social Casework,* 44:2:4-62, October 1963; and Jessie Taft, *The Dynamics of Therapy in a Controlled Relationship* (New York: Macmillan, 1933), p. 388.

146. Carol Swenson, "Social Network, Mutual Aid, and the Life Model of Practice," ed., C. Germain, *Social Work Practice* (New York: Columbia University Press, 1979), pp. 213-238.

147. Max Siporin, "Situational Assessment and Intervention," *Social Casework,* 53:5:91-109, February, 1972.

148. Urie Bronfenbrenner, *The Ecology of Human Development* (Cambridge: Harvard University Press, 1979).

149. Albert Bandura, "The Self System in Reciprocal Determination," *American Psychologist,* 33:2:334-358, March, 1978.

150. See, for example, Robert Morris, "Overcoming Cultural and Professional Myopia in Education for Human Service," *Journal of Education for Social Work,* 6:1:41-51, Spring, 1970.

151.   Ecological systems theory has been well presented in what is by now a substantial literature. See, for example, Carel Germain and Alex Herman, *The Life Model of Social Work Practice* (New York: Columbia University Press, 1980); Anthony Maluccio, ed., *Promoting Confidence in Clients* (New York: Free Press, 1981); Carlo Myer, *Social Work Practice* (2nd ed.; New York: Free Press, 1976).

152.   Andrew Shonfield and Stella Shaw, eds., *Social Indicators and Social Policy* (London: Heineman Educational Books, 1972).

153.   Andrew Shonfield and Stella Shaw, eds., *Social Indicators and Social Policy* (London: Heineman Educational Books, 1972), p. 14.

154.   Melvin Kohn and Carmi Schooler, "Class, Occupation and Orientation," *American Sociological Review,* 34:5:659-678, October, 1969; and Melvin Kohn and Carmi Schooler, *Class and Conformity: A Study in Values* (Homewood, IL: Dorsey Press, 1969).

155.   William Horner, P. Nelson Reid, and Marvin Okanes, "Manipulative Orientation and Social Insight: A Comparative Study of Social Work and Business Administration Students," *Journal of Education for Social Work,* 14:3:56-63, Fall, 1978.

156.   Richard Christie and Florence Gies, *Students in Machiavellianism* (New York: Academic Press, 1970), pp. 1-34;
       Niccolo Machiavelli, *The Prince and the Discourses* (New York: Modern Library, 1940).

157.   Harrison Gough, "Validational Study of the Capin Social Insight Test," *Psychological Reports,* 17:2:355, October, 1965.

158.   For example, see, Beulah Compton and Burt Galaway, eds., *Social Work Processes* (Homewood, IL: Dorsey Press, 1975); and Howard Goldstein, *Social Work Practice: A Unitary Approach* (Columbia, SC: University of South Carolina Press, 1973).

159.   Stuart Chapin, "Preliminary Standardization of a Social Insight Scale," *American Sociological Review,* 17:2:214, 1942.

160.   Alvin Toffler, *Future Shock* (New York: Random House, 1970), pp. 365-366.

161.   Eda Golstein, *Ego Psychology and Social Work Practice* (New York: Free Press, 1984).

162.   Joanne Miller, "Stratification Work, and Values: A Polish-United States Comparison," *National Institute of Mental Health American Sociological Review,* 46:6:720-744, December, 1981.

163.   Trudy Festinger and Rebecca Bounds, "Sex-role Stereotyping: A Research Note," *Social Work,* 22:4:314, July, 1977;

Jeylan Morimer and Joh Lorence, "Work Experience and Occupational Value Socialization: A Longitudinal Study," *American Journal of Sociology,* 84:6:1361-1385, May, 1979.

164. Robert Washington, "Social Development A Focus for Practice and Education," *Social Work,* 27:1:104-109, January, 1982.

165. Clyde Kluckhohn and Henry Murray, eds., *Personality in Nature Society and Culture* (New York: Alfred A. Knopf, 1953).

166. Morris Rosenberg, "Psychological Selectivity in Self-esteem Formation," in *The Self in Social Interaction,* eds., C. Gordon and K. Gengens (New York: John Wiley, 1968), p. 342.

167. George Psathas, ed., *Phenomenological Sociology: Issues and Applications* (New York: John Wiley, 1973).

168. Richard Zaner, "Solitude and Sociality: The Critical Foundations of the Social Science" in *Phenomenological Sociology: Issues and Applications,* ed., G. Psathas (New York: John Wiley and Sons, 1973), p. 28.

169. Leon Chestang, "The Issue of Race in Social Work Practice," in *Perspective on Social Welfare,* ed., P. Weinberger (New York: Macmillan, 1974), pp. 393-402.

170. Chester Hunt and Lewis Walker, *Ethnic Dynamics: Patterns of Intergroup Relations in Various Societies* (Holmes Beach, FL: Learning Publications, 1978), pp. 14-15.

171. Erich Fromm, *To Have or To Be* (New York: Bantan Books, 1976), pp. 57-115.

172. Jules Henry, *Pathways to Madness* (New York: Random House, 1964).

173. Inge Broverman, et al., "Sex-role Stereotypes and Clinical Judgments of Mental Health," *Journal of Consulting and Clinical Psychology,* 34:2:1-7, January, 1970.

174. Sandra Bem and Daryl Bem, "We're All Non-conscious Sexists," *Psychology Today,* 4:4:22-26, November, 1970.

175. Judith Lewis, "Counselors and Women: Finding Each Other," *Personnel and Guidance Journal* 51:2:147-150, October, 1972.

176. Nancy Schlossberg and John Peitrofessa, "Perspectives on Counseling Bias: Implications for Counselor Education," *Counseling Psychologist,* 4:4:44-54, October, 1973.

177. Joann Gardner, "Sexist Counseling Must Stop," *Personnel and Guidance Journal,* 49:2:705-714, May, 1971.

178. Linda Harris and Margaret Lucas, "Sex-role Stereotyping," *Social Work,* 21:5:390-395, September, 1976.

179. Trudy Festinge and Rebecca Bounds, "Sex-role Stereotyping: A Research Note," *Social Work,* 22:4:314, July, 1977.

180.   Benjamin Demott, "Hot Air Meeting," *Harper's Magazine* 84:2:23-26, July, 1975.
181.   Richard Cloward and Irwin Epstein, "Social Welfare's Disengagement from the Poor," in *Social Welfare Institutions,* ed., M. Zeld (New York: John Wiley, 1965), pp. 623-644.
182.   Max Siporin, "The Therapeutic Process in Clinical Social Work," *Social Work,* 28:3:193-197, May-June, 1983.
183.   Shirley Cooper, "Shaping New Methodologies," in *Perspectives for the Future Social Work Practice in the 80's,* ed., K. Dea (Washington, DC: National Association of Social Workers, 1980), p. 190.
184.   Max Siporin, "The Process of Field Instruction," in *Quality Field Instruction in Social Work,* eds,. B. Sheafor and L. Jenkins (New York: Longuian, 1982), pp. 178-179.
185.   Mary Richmond, *Friendly Visiting Along the Poor* (New York: Macmillan, 1899), pp. 179-218; Franz Alexander "The Principle of Corrective Emotional Experience," in *Psychoanalytic Therapy,* eds., F. Alexander and T. French (New York: Ronald Press, 1946), p. 66.
186.   Max Siporin, *Introduction to Social Work Practice* (New York: Macmillan, 1975), p. 264; Jack Rothman, "An Analysis of Goals and Roles in Community Organization Practice," *Social Work,* 9:2:24-31, April, 1964; and Neil Gilbert and Harry Specht, "Process Versus Task in Social Planning," *Social Work,* 22:3:178-183, May, 1977.
187.   Ruth Middleman, "Returning Group Processes to Social Work," *Social Work with Groups,* 1:1:16, Spring, 1978.
188.   Kurt Lewis, *Principles of Topological Psychology* (New York: McGraw-Hill, 1937).
189.   Allison Davis, *Social Class Influence Upon Learning* (Cambridge, MA: Harvard University Press, 1948).
190.   For a definition of "Macro-structural" Practice see, Irving Pergel, "Social Development and Social Work," in *Social Administration: The Management of the Social Services,* ed., S. Lavin (New York: Haworth Press and Council on Social Work Education, 1978), pp. 24-35.
191.   Stanley Cath, "Some Dynamics of The Middle: Later Years," in *Crisis Intervention: Selected Readings,* ed., H. Parad (New York: Family Service Association of American, 1965), pp. 174-192.
192.   Warren Bennis, Kenneth Benne, and Robert Chin, *The Planning of Change* (New York: Holt, Rinehart and Winston, 1961), pp. 11-59.
193.   Madison Foster and Lorraine Perry, "Self-valuation Among Blacks," *Social Work,* 27:1:60-66, January, 1982.
194.   William James, *The Principles of Psychology* (New York: Smith, 1890).

195. Gerald Gurin, Joseph Veroff, and Sheila Feld, *Americans View Their Mental Health* (New York: Basic Books, 1960).
196. Morris Rosenberg, *Society and the Adolescent Self-image* (Princeton, NJ: Princeton University Press, 1965).
197. Stanley Coopersmith, *The Antecedents of Self-Esteem* (San Francisco: W. H. Freeman, 1967).
198. Marian Radke and Helen Trager, "Children's Perceptions of the Social Roles of Negroes and Whites," *Journal of Psychology,* 29:3-33, 1950;
     Abram Kardiner and Lional Ovesey, *The Mark of Oppression: Exploration of the Personality of the American Negro* (New York: Morton, 1951);
     William Grier and Price Cobbs, *Black Rage* (New York: Basic Books, 1968);
     Alvin Poussaint, "A Negro Psychiatrist Explains the Negro Psyche," *N.Y. Times Magazine,* 52:5, August, 1967;
     William Hayes, "Radical Black Behaviorism," in *Black Psychology,* ed., R. Jones (New York: Harper and Row, 1972), p. 57.
199. Stanley Guterman, ed., *Black Psyche: Model Personality Patterns of Black Americans* (Berkeley, CA: Glendessary Press, 1972), p. 87.
200. Karen Horney, *Our Inner Conflicts and Neurosis and Human Growth* (New York: W. W. Norton, 1950).
201. Jean Piaget, *The Construction of Reality in the Child* (New York: Ballantine, 1954), pp. 349-361.
202. Frank Baker and John Northman, *Helping: Human Services in the 80's* (St. Louis: C. V. Mosby, 1981), pp. 18-37.
203. Jack Arbuthnat, "Error in Self-assessment of Moral Judgment Stages," *Journal of Social Psychology,* 107:289-290, April, 1979.
204. Lawrence Crabb, Jr., *Basic Principles of Biblical Counseling* (Grand Rapids, MI: Zonderman, 1975), pp. 22-25.
205. Lorna Goldberg and William Goldberg, "Group Work with Former Cultists," *Social Work,* 27:2:166, May, 1982.
206. Genesis 1:26-27 and Genesis 5:1-9, *Holy Bible* (Nashville: Omega Publishing House, 1963).
207. Lorna Goldberg and William Goldberg, "Group Work with Former Cultists," *Social Work,* 27:2:166, May, 1982.
208. Edward Canda "A Conceptualization of Spirituality for Social Work," (Doctoral dissertation, The Ohio State University, 1986), pp. 17-20.
209. William McDougall, *Religion and The Sciences of Life* (Salem, NH: Ayers, 1983), p. 87.
210. Erving Goffman, *Essays on the Social Situation of Mental Patients and Other Inmates* (New York: Anchor Books, 1961), pp. 125-169.

211.   Robert Lifton, *Thought Reform and the Psychology of Totalism* (New York: W. W. Norton, 1963), p. 429.

212.   George Beal and Everett Rogers, *The Adaptation of Two Farm Practices in a Central Iowa Community* (Ames, IA: Agricultural and Home Economics Experiment Station Special Report, 1960); and

    Edwin Flieschman, ed., *Human Performance and Productivity: and Performance Effectiveness* (N. J. Hillsdale, Lawrence Gilbaum Associates, 1982).

213.   There seems to be a clear conceptual relationship between the Protestant Ethic and a psychological "need for achievement." If different individuals, ethnic groups, and social classes within the same culture, as well as different national cultural groups, have significantly different levels of "need for achievement," there is an expectation of correlated variability in the role of objective achievement in building self-esteem.

214.   Charles Arlecton and David Klemmach, *Research Methods in Social Work* (Lexington, MA: D.C. Heath, 1982), p. 308.

215.   Joan Laird, "Sorcerers, Shamans, and Social Workers: The Use of Ritual in Social Work Practice," *Social Work,* 29:2:123-129, March/April, 1984.

216.   Many of the leading family therapists focus on a particular aspect of the family, such as (1) structure [see Salvador Minichin, *Families and Family Therapy]* (Cambridge, MA: Harvard University Press, 1974); (2) Organization [see, Jay Haley, *Problem-solving Therapy]* (San Francisco: Josey-Bass, 1976); and Jay Haley, *Leaving Home* (New York: McGraw-Hill, 1980); (3) Communication [see, Paul Waltzlawick, Janet Beavin and Don Jackson, *Pragmatics of Human Communication]* (New York: W. W. Horton, 1967); and Virginia Satir, *Conjoint Family Therapy* (Palo Alto, CA: Science and Behavior Books, 1964); (4) The "Family Game" or System of Rules [see, Maria Palazzoli, et al., *Paradox and Counter Paradox]* (New York: Jason Aronson, 1978).

    Also see, Murray Brown, *Family Therapy in Clinical Practice* (New York: Jason Aronson, 1978) for a discussion of family projection process and multigeneration transmission; for a description of unresolved indeogenerational grief see Ivan Boszormenyi-Nagy and Geraldine Spark, *Invisible Loyalties* (Cambridge, MA: Harper and Row, 1973).

217.   David Reiss, *The Family's Construction of Reality* (Cambridge, MA: Harvard University Press, 1981).

218.   Solon Kimball, "Introduction," Arnold VanGennep, *The Rites of Passage,* translated and republished in 1960 by University of Chicago Press (London, England: Routledge and Kegan Paul, 1909).

219.   Victor Turner, *The Ritual Process: Structure and Antistructure* (Chicago, Aldine, 1969).

220. Joan Laird, "Sorcerers, Shamans, and Social Workers; The Use of Ritual in Social Work Practice," *Social Work,* 29:2:123-129, March/April, 1984.

221. Sally Moore and Barbara Myerhoff, "Introduction: Secular Ritual: Forms and Meanings," in *Secular Ritual,* eds., S. Moore and B. Myerhoff, (Amsterdam, The Netherlands: Van Gorcum, 1977).

222. Van Cleve Morris, *Extentialism in Education* (New York: Harper and Row, 1966), p. 106.

223. Tony Tripodi, Peter Fellin, and Irwin Epstein, *Social Program Evaluation: Guide Lines for Health, Education and Welfare Administrators* (Itasca, IL: F. E. Peacock, 1971), pp. 3-23.

224. Ralph Turner, "The Self-conception of Social Interaction," in *The Self in Social Interaction,* eds., C. Gordon and K. Gengens (New York: John Wiley and Sons, 1968), pp. 93-106.

225. Van Cleve Morris, *Extentialism in Education* (New York: Harper and Row, 1966), pp. 101-102, Morris particularly stresses the environmental and cultural subjectivity of both actual and ideal knowledge in reaffirming the nature of education and learning as a "social undertaking."

226. Pamela Landon, "A Correlational Study of Diffusion Theory in Social Work Practice," (Doctoral dissertation, University of Denver, 1975), pp. 33-35.

227. Malcolm Knowles, *The Modern Practice of Adult Education: Andragogy Versus Pedagogy* (New York: Association Press, 1970).

228. Cyril Howle, *The Inquiring Mind: A Study of the Adult Who Continues to Learn* (Madison: University of Wisconsin Press, 1961), pp. 37-38.

229. Van Cleve Morris, *Extentialism in Education* (New York: Harper and Row, 1966), p. 106.

230. Robert Gagre, *The Conditions of Learning* (New York: Holt, Rinehart and Winston, 1965).

231. Claire Selltiz, Lawrence Wrightsman, and Stuart Cook, *Research Methods in Social Work* (New York: Holt, Rinehart and Winston, 1976), pp. 91-101.

232. Abraham Maslow, *Motivation and Personality* (New York: Harper and Brothers, 1954), p. 93.

233. Judith Nelson, *Family Treatment: An Integrative Approach* (Englewood Cliffs: Prentice-Hall, 1983), p. 21.

234. Dorothy Freeman, *Marital Crisis and Short-term Counseling* (New York: Free Press, 1982), pp. 2-7.

235. Cyril Howle, *The Inquiring Mind: A Study of the Adult Who Continues to Learn* (Madison: University of Wisconsin Press, 1961).

236. Van Cleve Morris, *Extentialism in Education* (New York: Harper and Row, 1966).

237. George Psathas, ed., *Phenomenological Sociology: Issues and Applications* (New York: John Wiley and Sons, 1973).
238. Charles Tart, ed., *Transpersonal Psychologies* (New York: Harper and Row, 1969).
239. Harry Sullivan, *Interpersonal Theory of Psychiatry* (New York: W. W. Norton, 1953).
240. Robert Gagne, *The Conditions of Learning* (New York: Holt, Rinehart and Winston, 1965).
241. Howard Rachtin, *Introduction to Modern Behaviorism* (San Francisco: W. H. Freeman, 1970), p. 60.
242. Van Cleve Morris, *Extentialism in Education* (New York: Harper and Row, 1966), pp. 101-102.
   Malcolm Knowles, *The Modern Practice of Adult Education: Androgogy Versus Pedagogy* (New York: Association Press, 1976).
243. William Eldridge, "Clinical Peer Group Evaluation: A Descriptive Analysis," *Alabama Personnel and Guidance Journal,* 9:1:15-28, April, 1983.
244. Martin Bloom and Stanley Block, "Evaluating One's Own Effectiveness and Efficiency," *Social Work,* 22:2:130-136, March, 1977.
   Charles Levy, "Inputs Versus Outputs as Criteria of Competence," *Social Casework,* 55:4:375, June, 1974.
245. Arthur Combs and Donald Snygg, *Individual Behavior: A Perceptual Approach to Behavior* (New York: Harper and Brothers, 1959), p. 149.
246. Robert Gagne, *The Conditions of Learning* (New York: Holt, Rinehart and Winston, 1965).
247. Joseph Schwab, "Problems, Topics, and Issues," in *Education and the Structure of Knowledge,* ed., Stanley Elam (Chicago: Rand McNally, 1964), p. 9.
248. Robert Woody and Jane Woody, eds., *Clinical Assessment in Counseling and Psychotherapy* (New York: Appleton-Century-Crofts, 1972), p. 316.
249. Cyril Howle, *The Inquiring Mind: A Study of the Adult Who Continues to Learn* (Madison: University of Wisconsin Press, 1961), pp. 37-38.
250. Arthur Combs and Donald Soper, "The Perceptual Organization of Affective Counselors," *Journal of Counseling Psychology,* 10:30:222, August, 1963.
251. William Fitts, *The Self-concept and Behavior Overview and Supplement* (Nashville, Dede Wallace Center, 1972), pp. 17-38.
252. Alfred Adler, *Practice and Theory of Individual Psychology* (New York: Haromt, Brace, and World, 1927).
253. Stanley Coopersmith, *The Antecedents of Self-esteem* (San Francisco: Freeman, 1967). See also, Joseph Marolla, "A Study of Self-esteem as a Two Dimensional Construct," (Doctoral dissertation, University of Denver, 1974).

Chapter Four

Clinical Inputs

Introduction

The topic of therapeutic inputs used in practice, is under-represented as a specific evaluative domain, in clinical as well as research literature. As the predominant independent variable for the clinician, however, there is tremendous need to study the general and uniquely-specialized impacts of this communication influence on clients, to understand interactive effects of counselors' and clients' investments of energy to produce change.

This unit of analysis is associated methodologically with various outcomes, but should also be compared to itself in various times of implementation, as used by different professionals in different treatment contexts; to include family, group, single client, crisis, long-term, short-term, co-therapy, and other situations. Each input should also be compared directly to the theory used by the counselor, to validate conceptual assumptions about client growth and change, to insure that theoretical prescriptions are operationalized properly and consistently via interventive skills, and to avoid effects of randomized inputs and reactive counseling.

This chapter examines categories of inputs, to illustrate questions and foci needed by clinicians, to comprehensively evaluate the impact of their input efforts.

Nominal Categories of Inputs

To understand complex therapeutic inputs, the words, feelings, gestures, and cognitions should initially be viewed as single units of behavior or non-behavior, irrespective of their specific real, symbolic, or imaged-by-counselor (or client) content or dynamic nature. In this conceptualization, an input's existence is assessed generically in terms of frequency of occurrence, positioning relative to other input units (pattern of initiation), relativity to client response, or its basic nature as verbal, behavioral, cognitive, or emotional stimulus.

Some clinicians may be unaware of the basic pattern of their input delivery, yet feel[1] that the nature, intensity, timing, and style of their comments or behaviors are related to theoretical specifications; and a determinant, in part, of effective outcomes with clients. This may be an incorrect assumption.

In thinking about frequency of occurrence specifically, therapeutic input is one operationalized example of an independent variable, and must be analyzed relative to the degree to which each unit stands alone, or exists in concert with multiple independent variables to produce a desired effect. Although some methodologists abstractly lump together large numbers of words and behaviors which represent lengthy time frames or holistic therapeutic gestalts, inputs must also be considered unilaterally, as well as collectively. This is necessary, since they can differ substantially from minute to minute concerning intention, dynamic nature, intensity, direction, growth-oriented impact, and quality of receptivity by the client; who may constantly change motivation, learning orientation, defensiveness, or adaptive posture in response to both internal and external input stimuli.[2]

Reiterating this emphasis, Hersen and Barlow[3] note that in experimental design, only one variable can be changed or manipulated at a time, before noting commensurate changes in client outcomes. When input, therefore, is not specifically defined and categorized, it is unclear why a client changes or regresses, or how much change in a targeted behavior, can be paired with similar units of amount or intensity of the interventive variable.

Despite clinical intervention as an ongoing process geared to utilization and capability attributes of clients, and inputs being phase-related and applied over repeated trials with cumulative effects (or withdrawn at selected intervals relative to client reaction,[4] and theoretical prescription); counselors must isolate as many active characteristics of inputs as possible, to form a plausible rationale for their activity.

This is, of course, complicated by intervening variables such as counselor expectation, client attraction to the therapist, nature of client problem, etc.,[5] as each factor influences input style which is selected. They collectively form a synergistic independent variable cluster, which also influences client outcome.

From a research perspective, although clinical treatment stresses individualization of diagnosis and therapeutic influence for idiosyncratic and unique client-counselor dynamics, the more input is unsystematically tailored to meet the client's needs, the harder it is to replicate findings related to targeted outcomes. It is necessary, therefore, to standardize inputs as manifestations of theoretical constructs.[6] A pitfall must be avoided, however, when holistic, integrated, and non-specific interventions are prematurely labeled as unilateral technological skills, since an illusion of specificity may artificially define inputs into behavioral units, which oversimplify and fail to capture their comprehensive nature.[7]

Counselors should understand the degree to which they deliver variously defined units of treatment, since this influences the following:

1. a client's temporal space to respond to any input; and degree to which multiple inputs control the therapeutic situation through the power of their presence alone, especially if linked together, so cumulative potency valences might overwhelm a particular client;

2. client responsiveness to specific words or behaviors, as a result of their singular influence as seen by the client separately from adjoining units of input; and as a function of time available for the client to receive a message, interpret it, and make a planful, rather than operant or classical, behavioral response;

3. the dynamics by which multiple inputs merge to form a new collective input, especially when units are delivered without opportunity to note singular, dual, triadic, etc. effects, as units are sequentially added with cumulating dynamics as they develop;

4. whether any input has a negative or neutral effect which, when merged with other positive units of input, catalytically diminishes or reverses outcomes of otherwise positive combinations of therapeutic stimuli;

5. use of inputs as planned responses to client stimuli, without allowing the client opportunity to behave independently, with sufficient freedom from input delivery to assess the stimulus from a client;

6.   potential for each successive input to be a dependent response to the immediately preceding input, or response to previous input collectivities with insufficient reference to the needs or response patterns of the client; which suggests that the longer inputs exist sequentially without environmental feedback, the more they may be perceived by the therapist as necessary, inadequate, or neutral.

As noted by one authority,[8] some workers do not analyze their input nature, presence or non-presence, syntax, positioning, or frequency, wherein they are operationalized relative to other associated units.   The dictates of interventive theory may, in particular situations, demand specific inputs or no inputs at all. However, with problems in viewing them during delivery, there is concern about the capability of any counselor to move sufficient distances from input behavior, to objectively assess whether those behaviors occur, conform to a theoretical design, and affect the client.

Evaluators may assume that inferences about the relationship between intent and content, or between content and effect, can be validly made. This can only occur, however, with a basic capability to categorize frequency, timing, and positioning of responses.   Also, autonomy of the input is critical, since units occurring shortly after client comments or client behaviors, may be conditioned responses to independent stimuli.   They, therefore, have fewer degrees of freedom to vary according to specific prescriptions of theoretical intent. Larger time frames of non-input behavior following client stimuli, on the other hand, suggest the counselor's ability to delay dependent inputs; or allow the client-stimulus situation to pass and then initiate a new, autonomous independent variable, which fits therapeutic theory and goal, rather than the client's predetermined counselor-response agenda.

One instrument for assisting supervisors and clinical students to become aware of absence of inputs and their specific nature, is the University of Michigan Practice Skills Assessment Instrument.[9] In this format, student interns are rated as to degree to which an input is present in their knowledge base or skill manifestation, to provide feedback about the basic nature of their activity. A generalized version of the scoring format follows:

- Behavior is totally present (or always present), when appropriate.
- Behavior is present to a large degree (frequently present), when appropriate.
- Behavior is present to a moderate degree, when appropriate.

- Behavior is present to a small degree (or is occasionally present), when appropriate.
- Behavior is not present in situations where the presence of the behavior is appropriate.
- Presence or frequency of behavior cannot be determined.

Although categories of inputs on the instrument deal with general qualitative dynamics of skills which will be addressed later in this section, they cover the following areas of client-related phenomena: personal attitudes and behavior, social roles, ethnic group influences, social conditions, problem presentation, client motivation, diagnostic statements, and treatment goals.

Other examples of specific inputs documented on the instrument, are these:

1.   "Uses the treatment relationship in order to promote rather than impede the achievement of treatment goals.
2.   Adequately recognizes the points of strain or harmony in the ongoing worker-client relationship, and relates these to his/her own feelings and those of the client.
3.   Provides support for desirable behaviors and expressions of feeling.
4.   Refrains from encouraging behaviors that are judged undesirable.
5.   Actively discourages behavior which has immediate and present danger for either the client or others.
6.   Anticipates difficulties in the client's environmental situations and prepares the client for them.
7.   Modifies interactional and structural patterns in relevant groups to which the client belongs.
8.   Uses existing interactional and structural patterns to facilitate the achievement of treatment goals.
9.   Effects appropriate changes in the individual's relationships to his/her external environment."

In considering presence or absence of particular skills or inputs, the counselor should remember that manifest skill units may not be parallel representations of units of their profession's base of knowledge, which suggests that clinical knowledge can be classified[10] to: (1) separate what exists, from values specifying what should come into being; (2) clarify separate domains and functions of information boundaries relative to outcome behaviors; (3) delineate dynamics of client states or conditions of existence, or client change; and (4) define degrees of empiricism related to input, process, or outcome. As practitioners view behaviors more precisely, they should vigorously examine domains of knowledge represented in the correlation between input and theory-related knowledge.

The clinical evaluator should also remember that absence of input at strategic times in the interview can have a significant independent effect, and there may be planned cognitive inputs (thoughts of the counselor) associated with a non-present behavior, which may require empirical measurement of a client response. Matarazzo, et al.[11] conclude that "non-content measures, either alone or more likely in combination with content-derived psychotherapy measures, appear to have a higher than average probability of furthering our understanding of process and related psychotherapy phenomena," with verbal conditioning often being a treatment procedure in its own right.[12] From a behavioral perspective, Bandura[13] demonstrates that modeling and vicarious learning modify responses, with a particular concern that client response may be predicated on simple presence of therapeutic input thoughts or behaviors. This activates an acute defensive response to unknown danger, or a predetermined area of client real or symbolic agenda, irrespective of specific nature of the input.

In any case, the counselor should develop awareness of the frequency, timing, and basic nature (behavior vs. verbal/nonbehavior vs. nonverbal) of their inputs, and their positioning relative to client behavior or response—not only on case-by-case bases, but also averaged over an entire caseload, to study systematic patterns. Possible input patterns are noted here, to help understand how important it is to profile this complex arrangement of significant therapeutic influences:

Symbol Legend

$CI_{(1-x)}$	= Client Input number 1, or any number through the last number manifested
$CR_{(1-x)}$	= Client Response 1-x
$TI_{(1-x)}$	= Therapist Input 1-x
$TR_{(1-x)}$	= Therapist Response 1-x
B	= Behaviorial Response
C	= Cognitive Response
NB	= Nonbehavioral Response
NC	= Noncognitive Response

Scenario #1: The therapist observes, or has systematic reports from an external observer, that input behaviors always occur immediately following client input:

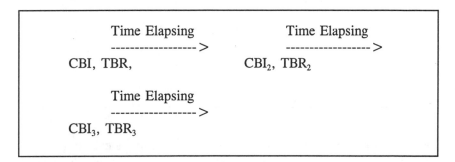

In this case, therapeutic interventions may be defensive **responses** to client challenges, or may be postponed until a behavioral response out of politeness, or some other deferential need, is rendered to the client. An example is this:

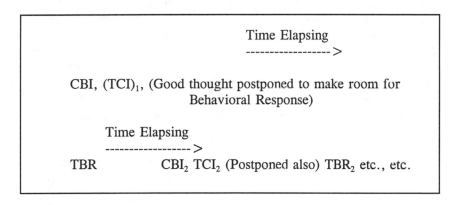

Scenario #2: The client makes inputs or responses, and there is a **delay** in therapist response or input. This represents a situation where cognitively planned inputs are not materializing (due to inexperience, ignorance of theory, defensiveness, fear, confusion over symbolic client messages, etc.), and their empirical manifestations may also not appear when useful. Also, there may be a theoretically sound plan to not respond to the client, allowing them to experience consequences of the behavior. This would symbolically be represented as follows:

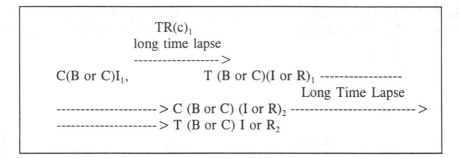

Cognitive responses may appear immediately, as noted by elevated TC (R or I), but these possibly correct cognitive plans may never materialize in therapeutically correct behavior; or may be the precisely desired input, without behavior, to help the client develop insight. The therapist or counselor, in any case, should understand the pattern in order to know what it means.

Scenario #3: In this case the counselor manifests a string of inputs desired to produce client responses, which may (a) lead to confusion about which input or combination of inputs have been causally linked to a desirable or undesirable response, (b) represent inefficiency in delivering a therapeutic payload, which could be handled in 1 or 2 inputs rather than larger frequencies, (c) represent progressive maneuvering to prepare the client for the eventual "punch line," or (d) represent therapist behavioral inputs or responses, to correctly or incorrectly perceived cognitive responses of the client, which are "sensed" rather than specifically observed. This process is graphically represented thusly:

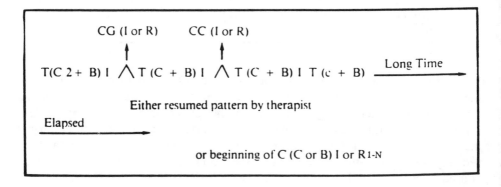

The possibility of client cognitive inputs or responses, is noted by elevated characters between the 1st and 2nd, and 2nd and 3rd therapist inputs, as discussed in (d) above.

Scenario #4: The therapist initiates a planned input and waits to note a client response, then initiates the same input if the response is not desirable; or initiates a new input relative to a different subject, to pursue an alternate goal (note that the counselor's thoughts occur and change intentionally between behaviors, to insure the most effective intervention):

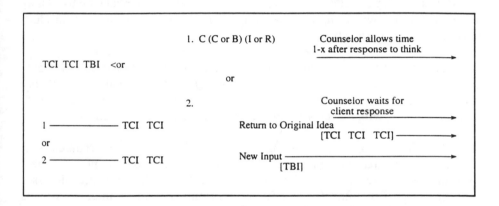

Although these represent only a few combinations of inputs or response patterns, they suggest importance of charting, or at least perceiving and explaining, processes of nominal input delivery, since this may have significant ramifications for effective service delivery.

The patterns of response can also be cross-tabulated with other theory, skill, or demographic variables, to note variations related to client gender, racial or ethnic groups, diagnostic category, time of day/month, nature of client problem, etc. Cross-tabulating response frequency and patterning, helps note biases exhibited with particular clients or under particular clinical conditions, also providing empirical data reflecting behavioral consistency with a treatment plan or theoretical model (i.e., less independent input in client-centered treatment, as opposed to analytic). By noting the observed frequency/pattern of inputs, counselors decide if there were corresponding or contradictory cognitive decisions related to their input behaviors, and inductively determine possible extraneous causes for any of their responses to clients.

One particular issue which should be mentioned, is the underlying value position of the counselor about the rights and options ideally available to the client.   Client **self-determination,** for example, might suggest that multiple proximate inputs by the counselor do not allow clients opportunity or freedom (because of input power and multiplicity), for a self-directed approach to their own development. In this case, spontaneous and independent client input may be reduced simply by frequency and positioning of counselor inputs.[14] If clients assume a passive role due to pattern of responses (also connected to attitudes of counselors), then information of significance to their problems may not emerge, because they have not physically (verbally and behaviorally) confronted and interdicted the input pattern. They, therefore, assume a deviant and possibly aggressive role, which may threaten relationship homeostasis and produce unnecessary client anxiety.

Another consideration in categorizing input, is the personal energy which counselors invest in therapy, as they interpret this to be correlated with theory and situation-related treatment effectiveness, concerning need to be energized to feel self-esteem, without regard specifically to treatment effectiveness.

Energy, non-energy, or contingent energy inputs can be important classifications to reflect goals and directions of work with clients, but may point to client resistance, transference, counselor bias, etc. Although the literature discusses "energy" in an often-undefined fashion concerning treatment intervention; its "capacity for doing work,"[15] or movement of any resting mass, translates to physical words and actions as the practitioner performs evaluative and therapeutic tasks. Energy, therefore, can vary in terms of direction, amount, consequences, and personally-defined value and utility, as clinicians produce evaluative questions or interpretive statements, or as facial expressions change to stimulate different responses from clients. The importance of differences among practitioners relative to type and amount of energy investment, is to learn why energy components are attached to various inputs, to understand energy-contingent values of work efforts, and to perceive practitioner assessments of physical or emotional resistance, leading to decisions to use certain types of energy.

With mental or psychic "energy,"[16] Jung[17] notes that flow of energy has a definite direction or goal related to decisions about personal competence, distinguished from the more circumscribed notion of tension discharge by the analytically defined "id." within the psychodynamic system.[18] The manner in which evaluative or therapeutic energy is allocated, expended, or reserved, contributes to decisions about potential effectiveness of specific interventions, and may be the foundation upon which professional self-esteem and personal judgments of competence are made.

As each counselor decides about effectiveness on the job, two dilemmas present themselves in terms of use of personal energy for self-evaluation:

1. Practitioners are encouraged by ethical norms and standards, to use substantial energy to solicit client feedback about outcome of treatment, make behavioral observations of client change, develop self-awareness of their own inputs into treatment, use research and evaluative methods to determine effects of treatment, and engage in relationships with peers, consultants, or supervisors who provide evaluative assistance. Although counselors may work hard (use energy) at evaluation, there is not necessarily a correlation between energy expended, and accuracy or effectiveness of evaluative activities. There are many factors, unfortunately, which limit the payoff practitioners receive for evaluative energy, including the fact that clients often do not change, or become worse, due to unknown characterological or environmental factors; or practitioners may lack skill for effective input, irrespective of the amount of energy used.

2. A second dilemma for the clinician, is to use personal energy in self-evaluation and intervention, which ultimately provides sufficient positive data to reflect competent service delivery, as well as self-esteem, professional worth, and personal competency. Although ethical professionalism specifies objective methods and interpretations of evaluative results, it is naive to assume that practitioners are completely objective in all evaluative circumstances, and do not actively seek and need positive feedback about performance. For practitioners with specifically pathological clients, or numerous uncontrolled environmental situations which make positive feedback difficult or impossible, there is concern about how to obtain evaluative data which is objective and valid, while also positive in nature. The practitioner who distorts evaluative findings, compromises personal ethics; while he or she who "tells it like it is," may be exposed to lengthy periods of negative feedback about interventive success. This is difficult with science's concern for treatment outcome as the primary index of client change and interventive success. In conducting competent evaluative procedures or seeking positive evaluative results; the nature, quality, and quantity of personal energy, are important components of overall success of self-evaluation, and should be used in categorization of various types of inputs.

As one example of energy utilization, the author found that clinical counselors he studied, made energy-related distinctions in evaluating input vs. outcome of treatment; with more energy invested in assessing input into treatment having little direct relationship to clients, but primarily involving practitioners' self-observations of what they did, said, or felt during interview sessions.[19] Saying or doing the right thing (which is good and presumably effective treatment), of course, also depends on how the client responds, and suggests an interactive effect between client and worker stimulus or response, as evaluative decisions are made.

In some cases, negative evaluative outcomes may be caused by practitioners saying or doing what they consider right, with little regard for appropriateness of these interventions with different types of clients. Processes by which practitioners invest effort in outcome or input are yet unclear, and it is uncertain how specific energy levels are used in either case. As long as energy is expended differentially along input and outcome dimensions, it serves the profession well to further understand dynamics and rationale for these alternatives; and fully appreciate efficiency and effectiveness, cost to the personality, payoff in self-evaluative results, and ultimate energy-related results of long-term service delivery.

Specific Types of Inputs

In addition to documentation of frequency of occurrence, positioning, and ostensibly independent vs. dependent nature of inputs, the counselor also should be aware of the grammatical nature of verbal comments (and cognitive internal "verbalizations" as well), and the nature of behaviors by which they are represented. This focus goes beyond mere presence, absence, or location of inputs, in describing their basic function in seeking verbal, behavioral, or cognitive reactions from clients; without addressing, yet, the quality or value/meaning of the response.

Verbally, the counselor may initiate declarative, interrogatory, exclamatory, positive, negative, conjectural, affirming, rejecting, assuring, skeptical, global, narrow, general, specific, long, short, fast, slow, focused, or unfocused inputs, etc., reflecting various natures and accumulations of words, end punctuation, and possibly category of response (verbal or cognitive answer, or another verbal or cognitive question when done rhetorically) desired. Several analytic dimensions of these statement categories will be discussed to illustrate their important connection to comprehensive input evaluation. Also, the reader should remember that nonverbal behaviors can be specified by type or characteristic, and convey messages to clients dependent on client selective perception and interpretation, concerning the effects of combining congruent or incongruent verbal and behavioral inputs, for the client to observe and plan a response.

Range of Input Types

Since each type of input (vocal statement or overt physical behavior) provides a variable stimulus for client response, the counselor probably desires the capability of implementing a wide variety of stimuli, to interact with differing modes, styles, characteristics, and problems of clientele. This is not positive in and of itself, irrespective of outcome; but suggests counselor flexibility in applying theoretical principles, by altering delivery of the independent variable in situations where desirable outcomes may not materialize. Assessment of various inputs allows open-ended content analysis of the full range of different categories, and tabulation of frequencies, means (averages), and other descriptive statistics to show which delivery style seems to represent the "nature" of the counselor, and which seem typically useful (due to frequency of use) for various clients. A narrow range might conversely suggest limited creative interaction or responsiveness with clients, or positively suggest the counselor has achieved standardized consistence with methods and theories, since the independent variable may not change significantly.

Dividing inputs into categories of statements or behaviors is significant, in associating specifics of client growth-related responses (insight, defense, conceptual change), with particular forms of stimulation (question, statement, etc.). Counselors, however, need to assess their baseline pattern prior to correlation with client outcomes, to make sure (a) clients are not selected who respond to a predetermined therapist pattern, and are a specialized sample, (b) clients respond to the qualitative intent of the input, rather than its consistency, stability, or wearing-down effects of perseveration (although this finding may be valuable also), and (c) therapists' range of inputs are not dependent reflections of range of client stimuli and, therefore, the client is conditioning the therapist, or preventing independent inputs. Input range should be based on client problems and theoretical goals, rather than how the client communicates messages and syntax, which are not necessarily the real problem.

Specific narrowing or enlargement of range of input types, also suggests that inputs are responsive to corresponding theoretical constructs which may be too narrow, broad, or confusing (possibly producing a more randomized dispersion of input statements or behaviors). A good exercise for counselors, is to randomly select any particular statement or question, and trace its origin to a particular purpose specified in theory; and then validate its grammatical form, based on nature of the client and goals of the intended therapeutic act. A theory suggesting confrontation for a particular defensive problem, when this problem appears in a highly-verbal client, may direct an interdictive and strong declarative statement; whereas the therapist discovers that a question might help reveal other ways of delivering effective units of treatment. The theory in use and nature of the client, should guide selection of input types, rather than the opposite, where the counselor "locks" onto a style; and either ignores input specifications of theory, conceptually makes it fit, selectively uses only parts of the theory, or chooses clients who fit the input style.

A rapid or highly variable change in input type (moving from rhetorical to real questions, to statements and back to questions, etc.) may provide a confusing foundation for the client's definition of self, relative to the counselor; or substantively alter the focus and consistency of the input philosophy, with no way of assessing whether the therapeutic vehicle is traveling down the main road or not. Even high correlation of input and client response (the client may be able to chase the counselor all over the territory, to generically match responses to stimuli), may not represent a healthy interpersonal relationship, or positive, planned therapeutic growth.

A wider degree or variability of the range of inputs also assists the counselor to associate or link unrelated thoughts or phenomena in the client's life, where they do not wish to envision an anxiety-producing connection. Sometimes (given insight and motivation of the client) this can be a direct connection between concepts A and B, by simple use of a straight content-seeking question:

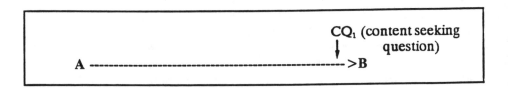

Other times, however, a wider range of question varieties might be needed to develop content first, and then rhetorically ask a second question to help the client reconsider the symbolic meaning of the answer (B):

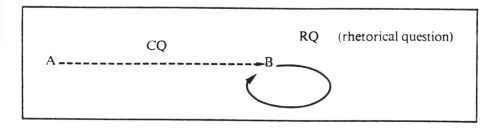

Some situations demand open-ended questions initially, followed by fixed alternative questions relative to several possible answers; and then a direct interpretive statement about one alternative, followed maybe by a command to force home a point about the process of even asking open-ended questions in one's life (this scenario has many different dimensions and meanings, which cannot be elaborated here):

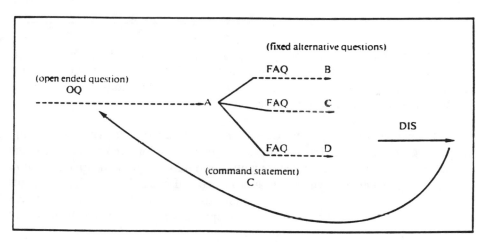

In the client's mind (and maybe in the counselor's), the route to connection between ideas is not always clear and linear, so flexibility in types of input communications may be necessary to help them associate ideas, or create new ones and test them for relevance within personal frames of reference:

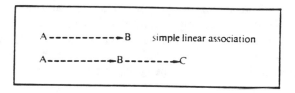

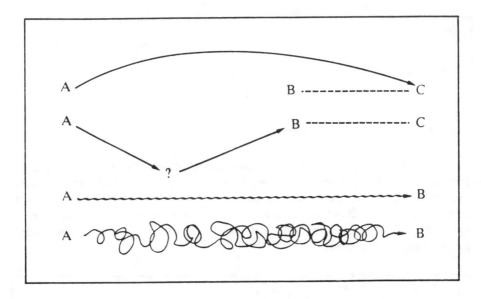

Clients respond differently, so communications have multiple, symbolic meanings. Each therapist does not necessarily deliver each input with the same degree of qualitative capability, so identically-worded questions sound very different, based on who makes the statement.

Many theorists believe in a direct correlation between the nature of facilitative conditions (types of inputs) offered by the counselor, and indices of client change;[20] especially action-oriented inputs,[21] providing communicative stimuli to induce change when and where it is appropriate and needed. A variety of inputs reflects a counselor's experiences, understanding and acceptance, rehabilitative ideas, powers of persuasion, and creative approaches to change—all important ingredients of the therapeutic experience.

Particular inputs may contain positive or negative denotations as a result of the words used, as well as connotations due to nature of the message or delivery style. Counselors might sound more supportive with statements and more formidable with questions (sometimes based on a client's previous experience with types of communications, such as a critically questioning father or mother), and need to understand typical stylistic patterns which accompany each input message. Frost, Becher and Graf,[22] for example, note that negative self-evaluative cognitions lead to depressed affect,[23] evidenced in laboratory analogue studies that induce moods via cognitive external manipulation. Velten's[24] mood induction procedure, requires the subject to read negative self-referent statements, whereby the subject experiences bodily sensations typical of depressed clients. The same mood induction can also produce elated or optimistic physical reactions. This includes development of new ideations, or the resurrection/confirmation of previously existing ideas,[25] from previous learning which could be a destructive process for the client, as a result of input nature rather than intent.

Another example of language style and nature comes from Eiser and Osmon,[26] who note "individuals may prefer to judge attitude statements expressing varying degrees of support for, or opposition to, a given standpoint in terms of response language which is evaluatively congruent with their own position on the issue; that is, they tend to make more extreme judgments when the term used to label the end of the scale closest to their own position, is evaluatively positive in connotation, and the term used to label the opposite extreme is evaluatively negative." Some authors[27] also suggest that evaluative language influences attitude, so units of client behavior are labeled (resistance, conformity, openness, anger, etc.), to give client and counselor a value position to which they are highly likely to react. This may represent a defense with motivational implications,[28] if they define inappropriate or biased encroachment through the labeling process.[29] The client may, therefore, spend time protecting the self, rather than in growth activity.[30]

Language containing some form of evaluative bias, may provide an unintended negative social stimulus in a relatively indirect, inadvertent, or subtle way, with the clinician having no intention of using evaluation input to exercise negative therapeutic power.

Frequency of Varying Types of Input Communication

Probably the most significant frequency-related issue for the clinician, is relative number of direct therapeutic vs. evaluative comments appearing in the context of counseling. Although it is certainly important to establish a congruent relationship between theoretical therapeutic goals and types of communicated messages to accomplish these goals, counselors must remember how easy it is to become preoccupied with orchestrated insight-producing words, phrases, sentences, and behavioral gestures. Meanwhile, they may neglect gathering progressive data from clients about how they perceive the inputs, and how they see their thoughts, feelings, and behaviors changing as inputs are received.[31] Although the counselor may analyze more general outcome behaviors, incremental data must be solicited from the client directly, to understand impacts of therapy; and monitor changes as viewed and defined by the client, as treatment progresses.

In previous research,[32] the author discovered that clinical counselors evaluated effectiveness most frequently by collecting behavioral feedback about outcome of treatment (mostly relevant to a priori behavioral goals for changes); but with little precision, standardization, method, or adequate instrumentation (see Figures 1 and 2).

The next most frequent source of information about counselor success was collection of verbal feedback, only 2 percentage points below the frequency of use of behavioral feedback. In this case, as with behavioral feedback, counselors most often (79% of the time) asked clients about overall clinical outcome, rather than collecting data about perception or effect of input into treatment.

Figure 1
Frequencies of Counselors' Responses Describing Forms of
Communicated Information Used in Self-Evaluation
(Total Responses = 288)

Form of communicated information	Number of responses	Percentage	Number of counselors responding	Mean/Mode/Median/Range			
Behavioral	121	42%	111	3.0	1.0	2.8	1-8
Verbal	115	40%	115	2.6	4.0	2.6	1-8
Cognitive	43	15%	32	1.3	1.0	1.2	1-3
Written	9	3%	9	1.0	1.0	1.0	1
Totals	288	100%					

Figure 2
Frequencies of Counselors' Responses Describing Verbal Information
Related Either to Outcome or Input of Treatment
(Total Responses = 115)

Purpose of Use	Number of responses	Percentage	Number of counselors responding	Mean/Mode/Median/Range			
Outcome	91	79%	44	2.3	1.2	2.0	1.5
Input	24	21%	19	1.4	1.0	2.0	1.3
Totals	115	100%					

In thinking about differential reliance on behavioral vs. verbal feedback by which counselors make self-evaluative decisions, and whether these foci are centered on outcome vs. input, some implications relative to frequency of varying types of inputs come to light.

One concern among counselors who primarily collect behavioral data, is degree to which input statements (or behaviors) have the proper nature and sufficient frequency, to produce behavioral indices of effectiveness. There may be an association between the types of statements used by counselors (statements about "acting" rather than "feeling," or comments vs. questions), and clients' association of those statements with either behaviors or less empirically manifested ideas or feelings, responded to with actions rather than words.

Conversely, high frequency of questions or comments relative to how one is feeling or what mental associations are operative, may be inconsistent with the counselor who avows interest in behavioral outcome data. This is particularly true if those inputs occur at a time (at the beginning or the middle) temporally and even conceptually removed from the phenomenon of client status, which exists behaviorally at the end (outcome) of therapeutic work.

In the author's research, behavioral outcome communication from clients, although valued by counselors for deciding competency, had an important limitation. Because information was communicated at the end of treatment, observations of client behavior were usually restricted to the final interview sessions, not incorporating long-term observation of behavioral change. Although counselors made decisions about treatment success, the validity of these conclusions lacked substantiating evidence once the client left the interview. None of the practitioners observed behaviorally communicated messages outside the treatment interview, nor questioned validity of "verbal" reports from clients, about treatment outcome.

In asking counselors to describe their "system" or "procedure" to analyze behavioral information, none presented standardized or systematic long-range procedures to compare behaviors, demonstrate degrees of change, or empirically decide about effectiveness. Decisions about communicated behaviors were subjective, arbitrary, and without clear process for conclusive decision-making.

The counselor, on the other hand, assessing self on the basis of client verbal feedback relative to inputs, might make decidedly different types and frequencies of input, along a fuller continuum during the course (not at the end) of treatment. These might be specifically worded (maybe as open-ended questions) to elicit information about the interpretation and here-and-now effect of other types of inputs made. Analysis of frequency and location of specific response-eliciting inputs, helps counselors confirm they are following their game plan for collection of self-appraisement data, but might also highlight discrepancies in this process.

Because counseling relies heavily on verbal interchange as the primary treatment technique, the 40% finding (Table 1) was considered low as an expected form of communication for evaluation. The author was surprised at the even balance between behavioral and verbal feedback (42% and 40%, respectively), particularly because many training programs emphasize that counselors elicit and analyze verbal information from clients.

The counselors surveyed seemed to balance use of verbal and behavioral information, although they questioned the relevance of clients' biased, manipulative, or defensive verbal reports of treatment outcome. They also need to develop alternate sources of verbal feedback from significant others, who possibly report more accurately on client progress. Over-utilization of supervisors and colleagues for this purpose is questionable, particularly because professional associates usually have little or no direct contact with the counselor's clients. Introduction of more co-therapy and supervision of interview situations, certainly might improve the relevance of this verbal information.

Finally, in situations where counselors are skeptical of the validity and reliability of verbal feedback from clients (select preferred behavioral indices, or adapt verbal feedback with various reservations or contingencies), there should be evidence of high frequency inputs designed to verify response validity (possibly more process- rather than content-oriented questions, or restatements of client responses rather than questions), and convert symbolically-coded (defended) client responses into positive and useful indices of change (or non-change) for direct determinations about value of inputs. Counselors, under most conditions, require a sufficient number of questioning-type inputs vs. content-delivery inputs (like confrontive or declarative statements), to collect data from clients about their satisfaction with treatment, and their perception of degree and adequacy of goal attainment.   On the other hand, if counselors believe clients offer sufficient numbers of unreliable and invalid responses, one must question the basic relevance of verbal media as a format for therapeutic delivery, since the verbalization of counselors may be equally suspect, and there would be no rational way of assessing effectiveness until the end of treatment, when final outcome behaviors are observable.

The Symbolic Meaning of Input Types

Each counselor must keep in mind that all communicative inputs are delivered from the context of the counselor's social role, viewed by clients as they have perceived communications in the past, and may have developed prejudicial mind sets. In this context, they assign to the therapist role: status, definitions of functionality, intention, and capability—related to what is said and how it is communicated through stylistic delivery, grammar, and context. Most authors agree that practitioners are not employed in totally circumscribed role sets[33] with predetermined outcomes (for self or client), but that there are a sizable number of variables[34] influencing eventual outcomes of roles, which cause some variability between different workers and between counselors and different clients.

Combs and Soper[35] note that "helpers" can be distinguished from "non-helpers" according to whether they:

1. have an internal vs. external frame of reference,
2. have a people vs. thing orientation,
3. view others as able rather than disabled,
4. view others as dependable, friendly, and worthy, rather than the opposite of these characteristics,
5. view themselves as identified with people,
6. see themselves as having enough, rather than wanting (in personal, physical or social attributes),
7. view themselves as self revealing rather than concealing,
8. see themselves as freeing of clients and not controlling,
9. view themselves as largely altruistic rather than narcissistic,
10. are concerned with larger rather than smaller phenomena in life.

Relaying information about these roles, comes through metacommunicative and symbolic nuances and patterns in the structure and delivery process, with further complications arising as multiple messages or inputs are sent simultaneously, nearly simultaneously, or with some form of command or aversive consequence message, which makes it improbable that clients will respond to clarify or question the intent of the inputs.[36] In this regard, the clarity with which a role is communicated to the client, may depend on types of input formats used, which in turn influence how the client views self as a responding and potential changer of thoughts, feelings, etc. Also, degree of flexibility the therapist has in changing roles (if this is therapeutically desirable), may also be enhanced or limited based on range, frequency, type, and symbolic undertones or overtones of message units.[37]

The important issue is internal validity for the therapist. Personality characteristics intended for therapeutic use, should be clearly and correctly represented within the style and type of communication, since these are not always congruent.[38] In many cases, the type of message conveys characteristics of the therapist which are negative to the client, and should be corrected if undesirable; or reinterpreted if style and type of input have incorrectly given a wrong impression.

The issue is illustrated by Duchn and Mayadas,[39] who note that understanding communication, demands characterization of configurations and behavioral sequences in interaction, in order to understand their variability. The therapeutic command to "begin where the client is" for example, has never been operationally defined, and offers no indices to help the clinician—if, when, how, or how much, this has occurred.[40] They go on to discuss stimulus-response congruence as a phenomenon representing accuracy of counselor responses to clients, in confirming or clarifying correctness of communicated messages, including symbolic and direct meanings of communication. This seems related to Thibaut and Kelley's points of view, that interaction is defined relative to the concept of behavioral exchange; with costs, rewards, and systemic outcome efficacy for each balanced exchange.[41] Congruence in clinical interaction has also been stressed by Richardson, Dohrenwend, and Klein[42] in their work on interviewing techniques, which cautions against clinical questions with no antecedents, or with predetermined counselor-determined antecedent agendas, resulting in confusing process and content in the relationship. They advise that counselors provide reactions to client messages, to increase interactive homeostasis.[43]

Correspondingly, research by Truax and Carkhuff[44] on processes of therapeutic intervention, discovered that content developed in highly-specific formats, was related to desirable outcomes in relationship interactions. Stimulus-response congruence can be coded as Substantive Congruent Responses (responses applying to immediately preceding response), Incongruent Responses (responses not containing content categories, relating to antecedent communications), or Nonsubstantive Congruent Responses (responses with no substantive subject matter, but providing feedback that the counselor was at least listening).

The concern for clinicians, is whether clients associate their own growth and defensive process with a change-orientation in the therapist, whether degree of congruence in growth energy is connected to congruence of communicated messages, and if this type of message format has a significant instrumental function in helping this congruence develop.

Often, clients want congruent communications as a form of dependency and defensiveness. For example, they ask "Do you think I'm a bad or evil person?" They expect a congruent and interdependent "no" answer as self-confirmation and parental approval; or a "yes" answer to affirm negative self-concept, retain the childhood safety of external parental judgment, or provide an aggressive object toward which anger can be externalized as an excuse for helplessness and fear. In both cases (yes or no response options), clinicians might refuse a congruent response, and either ask a question about process which is incongruent to client expectations, or make an analytic statement about process (why the question was asked) or conjecture about how defenses were used—to provide insight and learning.

In evaluating sequence of response or input types, a mismatch might be a positive index relative to some theories of intervention, yet a negative index if the client chose to view inputs as nonsupportive, nonunderstanding comments, not related to their agenda. Counselors may also make comments not correlated with the grammatical or behavioral communications from clients, and therefore miss the point by preventing even simple association between questions, answers, and body language. This could mean the counselor is not "hearing," or is responding to a personal rather than client agenda. The symbolism related to a therapist's characteristics of parenthood, capability, caring, attentiveness, or insightfulness, is always interpreted by the client. This is a coding model the therapist should uncover and understand, in order to know that when a question is asked, for example, the client may view this as parental manipulation and control, simply because it is a question, regardless of intent or content of the question itself.

Therapists who are newly trained may use lecturing or declarative statements as indices of their knowledge and skill, or rely on questions to cover up uncertainty about what to do in a counseling session, or focus attention off the fearful new counselor. Other types of statements or behavioral messages have similar or different symbolic meanings, and counselors should (through co-therapy, rehashes, and interactive awareness exercises) know their own category of input types, and understand symbolic meanings related to themselves and different clients.

It is also important, as noted earlier, that sufficient numbers of inputs be devoted to evaluation, to insure the counseling session is compared to some standard, and decisions about quality are made on this basis. Counselors should assess degree to which their comments or questions are designed to assess their own symbolism as a form of reflective or message-centered communication, as opposed to outer focused messages. It takes a special kind of message, delivered with unique denotation and connotation, to demand a response which may only evaluate the content of the message, but captures the symbolic and actual form in which the message is delivered.

For example, dealing with client anger may be very different, depending on arrangements of wording in a simple sentence, voice intonation, and follow-up message which expands, refutes, or attempts to evaluate the first message.

In one instance, the therapist question (TQ) "Are you angry?" not followed by any type of response (NR): (TQ-NR), may suggest to the client a diagnosis of anger, since an answer "Yes" without a therapist response, demands more client discussion; and an answer "No," followed by no response, may suggest the client needs to re-evaluate the answer rather than the counselor's question. Symbolic perceptions of counselor dominance, confrontation, or control emerge from this type of interchange, which may be good, bad, or neutral, when other dimensions of the relationship are taken into consideration.

In other cases, a therapist statement (TS) "You are angry?" followed by any type of question about anger (TS—Q Anger), may suggest some degree of control. It may simultaneously show, however, a willingness to relinquish therapeutic control to include the client as a participant in the evaluative process, although this option might have been denied with the initial statement about anger. The same initial therapist comment with a lowering of voice tone or inflection on the word "angry," may reflect more support, for example, than a stronger emphasis on the words "you" or "are," or no change in inflection for any of the words.

In another situation, the therapist statement "You are angry?" followed by a statement like "I just commented about a feeling you may or may not have," or a question, "Who defines your anger?" or even another statement which emphasizes the word "you" ("You agree with me that you are angry"); may be a two-part, associated message, which makes a content-oriented point about anger. This style, nature, and frequency, however, might also cause the client to reflect on the correctness of the diagnosis, the client's part in its development, the process of interchange between therapist and counselee, or other aspects related to the truth or validity of the first comment.

Although these differences might seem insignificant to some, many clients in heightened states of anxious sensitivity and awareness, attach entirely separate and very significant positive or negative symbolism to similar, but slightly different messages, which impact therapeutic progress or regression.

There is an important connection between therapist personality, interventive technique, client perception, and therapeutic outcome. The therapeutic climate is, itself, a potential change agent. Holt and Luborsky[45] isolate three sets of variables which influence outcome, that are communicated stylistically through technique and message construction: genuineness vs. defensive facade of the counselor, social adjustment, and freedom from status-mindedness. The Truax Accurate Empathy Scale[46] measures sensitivity to current feelings, and the verbal facility to communicate this understanding in a language attuned to the client's current being. This demonstrates a positive correlation between therapist empathy, patient self-exploration, and independent criteria of patient change. These messages can be communicated through voice quality, freshness of words, word combinations, and vocal modulation—all associated with differential outcomes, since they symbolize client and therapist values.

Although little conclusive evidence pins down the specific nature or outcome of client-therapist congruence (especially as developed, maintained, or terminated via language or syntaxical means), Borden[47] notes philosophically, that assessments of "compatibility" between client and counselor, when the counselor is using a diagnostic model that defines the client as pathological or dysfunctional, may imply that (a) the "patient" (Client) who is compatible with the therapist, is non-pathological as evidenced by ability to relate to a healthy counselor; (b) the counselor is really a "patient," no different in "pathology" from the client; (c) therapeutic power of influence, modeling, language, and communicational reinforcement may produce immediate client behavioral change; or (d) degree of congruence is the wrong assessment construct, and gives misinformation and distorted meaning to the relationship. Whichever is correct (there are undoubtedly more ramifications of this issue), the counselor must be sensitive to degree of congruence, how it is produced as a function of inputs, and its interpretation (or exclusion) as a meaningful dimension of therapeutic strategy and tactics.

These technical relationship concerns are extremely important, because "counseling effectiveness is determined to a large extent by the client's perceptions of the counselor's behavior,"[48] and as a "medium through which the client defines perceptions about the counselor, as well as perceptions the counselor acquires or experiences about himself (or herself)."[49] Counselors need accurate awareness of their own input dynamics, and client perceptions should match these, if positive outcomes are expected.[50]

Other research in this area resulted in confusing data, however, in that some studies find minimal similarity between counselor and client perceptions,[51] while others discern considerable similarity.[52] An important finding relates to discrepancies between the impressions counselors have of themselves, and high expert ratings clients make of these therapists, which may account for a higher degree of perceptual consonance, than when clients do not view similarly-high levels of professional expertise in their counselors.[53]

It is interesting to note, from data in one study,[54] that clients and supervisors agree more often about counselor behavior, than do clients and actual counselors who work with them. The varying potencies of client ratings can be viewed from a cognitive dissonance perspective, where they must cope with criticizing a helping resource[55] during periods of personal crisis. Other factors which influence symbolic congruence are counselor charisma,[56] power, mental transcendence,[57] parent-child transference, conflict and energy,[58] or natures of archetypes and mystical experiences.[59] The similarities and differences in perception of self and others, as these relate to content congruence or other therapeutic dimensions, provide important evaluative data which the counselor can use to understand the complexities of the counseling phenomenon.

Because so many theories are attuned to symbolic meanings of interactions, the type of input communication must allow various levels of symbolic definition to unfold, so these idiographic meanings can be interpreted correctly by clients and therapists, and meaning reinvested back into the treatment process. There should be sufficient degree of openness in hypothesis testing, as manifested by specific types and content of inputs; so interpretations of symbolism are accurate and avoid prejudicial error, through excessive loyalty to past diagnoses which may be incorrect for a particular client. Also, alternative hypotheses should cautiously be labeled as resistance, "lack of motivation," or "manipulation"; and must give clients room to think, feel, or behave in a style which is genuine for their life values, rather than being predominantly reactive to therapeutic inputs. Some layers or stages of symbolism within the interactive therapy relationship, are noted in Figure 3.

Evaluatively, at each stage of this model, the therapist's inputs with words and other physical, cognitive, and vocal "language," must check out the return or independent messages from clients. They should also lead them to successive steps in the sequence, so more symbolic messages do not cloud the scenario, and clients can clearly trace the steps they experience in the goal-directed continuum from initial coded message to final uncoded, more positive behavior. As the therapist makes an input move (as in a chess game), she or he must anticipate degree to which the move facilitates or hinders the next move on the client's part, while correcting distorted symbolic perspectives of either party along the way.

Figure 3
Symbolism in Clinical Counseling Relationships

T = Therapist Communication
C = Client Communication
Lines = Sequence of Progress
small letters = subcategories of symbolic impact
I = Input
O = Potential Outcome

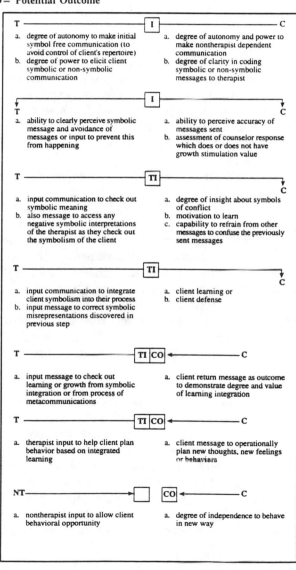

T ——————————[I]—————————— C

a. degree of autonomy to make initial symbol free communication (to avoid control of client's repertoire)
b. degree of power to elicit client symbolic or non-symbolic communication

a. degree of autonomy and power to make nontherapist dependent communication
b. degree of clarity in coding symbolic or non-symbolic messages to therapist

T ——————————[I]—————————— C

a. ability to clearly perceive symbolic message and avoidance of messages or input to prevent this from happening

a. ability to perceive accuracy of messages sent
b. assessment of counselor response which does or does not have growth stimulation value

T ——————————[TI]—————————— C

a. input communication to check out symbolic meaning
b. also message to access any negative symbolic interpretations of the therapist as they check out the symbolism of the client

a. degree of insight about symbols of conflict
b. motivation to learn
c. capability to refrain from other messages to confuse the previously sent messages

T ——————————[TI]—————————— C

a. input communication to integrate client symbolism into their process
b. input message to correct symbolic misrepresentations discovered in previous step

a. client learning or
b. client defense

T ——————————[TI][CO]◄—————— C

a. input message to check out learning or growth from symbolic integration or from process of metacommunications

a. client return message as outcome to demonstrate degree and value of learning integration

T ——————————[TI][CO]◄—————— C

a. therapist input to help client plan behavior based on integrated learning

a. client message to operationally plan new thoughts, new feelings or behaviors

NT——————————►[ ] [CO]◄—————— C

a. nontherapist input to allow client behavioral opportunity

a. degree of independence to behave in new way

Content Orientation of Input Types

The content of inputs represents topics or subject matter which the therapist introduces, allows to be introduced, or responds to from the client. The therapeutic dynamic change nature of inputs will not yet be discussed, although it certainly incorporates content subjects, but goes beyond this to affect client processes of dealing with specific developmental or conflict subject areas. This will be discussed later in this chapter.

In considering content of inputs in detail, each of the following content characteristics is important, and will be dealt with successively in this section: content relevance; content rationality; variability, stability, and timing of content delivery; time frame of content placement; internal vs. external locus of content; tactical or strategic goals of content use; individual or shared meaning of content; normative/deviant content orientation; interventive and evaluative content; and degree of congruence between content and theory.

1.   *Content Relevance:* Whether topics of discussion in counseling sessions are relevant, depends partly on the theory of growth and development which (a) is espoused by client and therapist; (b) describes and predicts client past, present, and future behaviors; (c) presents categories of significant reality, which the client conceptually possesses and potentially can use; and (d) factors in the client's degree of selective perception of content areas he or she feels are related to processes of change. Although there are many abstract conceptualizations of reality which represent growth-conflict phenomena relative to the client, evaluation is irrelevant if the client is not a full participant in the process. In this role, clients must perceive that specific inputs fit into their frame of reference, which describes their development and dynamics of thought, feeling, or behavior that must be activated for change to occur.

As noted previously, one evaluative dimension is degree of congruence between counselor and client perceptual formulations. A significant index of change, is extent to which the client accepts and utilizes a meaningful and relatively correct framework for explaining and changing their uncomfortable reality, or redefining self or environment so that more external changes are not necessary. In any case, the counselor must engage clients with content they can relate to, and either develop self-diagnostic and change capability within their own conceptual and lingual world, or begin a systematic transformation process using client-relevant concepts initially, replacing them incrementally with new concepts over which the client can eventually maintain perceptions of personal ownership.

Thaibout and Kelly[60] define content relevance as extent to which a counselor's response (defined as independent or reactive input) is perceived by the client as relevant to their substantive concerns in treatment. This assumes that clients' content reactions develop from, and are enhanced or limited by, their individual or cultural response repertoires as specified in their perceptions, expectations, domains of interest, and goals.

Also, Lennard and Bernstein found that similarity between client and counselor situational definitions, is crucial in therapeutic interaction:

> "When both members of a dyad are in agreement regarding their reappraisal obligations and returns, there is consensus or similarity of expectations, and harmony or stability occurs in their interpersonal relations . . . But when there is a degree of discrepancy or lack of consensus between participants, and these expectations are dissimilar . . . manifestations of strain appear in their interpersonal relations. If expectations are too dissimilar, the social system disintegrates unless the differences can be reconciled."[61]

In conjunction with this, when content expectations are not reconciled, clients discontinue treatment before goal achievement.[62]

A major concern here, is how the counselor makes accurate interpersonal discriminations related to contextual process, and client life concerns and frameworks. The counselor's cognitive framework and complexity are one dimension of perceptual structure, that relates to the ability to negotiate synthesis with clients. Some studies demonstrate, in the process of making clinical judgments, that practitioners who have high levels of cognitive complexity,[63] tend to collect, process, and use significantly more information "bits" than do their less complex counterparts. This presupposes that more complex practitioners assume few commonalities, and make fewer unwarranted assumptions about their relationships with clients, using a wider array of data for evaluative decision-making.[64] As practitioners collect comprehensive data on clients (information seeking inputs), they should understand personally how this information is organized and reflected back to the client, to check accuracy of content-related assumptions, and gauge client ability to validly envision and accept responsibility for ownership of material communicated by the counselor.[65]

Further, cognitively complex practitioners base their therapeutic responses on immediate rather than outdated client information, or stereotypical classifications. They flexibly shift content to correspond to client focus (which may be a detriment, if consistency with theory is maintained), and have a broader battery of input therapeutic skills.[66] In this regard, it is important for clinicians to develop awareness of the complexity of their own thought, awareness, and assessment processes. They should carefully review data they collect, to corroborate this self-awareness and professional style; or be more aware of areas where they need personal learning about their levels of discrimination, differentiation, and complexity, to avoid oversimplification of client content.[67]

In considering content relevance, there may be circumstances in which conceptually, client and counselor match up adequately, but one or both have difficulty communicating their convergent ideas grammatically (verbally) or behaviorally. In another instance, the therapist may not use inputs which have clarity or capability to define discrepancy, as the counseling interchange unfolds. This requires a structural input format by the professional, to check the meaning of words and phrases through questions, rephrasing, explanation through examples, narrative stories, analogies, and other comparative examples; and even direct confrontational challenge of the correctness of statements, to be sure of the client's idiosyncratic meaning. Some forms of therapeutic language may be highly specialized, "gimmicky," or specifically related to particular personality constructs, with little inherent expectation for the counselor to step back from this grammatical framework, to view its relevance to the client; or determine if the client can reword therapeutic concepts into his/her own psychosocial cultural framework.[68]

An additional contributing factor to the relevance of context, is ascription or attribution[69] of characteristics to the client, which may be based on having gathered incorrect or symbolically-misleading data, or may reflect personal designs and needs of the counselor, with little opportunity for the clients to refute definitions of their selves. Because of the linearity of many approaches to treatment, step #1 may have an incorrect major premise, leading to steps 2, 3, and 4, wherein each subsequent input may in itself be correct, but based on previously incorrectly defined parameters. On the other hand, all steps in counseling may inadvertently distort major cumulative parts of reality, toward the therapist's perspective and self-defined best (albeit defensive) interests. This sequence requires periodic pattern disruption to assure comprehensive[70] and objective points of observation, and to retrace steps to beginning assumptions—to detect errors in sequence or expose flaws in basic assumptions or conceptual formulations.

Narrow or incorrect perspectives of irrelevant content, may also be related to stages of role performance,[71] psychological status, regression, or growth, through which the practitioner passes in the intervention process; as they see themselves at various levels of success in negotiating engagement, being accepted, or making/facilitating change—which might even be a process of clients' shaping content of the therapist.[72] In this context, content irrelevancies may lead to client changes in behavior or role performance,[73] as a result of their modeling or social/behavioral learning. This may produce phantom content relevancies within an artificial therapeutic situation, not necessarily preparing clients to replicate their behavior (even if it is desirable), or understand decision-making in the outside world. Other variables noted by Rothman,[74] influencing roles and role outcome relevancies of clients and counselors, are (1) differential opportunities available to meet needs (real or symbolic) through expectations for role performance, (2) the ways time is used in the relationship, as this fits philosophically with reality and goal orientations, (3) various perceptions of ends vs. means, (4) viewpoints of non-goal attaintment and its meaning in the ongoing relationship, and (5) prescribed cultural behaviors and states of existence, for client and counselor separately and jointly.

The locus[75] of evaluation or perspective from which the counselor views the client, and which contributes to the relevance of input content, is partly reflective of whether the counselor thinks with or about the client. Thinking with the client allows room for their perspectives in (1) defining the problem, (2) articulating short/long-term goals that are attainable, with their motivation and energy investment, (3) clarifying perceptions of needed ingredients, to attempt problem resolution, (4) differentiating expectations of the counselor/client role performance, as part of the therapeutic contract, (5) insuring discussion of rights of the client for confidentiality, and protection from potentially damaging outcomes of therapeutic work (or nonwork), (6) eliciting input from the client about external influences or internal defenses, which they feel will impede progress, and, finally (7) maintaining final client-centered control of the intensity and length of treatment, including self-determination related to subsequent termination.

There is concern, of course, how inputs remain consistent with the counselor's internal and theoretical concept of the world, and whether dissonance occurs as the practitioner reorients her or his thinking, to match conceptualizations (increased content relevancy) of the client. Content relevance, wherein the practitioner has a theory and set of internal perspectives and principles, may ideally and effectively occur when certain conditions are met.

First, the practitioner flexibly moves from content to process and back to content, so central focus or balance can always be maintained, and goals are met by either method of delivering inputs.

Second, the practitioner uses intersecting vectors of knowledge, to match client and counselor perspectives along anchor points involving converging ideations, and some form of transferential indexing; so that the client has assurance that the counselor understands that they have a position, but can also perceive parts of it the same way.

Next, the practitioner develops inputs which transcend both client and counselor conceptual limitations, to evolve new concepts or shared cognitive positions in a relationship-oriented framework. Each gains security, by having a common base when they give up or modify parts of their perceptual framework.

Finally, the counselor uses inputs that insure analysis of processes of thinking, which view the negative and positive effects of working to develop cognitive convergence, and analyze how they individually and collectively handle differences in conception which cannot be relinquished, amalgamated, or otherwise converted.

The only other alternative, is for the counselor to be a-theoretical and devoid of personal positions and explanations of reality and psychodynamics. This raises questions about the possibility of any systematic evaluation, with no rationale for standardizing inputs or assuring a base of professional self-esteem and psychological comfort, with a highly amorphous and confusing basis for working with clients.

As noted earlier, some authors suggest that relevance of content is also determined by social and therapeutic roles of the practitioner. In cases of limited role set and inability of the practitioner to use a variety of sub-roles,[76] there are evaluative questions about ability to relate to a wide range of client perceptions, based on myriad roles they bring into the clinical setting. There is also concern about expectations that clients relinquish some or all of their role identity, to help bring content of the interaction within reasonably mutual areas of perception. Of course, for the client to relinquish unhealthy behaviors or perceptions, some change of role identity is traditionally expected; yet it is important evaluatively, to insure that the least amount of change occurs in the direction of the therapist's life arena, unless this is a role position which the client freely chooses as most appropriate.

Conversely, when practitioners exhibit wider variability of role repertoire, there may be danger of too much movement of the foundation from which inputs are delivered, causing confusion in adjusting responses to stimuli. Also, excessive change in the independent variable, makes hypothesis testing and cause effect analysis impossible. Practitioners who define themselves too unidimensionally, may "perform ineffectively by constricting the boundaries of their potential role repertoire."[77] Sometimes such limitations are intellectual in etiology (being familiar with only a limited number of specific roles), sometimes they are ideological (only certain roles are considered appropriate from a value standpoint), and other times they are part of stimulus-response negotiation of mutuality (or intended role convergence), in dyadic role interchanges with clients. One evaluative question relates to practitioners' flexibility in expanding and contracting their roles, and understanding reasons for manifestation of any role at any particular time, especially relevant to client stimulus or need. Content relevance is affected by the fit between role foundations and ability of counselors and clients to negotiate enough congruent stability, to allow the only variability to come from difference in content, rather than differences in positions from which content messages are sent or received.

A good example of this was observed in a phone call from a listener to the author's weekly radio broadcast on family dynamics.[78] The caller presented a problem in her family, relative to chronic disagreements between parents and adult children about religious preferences. The problem appeared to be role conflict related to communications of acceptance and love, and fear of role deviance and loss. Because of role differences, however, the family was not able to resolve issues about the content of various religious beliefs. Additionally, role conflicts were more anxiety-provoking, so the family displaced the conflict into religious doctrine, which kept them negotiating (or fighting), but insured continuation of the relationship. In this case, content relevance may have a defensive posture for fear of relationship and role disintegration; and agreement about content may not have resolved role and interpersonal relationship issues.

The evaluator must, therefore, be careful about which aspect of reality is dealt with, and be sure that alignment relative to one, does not become a smoke screen to avoid dealing with the other. They must also insure that either content *or* process be held relatively constant, for variability of the alternate one to be assessed.

When roles between practitioner and client are in conflict, one author[79] delineates possible strategies to help control negative influences: (1) emphasizing only one set of role expectations, (2) balancing competing expectations (compromise), (3) withdrawing from role performance, (4) changing the role definition, or (5) using aggressive and symbolic adjustment patterns, where lack of clarity and role syntonicity directly impact outcome effectiveness.[80]

In some cases, practitioners will necessarily stimulate or perpetuate conflictual conditions which produce conflict, because of their need to be analytical, assessment-oriented, and interactional.[81] In order to view the relevance and nature of content, they need to step back from both content and process into relatively autonomous[82] roles. However, this role movement or change may impinge on perceived or real relevance of roles as representations of concrete reality, or the client's ability to view the therapist in a trustful context, serving as the backdrop for real or perceived states of content relevance.[83]

As the therapist becomes devoted to the evaluative role, content may deviate from the client-therapist interactive and strictly therapeutic mutual mean, moving toward the clinical researcher's more abstract and/or methodologically engendered themes, so secondary threats to treatment might also occur. Some examples of these effects are noted by Thomas,[84] who emphasizes that demands of research and evaluation limit or interfere with the service nature of counseling; since design, orientation, or methodology intrusiveness, raise questions of content and process relevance. Some forms of intrusion which Thomas delineates, are paraphrased below:

a.   Delayed service. "The requirements of evaluative study may cause a clinician to postpone or interrupt service to obtain a baseline, to withhold or reverse an intervention instead of moving into maintenance, to delay work on important target behaviors while carrying out experimentation with other target behaviors, or to collect data to the point that inputs are delayed."

b. Incomplete service. "Clinicians may emphasize experimental criteria of change, but not service criteria; restrict behaviors targeted for service to only a few; restrict amount, type, and variety of intervention for the sake of the evaluative requirements; or restrict target responses to only a few of those that would ordinarily be addressed in service."

c. Imposition of extraneous requirements. "The research regimen often requires the practitioner or client to devote additional time and effort to activities necessitated solely by the research, which include measurement and data collection beyond what would ordinarily be required in service;[85] (sometimes accompanied by) an objective, scientific stance on the part of the practitioner when this runs counter to service requirements and is achieved at the expense of the client-helper relationship."

d. Adverse client reactions. "This type of threat to service includes a variety of negative reactions on the part of the client, that are occasioned by the research requirements. These might be resentment, disaffection with the helping person or the service, reduced motivation, or premature termination."[86]

Ways to avoid experimental negative effects, include sharing with clients that counseling or casework are also experimentation, evaluation, and theory building (so they can be research collaborators); and explaining the idea of manipulating independent variables, and noting effects on dependent outcomes within their own psychodynamic processes,[87] as part of experimental explanation[88] for growth, development, and goal attainment.

Evaluators sometimes have the flexibility of reducing the complexity of a formal evaluative design,[89] or reducing the stringency of their clinical data and assessment standards, to fit more practically into any client's agenda hierarchy and exploratory tolerance level.

In these cases, compromises may be made to retain clients in counseling, rather than deny them service because they cannot fit the demands of informal or formal evaluative methodology. However, this usually reduces the power of the design to accomplish scientific evaluation.

2. *Content Rationality:* The previous discussion of content relevance, pertained to the fit between the specific conceptual styles and agendas of the

practitioner and client.   This section is similar, but more philosophic, addressing concerns about overarching idealistic therapeutic goals, and representing life spaces within which clients safely function after therapy, without serious risk of deviance or threats to psychosocial survival in their real world environment.

This discussion concerns social responsibility of counselors conflictingly caught between their roles as idealistic social advocates, and technicians, to improve client processes of adaptation to the environment.

There are always conflicts between loyalty to self, client, professional norms, and social obligations, all of which demand deferred gratification, alteration of personal need priorities, handling frustration, and engaging in agonizing inner debate over right and wrong interpretations of practice:

"Part of the neglect of the concept of responsibility in therapy may stem from current social pressure to 'do your own thing,' to 'let it all hang out,' and possibly from some tendency related to increased urbanization and depersonalization, which may promote callousness or indifference to the suffering of others.   Part also may be due to the therapist who, after coping with considerable resistance on the part of the client, will settle with a sense of relief for a breakthrough in self-awareness as though this were an end in itself.   Part of this neglect of responsibility may come from the unconscious alignment of therapist with client in an attack on certain key figures, and part may come from a mixture of inexperience and fear—an inexperience that has not yet given the novice therapist sufficient opportunity to see how actions must be connected to feelings, and the fear that demanding that the client be responsible for the effects of his/her feelings, may be too threatening, and the therapist will therefore 'lose the client.'

In fact, it is not always easy, especially for a beginning therapist, to reach and stay with the client's strong feelings, which may be experienced as overpowering to the therapist.   Therefore, the therapist may view the mere expression of feeling as a triumph in itself and not think of how the client will then use (or misuse) the newly released feelings."[90]

Also, professional orientations toward engagement between therapist and client in process, suggest some exclusionary attitudes about final outcomes, and result in some irresponsibility and neglect relative to therapeutic effects:

> "Patients, it should be noted, perceived the analytic alliance as newly acquired 'power' to gratify themselves, and some patients exploit this new tool at their disposal to manipulate their environment, thus exacerbating the distress to the family."[91]

There must always be concern about the possible myth concerning the counselor's objective position or neutral value investments,[92] as well as awareness of ways this bias evolves into communicational content, to influence nature and direction of therapeutic work.[93]

Reactions against this judgmental process may be equally irresponsible, in the case of a counselor's assumption that nonjudgmental questioning or conjecturing to identify issues or conflicts will, in and of itself, produce insight; while neglecting to point out client behavioral or attitude destructiveness which may require some form of judgmental definition. Also, client development requires longitudinal interplay of therapeutic perceptions and interactive behaviors, which can probably never be measured accurately, on any one scale or circumscribed observational paradigm.

As clients expand therapy-related influence into their own social network, the number of influential variables expands, and may complicate the assessment and interventive picture due to geometric enlargement of actions, reactions, and counteractions, that may have been due to specific counselor input.

Regarding the responsibility that each counselor possesses relative to therapeutic power of influence (also to be addressed in a later section), some thoughts about the macro environment may be helpful as a comparative mirror for therapeutic inputs. In today's world of harsh realities, adaptation to the real world may require attitudes, feelings, and behaviors, much different from those taught in idealistic therapy sessions. The humanistic qualities of honest relationships, interpersonal trust, clear communications, and absence of defense, to mention only a few, may be the least desirable, practical, and effective modes of survival for clients. For these individuals, application of psychologically "healthy" behaviors, may create dysfunctional situations or even failure, in organizations or social situations not operating on similar idealistic principles.

In addition, philosophic values and reality interpretations of the therapist, may not even corroborate clients' own experiences of growth and development in the world as it actually is for them, in past or present dimensions or psychosocial representations.

How clinicians integrate their own real or ideal concepts of the world in relationships with clients, and define "adaptation" within social environment, lays the rational content-oriented foundation for the client's learning, skill development, attitude adjustment, and overall successful therapeutic experience.

The counselor must scrutinize direct or indirect communication of values to clients within characteristics of feeling, cognitive, or behavioral options, which the therapist supports as legitimate therapeutic goals, and which contribute to the definition of health or pathology as a diagnostic cornerstone of clinical counseling.

Content rationality should be examined in several areas:

The first and most basic, is communication of unrealistic hope or optimism to reassure clients,[94] when there is a questionable assumption that the environment will yield opportunities for them to achieve fantasized hopes.

Another situation occurs when counselors work with clients to identify, express, understand, accept, or change conflictual, hidden, or unacceptable feelings, to enhance self-management and develop insight.

In processes of freeing feelings and emotional expression, however, the counselor exercises considerable authoritative power in loco parentis,[95] of "inducing or reinforcing attitudes" associated with emotional discharge; and at least tacitly suggests that the client's social environment might be interested, supportive, or positively judgmental about affective expression:

> "The counselor offers a corrective experience to his (her) clients when he (she) demonstrates that such things as anger, sexual drive, feelings of inferiority . . . will be understood, not condemned or rejected."[96]

Although free healthy expression of feeling may enhance relationships in close-knit primary groups and families, today's often-impersonal world may discourage sensitivity of self-disclosure:

"The disorders of our society, resulting from radical change, invade and infect our daily family and community life. These disorders include the combined impact of technology, a state of continuous war, racial conflict, crowding, violence, the invasion of personal freedom, the decline of humanistic and spiritual values, and the loss of human connectedness. From these influences emerge the 'mass man,' the orientation to power, manipulation, acquisition, and a trend toward depersonalization . . . People are being mechanized, dehumanized, brutalized . . . and they no longer seem to care."[97]

The counselor who fosters emotional self-expression in clients, without introducing honest orientation to environmental limitations, and teaching guidelines for selective emotional response (survival skills), may provide detrimental services to his or her constituents.

A final component of clinical counseling, necessitating a rationality content screening, is the client's restructuring, clarification, testing out, modification, or relearning of cognitive thoughts or thought patterns—to produce more "rational,"[98] less constricted, conflict- or guilt-free,[99] more conscious (not repressed),[100] or less transferential[101] ideations, which improve psychosocial adaptation:

"It is a premise of counseling that the intellectual and emotional understanding that the client works out within the therapeutic process will carry over to current and future life experience . . . with the assumption that what is learned will have general applicability outside the counseling situation."[102]

Clients who are not severely pathological or psychotic, may become frustrated seeking sensible explanations of the world's multicausal and multicorrelated events, many of which are incorrectly distorted or dishonestly portrayed to the public.[103] On the other hand, clients also suffer from awareness of true but painful reality, from which they could possibly escape through their creative delusions, and conceptual alterations of personal circumstances. Cognitive restructuring may remove defensive thought content or processes, which could be necessary for survival in environments which are hostile, personally degrading, or otherwise anxiety-provoking.

For the clinician, the ethical dilemma involves competing personal and professional needs to reduce suffering on the one hand, and to help clients develop less "pathological" perspectives about reality (as one symbol of psychic health) on the other:

> "The real problem has to do with the revelation or protection of ourselves and others, leading them (children) astray or enabling them to walk in a clear direction. The fundamental question is, under what conditions do we abandon shame and allow the truth to come out?"[104]

In concluding, emotional or cognitive work with clients resulting in specific behavioral changes, in which client visibility and interconnectedness in social systems impact the equilibrium of other individuals; may significantly influence the client's opportunity to adapt and fully benefit from counseling outcomes. Obviously, some clients who occupy more public[105] social roles through employment, community activity, or school, may have less opportunity for realization of idealistic and unrealistic thoughts, feelings, or behaviors. This is because an increased number of individuals (social roles and positions) contribute to definitions of reality and the power of social systems, to control identity and reality of individual constituent members. A client who follows idealistic and unreal therapeutic objectives while occupying highly-social roles, could threaten the security of other individuals in the system who must also survive, and who reciprocally meet the emotional needs of the client in nonthreatening situations. The client risks assuming overt deviant roles within the system, whereby expectations and outcomes are predetermined by formal or informal norms, which disadvantage clients who attempt to "grow" beyond tolerance limits and boundaries of their respective social environments.[106]

Individuals more isolated from these complex interconnected roles, may have an easier time developing "ideally healthy" feeling behavior configurations, with less reliance on pathological societal institutions for meeting emotional and survival needs. Additionally, their distance from these systems allows deviant "healthy" roles, without negative repercussions and punishment from systems defending their own equilibrium and existence.

3. *Variability, Stability and Duration of Content:* Association between scientific theory and clinical practice, is partly formulated through use of experimental philosophy to help define specific target behaviors, learn what factors control those behaviors, and determine the best technique to bring about immediate and long-term success.[107]

These scientific and evaluative processes have requirements and consequences which impact both client and counselor,[108] and inherently involve alteration, manipulation, introduction, withdrawal, and modification of inputs as independent variables; to create differential conditions under which outcomes can be measured and decisions made about them. Evaluation of psychological and social adaptation is designed to insure that desired change does occur, but also to demonstrate which interventions work with particular counselors, clients, and targeted behaviors.

With consumer-related service demands of clinical practice, the therapist, caseworker, or counselor may try a variety of different techniques (jointly or in serial fashion) to produce results;[109] and may be pressured to make rapid or increased numbers of changes, when preliminary clinical data reveals that desired results are not produced,[110] or clients actually regress. These changes include alterations in content components of inputs, where alternating designs to find the right input content for a particular client in his/her unique social setting, often compromise goals of both practice and research. This happens through the confounding effects of multiple inputs occurring at the same time as a result of uncontrolled development with cumulative input effects, or client idiosyncratic response to contradictory inputs, which are initially exclusive or cancel each other out.[111] This is complicated by a tendency among some counselors to employ different, eclectic techniques to suit different problems,[112] or to select clients to fit the method, rather than adapting the method or using consistent methods, and allowing variation to occur in actual valid outcomes (good or bad).

In addition to rationales for varying the nature or presence of the independent variable, counselors also consciously or unconsciously vary their content (inputs) in response to client communicative stimuli, or decisions about effectiveness of, or need for, particular interventions not necessarily associated with outcomes. Some research finds an association between timing of response to clients, and perceptual field of the therapist,[113] which suggests timing and nature of content may be related to perceptual, rather than theoretical or methodological agenda. This brings up concerns about congruence between client-therapist perceptual fields, influencing selection and manifestation of both independent and dependent variables, and the possibility of viewing content as to its relationship to client need, agenda, and therapeutic goal.

Lack of content stability (including stable transitions) between topical areas, may sufficiently confuse the client to (1) produce artificial outcome responses, to control anxiety relative to the therapeutic relationship, (2) cause deceptive variability in client content, leading to incorrect diagnostic impressions as the client attempts to follow confusing (maybe random to them) cues of the therapist, or (3) inhibit relationship bonding and trust, as the client envisions his/her own instability in the therapist (not necessarily a protective defense, but correct identification). This also occurs when the client correctly realizes that the counselor does not have a systematic plan or direction, to formulate an effective helping effort.

Content which is unstable, is difficult to associate with prescriptions of a theory of intervention, and is equally unreliable as a correlate or causal factor in dependent variable outcomes. This is true because this content may be confusing for the client to think about, internalize, and plan an adaptive or maladaptive response; which can then be analyzed as an index of change in association with some factor of intervention. On the other hand, there may periodically be a rationale for varying the content in rapid fashion, to test the client's perceptive, receptive, cognitive, and communicative ability, or provide therapeutic experiences relative to some conflict-oriented goal. In these cases, the counselor should have a clear rationale for content variation, and identify empirically and theoretically the principles and exact dynamics involved, so this process can be consistently followed to produce valid and significant outcome client responses.

Length of content (duration or repetitions of the same object, or length of silences after subject introduction to communicate its continuity through time) is equally significant, as it does or does not allow clients opportunity to consider its meaning and implications. It is also important relative to client response, which gives the counselor reasonable grounds to assume accuracy of therapeutic communication, correctness of message reception, and significance of response as a reflection of relevant concerns. Counselors can obtain feedback about the stability of content, by doing a content analysis of audio tapes to document numbers and types of content used in a counseling session, and empirically record the number of changes and the times and circumstances of change. These therapeutic inputs provide backdrops to measure client response and interpretive decisions.

Qualitative interpretation of clinical phenomena appears to be some function of the extent to which the therapist controls, organizes, plans, places limits on, or holds constant the vast array of verbal and behavioral responses or inputs,[114] from which the client chooses and reciprocally selects a response.[115] In an article on task-centered casework which focuses on specific problems, Blizinsky and Reid[116] note that direct attention to the problem, is directly associated with positive change in the target phenomenon, which presupposed convergence of client and counselor perceptions of therapeutic, behavioral, and attitudinal domains;[117] where discrepancies have been resolved in dynamic interactions[118] and therapeutic socialization.[119]

In analysis of case situations with a topical coding scheme, Blizinsky and Reid found that counselors and clients demonstrated congruent task-centered discussion 53% of the time, with 17% of communications not related to client problems at all. They also note that counselors introduce more counseling and theory-related topics than clients, with 62% of worker-related topics related to the task-centered model. There is a significant correlation between degree of focus on target problems and degree of change in these problems, as corroborated by counselors and independent judges. However, continuity (time spent on topic) of problem focus is not significantly correlated with problem change.

Some interesting variants of these findings are that clients and counselors may be inclined to discuss problems already in process of positive change; and perception of target change may be related to amount of time spent dealing with the target in therapeutic discussion, not directly linked to objective criteria of behavioral improvement. It is also interesting to speculate about different effects of cumulative focus on problems, as opposed to continuous concentrated focus at singular times.

In some cases, due to practitioner hypothesis, accurate data about ineffective treatment outcomes, or concerns by self or agency about treatment cost efficiency; content may receive alternated or reduced time (either fewer separate content introductions, or reduced longitude of each discussion). Issues of depth of client integration, potency of influence, or communication and awareness of issue seriousness, are jeopardized due to lack of topic continuity. Of course, there is no certainty that length of content manifestation insures client change, particularly because resistance to "parental" domination, cognitive overload, or some other defensive factor, may lessen the effect. In some cases, the therapist may feel that the intermittent, pulsating effect is better, where content introductions are timed to relate to points in the client's agenda where insight is deemed more probable, and/or where defenses are reduced. Ostensibly, this may appear as uncoordinated and unstable content, *due* to changes during time out periods where content is not being introduced. It may, in fact, be an example of sophisticated and intricate planning, with comprehensive knowledge of client agenda, style, and receptivity.

One question about efficiency of treatment concerns the cost, relative to time and energy, to attain a distant vs. immediate goal.[120] Although achievement of desirable behaviors within a short time, appears theoretically and practically reasonable, energy expenditure should also be predicated on data which suggest probability of success relative to actual empirical outcome, rather than symbolic long-term meaning of behaviors exclusively. Deferring gratification (of positive data) in clinical counseling may result in allocation of energy in the wrong directions, with possibilities of having to begin all over again, to initiate a route to more ensurable behavioral changes.

Concern with practical relevancy may cause the counselor to be reluctant to push the vulnerable client, although some gambling may be required to formulate and test a clinical hypothesis, especially since growth means movement to a higher and unknown level of thought, feeling, or behavior.

4. *Content Time Frame:* In considering the period of time (past, present, future, or some less traditional time/space dimension) denoted by words or phrases that make up content of the therapist's input, the evaluator examines a critical factor relative to input effectiveness and probability of effectiveness of outcomes. Certainly one issue of time dimension, centers on congruence between content-time and theory-specified time. The theoretical orientation should guide comments about periods of the client's life within which problems were caused, are maintained, or are manifest; and where actions are necessary to result in solutions. Therapists should understand the extent to which they behave consistent with theory, as well as assess the temporal location of content messages, to understand the interpretive meaning assigned (but not always communicated) by the client.

From a diagnostic perspective, many therapists affirm the need to thoroughly know the client's past history in order to unravel present forms of distress and conflict, as old role patterns re-emerge in present relationships.[121] This includes attention to the procedural dynamic process of parent-child past relationships, since psychological internalization causes these relationships to be preserved in the minds of clients, who are working out conflicts in the development process.[122] In some cases, a genogram or sociogram history of a client's social network from the past and present, connects end points of expansive time frame domains of content. Genograms also show clients' content-oriented status and states of being categories, relative to other components of an interlocking system of functionality for them and others. Family sculpting is one way to use present physical positions of individuals, to demonstrate relational emotionality as it has transcended developmental time, and has been an outcome product of this longitudinal dynamic.

Another concern with past references, relates to the research concept of sampling error.[123] The counselor needs a fair, correct, and representative sample of the client's behaviors or feelings, to make proper diagnostic assessments and correctly plan treatment. This means paying attention to time, space, and location dimensions within which particular behaviors occur and are reported, since circumstances of occurrence are characteristics which give meaning to any attitude or behavior, and insure validity of the counselor's observations and decisions.

Some clients view the content attention to historical data as a significant index of counselor depth, interest, comprehensiveness, and caring; and may, therefore, develop a more solid and trusting relationship for additional therapeutic work to come. A form of positive narcissism may also be stimulated, as clients tell their story, which confirms the value and longevity of roots, and focuses on the personal strength of having survived adversity, when presently the client may experience devastating failure.

Past time is the context in which many psychodynamic, ego-oriented, and analytic theories believe transferential conflict is elucidated, and the location where some relearning occurs. Clients presumably need to hear recurrent past time content discussions, therefore, to avoid escape from this area of past and re-enacted present conflicted functioning. They must be conditioned by content nature and time frame, to conceptualize themselves in this time dimension, and believe that they are undoing, redoing, or re-experiencing past growth patterns in a more positive way. A counselor who negotiates change from this viewpoint, should seriously question the use of content (especially large amounts) in the present, and justify this variation as to potential impact on, or neglect of, defined areas of problem origin and resolution.

Task-centered, behavioral, and crisis-oriented techniques and theories might manifest a preponderance of content—tenses in more immediate time, or future time, as a reflection of their particular orientation to helping. In these cases, clients' interpretations of content time frame are critical, since they have beliefs about the origin and location of resolution factors, and need to be consistent (time-wise) with the counselor, or convert counselor time into client time, for positive change. Just as in jet lag, there are evaluative issues as clients move from one time to another, including delays for client input systems to begin functioning, or for outcome indices to materialize.

Most therapeutic models and humanistic social scientists, also use future time in various ways to give hope, model hypothesis testing, teach planning techniques, or literally move clients to a more independent, conflict-free sphere of transcendental existence.[124] This process occurs so clients can envision more rational thought (for themselves) without its fantasized destruction and then, with the cognitive image in place, correspondingly fashion empirical behaviors.

Counselors should be aware of content related to the future, and understand whether clients are able to envision for themselves the "giant steps" to move from past entrapment, through the present, and into a future. An associated question, of course, is how these transitional steps are actually measured or evaluated as to therapeutic significance. Therapists can gain valuable feedback from clients by inquiring about their awareness of content time frames, and eliciting cooperation in defining how they use energy to engage the content, and change.

A last dimension of time relates to transitional change (neither A nor B, but A approaching B), discussed relative to "disorders of change" by David Kaplan.[125]

Disorders of change are relevant to the present discussion, since they constitute conflicts by individuals. Their relevant social systems negotiate real movement along lifelong[126] behavioral-psychosocial paths, where specific stimuli precipitate the change event.

5. *Internal vs. External Content:* Comments made to clients by therapists are important directional devices in locating sources of problems, contexts for solutions, and gestalts within which healing communications and relationship dynamics occur. The simplest dichotomous framework differentiates content introduced relative to the intrapsychic life of the client, as opposed to the external part of the client's symbolic psycho and social functioning. From an evaluative standpoint, content focusing on behaviors, external systems, and objective phenomena (outside the client's head), may be more easily translated into operational definitions and empirical measurement schemes, for methodological competence. Regardless of the clinician's theoretical orientation, methodology, or preference for skill utilization, some determinable event (as externally verifiable as possible) should be defined into units of behavioral activity, so observations over time can be compared to one another to note directional changes.

    Behaviors can be "tasks" in task-centered frames of reference, "targets" in behavioral terms, "irrational ideations" in cognitive therapy, "conflicts" in analytic terms, or "states of being" in existentialism; as long as there is some attempt to connect internal and external content, to cross-reference any event in the client's plan for psychosocial change. This means thoughts, feelings, and behaviors should be assigned quantitative as well as qualitative dimensions, and assessed in temporal and internal/external frameworks, which represent their nature and interactive dynamics.

    Empirical practice necessitates, to some degree, externalization of phenomena for systematic collection and evaluation of data, and specification of problems and outcomes in terms that are concrete, observable, and measurable. An operational definition delineates characteristics of an abstract idea or component of reality, as a set of observable and verifiable indices, to insure that errors and misrepresentations do not contaminate the clinician's efforts to control as much of the evaluated therapeutic environment as possible.

    Some dilemmas, herein, are related to errors of interpretation of psychosocial phenomena, which create confusion about internal or external domains of reality. Evaluation and practice can both be founded upon principles of inductive and deductive logic, which insure rational systematic reasoning and consistency. This is especially true for the "post hoc fallacy," which defines a causal association between two events (internal-external) that may be only correlated, or not associated at all. In cases of internal relative to external changes in the client, the therapist may not have fully explored each separately, and the relationship between them, prior to making evaluative judgments.

Another example of internal-external fallacies, includes erroneous reasoning, that individual and group characteristics are the same, and can be interpreted by studying empirical outcomes from either domain without constructing interactive behaviors indices. This reasoning leads to errors when translating internal and external phenomena into their empirically-symbolized counterpart in the alternate domain. Comments (input content) which denote that external behaviors are the crux of the maladaptive problem, may suggest to clients the futility of analyzing internal a priori dynamics; while placing stronger evaluative emphasis on inputs into relationship systems (i.e., saying and doing things which the system defines as appropriate and valued, to maintain boundary integrity, role stability, interactive functionality, and negotiated norms).

The diagnosis in this regard, should be different from intrapsychic frameworks; and therapeutic input content should consistently focus on topics related to variance from alternative proactive or reactive behaviors, which have critical criteria of effectiveness closely associated to homeostatic or transitional states of the external system, or individual dependence on the system. This means external behaviors as causes (i.e., job stress), might have predetermined categories of average expected influence on the individual; and reactions to this stress are assessed as outward signs of non-stress or expected stress behavior (e.g., grieving a loss). These may not be capable of modification until there is reduction of the external stimuli, or increased distance or time between stimulus and response. The client attempting to understand interactive outcomes and choices may, therefore, be confused if an external content-oriented counselor chooses to also deliver internal content (e.g., discuss states of awareness or irrational childhood fantasies), without revision of a formula to explain why and how this domain variation occurs. The counselor using a reference locale, should explain to the client when shifts in perspective occur, and how this different data should be used for therapeutic advantage. The author has witnessed student role-plays in which the pretend therapist vacillates between comments about "angry responses to spouse" or "assertive provision of structure to child," and "internal self-perceptions of entrapment" or "narcissistic needs for stimulating attention"; to the point that the client struggles to understand what is to be done with each different piece of reality-defining data, and how one type (internal) relates to the other (external).

There is no question about the theoretical and practical advantage of therapeutic efforts around external goal analysis and attainment. However, the counselor must be cognizant of how input content allows the client to journey to this realm of perception for sufficient periods of time, to make use of the insights that are available,[127] and then return to the internal world for associated decision-making as well.

As clients experience conflicts related to important life goals as part of the interplay between external social stresses and internal conflicting values, their reactions do not necessarily manifest a clear and logical path of approach, to monitor relevant identity-related interchanges between inner and outer life.[128] They may shift their focus in seemingly-random attempts to defend against demons (conflicts), who attack from both inside and outside simultaneously, or in alternating fashion.[129] Freud[130] summarized, in fact, that frustrating situations[131] do not singularly explain adaptation, but the important fact is the interplay between inner and outer[132] dimensions of life, which are reciprocally deterministic. Input content, therefore, should help clients define treatment goals,[133] not only abstract or specific, short or long-range; but also related to internal or external sources of stress, and dynamic potential for problem resolution.

"Accurate assessment of the sources of blocks to goal attainment is necessary for selecting targets for intervention. Intrapersonal or intragroup blocks to goal attainment may relate to deficiencies in knowledge or skill, conflicts, or emotional and behavioral disturbances within the client system. Blocks arising from the intraclient system suggest aspects of the client system's functioning that may require modification for effective goal attainment. Interpersonal or intergroup blocks may suggest the need for the use of cognitive restructuring or behavior modification techniques to change the behavior of specified individuals or group members. Blocks arising from the physical surroundings may suggest environmental modification procedures to facilitate the attainment of goals.

Assessment of blocks to goal attainment should include an estimate of the degree to which specific impediments reduce the likelihood of goal attainment within the time frame desired by the client system. To identify the sources of the blocks, their characteristics, and an estimate of their importance in thwarting goal attainment, the worker must consider data related to the client system's objective and subjective perceptions of these factors. If the worker does not verify the client system's subjective perception of blocks, he or she may agree to work at influencing inappropriate target systems."[134]

In a more removed or intimate spectrum of external-internal domain, the practitioner may use content related to the client's spirituality, relationship with external forces in nature or the cosmos, or other dimensions of reality, which are outside the realm of traditional intrapsychic existence or external interpersonal reality. In these cases, there may be absence of empirical verifiable outcome evidence for both client and practitioner (e.g., God's will, manifest in a reality situation), or absence of data for the practitioner; but very clear perceptions of spiritual messages, signs, faith perceptions, or feelings on the part of the client, actually living within the system of this external (or ultra-internal), spiritual, transcendental, psychic, or metaphysical existence.

When the therapist is not able to perceive or understand outcome-related data of this nature, a professional consultant can help in planning inputs that are logically related to external or spiritually internal content of the client's reality domain, especially when outcomes are likely not perceptible to the counselor. This is like teaching a sight-impaired person (the counselor) to hold a pistol and hit a target (dangerous wild animal) that only the client can see, yet the client depends on the therapist to aim and shoot accurately because he/she is unable to do so.

One example of unique perceptions of clients can be seen in the Hispanic culture,[135] where concepts of magic and religion have functional meaning and purpose, in crisis-type personal and social situations. In fact, they provide opportunities and conditions for handling certain conflicts which are empirically non-resolvable, except via belief in, and relationship with, the supernatural[136] and cultural context of the belief system.[137]

Because of the significance of these cultural and spiritualistic perspectives, consultations with Hispanic folk healers might be useful in planning appropriate and effective interventions; and help the non-spiritualist clinician understand various states of existence of Hispanic (or other cultural) clients. They could also rely on authority to assist in developing operational and empirical definitions of significant phenomena, so changes in clients' spiritual selves (if this is possible, via an interpersonal medium like psychotherapy or counseling) could be effectively documented and assessed.

In the Puerto Rican culture, there are four separate healers who are necessary to understand and assist with differentiated realms of internal, external, and qualitative spiritual needs. The types are: (1) spiritualist, (2) Santero, (3) herbalist, and (4) Santiguador. The spiritualist helps the individual deal with good and evil spirits in the invisible world contained in the empirical world, but where state of being outcomes are assessed within eternal reality domains.[138] The spiritualists precipitate and prevent illness, manifested in both physiologic and social pathology.[139] The Santero uses African methods combined with Roman Catholic beliefs to diagnose illness, which is the relative influence of spirits incarnated in human bodies, as a function of trials they must endure as ordained by God.[140] Herbalists[141] use a "naturalistic"[142] orientation of physical causality with criteria of holistic balance, indexing adjustment success. They diagnose imbalance and then prescribe special remedies, to return the body to its adaptive state. Finally, the Santiguadores emphasize chronic and intestinal diseases, orthopedic problems, and muscle aches and pains.[143] Their orientation to rehabilitation involves God's will,[144] and ritualistic intercession of laying on of hands, massages, herbs, and prayers, to win back the creator's favor.

Clinicians dealing with external (or extra-internal) content that is perceptually, culturally, or intellectually removed from their typical realm of thought, need inputs designed to engage the real dimensions of this phenomenologic, cultural, or spiritual domain. Additionally, they need precisely formulated operational definitions developed with the assistance of the client and significant others (possibly spiritualist consultants), to identify circumstances, behaviors, nonbehaviors, thoughts, environmental occurrences, relationship patterns, or other observable phenomena; which are illustrations of various outcomes which may occur outside the direct receptivity range of the therapist. Inputs must also differentiate internal from external domains, and have validity correction perspectives, to alert the counselor when and how they may have crossed over the boundary, from one to the other.

To illustrate the complicated integration of internal and external life, with emphasis on the internal as the domain of understanding the self, Frankl[145] writes that meaning is found in everyday life through the daily process of change, and cannot be defined in a general way. The counselor, obviously, has a difficult challenge to decide whether there are unifying principles[146] which perceptually or methodologically integrate internal, external, or other domains; and further, to understand that the order imposed by evaluative theory or method, may distort or negate the true nature of internal or external causality, or variations of either.

6. *Tactical vs. Strategic Content:* The latter part of this chapter discusses general and specific purposes of therapeutic inputs. This section addresses the preliminary point, that counselor input content contains a frame of reference or arena of action, at a locus of specificity or abstraction, relevant to client life-dynamics. It ultimately has impact on the power, intensity, and purposefulness of inputs, affecting desired outcomes. Often the counselor assumes that input is interpreted by the client productively, and transformed/transported to the right level of significance for its effect to take place. This is like assuming that a medical patient can select sequences of treatment for an illness, without consultation of medical staff to pinpoint (a) immediate steps to reduce swelling, (b) secondary steps to improve circulation, (c) intermediate steps to curb infection, (d) sub-intermediate steps to reduce pain, (e) long-range steps to rehabilitate injured areas, and (f) long-range steps to improve self-care attitudes, perceptions, and behaviors, to reduce susceptibility to recurrent injury.

In clinical psychosocial practice, the same problem occurs as the client relates interactive and dynamically-related characteristics and symptoms to which the practitioner responds; with inputs designed to focus attention, illustrate realms of causality, and point directly and inferentially to processes of resolution. An example of the complex use of inputs (see Figure 4), further illustrates the dilemmas faced by the therapist, in locating the proper strategic or tactical arena of influence. After each discussion of content, a line is drawn in the table to suggest the focus which input comments might relate to, including potential therapeutic goals which might be associated to each dimension. Each line is extended into each relevant box and ends with a perpendicular line, to illustrate the end point of therapeutic goals or intentions. The example relates a therapeutic interview between the author and a client involved in psychotherapy. It is simplistic, but the frameworks for actual intervention can be more sophisticated and different in myriad ways.

In the example given, specific words used by the counselor help the client respond to tactical or strategic goals of their therapeutic work, with implications for amount and type of growth achieved. Counselors must be careful, due to inexperience, ignorance, theoretical orientation, or personal discomfort; to not maintain the client's realm of response totally in the tactical domain, to the possible neglect of higher level abstract and strategic

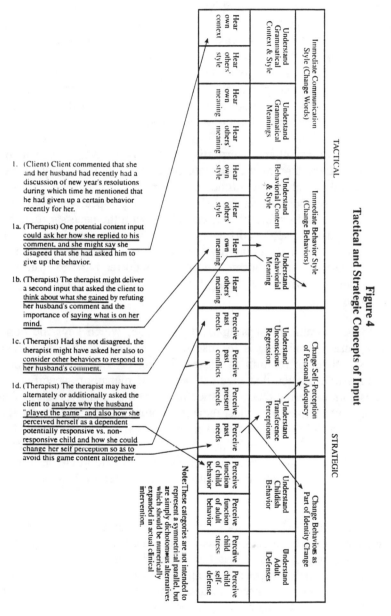

Figure 4
Tactical and Strategic Concepts of Input

1. (Client) Client commented that she and her husband had recently had a discussion of new year's resolutions during which time she mentioned that he had given up a certain behavior recently for her.

1a. (Therapist) One potential content input could ask her how she replied to his comment, and she might say she disageed that she had asked him to give up the behavior.

1b. (Therapist) The therapist might deliver a second input that asked the client to think about what she gained by refuting her husband's comment and the importance of saying what is on her mind.

1c. (Therapist) Had she not disagreed, the therapist might have asked her also to consider other behaviors to respond to her husband's comment.

1d. (Therapist) The therapist may have alternately or additionally asked the client to analyze why the husband "played the game" and also how she perceived herself as a dependent potentially responsive vs. non-responsive child and how she could change her self perception so as to avoid this game content altogether.

Note: These categories are not intended to represent a symmetrical parallel, but are simply dichotomous alternatives which should be numerically expanded in actual clinical intervention.

perspectives about developmental process, and past dynamics of conflicts (meaning) relative to current behaviors. This is a function not only of philosophic orientation, but also words and tenses that comprise clinical inputs: say vs. feel; is vs. was; how vs. why vs. what; am vs. used to be; need vs. want; will see myself vs. will be seen by; did vs. considered status related to doing, and so on. This framework is also relevant because it relates to formalized phases[147] of theory-specific treatment and evaluation, having distinct tactical or strategic outcome goals, guided methodologically by the nature of inputs and target agendas.

The assessment and interpretive process is complex, however, because inputs for treatment, as well as data-collecting activities, may alternate the focus of target behaviors, attitudes, or identity states between various levels of specificity and abstraction. Continuity of perspective about outcomes may be obscured or totally lost, especially with the necessary use of client observational and self-report data outside counseling sessions. Because of the importance of data stability[148] and reduced variability, treatment and evaluative inputs must locate data domains correctly,[149] to insure validity and reliability, while accounting for effects of developmental learning and modeling.

One example illustrating input language, which keys the domain of therapeutic orientation, is the use of metaphor[150] relative to the medical disease model in relation to the counseling process. The author of the above article argues that medically-oriented metaphors specifically teach counselors to define characteristics and psychosocial dynamics of clients, in ways which may not reflect their true natures. Although model A (medical) and model B (psychosocial) may exist as separate realities, language may be used for "sort crossing,"[151] which compares aspects of classes A and B, does not isolate perspectives exclusively within either domain, and facilitates the process of integration. A number of language dilemmas exist.

More may be known about one class of events than the other, and this knowledge may even be spurious.[152] The metaphor establishes an illusion that connecting them provides the same or similar degrees of knowledge about both domains, especially the less empirically-evident aspects. As this principle is applied to previous discussions in the text, an input comment related to an abstract or strategic domain of reality (e.g., transferential regressive identity state), may not accurately apply to a more concrete (possibly symbolic, but whose symbolism is unknown) area of tactical performance (client asking a specific question).

Also, connective language may bridge the gap between incompatible reality domains, which might only be considered together as subcomponents of a third reality; therefore, they do not need connective language, but rather definitional or associative language, to see similar and dissimilar aspects of their integrated existence. For example, if a client is culturally and economically deprived, and performs the act of stealing food; discussing this phenomenon in relation to analytic concepts of oral dependency, aggressive acting out, etc., may be an incorrect interpretation of several separate reality domains (cultural deprivation, physical hunger, social power, psychological trust, or self-confidence). For this particular client, insight or awareness might require a concept which merges each sub-reality, into a new and separate domain of A, + B, + C, + D, = E. . . . [153]

In this regard, inputs should be accurately keyed to domains they represent; and integrative options or verbal crossover perceptions stimulated by behavioral or verbal input, should be carefully checked for validity. This is especially necessary since inputs imply definitions of causality, motivation, outcome probabilities, or status, and can appropriately expand or reduce data about client problems.[154] This problem is noted interculturally, where social service orientation, diagnostic perspective, input language, or outcome expectations, misinterpret knowledge, art, beliefs, and customs in terms of strategic mal-transformations from one culture to another, but also incorrectly transform strategic to tactical (or vice versa).[155]

Differences in evaluating African-American clients, for example, include some major components of childhood (as dimensions of growth and development) which are different from other cultures, related to dependency characteristics,[156] and consequent alterations in maturity attributes of the developing parent-child relationship. Another difference is emotional preconsciousness needed by many black children in the illegal, amoral, and violent community environment where they survive; with unique stress management abilities, role flexibility, strong religious orientation,[157] and powerful friendship bonds.

One final difference, relates to concepts of time among African-Americans:[158]

"Time, in the African framework, is phenomenal rather than mathematical. That is, in the traditional African sense, time is not a precise mathematical entity around which an event is developed, but rather a flexible notion that is determined by when the event (phenomenon) occurs. For example, a party is scheduled to begin at 9 P.M. Most likely, the Anglo-European host would feel that around 9 'it's time' for the party. People of African descent would not be expecting anyone at 9 and would feel that 'it's time' for the party whenever guests arrive. Nobles has aptly suggested that a more appropriate enunciation of CPT is 'communal potential time.'"

The counselor must always remember to interpret translated dynamics, relative to environmental stimuli impacting the individual's cumulative developmental history and behavioral experience;[159] as opposed to immediate events, conditional situations, and nature of therapeutic situation.

It is essential that clinicians translate system-client interaction into intra- and interpersonal terms, and incorporate these dynamics in indexed categories of psychosocial assessment, to reflect comprehensive understanding of psychological and social determinants of client functioning.

7.   *Individual vs. Shared Content (Therapist vs. Client vs. Dyadic Agenda):* As each counselor interacts with clientele, incongruences in concepts, semantics, operational definitions, and other philosophical or concrete perspectives differ, so therapeutic effort must improve communicative sharing, and develop associational overlap in key ideas related to client development.

A particular issue is that the therapist's personal life agenda, may be reflected in conceptual input framework that purposefully (in a healthy fashion), inadvertently, or pathologically (as an ego defense mechanism) in whole or part, excludes the client as a significant object of attention. The client may do the same relative to the therapist, or dyadic relationship, as it constitutes a third entity which may be synergistically powerful and systematically bounded enough, to produce a microcosm of reality which excludes relevant dimensions of either separate involved personality. This is not an argument against each existential (unique, separate, autonomous) identity, but concern with the psyche's proclivity to seek unilateral self-actualization, relative to the personality's trust in relationships and dynamics of others for mutual survival. Complicated alternating, non-differentiating, or non-integrating cognitions that incorporate or exclude the reality of an external object (client or counselor), can negate or distort evaluation of conceptual products (synopses, thought content, energies, etc.).

Although research is limited and inconclusive in this area, differential outcomes may result from introduction of genuineness, warmth, and empathy[160] (as core conditions) in the therapeutic process. This suggests client-oriented content might be paired with affect on the part of the therapist (integrating cognitive agenda and feeling content), for relevant client-guided empathic responsiveness; although this outcome does not necessarily have to be intended by the counselor, or perceived by the client. Also, data about therapist attitudes and values concerning the client,[161] suggests that input may have to be intricately content-connected, in order to presume reasonable probability of successful outcome.

Results and decisions must meet "therapeutic"[162] criteria, when outcomes are psychosocially relevant for the client. However, they must also take into consideration, social values and appropriate professional goals held by the counselor; and personal agendas counselors integrate into practice, to maintain a sense of their own utility, relevance, and self-actualization. The clinician is challenged to monitor the processes of emergence of client content, including factors in counseling which alter, distort, negate, or prohibit content not directly representative of the client's gestalt, or indirectly transferable to their domain of functioning. This threat to evaluative research might be labeled a misrepresented intervention, which is a discrepancy between the label given to an intervention, and what the intervention, in fact, consisted of—which could represent negative or spurious positive results. Another threat to standardization of evaluative findings, is the idiosyncratic, individualistic (rather than shared) intervention, closely attuned to the practitioner's personal agenda at a given time. Thus, it could not be considered subsequently for replication with similar clients, because it is a biased data situation (if the counselor agenda remains constant); or an independent and totally different clinical situation, if the agenda is not present (even if the client is identical in the replication situation) at a later intervention phase. Any input not adequately labeled and described to enable another matched clinician to implement it in approximately the same way, closes the door on comparisons of effectiveness of inputs, with different clients at different times.

One other bias, even if the practitioner is aware of the circumscription and personal nature of their input content, is viewing this content in stereotypically patterned fashion. This could be based on culturally learned theoretically/methodologically dictated assumptions that reflect fixed diagnostic preconditions, reactive responses to client stimuli (anger, resistance), or some other type of client status; contingently placing counselor input content secondary to, and reflective of, client action or reaction.

In one case of self-ratings,[163] researchers note that client (in this case, children) ratings of positive and negative personality traits of professionals, were generally more positive than self-ratings, which at one level reflect differential identity assessments, possibly contingent on individual or shared input. There was also lack of clarity of how self-assessments materialize, vis-à-vis the nature of content awareness and integration.[164] The study illustrates that workers and clients may not agree on ratings; therefore, inputs may be seen differentially and skewed in many directions, if congruence is not reached while also retaining the individuality of both perspectives. This may represent incompatible but relevant reality domains that may not be bridged, due to limitations of the input medium. In sharing perceptions, however, workers can be hurt by negative feelings of clients, which suggests they purposefully downgrade their perceptions of self and input content defensively, or rely more on self rather than client content, to hedge bets in looking more positive.[165]

Counselors may experience a paradox in evaluative activities, since data results designed to help them may, in fact, elucidate input ineffectiveness which diminishes self-esteem. Some, therefore, may respond to this conflict by viewing multiple domains of personality to make adequacy decisions; concomitantly selecting multiple input contents and formats of individual and shared nature, to accomplish their assessment goals.

Actual decisions about professional capability may be partly based on assessment of counselors' performance in personal roles and experiences,[166] which include roles as spouse, parent, child, peer, good neighbor, political constituent, lover, and others which can be cognitively transformed into individual effectiveness indices, without sharing this process with the client.

Sometimes, personal areas of performance yield accurate and valuable feedback concerning counselors' basic qualities as effective human beings, especially when distortions and input-feedback systems of communications with clients, relate more to specific input techniques:

"In general, inquiry has its origin in a conceptual structure. This structure determines what questions we shall ask in our inquiry; the questions determine what data we wish; our wishes in this respect determine what experiments we perform. Further, the data, once assembled, are given their meaning and interpretation in light of the conception which initiated the inquiry."[167]

Throughout the literature, personal attributes seem to be essential dimensions of the counselor's therapeutic skills, and are significantly integrated with professional values, attitudes, and orientations. In a recent article, Rhodes,[168] stresses the following:

"The therapeutic relationship is as much dramatized by the worker's personal attributes as it is by technical expertise. It is this combination of personality and professional competence that charac- terizes the worker's therapeutic style, (and constitutes) the configu- ration of unique personality traits that represent a convergence of bio-psychosocial experience."

These combined personal and professional attributes in the counselor's "total self," become important when associated with clients' input into treatment. As the therapist's personal feelings, relationship skills, values, and life experiences are activated in the relationship, they become dynamic parts of the therapeutic gestalt:

"The range of interaction within which the therapist's experience is pertinent—even indispensable—to full therapy engagement is very large. Recognition of the centrality of the therapist's own experience exists not only within gestalt therapy, but also . . . (among all those) whose therapy is a two-way human engagement. Within this frame of mind, to include the therapist's experience is as simple as one and one equal two."[169]

Other authors emphasize psychological maturity, social adaptation, self-reliance, capacity for intimacy, cultural values, personal sensitivity, and healthy personal relationships of the competent counselor, as prerequi- sites or accompaniments to primary knowledge and skills of direct treat- ment intervention.

In discussing the critical relationship between counselors' personal attributes and life experiences, and methods or attitudes of self-evaluation as they relate to these factors; traditional research evaluation literature stresses that self-evaluation is not direct assessment of the counselor's self, but focuses on the client's behavioral or attitudinal change, as a result of counseling interventions. Single subject ($N = 1$) evaluation or other quantitative designs, sometimes imply secondary importance of the counselor's personal characteristics, while stressing client behavioral outcome as primary focus of assessment. Although the counselor's input on knowledge, skills, and personal characteristics is an important ingredient of effective treatment, personal input factors are often not discussed, as offering primary data for self-evaluation.

It is unclear how clinicians use or interpret feedback from personal experiences affecting their feelings of professional competence, or how this individual judgmental information becomes shared with clients' (directly or indirectly) evaluative perceptions, for integral and systemically valid outcome assessment. In some parts of the literature, counselors' input into treatment, reflecting personal capabilities and experiences, is sometimes considered a phenomenon to be controlled, held constant, or corrected, as a potential negative influence on treatment. Dynamics of the counselor's cultural or personal background, are often labeled as contaminating intrusions upon the objective use of knowledge or professional skills.

Countertransference is one instance where the counselor's personal relationships reflect negatively on objective interaction with clients, and counselors are cautioned to avoid this pitfall of therapeutic treatment. Guidelines for self-awareness require that clinicians be acutely conscious of specific responses to a client, to separate professional relationship dynamics from actions which are personally motivated to fulfill the clinician's personal drives. Another negative influence of personal experience is discussed by Williams,[170] who recognizes that "therapists' personal and professional backgrounds strongly influence their preoccupation with (therapeutic) roles that are facilitative or nurturing." But, he warns that ". . . personal background has led most therapists to fear, distrust, or discount the possible therapeutic value of group processes in their relationships with the individual members of the group." Although Williams is specifically commenting on therapy with groups, he echoes a significant concern about all forms of counseling.

One modification of restrictive use of personal factors for professional self-evaluation, occurs if personal relationships are with professional peers, on or off the job. These relationships are considered by some to provide useful evaluative feedback; integrating peer evaluation, the counselor's self-assessment, and outcome data from clients, in the context of an external and possibly more objective social unit. Unfortunately, there is little guidance from the literature on how to correlate this information for evaluative judgments, and the data itself is of questionable validity for systematic evaluation. Examination is therefore required, concerning actual and subjectively-perceived convergence formulas for each counselor-client dyad, as personal and professional factors interrelate and represent subsequent introduction or withdrawal of therapeutic inputs.

Theoretical conceptualizations of cause and effect linearity, between therapist input and client outcome, should take into account complex matrices of data which evolve from professional or personal arenas of the counselor's life:

> "The process of evaluation is highly complex and subjective. Inherently it involves a combination of basic assumptions underlying the activity being evaluated and of personal values on the part of both those whose activities are being evaluated, and those who are doing the evaluation. Evaluation is a continuous social process rarely stopping to challenge these assumptions or bring the values into the open."[171]

8. *Normative Nature of Content:* In considering relevance of input content to any conceptual framework, as well as developmental deficits and goals of the client, it is important whether comments, words, or phrases fit a traditional value framework for culturally approved norms, or deviate from commonly-expected reference points. Cultural relativity and attention to human diversity must be evaluated vis-à-vis intended or inadvertent impact on clients' assessments of their own self-esteem, or any anxiety created about need to change, range of perceptions about life meanings, and degree of awareness of correct or incorrect (for the client) alternatives to problem definition or resolution.

Counselors in this situation, are faced with a complicated evaluative agenda which addresses philosophical, social, and ethical issues, as they decide what to save or delete in discussions with clients. They must consider some important questions:

First, is a counselor (particularly within a public agency) expected and legitimized through funding policies and administrative procedures, to support traditional democratic and humanistic norms, and is degree of normative congruence an evaluative criterion? A good example of this controversy is the pro-abortion counselor in a Catholic Social Services Agency, whose content may or may not allow room for the client to perceive "acceptability criteria," based on a variety of norms for abortive behavior relative to interpersonal relations. In some cases, counselors feel there is therapeutic benefit in presenting content supportive of a wider range of socially, spiritually, or philosophically acceptable alternatives. These help the client concomitantly expand conception of self, via association, identification, or modeling. Alternatives also precipitate existential crises, to produce anxiety to grow and possibly change; or help clients test commitment to avowed standards, to consolidate previous thinking, feel confident, or consider perceptual and cognitive modifications of traditional values.

Further, is the social scientist expected to be an advocate or critic in terms of class actions;[172] and, in fact, develop evaluative criteria relative to leadership in changing norms, values, or practices which individuals, agencies, or professional groups feel are unjust, discriminatory, or otherwise limiting?

This concern with counselors' identity with their profession and extent of allegiance to human rights, social action, or other philosophical commitments of a normative nature; has evaluative implications for input and client outcome. This depends on if and how the counselor ratifies professional pledges to social justice, or actually employs normative principles through deliberate use of clinical techniques. Diagnosis and attempted remediation of human problems represent normative positions, and are activated and symbolized in thoughts, feelings, or interactions of clinical clients. This does not imply counselor intervention with large social groups, but refers to the planned use of clinical skill and knowledge, within intrapsychic and interpersonal boundaries of counseling relationships with individuals, families, or therapeutic groups.

One area where input may include particular dimensions of normative content for the client, is teaching and role modeling during counseling, especially where clients' respect for knowledgeable experts and dependency on "parental" rewards (transference), suggest both susceptibility and motivation for learning. Social values can be taught pedagogically, or indirectly inferred, through provocative questioning, rhetorical conjecture, or role modeling in response to ideas or behaviors generated by clients.

Counselors might inculcate or control their influence about racial equality, women's rights, war, gay liberation, religious freedom, or other situations, depending on their orientation to the role of normative content, relative to client psychodynamics and overall developmental human process.

The author recalls numerous psychotherapy interviews in which his reluctance to actively educate, resulted in tacit approval of sexist, racist, or inhuman behavior of clients. A particular view of therapeutic objectivity and concentration on neutral "process" techniques, allowed noncommittal acceptance of specific client values and goals. This negligence also contributed to analytic and evaluative submersion in how clients were behaving or communicating, rather than attention to content of the normative value-laden message, or nature of behavior or attitudes. It is obviously possible (and maybe desirable) for the practitioner to apply acute, situational methodologies to specific client process, yet ignore broader strategic issues relative to service to the "community" (and its social norms), which legitimate some or all aspects of counseling activities.

In discussing orchestration of clinical skills and philosophical social values, Lifton recounts the inseparability of political-ethical and therapeutic ideologies in working with Vietnam veterans. Conflicts between his anti-war social advocacy role, and psychiatric commitment to client healing through therapeutic techniques, caused the following dilemma:

> "Most of the professionals took the position that we were . . . offering necessary therapy to veterans who were our clients. The minority view . . . was that we were trying to create a new institution . . . (that) could be better described as a dialogue between professionals and veterans, beginning from a common stance of opposition to the war . . . (with) greater emphasis upon . . . ethical and political commitments of professionals."[173]

A second source of clinicians' power for regulating normative, deviant, or neutral input content and client outcome phenomena for social action, is the judicious use, or purposeful omission, of individual or family diagnosis. Diagnosis as a process in and of itself, focuses and defines pathology or deviant roles, and the part of society which may deprive clients of acceptable outcome options. It may also negate their right and expectation for some self-diagnostic opportunity.

This reaction to labeling or not, can be seen with the clinician supporting women's rights. He or she may curtail "hysterical" and "dependent" traditionally feminine diagnoses as personally demeaning sexist labels, which ignore socially unjust circumstances where feminine inadequacy is expected. The counselor could also place positive emphasis on assertive, controlling, or other nontraditional feminine characteristics, allowing clients to struggle with the process and outcome of integrating potentially divergent normative perspectives, within their psychosocial frames of reference.

Another example is the parent who diagnoses children's independent and self-reliant behavior as wrong or deviant. The therapist who supports children's rights might block, contradict, or redefine parental labeling, even if it disturbs family equilibrium; to exercise professional diagnostic leverage in support of a social value.

A third clinical power related to diagnosis, is the counselor's analysis or interpretation of clients' psychological and social experiences. This exposition of meaning, cause, and implication of thoughts and behaviors, can forcefully translate individual subjective experience into an officially sanctioned commentary on reality. The therapist exercises substantial control in portraying dynamics of clients' lives as consistent or conflictual scenarios of social justice, humanism, and democratic freedom, or other philosophical perspectives. Also, clients' perceptions of the quality of their social condition and goodness of their intentions and interactions, are significantly correlated with the clinician's evaluation and annotation of these phenomena.

Therapists may help family members interpret their relationships in a normatively different light, or modify broad conceptions, attitudes, goals, definition, affective reactions, and hypotheses they form. Conversely, they may support overall viewpoints they hold about life and its various sub-dimensions and ramifications. Some authors suggest that therapists deliberately employ interpretive prerogative to accent socially-generic (rather than individual or ethnic) attitudes, feelings, and role options, which are typically censured through prejudicial discrimination. By employing analytic interpretations which cogently pinpoint social values, especially with commensurate confirming or deviant behaviors, the counselor may discover greater awareness or social consciousness in psychotherapy, and feel heightened satisfaction with evaluative results that flow from this orientation.

A final example of clinical power is communication technique, in which the therapist selects supportive or dissuasive words/tones/behavioral gestures; autonomously directs or interjects messages at opportune moments; or authoritatively asks for silence, interrupts, defines, expounds, ignores, or otherwise manipulates communicative content or process, to enhance consideration of broad or specific concerns. Carefully engineered information management, can assist development of self-awareness and create growth-inducing or destructive anxiety to challenge or support values, and reveal moral issues about right and wrong social attitudes: ". . . man's search for meaning and values may cause inner tension rather than inner equilibrium . . . (which is) an indispensable prerequisite of mental health."[174]

Sensitively empathetic expressions from counselors support debilitated identities and discourage defeatist behavior, which are often self-inflicted and culture-enhanced ailments mirroring societal injustice. Also, positive communications can simultaneously block destructive messages from spouse or family, and reinforce attitude and behavioral changes actualizing particular human philosophies. The client has the opportunity to investigate untried social roles and actions offering more power, autonomy, influence, status, dignity, equality; or the social advantage to discover new channels, or activate existing avenues of communication, social transaction, and philosophical self-actualization.

Scrutinizing the nature and social consciousness of clinical theories and techniques, challenges the real world orientation of a relatively isolated form of social service. It places client self-determination and therapist objectivity in question, since specific values (not comfortable to some clients or therapists), undergird methodology. Without awareness of the normative nature of words, sentences, gestures, or expressions, however, the counselor may succumb to myths and delusions of effective practice, or retreat to the neutrality of the objective-but-distant expert, who does not really get psychosocially involved. This may lead to the technician's disciplined unconcern for the client's social rights, dignity, questions, conflicts, or opportunities.

Although pressure on clinicians for scientific accountability seemingly encourages sterile methodological automatism, most would agree that human norms and values are the cornerstones of democracy and responsibility, of all social scientists. The clinical practitioner may be ethically obligated to transmit these values and human rights through the powerful use of therapeutic knowledge, skill, and influence.

A final question clinicians face as they develop a therapeutic agenda, is whether evaluative criteria are flexible enough to change, for idiosyncratic situations. This change allows normative content to be evaluated positively as input, in cases where the client cannot or will not change basic social value perspectives or behaviors. Still, it could be assessed as negative content, where the client "needs" encouragement to broaden his or her horizons. If this flexibility is viable, counselors must also develop evaluative self-awareness of their changing vs. stable needs, to manifest a social identity; and decide whether they can vary the normative vs. deviant nature of content, without sacrifice to other areas of needed consistency in affect, personality style, conception, or image. As one variable has greater or lesser degrees of freedom within the professional's intrapsychic system, it may impact corresponding degrees of freedom (or inertia) afforded other intrapsychic functions. This interdependency must be examined in terms of personal right-wrong (conformity/deviance) structures within the therapist, which may be acted out via the client.

The counselor is also evaluatively required to help clients step back from value-laden content, to assess methodologically and theoretically, what is occurring therapeutically, so they can see their own progress or regression, without confounding effects of value or philosophical content overload. The counselor at either end of the normative continuum (normative-deviant), or fluctuating somewhere in the middle, should share this with the client to understand the relativity of therapist prerogatives, and make a conscious decision about how to handle the content.

One example from the literature discusses treatment of the female alcoholic client,[175] whose alcoholism comprises two distinct sets of problems, which are significantly differentiated relative to gender. The authors criticize traditional treatment programs as male-oriented, noting sexist stereotypes of women as nonindividuals through secondary self-definition in association with, and dependent on, men; and obscuring separate feminine identities in lieu of dyadic concern for the woman's child or family.[176]

In considering therapeutic input content with these clients, the therapist's "social attitude"[177] is an important foundation, especially considering notions of conservatism and liberalism of a host of social attitudes and positions. Counselors may assume that low self-esteem is predominantly connected to psycho-pathology, rather than to sexist value decisions and boundaries. As Peak and Glankoff note, "Rehabilitation, resocialization, call it what you will, is often for women a question of reorientation to the servant role, not for open-ended self-fulfillment with all its many possibilities."[178]

Broverman,[179] et al. also reveal that professionals' clinical assessments differ relative to client gender, and further note that their health-related models of evaluation, irrespective of client gender, conform closely to male health and adaptation orientation.[180] The counselor must be aware of normative messages contained not only within linguistic and communicational patterns,[181] but also in theoretical frameworks providing overarching definitions of reality. Another example occurs in marriage and couple counseling, with the introduction of content about extramarital relationships, which may be considered deviant by the client, some social groups, or both. While social changes encourage numerous variations of non-marital, cohabitational associations, culture has neither strengthened the bonds of marital union in resisting these allurements, nor assisted matrimonial pairs in integrating more liberal perspectives and values, to successfully negotiate open marriages and alternate lifestyles. Marital partners who become dissatisfied, or seek a wider range of relationships, are often simultaneously: (1) attracted by society's liberated relationship alternatives, (2) guilty in feeling trapped by traditional expectations for marital loyalty, (3) suffering with specific conflicts or deficits in present relationships, (4) pleased with the comfort or protection of extramarital unity, (5) fearful of personality destruction or devastating loss, due to myths of lifelong scars of unfaithfulness (as perpetrator or victim), and (6) unskilled in dealing with complex feelings and behaviors in any of the above dilemmas.

The problem for therapists, therefore, is how to view extramarital relationships in a way which does not further hamper their marital clients, and restrict options for client growth, by: (1) unnecessarily defining the external relationships as pathological, (2) excessively focusing attention on the marriage, and invalidating one or both partners' need for defensive space, or (3) imposing inappropriately restricting judgments on individuals who have found meaningful connections beyond limited capacities of their spouses. The therapist is challenged to discover significant positive dynamics and personal attributes in extramarital situations, otherwise defined negatively without redeeming value; and from that, to creatively use this information about human interaction to foster clients' positive self-awareness, growth within the marital dyad (if possible), and development of new relationships and personal horizons beyond the marriage (concurrently or subsequently), if indicated.

Some marital relationships, excessively responsive to social pressures for romantic and emotional exclusivity, and mirroring legal and religious codes using relatively tight boundaries; contain individuals with constructed perceptions of their full range of emotional needs, personal capabilities, and total identities. Extramarital activities and outside interpersonal relationships with men or women, are typically prohibited as potentially damaging to self-concepts and security of these partners. Occurrence of an outside relationship, however, can sometimes ironically provide the arena for expanded awareness and perception, especially as therapists analyze components of the extramarital experience from alternate or neutral normative perspectives. In fact, self-discovery may only come in response to crisis, when individuals are forced to risk stereotypical and narrow normative perceptions within which they imprison themselves. A fuller range of needs, feelings, and personal capacities may only enter awareness, as multiple relationships and interactive problems attack the defenses of the traditional marital and social system.

Unfortunately, many childhood socializing experiences and prohibitive adult norms, censor free use of cognitive originality, so some relationships inherit the sterility of this perceptual and emotional constriction. Many married couples unnecessarily fear gross pathology or repressed sexual or aggressive imagery; or avoid social or spiritual deviance, which they assume will evolve if they stray from mature, sensible thought and action. The therapist who sees extramarital relationships as self-actualizing attempts to discover new roles, embellish desired character traits, or inject excitement into dreary lifestyles, can help couples attack their aesthetic rigidity, and jointly inflate their sagging marriage. As the couple study and map out autonomous relationship dynamics noted in the peripheral liaison, they begin developing a focal point and new normative criteria to define competent, qualitative, and adaptive behaviors, which serve as a model for their own interactions and system realignment.

Therapists who work with these clients at critical junctures of relationships, must also assess their own philosophic values, and corresponding input style and content about extramarital associations. This includes biases concerning marital loyalty or disloyalty; diagnostic predispositions favoring traditional or liberated relationships, in assigning dysfunctional or pathologic labels; and narrow viewpoints preventing deployment of therapeutic knowledge and skill, to build upon strength and utilize all facets of personal and relationship dynamics. Each therapist must consider unique values, skills, cultural backgrounds, and preferences of clients in helping them retain personal self-determination, and guiding therapeutic intervention to meet their special needs.

Theoretical orientation and agency setting for the therapist's intervention also guide selection, time frame, scope, and delivery of varying techniques and strategies—including specific skills in dealing with crisis or deviance situations and dynamics.

9. *Interventive and Evaluative Nature of Content:* A major component of the therapeutic endeavor should be devoted to evaluation and objective stepping-back from the process, to accurately and meaningfully perceive its nature and influence.[182] In fact, outcome effectiveness studies show that planned, systematic efforts to facilitate change,[183] lead to more positive outcomes, as opposed to unplanned treatment, informal assistance, or no help at all. There is a tremendous rationale for evaluation somewhere within the treatment process.[184] Also, within formalized evaluation procedures, evidence suggests the assessment process itself (in addition to the independent treatment variable), affects client perceptions and outcome behaviors; especially when there is lack of systematic planning and control of measurement procedures, multiple evaluators, instrument stimulus power, or evaluative social environment.[185]

The practitioner is in a methodological, as well as a philosophical, dilemma. Methodologically, evaluation (which includes introduction of input, ranging from empirical self-assessment questions, to provision of research instrumentation) is essential and provides rationale for the existence of treatment. As this occurs, quality of evaluation demands precision and rigor, which may be difficult for counselors to produce. Also, efficacy of the therapeutic approach itself may be hampered, delayed, or even reversed/repressed; depending on impact, saliency, symbolism, and client interpretation of the evaluative process.

The objectives of counseling and research also involve different perspectives about outcome goals for change, with questionable ability of either to be directly translated into relevant units of the alternate methodology, for scientific relevance. Counselors must be particularly sensitive, therefore, to the possibility of mutually-exclusive domains or entirely different independent variable effects, which cannot be compared equivocally in viewing common outcomes. There may, however, be instances in which domains and criteria of clinical and evaluative outcomes are identical. This does not pose a major problem for the evaluator, as long as these times, client statuses, or unique conditions can be clearly identified.

In considering this dilemma, one example of difference, is alternating usage of different treatment approaches, when (a) the client situation does not allow for free manipulation of some inputs, to test outcome reactions, (b) evaluative demands on the professional, necessitate withdrawal of the independent variable to determine its short- and long-term effects, and (c) there is no overlapping domain, in which both treatment and evaluation can be subsumed under a more general category which allows them, by design, to be altered.

In a common A-B-A-B design containing a baseline measurement (A), intervention (input) (B), and assessment of outcomes relative to baseline (A); introduction of the intervention (B) may not be practical in many settings, because the intervention cannot be altered or withdrawn—yet this is necessary for evaluative inputs to be employed with reasonable proba-bility of success.

The above example, as well as other situations where evaluative and interventive inputs are used in interactive and related fashion, raise a significant question as to whether any single case treatment/assessment, can be conducted without seriously compromising the validity and effectiveness of either. The other alternative, is to view treatment and evaluation as subcomponents of a broader perspective ecologically on clients' and coun-selors' dimensions of existence; so longer durations can be tolerated for alternating treatment, treatment-evaluation, and evaluation designs, before the entire sequence has run its course.

Philosophically, the practitioner is confronted with an input dilemma, because many (if not all) theories of intervention suggest evaluation is a central theme of client learning about self-government. Input must contain evaluative content, yet this content may need differentiation from, or assimilation/integration with, more formalized evaluative content for research purposes. The counselor is concerned with relative qualities and amounts of client-evaluative, research-evaluative, or direct treatment input, and decides if these inputs are different and why. Therapeutically, clients struggle with the nature and dynamics of self-assessment, and may benefit from affirmatively stated opinions ("You are a very capable person, Bob"), by which they experience positive results (versus negative and traumatic ones, experienced earlier in their developmental history) of evaluation. They learn to do this at a later time for themselves via modeled learning. The input may not be strictly evaluative in nature of content, yet have a goal relative to evaluation.

Within a behavioral theoretical context,[186] there may be a learning advantage in delivery of reinforcing statements, rather than evaluative questions, depending on nature of the problem.[187] This calls into question the relative power and function of the counselor versus the client. The professional may become a parent substitute[188] and make evaluative statements, without necessarily directly or concurrently involving clients in their own evaluation.

Client dependency on external control may be a by-product or even purpose of counselor evaluation, yet the client and counselor must depend on evaluative process and findings, to guide them toward goals and objectives they might not reach otherwise. Over-dependence or excessive energy investment in the value of evaluation, can sometimes obscure a flexible perspective about client change, selective perception, or idiographic developmental dynamics. The counselor's introduction of evaluative content as communicated input, must deal with the process by which the evaluative framework may be a stimulus for specific negative client responses, symbolically or directly reflecting developmental conflicts. Also, whether counselors make direct evaluative comments or not, they must consider input content suggestive of positive or negative classifications of results, since this impacts client self-image within the interventive theory's philosophy of helping.

In an article related to policy, Neil Gilbert[189] suggests the importance of identifying "at risk" populations relative to a social problem, yet reminds the professional of the stigma and client resistive reactions, to the evaluative assessment itself.[190] He notes: "Many social problems attach both stigma and, in the public eye, some degree of individual responsibility to people who are experiencing the problems or who are somehow judged to be at risk of getting (or retaining or becoming worse) them." Since evaluative theory and method cannot guarantee reliable and correct classification of client adequacy relative to secondary impacts, the client is always vulnerable to negative and developmentally-damaging progressive con-notations associated with evaluations.[191]

There is an issue here also, of universality vs. specificity of evaluative categories, since they may represent differential self-perceptions of either positive or negative dimensions. If the client perceives that an evaluation has emerged as a result of worker input content, that places them among a large population of good or bad individuals; the counselor must consider how the client uses this supportive ("I'm glad other people are this fright-ened of control by outsiders") or indicting ("I am sicker than I thought, and part of a population of nationally defined pathological characters") data, to help or hinder their participation in treatment. As clients envision their relationship to a population group, they make decisions about the character-istics of this universe,[192] and their deviation from its central tendency dimensions.

More specific evaluative criteria, on the other hand, might control clients' goal assessments and any consequent stigmatization. These criteria may also curtail unrestrained abstraction that occurs, making evaluative self-perceptions more empirically relevant, grounded, and possibly less pro-nounced in the client's mind. There is always danger, however, that increased evaluative content specificity, may be more pointedly painful and closer to home, so the client might better withstand stigma, with universal abstraction to reference groups. It may also be encouraging for clients to take on evaluative characteristics of some reference groups as a temporary process of belonging, even if the subcultural, evaluatively-referenced group, may be negatively defined as deviant within "mainstream" society.[193]

As evaluative content ranges in degrees of specificity and generality, the practitioner should be sensitive to the quality of classification which the client attaches to the evaluative process. Hereby, the counselor helps the client: (1) identify a starting point which reflects a view of evaluative statements, and classifies decisions about self as this occurs; (2) expand this decision, to trace its ramifications through inductive extrapolation of further dimensions of the evaluative content-induced decision; (3) determine if general self-revelations occur, and what they mean to the client, as they deductively imply specific perceptions of the self-in-situation; (4) see if there is a patterned process of movement perceptually, from general to specific; and (5) note movement back to a previous evaluative generaliza-tion, to another generalization, or to another specific conception, impacting level and significance of awareness, and positive vs. negative perceptions of status:

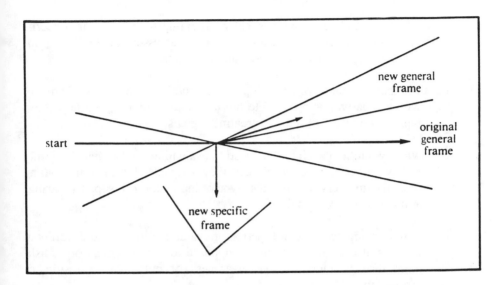

It is critical in any scenario, that the client take an in-depth look at evaluative process and content, so decisions about them (and antecedent perceptions) are clearly understood, and therapists gain feedback about how their evaluative or interventive content work independently, alternatively, or jointly in the helping effort.[194]

Each time content emerges in input speech (or is inferred symbolically from behavior), a choice[195] has been made as to the content's evaluation or interventive orientation and propose. These choices relate to domain categories by which reality is classified and understood; including its specific nature, logic which explains the content, its action component for decision-making and causal influence, level of abstraction and explanatory power, intensity and influential power, the nature of its relation to other variables within the ecological reality, and its symbolism.

In an article about evaluation as a "performance-focused" phenomenon, Pool[196] notes that anxiety has an ever present association with the concept of evaluation, and has negative social connotations. Still, it can be more productive and less fearful, if the process begins with the person to be evaluated, rather than originating externally to them,[197] as a way of developing responsibility and commitment. The counselor choosing evaluative versus non-evaluative input content must, therefore, consider:

a.   whether the client is diagnostically struggling with issues or concerns of self-assessment, or is a relatively good assessor, given the contingencies of evaluative or non-evaluative input;

b.   whether the client will develop differential levels or types of anxiety with evaluative, as opposed to non-evaluative content, and how these types of inputs contribute to treatment goals;

c.   what symbolic meaning is attached to evaluation by the client, not only in key words or types of phrases they associate, but also in meaning of evaluation versus some other type of input (control, support, caring, ambivalence, etc.); and

d.   how learning occurs as a function of evaluative input, and differential benefits of learning by doing, as opposed to reinforcement or punishment through more passive awareness of outcomes or results of evaluation.

Some authors argue that excessive and illogical evaluation of the client result in blaming.[198] This is a fallacy in social reasoning that makes those who suffer from social problems, the cause or part of the cause (including not having arrived at a solution, given their apparent or ideally-conceived free will);[199] rather than using evaluation to differentiate external causes or characteristics of client risk or susceptibility.

In 1973, Caplan and Nelson[200] found that psychologists who used person-centered orientations, gathered information predominantly on person-centered variables, with limited evaluative outcome findings supporting these prior classification biases. These definitions were also related to their skill capabilities, rather than other considerations of client need or projected goals for change. The biased judgments were further associated to methodological and theoretical aspects of the scientific philosophy; including specificity of measurement, methodological controls, and unidirectional assumptions of causation. Because specificity is one methodological goal, its transference to the treatment situation may result in excessively narrow definitions of the problem, client characteristics, outcomes, and inputs.[201]

Mishler[202] criticizes the process of "context stripping" research methods. which retract and place boundaries around variables, to isolate them from the domains where they are interactive. This may provide a simpler type of therapeutic logic, but may not be an accurate representation of reality,[203] representing a serious fallacy of reductionism for efficiency and simplicity. The selection of treatment or evaluation inputs which limit the scope or complexity of the client/situation phenomenon, may also be a projected function of awareness of limitations in evaluative technology,[204] such that the technique's "vision" becomes that of the counselor.[205]

As noted previously, evaluation can be significantly connected to the client's individual growth and development, with various evaluative inputs (content), teaching them the autonomous process of independent and accurate decision-making. It is plausible to assume that the client models this behavior relative to the degree of its visibility, and to reinforcements following client manifestations of approximations or duplications to what the counselor exhibits. Structurally, for the therapist to have evaluative reinforcing capability, some definitive evaluative content may need to precede open-ended modeling opportunities as follows:

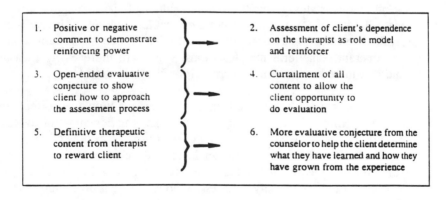

1. Positive or negative comment to demonstrate reinforcing power

2. Assessment of client's dependence on the therapist as role model and reinforcer

3. Open-ended evaluative conjecture to show client how to approach the assessment process

4. Curtailment of all content to allow the client opportunity to do evaluation

5. Definitive therapeutic content from therapist to reward client

6. More evaluative conjecture from the counselor to help the client determine what they have learned and how they have grown from the experience

As the client increases proficiency in asking evaluative questions, the counselor should reduce direct reinforcing or therapeutic comments, as well as evaluative questioning; and the client should ultimately move from evaluative questioning, to content that is more direct in its nature and impact.

It is important for counselors to decide if growth comes from the evaluative assessment process, or other direct decisions emerging from that process.   As the client, for example, decides to be affirmative and less passive in communication with an employer, is he/she simultaneously able to evaluate the action and its effects, or do these areas of content appear sequentially following rules of grammar and logic, to be therapeutically and evaluatively meaningful?   The evaluative and direct decision-making acts are complicated, and must be considered separately as well as collectively, for each counselor to understand their function and utility.

Some practitioners, on the other hand, feel too much content related to evaluation ("What do you think of this feeling? Why did this sequence of events occur? Who am I? Is this a relevant choice for me?" and so on), providing an inadvertent escape from here-and-now living and acting. Evaluative content (not necessarily resultant decisions) may be a cognitive exercise that delays or prevents acceptance of one's feelings, and delays action, especially if it occurs before rather than after, critical actions or target behaviors. Counselors who place high value on affect and feeling, may believe cognitive assessment is conceptually and philosophically incompatible with authentic insight and experience of being. This may be true, especially when evaluative content and energy compare ideal with real or other ideal states of identity, which build artificial perceptual structures that inhibit realism and actual decision-making and action in the present. Evaluative content may move the client farther from basic communicational and operant behavioral manifestations, which are more easily measured, and considered by some, as more helpful in counseling.[206]

Criticisms of the ineffectiveness or excessively-delayed effectiveness of long-term psychotherapy, may relate to lengthy demands for evaluation of child and adult developmental status continua, as well as client manifestation of new behaviors at a higher level of development. In these cases, comprehensive evaluation necessitates abstract and multilevel assessments, as opposed to behaviorally-oriented (although evaluation is important here also) treatment models. In considering therapeutic effectiveness, some counselors may be reluctant to accept the concept and practice of planned short-term intervention,[207] despite outcome research illustrating its effectiveness. This may represent their attachment to tradition, preference for interventive theory, or a decision about the relative effectiveness of evaluative process and outcomes, within either orientation.

Two issues here, are how the client decides to change a thought or behavior; and how evaluative content by the counselor, functions in setting the stage for inherent self-awareness and insight process to emerge. Other issues involve communicating to clients that new stages of developmental capability have been reached or are expected; and reinforcing the status or behaviors clients have already achieved, while using evaluation as a tool to help explain and validate these changes. Counselors are challenged to be cognizant of direct treatment content they deliver, as opposed to, or associated with, evaluative content. Further, they must determine how these are similarly or differentially perceived by clients, and similarly or differently functional as part of therapeutic change and goal achievement.

10. *Content and Theory Congruence:* Another benchmark in assessing effects of interventions, is the theory which explains the nature of human growth and development, including conflicts when development is not ideal. Theory guides thoughts, words, and behaviors which engage clients dynamically in a therapeutic process of change;[208] relative to their knowledge, experience, self-image, culture, functional skill related to task accomplishment, status attainment, or state of being satisfaction. For the professional, this means attending to immediate behavioral manifestations, while abstracting situational elements and reformulating a richer symbolic and referential meaning, that provides an accurate comprehensive guide to therapeutic action. It may be easy to view practice procedures as generally or strategically aligned with theoretical prescriptions from a broad perspective. Yet, the counselor may overlook specific applications or variances, reflecting specific content inputs that are empirically[209] non-normative (wide variance from the mean expected performance); or are components of subgroupings of tactics which have specific purpose, but are not necessarily contained within the theory's guidelines or expectations for overall interventive performance.[210]

It is conceivable that theory may not provide an accurate road map into the inner confines of the client's psychic, interpersonal, or social territory;[211] and content deviations may be necessary to informally modify the theory, as a useful guide for action. In this regard, observations of specific negative or alternate positive client outcomes suggest a new classification or descriptive model which, via the stable channels of controlled input content, becomes representative of conversely independent variables, with the theory then being viewed dependently.[212] This process works both ways, if degree of congruence between input behavior and theory specifications leads to positive client outcomes, and vice versa.[213] Also, counselors should hold constant their regular content concepts, so new data which emerges in theory, can be evaluated so it fits pre-existing theoretical formulations, or represents reality which has not been defined, but can be seen more clearly if theory and input content are consistent. Together, they form a static backdrop against which to compare new data,[214] and formulate new hypotheses.[215]

In any of the above cases, theory should be behaviorally and experientially specific enough to let the user know exactly what content fits and does not,[216] while reflecting input requirements and expected client outcomes. This is necessary because clients often do not demonstrate desirable or immediate outcomes, and the practitioner needs consistency of the independent variable long enough to study variations of the client's agenda. This helps them understand reactions to stimuli, without making the client confused, relative to excessive mobility of the input technique. In many cases psychotherapeutically, it is necessary to repeat specific types of content, verbatim, over repeated periods of delivery. This communicates to the client its significance, and insures that alternate theoretical prescriptions do not creep in. This is important, since the therapist might encounter resistance and feel pressured to move ahead, before the client has gained a critical element of self-awareness, demonstrated a behavior, or changed in a critical developmental area.

Pushing for high content correlation between input and theory, also forces practitioners to be acutely aware of their own behaviors, and stimulates thorough understanding of the theory. Each comment in a treatment situation should have direct linkages to theory, and theory should deductively have each of its elements operationalized empirically in the clinical interview.[217]   From a behavior modification, role modeling, or social learning perspective, therapy may be conceived as a process of conditioning the client to think and behave within the confines of a new realm of existence, so content congruence with theoretical constructs, may also serve as an index of shared communication and client acceptance of a change-oriented model of living.[218]   Noticing the differentiation or amount of incongruent content between client and counselor, and between either client and/or counselor and theory, provides valuable data about discrepancies in the social relationship, and social change process. The therapist, of course, must not be deceived into thinking that production of content relevant to her or his own theoretical system is, necessarily, evidence of the validity of that system.   Effectiveness of theoretical classification systems is determined and tested, via content bridges that are built by the counselor.

It is a sufficient problem in and of itself, to determine if client character-istics and theory match up, without also worrying that these two domains bypass each other, because language and grammatical content do not pro-vide consistent and correct communicational linkages, to match up the real (client) and synthetic (theory) models of reality.[219]

The practitioner, in associating theoretical concepts to pragmatic content of intervention, must also remember that some content areas of theory are abstract, and include interactive or associative relationships between subunits (for example, the theoretical concept of confrontation may suggest a special relationship between trust, degree of force, and type of resistance blockage). While the therapist uses content which seems to match the notion of confrontation, he or she may only see its singular characteristics, and fail to understand that relationship is implied, particu-larly because of the imprecise and variable nature of language systems to accurately represent reality.

An example of this emerges when working with clients who previously experienced more behaviorally-oriented alcohol and drug treatment, who may interpret the term "acceptance" (content) of one's alcoholic nature, as a critical initial step in treatment; and who employ confrontational tech-niques to break down resistance to saying publicly: "I am an alcoholic." When these clients believe that acceptance has been a critical therapeutic step, yet continue their pathological syndrome which sometimes includes substitution of other symptoms to replace alcohol consumption, the coun-selor must consider whether "acceptance" implies a complex relationship between security in a helping relationship, cognitive awareness of strength, movement through adolescent rebellion, and/or some level of autonomy. Admission of alcoholism conceptually, therefore, does not simply become another form of dependence, which might be contradictory within the developmental theory.

Practitioners must be aware of various typical levels of abstraction which are part of their cognitive repertoire, understand when and why they move between them, and determine how to assess where they are concep-tually, at any one time. They must insure theory and content relevance at the same level of genus and species as that of the client, so content variations can be measured on the same scale. If the client conceives "inches," the theory means "pounds," and the therapist delivers content relative to "softness"; then the same object can be discussed, but variations appear on entirely different planes of reality, unless a broader construct allows all three dimensions relevant[220] meaning. Therapists must consider whether content accounts for the stability and continuity of events in addition to their dynamic inherent motion, or their catalytic outcomes secondary to interaction.

The stabilization of input content elucidates problems with internal consistency of theories (as inner constructs may contradict one another); and congruence between personal philosophy of being, and the formal theory description of this phenomenon. Assumptions or views of events in the clinical milieu are often implicit theories of personality, which may be hard to distinguish from content reflecting idiosyncratic personal bias and conflict on the part of the counselor, or from more formalized theory.[221] An important question emerging from this, therefore, is whether theories emerge from practice experience, or serve as post hoc explanations of practice observations and outcomes; and whether separate theoretical and experimental practice frameworks are translatable via current systems and procedures of conceptual input content.[222] If the counselor notices ongoing inconsistencies between input content and theoretical constructs, does lack of confidence develop in theory/self/client, or push the practitioner in the direction of artificially forcing perceptions of congruence (based on degree of dependence on theory, as a guiding "parental" security force in one's professional life)?[223]

Process and Inputs

Introduction

In previous sections, specific types of inputs and their content were discussed, with attention to categories and frequencies of topics appearing through the medium of grammar and behavioral referential symbolism. It is critical for the clinical evaluator, in this regard, to understand what is being discussed or jointly perceived by counselor and client, and how various appearances and connections (relationships between ideas, natures, timing, and differential relevances of these clinical topics) are part of the foundation for change. Content is the subject matter which localizes and identifies issues through which the client moves enroute to change: it is similar to the "noun" in grammar, which denotes person, place, thing, action or quality. The limitations of noun-like elements of clinical practice, however, occur in their nominal, classificatory, or taxonomic nature; where they are deficient in ability to connote how any particular phenomenon came to be, or the action-oriented process by which it might change. The "verb" in clinical practice, therefore, is needed to provide a framework and operation for movement, change, progression, regression, or other procedures; for attaining, maintaining, relinquishing, or modifying any status attained. The author chooses to call this "process" in clinical practice, and will discuss significant evaluative questions and issues, which concern use and assessment of these action-oriented inputs.

In some cases, therapists might be confused about the difference between content (the "what" of treatment) and process (the "how" part), and incorrectly or prematurely believe that awareness of a particular topic by the client is, in and of itself, sufficient for change. Therapists must focus on clients, and solidly perceive a particular subject matter which represents a critical domain of reality or competing realities. However, clients also take action (whether overt behavior, cognitive decisioning, or evaluative feeling and awarenesses) which causes them to reduce symptoms, value differently, or change behavior which they antecedently and consequently would define as good, better, or not as bad, for their immediate or long-term well-being. Counselors who fail to recognize the action component of client progress or regression may, therefore, not recognize the concomitant component of their own action, which helps the client both energize and act—and miss critical evaluative questions that are unique to this change component of treatment.[224]

Conversely, focusing only on changing, involving, doing something, making decisions, feeling, talking, and so on, without interactively considering the content islands in the movements of change; may result in clinical process with no outcome objectives, and no temporary or permanent resting points for clients to define states of adequate being. This may eventually exhaust client or therapist, or cause the client to define adequate life status only in terms of continual movement. The ideal evaluative spectrum includes equal consideration of both content and process, as they interactively provide the client thoughts, feelings, and personality categories to maintain integrative and functional balance in the psychosocial system.

Process and Functionality

As counselors interact in various ways with clients, evaluative questions center around specific dynamics of intended client action, as a function of a direct or indirect relationship to therapist activity. If client and worker actively are both measurable, or at least observable as distinct behaviors; there may be a catalytic, action-oriented, dynamic, propulsive, energetic, magnetic, repulsive, integrative, or other functional relationship between client and worker behavior, through which interstitial action takes place to link therapist input to client outcome.

Within this focal area of action, various client characteristics are significant contributing factors to reception of intended input process (like motivation, attention, anxiety, family supports, etc.). Input purpose can be conceptualized also, at several levels of outcome and developmental functional intent, having direct and indirect significance for the client (see Figure 5).

Figure 5
Impact of Inputs on Client

Counselor Action Input

Diagnostically Correct	Diagnostically Incorrect
Theoretically Congruent	Theoretically Incongruent
Technically Correct	Technically Incorrect

Direct Impact
- Cognitive Client Reaction Intended
- Behavioral Client Reaction Intended

Developmental Impact
- Cognitive Client Reaction Intended
  - Secondary Stimulus from Client or Counselor Expected
  - Client Decision — yes | no
  - Client Corrective Action — yes | no
  - Manifestation of New Developmental Level
  - Reduction of Original Presenting Problem Systems
  - Client as Independent Self-Therapist
- Behavioral Client Reaction Intended
  - Secondary Stimulus from Client or Counselor Expected
  - Client Decision — yes | no
  - Client Corrective Action — yes | no
  - Manifestation of New Developmental Level
  - Reduction of Original Presenting Problem Systems
  - Client as Independent Self-Therapist

Because they must understand the scope of their own abstracted perspective about intended client outcome, counselors should use a comprehensive system of taxonomy or classification: to know what the theory tells them to do, whether they have correctly assessed developmental and problematic status of the client, the degree to which client or therapist bias/distortion/intervening variables are dormant/constant/controlled, and specifically what behaviors occur as input and what they are intended to accomplish in operationally-defined terms. This process cannot be overemphasized, particularly since counselors deliver inputs intended to produce client self-awareness, develop insight, and help the client to be stronger, more caring, and less manipulative.

These transformation processes connect thought and behavior, and ensure that theoretical intentions are actualized in (outcome stimulating) behaviors. For example, Gibbs, et al.[225] found that individuals with developmental deficits, manifested age-appropriate levels of cognition at different times, potentially predicated on alternative action stimuli (internal or external). Redl and Wineman[226] reported that young men with undersocialized behavioral disorders, experienced extreme difficulty in grasping social relations at some times of observation, but demonstrated superb social manipulation skills to meet their needs at other times.[227] In these cases, it may be unproductive to discuss inputs in terms of global constructs relating to adaptation or ego strength, since specific pinpointing of effect is necessary, to parallel the client's ability to differentiate thoughts and feelings in very minute ways. This is always complicated, of course, by confusion about the nature of cause-effect relationships within and between intrapsychic and social realms of existence, because of the complexity and deficits within models or theories, to explain influential action. To provide a fuller understanding of input functionality, major categories of inputs will be discussed separately, with brief analysis of each as presented.

Categories of Action Inputs

There are separate, concurrent, overlapping, joint sequential, and other unnamed types of specific input actions, which reflect different theoretical approaches to practice, varying client styles, and counselor interest and abilities. No text, even those specifically teaching counseling, therapy, or casework, lists or discusses all inputs, especially as a reflection of individual counselor approach to practice. With this disclaimer in mind, an outline follows which highlights action categories of inputs that theoretically provide cognitive and behavioral influences on client conditions, as derived from a comprehensive review of the literature.[228] These inputs are both generic and specific, and relate to various levels of psychosocial person/problem/situation domains, and functional dynamics of adaptation.

These categories are not presented in particular order, and have been coded with letters to remember their key active ingredients, as they operate on the intrapsychic, interpersonal, or systemic environment. This also suggests that theoretical statements and action statements can be connected through operational labeling processes, adding numbers or other codes to subsequently represent priorities, potencies, or other factors to pinpoint the process and context for their use. Each practitioner should be aware of specific action inputs, if evaluation of related client outcome is to have relevance.

Pattern Interruption (PI)
1. Divert attention to alternate stimulus
2. Create overlapping simultaneous messages
3. Redefine primary/focal content
4. Initiate forceful threatening stimulus
5. Suggest potential negative reinforcement
6. Confirm but redirect message directions
7. Create spectator role for client and incompatible self-awareness
8. Offer positive reinforcement for alternate pattern

Judgment or Diagnostic Assessment (JD)
1. Confirm identity status
2. Suggest missed options for positive reinforcement
3. Suggest potential occurrences of negative punishments
4. Create fear of child-like deviance
5. Suggest antithetical or incongruent perceptions between counselor and client and therefore diminished opportunities for relationship stability
6. Provide "parental" approval or direct disapproval

Increase Variables (V +)
1. Postulate new concepts
2. Force deductive or inductive logic and block previous conclusions
3. Withhold reinforcement for specific conclusions but not decision-making process
4. Question conclusions
5. Exaggerate negative conclusions
6. Reiterate paradoxes
7. Support hypothetical conceptions of altered states of being
8. Expand range of inclusiveness of one variable

9. Challenge judgment anchoring (comparing evidence)
10. Show transition points in life processes

Decrease Variables (V -)

1. Accent specific foci to diminish excessive expansion of awareness
2. Force prioritization of content
3. Reduce anxiety by decreasing perceptual/cognitive stimuli
4. Develop category system to group variables

Create Causal/Correlational Linkage (CCL)

1. Provide modeled stimulus behavior to which client is highly likely to react
   a. to see negative consequences
   b. to see control dynamics
   c. to make value judgment
2. Infuse causal diagnostic feedback to provide behavioral rationale with positive connotations
3. Define consistent patterns of relationship dynamics that can be altered by (a) redefinition or (b) behavioral alteration
4. Reduce degree of conceptual-behavioral dependency through location of priorities, redefinition of degree of positive/negative consequences
5. Redefine independent/dependent nature of variables
6. Interchange independent and dependent variables
7. Pressure alternative causal hypotheses
8. Identify intervening variables and their effects

Differentiate Time/Space Dimensons (TS)

1. Change time reference between past, present, future; conscious and unconscious
2. Associate differential value interpretations for alternate time frames
3. Hypothesize future outcomes and ramifications
4. Investigate differential growth patterns per unit of time/situation (alternate developmental models)
5. Differentiate normal and pathological fixations and regression behaviors
6. Teach conceptual change of time focus

Evaluate Needs (NA)

1. Create awareness of stress, esteem levels and need content
2. Define quality of object relations
3. Stimulate conclusive decisioning relative to outcomes

4. Differentiate primitive separation of primary anxiety from signal anxiety (internal changes)
5. Teach behavioral self-monitoring

Redefine Crisis (RCr)

1. De-emotionalize volatile issues
2. Emphasize time-related decreasing energy
3. Build self-esteem about survival
4. Define non-victim roles
5. Plan death/loss
6. Maximize perceptions of choices
7. Link clients to support systems
8. Develop reconciliation framework to reconceptualize with the past
9. Identify gains
10. Confirm and explore alternate views
11. Balance success and failure
12. Integrate past with present circumstances
13. Stress value of conflict for normal growth
14. Increase tolerance levels

Denote Repetition (DRep)

1. Create awareness of meaningful occurrence frequencies and interpret levels
2. Communicate negative value of inflexible repetition
3. Identify causes for repetitive behaviors or thoughts
4. Stimulate time distancing
5. Connect compulsive behavior manifestation to thought/feeling preoccupation

Differentiate Symbolizations (S)

1. Identify labeling and classification schemes
2. Define images of strength vs. weakness
3. Reframe confusing or negative content
4. Stimulate self-recognition
5. Create visual images and clarify cognitive images
6. Differentiate images that are reactive to therapeutic inputs in progress vs. stationary and non-movable images
7. Give concept of mobility to images
8. Give images representational form
9. Connect process and content symbols
10. Recognize psychological nature of symptoms

Develop Projection (Pro)
1. Produce external anchoring points for judgment and coordinated perceptions
2. Create awareness of incremental decision adjustments for information input
3. Teach perceptual consistency through information comparisons
4. Extrapolate and interpolate data (infer value beyond or within known range)

Coordinate Inner Emotions with External Stimulation (I/O)
1. Change role expectations
2. Teach problem-solving
3. Substitute affective experience for intellectual processes
4. Stimulate intellectual integration (working through)
5. Heighten feeling sensation
6. Explore broader range of feelings
7. Compare effects of personal and social standards and rewards

Dissociation and Distancing (DD)
1. Define variable stressors and simulate physical, conceptual, and emotional distancing
2. Develop concepts of intervening units of time, behavior
3. Teach independence vs. dependence of cognitive processes
4. Teach self-perception—self-observation in absence of external cues
5. Explore extent and process of developing conceptual autonomy

Differentiate Socially Efficacious (Situationally Functional) (E—D) From Deviant (Idealist Normality) Perceptions
1. Produce comprehensive understanding of social contexts
2. Define positives in feelings, behaviors, and situational positive/negative influences
3. Define deviance as joint victimization
4. Explore preconceived values
5. Encourage deviance to foster creative exploration/expression
6. Teach that internal emotional experience and external expression of affect need not correspond and are not necessarily identical
7. Create awareness and acceptance of harmfulness of negative behaviors

Change Learning Model (L—L)
1. Attach reinforcing power to alternate stimuli
2. Change targeted behaviors of interest
3. Increase or decrease reinforcement schedules, intensities
4. Integrate monitors or reinforcement controllers at various points in the system to alter its function

5.   Teach developmental causal and trait theories
6.   Create achievement standards and self-administered rewards
7.   Assess current performance relative to criterion and formulate evaluative judgment

Internalize Process (IP)

1.   Develop self-dialogue, stress desensitization, behavioral and cognitive rehearsal, internal decision-making
2.   Create awareness of negative dimensions of abuse, limiting negative self-dialogue
3.   Create awareness of fixed and transient conceptual sets or categories, and their function/maintenance dynamics within systems
4.   Enhance personal responsibility
5.   Interdict negative or angry self-talk
6.   Encourage "I" statements
7.   Internalize past, present, future expectations as personal agenda

Externalize and Redefine Feeling (ERF)

1.   Differentiate self from others and various identity statuses
2.   Teach displacement and projection
3.   Create awareness of overperception of self
4.   Change cognitive bias of "ego-centricity" for realistic perceptions
5.   Link client behavior with significant other people

Develop New Concepts of Life Survival (LS)

1.   Create optimism, hope, and positive orientation
2.   Develop bilateral measurements of gains and losses of power
3.   Analyze belief systems, values, opinions, stereotypes, expectations
4.   Develop client motivation

Conceptualize System Concepts (Sys)

1.   Develop concepts of mutuality, synergy, collectivity; cohesion, support
2.   Create awareness of boundaries and their function
3.   Demonstrate conjoint problem-solving
4.   Differentiate original from present systems
5.   Develop structuring
6.   Conceptualize and design variations in composition and function
7.   Integrate new roles
8.   Teach conflict models
9.   Differentiate independence and dependence within system
10. Teach achievement-orientation within systemic contingencies

11. Identify the world as structured, ordered, understandable
12. Differentiate view of self, external system, and synthetic view of both together, relative to process and content
13. Teach functions and values of cultural influences

Use of Negative Traits and Defenses (UD)
1. Reinforce character traits for altered rewards, outcomes
2. Create comparative decision-making to form perceptions of options and new behaviors
3. Intensify feeling and emotion to increase psycho-tension and mobilize unconscious material

Redefine Deviance (Functionality) (+ D)
1. Create appreciation of balance and stability functions
2. Identify themes
3. Operationalize definitions of problems (consequential thinking)
4. Stimulate creativity

Relive Growth Stages (RG)
1. Enforce ownership of phenomenon (not projection, displacement, denial)
2. Broaden experience by encouraging movement horizontally and vertically
3. Promote regression to conceptually and emotionally relive positive past experiences
4. Teach developmental theory
5. Pursue movement to stimulate graduated, progressive, anticipatory stage appropriate behavior
6. Re-expose client, under favorable conditions, to transference relationship
7. Create awareness of dependencies
8. Uncover and re-experience repressed emotional conflict
9. Connect present conflict locus with early childhood emotional conflict and defensive decisions
10. Interpret transference

Take Parental Control (by counselor) (PC)
1. Teach assertiveness
2. Protect client
3. Offer forgiveness, permission
4. Become less active to allow client activity, thought

5.   Mediate conflicts and advise
      a.   reframe
      b.   redefine
      c.   partialize
6.   Establish rules and structure
7.   Reinforce client value
8.   Provide escape value for feelings
9.   Expect change
10.   Allow "freedom" of expression without judgment
11.   Provide symbolic activities to enhance awareness of conflicts
12.   Create awareness of universality and human commonality
13.   Provide platform in transition from old to new principles of living

Produce Associative Connections Between
Attitudes and Behaviors (A + B)

1.   Show causes of non-correlation between verbal and behavioral stimuli
2.   Demonstrate specific associational linkages
3.   Illustrate differential activity to situational pressures and social norms
4.   Correct irrational or erroneous processes of attitude formation
5.   Stimulate self-reflective process and analyze corrections of incorrect self-perceptions
6.   Describe internal states of being
7.   Examine effects of self-analysis of attitude/behavior matrix
8.   Compare degree of awareness of behavior versus other criteria for determining behavior
9.   Analyze confidence in attitudes
10.   Differentiate observations and analysis of thoughts
11.   Connect therapeutic concepts with life agenda concepts
12.   Interpret status fluctuations as ratio between ego and personality stability

Clarification (CL)

1.   Elucidate real client-stated/perceived conflicts
2.   Define meaning of symptoms and impulse-anxiety-defense triad
3.   Differentiate individual from relationship issues
4.   Create awareness of conflict between unacceptable wish and defenses against the wish
5.   Clarify dynamics and meaning of communication interchanges
6.   Stimulate awareness of goals and life view
7.   Maintain focus
8.   Rephrase communications

Behavioral or Cognitive Directedness (B/CD)

1. Recognize negative cognitions
2. Conduct empirical reality testing
3. Examine distortions
   a. overgeneralization
   b. catastrophizing
   c. dichotomous thinking
4. Provide correct emotional experience
5. Correct distortions
6. Provide structured problem-solving models and skill training
7. Utilize contingency contracting
8. Desensitize client
9. Conduct role-play
10. Teach effective communication
11. Provide homework assignments to promote generalization
12. Teach relaxation exercises and cognitive-behavioral techniques of stress management
13. Teach and demonstrate self-observation
14. Interpret conflict (cognitions)
15. Assess function of negative cognitive/behavioral processes
16. Identify and prohibit resistance
17. Simplify complex problems through behavioral specificity
18. Reward performance of feared positive behaviors
19. Prohibit negative behaviors

Support (SP)

1. Reinforce humanism and idealistic phenomenology
2. Give summations
3. Demonstrate warm, non-blaming, positive image
4. Validate feelings
5. Express love
6. Use humor to diversify perspectives on conflict
7. Teach client to view encounters with others as non-hurtful

Confrontation (CF)

1. Interpret and challenge resistance and defense relative to contexts of past, present, and transference
2. Help client accept responsibility for actions (blame, fault)
3. Clarify underlying conflicts as differentiated from stated conflicts
4. Delineate ways conflicts are played out in relationships
5. Use time pressure to enhance crisis and motivation

6.   Encourage choosing and decision-making
7.   Be antagonistic to get client to defend and test out adequacy of decisions—create existential crises
8.   Promote anxiety so client will examine avoided issues and increase emotional intensity
9.   Expose patterns that are repetitive, self-punishing, and self-defeating

Reflective Feedback (NO interpretation) (RF)
1.   Stimulate interaction via reflection and directive statements
2.   Clarify levels and types of motivation
3.   Show effects of client stimulation

Model Behavior (Mod)
1.   Increase frequencies of positive and adaptive behaviors
2.   Make decisions and evaluate outcomes

Facilitate Analysis and Planning of Goals (PG)
1.   Increase goal awareness, commitment, and contracting
2.   Encourage participation in setting goals
3.   Encourage and reinforce goal-related actions

Reduce Anxiety, Produce Relaxation (A})
1.   Conduct meditation, cognitive relaxation, and muscular relaxation exercises
2.   Create awareness of anxiety-associated cues for physical process
3.   Behaviorally extinguish conditioned anxiety-reactions
4.   Expose, densitizate, and change internal states of sensitivity

Promote Health Practice (HP)
1.   Encourage holistic self-perspective
2.   Create awareness of "mediating" processes in somatic illnesses
3.   Define defenses and coping mechanisms associated with physical adaptation
4.   Discover dual nature of mind-body equation (functional unity)
5.   Stimulate insight into control of physical and mental process
6.   Connect inner and outer excitement via insight or behavioral change
7.   Conduct evaluation of client health status and practices and make recommendations
8.   Teach right and responsibility to achieve physical pleasure

Metacommunication and Communication (MTC)
1.   Reconstruct communication patterns
2.   Analyze syntax, process, and pattern

3. Identify organizational and relationship framework for communication and its symbolic meaning
4. Analyze communicational aspects of defining and deciding actions
5. Discover internal connection between motives, reasons, and actions
6. Develop categories or classifications of actions
7. Teach intuitive versus non-intuitive analysis
8. Control functions of properties of communication (context)

Education (ED)
1. Teach problem-solving skills
2. Plan constructive activities   •
3. Utilize role-playing techniques
4. Teach assertion and provide practice opportunities
5. Examine motivation and teach social skills
6. Educate clients on effects of problems, symptoms, and defenses
7. Teach social (empirically verifiable) discrimination of level of dysfunction/ change
8. Teach self-monitoring and self-management skills
9. Enhance information acquisition skills and content skills
10. Teach information extrapolation/interpretation
11. Coordinate symbolic referents applied to concrete facts
12. Facilitate application of facts to social and individual situations
13. Teach learning themes and principles

Self-Efficacy (SE)
1. Instill and strengthen self-perceptions of coping efficacy and awareness of weight placed on efficacy decisions
2. Demonstrate awareness of performance accomplishments, structure-guided mastery experiences, and behavioral approximations
3. Provide alternate self-enhancing definitions
4. Help client accept and use power

Preventive Diagnostic Skills (Prev)
1. Review incidents of deviance, anger, loss of control, to identify early warning signs, analyze client interpretations, and develop a framework with alternative options
2. Encourage role choices consistent with self-concept by encouraging definitions of self-concept and classifications of roles

Introduction of Placebo (P)

1. Initiate input skill as placebo to allow other significant variables time to activate

System Management (Per + Sys)

1. Operationally define person and situation interaction and match-up (situationism)
2. Arrange and analyze concomitant variation
3. Demonstrate reciprocal causality
4. Facilitate personality related choices of situations to produce congruence
5. Create awareness of degrees of freedom of choice
6. Allow pressure from environmental variables
7. Demonstrate variability of self-referent cognitions in external or internal environments
8. Mitigate vivid cognitive self-structure
9. Create awareness of social comparisons as a learning phenomenon
10. Analyze need satisfying roles
11. Teach responsibility for identity (counteract dependency)
12. Shift needs outside of conflictual relationships
13. Encourage relinquishment of childhood conflictual roles
14. Direct congruent messages
15. Coordinate behavior exchange, cognitive and attributional changes; instigate parallel but non-contingent changes
16. Teach communication skills to handle conflict and achieve problem resolution
    a. use behavioral rehearsal, repetition, and response generalization
    b. analyze the state of the relationship
17. Create awareness and control of environmental reinforcement contingencies
18. Rearrange ratios of adaptive to defensive behaviors
19. Teach the system to interrupt itself positively

Cognitive Restructing (CR)

1. Create awareness of outcome expectation hierarchies and behavioral results and implications
2. Create awareness of inner monologue and influential input media
3. Enhance performance accuracy and awareness of cognitive ability (level of performance) and cognitive style (manner of performance)
4. Assess field dependence and independence
5. Help client differentiate:
    a. accuracy versus inaccuracy of performance
    b. value dimensions of performance

      c.   effectiveness versus ineffectiveness

      d.   behaviors from being states

6.   Create awareness of incorrect cognitive linkages

7.   Develop foci that can be separated from conflictual spheres of cognition

8.   Define cognitive perceptual categories of gain rather than loss, and self-diagnostic categories

9.   Define major and minor premises of client-relevant syllogisms; fixed and variable conclusions

10.   Link parallel contexts

11.   Increase frustration tolerance

12.   Disrupt irrational messages

13.   Develop images of adaptation

14.   Develop behavioral referents for intrapsychic process

15.   Create implosive activity

16.   Encourage risk-taking

Paradoxical Measures (Par)

(A contradiction following a correct logical deduction that results from consistent major and minor premises)

1.   Employ symptom prescription to develop self-control

2.   Create cognitive positive images associated with aversive situations by pairing noncompatible stimuli desensitization

Environmental Manipulation (EM)

1.   Redefine client discrediting evidence from environment

2.   Close avenues to rationalization and environmental attribution of success

3.   Remove strong internal or external constraints to enhance self-inferences for development of dependable source of assessment information

4.   Physically separate enmeshed clients

5.   Facilitate decision-making about discrepancies between behavioral standards and self-expectancy

Self-Disclosure (SD)

1.   Teach self-disclosure as a form of modeling

2.   Develop favorable impressions of the therapist

3.   Speak honestly about self and client

4.   View problems in emotional terms

Adult Development (AD)

1. Identify tasks and convey confidence in inner sameness and self-continuity
2. Stimulate intimacy and commitment to affiliations
3. Create awareness of generativity, responsibilities, and opportunities
4. Facilitate ego integrity and structural unit (order and meaning in the inner world)
5. Create awareness of structure-building (stable) and structure changing (transitional) periods
6. Help client reject false assumptions rooted in childhood experience
7. Increase complexity and differentiation to produce ego development
8. Encourage impulse control
9. Control stereotyping, encourage appreciation of uniqueness, and define conceptual clarity and multiplicity
10. Differentiate self from nonself
11. Differentiate autism, symbiosis, and exploitation
12. Facilitate internalization of blame and handling guilt
13. Create assessment of opportunism by differentiating manipulation and exploitation from self-fulfillment
14. Create understanding of conformity to external rules while setting self-evaluative standards
15. Differentiate norms from personal goals
16. Create self-awareness in relations between self and relevant groups
17. Define adjustment and adjustment problems
18. Differentiate feelings from motives
19. Create understanding of conceptual patterning
20. Stress dependence versus independence as a problem in cognitive awareness
21. Encourage tolerance for ambiguity, conflict
22. Teach skills to cope with conflicting inner needs
23. Help client renounce unattainable goals
24. Integrate affect and cognitive structures
25. Define aspects of earlier stages that can be retained within adult roles
26. Understand interpersonal connectedness, collective rewards, and joint gains
27. Pursue development of a specific self-concept
28. Contradict previous negative parenting

Expectancies (Ex)

1. Offer attention
2. Help client acquire expectancy of increased personal effectiveness
3. Expose client to stressful situations to produce change by itself
4. Use cues to indicate change dynamics related to expected outcomes

Milieu Treatment (Mil)

1. Link developmental deficits to phase-specific tasks
2. Define internal and external systems of consequences and rewards to build socially and personally acceptable behaviors
3. Understand interpersonal expectation and limits
4. Involve significant others in treatment
5. Facilitate role reversal for learning new role conceptions
6. Differentiate self from others
7. Resocialize the client
8. Develop awareness of need-meeting motives of behavior, especially hostile and disruptive motivations
9. Encourage expression of anger in less destructive ways
10. Provide behavioral limits and controls
11. Reward verbal communication of needs, anger, distress
12. Provide alternative objects of aggression other than self
13. Provide alternate forms of sensory stimulation
14. Create phenomenologial congruence (extent to which a person sees the self as others see him/her and sees others as they see themselves)

Dialectic (Dial)
(A developmental transformation via constitutive and interactive relationships)

1. Divert attention from conception of external forces in environment causing activity of discrete, independent, unrelated, separate, inert, passive parts or reality
2. Stress activity or process where motion is inherent in developmental terms and outcomes are related to this interactivity process
3. Realign concepts in conjunction with unfolding emergence of thesis, antithesis and synthesis
4. Emphasize structure and function
5. Teach principles of evolutionary truth
6. Teach interactive and reciprocal processes of relationship definition and resultant homeostasis
7. Define the problem as an attempt at resolution and also as a solution
8. Teach relational ethics
9. Use logic to solve double-bind conflicts by establishing one of the contradictory messages as "correct"
10. Integrate contradictions by moving to metacommunicative level synthesis
11. Teach reciprocal causation
12. Associate correlativity of knower and known

Mediation (Medtn)

1.   Create awareness of conflict-solving techniques
2.   Manage relationship behaviors
3.   Withdraw force, compromise, confront, maintain neutrality
4.   Depersonalize problem foci
5.   Teach timing of communication responses and stimuli
6.   Create awareness of deeper interests and needs
7.   Create options for mutual gain in client systems
8.   Seek objective standards rather than personal wills
9.   Develop awareness of power imbalances
10. Define differences between substantive and symbolic issues
11. Employ retroactive experiences
12. Create awareness of tactics versus strategic philosophies
13. Empower the weak client
14. Assert scientific basis of rational thought; teach client applicable research findings
15. Develop awareness of linkages
16. Serve as receiving mechanism for venting of feelings
17. Reframe questions so no one loses
18. Teach client to speak and think through a buffer or rational filter
19. Recognize negative feelings and ideas existing simultaneously
20. Utilize role reversal
21. Broaden field of acceptable ideas and feelings
22. View separate parts of personality
23. Break down issues and explore their meanings
24. Partition the conflict
25. Link issues into constellations which later submerge them and reduce their negative impact

Communicate that Change is not
Feasible-Disengage (D)

1.   Reflect client efforts to solve unsolvable problem
2.   Diagnose client motivation and decreased desired outcome potential
3.   Share own (counselor's) skill and knowledge deficits

The previous listing of input dimensions, represents a variety of formats, theories, and comparable as well as unique styles, to categorize the "verb" or action component of therapeutic work (the reader will know other ways to present, subdivide, or combine categories—or even represent their nature in totally different fashion). They illustrate some forms of change-oriented dynamic activity, that can guide counselors in developing their own lists, as a prelude to planning evaluation of their presence within counseling, and assessing their outcome effect.

The important point in evaluation, is that practitioners must understand the nature and purpose of each separate, as well as coordinated dimension of input, to operationally define precise action that is taken. This is critical to trace effects on clients' bio-psychosocial functioning, note long-term developmental change, and differentiate specific units of intervention which were or were not helpful in assisting clients to rearrange patterns of adaptation, so change occurs.

Failure to define inputs as having specific action identity, questions the defensible rationale for any action. It blocks comprehensive understanding of client outcomes as anything other than random or serendipitous combinations of variables, not related logically to overriding principles of personality functioning, or psychic and social structure.

To demonstrate one perspective and approach to this evaluative process, and identify key questions about input effectiveness, this section discusses selected individual and combined inputs within the context of abstracted definitional categories, representing dimensions of action. Categories which follow, were derived from analysis of specific types of inputs discovered in the literature, providing a framework to scrutinize specific interventive functions.

Interdictive Inputs

Numerous authors discuss one purpose of inputs, as simply blocking or providing interruptive wedges to delay, disrupt, or stop destructive client cognitive or behavioral processes. In evaluating these inputs, it is important to establish baseline frequencies of client behaviors, to supply the interdictive stimulus and encourage continuance, delay, or disappearance of the previous patterned response.

There are benefits in the here-and-now therapeutic environment when habituated repetitions are lessened or discontinued, but it is equally important for counselors to monitor their behavior after the interruption has occurred, to insure that additional planned therapeutic goals are pursued during the interim period, when client behavior has been altered. It is important to establish parallel measurement models for clients when not in the counselor's office, so they can assess degree of learning, and determine if internal or systemic self-reinforcements have been transplanted to produce similar or alternate pattern interruptions.

The clinician measures effectiveness of these techniques relative to the recurrent numbers of interruptions needed, the force and persistence of technique application, length of time the pattern remains broken, and types of client activity which occur before and after successive therapeutic interruptions. Some patterns might be graphically symbolized as follows:

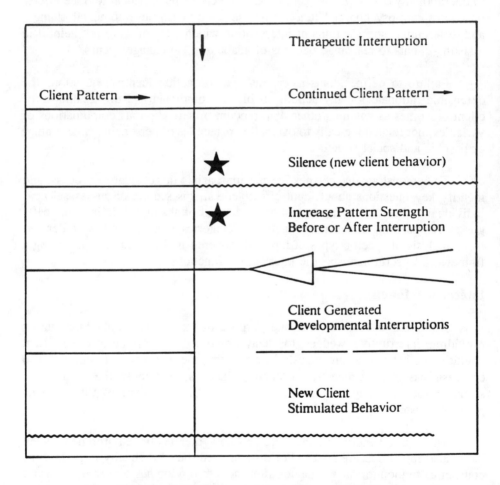

Hypothesis that this was the **pattern** originally
and first behavior interrupted was acute,
situational deviant reaction

The dynamically-oriented clinician must, of course, be concerned about concomitant assessment of clients' perceptions about therapeutic interdictions, not only to assess whether they even perceive the interruption, but to determine significance they attach to this particular input behavior. Interruption may be a valuable prelude to a subsequent therapeutic tactic (so degree of interruption and effort of following activity, would be assessed), but may also have positive or negative ramifications, independent of inputs which follow. Some clients, for example, view the interruption as a devastating invasion of their psychic or socio-metric space (identity); and developmentally regress, passive-aggressively continue their pattern silently, or temporarily delay it with defensive behaviors, so no interruption has actually occurred at all. Other clients may be confused by the process and neither gain nor lose momentum, but simply waste time responding randomly, neutrally, or in crisis fashion to a stimulus they do not understand. Others learn from the technique, see the compulsive and ineffective nature of their patterns, and realize that other more efficacious activity must ensue. The clinician must evaluate the client's interpretation after interruptions, to definitively know if learning occurred, or whether additional techniques must be appended to the interdictive behavior (coordinated input package). Client self-regulated interruptions can also signal compulsive ritualistic dependency, rather than autonomic growth toward maturity.

In some cases, the counselor may decide that interruptions be intermittently introduced, so the client developmentally benefits from the autonomy or protective defensiveness, of having control over intermittent segments of daily life, to defend against "parental" intrusions. In this case, effectiveness of interdictive inputs may emerge in their interwoven juxtaposition and interdependency with client patterns of action or inaction, in time-out input periods. A behavioral approach might also include pattern interruption, as well as distinctive reinforcement of mutually-exclusive and positive alternate behaviors, which the client explores during time-out periods following interruption. Operationally, this looks like a laddered progression of approximations to desired behavior, as follows:

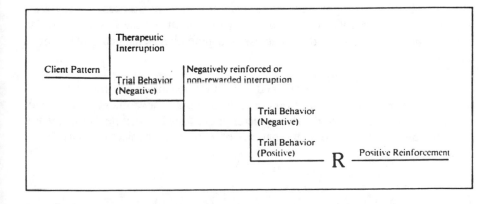

One implication of this approach, is that the client may be a receptive and motivated learner either before or after the interruption of negative patterns, but it is important to assess learning potential as early as possible, so hypotheses develop even before the "trial and error" interruption occurs, to prevent nonproductive or regressive consequences.

Gestaltists might feel that pattern interruptions help clients become aware of their activity which needs specific evaluation, separately from assessing the interruptive behaviors themselves; and these same activities might require more comprehensive analysis of degree of awareness, regarding childhood or adult functionality. This "degree of understanding" variable, however, does not necessarily suggest commensurate degree of behavioral change. Both may require additional inputs before or after the blocking stimulus.

Connected with the strategy of pattern interruption, is the function of helping clients become aware of the nature, repetitiveness, and solidarity of their behavioral, affective, or cognitive repertoire. The developmental goal may be to define and exercise autonomous evaluative and self-governing responsibility, through assumption of external platforms of perspective, to see one's behavior and decide about it at the same time. There is philosophical concern about whether clients can meaningfully envision a repetitive pattern within which they are embedded, functionally dependent, and synchronized, since the nature of the pattern suggests linear viewing of successive expected behaviors, to avoid anxiety. External perspectives demand extraction from this binding chain reaction, without occupying a proven structure of equal or superior psychic and emotional safety.

One chain reactive pattern may be substituted for the other, with a definitional contingency in the second chain that demands awareness and viewing of the first; but in any case, counselors have a complex evaluative mission, to understand how they might have stimulated this new awareness. They then decide if it is functionally or developmentally different from the first pattern, and determine how to assess its differentness and potentially-changed psychosocial functionality and outcome.

Assuming there is dynamic and structural meaning of "awareness" of patterns, another evaluative question concerns amount of awareness, and categorization and documenting of decisions the client has made, relative to this awareness. In this scenario, the input pattern of evaluative conjecture may be as follows:

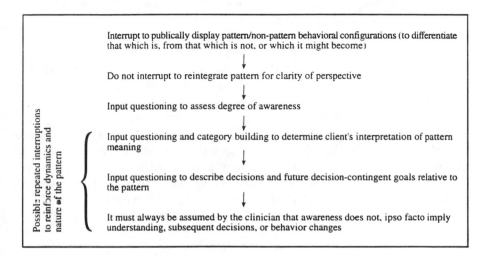

Clarification and Reflection

Another clinical input which nearly all theories and even eclectic methodologies value, is counselor reflection of identical, similar, exaggerated, or diminished manifestations of a stimulus the client has been, or is currently demonstrating. This can be active repeating of verbatim client responses, or silence to signal an expectation to think about and re-experience that which has just transpired. Reflection is a "mirroring" process, evaluated in terms of congruence of client image of themselves before and after the reflection, requiring pre- and posttest assessments. The mirrored reflection is compared to an indexing standard along some diagnostic or developmental continuum. Evaluative perspectives should focus on before, after, and a third position, to further clarify ranges and boundaries of the triangulated perspectives. One theoretical approach to the reflective process maintains that awareness is predominantly relative to the client's gestalt, and is not designed to be thrust into the external arena of the expert's opinion, or compared to other external qualitative criteria. When reflection is primarily for the client's benefit, a sound evaluative approach assists the client in developing a taxonomy of a full range of "self-reflections," building a blueprint of personality, and providing grounding points from which to assess variations of self-perceptive positions. As the counselor plans to reflect back, evaluative questions should follow, giving the client time to act independently on this awareness. These questions assess client reception of the reflected image, determine whether the image has changed as a result of the reflection process, and assess what the perspective or focus means, as the image assumes some position of value in cognitive structure.

Sometimes a stream of consciousness or free-associative experience after the reflective input, reveals a parade of image foci. These patterns or symbolizations assist the client in analyzing behavior, and sometimes set in motion a chain of client image-to-image self-reflections (excluding the theorist), which provide a richer array of data for comparison. The counselor can continue to use the reflective process to create awareness of constellations of images and image associations (as categories of images are compared to each other), as well as individual image comparisons to normative or deviant categorical patterns. When there are external images which the counselor believes serve as positive, negative, or different variations, the reflective process may involve behavioral control and reinforcement, through anticipatory rewards or punishments for altering patterns.

The counselor needs to be aware of differences between open-ended reflections and relatively fixed-alternative (usually controlled by the expert or the treatment goals) reflections, because the outcomes may be different, and assessment of effectiveness will vary accordingly. In the case of clarification as an input, the counselor should evaluate ability of the client to produce clear messages or behaviors, the client's progressive changes, and reduction of other factors which confuse communications or aid in the functional defensive necessity of unclear client behavioral or verbal manifestations. Therapists should separate concerns for achievement of clarity, out of situations where clients feel they are clear (and may be correct in this assumption), but where the counselor misrepresents clarification for alternations of imposed transformations of the client's communicated image, agenda, or message. In interpersonal situations there is a particular dilemma, because nonresponse from others sometimes leads to the incorrect assumption of clarity in message reception, which may be followed by correct or incorrect response regardless of the message clarity. The evaluator must monitor each contingency as a separate entity, to factor out causes of variations, illustrated in Figure 6.

One concern here is whether clarity was achieved and what, if anything, the added clarity accomplished, relative to other criteria in the clinical milieu.

Variable Manipulation (Increase/Decrease/Modify)

Many theories suggest that counselors help clients broaden their perceived and acceptable options for thoughts, feelings, or behaviors, or develop a wider or narrower perspective about certain aspects of their lives. This structurally may

Figure 6
Message Interaction in Counseling

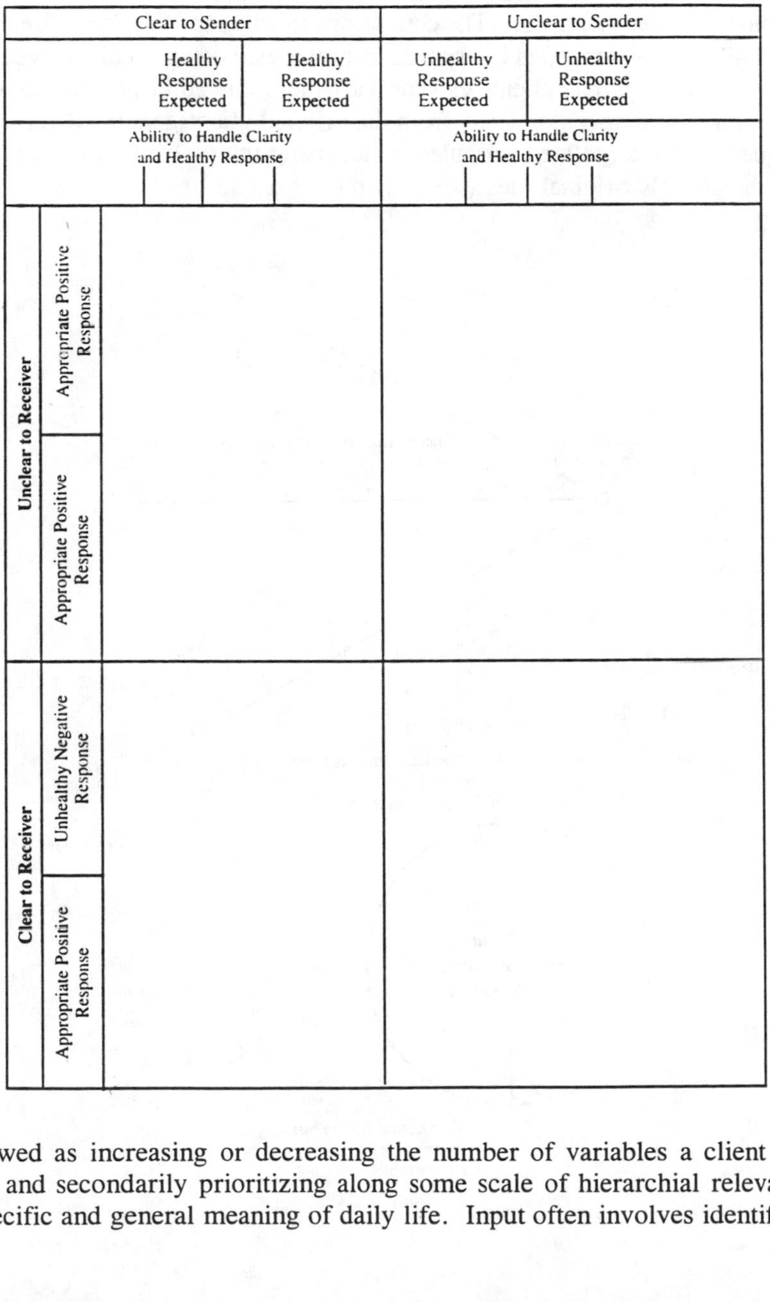

		Clear to Sender		Unclear to Sender	
		Healthy Response Expected	Healthy Response Expected	Unhealthy Response Expected	Unhealthy Response Expected
		Ability to Handle Clarity and Healthy Response		Ability to Handle Clarity and Healthy Response	
Unclear to Receiver	Appropriate Positive Response				
	Appropriate Positive Response				
Clear to Receiver	Unhealthy Negative Response				
	Appropriate Positive Response				

be viewed as increasing or decreasing the number of variables a client knows about, and secondarily prioritizing along some scale of hierarchial relevance to the specific and general meaning of daily life. Input often involves identification of additional thoughts, feelings, or behaviors which are linked according to some explanatory principle, to those which are previously known or communicated by clients (for example, a feeling of aspiration rather than anger, when confronted with a block to need-meeting). The counselor can measure this input function by simply noting its presence, as a response to previously categorically-keyed manifestations of a negative client-relevant variable. In addition, the counselor observes amount of variation away from the original client-generated variable, or the frequency of interpolated variables at increasing intervals of conceptual closeness to the client's original idea (see Illustrations a and b).

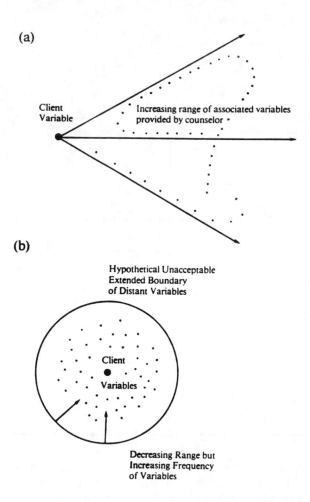

(a)

Client
Variable

Increasing range of associated variables
provided by counselor

(b)

Hypothetical Unacceptable
Extended Boundary
of Distant Variables

Client

Variables

Decreasing Range but
Increasing Frequency
of Variables

The counselor can also help the client decrease the number of variables in the perceptual or behavioral arena, by combining two or more into consolidated variable clusters (which may be redefined as single units of reality), or by using reinforcement and selective attentional mechanisms to attend to particular types, or reward a client's consideration of fewer numbers (see Illustration c).

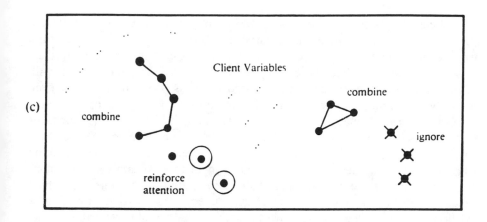

Evaluation here is complicated, because it is initially difficult to measure the extended or diminished nature of the client's universe of variable units; and confusing to decide about associative relations between numbers of variables, values placed on these variables, energy or direction for action-inherent in particular variables, and overall relevance within corresponding states of developmental, adjustment, or adaptive adequacy in the client's and counselor's framework.

As counselors become involved in this increase/decrease process, the evaluative focus must be on whether former states of being (with one index being numbers of variables) have actually changed as a result of frequency alterations; and at which point the inflation or deflation saturation, or systemic disequilibrium, sets in, without associated abstract redefinitions of reality, self, or both. The counselor who helps Ms. Jones consider more options in her life, can cross-reference each option-increase with some index of developmental change (movement toward autonomy, flexibility), and examine different dimensions of personality self-awareness, as each new variable positively or negatively interacts with those previously open for consideration. Geometric properties of expanded outcome products, however, may emerge as a client-centered critical mass, which may cause regression rather than progression. An example, is work with passive and dependent women in traditional marriages, who feel general security in their social roles, but acute stress in the quality of the relationship. As variables are expanded to consider nontraditional female social, sexual, and/or economic roles, some clients become overwhelmed and further regress (not only with variable reductions, but also with added strength to identity decisions) to perceived safe confines of their psychosocial or perceptual milieu.

Clients may also have conceptual, cultural, and social boundaries placing limits on additions or subtractions of variables, as their degree of variance from norms becomes involved. Sub-boundaries may cluster certain variables together, as do county and city boundaries within states. Increases or decreases with cross-cultural boundary lines can be assessed in terms of the meaning (or even possibility of crossing) to the client, and relative future conditions of normative person-in-culture adequacy, as resources are modified, relocated, added, or deleted. This can be particularly problematic when the counselor feels the client is overwhelmed by too much data impacting his/her stressed decision-making apparatus. This may necessitate provision of input to eliminate some variables from conscious awareness, or to suggest a revision in the value framework which defines certain facts as more significant than others. As variable extinction or alteration progresses, the counselor needs to insure that variable remnants are not retained somewhere else in the psyche or unconscious. These remnants can also become reprioritized in current operating cognitions or behavioral patterns, without adequate analysis of concomitant or developmental changes in structures which authorize and support the original or newly-prioritized variables. Increases or decreased in variables may cut across lines of real or symbolic abstraction, so the counselor must be evaluatively sure (and help the client understand), when horizontal or vertical changes have been made or attempted:

Horizontal Variable Changes	ABC → ACK
	↓ ↓ ↓
Symbolic Boundary	————
Symbolic Changes	XYZ　ZZZ

When horizontal distant changes have been made:

ABCDEFGHI	Variables
XXXXXXXXX	Symbolic States
ABCDEFGHI	Variable Changes
XXXXXXXXX	Symbolic State Changes
Eliminated	

When vertical changes have been made, placing less abstract variables at too high a level where they do not fit:

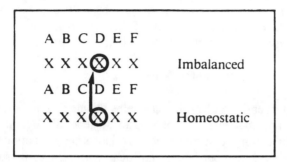

When higher-level variables are placed at lower echelons, have no meaning, or engulf the other variables within their definitional power of abstraction:

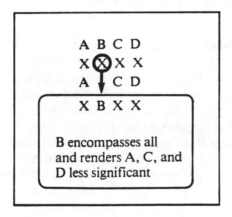

Numerous known (as well as unknown) factors in the client's ideational or behavioral system may be intricately related, so these relationships must also be evaluated, as frequencies or valences (philosophical or social values) of individual variables are altered. This includes the long-range effect of increasing and decreasing the field, since the client may situationally respond to the variable changes, additions, or reductions; but may not have learned specific mechanisms to reintroduce or continue the addition/subtraction processes, independently outside therapy.

Also, developmental advancement may suggest rapid addition or subtraction of outdated thoughts or feelings, or combinations of variables to produce new singular conceptual units which look like reduction, but may symbolically represent increase or expansion. The counselor must constantly compare developmental indices to the here-and-now parameters of change, to know when to facilitate increase or decrease, and correctly evaluate immediate and long-range results.

Awareness/Control of Intervening Variables

In many interventions, the clinician helps clients develop understanding of the nature, meaning, and outcomes of variables, generally outside the realm of their psychic or behavioral control. These variables may function to complicate client adaptive process without being significant, necessary, or sufficient; with active ingredients to influence conditions, growth, development, or life satisfaction. Some examples include maturational or transition dynamics in one's life, social conditions in the environment, extended family interference in nuclear family adjustment, or personal values which are inflexible or not suited to current situations.

In some cases, the clinician may assume responsibility for parental protectiveness or management dynamics involved in controlling the outside influence (meeting with grandparents to encourage more tacit influences on nuclear family's child-rearing struggles), prohibiting its influences on nuclear family, or prohibiting its influential nature during therapeutic sessions (refusing to discuss client's alcoholism without discussing psychological fears, dependency, or anger which, according to some theories, must be dealt with first). If this input is a process of reducing noise or interference irritations which distract the client from important work to be done, evaluations should include the client's amount and strength of disengagement from peripheral stimuli, as well as other qualitative indices of continuing ability to split off from distractions (focus, attend, and pursue); to understand benefits received from allowing intervening variable influence. This assessment includes goal identification and directedness, with associated cognitive management skills to divert or deflect incoming irrelevant or lower-priority stimuli, into other acceptable (cognitively consonant) categories of states of being (e.g., "I am a person who has back burners, and can live with some issues temporarily sidetracked; but I also have control of the switching process, to add or subtract burners, and relocate variable topics or areas of content based on a predetermined system of priorities").

Another index, is the decreasing frequency of therapist involvement, and increasing ratio of therapist/client inputs to control distractions. Clients who need intervening factors may be evaluated relative to their ability to recognize specific times of stimulus presence; awareness of decisions which choose one stimulus vs. another; and eventual connection of this choosing or prioritization of previous life conflicts, erroneous or correct beliefs, or personal or sociocultural values.

Therapists may deliver inputs which specifically recognize two or more potentially equal pieces of data (one might be defined as the intervening variable, and the other either an independent, dependent, or another intervening variable), and insist on continued recognition to precipitate conflict (and anxiety), to the point where the client is forced to deal with a decision. Clients can be evaluated on this balancing or conjectural component of their process. This includes ability to: assume the neutral posture to honestly debate these conflicts, use the counselor as a natural pivotal point from which bivariate perspectives can be considered, and explain and justify subsequent choices or non-priority non-choices, as a form of conflict acceptance and deferred gratification/pain. Therapists can assess their own input, as ability to see multivariate situations, and remove themselves from entrapment in specific partisan content concerns, in order to see the process of additional (possibly undefined or non-understood) cards placed in the psychosocial deck.

Where counselors do not take active charge of the "holding-constant" process, they may assess their ability to thematically interweave emerging variables into the client's decision-making channels; encourage client consideration; and evaluatively monitor (and analyze with clients) influences each new or old-but-reintroduced ingredient has on symptom sub-outcomes, or variables themselves as they merge with or cancel other content areas. An analogy to this, is a super freeway controller who manages access to all on and off ramps, so different types, colors, sizes of vehicles, are introduced to the moving mainstream at various locations in varying combinations; and who then monitors changes in the main traffic pattern, as different vehicles (variables) are factored in. For example, allowing only trucks at each on ramp, eventually transforms the nature, style, and type of mainstream traffic. This traffic control function requires recurrent evaluative questions to clients about ways they see their own traffic flow, and changes of freeway definition as operative units change. It also requires analysis of dynamics by which clients can incrementally assume these traffic control functions themselves.

Environmental Manipulation

Some discussions in the literature suggest that clinicians have a dual responsibility for intrapsychic psychological intervention, as well as correlated action in the client's social milieu. These perspectives appear predominantly in social work, community psychiatry, social psychology, and clinical sociology professions, suggesting skills and rationales for varying subtotal interventive efforts on behalf of individuals (excluding macro-level attempts to influence broad social policy/law, organizational structure, or general sociocultural norms or practices). Examples include work with teachers to modify a classroom situation or student-teacher relationship problem, work with extended family members to reduce negative impact of their family system, or advocacy with employers to retain an effective employee (the counseling client) struggling with acute stresses which will be therapeutically alleviated, or to provide a longer period for attempted mastery and change. The author used this technique frequently in military mental health work, to encourage unit commanders to provide flexible opportunities for individual rehabilitation in lieu of service discharge, punitive court martial, or administrative punishment action.

The initial evaluative question in these cases, is how counselors currently diagnose the problem, since the treatment rationale suggests an interactive (very probably synergistic) relationship dynamic, between (a) individual perception of self, (b) individual perception of self-in-situation, (c) individual perception of situation, (d) individual situation determined or situation-specific action (indepen-dent) or reaction, (e) situation independent influences and power of control, (f) situation reactions to individual behavior (and underlying attitudes and percep-tions), and (g) holistic need-meeting configuration of individual and environment, in the process of interactive struggle with each other.

Simulations and guided exploratory evaluative procedures must be under-taken before input is delivered, to assess the ratio for this systemic relationship condition (including degrees of freedom of either phenomenon to change), so inputs have a reasonable probability of impact. This is especially important due to unstated, informal needs of either part of the system, to benefit from current specific dysfunctional patterns, which may be functional for other or more general aspects of holistic person/situation performance. Any inputs relative to environ-mental manipulation, may have direct one-to-one translation into the client's life or adjustment scenario. Too, they may have a longitudinally-delayed develop-mental impact or a geometrically-expanding or diminishing influence, when combined with energy from other parts of the ecology, with lengthened dif-ferentiating influences after the "tidal wave has hit." Finally, inputs may alter (to varying degrees) behavioral patterns or options available to other individuals within the system, with whom the identified client interacts and potentially collaborates for mutual adaptation and survival. In some cases, changes in environment rob the client of necessary defensive excuses, actually increasing dysfunction (and anxiety and defense) rather than opening a door toward solution. Environment may passive-aggressively resent change and exercise negative retaliatory stimuli, which further confuse or block goals of the client. Also, changes in the environment, may lead the system's positioned "representatives" (teachers, employers, etc.) to expect immediate commensurate and "appreciative" changes in the client which may not materialize. Consequently, input may be wisely geared toward gradual increments of negotiable change, with indices of quality of client-plus-environment-discussion about potential and planned changes, as important as the actual outcomes. It is also important for the client to understand why and how reciprocal expectations are developed, and learn that change in the environment may necessarily require change for them also, while avoiding the idea that this means more external control or dependency on the environment.

Clients could do better after change, if they feel they had architectural and authorship power in creating the change philosophy, or actual behaviors. Evaluation looks at the process by which any mutual change occurs, assesses qualitative parameters of this "mutuality energy," and monitors changes in perceptions of either party, as the change gets underway. Changed perspectives by either party, mean that the system actors and themes are, in fact, different, new problems which may continually emerge. Awareness by all parties of small incremental change approximations of desirable outcomes is critical, so the often-imperceptive or more distantly (globally) perceptive system can positively register successes for relevant participants.

As positive changes occur, it is critical to evaluate: (a) degrees of variation between perceptions of current positive data (the boss did, in fact, praise the employee for a formerly-ignored behavior), as both parties deal with convergence in this congruent, but not identical awareness; (b) comparisons of the present positive perception to past negative perceptions, and individually-perceived or shared accounts of deviation (in behavior, affect, and cognition), along with definitions relative to self-actualizing intentions; and (c) convergence relative to perceptions of diminishing standard deviation (their averaged deviation scores), as conjoint agreements representing collective collaborated movement of the system.

The important point for the practitioner to remember, is that separate outcomes as a result of environmental manipulation, may not necessarily mean that a significant positively-intended change (growth) has occurred, for either the system or the individual within it. Also, the therapist must pursue evaluation which checks out various contingencies so input efforts are not wasted or submerged, in a person-plus-environment dynamic configuration of perception, feeling, and behavior, which could prove innocuous or destructive for either faction.

Development of Systemic Conceptualizations and Behaviors

Most therapeutic approaches help clients understand structures and dynamics of social systems (especially nuclear, original, and extended real and symbolic families), and develop behaviors to grow or at least survive, as group members therein.

A preliminary dilemma concerns assessment of the degree to which each client is actually influenced by dynamics of any system (symbolic past, present, or future anticipated), in conjunction with extent of feeling like a dependent variable phenomenon, within these systems. Inputs directed at the individual client strongly influenced by the system, may delay some principles of social learning, behaviorism, and collective group behavior; because the input thrust suggests an individual may have perceptual or physical control over behavior, while defining the controlling system as necessary to the survival of individual members. The clinical evaluator must be clear about personal theoretical orientation initially, later assessing specific areas (operationalized into particular outcomes) where clients have a reasonable probability of autonomous self-control (resistive deviance, or autonomous unilateral directionism within the system). The counselor may only evaluate efforts in areas which (according to some strict behavioral propositions) include only domains of thought, feeling, and behavior where the system has declined to exercise control; or areas where the system has defined options for individual control, which either conform to the system's norms, or are deviant (scapegoated acting out or negative behavior) but necessary to the system's survival.

Where the client is fully dependent, input may have to be partialized into understanding the system's "dynamics" component, and an "acceptance of inability to escape" component, if the system has strongly defined basic identity and thought/feeling structure of the client, during key developmental experiences. The individual may never extract the "system" from the "self." This might be seen for example, in regressed schizophrenic clients and character and behavior disorders (not so much in neurosis, where the battle still rages and neither side has yet won). The clinician must be clear concerning which types of evaluative answers are sought (or allowed), based on the theoretical framework that determines which evaluative outcome categories (of self, relative to system) become defined as logically allowable in the clinical assessment.

In helping clients understand the structure and operating principles of systems which are significant to their lives, evaluation should clearly differentiate the following levels of understanding:

1. the client's demonstration of understanding, based on confidence in the counselor's alleged knowledge and teaching of these principles, in subcategories where (a) the client is in a systemic dynamic with the counselor (transference), and must understand; (b) the system has defined itself and/or socialized the client to believe that it is not understandable, or exhibits confused or random patterning so the client has little chance of correctly seeing the pattern; (c) the client manifests understanding to reduce current anxiety; (d) the client understands a system which is understandable, but refuses to change because alternate, more positive understandable systems, are unavailable or imperceptible;

2. the client's understanding of parts of the system, but inability to see its totality; or understanding general totalities, but having ignorance of, or very personalized (private/secret) understanding, of finite dimensions of specific structure or operation;

3. the client's understanding of the system where: (a) the client represents a dependent or independent variable component of the system; (b) he/she is an outside observer, with a state of mind of being external to the system (e.g., in a healthy foster home, viewing a pathological family of origin), and away from the system's influence, with contradictory positive system forces in operation, and the client has (i) no alternate options to return to the system and expect change, or (ii) no reasonable chance of fully or partially extracting him/herself from the system, or (iii) absolute certainty of having to return to the system;

4. the client's understanding of the system as a result of developing hypotheses about its nature (based on hypotheses of the therapist, or teaching of group dynamic facts), and then conducting empirical tests by varying behavior or negotiating the variance in some independent system component, to observe actual effects and build understanding from an empirical standpoint (a therapist can ask questions like, "What happens when you do this differently?" or "Why don't you change one part of your behavior and note the effects?" etc.).

This approach assumes input which provides a temporary, supportive, and exploratory structure within the counselor-client system, and which pushes the client in and out of the boundaries, by providing propellant and a supportive bridge to cross these boundaries. The approach evaluatively collects data when the client is on both sides of the fence, and enroute. The input must then compare the data, to arrive at a mean/average understanding, divided by the number of different perspectives, to control for wide variances of the data. This process helps clients differentiate their perceptual position relative to any one system, and makes sure they realize that extraneous positions in one system, may simultaneously represent central positions in another interlocked or adjacent system:

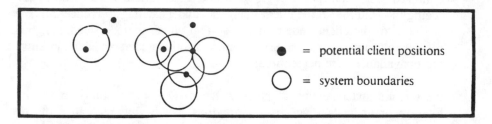

In all of the above, evaluators should be concerned about quality or quantity of understanding necessary, to produce a conversion to behavioral change. This concern extends to whether understanding of one system's dynamics necessarily implies that another system that has differing dynamics, could be understood or negotiated. A final concern, is the differential effort of understanding a system retroactively (knowing how one developed excessive childhood guilt as a result of certain family dynamics) from the current position of an adult who behaviorally confirmed these perceptions throughout life, as compared to the original childhood understanding, which contributed to definitions of the presently perceiving adult. There is undoubtedly a transformation process, as different levels of understanding and different time frames for the behavior of understanding occur. These must be sorted out evaluatively, since the system one tries to understand, may be near or distant, and have varying explicit or implicit effects on the perceiver and current or future systems.

From a synergistic perspective, inputs might only be evaluated and delivered to jointly interacting units, where the unilateral assessment of any individual unit (the client), must subtract out the independent effect of other persons' energy, which combines with that of the client to produce an outcome norm, collective perception, or behavior. On the other hand, a systems perceptive might suggest delivery of input to the individual client, with subsequent evaluation of how and to what degree, that input modified interactive dynamics. The clinician could document degree of autonomy the client has, in retaining ownership of the input result after it has been reflected from any significant other, and possibly modified in its return trip to the client, concluding with comparison of the joint outcome as the client factors out a personal perspective of unilateral benefit-in-context-of-association.

The selection of these inputs, obviously, demands analysis of interactive relationship and the degree to which the dyad, triad, or system jointly receives input (what are the collective and mutual categories which define receptors of input of the unit), and mutually produces simultaneously-changed or correlationally-linked, reciprocally-dependent behavior. If this is not possible, then inputs must be evaluated in singular units only, with assessments of the developmental impact of inputs, as they are transformed into the system's language and operations. Mutually shared input evaluations require questions demanding convergent awarenesses. Multiple pieces of data (feelings from each member, for example) must be solicited, examined, compared, and re-entered into each unit, for congruence and cognitive consonance checks. Additionally, those data must be re-exhibited externally for joint assessment, and then assessed in terms of joint behavior empirically observed collectively or separately, but definitively linked by the behaving parties and observer, as part of the systemic whole. These operational definitions are difficult, but must be accomplished if inputs are related to systems.

Any individual variation from predetermined norms of the system, must be evaluated concerning the individual's position relative to the system (even if therapeutic input is intended to produce client-approved deviance), since potency, frequency, duration, and value of the behavior (conforming or deviant), are partly determined by the nature of the system and its definitions of the client.

Inputs have various stages of potential retroflective redefinition by the system, and the client-viewing-the-system-viewing-them. They cannot be simplistically circumscribed with a finite nature at time and delivery of input, for they constitute a continuous variable (not finite) progressively and regressively redefined by its products and, therefore, may require some optional variation format, so clients can use it in the most effective way, once they see how it unfolds. A physical example is a medicinal time capsule where main effects are predicted, but whose side effects are chemically and psychologically dependent on main effects, at the same time altering the main effects because of the body's and mind's reaction to itself in process, and its intersystemic organ relationships.

Evaluation should show how specific parameters of systems, to varying degrees, produce or contribute to different influences of inputs, and define the system's capability to receive an input even before counseling begins. Inputs may be relevant and have impact value, for present client-associated systems in which modification is possible. They may apply more appropriately to other systems which exist only in the client's mind (hypothetical ideal), yet influence client behavior if the input does not really change the real present system. Correctly, inputs may be neutral in nature relative to all systems, and cause neither progression or regression, although their delivery may waste valuable therapeutic time which might be more productive with other input usage.

In mediation counseling, for example, the contents of discussion are systemically linked into constellations to submerge their independent negative or exaggerated impact. The issues can also be subdivided into smaller distinctive parts to separate out the collective effect, and clearly see the independent energy of unitary factors. These processes occur with the interactive/independent role occupants, and include separating parts of the personality for individual and collective analysis.

Evaluation concerns whether the therapist actually rearranges cognitive reality structures and client perceptions of interconnective linkages, to accomplish the separating, joining, defining, or expanding which is intended. It involves detached comparison of the new dimensions to the old, at various levels of closeness to the manipulated ideas, to determine structural realignment or developmental changes. The clinician who helps clients manipulate associational linkages between content domains in systems, or their degree of specificity or abstraction, should also take repeated measures of changes. This is necessary since, for many clients, the rearrangement of habituated patterns is a complicated process, which can be validated to some degree, by some pressure on clients to return to previous patterns publicly (not defensively in private where evaluative focus is absent), to determine the comfort, facility, or difficulty they have in maintaining any position within a system. Within a milieu or family systems perspective, a common technique is to provide clients with direct experience performing alternate, reciprocal, or nontraditional roles. Another, helps them conceptually understand or image thoughts and feelings involved in others' assumptions and performance, or the system's interrelated roles and positions.

Several issues emerge as these techniques or similar exercises, are therapeutically instituted in social systems. Although clients may ostensibly go through role-reversal motions (e.g., children direct a family meeting), or actually agree in counseling that they feel what it's like on the other side of the fence, the evaluator is wise to skeptically view potential artificiality. They should rigorously assess how, and in what specific ways, these attitudes or awarenesses might be tempered or altered by the system, supported and rewarded by interactive norms and processes; and behaviorally played out within the roles, as they are anticipated to change. Outcome evaluation can get a head start through progressively-demanding simulation and problem-solving exercises, to test the staying power and developmental effects of any alternative positions explored.

Also, change in any one position or role within a system, may produce changes in other interactive elements, so evaluation must consider relative stability of changes throughout the network (e.g., Johnny is behaving in school, but has the teacher really changed position relative to deviance, independence, etc. for sufficient periods of time to allow any newly changed pattern to emerge and, therefore, represent a new identity for the whole system?). Many changes, even if all roles and positions are surveyed to determine the effects, are only temporary, or have permanent potential but are untried (due to their immaturity of existence). Different hypothetical perspectives and models help the clinician assist the family to test possible longitudinal impacts or implications, and make anticipatory judgments of expected outcomes.

Dissociation and Distancing

A number of input techniques help clients behaviorally, affectively, or cognitively distance themselves from fixed symbols of traumatic pain, representations of need deprivation, or fearful stimuli (conscious or unconscious, real or imagined). It is difficult to determine precisely how the therapist facilitates this transcendence, but there are important evaluative implications for each therapist option.

Dissociation or distancing may partly be the facilitated awareness or allowance of the passage of time, wherein recollections (as in death of a significant other) fade with no concerted efforts to purposefully help the phenomena become energetically active, in the emerging present-time dimension. Evaluative emphasis includes identification of numbers of new referents in present and immediate past reality, and assessment of client efforts to move defined concepts into future developmental time perspectives; and return only to immediately preceding ideas or units of time, indicating spiraling growth away from the original representation. There may be a relationship of time passage to concept attainment, and return to original negative stimuli. The counselor can help the client construct nominal classification categories into which new and recently-old references are placed, to represent new global assessments or domains of reality, ideally excluding a significant position or role for previous traumatic stimulus ideas. However, amount of time as a frequency measurement, without concomitant assessment of symbolic distance and perceived experience of symbolic travel or movement, will probably not show relevant dimensions of evaluated distancing.

Clarity or fading of images of pain and trauma are important reference points, but must be evaluatively anchored in empirical referents, which include icons, paintings, songs, drawings, or other elements encountered or perceived at the time of trauma (or conscious adult awareness of childhood trauma). These referents can repeatedly be monitored by the client as to clarity, distinctiveness, value, or other measures of potency; and compared to current symbols produced or experienced, to represent past or present alternate reality. Distance, therefore, can be the emerging clarity and value of new images, the fading clarity or potency of old ones, and the degree of difficulty clients have in conceptualizing or re-experiencing earlier negative experiences.

Another influence on distancing is similar to input techniques discussed relative to systems, and includes the inductive/deductive process of extrapolation and interpolation, which divides conflictual reality into smaller and more manageable subunits. The process is interpolated by placing entirely new pieces of connective reality between existing units, and extrapolating by inferring other values beyond the known range of the client's painful traumatic reality. Evaluatively, concerns are whether the client has a sufficiently rigid and centralized reality base to never lose sight of painful life phenomena (thematic stability, concreteness, centrality, predominance), which can be measured as therapeutic probing tries to penetrate this reality, or as life events and behaviors are observed with sufficiently strong connective linkages, to constitute a powerful synergistic system. Also, the clinician needs to classify interpolated units of reality concerning their philosophical congruence with previous and present ideations, and extent to which each could represent an independent variable that does not need to occur in any linear chain, between previously-existing perceptions. Interpolation may be reproduction of already-existing reality with different labels, so there should be analysis of the probability of new ideas occurring in a normative set of adjacent ideas, representing either a deviant idea in the same set, or a conforming or deviant (standard deviation) concept in some other population of ideas.

Several populations of typical and atypical phenomena must be created, so separate interpolated or extrapolated ideas can be compared to normative groups. This comparison determines whether they represent stepping stones away from the client's traumatic representations of trauma, or to what extent they may still be representative samples of the existing population of ideas. What appears as distancing, could be the presentation of more self-confirming data, which can also be cross-tabulated with amount of anxiety generated by new-versus-old thought, and subsequently-linked behaviors. The counselor must beware of excessive focus evaluatively on the events of interest (especially if they are positive), because of the possibility (watch any good magician) that other activity takes place out of sight; and this activity becomes invisible when the illusion is focused on but, in fact, is the foundation framework for growth or regression in the clinical situation. The evaluator must look forward and backward, since activity goes on in both directions.

Another approach for distancing, teaches or models both independence of separate thoughts and control over self-evaluative judgments, about the significance of independent events (e.g., "You are choosing to define this event as a failure; let's think about other possible definitions and, given these alternate judgments, could you perform the consequent success-related outcomes, and then think about the contradictory evidence you have produced?"). The evaluator should collect considerable self-awareness and self-report data from the client, about feeling free to think a particular thought, which includes definition of associated behavior correlated with a feeling of developing independent identities, which further authorize independent thoughts. In some cases, the less obvious identity domain shows more progress (higher empirical frequencies) than overt behaviors.

The opposite, of course, where independent distancing occurs in entirely new or unplanned populations of ideas, that do not actually represent improvements in targets of interest (conflict); constitutes changes in alternative life domains. Distancing in separate reality domains may also be defensive, but the evaluator is obliged to identify entry into new territory, and assess the client's valuation of the advantages or disadvantages.

In reprioritizing values ("I guess I will just have to see my mother as less important to my survival, now that I am supposed to be an adult"), the evaluator helps the client undergo a comprehensive and detailed cost-benefit analysis of gains and losses, to understand how much self-image investment in past object-value allocation must be relinquished, and what potential gains become available as this energy is progressively freed to seek other objects of attachment. This analysis includes losses which occur, as significant others realize they have been reprioritized and, therefore, react to the client by rejection, withdrawal, etc. Distancing from one value investment may concomitantly mean increasing nearness to another ("I guess I can use my wife's family to meet some of my needs"), so the evaluator should comparatively assess degree of movement, as well as the functionality of the object of movement, in terms of its capability to validate continued independent movement of the client ("I will make love contingent on my child's increasing autonomy from me as a parent").

Relive Growth Stages

Although most psychodynamic theories discuss the therapeutic advantage of clients' relearning or undoing previous growth and developmental deficits, it is complicated to discuss this as a separate entity from other related input dynamics.

One salient dilemma, is that inputs to help clients regrow (experience more positive parenting, take responsibility for actions, make their own evaluative judgments and plans, etc.) may occur in an integrated and interactive fashion, giving them a seemingly random appearance. This happens as they frequently alternate between therapeutic action and inaction, and require accompanying negative outcomes in clients' lives to give them the opportunity to struggle, fail, evaluate, or plan, as part of relearning within the context of a more supportive relationship. In many cases, inputs are reactive to client developmental needs which are changing; therefore, they vacillate between frequently-divergent polarities. So, there is a question of whether the input has actually become a client-conditioned and manipulated dependent variable, whose dimensions must be predictable and trustworthy in order for clients to grow on their own.

Because of highly variable time dimensions within which these inputs can be delivered (as with first-time parents, when the good parent supports sometimes, criticizes sometimes, ignores sometimes), evaluation requires remembrance (documentation if possible) of staggered inputs, with periods of time (including variables) intervening; but with some capability of associating inputs of similar intent (supportive inputs, critical inputs, etc.), so they can be standardized and compared, to separate singular from collective input effects.

Although some counselors argue that specific re-parenting inputs cannot be factored out to this degree of specificity, this process must occur if there is to be any rationale for successive delivery of theoretically sound inputs. Otherwise, the counselor could logically be required to deliver input A_1, allow passage of time (with presumably the presence of other inputs B-D, and potentially-associated client outcomes), then reach the point of possibly delivering A: but (1) either deliver this input and note the outcome, and not decide what caused the outcome (thereby suggesting that almost any non-aversive input could have been delivered); or (2) not deliver input A_2 to see what outcome occurs without it (and make some assumption that any observed outcome may be associated with or at

A, rather than A_2, A_1, and further assume that a negative client outcome might support the idea that A_2 was necessary; or (3) see if the client delivered the input her or himself, to substantiate that it was necessary; or (4) refuse to deliver any but neutral subsequent inputs, allowing the passage of time to sift out and naturally differentiate which inputs may be significant, but noting if outcomes or outcome needs had lasting positive, negative, short-, or long-term effects.

Counselors must bear in mind the tremendous effort they expend in input delivery, which may be necessary if inputs are sufficiently potent (quality vs. quantity) to do the job, or if there is a cumulative effect of a large number, none of which may have to be delivered with much potency.

As each input may have a developmental history and future of its own, and therefore unfold after delivery, the counselor must be acutely aware of the client's gestalt and existential and phenomenologic perspective about the input as it is delivered. This is important since regrowth, by definition, implies that the client in some fashion is transported, together with the regressed or traumatized child, into the past to some extent. They logically need to acknowledge (at least unconsciously) that he or she is in the right time and dimensional space, to receive the influential inputs. Directly re-parenting the adult who is running away from or denying the injured or helpless child, suggests that inputs may be registered (if they are received at all) by an adult decisioning system (defensive and without the child necessarily in the receiving mode). This system then, transports the input to the secluded child, delivers the input, and then re-defends until the seed grows. If this is true, evaluation necessitates following this procedure along some conveyor transport system to establish indicator points along the way, and then assess experiences of the inner child, as indices may change on the lengthy growth trip.

The developmental scenario of effects of any or all inputs suggests, also, varying direct and inverse indicators of the growing child inside the defensive, conflicted, or regressive adult. Manifestation of negative outcomes suggests the child is testing limits and experimenting with previously-avoided consequences, which may produce other negative consequences with which others must deal, which may have backlash effects, to further endanger or traumatize the child. The evaluator must have a good handle on variations in growth manifestations experienced by normal children, so expectations for increasing or decreasing frequencies can be indexed for valid meaning. Both increases and decreases in some goals might be seen together as an interactive pattern, whose fluctuating nature also suggests that inputs must vary in their own nature developmentally. From the input side, this means careful and rapid analysis of emerging outcome patterns, capability for a multiplicity of types and degrees of energy attached to inputs, and rapid delivery of some inputs which are capable of split-level delivery. One is energy input, to reinforce positive intended increases; another, energy withdrawal to support, but not directly reward, necessary negative directions which produce negative outcomes, but are positive on ex post facto decisions. A third type, intermittent energy, inputs again to reinforce client growth acts after negative consequences have been manifested. The input foundation may be analogous to a river whose powerful molecular forces keep constant pressure on a dam which defends against the water: as it alternatively moves through any flood gates in the dam that are opened by intent or through pressure; moves around or over the dam to eventually continue the progress; assumes a temporary placid nature while the necessary (but not limitless) defensive functions of the dam are operational; or can split itself in many directions to seek new uncharted decisions, yet also re-emerge carrying material (sand, debris, fertile soil) from its separate paths. Evaluatively, the river must be viewed holistically as partly dammed, wholly in movement, and separated into segmented movement dynamics, relative to separate and total ecological outcomes.

As noted earlier, awareness by the client of the re-parenting process, is also an index to be charted. It includes the client's progressive version of the input phenomenon as it grows, merges, or separates, so specific behavioral outcomes can be directly related to client recollections of parent-child interactions the original time: (e.g., "What is it like when I suggest to you that you can make up your own mind about this issue, and how does this feeling compare to the time you told me about with your father; and with this piece of information I have given you, where will you store it and what do you see as its next step?"). If a client lacks awareness of the re-parenting input, then the first evaluative index should be awareness of the re-parenting input, then the next index should be awareness of this moment of parenting, unless a more flexible index of referent behavioral changes can be developed, to suggest that somewhere (unconsciously perhaps) the message is being received. For messages not received, the only indices which may be helpful, are indicators of desirable behavior based on environmental control (strong contingencies in behavior modification program) or reduction of defenses, which are probably impossible if supportive parent messages are not received someplace. Possibly the only alternative is chipping away at defenses via frontal assault, which represents questionable humanistic ethics, since the client is changing as a result of increasing need for exhaustive defenses; or loss of energy through fatigue and exacerbation of trauma, which forces a panic-induced change in their posture of awareness and receptivity.

Also, as noted earlier, some parenting inputs do not seem to be inputs at all, but are absence of activity whose presence the growing child might interpret as controlling or producing dependency when, in fact, independent behavior is either desired or deemed necessary, in a growth continuum. Withdrawal of overt activity, which theoretically may be an active input as the child uses this catalyst to invest his or her own energy, is difficult to measure, particularly if the client does not have a structure with which to guide investment of energy. It may also lead to confusing conclusions, since amount of withdrawal may not provide clear empirical phenomena from which measures of reactive beginning and ending points, are determined. With input withdrawal, it is also hard to monitor interventive data arising from anxiety defenses, or other client self-imposed inputs placed into the often envisioned empty space. This is true since the space may not be empty at all from an input perspective, but is empty because the client has not been provided with more elementary stimulus-response conditioning, to know at least approximations of what reactions should occur.

The author has made, for example, periodic judgment errors in his heuristic teaching approaches, wherein he has not provided answers or even structure to some aspects of student learning, in hopes that building anxiety in the open space (absence of clear, empirically-specific inputs), would lead especially dependent students in the direction of more independent learning. What typically happens, is that independent students zoom ahead with free reign, some students on the fence move ahead slowly, and most dependent students fill the empty space with resistance, anger at the professor, alternate learning, or some other form of withdrawal. In response to this, the author might confront this resistance and again individualize awareness of the growth opportunity, realizing many students repeatedly will not use the available opportunity—sometimes because they have no models as examples or concrete frameworks, with which to replace the emptiness they fearfully perceive. The withdrawal of inputs should be accomplished by designing a classification system to define not only amounts of withdrawal (duration, intensity, abruptness, timing), but also correlated categories of client response, so excessive or poorly-timed withdrawal can be slowed or reversed (not measurably with the antithetical or converse introduction of inputs), producing indices of client awareness of opportunity and self-structure.

Finally, as developmental changes occur, the client may see categorical patterns of constellations of identity domains which are separate from, and more abstract than, specific behavioral referents or even groups of behaviors, which correctly or spuriously give the impression that behavior corresponds to image. Inputs, therefore, should be assessed relative to specific behaviors, designed and evaluated as they stimulate the client's more global identity, in which the magnitude of their direct impact may be reduced, but the cumulative effect, added to numerous other positive dimensions of client identity, causes a significant effect. This is the big fish in little pond vs. little fish in big pond issue, where some inputs need to be increased or decreased, based on perceived domain of interest and growth (or regrowth) of the client. The outcomes observed to assess input effectiveness, may have to be indexed (and not necessarily synonymously with inputs) to relate to the client's "ponds," and the client's movement of inputs between ponds, as part of their development.

Development of Client Projection

Some theories of clinical input suggest a process similar to the defensive mechanism of projection, which enables the client to gain better perspectives of how he or she appears to others (and what they experience in the process). This happens by hypothesizing an external perspective, opinion, or value, and making decisions from personal frameworks in response to this image. The client is expected to achieve a viewpoint whose domain is external to him/herself, and whose content may be identical or similar, but probably is different. The client is expected additionally to derive meaning or value about this perspective, and apply its significant elements to themselves, related to subsequent personal decisions based on the relationship between internal and external data. This technique helps clients: understand their impact on others who, in turn, reward or punish them; see parts of themselves which internal defenses may not allow; appreciate needs of others as screening mechanisms for actions of the self; and broaden their range of cognitive, emotional, and behavioral functionality, creating greater numbers and qualities of adaptive opinions.

The clinician is concerned that clients develop anchoring points outside themselves, and should assess degree of flexibility a client has, moving from inside to outside looking back, and should help the client measure the relative degrees of security felt, at various points in this movement process. Cognitive and ego-oriented theorists might suggest behavioral pairing of self-reinforcements for the movement or planned projection itself, and measure frequencies of self-talk or self-imposed positive messages, for the projective process. There are possibly diminishing degrees of security clients feel as they increasingly perform this process independently, but they may initially accomplish it only to please a counselor who suggests it is a useful tactic. Categories of positive vs. negative uses of projection must be developed, so client and clinician can determine when appropriate vs. escapist use of this technique materializes. This should be correlated with level of anxiety, except that sometimes, an inverse relationship occurs so that high anxiety precipitates or is associated with projection to further understand, rather than avoid, inner feelings and decisions. The indicators here are frequency of response; cross-tabulated with situation, level of anxiety, and presence of other regressive symptoms; further cross-tabulated by uses of key personal feelings during and after the projection occurred; and finally cross-tabulated by presence and type of decision-making and subsequent behaviors, after the protective maneuver has been accomplished.

Analysis might also differentiate pseudo-factual projective statements made to self ("You definitely are this kind of person"), from conjectural hypothesis ("You might be this kind of person, and you may have alternative choices relative to what you learn about yourself"), through comparison of multiple sources of client-elicited feedback, therapist feedback, and observations of behavioral referents. This is equivalent to the statistical calculation of means, medians, modes, variances, and standard deviations, so the client can construct an external reality set of criteria as one population of identity indices, compare this to the internal one, and then attempt growth behaviors, in order to negotiate convergence. Clients can also build a simulated behavioral model for themselves with the help of the counselor, categorizing various internal states of being in their normal to abnormal (secure to threatened) gestalt, and then experimentally attempt the projection process relative to each state, to note changes in the dependent variable self-state, as a result of moving away from the center of the state for a more objective view.

The counselor can evaluate the input by noting degree of comprehensiveness with which the client observes and understands the movement process; state-of-being frameworks from, and to which, movement is negotiated; and the clarity, frequency, and ease of evaluative judgments and decisions made by clients. This evaluation includes factors relating to client processes:

1. completeness of data gathered
2. use of all data in the decision formula
3. logic and rationality of deductive conclusions
4. clarity and operational specificity of plans, based on decisions and correctness in differentiating one framework from another
5. ease and correctness in differentiating one framework from another
6. capability to prioritize frameworks and loci of movement
7. strength of perceptions of independent choice, in starting and stopping projective movement activities
8. awareness of specific incremental and summative decisions made, and the data-based projectively grounded rationale for decisions

9.   degree of consistency in repeating the projective process (identical replica-
     tion), when desirable and positive results have been achieved
10. ability to decide when negative results of protection have occurred or
     recurred, ability to check out all parts of the system for malfunction, and
     ability to take perceptual correcting action.

Therapists have to be concerned with dependency, and should envision the
points, duration, and direction of their conduit role and function, gradually
decreasing the amount of time they sustain the client, before the client disembarks
at each projective point. They should also be aware of the frequency with which
they are required to assist the client on the return trip, with their newly-acquired
data baggage (the projected idea). In cases where the client discovers a congruence between multiple sources of projective data ("I expect that most of my
friends don't like me when I get drunk and disorderly so frequently"), the evaluative process involves checking out these ideas with open-ended solicitations of
feedback from significant others. This can be assessed in terms of the client's
capability not to bias the question, with preconceived fixed alternative question
formats.

The counselor and client can also evaluate degree to which feedback may
be altered or distorted as it enters personality systems, with indices of defensive
maneuvers, childhood data (e.g., negative parental injunctions), or cognitive
distortion frequencies (helpless beliefs about self). Evaluation can then assess
types, clarity, and implications of value judgments the client does or does not
apply to the projective, but now-validated data. Then, assessments of behavioral
goals and their correlations with the projective and real feedback data, can be set
up in a multiple baseline design format, in which the client measures (1) frequency of specific behaviors, (2) persistence of projected hypotheses, (3)
persistence of feedback collecting qualitative attempts, (4) degree of change or
loss of strength of real opinions of others, (5) actual frequency of new and more
positive perspectives, and (6) eventual decrease in dependence or need for projection, evidenced with increased positive self-rewarded behavior and independent
confidence in self.

Develop Associational Linkage Between Cognitions, Feelings, and Behaviors

Because many clients experience difficulty associating some of their ideas
with each other, or understanding the relationship between particular thoughts and
feelings; psychodynamic, analytic, and cognitive therapies suggest that this connective linkage be an important therapeutic input goal.

From a psychodynamic view, the counselor should first identify clients who have adequate intelligence and self-awareness to associate variables in their lives, but are unable to do so due to excessive acute anxiety (certainly relative to conflict between some of these ideas), which places physical or mental overload on their systems. In these cases, it is assumed that the individual could make adequate associational connections and render appropriate decisions, if anxiety were reduced to a manageable level. There is some question whether the input should be directly aimed at conflicting ideas themselves (which are not being connected, especially since nonconnection is also a desirable self-protective state), or more pointedly leveled at the defense or anxiety-related ideas as a preliminary or sufficient step, to allow the client to then take charge of personal associational affairs.

Evaluation considers a field of variables, with the following characteristics: (1) at least two conflicting phenomena C_1 and C_2 (which can be two cognitions, a cognition and a behavior, or two behaviors having corresponding cognitions); (2) a cognition which encapsulates the conflictual domain and provides an overview of it (including a definition O_1); (3) a cognition which defines the anxiety overload (A) itself; (4) at least one other cognition relating the anxiety to the total personality system (B); (5) additional cognitions concerning other intervening variables (the counselor, the counselor's ideas, etc.), and the functional purpose of defenses raised to control anxiety (D); and, finally (6) an additional cognition representing an integrating function to serve as a "workshop," where two or more ideas are put together to produce some synthetic third idea, or where a third abstraction allows them to exist simultaneously in harmony, because of a definition which authorizes their new or different association. This field of variable relationships is depicted in at least one potential scenario in Figure 7.

In the scenario depicted, the evaluator first outlines the full range of ideas and behaviors in the client's field of activity, and specifically goes through both inductive and deductive processes to discover higher or lower levels of abstraction. These might represent thoughts or behaviors that have clearer or more significant linkages. This is essentially a nominal level data categorization, so all separate potentially-connected or disconnected units can be placed in categories which define their natures, as well as the type, time, place, duration, and value of other categories. As noted earlier, the counselor then considers whether the connective linkages should be made relative to the relationship between present anxiety manifestations and the total psychic system under attack, because changes in conflictual ideas may be more appropriately measured relative to anxiety-reduction. One dilemma, however, is that some conflicts return to baseline unconscious or other protective environments, and, therefore, anxiety-reduction may be a spurious measure. Some theories suggest that connective linkages do not occur during periods of excessive anxiety or psychic disequilibrium, so inputs consist of pseudo or temporary connections (as seen in relaxation techniques, support, etc.) between perceptions of psychic disintegration, and a protective tranquil state of being. Some clients only "hear" about perceived negative cognitive connections when anxiety is perceived at a manageable level, so the only connections allowed are between perceptions of flight and disintegration, and the ability to select and control a defensive process.

Figure 7
Ideas in Conflict
Two Ideas or Cognitions (or Behaviors)
in Conflict

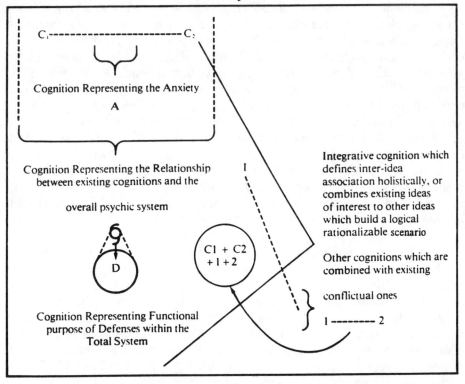

The input essentially sets up an hypothesis of controlled retreat, and connects conflict with the counselor's parental control, which takes temporary cognitive control of the anxiety (almost like providing a temporary host organism), so the client can "pretend" to be comfortable enough to test out the hypothesis, and hopefully take control of perceived disintegrative process. Evaluation here seems paradoxical, since it includes assessment of increased dependence on authority for protection, irrational reliance on pretend fantasies of a safe world, and use of behavioral indices related to anxiety-reducing behavior and degree of distance achieved temporarily from the real conflictual issues.

One case is where the counselor helps the client connect ideas directly (e.g., "I can disagree with my parents' values, and at the same time [connective link] fear childhood survival, without the love or support they might withdraw; and recognize passive-aggressive reactive behavior as a symbol of this conflict [another connective link], and self-define any adequacy as one example of a change in other behaviors" [another connective link]). The specific input is hard to define and operationalize, but seems to bring two ideas together, hypothesizing an association between them, as opposed to some association the client is making or has made in the past; and then relying on forceful energy to push the client in the direction of the new association, which he or she otherwise would not desire to entertain. This energetic power may be accumulation of previous extreme feelings, then associated with the idea that is intended to be considered as true, or the heightened awareness of negative punishments which occur if the client does not accept or consider the new belief (learning contingency management).

An example was one of the author's clients, who had performed a series of avoidance and passive-aggressive behaviors toward a work supervisor, connecting these behaviors with her self-depreciated image or extraneous circumstances, but not considering they may have been symbolic acted-out representations of feelings about her father. Repeated attempts to cognitively connect these disparate domains failed, until the therapist helped the client build up a reservoir of negative feelings about the father; so when the most recent acted-out behavior occurred, the powerful energy of this accumulated and now-overpowering data flooded into awareness to cause crying and release, and consideration of the new connected information as true, because of the force associated with it.

Evaluatively, the focus may not exclusively rest on the behavior or thoughts to be connected, but may increase in behind-the-scene energy (which can also be created with withdrawal of therapist approval, or reward for selected awarenesses, as a boiler engineer might measure pressure as one index of the machine's increasing capacity to perform work). Inputs may take the form or suggestive enticement, exacerbation of feelings, or blockage of defenses; so energy build-up might occur. From a structural perspective, the counselor can develop inputs which are architectural in nature, so several options for defining connective linkages are developed as suggestions, and the client is measured on their ability to trace each possible explanation to its eventual conclusion, if all syllogistic components are played out. Measurement perspectives include variance of all outcomes relative to each other from the original connective, problematic link; and from some normative criteria in the client's philosophical and cultural life perspective, which define categories and degrees of acceptable existence.

In the case of cognitive restructuring, some clients have simply not learned to be sufficiently aware, have limited appreciation of their powers of association, lack intellectual capacity to perceive associational matrices, have developed habituated domains of self-reinforcing awareness wherein they do not know of the existence or associational dimensions of certain awareness, or have not had experiential exposure to process or outcome consequences of various connectedness positions.

Evaluation in this light, may center on inputs which call into question, discredit, or create dissonant values or images relative to traditional associative connections, or traditional patterns of unilateral domain awareness which exclude dynamics of associational history. Prior to the development of new corrections, clients may be assessed on increasing degrees of skepticism, increasing conjectural statements, or hypothesis manifestation of what they think, feel or do. Paradoxically, this means they have probably made other atypical (for them) associations between their adequacy and reality-questioning statuses, due to associative connection with the therapist. As degree of skepticism increases, an inverse indicator may be dependence on the counselor's support; so at some point, inputs relative to dependency produce minimal to moderate reversal of the dependency frequencies, with initial losses in degrees of skepticism, but collateral increases in perceptions of self-control or decision-making power of these interactive indices. Cognitive restructuring may then be assured relative to numbers of explored or considered associational variables and relationships between them, and assessment attempts to "walk through" various options to determine reasonably expected outcomes, and decide about their desirability.

Once a new structure (with new relationships) is created, evaluation centers on the strength of this structure. Inputs might be delivered to test its strength (create anxiety relative to its solidarity or functional efficacy); and be evaluated concerning processes of utilizing the new structure, and making decisions about its outcome ("I can say 'no' to authority figures, and they may not reject me") and other criteria of personality status ("I need to say no in my life, so I can say yes to other priorities for myself, and I am better off saying no at least some portion of time for functional purposes, or on principle alone"). Inputs might be designed to help clients do comparative evaluation of behavioral sets of normative standards already in existence. They can also inductively emerge as various new behavioral sets; then, categories of personality status are constructed by the client, to substantiate their existence and support continuation through recurrent client-centered awarenesses of normative conformity and deviation.

Concerning normative behavior, the clinician may help the client view various behaviors as samples which may or may not represent the same population of events or phenomena:

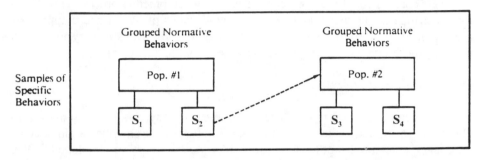

These may help the client understand what types of behaviors or behavioral connections exist, and also compare any specific behavior to general and specific characteristics of the population; to decide if it belongs, or, as noted in the diagram; to decide if a sample may belong to another population. Clients may be evaluated on ability to decrease or predictably control error in associating samples to population categories of phenomena, as they develop heightened awareness of the ranges of behaviors they can allow to exist in the population, and the decreasing probability of population-related identity, as specific behaviors deviate from the expected average.

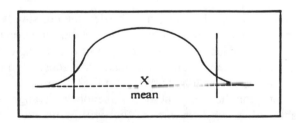

Small probability of sample behavior
existing confidentially within population—
decreasing confidence in predictably
controlling error

Clients may also be evaluated on ability to observe any behavior or thought, and move from a descriptive analysis, to an inferential, causal, and decision-making mode. They can learn to assess fluctuations in anxiety or psychosocial status as a result of the changing ratio of connected to disconnected ideas or behaviors, or as a function of the ratio between those connected in one way, as opposed to some other fashion. These include degree of awareness of causes for the dissociation of some behaviors or cognitions, which might otherwise be associated.

Of course, cognitive restructuring has a developmental process as well, so inputs change in frequency and nature, as new stages of the structure appear or are intended to develop. The counselor needs to know ways to vary inputs, to produce more qualitative connective behaviors on the part of clients.

Differentiate Symbolizations

Evaluation relative to presence and relevance of symbolic representation in clients' lives, initially takes the form of exploratory research, since a glossary or dictionary of symbolizations and empirical referents must be developed. The counselor and client together, conduct a progressive content analysis of behaviors, verbalizations, appearance configurations, and other data to understand which components of living are represented symbolically, and how they can be attached to empirical referents, so occurrence can be documented for subsequent outcome decisions, and determination of therapeutic inputs. Once symbols and referents are discovered, documented, and categorized, frequencies of occurrence can be tabulated, along with other annotations of time of occurrence, psychic state during which they occur, functional utility, consequent symbolizations, and thoughts or behaviors which manifest themselves, after any particular symbolic representation has emerged.

The initial input of the therapist, may be designed to simply create aware-ness of the presence and value of symbolic representation in psycho-sociocultural life. Input can take the inductive-deductive form of examining empirical behav-iors to see if they have symbolic referential imagery associated to them ("Do you suppose this behavior might have any other meaning?"); or beginning deductively with a typical client symbolic representational phenomenon (anger at your father), to help the client explore whether this conflict will be manifest in cryptic form in the future. The therapist can measure how the client conducts this examination procedure as the field of symbolization begins to sharpen and become more predictable. The counselor can also measure effect of inputs based on the quality of client proof that one symbolic representation is different from another, including the client's ability to document differences of degree in variances between empirical indices, and ability to trace each symbol back to its roots.

Another input helps clients substitute different, but equivalent, symbolic referents, to prove they truly understand the principles or dynamics inherent in the image, which is somewhat parallel to analogue exercises in thinking or learning. This may reinforce symbolic flexibility, often neglected by clients who see themselves trapped in narrowly-confined symbolic worlds. The frequency or referent substitution may be similar to response generalizations, where the client gains greater confidence (degree of this confidence can be assessed) in manipulating their symbolic world, but also may eventually change negative or conflictual symbols, including elimination of some representational patterns.

Clients can explore a wide range of symbols in the broader context of their milieu; and the therapist can assess how inputs result in occurrence of this exploratory process, degree of distance clients achieve in moving away from their own symbols, and closeness with which they approach symbols in other (other individuals,' or other cultures') domains of represented reality. The therapist might employ question content, for example, containing spatial or temporal gradients to move clients any number of variable units of distance away from their traditional concepts, and closer to awareness or understanding of alternative symbols.

An example of this mobility process occurred with an anorexic client with whom the therapist worked. She collected referents from her world (magazine pictures, records, environmental artifacts, etc.) which represented repressed identity images not discovered, or defined as simply antithetical to a negative and conflict-ridden body image she currently espoused. Therapeutic inputs helped her identify new images, and relate them qualitatively and quantitatively to her current concepts. One example may be the concepts of soft versus hard: therapeutic comments incrementally suggest that the degree of difference between these be envisioned, along with the associated variances in personality attributes, and fluctuations between overall life values and implications for each in terms of relationships, goals, and aspirations. The focus can be closer or more distant to keep them engaged in the differentiation process, with corresponding movement and respective distances, as one evaluative index:

1. "What things about you are either soft or hard?"
2. "How do you know the differences between these two?"
3. "If you wanted to make this soft component of your identity (appearance, speech, perception, etc.), even softer, what would you do?"

4.   "How do you feel when you think of the space in between the soft and hard? What could you use to measure the distance?"

5.   "Give me one other example of how these two soft-hard parts are truly different."

6.   "How does it make you feel when I suggest that these soft and hard parts you mentioned, are closer together than you think? What ways show their closeness of similarity?"

Inputs can be designed to produce movement in images, but movement must first be produced in the point of focus on each image. This provides assurance that the client is truly changing, rather than remaining sedentary and supplying new referents to represent old conflicts, which gives the appearance of movement. An example is a parade: the client envisions the linear passage of differentiated units, but does not necessarily conceptually move to a new awareness with each one. On the other hand, being in the parade can mean that each unit sees only itself, and cannot recognize other units ahead or behind.

Inputs should insure that the client can move along with each unit, to truly experience its essence, and yet stop periodically to allow the next unit to come into view, then moving along for a while with that unit. The client can be alternately a parade spectator and participant, and the stopping and going can be measured by the clinician through comments to the client from each different perspective. The counselor assesses whether the client is drawn toward the therapist along the perceptual vector, returns to the same or a different spot when the input is withdrawn, or recognizes degrees of difference in positions, and empirically documents degrees of difference.

Parental Surrogate Control

There are times in each client's psychosocial life, when the therapist feels parental (superego, supportive, directive, influential, suggestive, expectative) control is necessary to manage the regressive process, crisis, or personality disin-tegration. They may re-educate or redevelop the conflicted, fixated, injured, traumatized, or underdeveloped "child" inside the adult, or teach the adult a new type, range, duration, or intensity of behavior.

First of all, parental control in any manifested forms, is a temporary phenomenon, which may have strong intensity initially (in response to client crisis), with diminishing power as the client grows and assumes this responsi-bility. Also, support may be of mild to moderate intensity, with possibly a gradual increase in power followed by decreasing intensity, as the client begins to change. In the first instance, where strong parental influence is necessary, the counselor must be careful to correctly assess degree to which client anxiety (or any one of its associated symptoms) is a function of perceived entrapment, within a childhood transaction (real or fantasized) of parent-child control. Therefore, despite the deterioration of the client or extreme nature of the crisis, a massive dose of that dynamic, from which the client is already suffering, may cause greater overt manifestations of crisis; or provide an external decrease in the deteriorative process while internally, unconsciously, or defensively causing greater loss of client baseline levels of self-esteem and dependency.

The therapist may approach this by initiating more, and then withdrawing all, parental inputs, to determine the sustaining effects, and note impact relative to re-traumatization. The therapist should also decide about the client's perception of "parenting," as either a positive and necessary temporary rescue attempt, or a more serious threat to identity. An incorrect massive dose, once delivered, is hard to retrieve; but can certainly be followed by additional corrective inputs to explain the error, provide checks and balances on irrational assumptions about it, or spread out the effects, by drawing in other awarenesses or benchmarks of strength to mitigate the impact.

In some cases, the client may need, but not receive, a sufficiently powerful dose of parenting, so its effectiveness may be lessened or eliminated, suggesting that the counselor know the client's level of need deprivation, and perceived function of the input, as the client idiosyncratically perceives it. If the input is effective, the therapist should define various indices of its effectiveness, which are related to the cognitive, behavioral, and emotional functions of childhood, contained in the particular developmental theory employed. The counselor can ask her or himself how a child at a specified stage of development responds to a particular type of needed parenting, and then index this as an outcome measure or ratio of child-to-current-adult status. This necessitates a bimodal input approach, viewed (or rejected) by both an adult and a regressed child simultaneously. There may be differential and even contradictory effects as the child views the input positively, but the adult resents it; thus, dialogue between parent (counselor), adult (client), and child (also client) must occur, to decide how much parenting is necessary and welcome, and whether or not it is, was, or might be effective. Once the counselor is in the parent input mode, cognitive consonance and repetitive patterning principles may make it difficult to rapidly discontinue a thrust which is highly valued. The counselor may not even be aware of the continuing delivery of the input, because its power produces a controlled client phenomenon, which further appears to validate its necessity. This is particularly true when the very status of the professional role and position has some parental characteristics, regardless of deliberate or inadvertent parental behaviors.

In cases where a smaller initial dosage avoids overwhelming the client, the counselor needs a sensitive touch to correlate input with receptivity and incremental functionality for the client. The counselor must hypothesize and define the exact point at which additional increases in parental input, block emergence of self-parenting from the client; although increases in self-parenting (e.g., integration of ego-superego capability) as a result of therapist parental input, may become increasingly fearful for the client, and necessitate reinitiation of the therapist input as a booster dosage.

In some instances, parental-type inputs are not necessarily designed to forcefully alter a specific negative behavior (provide injunction or interdictive blockage), or behaviorally mandate (or increase the probability of occurrence) a reinforced positive behavior. They may, however, provide a backdrop or permissive atmosphere for the child-in-the-adult client to experiment with new thoughts, feelings, or behaviors, to decide about their functional value. Appropriate supportive and facilitative inputs must communicate to the client that a protective wall has been constructed, but that it has occurred through that client's approval, and can be removed, altered, or modified at will. This can be accomplished as the therapist forcefully assumes a position of questioning or examining, via rhetorical questions, conjectural words, hypothetical examples, and explanatory or interrogatory intonation ("What do you think would happen if you tried being honest, and what are some statements you might make to your son, which you have not tried before?"). The difficulty with this input, is that some clients immediately respond to the counselor stimulus with either a positive effort to explore, or a defense. This misleads the counselor in determining if clients respond on cue. If they define their response as one characterized with sufficient degrees of freedom, autonomy, and self-control that the supportive and stimulating parental atmosphere communicates to them, they can try something new as part of a learned repertoire, which includes parental perceptions that they (clients) are also able to evaluate effects of their self-selected actions. Parental input in the form of a statement from the counselor, should be accompanied at various points by questions about the growth and learning atmosphere, so the client provides evaluative feedback of performance of a specific behavior, and permission or freedom to perform the behavior as a projection of future identity. Provision of a parental milieu is deceptive from an evaluative standpoint, because it is often without a focal point that allows the client room to maneuver, while maintaining a sufficient image of safety.

Recurrence of intended specific behaviors can be one cumulative index of existence of the atmosphere, but to test real growth of the client, some counselors want the client to also perform deviant or non-"good" child behaviors, to demonstrate the true degree of freedom to deviate (a wider range of behavioral variability). This is similar to some parts of adolescent rebellion, in which decisions confirm or change behavior based on personal security (self-initiated parental atmosphere), rather than continued exhibition of conforming behavior without the healthy option to deviate. The parental boundary should progressively fade away, replaced by a client-designed and engineered boundary, which the counselor tests to insure that, although the dimensions and appearance may be the same as the structure provided by the therapist (it can also be different, of course, based on client preference and personality style and needs)—authorship must necessarily have changed hands.

In many cases, parental input is not specifically designed to produce particular behavior, or result in a specified outcome; but more globally enhances self-esteem, offers attention, and confirms the significance of the client. In these cases, input takes the form of direct praise or compliment, or is more subtly behavioral expectancy that the client cognitively or emotionally registers. Because these inputs can be immediate in their behavior orientation, and developmental as a part of personality foundation reconstruction, the counselor has a difficult evaluative task concerning them. For developmental goals related to self-image, it is hard to define specific outcome indices of change, and hypothesize degree of receptivity of the client as a self-perceived needy child. Inputs, therefore, may have to be (a) sustained over a lengthy period of time, with no empirical indications of identity change; (b) sustained through periods of intermittent progress and regression of positive image behaviors; (c) accompanied by careful analysis, or the changing frequencies of indicators, where solidarity of these indices represents identity change; and (d) assessed concerning decreasing ranges of variability, as they settle into a more close-knit pattern. The counselor may not be able to predict number of inputs that must be delivered, or accurately associate behavioral indices with identity changes, particularly in the early stages of therapeutic input, except as clients report their own interpretations of the relationship between specific behaviors and identity attitudes. There may be confusing or curvilinear correlations between attitudes and behaviors, which will not provide much help initially, in planning inputs. The counselor must differentiate inputs that truly improve self-perceptions, from inputs which infantilize, confuse, or overwhelm the client.

In some cases, the client compares current inputs (with extremely high emphasis on client interpretation) to previous parental inputs (not current therapeutic substitute), so the counselor can make decisions relative to comparative ratio and impact; and alter inputs based on type, degree, and result of conflict, which is set up and monitored as the client thinks about the outcomes (past, present, and future). Sometimes, withdrawal of parental support which creates anxiety and opportunity, may have a more significant impact itself, so the counselor may be more attuned to times when inputs are not delivered, and compare the client's changes with each successive withdrawal. For the withdrawal to be the independent variable here, deliveries of the input must be controlled and held relatively standard. Thus, change in outcomes is not related to varying amounts or intensities of parenting, but to parental expectations that the child develop self-control in the absence of active parental inputs. Intermittent inputs may be more helpful than standardized and consistently-delivered units of parenting, since parental support may not allow the client sufficient unsupported opportunity to respond. Without the support, however, the client may be unable to respond, so having intermittent inputs provides both conditions, compared by noting differential client outcomes within each one. The problem with measuring or accounting for inputs, however, is that they must be delivered in some discernable or measurable pattern, if any decision is to be made about their specific effect. Using them excessively or too randomly, confuses the counselor as to which specific input thrust had a significant effect; how much was waste; what unnecessary and possibly delayed progress resulted, as input continued after the client had already made progress; and how much is completely unsuccessful, with positive or negative change resulting from other phenomena, which may remain hidden as long as the powerful parenting input continues to be delivered.

Sometimes, parental input might be more effective as a response to client stimulus (approval of a behavior or activity), where the counselor wishes to assess decreasing frequency of the response (R), relative to increasing occurrence of qualitative client behavior (B), along a categorical criteria continuum divided by (or otherwise accounting for) this relationship, between quality client behavior and requests for parental response, compared to need for parental response (RPR) to sustain the positioning behaviors.

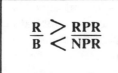

$$\frac{R}{B} \begin{matrix} > \\ < \end{matrix} \frac{RPR}{NPR}$$

These indices say little about input relative to outcome, but some combination gives a better index not only of occurrence of the input, but also their effectiveness, when considering need. Other formulas, of course, could be envisioned, any of which should alert the practitioner to the presence of relativity of inputs to needs, their own potency and frequency, and differential outcomes.

Parental inputs may also be designed to redefine or reframe a particular situation or perspective, or separate an issue into smaller or larger manageable parts. The counselor must remember that reframing is typically hypothetical or conjectural for many clients (sometimes seen as a pretend or fantasy game or exercise), so an outcome within the reframed scenario must be measured longitudinally relative to the stability of the behavior, and stability of the reframed cognitions. This insures that positive behavior does not obscure slippage in the reframing arena, which might alter the behavior in the long run, or modify it unconsciously, privately, or defensively, in its more immediate period of manifestation. The input should be assessed relative to adequacy and significance of the reframe, and if the client returns to the original frames or definitions. Sometimes the danger is that the reframed respective is artificial, but the resultant outcome is positive. This leads to the question of whether inputs are positive or helpful, if a false minor premise leads to the correct conclusion, but only leads to that conclusion as long as the cognitive error is not discovered. Reframing may also distort a more complex conflict which, in the client's symbolic referential structure, only makes sense in this integrated form. Disintegration and separation actually produce a different reality which appears to be resolved, but provides an answer to the wrong, or a partial question. The counselor can use this input in a point/counter-point or thesis/antithesis fashion, wherein parental input initially reframes and determines consequent outcomes, but is then contradictorily used to pressure return to the original frame, with the benefits of the now-antecedent reframe to obscure the outcome, and compare it to the first outcome with the initial reframing. This is similar to tearing down a machine and observing each part separately, putting the machine together in different ways, then returning it to its original configuration to insure it was not changed for the sake of change alone, and that the original frame was perhaps the best one after other alternatives were considered.

Enhance Client Self-Evaluation

Some inputs, whether more directive in nature or part of existential, client-centered, or non-directive therapies; assist clients to develop awareness of their needs, and evaluate or diagnose various aspects (sometimes all aspects holistically) of their bio-psychosocial status and adaptation, which also includes planning future activities, growth endeavors, and changes.

The initial problem with making statements or asking questions of clients to help them develop diagnostic awareness, is that they often do not have a data base from which to draw cognitive constructs, or do not have skills to perform actual comparative assessments, even if data bases exist. This obviously occurs working with children and adolescents; clients with intellectual and cultural deficiencies; clients with severely impaired, inadequate, or schizoid personalities; and others who are well defended or simply have not learned psychodynamic frames of reference. Input must be assessed, therefore, not entirely in direct relation to the quality of open-ended response ("I feel frightened"), but in relation to this response relative to potential to respond at all, and to differential criteria of correct response according to theory and the value of the evaluative perspectives, as this has (or does not have) meaning for the client.

In some cases, input may be more appropriately delivered in a fixed alternative format with clients having a limited baseline awareness repertoire. This forces the client into awareness categories which do not represent exhaustive or mutually exclusive arenas of status, or represent combined categories which the therapist has not envisioned. In repeated administrations of the input, the counselor should help the client use the same categories, so change within any one categorical response can be assessed, rather than changes between categories. The unplanned mixture of evaluative categories used for the client's own assessment, may mean that the counselor is never sure whether change in any one category has occurred. The way the input is handled, and not the way the client defines or manifests the outcome, will address this. Also, input must flow upward in either increasingly more specific subsets of evaluation (e.g., regarding holistic stress, reduced to specific stress in one life, reduced to stress in a particular muscle group); or multiple indicators, so the client does not get trapped in doing massive global assessments with little anchorage to specifically correlate them to, and no particular consequent direction for change. The more the counselor sets up bivariate analytic models for the client, or multivariate levels of assessment, the more precise the answer will be, and the more accuracy the therapist develops about whether the client really makes accurate and specific assessments.

It is hard to plan interventions for clients who might, for example, be good at evaluating themselves as "highly stressed"; whereas more mileage may be possible if the client assesses stress, cross-tabulated by biological reaction time of day, interactional dynamics, specific irrational cognitions, hypothesized fearful outcomes, and degree of real social support. This means that inputs require successively smaller subunits to achieve specificity, supplemented by a checks and balances system to move back and forth from any position (inductive and deductive), to assess correctness of proceeding or following categories as they are determined in process of development.

A problem develops if the client's assessment does not match the counselor's, where the therapist has a predetermined model for client functioning and dysfunctioning (which most therapists do). Left with two divergent evaluative perspectives, the counselor must decide about the input which produced this divergence. On one hand, the counselor might believe that the client's process of making evaluative judgment is most important (usually for developmental advancement purposes), and feel that evaluative outcomes are normally distributed. If the client makes enough of them, they become more accurate (by change alone and also by learning), and larger samples of data used by the client, "naturally" result in correct assessments. If this is the counselor's perspective, then continuation of the same input should produce eventual desirable results, even to correctly refute the counselor's diagnostic perspective.

In other cases, the counselor may believe that reality testing is a process of comparing evaluative perspectives, and that congruence of assessed status is crucial. This requires inputs to elicit judgments on the client's part, as well as making explicit contradictory judgments, to then stimulate assessment of the convergence. This implies that the therapist uses input on the self to insure that the counselor's perspective also moves toward congruence, rather than remaining fixed and waiting for the client simply to agree. This process should be openly shared, so the client sees the counselor also exploring ways and outcomes of assessment.

In another model, input develops a questioning attitude on the client's part; however, it assumes that the actual content should be determined by the counselor, and evaluation on the client's part should place high emphasis on evaluation of resistance to the correct awareness. This directive approach suggests that the input may not be most effective if presented first ("What do you feel?"), but may be more appropriately placed after a judgment is given ("You feel angry—do you see this or what is getting in your way of seeing your anger?"). There may be fewer degrees of freedom for the client to perform open-ended categorical assessments, but more opportunity for them to learn evaluation by disputing the judgment of the counselor, and gathering supportive data to prove he or she is not angry (if this is the assessment in question). If this happens, the counselor decides whether the goal is to help the client play out the selected hand through adversarial evaluation (with gains in other areas of assertiveness or autonomy), or whether evaluative input serves as a blockage, and should be readministered until congruence is achieved or transference, superceding the original evaluation.

Premature employment of this input sometimes overwhelms or confuses clients, especially if deductively employed (What do you think and how do you confirm it?). It may be more successfully used inductively, by helping clients identify behaviors and then piece together more comprehensive assessments, as they go along and have mounting evidence to make a point they have not yet considered. This can be done by helping clients define behaviors, measure or assess frequencies of occurrence and potencies, and then subsequently decide if higher frequency behaviors or behavior constellations, suggest a definitional category. Also, especially with children, teenagers, and impulsive, immature adults; counselor evaluation may make the client feel resentful, controlled, helpless, or confused, so abstract evaluation may be temporarily or permanently impossible. The counselor may be required to set up a range of outcomes which would result from the evaluation if it were present (phantom evaluation), and concretely construct a set of linearly-complete separate contingencies, to include all possible behavioral outcomes which the client cannot independently envision as a result of abstraction, but can role-play or conceptualize concretely. This is akin to task-centered, behavioral, and other contingency learning models, in which there is no one comprehensive evaluative structure or moment, but rather a set of sometimes disjointed minuscule pleasure/pain assessments which the client makes. In these, results of evaluation reflect the nonexistent evaluation, which will often only be registered in the counselor's mind.

The counselor should always envision both the home base (primary evaluative structure and accumulated outcomes) and the progressive comparisons of data A/B, which occur as the client deals rapidly with vast amounts of information. It is confusing to assess effectiveness of this input with so many assessments occupying a multitude of cerebral synopsis and energy surges, so one perspective uses the input only for dyadic comparisons (A/B), so decisions about at least two alternatives become cumulatively associated with only one other item (including one item which is the holistic composite of all previous decisions). In this case, there is only one up-to-date baseline which is congruent and as cohesive as possible, to compare to only one new piece of information at a time. An evaluative decision which does not seem consistent with accumulated previous decisions can be retraced, dyad by dyad, back through a system, as a result of therapist directive or client discomfort with conflictual behavioral outcomes. This narrowing of the field provides specific feedback to the counselor about specific evaluative processes, which may obscure effectiveness of this input, if the field of action becomes too cluttered with comparable facts or bits of data.

In considering processes to help clients retrospectively pick up warning signs relative to present problems or stress, the counselor must spend considerable energy teaching the client empirical processes of behavioral recognition and descriptive classification. Input simultaneously assists the client in disengaging from the powerful control of those symptoms which are indicators of stress, and symbolically-regressive attempts at conflict resolution and adaptation. Outcome to assess efficacy of inputs can be measured in frequencies and degrees of accuracy of symptom recognition. They also differentiate symptoms having different causes, or symptoms which are relatively healthy indices of non-neurotic stress, and adaptive behaviors which are not symptoms at all. Inputs teaching this self-awareness, especially among clients who lack this affective sensitivity or who are heavily defended, often require considerable flexibility and elongated time dimension for delivery. This is because they must be activated when symptoms are present, in order for the client to gain experiential sensitivity. They continually assume a regressive, backward-motion perspective, to stimulate clients to pick up cues at earlier and earlier periods in their symptom's pattern of manifestation. Sometimes these inputs must abandon specific content areas of discussion, in order to respond to an immediately emerging behavioral cue in the client's repertoire. These inputs are more effective making associational links between present content and process, or linking current and past awareness of processes, with future plans to make decisions about symptoms as they occur. The most obvious evaluative danger, is that the inputs will create awareness of symptoms as ends in and of themselves, without pushing on to expect the client will make additional decisions about the awareness, once it has occurred. The author frequently hears new clinical practitioners describe therapeutic goals relative to "getting in touch with feelings," period—without acute awareness that the input statement or question must move past this point to other frameworks for action. This is true even in client-centered or existential approaches in which the counselor is possibly less active, and the work is done largely by the client, but with a stimulus or expectation, indeed, that the work be done after the awareness has been achieved. Some counselors also lack awareness of where this experiential awareness fits into therapeutic frameworks for change, so they often do not parlay initial input results into a more significant advantage for the client. This input, therefore, has at least a two-stage impact, which cannot be evaluated unless both stages and their corresponding outcomes are assessed holistically.

Inputs related to self-assessment, which emphasize behavioral manifestations of conflict/stress (anxiety, compulsions, withdrawal, specific expressions, or verbalizations), must also be finely tuned through awareness of levels of the counselor, to help clients perceive specific, often minute, aspects of their behavior or expressions. This means degree of specificity and precision with which input focuses the client, is an invaluable index of its success. Sometimes this is as specific as the movement of a client's eyes from center to peripheral vector, tightening of stomach or neck muscles, or curvature of lips, which, if missed by the therapist and client, neglect significant areas of awareness. In these situations, the input is measured or assessed initially in terms of its presence (the counselor did comment to the client about increased muscle tension), but secondarily relative to subsequent occurrence to reflect its repeated absence in the client's own input repertoire, and also in terms of whether the awareness (once achieved or recognized by the client) was also valuable in other arenas of therapeutic gain.

When self-assessment on the client's part also includes awareness of esteem or nurturant needs, levels of fear or anger, desires or longings, or perceptions of the various possible natures of reality; the counselor often enters an arena of awareness with the client that is amorphous, confusing, uncertain, or symbolically referenced or indexed. This lack of definition requires that the input have enough persistence and intensity, to keep the client cognitively engaged in pursuit of a slippery and elusive object of awareness. The input must also have the strength and circumscriptive capacity to isolate the perceptual and visual arena, and exclude extraneous perceptual or cognitive/emotional awareness. It must be precise enough to insure that the client really "sees" what he/she and the counselor believe may be there, or what the counselor feels the client should see. The author recalls work with some clients or students where extremely intense eye contact, accompanying touching, accompanying voice intensity and tone, and sustained modulation; were all necessary to help the person engage anxiously/ excitedly in pursuit of an awareness of "need for father's approval as seen from age 13 or 14." This may never have been achieved and experienced in its proper traumatic intensity, without the combined effect of the eyes, hands, voice, etc., which comprised the input delivery package. Awareness of feeling and identity states, of course, is difficult, so inputs often are delivered in repeated and either successive or intermittent occasion, to progressively circumscribe the object to be perceived; but also cross-reference it and clarify its validity. The degree to which this task is assumed by clients marks its success, given the occurrence of meaningful decision-making by the client unilaterally, in conjunction with the awareness.

This input may also be retroflective to help the client review previous incidents of destructive, conflictual, or otherwise problematic behavior. In many cases, it purposely places controls on all other input behavior, as previous awarenesses are being recollected or re-experienced. This is necessary so the client can experience them in the absence of symbolic or actual parental or societal reaction (which could conceivably alter or prevent the experience from occurring, since many clients don't trust that they can hurt again, and survive the experience). All of this may appear to be wasting time in pursuit of experience rather than change, but it may be necessary if the client is theoretically expected to develop and use self-awareness perceptions. The therapist often has to use probing input to elucidate the experience, and follow this with supportive explanatory input to help clients understand it. This must be followed by supportive input, to return painful awareness to a position of non-aware safety temporarily, followed by more probing to help clients make decisions and changes. Alterations of these sequences of input are certainly possible, but each new sequence must assess its relationship to theoretical expectations, and resultant client-related outcomes.

Confrontation

Confrontation has always been a mainstay of most clinical psychodynamic intervention. This technique, if used and evaluated properly, can be extremely functional in helping clients increase informed self-awareness, and behaviorally, cognitively, and emotionally interrupt destructive patterns to allow room for improvement.

Effectiveness of confrontation should be assessed as (1) ratio between parameters of relationship trust, (2) block or delaying nature of the confrontative technique, (3) client perception of the structure and process of their psychodynamic behavior, and (4) availability of positive options for the client to initially protectively cling to, and subsequently embrace, as a new adaptive pattern. The nature of confrontative behavior and style of delivery are also significant, since the client may not view them as helping/caring/interventions, may not even know that they exist at time of delivery, may not feel they are significant enough to attend to with sufficient psychic energy/anxiety to learn, or may not realize their interconnectedness to other dimensions of psychodynamic process. Counselors get the most reliable feedback about confrontative style through co-therapy, in the presence of an outside observer, or with clients who are sensitive, honest, and relatively sophisticated in their feedback capability. Feedback styles can be categorized via content analysis of therapeutic communications, and their effectiveness assessed with reference to qualitative and quantitative responses from clients.

Probably the most important index of confrontational input, however, is ability of the input to manifest self-contained examinational stimuli, to help the client understand the purpose of the confrontation before, during, and after its manifestation. This index also guides him/her to make conceptual associations between the function of antecedent behavior; the opportunity and stimulative gap in process engendered by the confrontative input—usually occurring immediately following a client behavior or word that is dysfunctional; and the range and quality of valuable client responses in the future, with and without the presence of the confrontational input. The literature, in this regard, discusses interpretive subcomponents of the input to include elucidation of conflicts between forbidden wishes and defenses against them; needs which have been avoided and values about these needs; repetitive patterns and psychic costs relative to pattern maintenance, and other needs which the compulsive patterns exclude; and symbolic forms of adaptation from the past, acted out in the present as part of historical reenactment, as well as transference.

The counselor must be alert to the interpretation the client places on the confrontation, particularly because it may closely resemble some form of social rudeness, ignoring, attacking, or provoking, not only having socially normative connotations of unacceptable assault, but compounded by the client's need for parental or authoritative approval, and his/her sensitivity (probably with different goals and intentions) from the past. The effectiveness of this input necessitates examination with the client, of how he/she perceived its occurrence, and how its delivery has affected him/her, so positive intentions can be highlighted and defensive responses or resistance can be analyzed, and a decision made about differential future options.

The input is only effective if it truly interrupts, so that disequilibrium is created in the patterned system of client habituated behavior. Also, decisions the client makes during and immediately after the input, must be identified and analyzed, so the counselor/evaluator can decide if the confrontative input actually had an effect in producing new behavioral systems or configurations (or approximations thereto), which fill the emptiness when stoppage occurs.

In this regard, another focus of evaluation is whether the input has placed the client in a learning mode, and true opportunity for growth has been carved out of the array of thoughts and feelings which often interact, without overt reflection of their meaning or dynamic. This is similar to the unexpected discovery of a clearing or open space after traveling through a dense, possibly frightening, and confusing, jungle; it gives the traveler a chance to rest from the burdens of travel and battle with the terrain, before entering the forest again on the other side of the clearing. The problem is that most clients need some aspects of the forest struggle to symbolically define their identity, and keep them afloat in life. They may not ever see clearings which periodically emerge, and are uncertain how to use them. They may move through time quickly to re-enter the forest, circumnavigate the clearings to anxiously avoid dangers, or use them for minimal rest, but spend too much rest time worrying about their impending re-entry into the forest. Although the counselor may "see" that the forest has been brought to an end by the confrontive input, the client may not share this perception, and walk into the open while remaining cognitively and emotionally engaged with the forest. The opening is only a small part of the confrontive input, while the client's behavior and decisioning in the middle of the clearing, and how they see the forest and the clearing collectively; are also key evaluative questions.

What should occur in the clearing is largely determined, and specifically defined by theory, but should contain:

1. dimensions of understanding systems
2. connections between past, present, and future
3. acceptance of responsibility for actions and subsequent learning
4. clarification of both symbolic and actual reality
5. connective linkages between behaviors, thoughts, and feelings
6. association between individual agendas and dynamics of relationships
7. awareness of, and rationale for transference adaptation
8. decision about the existence of anxiety relative to the confrontational behavior, and a conclusion about how to handle it
9. a plan to establish goals and objectives for the future
10. clear decision prior to re-entry to the forest on the other side of the clearing, and
11. analysis concerning adequacy of previous life decisions.

An example of part of the process comes up in the author's clinical classes with some masters degree students who, in the teaching viewpoint, are either protecting/insulating themselves against uncomfortable learning, or acting out symbolic parent-child agendas transferentially with the faculty person. One student asked a values-related question. The instructor believed the student knew her own answer to this and wanted confirmation, or wanted to make the instructor commit himself to a controversial perspective, so the student could displace or project anger through rejection of the opinion (father figure), and prove one more time that adults (parents?) are incapable of genuine caring for her, and that she dare not risk being different. Answering the student's question would have contributed to playing out the scenario, wherein everyone (parent, student, instructor, other students in class) was destined to lose. The instructor decided to confront this issue, partly to help the student learn about her own process, but also to clinically illustrate the confrontational technique to anyone in class who wanted to learn it. The author refused to answer the question (which would have been quickly addressed in a nonconfrontational situation), and created the open space discussed earlier. This was quickly followed with some structure to guide the student into the frightening open space, to help her examine what she had just done, and conceptualize different outcomes which might result with and without the author's response. It also allowed her to consider potential responses the author might have given. The effectiveness of the input must be determined after the struggle of the open space occurs, so one can decide if the confrontation which made the space, also followed up to make it a "functional" space as well.

Some confrontational techniques use paradoxical intention, or symptom exaggeration or cuing (prescription to produce awareness, and consequent learning and self-control to illustrate choice). The important evaluation of this strategy is whether clients differentiate the actual "game" of symptom manipulation from a perception they may have of the counselor's possible lack of concern (which many clients perceive relative to this technique), so the confrontive role assumes a negative social definition. This confrontational technique, when used without an analytic structure to understand its function, can lead to anxiety/crises or regression in some clients, who see only their entrapment and vulnerability to a past reality. The counselor is advised to assess the client's degree of regressive potential, along with ability to abstract beyond the technique, to perceive its superordinate functionality. The technique might therefore be evaluated relative to its ability to either converge perspectives of reality, or differentiate them, whichever the client is most in need of experiencing at any particular time.

Develop Causal and Correlational Linkages

Considerable therapeutic time is spent assisting clients develop conceptual (and corresponding affective and behavioral) connections between divergent areas of their identities and behavioral patterns. This is a difficult task to accomplish and assess, because the connective linkages are often unknown to the counselor as well as client. A series of hypotheses have to be postulated, for the client to construct dyadic comparative models for any two ideas at a time, to compare areas of identity which are similar and different, and construct abstract categories containing the separate yet possibly-related subsets of reality, under one associational category (e.g., dependence, aggression, running away). Evaluators must avoid forcing the client to assume connective linkages which are not actually correct, or to abstract too broadly to include relationships between ideas or feelings which are too tangential or circumstantial.

Evaluation insures that the client has not "seen" a relationship ostensibly between A and B (which might correspond to the counselor's perspective about the client's dynamics) when, in fact, the client either sees a relationship between A and C; B and C; a specific subset of A and all of B; a subset of B or a subset of both A and B; or even a relationship between A and not A, which the client inadvertently or conveniently attributes to B, which is not B at all. There are also different temporal and spatial dimensions within which A's and B's exist, wherein they are constant in some arenas, but actually become different variables as time advances, regresses, or as spatial configurations change (e.g., closeness to a stimulus, distance from an event).

Also, the client may perceive that specific relationships between phenomena do, in fact, exist, but the evaluator must design input to determine the exact nature of that relationship as seen by the client; while affirmatively proving that the client's present type, nature, and degree of problem are definitely related to the relationships which the client sees as governing his/her life. The client and counselor will also see different associations between phenomena, and evaluation of the success of the input must consider the counselor's ability to help the client define and pinpoint different, but specific, qualities and quantities of association or causality, so similar amounts of therapeutic inputs can be applied in the change process. For example, clients severely traumatized as children in a strong associational linkage between parental disapproval and self-confidence (which, of course, must be more specifically defined in the actual therapeutic process), or in the linkage between maternal or paternal sexual seductiveness and pathological sexual sadomasochistic fantasy; may require similar or greater degrees of therapeutic change-oriented stimulative power, compared to the amount or quantity of therapeutic energy necessary to correct or otherwise deal with a possibly less powerful connection between image/fantasy, and failure of a course in the client's college years. In cases where the client does not see the linkage, the input must continue the same process of connective association, but persevere to elucidate other single or multiple sets of unknown variables, which are similarly connected to the process of not seeing the connection between A and B.

Since most bio-psychosocial phenomena are multivariate, the evaluative process is likewise confounded, since all pieces of the puzzle must be put together in specific ways. The input must contain sufficient energy or attractiveness to engage the client in the puzzle-solving process, so the quality of its appeal characteristics or attention-getting dynamics, must be assessed relative to the attention span of the client, quality of the client's engagement, and consequent correctness and functionality of decisions after their interest has been peaked.

In some cases, before clients engage in the exploration of new reality sets, they need to be convinced that their present perceptions or connective linkages are sufficiently incorrect, burdensome, or dysfunctional to be the predominant or strongly contributory cause of current pain, or the potential cause of painful consequences in the future. In many cases, clients will not believe they would be better off with new linkage perceptions. The input must have a built-in dual retardation or "patience" quotient, to allow the client to progress so that empirical consequences, which the therapist can then suggest as also associated to their a priori associational patterns and scenarios, actually develop. This is a series of regressive associational linkages which keep moving farther back in time, to eventually reach a causal or prime linkage association, which can be altered to produce changes as time progresses again. There is no clear linear pattern necessarily, so counselors need to insure that once entry on the continuum has been negotiated, they help clients move in the appropriate backward or forward direction, to come upon additional necessary linkage points which may be critical elements in the holistic causal or correlational formula.

Clients must consider whether they have the ability to alter any associational perceptions, which in itself is an additional linkage between variables of autonomy, relationship, strength, or options. Redefinition is one part of this capability, while behavioral change may be an associated or subsequent dimension that does not necessarily go hand in hand. In causality, the general nature of variables must be discerned, along with specific situations where their basic nature might be interchanged, or where typical degrees of independent influence or dependent receptivity change.

Differentiation of Inner and Outer Spatial Dimensions

Many therapeutic approaches deal with client problems related to inability to associate inner feelings or states of being (presumed being), with external antecedent, concurrent, or consequent behavior. This is an addendum to internal states or a symbolic manifestation of, reflection of, or reaction against them. Conversely, many clients have difficulty observing external behaviors and tracing the causal linkage into the inner domains of their personality, sometimes because they have never learned to do so, or because it is painful. In addition, many clients struggle with developing capability and flexibility to change emphasis from inner to outer space or vice versa; and lose adaptive creativity and opportunity, since this inter-spatial movement may be necessary to handle particular types of inner or outer stimuli, and deal with self- or other-generated conflict.

One of the first evaluative questions, is whether the client can even differentiate various inner vs. outer life spaces (certainly a problem with chronic or acutely-psychotic clients, and children at certain ages), and determine degree of stabilization of these life-space perspectives. This may be influenced by the stimulus and disruptive effect of anxiety, drug or alcohol use, or growth stages and dynamics, in which clients perceive inner and outer dimensions within a general range of vision which is cultural, age related, intelligence related, or diagnosis related; and therefore idiosyncratic, but also culturally nomothetic, for each individual. The counselor needs to establish an initial baseline range of past perceptual variation, then hypothesize an obtainable and incrementally adjustable variation goal which is best suited to the problem needs and success capability of each client. Degree of exchange between outer and inner, and length of perceptual stability within any one domain, are critical patterns to establish. With this accomplished, the process of teaching, confronting, or calling attention to these phenomena begins with subsequent assessment of amount of learning about the life spaces, ability to recognize examples of each type, and ability to see movement as it occurs, to improve anticipation or *ex post facto* decisions about the event. This assessment also includes measurement of the time clients spend thinking about, or actually existing within, inner or outer fantasy time; or percentage of responses they manifest (words, reactions, thoughts, appearance and attire configurations) which existentially occur in any of these locations.

Specific input may be problematic if there is low correlation between the client's and counselor's "space," and there may be conjecture about whether any input-related change can occur, if client and counselor are literally dwelling in two separate and potentially mutually-exclusive "spaces" of reality. Another question, therefore, is whether the client can accept differences between self and therapist, and, in fact, actually consider the possibility (implying some cognitive dissonance, deviance, or nonconformity to self-images) that different reality domains exist (inside-outside, self-other, past, present, etc.), and alternate outcomes may be associated with their presence in some other domain. This also includes, as noted by recent psychic research, the domain of the transcendental, super-psychic, transpersonal, or, as noted in many religions, the ultra inner world of awareness of the spiritual realms of relationship communities with a God-head. For all the above, evaluation includes the client's ability to define and recognize indices of inner vs. outer states of being (e.g., "Are you behaving in a peaceful way, but feeling angry?" and "How do you know you are doing either?"). Measurements include changes in correctness (validated partly by counselor observation, but also through feedback from significant others or environmental outcomes, coded to represent feeling states) of recognition, or speed of state-of-domain identification. To view the effectiveness of the input, counselors must assess their ability to assume a metacommunicative posture to move away from the specific content, toward questions or other stimuli which (a) keep the content on hold, and, therefore, valid and significant for the client and (b) focus attention on the framework underneath the content, which gives energy to this inanimate phenomenon of existence. The inability of the counselor to match inner or outer worlds, with real objects of reality (personification or reification, to which the client attributes value, cause, content, and functionalism) will probably mark the failure of this input. The counselor's input is assessed relative to capability not only to interrupt ongoing linear or circumscribed aware-nesses of an ultra-status thought or act, but also to posit believable structures which the client may not see. The input may include the establishment by the counselor, of scenarios which support the very definition of the structure by indirect, *ex post facto* awareness of consequences, from which the client can assume there must have been an antecedent significance rationale, from which positive or negative results emanated. The input technique may also involve the process of ignoring all previous existing benchmarks of reality, to help the client look past them to empirically build structure or categories of reality, supported by the ability on the part of the counselor to reward or emotionally reinforce this exploratory architectural process, at a time when the client needs to feel suc-cessful at something.

The counselor must remember, also, that the client may not yet understand the need to construct a new building, and what the separate rooms are to be used for in the future. The input is related to incremental construction or building techniques, and might even use concepts and language from physics, engineering, mathematics, geology, or architecture; to help clients envision separate domiciles into which they may eventually move, to decide if they have ever been there before, and what significance their presence within and without various structures, might mean.

The significance of client valuation of perceptions, behaviors, or events from their inner or outer worlds (past, present, or future), is a second major evaluative issue. This, of course, comes sequentially after concerns about whether clients can even identify and differentiate variations in spatial domains of their lives. The reason that values (or levels of significance) are so important, is that they represent (symbolically and actually) specific points of fixation or regressive status, since the adult client who has been traumatized or has had special needs met at particular times, may repeatedly return (cognitively, behaviorally and emotionally) to these times through the valuations placed on them. The very act of valuing and spatially returning, has functionalism all its own in the past (to re-enact unmet need situations, for example); and meets manipulative, defensive, or other needs in the present external social relationship domain of the client. Differential valuation of spatial locations is not only significant as it relates to the efficiency and energy of client time and awareness investment, but also because these valuative perspectives are often correlated—they partly control the status definitions or self-image/identity diagnoses the client makes about her or himself. Consequently, they become a stimulus which significantly effects other outcomes in the future.

An example is a client who had been, or perceives herself to have been savagely rejected by her father at a time in her life when she wanted to replace her mother as dad's caretaker; and when confusing identity and self-esteem questions necessitated the external security of her father's love and support, which she described as having been siphoned off into his work compulsions, and blossoming love relationship with her eventual step-mother. The resolution of this dilemma for her at that time, was to fully internalize this scenario so she could act out both hurt and fantasized functional resolution of her existential dilemma. The inner scenario has the following components, summarized here to give a general impression of the process:

1. father is perceived as a horrible monster who relentlessly persecutes her for her badness (inability to earn his love), so she has an innoculative dose of poison which is less than (compromise) that of total rejection, and her system builds up psychic immunity;
2. she maintains closeness and erotic attachment to the monsters, to always retain the relationship (which never was, or never reached fruition as she defined it), so she and her father will forever be together;
3. she attaches many inner perceptions to the cleansing nature of water, so she can be exonerated from guilt, and reborn as a healthy and happy child;
4. she fantasizes numerous dimensions and specific characteristics of the monsters, and reinforces these images to externalize blame and avoid responsibility—making her father the continual villain;
5. she envisions (through dreams mostly) many specific dynamics of this relationship, gains reward for the secret persecution she suffers, and sees this martyrdom as her virtue and eventual salvation; the martyrdom experience is a place to escape external pressures of the world, and the uncertainty of failure outside, that could even be worse than her inner suffering.

The counselor must precisely understand where values are placed internally (or externally); the potency of these spatial valuations (in the example above, the client places enormous significance on the sanctity and necessity of her inner world, as a critically-functional life survival phenomenon); differences in types and amounts of valuation; and amount of valuative loss envisioned by the client, as she considers the option to change perception to a new domain. For many clients, habituated value allocation patterns will never substantially change, because of the inherent functionalism of the scenarios played out, and the length and amount of value energy invested. The counselor only looking at functional or dysfunctional relationships acted out, may make one diagnostic decision about the need for client change, but neglect to consider the degree to which this is affected by value investment. The counselor should decide what modifications would be feasible within spatial domains, rather than assume the client can tolerate the loss, to negotiate between domain perceptual or behavioral readjustments.

Also, considerations of the amount of value placed on any one existential domain, suggest therapeutic work to consolidate, expand, decentralize, or otherwise alter the placement of value. Inner or outer spatial perceptual frequencies and scenarios remain the same quantitatively, but a qualitative change occurs in the degree of psychic energy invested (more energy can be used elsewhere; while maintaining past spatial patterns or changes in value investment, might eventually extinguish constructs which comprise and sustain the inner or outer system).

A third part of this evaluative picture is described in the literature as helping clients develop a form of projection, to understand others with whom they interrelate and, therefore, better plan their own actions as both stimuli and responses to valued love or relationship objects. This is also a spatial movement from inside the self to inside another, inside another looking toward the outside of the other and the self, and looking at the inside of the self from the viewpoint of the other. Assessment of this technique involves helping clients (who need to correctly project) develop anchoring points to which they safely attach themselves within the other's perspective, which relates back to a position of reward or security for them. This allows them to occupy this perceptual position long enough to more fully experience the ramifications and manifestations of its existence. Counselors can evaluate their own effectiveness in helping clients identify common denominators, their ability to channel some energy into this position, and tenacity in helping the client maintain contact for a sufficient time with self, to feel comfortable enough to transport this safe haven into the domain of the other. It's almost like discovering a pearl in the client, building an oyster around it, creating a conveyer belt to take it into the world of the significant other, and opening the oyster and joining the original pearl with a similarly-valued pearl, in the new host environment. Many clients resist seeing the fear in others (maybe manifested as violence or abuse toward them), because they have not seen their own fear, and the therapist needs techniques to heighten awareness of the client's own fears, to reinforce some value for attaining this awareness (so it is intrinsically valuable to the client). At the same time, the therapist helps the client block perceptions of heightened levels of need deprivation from the significant other, so the projection does not compromise the independence-dependence struggle. One technique points out mutual outcome benefits, and then works backwards to illustrate for the client what gains will be made, by understanding the significant other. It is important, too, to show how the significant other, once understood, contributes to a gain for himself/herself first, and then for the client, so the client feels stronger and reciprocates with more positive feedback. This input is an outcome-regressing-to-input-model, as opposed to a self-actualization-progressing-to-outcome model. Evaluation assesses ability of the technique to arrange intensive focus on self and other, the length of assumption of alternate perspectives, and ability of clients to extrapolate from intensity of their perspective in someone else's shoes, to the parallel quality or quantity of their own resultant growth. This occurs either through changes in the behavior of other, or changes in the self, through self and other (general) human understanding. Therapists can assess their ability to help clients see areas of actual gain, or develop fantasized constructs which hypothesize a reciprocal give and take, as long as the client begins the projective process in good faith. This is necessary even though the significant other may initially have no plans to change, because he/she is locked into a narrow self-image by the client's inability and previous unwillingness to "see it their way." They cannot change until the world has been seen that way long enough, so the client, in fact, has a changed image of self. If this outcome does not materialize, however, the therapist needs a back-up plan so the client wins individually, even if the significant other does not reciprocate: "I will reach out my hand in future hopes that being understood will help my friend reach back, but I will also value the reaching out in and of itself, even if my hand gets slapped."

As clients project into the space of someone else, there are also important evaluative questions about incremental decisions they make about themselves (as well as the significant other), as they longitudinally dwell within the perspective of the other. This relates to ways they see themselves more positively for their perseverance and qualitative efforts, and to new viewpoints they discover, as they see themselves as others see them. These decisions, for evaluative purposes, must be documented so their frequencies (whether positive or negative) can be tabulated as the client's overall growth process continues; and so the counselor can evaluate degrees of discrepancy between old and new perspectives of the self moving into the domain of another, as this represents a personality strength of flexibility, benevolence, caring, or leadership.

Another significant component of spatial configurations, applies to input which helps clients correlate or define associational linkage or transportative psychic media. Inner can be connected with outer ("He says A, I feel B"); two or more inner processes can be connected to each other ("When I feel sad, I also feel angry at myself"); or two or more outer phenomena can be connected—although this is both a psychic as well as behavioral connection ("When I lose my temper, I lose behavioral control in other areas as well"). The reason for the input, is to help clients define the connective psychic tendons but, more importantly, to make an evaluative decision about their rationality or efficacy to consider other options ("When I feel sad, I do not have to also feel angry, but can alternately feel pride in the richness of my emotions").

One part of this input establishes a boundary around each separate event, so the client learns to see each event's circumscribed limitations, to differentiate the exact point and process by which the event ends. A linkage avenue is set up to carry its essence (or part of its essence) into a new and not necessarily identical, relevant, compatible, or separate domain of reality. The clinician helps accomplish this by working with the client to more precisely define and focus on each event, to define their unique differences. Further, the clinician must refuse to accept linkage perceptions until the client has considered each domain separately, and identified extrapolated empirical manifestations, consequences, or antecedent events, that are directly linked. The clinician documents frequency of times a client "jumps to conclusions" (establishes connectives links), without first acknowledging that a linkage process has occurred.

A second part of this input considers the intervening connection between ideas, with particular reference to the client's ability to recognize it as a separate

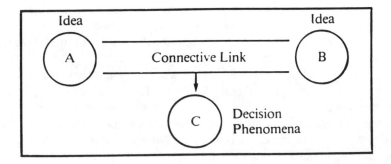

variable (that can exist or not, change, be modified, etc.); and neither an intermediary constant, nor an inherent part of either separate idea (A or B) which it connects. Counselors can certainly measure the ratio of times they have to point this out, versus the number of times clients do this voluntarily; but they can also assess comprehension of differences as symbolized by ability in other decision-making areas of life, degree of acceptance, and comfort with awareness of the essence of the connective linkage phenomena. Further, more advanced evaluation includes the quality of clients' analysis of the rationale for setting up major linkage associational units, with categorization of positive and negative benefits they achieve with the linkage in place. They may note that their linkage of here-and-now phenomena (as a separate entity which can be assessed individually) is connected to other sets of linkages in childhood or past regressed conflicted areas of identity formation, so that the linkage system assumes a more complicated structure.

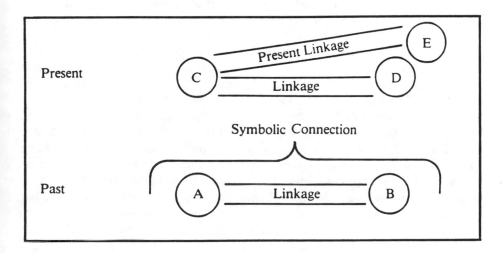

Since adult life has its options for learning, however, some linkages are related correctly to the here-and-now, and not directly associated with ghosts from the past (noted by circle E). The nature and functional meaning of those linkages between different ideas and possible life spaces is important to evaluate, so the client can develop a blueprint profile of: which spaces are linked, which commonalities exist in the linkage phenomena, what differences there are, what outcomes result, how they affect the total system, what types and degrees of control can be exerted (by the client) to sustain positive spatial connective processes, and what changes should be made.

Sometimes this evaluation can be more effective if the client actually draws a diagram of ideas, behaviors, and interconnections; complete with boundary lines to illustrate inner and external separations, and past/present/future differentiations. Since this is an exploratory or discovery process, the counselor assesses his/her own use of questions and interrogatory statements; the changing interest of clients in this problem-solving or puzzle construction process; and ability of clients to see various domains with vivid and animated clarity as significant, "alive," and energetically dynamic moving parts in a complex system.

One technique especially recommended for dealing with the meaning of internal vs. external process, particularly as clients are encouraged to take responsibility for their *own* interpretation and control of the world (through existential perspective and gestalt awareness and cognitive control), is the self-dialogue technique of creating a complete, self-contained inner conversation. The subject, predicate, and adjectives/adverbs of sentences must all be related to, and emerge from, the client's inner world, rather than including other domains. Some counselors evaluate their performance by forcing clients to use the word "I" at the beginning of sentences, but evaluation also concerns the application of other words as well. An example is the statement, "She betrayed me when she went to work and relinquished her traditional homemaker role." This statement connects outer and inner in a way which prevents understanding of either, suggests excessive responsibility by other for self, and ignores other decisions about feelings and self-perceptions. Therapists might assess their ability to help clients convert outside to inside by changing words and noting implications, or analyzing the connective linkages irrespective of either the other, or inner specific content. Changing the words could involve the therapist's substitution of words in reframing or restating the sentence: "I chose to feel————when I perceived her behavior as————relative to my image of myself as————." Evaluation here demands assessment of the actual sentence restructuring, as well as the ability of the client to fill in the words; relative to the ratio of resistance, length of time the client maintains the new structure as a component of learning, frequency with which he/she can back away from the original or changed statement to analyze it, and the range of varying interpretations the client allows him/herself to have, relative to various degrees of satisfaction as they hypothesize different options.

Evaluation can center on the connective linkage (e.g., "The statement I make to myself says that other people are responsible for my happiness, which is the reflection of my relationship with parents, in which I incorrectly assumed I had to give up certain aspects of my individuality to make them happy") relative to its ability not to include specific content, but remain centered on the process by which particular areas of content are drawn into various domain areas. The counselor notes the frequency with which the client returns to external content, and progressively evaluates the quality of the analysis of why and how this transportative process occurs.

Also, feelings of emotional security, control, or anxiety-reduction connected with either internalization or externalization can be documented, and these feelings assessed in comparison to similar feelings from the past, or perceived fantasy feelings envisioned for the future. Also, they can (in their positive dimension) be associated with antithetical negative feelings from childhood about non-security. Hereby, degrees of inverse connection can be measured, as feelings from the past or present are compared to themselves for degree of potency; and this positive/negative association moves more closely together to become the same, or reverses itself completely, so the denominator and numerator eventually exchange positions.

Metacommunication (communication about one's communication) is also a process to approach a change in either internal or external space, since one has to assume an external position to use the self-in-action as the subject of attention, and grammatically as the subject of a sentence. It is fairly simple in this regard, to evaluate utilization of this technique, and to set up categories of various results which metacommunication produces; and of specific qualities (feeling states, behavioral options) directly linked to the movement to, and results of, meta-communicative technique.

Change the Learning Model

Many theoretical approaches to clinical practice suggest that clients experience psychological and social dysfunctions as a result of adherence to particular models of learning, behavioral self-reinforcement, social system contingencies, and philosophical deterministic mandates. Although many models are remnants from traumatic or distorted childhood experiences, client change can occur with more immediate attacks on the model itself (including some of its operating rules and propositions); in addition to, or sometimes as a substitute for, more remote efforts to re-parent or otherwise correct the distortions developmentally, throughout post-childhood symbolic experiences. Some argue, of course, that more immediate changes in learning models provide only temporary or less comprehensive changes. Others contend, conversely, that changes in the here-and-now configuration of the learning model (with its combined past and present dimensions), begin a new process of self- and significant-other reinforcement, that does correct some childhood distortions with new experience, or outcome data providing healthy roles, into which the client can quickly move to receive rewards these roles offer.

To successfully negotiate and evaluate this input, the counselor is first pressed to insure that the client perceives the functional principles of learning (reward, anxiety over status repetition, rehearsal), and recognizes essential components of the learning system (social and nonsocial reinforcers, behavioral outcomes, criteria of adequacy, and other elements). This may necessitate an early educational effort on the part of the counselor, to teach facts about learning. The evaluative efforts determine extent to which clients actually believe in principles and processes of learning intellectually (as a part of living), extent to which they understand specific processes of learning and behaving models, and whether or not they operate under the auspices of competing models of learning, which defensively mandate that they do not recognize other forms of learning or changing, which they find traumatic or frightening. Some efforts to alter sub-components of learning models fail, because clients do not philosophically accept traditional learning or behavioral principles as a key life process, or really do not understand the operating mechanisms. In some instances, the client may tenaciously cling to hereditary, constitutional, deterministic, ecological, or other models of existence, so input cannot be delivered without certain failure, since it does not philosophically fit the client's perspective. Counselors must insure a relatively-congruent interpersonal philosophical perspective if they desire to evaluate true integration of new learning models, and should cross-check to be certain they are not altering the congruence or compatibility data.

In cases of philosophical incompatibility, evaluative questions and foci change to center on definitions of any areas of congruence, and to determine if there are dynamics of interpersonal influence (independence-dependence, leader-follower, teacher-learner, joint change, etc.) which could serve as a rationale for continued therapeutic interaction. A good evaluative question here is: "What is the specific nature of our relationship by which either of us expects reasonable probabilities of change?"; or "If one of us behaves, thinks, or feels in a different way (from our resent agenda), how will this occur?"; or "What is it about the way you view (or interact with) me, or I view you, that may cause you or me to change something about our lives?" The counselor must, of course, work out the specific details of this dynamic relationship (if it exists) in order to have hope of eventual outcome assessment.

If the client does recognize a system of learning, the counselor can make preliminary assessments of the value of legitimacy placed on this process. In addition, the counselor can correlate changes in this value perspective, with client increases in (1) exposure and control in manipulating their system, (2) client successes in using the system to produce new behaviors, or (3) understanding of the system without necessarily resultant changes. Also, counselors must assess their own input relative to their ability to help the client define specific, circumscribed, and operationally-definable units of the learning system (Figure 8).

Figure 8
Influential Values and Clinical Learning Stimuli

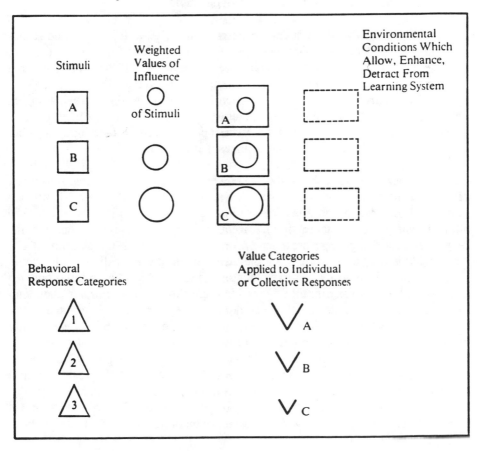

The inability of practitioners to help clients define the component independent and dependent variable units of the system means, initially, there is no way to insure precise conceptualization of this (or any) reality domain. Secondarily, it prevents hypotheses of systematic outcomes, as a result of relationships between these definable elements of the learning domain.

Once specific learning model change inputs have been provided, one approach the clinician may use, is to negotiate attachment of reinforcing power of an alternative stimulus, to the one to which the client is presently responding or has previously responded. One way to do this is for the counselor to introduce a new stimulus in the client's milieu, modeling behavioral responses while concomitantly ignoring a present stimulus (energy divestiture), which therapist and/or client feel is less functional than optimally desirable.

The process by which clients respond to the original to-be-changed stimulus, may be the same dynamic process by which they attend to, invest energy in, and use for reinforcements—the therapist as a role model. If these processes are not the same, then the input must be examined to insure that the modeling does, in fact, have learning relevance to the client, or to validate the real vs. assumed learning value of the stimulus to-be-changed. One or both may not, in fact, be correctly defined as significant parts of the client's learning paradigm, so other variables and dynamics might require investigation.

Another way to attach reinforcing power to a substitute stimulus, is to block clients' ability to respond to that stimulus (e.g., therapist refuses to listen when clients talk in baby talk to a latency-aged child, or the therapist talks to child in adult language at the same time), providing negative reinforcement for the responses as a competing phenomenon, or to directly attack the stimulus itself. This attack is hard to measure since the therapist can discredit the stimulus situation, diminish its power ("Your mother's opinion may not be as important for your overall welfare as you think"), or highlight flaws in the stimulus phenomenon which undermine its sanctity, autonomy, or legitimacy ("Your father criticized you because his wife criticized him, and he felt helpless, weak, and afraid"). The evaluative challenge is to establish a clear picture of the client's protective barrier which insulates the stimulus, and to measure gaps which appear in this structure as the client changes degrees of value attachment, weakens causal linkage connections, accepts the presence of more mitigating intervening variables between stimulus and response, or changes degree of attention to other stimulus situations, people, or events, which may be competitors for the client's affections or dependence.

Another approach inserts governing monitors or regulators within the S-R linkage system, to reduce the "psychic voltage" transmitted between stimulus and response. In communications and systems theories, this input reduces the strength of the relationship between stimulus and response, setting up a dissonant conflict for the respondent in terms of rationale for their time and attention, while creating a progressive extinction process, eventually causing the stimulus to drop out of sight. If this happens, the client is left with either an unsupported response; or the option to identify other stimuli which meet the need for maintaining a system of goals and objectives, and the security of S-R cognitive and behavioral connections. The counselor must remember, of course, that many S-R connections are alive and functional with past unconscious, repressed, fantasized, or otherwise maintained systems of earlier living. Theoretically, therefore, the clinician may need to determine whether the S-R relationship bond can accept the monitoring or regulating function in present time, or whether these connections need to be transformed by the client (traditional transference phenomena) into a past time and life dimension.

This input, in any case, frequently provides filler between S and R, which might be time spent not talking (which could, however, conceivably heighten the sensitivity and impact of the stimulus, and accentuate rather than diminish its potency). Other filler might include use of analytic words or explorations, change of focus of attention, or other ways to disrupt or divert the direct communication line between stimulus and response. The evaluative focus is on the consistency with which this input is delivered, and its correct placement between the right S and R, as the client sees this critical connection. More importantly, it must focus on the evaluation of amount of delay in response, saliency, and power of client response (since this is expected to increase resistance initially, and maybe decrease with progressive decline in reinforcement and client perception of the clarity, strength, and amount of correlated connectedness between the response and the stimulus condition).

The counselor can purposefully direct or assist (or indirectly model) the client to reduce emotional excitation or salient sensitivity which occurs after the stimulus, and as a necessary condition for the response (via relaxation techniques, soothing commentary, slowed pace, etc.), which can be assessed with biofeedback monitoring devices or observations of visceral or physical responses. Decreases in client anxiety reveal that inputs may be intervening with noticeable impact, but they must also be checked by eliciting client reports on how the occurrences are perceived, prior to the response of interest. The degree of description in typical patterns helps show the input has been delivered, but further investigation is needed to discover whether the client, in effect, sees this particular model for learning and responding as undergoing any modifications, and to categorize their perceptions of what this change means for them.

The counselor can vigorously apply evaluative criteria to specific outcome responses, in an effort to alter the client's sensitivity to the "so what" of his/her behavior, but also to ensure that all behavior achieves its highest level of meaning and emotional payoff, relative to criteria applied to those behaviors (singly and in combination). This includes comparison of emotional payoff between the use of client-generated criteria vs. external criteria, in which there is divested ownership.

One way of using this input, is to give clients repeated exercises to explain a particular outcome behavior along multiple standard criteria of adequacy, and to push them to make a comparative judgment based on the criteria and behavior, rather than on the behavior's comparison on only one standard and its behaviors, or simply on the behavior compared to its nonexistence. This means, for example, rather than working with a client who talks about overeating relative to dieting, which is a learning model of relatively limited symbolic significance; the counselor encourages the client to compare eating various amounts to some other significant criteria (see the multivariate Figure 9 as an example):

Figure 9
Bivariate on Clinical Phenomenon

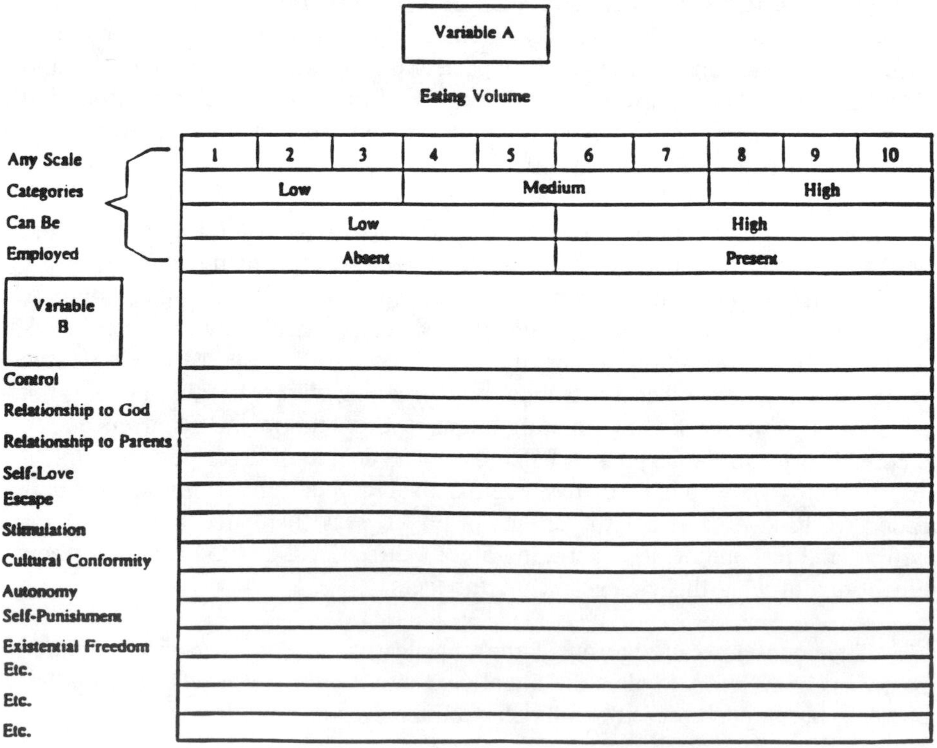

Variable A

Eating Volume

	1	2	3	4	5	6	7	8	9	10
Any Scale	Low			Medium				High		
Categories	Low				High					
Can Be	Absent				Present					
Employed										

Variable B										
Control										
Relationship to God										
Relationship to Parents										
Self-Love										
Escape										
Stimulation										
Cultural Conformity										
Autonomy										
Self-Punishment										
Existential Freedom										
Etc.										
Etc.										
Etc.										

The client can then comprehensively examine the learning model through awareness of multiple alternative models or variables, and subsequently look at relationships between these variables, so a definite decision shows what the client is learning, and how it is perceived.

Another component of helping clients assess and apply evaluative criteria, is direct judgment (counselor generated criteria) from the clinician; as long as clients are also encouraged to examine their feelings about these criteria, as they consider other criteria as well. These judgments can be employed to validate identity status ("When you do this, Mr. Jones, you are running away"), ("This was a kind gesture on your part"), or confirm deviance ("I don't agree with this behavior"); and may include judgments about clients' process of using criteria to understand and make decisions about their learning models ("You're not considering all the different ways you can define your boss's intentions or feelings, when he snapped at you"), ("When you say this to her, she will probably strike out at you").

The important point to remember when making a direct judgment to a client to change learning models, rather than simply producing a new response to an old

Variable A	Eating
Variable B	Other Factors

Possible Relationship Connections:
A causes B (always, sometimes)
B causes A (always, sometimes)
A and B are directly correlated
A and B are inversely correlated
A and B are not associated
A plus unknown X causes B
A adds power to B which causes
C to have retroflective causal connection on B
Etc.
Etc.

dependency model, is that the input is delivered within a system of inter-dependent contingent phenomena. A change in response based on a direct judgment is one measure of effect, but an equally valuable assessment perspective, involves how the client who is responding (or resisting response) actually views and defines the response relative to other responses, and to stimuli which may or may not change concomitantly. If the model changes, the change must be assessed considering all components of the system in all its conditions, rather than viewing only part of the system, as it responds to an extraneous outside influence (see Figure 10).

The evaluative perspective goes beyond what is said by the therapist, and how the client responds. It must include how this connection fits into the total picture (possibly a very minimal and insignificant part, relative to the whole), even though the therapist may subjectively see the S-R relationship with the client as much larger.

Sometimes, judgments or realignments of learning systems include introduction of new criteria; as philosophical concepts of the meaning of life which are related to the counselor's optimism and are, in fact, new or distant perspectives for the client. Wherever a counselor introduces philosophical (and especially ego or cultural dystonic) input and evaluates it, there are several concerns to keep in mind.

Counselors must first assess degree of reasonably-expected congruence between their perspective and the "average" viewpoint of the client (exclusive of crisis attitudes, acute psychotic periods, or attitudes maintained by brief, but severe interpersonal dependency contingencies). Many clients continue, generally, to explain reality through formulas which are habituated and relatively stable aspects of their idiosyncratic, but also group normative world; and are often not capable of drastic variability from this pattern. Some clients are uncomfortable with perceived deviance from the counselor's philosophical perspective, and pretend (and genuinely try) to integrate, accommodate, or assimilate the optimistic constructs. However, this will lead the counselor off base, unless they include, as part of the input, an opportunity for the client to provide a checks and balances type of feedback, to help the counselor monitor and control excessive, emotionally-laden philosophical perspectives. This feedback helps clients examine how they are affected by what can easily become sensationalistic, charismatic, or entertaining inputs, which may have initial heightened appeal, but diminishing long-range return.

In some cases, the input will have a definite beneficial effect on clients, and it will sometimes appear to jostle them out of depressive episodes or lethargic inaction. Evaluation can include an assessment of the particular style, timing, or pattern of words, used to produce the greatest movement away from predetermined definitions of negative behaviors. The counselor must realize the reinforcing power of these stimuli, and assess any changes in the therapeutic relationship following input, and longer-term independent change by the client.

Figure 10
Client Learning Model System

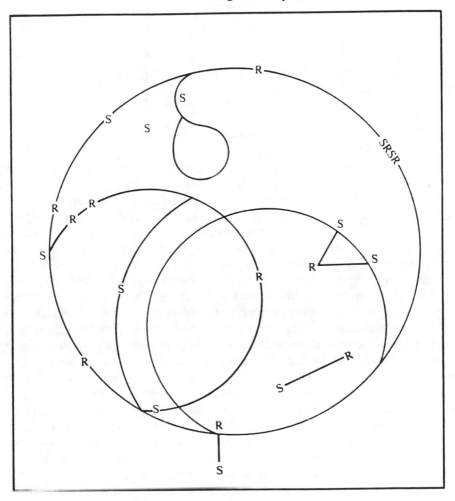

S = Stimuli
R = Responses
S←→R = Cognitive/Behavioral Relationship

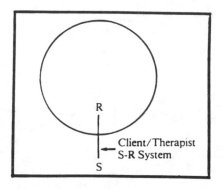

If the client begins revising or creating new concepts of life survival or meaning, the counselor should continually help him or her play out the value position within numerous behavioral scenarios, relationships, and work situations, to help the client decide on "goodness of fit." The counselor should also help the client systematically compose new concepts to compare to pre-existing ideations, to see if they are compatible, if any have to be eliminated, or if they can coexist or be integrated. As new life philosophies are compared to other ideas (e.g., feminine power with dependence), behavioral modes can be developed and tested. The client and counselor can discuss how much forced conceptualization ("Make yourself think in this positive manner") or trial behavior ("Keep behaving as though you feel attractive") may be necessary, to analyze incremental results and, therefore, forecast overall outcomes. As adult or child reactivated learning occurs, this bouncing back and forth cannot always occur in the natural lengthy format which should have occurred during childhood, and the counselor should understand the client's developmental stages, to determine how many actual learning exercises are needed for a new, revised, or reactivated concept or construct to develop as a solid personality cornerstone. These new concepts should also be compared to other concepts within the client's gestalt, to show balances and disproportions which cause stability or disequilibrium in the system. As the client begins to notice this disequilibrium, the counselor may sense "pathological" defense, and increase efforts to drive home certain life perspectives which then result in more defense, even though a temporary and moral imbalance previously related to the input and its new dimensions. The client may also respond with excessive positivism as he or she experiences an overdose which alters some parts of their conceptual world permanently, or will fade out of the cognitive bloodstream, to give a spurious readout on outcome and input. The client should also examine the negatives related to the espousal of new concepts of life. One form of input which may be helpful, is a devil's advocate approach, so the client is pushed to consider pros and cons.

Sometimes, inputs to change the client's learning model, involve reconceptualization of negative situations (depression, death, loss, loneliness, anxiety, failure) to discover their beneficial qualities and gains. In some cases, the reader may feel that this input involves a distortion of reality to help the client tolerate pain of a negative condition, until time reduces this memory energy, or new and different positive events (gains) are substituted. If this is true, the counselor's input involves tenacity in maintaining a false perception as a stabilizing factor, with concomitant input efforts aimed at future planning, given the nature of "presumed" gains in the present negative condition. This input involves helping the client define the strength obtained (e.g., emotion in human suffering), and postulate subsets of this condition which are similar or identical to future desired behavioral categories ("You are already a success in some life areas, because of the richness of suffering you have previously or are currently experiencing"). The client may also derive action conditions emanating from the negative condition, and subsume behaviors necessary (as process, and not an existential condition of status as noted before) to achieve desired status in the future ("Undergoing this loss means you have the tenacity to go out and seek another friend, job, or achievement, because you have overcome resistance"). The counselor assesses input as a proactive and regressive multitiered developmental process which holds the client in place (prevents regression), and focuses on a future status or behavioral activity. This process focuses back from the reinforced process (which cannot be rewarded without having the negative antecedent condition neutralized, or as a reflective mirror to watch the self) to the negative foundation, which provided a change arena; and then refocuses the original negative phenomenon, so current success becomes the new central focus and foundation, so the client does not return to the suffering mode to achieve success.

If there is benefit from negative or painful life experience, the input is different, in that the counselor helps the client develop a deeper, more intense focus, and positive categories of valuation for defined negative experiences. The input, however, will not necessarily focus on specific future behaviors, since this may mitigate the true richness of the present or past experience. As new cognitive associations are attached, and efforts to escape the negative phenomenologic condition are decreased; behaviors aimed at movement onward may not be a positive index, whereas nonprogressive behavior and sedentary reflective experience (although less empirically verifiable), may be evaluatively more desirable.

In redefining crisis, the therapist may use input which does not change or block any crisis dynamics themselves, but attempts to cause redefinition of the self, which represents fewer degrees of identity depth or potency in negative self-concepts of victim: helpless, trapped, out of control, rejected, angry, inadequate, or tolerant. One way this works is through the counselor's simultaneous experiencing or sharing in the force of the crisis event with the client, while modeling more desirable behavior connected with a new identity or self-definition, and teaching the client behaviors, thoughts, or words which are manifestations of the identity state. As the counselor begins this vicarious experiential process, evaluative questions consider the client's engagement as a learner in this process, which psychodynamically means developing concern about whether the client views the counselor as a significantly powerful influence, to relinquish childhood fantasized benefits (e.g., helplessness leads to parental rescue, and gives the child power and opportunity to reject his/her neglectors), in order to learn new behaviors. Secondly, the client should see that a reconstructive process is going on, wherein a new identity perspective is being created.

The author, in earlier years of clinical practice, remembers crisis counseling sessions where he assumed clients were relinquishing secret rewards. He did not pursue this evaluative concern directly, at the time modeling inputs were delivered; only to find out that clients responded identically to other subsequent crises and, in fact, needed to experience crisis to complete their alternate picture of adaptive, but regressed and symbolic lives. Sometimes counselors spend so much energy on input delivery to calm the client, or superimpose temporary rational cognitive or behavioral structures, that they assume (because their work has been exhausting) that something positive is happening for the client's benefit. The counselor must continually assess whether a progressive building process is, in fact, underway, and specifically examine if clients are temporarily or permanently removing decayed or outdated foundations, replacing them with new structures as a substitute, rather than maintaining interlocked or parallel structures for crisis and noncrisis identities.

In other cases, counselors work to extract a highly-volatile emotion, perception, or identity component from a constellation of these emotions or experiences, wherein the volatile factor causes, or is a significant contributor to, the emergent or crisis-like valuation of the circumstance. An example, would be to extract the personal degradation ("Parent doesn't love me, and I might be abandoned and remain unloved forever") factor from a consideration of someone else's behavior ("Pulling too close to me in a traffic situation"). In this case, the intent is to see the current situation in a different light, and understand dynamics of previous relationships (or qualitative absences thereof), as they are paired with, and strongly influence, current processes of living.

The evaluation of this factoring-out process, involves coordinated input subparts. The counselor must ensure tenacious blocking and non-reinforcement of the paired consideration ("We will not discuss traffic and your identity concurrently"), with evaluation of extinguishing behavioral and cognitive responses, by the client. There must also be fairly-rapid movement along a logical path of analysis, so positive meaning can be derived from separate consideration of both scenarios (traffic, ego), while linking one idea to another (decreased variability and increased connectivity within scenarios); so an overall holistic spectrum is built to withstand attempted invasion of ideas from the alternative thought pattern. This movement includes evaluation of the strength and continuity of the new stream of thoughts, and the solidarity of their connective feeling tissue.

Another input subpart is stimulation, to place each specific scenario within a broader spectrum of balanced life experiences, incorporating a measurable decrease in weighted or seeded value, as specific experiences are entered into the holistic spectrum for consideration. Here, the crisis counselor may be interested in expanding the data field initially, and defocusing attention from one aspect of data, intending to refocus later when a more accurate and less emotionally charged version is possible.

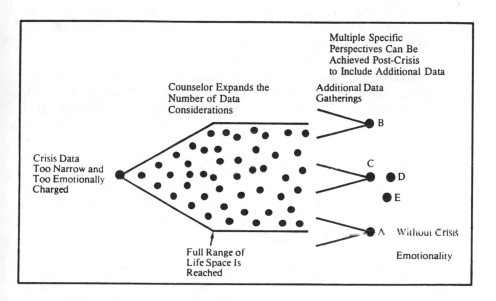

The final subpart uses forceful suggestion and recollected correlated data, to illustrate to clients the infiltration of past relationship conflicts within present domains, placing negative value judgments on the inappropriateness and negative consequences of this in adult life, and consequently evaluating the acceptance of:

the "truth" of this negative information about past life experiences, the motivation to attempt separation of past from present, and the ability to envision positive benefits (including self-reinforcements) from this process.

In the long run, this evaluation includes the client's reconciliation with the past, wherein the counselor measures the client's reconciliatory input. This reconciliation suggests that a balance of acceptance and rejection of the past can simultaneously exist, and creates awareness of strength or other positive experience, as a result of having survived a negative experience. Additionally, it supports acceptance of the client's own humanity and ability to accept parents' mistakes (real or imagined by the client), as a necessary and unavoidable component of living. Finally, this reconciliatory input fosters identification of future goals and objectives to compensate productively for past losses, substitute as penance for past unforgivable errors, or pass on a new legacy to children envisioned as part of a re-parenting vicarious experience. This planning process can also be carried out as a more autonomous input, to deflect energy from conflicted areas of living, and sublimate it into productive activity. In this case, the counselor should evaluatively assess changes in energy focus/direction, and amount and cost effectiveness/efficiency, as planned goals result in outcomes which the client should be assisted in evaluating, relative to other outcomes resulting from different energy investments.

In considering changes or redefinitions of client growth and learning models, the counselor often deals with the issue of socially deviant behavior, especially with involuntary clients. An important first step in evaluating inputs relative to deviance, makes a determination about the client's status relative to normative or deviant criteria, and places the client within one of several categories. In one, the client is inadvertently deviant with external behavior as a secondary manifestation of ego defensiveness. The client recognizes the deviant behavior and wants to change it. In another, the client is inadvertently deviant with external behavior, with secondary intentions for goal accomplishment and recognizes the deviant behavior, and does not want to change. These and other possible categories appear in Figure 11.

Until the client is categorized or placed in a contingent status relative to deviance, the counselor cannot choose a treatment goal or decide on proper input. This is because the deviant behavior itself, constitutes either a stimulant or respondent focal point around which some usually-significant component of the client's life revolves; which is used as an idiosyncratically and culturally-determined index of personal and social inadequacy and, therefore, as a guide to future decision and action.

Figure 11
Client Deviation Status

1. Association with Deviance	
a. Direct	b. Inadvertant

2. Type of Deviant Activity	
a. External	b. Internal

3. Centrality of Functional Manifestation (Goal Accomplishment)	
a. Primary	b. Secondary

4. Client Recognition	
a. Aware	b. Unaware

5. Client Motivation to Change	
a. Motivated	b. Unmotivated

6. Client Need for Conformity		
a. Necessary	b. Optional/Situational	c. Unnecessary

Other input examples, differentiated by client category, are as follows:

Category 1a: With clients who are highly involved, integrated, embedded, and/or solidly entrenched in a collectivity of deviant behaviors, (criminals, psychotics, severe character disorders, delinquents, some forms of creative artists) and who interface with deviance in a fairly regular pattern and with potency of deviant action; the counselor must select relatively-forceful inputs to block entrenched patterns of behavior, to strongly control reinforcements, and provide clear and positive incentives. The counselor may need to be strongly judgmental to provide interdiction of patterns, or may be substantially non-directive (avoiding particular theoretical orientations), to avoid driving the client more deeply into a defensive posture, and to provide a highly visible and potent antithetical stimulus to get the client's attention. The therapist may also connect client inputs with destructive deviant outcomes for their victims, using guilt as a wedge. Also, dealing with maintenance systems in the community, and assuming a more decentralized treatment thrust, may be essential if clients strongly conform to peer groups or community norms.

Category 1b: If clients are tangentially associated with deviant groups or activities (acute psychotic episodes, pre-delinquent kids, some professional social activists concentrating on specific issues, angry acting out, or explosive episodes), the counselor may select inputs to help them understand their level and degree of deviant involvement (which may not be as functional for clients in category 1a). They also assist clients with operational definitions of deviant vs. nondeviant external actions, differentiating points at which they move from one category to another, and to help them clearly define social consequential behaviors which result. In some cases, the client may have a less serious and possibly easily-reconcilable inner conflict which manifests itself tenuously as external deviance, wherein simple educational efforts will reduce the external behavior, and then more detailed inner analysis techniques become useful for the inner conflict.

Category 2b: In cases where clients "feel" they are deviant, bad, or pathological, inside, but may or may not demonstrate external deviant behavior, inputs may accentuate external behavior (which may not help with previous external categories, who need more inner strength and awareness) and create awareness of its positive nature, and the differences between inside and outside. Input may also be used to help clients understand the unique symbolism of inner deviance and outer conformity, as separate or interconnected phenomena. Cients might also be encouraged to experiment with more external deviance to produce a shock effect, to emphasize the destructive nature of their inner world, or help them externalize conflict as a less destructive outlet than the inner battles they wage against themselves. Evaluative questions, therefore, are dependent on the nature of these inner relative-to-outer domains, wherein one domain may be a primary area of client goal accomplishment (internally to punish the self, in hopes of improving to please parents). Externally, however, the goal may be irrelevant and possibly inconsequential to the psychodynamic problem. This is different from clients whose primary thrust may be to manipulate for external recognition, while feeling less conflict internally. The important point for clinicians is that the interface between inner symbolic goals and objectives, is differentiated when external behaviors come into the picture, and both inner and outer worlds can be reciprocal independent and dependent variables which influence each other's nature. Therapeutic foci are predicated on these categories, as they are interpreted by both client and society.

In some cases, the counselor provides input which helps the client separate inner from outer worlds, so the client learns a mixture of behaviors: to be externally conforming and internally deviant, relative to society symbolically; to be internally conforming and internally deviant to society symbolically; and, to be internally conforming to expectations of self having some degree of autonomy, rebelliousness, or obstructionism, which may not be defined as deviant unless manifestations become external and publicly noticeable. Based on categories of association, functionality, recognition, and motivation (and others not listed), the evaluative questions change as each outcome (predicated on input) simultaneously registers on several scales, having different combined meanings to clients, depending on which scales and scale values are activated.

Provide Psychosocial Support

The provision of supportive therapy is frequently-mentioned among most theoretical frameworks, yet may be one of the most difficult to properly execute and evaluate. There are numerous subdimensions of this important process, relative to the question of evaluation.

1. **Acceptance and Non-blaming.** Because many clients are traumatized early in childhood with actual or perceived harsh, limited, irrational, inconsistent, or excessive judgment and control by parents, creating negative self-image limitations on risk-taking, or constrained lifestyles; one obvious problem with evaluative input, is that it represents a clear and often substantial contradiction to previous client-patterned learning (original learning in family of origin, as well as learning from symptoms and defenses used throughout life to make neurotic or psychotic compromises, control anxiety, etc.). As a contradictory response, input may be delivered in dosages which are unrealistic, overwhelming, or incomprehensible to clients who have not experienced it from self or others previously, and who may be ignorant of its safety and functionality. Some clients have modeled or learned external, socially-approved forms of accepting support, but are incapable of such substantive change. In fact, they alter many units or dosage amounts of supportive inputs, to represent other more familiar phenomena which are often negative (e.g., control, paternalism, mockery, weakness on the part of the therapist). Counselors may need to offer a more realistic dual input of both support and nonsupport (or some other input expected by, and more familiar to the client), and gradually increase the ratio of each, so the client more calmly and incrementally learns.

   Sound evaluation demands that the counselor seek feedback from the client to assess exactly how they perceive acceptance which is delivered, and what decisions they make about it; how they assess the differences between acceptance and other types of stimuli or responses; and if they differentiate the acceptance/nonacceptance continuum, based on who delivers the input. In some cases, as clients perceive acceptance, they feel insecure about placing excessive demands on their frail autonomous systems, and the counselor needs to differentiate insecurity based on a semi-positive (but not fully a positively-perceived) environment, from insecurity based on a previously negative (but now perceived as positive, or at least familiar and safer than the unknown) environment.

If clients indeed, experience acceptance, there are some idiographic conversion tables which the counselor must discover, to understand how much acceptance is necessary to be perceived and incorporated by the client, in order for them to feel there is opportunity to have a positive self-image. Also, there will usually come a time where acceptance will set the stage for, but not necessarily provide, a sufficient force to dislodge seriously-regressed defensive fortifications, or motivate the client to take action. As each client accumulates various amounts of acceptance units, the therapist should evaluatively ask "What happens now," and determine if acceptance allows a natural unfolding process of personality development; or if power, control, and judgment (which produced the trauma in the beginning) are necessary to facilitate a definitive and directional personality thrust (albeit negative), as opposed to a neutral outcome. The counselor must be aware, also, of when to withdraw acceptance which infantalizes clients, at points when they accept their "selves," even though some clients question which judgment of them (the new positive one, or old negative one) is the illusion or delusion.

2.   **Validation of "Feelings."** Another aspect of support is validation of client feeling, although evaluatively there are important differentiations between feeling content, and the right or option to "feel" anything at all. Some counselors become confused assessing different feeling contents, or feel stuck with clients who express a narrow range or rigid pattern of feelings when, in fact, evaluation might more appropriately be centered on the client's changing perception of self-as-feeler. The validation process of feeling, per se, may be more basic than the nature of feeling, so counselors should insure that its baseline nature is not distorted, by the particular positive or negative character of any specific type of content. In this case, average amounts of feeling (to correct for very little feeling with negative content, or a lot of feeling with more comfortable positive content) must be balanced against the most and least frequent amount of feeling, along with

perception of feeling and feeling opportunity, not necessarily measured relative to its verbal or overt expression.

The counselor may dig deeply to discover hidden desires to experience masked or symbolized feelings, and actual non-expressed feeling, to establish a baseline. He or she might also use degree and type of acted-out feeling as one index of feeling capability, in addition to attention to more socially-accepted and public traditional feeling expressions. Clients can conceivably develop a relationship with therapists in which they explore qualitative and quantitative changes in perceptions of the right to feel, yet do not get to the point, for an extended time period, where they can be displayed publicly. Very often, the counselor provides input which defines aspects of the personality as feeling components, which had not been so defined previously, or are only approximations to a full and healthy feeling phenomenon. The counselor must provide this input carefully because of the subjective interpretation of feeling, feeling opportunity, or feeling authorization, and because the client's social situation may not yield opportunities compatible with perceptions. In fact, opening up opportunity may be traumatic, as feelings move into newly-developed psychic roles, but may overwhelm a system which could incrementally handle only a small dose initially.

Measurement of client changes in perceptions of the valid "right to feel," may be a slow process which parallels growth in perceptions of other rights (think, explore, retreat, fail, perceive, distort, misinterpret, etc.). The counselor's input may have to be mobile enough to recognize this pattern and range, and leave the ability to connect feeling to other human experiences, in ways that, although content may be incongruent, allow the client to see that the process and nature may be similar or identical. This includes input which defocuses specific rights or feelings ("I'm not concerned yet with what you are feeling, but with the fact that you do feel something, anything at all"). This is important so clients do not assume measurement is predicated on their ability to display particular natures of feeling. A positive index of change, therefore, might be the ability to develop a wider range of brief feelings, and move from one to another; or to develop a strong state of readiness to feel, without necessarily being compelled to put any particular feeling into the open.

Clients may accept their right to conversely not feel, if control and autonomy are the issues, so the correct measurement of input may have nothing to do initially with feelings, but with a more generic definition of the non-feeling-being-with-a-right-to-choose. The anxious counselor needs patience as the client gets better at not feeling, as a function of learning that he or she can feel or not feel eventually.

There is another problem altogether with clients who allow their cognition-emotional computer to be programmed for feelings, but who struggle with the adequacy or acceptability, correctness, or recognition of a specific type or amount of feeling (anger, fear, love, etc.). A counselor attempting to "validate" or "accept" any specific feeling is on precarious therapeutic and evaluative ground, because this may set up a contradictory reinforcement contingency between the counselor and parental symbolic substitutes. Further, it may precondition what he or she thinks a client might feel, based on a subjective and idiosyncratic theoretical model which may not relate to the client's agenda or philosophical life interpretation ("Are you feeling angry?" or "You look angry or afraid"). It may also give permission for a feeling to be recognized and accepted which is not the correct feeling, or is a dangerous feeling for the client, given particular survival contingencies ("How can I be mad at God and still be a good and appreciative Christian?").

Also, the focus on validating a particular feeling, may suggest that measurement of adequacy or inadequacy revolves around degree of clarity or strength, or prominence of this feeling (especially if not recognized or expressed previously). Herein, evaluation runs into a temporary dead-end because the feeling, in and of itself, may not necessarily be an action or behavioral phenomenon. Validation of any feeling may obscure the client's view of antecedent rational or irrational formulas (cognitive or relationship formulas), which produced the feeling. Also, other feelings which may be more basic to the personality (fear expressed as anger), or which logically follow the feeling (anger at another, followed by need for them, followed by reacting to compliment or confirming the adequacy of a significant other), may be predicated on the initial expression of the feeling itself.

As an input, validation of feeling requires evaluative measurement of how the client accepts the validated posture assessment of philosophical congruence of any and all specific feelings between counselor and client; and assessment of the client's movement, decisions, or actions, which revolve around, and are reactions to, stabilizations of a feeling impression. The counselor must also learn how this impression longitudinally interacts with behaviors it has stimulated, through its own existence and nature.

3. **Expression of Positive Feelings Toward the Client.** Expressing positive feelings is a complicated evaluative problem for some therapists (each theory of intervention places differential emphasis on this input), especially with clients whose behaviors, feelings, attitudes, or lifestyles are filled with socially negative characteristics, and who become unlikable in many respects. The counselor is in a dilemma since he or she may theoretically desire to honestly evaluate the client's behavior ("I like you, but don't like your behavior"), while showing positive concern for the pain, anxiety, or tragedy a client experiences in arriving at, or maintaining a current lifestyle; or offer positive reinforcement for the new person (in some respects) the client can become.

When counselors provide honest (hopefully correct/helpful) inputs, which elucidate that (a) they do not like a particular behavior/attitude/feeling, or which suggest that (b) a particular B/A/F may not be acceptable to other people, or is considered bad according to some perspectives; they may notice that some clients, in fact, find the feedback helpful, but may not mention it directly. Success, however, might be measured through their public or privately reported efforts to change, or may be seen in their inadvertent increased efforts to defend themselves (even including attracting the therapist), which symbolizes sensitivity (feeling) to closeness in the therapeutic alliance, a deepened awareness of their need to change (which they may have a denied), and a supportive sense of honest connectedness to someone who cares enough to be honest.

Clients may even exaggerate symptoms to show they have heard the message, and to signify that the counselor is significant to them, or even to elicit more support (also seen by them as provision of structure, control, or security). The counselor noticing any of these variations in symptoms, certainly should note their intensity and duration, but conservatively interpret their meaning, until such time as they see if a new pattern has developed; to learn whether an increase will be followed by a decrease, or whether a client actually reports how he or she feels about the supportive components of counseling.

Other times, the pattern which emerges will be identical to previous patterns, or not have a sufficiently clear or meaningful identity, to clue the counselor with any evaluative feedback about the supportive nature of what was done or not done. This suggests, therefore, that additional input is necessary to follow the delivery of honest feedback. This added input may be supportive in showing the client there is hope for change; illustrating specific ways to change; showing the client that the counselor understands he or she is not behaving negatively, totally by rational choice (this becomes a problem, however, with behavioral, gestalt, or reality-type therapies, in which excuses are not seen as supportive or helpful in some circumstances); suggesting that support is available to a new personality who can change the negative behaviors; or affirming that a human being is worthy, regardless of any behavior, attitude, or feeling.

In these cases, evaluation has at least two levels, wherein the counselor determines "how" the client heard the initial honest feedback, and also how the client perceives the secondary installment relative to the first. In some cases, clients will not hear the first honest feedback, and a secondary support unit may not be sufficient, because so much defensiveness has collapsed. Several supportive input units may have to follow, with careful attention to the possibility that the initial behavior was manipulative to get the support (the counselor is the mouse pressing the mechanical bar, with the client dispensing the reinforcing food pellet). Once support begins, its repeated occurrence and cumulative intensity may cause the client to forget or negate the original honest, but hurtful/fearful feedback.

There are other circumstances in which the counselor may not wish to attend to the negative client characteristics, and will make direct statements to the client relative to strength, survivability, courageous suffering, or fear. Some clients will reject this support because they feel it contradicts a self-image, or they feel manipulated. The counselor, therefore, needs to develop a keen awareness and precision taxonomy to quickly define rejecting behavior (twitch of an eye, hand movement, specific words, etc.). The counselor also needs to decide what to do if the client is rejecting— whether to deliver a stronger support message, to withdraw support, provide analysis, confront, and so on. Many counselors routinely determine simplistically, that clients are not "hearing" the support; but they may take this data finding one step further to make a decision of specifically what should be done next, or how long negative feedback should be allowed, before it becomes an index requiring the counselor rather than the client, to change. Some philosophies weigh inputs by the pound, and assume the more weight one accumulates, the greater the eventual effect. Others suggest that this is inverse, in that the more weight (of specific input units) accumulated, the more weight is required in another input sector, to balance the scale and undo the bottleneck. Clients' self-perceptions are extremely helpful here, to monitor their decisions as more or less input is provided.

In conjunction with investment of positive statements about clients, the counselor should determine not only if the client can say, "I feel your support to the Nth degree," but truly understands the function of support. The counselor should ask the question, "What does the support you feel now enable you to do, which was not possible before the support arrived?" In some cases, clients feel that empathy provides considerable positive outcome benefit yet, once it is withdrawn, they learn they have not converted this emotional benefit into any new or different energy form, which allows them to provide other stimuli to their system, or free other feelings which, in turn, facilitate growth. The emotional closeness frequently feels good to both therapist and client, yet does not necessarily cause scaled change in additional outcome indices. If it does, the counselor may not recognize it. If it is sufficient in and of itself without connection to other variables, then the counselor may not have a clear rationale for providing other inputs, which may not be necessarily helpful to the client.

Sometimes the counselor may view support as positive reinforcement for specific client behaviors (usually new and experimental ones), which can be a therapeutic quagmire because this type of support is usually definitive, directional, partisan, subjective in its idiosyncratic (but sometimes incorrectly assumed generic) nature, is delivered before outcomes can be empirically tested, and is based on theory of "common human nature" or the counselor's experience. Therefore, it may not have the systemic or individual outcome anticipated, and causes clients to lose faith in the counselor or in themselves. This is especially true if they are not really making an independent choice, but a clearly unidirectional response to counselor control (which will probably not register anything positive in the client's cognitive and emotional computer, anyway).

Some counselors decide that support of this type has to be extremely conservative, tentative, and delayed, so the client has an opportunity to develop autonomy in behavioral choice selection. The client may need time to experiment with actual varied outcomes, make a decision about them, and then receive support; not for the behavioral choice, but for having (a) behaved somehow, (b) made a decision about it, and (c) accepted the consequences (positives and negatives).

Counselors may measure nonpartisan or nonbiased nonsupport initially, and view themselves as directly more successful the longer they delay any supportive input. This allows commensurately increasing amounts of experimentation (including painful struggle and ambivalence on the client's part), to provide the greatest possibility that the client makes a support-worthy and field-tested decision, or handles affairs without any support at all. Some clients in these situations, however, will not take action without committed investment of support capital, and feel abandoned and alienated without strong doses in the beginning. The counselor might decide in these cases, to provide the support, but include a gradual withdrawal clause, determined by a combination of interlocking events:

a.   passage of time
b.   increases in support-residue
c.   increases in client dependency
d.   increases in client independence
e.   difficulty of the environmental situation
f.   support from other sources
g.   client decision-making about support received incrementally
h.   client cooperation is self-supportive partnership with the therapist

4.   **Therapist Self-disclosure.** In some instances, counselors feel that self-disclosure (to a limited degree and with specific goals) improves emotional bonding with clients, and enhances empathetic sharing and provision of support. There may be an assumption that modeling, identification, or mutuality occur between client and therapist, which require clarification from the counselor, particularly in terms of the degree of congruence they perceive between life circumstances, their abilities, or the possibility of personality image sharing or incorporation.

If the therapist details an event similar to that experienced by the client, without discussing associated resolution or irresolution, the client may be left with an incomplete puzzle to piece together. They may find difficulty understanding the principle or process of resolution itself ("How did the counselor do it, since I can't or haven't yet?"), ("I wonder why they haven't resolved this problem yet, and is it a function of the problem or the therapist?"). The client might also experience parallel confusion in comparing personal units of reality to those of the counselor, and may not understand the current interactional pattern ("Why are they telling me this?") as it unfolds to detail the shared event. This model is depicted in Figure 12.

Figure 12
Differential Problem Resolution Formulas

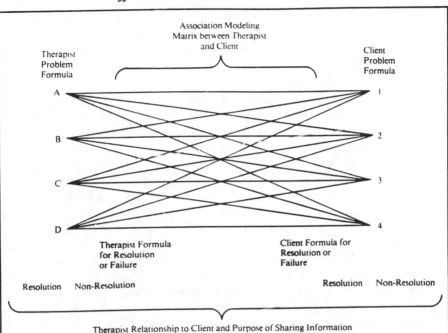

Clients have to make decisions about each area of the domain, as well as consider the overall therapeutic relationship. They will need to be evaluated not only on whether they have learned anything from the example or shared event itself, but also if the act of sharing (with various degrees of relevancy of content) provided supportive input leading to an eventual outcome or other decision. Many clients may not understand the example at all. This situation requires evaluative consideration of whether another example would have been helpful, whether the timing was right, or if there was any supportive outcome, regardless of the specific example content. In other cases, however, clients benefit from analogies which are self-reflective to some extent, but do not have added baggage of therapist idiosyncracy, relative to problem focus or resolution/irresolution formula. Analogies may also help clients understand their reality, by explaining it in nontypical and more ascertainable terms, which may be taken from their particular cultural domain (e.g., analogy of electrical circuits to help an engineer understand family systems).

The client's identification of the counselor simply as a human being, or an accessible resource through their common experiences with problems, may not be supportive, given other visible sources of power and control and ultra-human discretion, held by the professional helper. Further, clients may need to see differences between themselves and this helper, in order to be dislodged from their defensive and habitual patterns, to learn, change, and grow.

5.   **Use of Humor in a Supportive Fashion.** Many counselors consider humor or joint humorous sharing as a significant addendum to input intervention. In some cases, the humor (as well as other non-humorous diversion techniques, such as discussing the weather or a new movie, at either beginning or end of the counseling session) is used simply as a relief or pattern interruption to help clients rest, regenerate energy, or recompose themselves, when emotionally-draining topics occur. In this regard, the counselor has a difficult evaluative task deciding the degree of anxiety which is tolerable to the client, and whether it is beneficial to allow or expect the client to "live through" fearful experience and conquer irrational beliefs, in an effort to rearrange conceptualizations. Also, the time allowed for this type of support is important, since the client's "critical mass" for therapeutic change may be reduced during diversions, may not be reconstituted during a particular session, and may not reach optimum change potential for many sessions to come.

How clients use diversion is also a significant evaluative question, since their perception of diversion is also a self-image perception, relating to issues of self-control, identity definition ("Am I a person who can ever escape, have refuge or relaxation?"), ego integration, and life philosophy. Relating current diversionary experiences (either counselor- or client-induced) to other opportunities or past/future potential occurrences of diversions, can also be evaluatively useful to understand dynamics by which these opportunities occur. This may help clients understand their past or present decisions about them ("Why don't you reduce the intensity of arguments with your daughter?"), and encourage learning of cognitive and behavioral techniques to create their own diversions, as a self-induced anxiety-reduction mechanism.

Humor as a diversionary tactic can be measured relative to relaxation and tension reduction, and scaled relating to changes in muscle tension, facial tightness, nature of expression, cardiovascular and pulmonary changes in intensity, pace or duration of stressed responses, or speech and gross body movement. Also, clients can be monitored on the functionality of efforts they personally arrange, to create diversion for themselves.

In cases where diversion or humorous inputs are used defensively, inappropriately, or exaggeratedly, frequencies of these events can be monitored, along with the client's perception and degree of understanding of precipitating events (cognitive predispositions to make this defense highly probable); and processes/dynamics by which the use of this technique was considered necessary to produce fantasized or destructive functional outcomes. Assessment includes clients' capability to change components of their decision-making formula, and behavioral manifestations of cognitive-emotional decisions which perpetuate the compromising pattern.

A second area involving humor is not specifically diversionary (although may have an intended secondary effect, or unintended primary effect), but directly uses humor for primary therapeutic impact. In these cases, humor demonstrates contradictions in reality; illustrating selective, unilateral, excessively broad or excessively narrow perspectives; pointing out deviant idiosyncratic behavior, often through exaggeration; suggesting the commonality of experiences of human conflict and suffering; and showing the rigidity of cognitive process or social custom.

As this technique unfolds, important evaluative concerns can often be ignored or inadvertently neglected by the counselor, who is not certain why or how humor might be specifically used as an input, or does not take the time to use the experience for more potent therapeutic gain. Evaluation insists that clients (at some point) specifically discuss a humorous episode which has recently occurred in counseling. This helps the counselor assess the meaning attributed to it by the client, and explore its symbolic meanings, so understanding and awareness can be increased as a direct result of the experience. Clients might be encouraged to define the role of humor in their lives, and compare their idiographic utilization (or non-utilization) to other traditional uses of humor, to understand how they conform or deviate, and why The question here is, "How do you compare with others in the ways you use humor, laughter, fun, etc., in your life, and what do you think about it?" The counselor explores specifically what happens in both process and content during a humorous experience, and how clients learn as a result of the experience. Subsequent evaluation can monitor frequency of recurrence of client-initiated humorous incidents, and evaluate assessment of learning and learning-induced behavioral change which ensues.

Counselors can do comparative analysis of psychosocial-behavioral dynamics uncovered within the confines of a humorous episode, and help clients draw parallels or contradictory analogies to other arenas of their functioning. Therapists can also determine reasons why this learning was not available previously in the processes of other behavioral patterns (ones not related to humor), helping clients decide why they might be able to envision self-awareness in other areas, and not see their meaningful parallels in the humorous process.

Counselors can take a more global and abstract approach to evaluate how clients feel after an experience involving humor, and examine longitudinally differences, similarities, increases, or decreases in these post-humorous states of being as time passes, and as more or less humor is introduced. They can also help clients compare past humor states with their predispositions, prior to the onset of humorous experience. This helps them determine if a set of circumstances accumulates to the point of causing or necessitating a humorous response, or if clients either manipulatively bring about humorous acts or responses when they see certain indicators in their patterns of thinking or feeling, or could bring about alternative non-humorous responses which might be even more helpful to them.

6. **Contradiction of Harmful Effects.** One frequently-employed supportive strategy, is for the counselor to directly or indirectly redefine pain or harmful effects clients feel and believe are associated with their various life statuses and decisions. Frequently, this takes the form of initially accepting or affirming client perceptions of pain or harmful consequences (which many strategies suggest is a supportive mechanism that stands alone), but is followed by efforts to help clients redefine type or degree of physical/ psychic danger they perceive for themselves. This reduces the pressure of crisis perceptions, and teaches clients ways to control emotional outcomes in their lives. This technique is typically accompanied by efforts to help the client change antecedent thoughts or behaviors, which directly or indirectly cause negative and painfully perceived results. Sometimes this does not directly address the potency or rationality of the pain itself, but does allow clients to maintain their pre-existing conceptual structure of rewards and punishments, with modification of only the stimuli.

The counselor must always be wary of seriously-disturbed clients who have nothing but painful outcome categories from which to "choose" (or in which they are perpetually trapped), or clients who adapt to life by enjoying or needing painful experiences for self-punishment, reconciliation, or identity confirmation. In these cases, changes in the antecedent precursors will not result in substantive differential outcomes, since the client fulfills his or her own symbolic destiny, and perceives what must be perceived to avoid regressive ego deterioration. Supportive redefinition probably will not work; or more pointed, developmentally-directed, and forceful inputs may be necessary, to change a strong-entrenched past reality.

In the supportive component of contradicting harmful effects, the input strategy includes modeling a response pattern which is, to varying degrees, not responsive to painful cries, or ignorant of painful definitions of outcomes or agendas. These set up contradictory cognitive conflicts that ideally communicate to the client that there are alternate perceptions of reality, and maintenance of past perceptions may place him or her into some form of deviance, relative to the counselor's (the social world's) normative expectations. This may be construed as a differential, but modified and controlled use of pain, so it does not necessarily reflect a contradiction of reality. In other words, the counselor may directly comment to the client that, although the client feels or perceives great pain or danger at the present time, this is a function of special alignment of perceptions; and with realignment or returns to post-crisis perceptions, the client will probably no longer experience the pain (the counselor may encourage the client to role-play recollected past experiences, where lesser pain was evident). The counselor may sympathize with the pain, affirm it, and then ask the client to conduct specific meditational, relaxation, gestalt imagery, or other forms of activity to "place" him/herself in a less painful or actual pleasurable circumstance. The therapist may also distract clients periodically from direct awareness of painful phenomena, or simply be more directive with clients, telling them that they are not really in as much pain as they believe, and that they are stronger and more capable than they are allowing themselves to see or believe.

Evaluatively, this supportive technique is assessed in several ways. The counselor can help the client determine the degree of faith they have in the contradictory perspective; and parlay this into commensurate degrees of awareness about the self, the incorporative characteristics obtained, or shared positive energy transformed into unilateral energy and ability (for the client only) to perceive "positives" (less painful or less harmful) in their life circumstances. The counselor can define baselines of positive viewpoints, noting increases in non-painful perspectives or definitions of situations which do not have integrally-attached harmful effects, as these changes are correlated with supportive inputs directed at the painful perceptions, which do exist. Analysis of the client's thinking about the differences between pain-indexed effects and pleasure-indexed effects, can be evaluated, particularly to identify differences in cognitive or behavioral formulae which are selectively used. This analysis identifies numbers of irrational assumptions, or non-empirically supported assumptions which are made. The counselor can also assess changes in the frequency of these occurrences, as concomitant supportive inputs increase in duration or intensity.

Clients can directly report on their subjective impressions of lessening amounts of pressure, fullness, intensity, or power of harmful perspectives (which they frequently have difficulty conceptualizing simplistically); however, they can be assisted in expressing these feelings, via self-anchoring attitude scales or other representational measures. They can put their perspectives of pain measurement into some form of analogy (e.g., "I feel like I am falling down an elevator shaft with no bottom"), that is changed with effective support to another framework ("I still feel like I am falling, but the rate of speed is slower and I can see the bottom, and I don't think it will kill me when I hit") for further learning.

Oftentimes, evaluation includes notations of the client's ability to change focus away from a negative emotionally-laden arena of living, wherein feelings of pain connected with general feelings states, can be mitigated by concentrating on positive aspects of behavior; and fearful behaviors can be contradicted, by positive mental or nonbehavioral psychic activity. The counselor must, of course, ask the client if he or she agrees with a viewpoint that an event is not as painful or lethal as it seems, and evaluative data can be useful as clients work on why they do or do not agree with the supportive input of the clinician, and discuss how agreement could conceivably be reached.

Anchoring indices in other functional areas of the client's world are useful, since each time the counselor determines if less pain is perceived, the client will also linearly respond to expectations, patterns, and structures within a pain- or suffering-oriented scenario, and may be inclined to provide contaminated data. Laterally connecting pain perceptions to outside factors helps correct this bias, and provides a supportive input in and of itself (see Figure 13).

Figure 13
Anchoring Indices in Counseling

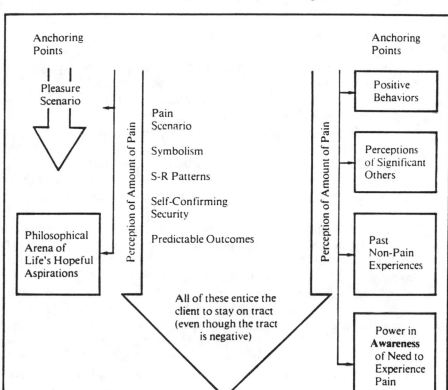

7.   **Summarizing as Both Support and Input Planning.** In many cases, counselors provide supportive input in the form of summaries or overviews to clients within, and at the conclusion of, their counseling sessions. Sometimes, this reflective feedback may be considered a more active and aggressive strategic and tactical input which creates new learning, and sometimes it generates stimulation for change and actually moves clients from one status category to another, as units of reality which are summarized are put together in new ways.

One example is Rogers' client-centered therapy, in which repeating or reflecting clients' expressed ideas, provides empathic support, but also blocks typical escape routes (rationalization, denial, intellectualization, projection, etc.); and plunges the decision-making process back within the client's own inner circle of perception. This forces the client to struggle with the formula by which he or she arrives at less desirable (or lesser degrees of right/acceptable) answers.

In thinking about the support summary process, the therapist may prematurely assume that wrapping up the session (this does not mean smoothing over areas of conflict or emotional turmoil, which have developed during, and will continue after the session) has a beneficial effect for the client, in producing greater understanding or integration of previously exposed content. The counselor may also assume that summarizing serves as a prelude for clients to develop direction and planned goals to continue therapeutic work before the next session, to also provide a preliminary framework to begin work during the next scheduled appointment.

These assumptions must, however, be documented, because summaries may superimpose a conceptual structure which has myriad effects. This structure can provide an opportunity for the client to retreat into more emotionally-safe abstractions, providing an excuse not to continue to struggle until the next session; furthermore, it may provide a perceptual stopping point, and inadvertent suggestion, that the work is temporarily over and will be left in a neatly tied up package at the agency or clinical office, not to be reopened until the next session. It may also suggest a simplistic integration of complex psychosocial content, which provides one level of pseudo-resolution of problems (the summarizing becomes a defense). Hereby, the client experiences a reduction of conflict and anxiety at some level, but makes decisions (based on strength and frequency of summaries, as well as their symbolic meaning to the client) about levels of adaptation which the client will not pursue. The structure may confuse the client, by using concepts and constructs which are not true representations of reality as the client sees it. This, of course, depends on the client's capability, motivation, and the length of time working with the therapist. These constructs may also obscure specific lines of reasoning which the client is successfully pursuing, and needs to continue to think through and struggle with, rather than make final decisions at a remote level of understanding. The summary may be totally incorrect and constitute a figment of the counselor's imagination concerning holistic integration, having limited application to the client's life. Finally, the summarizing may not be supportive. The client may experience an increase in anxiety, since the summary may suggest a more global problem than the client wanted to perceive; may cause them to assume the problem is excessively complex, so as to reduce the probability of its resolution; or causes the problem to appear so abstract, that a direction for change becomes more obscured. Some clients feel clear and optimistic about a therapeutic process which has occurred, only to report confusion about what had just happened.

The counselor must specifically inquire about the benefits of summarizing input, to elicit rewordings of the summary from the client, and compare changing reactions to this component of the sessions, as the client moves from one session to another. Specific questions can be asked about how the client perceives the wrapping-up process. These questions should be specifically aimed at eliciting comments on the client's decisions, assessments, and impressions during this phase which, when regressed or retrospectively overlaid on past sessions, may have a particular growth-oriented meaning, or provide guidelines or new growth dimensions in anticipation of the future.

Another evaluative approach is for counselors to refrain from summaries, and provide open-ended questions (and stimulation) to clients, to help them do their own wrap-up, and subsequently develop categories to describe and explain how the client closes the session. This enables the therapist to compare changes in frequency and style of summarizing, correlated with the previously-mentioned decisions for future action.

Another related area of summary impact, is the process of planning goals and objectives for subsequent sessions, or for more generalized areas of the client's life and struggle for adaptation. In some ways, engaging the client in planning can be considered a more forceful and direct input that makes the planning cognitive process a direct contradiction of previously held reality constructs, and even necessitates the client's exploratory and venturesome adaptation of new self-image statuses ("I am a planning person, as opposed to————"). In such a situation, the counselor should evaluate the existence, frequency, and quality of the plans themselves. They should also help the client regress and progress back and forth from the completed plans, to the a priori state of having no plans. This helps determine differences between plans/no plans, and correlates this with differences in personality planner/non-planner, and associated perceptions of the world. In some cases, clients develop plans, not realizing (or afraid to realize) that they are, in some aspects, a truly different person (who now plans); and that the plans themselves may be much less significant than the changing psychic material from which the plans emerge, as an outer and inner reality orientation.

Carrying-out of plans is another fruitful arena of evaluation, but the counselor must realize that overt action may be frightening to some clients, so cognitive, as well as behavioral approaches or approximations to completed action, should be measured. Also, the completed action itself should be assessed, followed longitudinally by evaluation of sustaining characteristics and plan maintenance behaviors of clients.

Clients sometimes readily adapt the planned behaviors and, although dramatic evaluative results might ensue, the counselor should also measure the behind-the-scenes posture of the client. An inverse relationship may exist between behavior comfort and outcome behavior, and it may be defensive or dependent on the supportive structure, rather than having independent meaning relative to the client's change. Therapists must also assess whether resultant plans come from within the existing reservoir of client constructs. They should consider how suggestions for planning, vs. suggestions of plans, vs. noninvolvement to elucidate planning gaps; motivate clients to reach within themselves for images of the planned outcomes. Evaluation includes how successful counselors are in pinpointing the bridges which connect various structural images (planned phenomena and planner identity), and how successfully they help clients focus on these important therapeutic interconnections.

In cases where planning takes on a more supportive character, the counselor may find that most ingredients for a planner self-image, and for the planned structure, already exist (even in seedling form) within the client, so input suggests discrepancies between planned vs. non-planned status, to stimulate the client's own self-correcting anxiety to "kick into action." The counselor may also pinpoint ways the client blocks his or her own potentially-emergent planning endeavor (through one irrational assumption, the absence of one piece of information necessary for planning, or through existence of excessive data which confuses the planning process). The counselor can then step out of the way to allow the client to make plans.

Sometimes, support comes after the plan has been developed, in which case clients may need "parental approval" of the plan itself, or the planning process. Here, evaluation of input involves not only whether approval is given, but also how clients were or were not aware of need for approval (and concomitant efforts of this need, despite actual approval maybe provided by the therapist), how clients communicated their need, and any decisions about goals or goal-setting processes after approval is received. This includes assessment of degree of client commitment to goals before and after supportive approval, as well as measurement of changes in this commitment, as clients gain awareness of the function of therapeutic approving support. Also, it may include degree of client and counselor participation in the goal-setting process, and awareness of the meaning of the counselor-client relationship, since approving support is contracted as a part of mutuality vs. parent-child dependency/manipulative relationships.

In some cases, the counselor may stop the goal-setting approval-requesting process, to retrace steps the client pursued (summarizing) in arriving at the approval-request stage; and help the client make comparative analyses of their identity in the non-requesting planning mode, the requesting end-of-planning model, and the pre-activity (pre-judgment of outcome) mode, to determine what, if any, differences exist. The counselor's therapeutic input might progressively consist of helping the client envision the outcome scenarios of approval vs. non-approval, if the therapist "hypothetically" acts in either capacity. Input can continue to involve support for the client, providing support for "experimental" plans followed by support of the client's efforts to evaluate the plans, and their operationalized outcomes. This can then be followed by more definitive counselor support, after the client has "walked through" the stages independently. If definitive support is decided upon and given by the counselor earlier, evaluation assesses how the client feels about the support as it occurs; what decision-making or identity-defining meaning it has as it occurs, and after it has fermented in the client's mind; and how specific gains or losses in client growth occur, as a result of the presence or anticipated presence of the supportive input.

On some occasions, if transference is intended by the counselor, disapproval of the plan may be the intended nature of the input, so the client is forced to deal with fears of disapproval, rejection, or individual deviance. The evaluative thrust comes via assessment of types of responses, changes in response with repeated rejections (certainly under progressively incremental, controlled, and supportive circumstances within a protective therapeutic alliance), and client ability to step out of the present rejection action, and abstractly deal with its overall past and future meaning relative to basic identity issues.

Direct Client Education

Most treatment approaches either directly employ or philosophically value, providing direct training or education to clients. This can take the form of teaching cognitive decision process (rational emotive therapy), showing clients how to "experience" the self (gestalt therapy), or teaching specific actions as part of a self-imposed reinforcement program (behavior modification).

The initial evaluative question here, is degree to which the client is in a sufficiently productive/receptive learning mode. This determines that they perceive a need for the new learned content or process, and will not misinterpret it or pathologically symbolically represent the content. Additionally, it shows they are capable of avoiding excessive learning defenses, and know how the material should be used for future thought, feeling, or action. In some cases, initial input may require withholding actual educative action on the part of the counselor, to allow the client to experience consequences of a perceived or therapist-defined learning deficit, coupled with evaluation of the client's degree of anxiety/cognitive dissonance, relative to discrepancies between current and potential states of being. This assumes that learned content will be added to the equation, and is also the correct and valid addition. Some education occurs in teaching the client about gaps in their adaptive repertoire, and how to evaluate the results of various types of learning-deficit outcomes; however, the counselor must always remember that the most important evaluative set of questions, revolves around clients' decisions about what they do or do not know, and how new learning will be used.

Because the client is dependent in the counseling situation, there may be a strong external facade of learning readiness, not supported internally (cognitively/ emotionally) with perceived need, motivation, and intent for action. The counselor must test and retest the waters to assess learning probability, and determine whether the outcome is positive (high learning motivations), so results can be recycled into the client's awareness, and used as part of the psychotherapeutic gestalt to analyze developmental arrests, misconceptions, regressions, defenses, client games, excuses, and fears.

When actual facts or skills (any area of new knowledge) are taught by the counselor, the client must be tested as to immediate reception and preliminary integration of new information, so when the client does not learn initially, the counselor can reintroduce the input, to insure the material has registered in some level of awareness, in the client's perceptual scope. The counselor can also longitudinally assess any slippage or learning loss, with verbal questions or behavioral/cognitive exercises (tests) administered to insure that the client has learned the new content, and to plan for intermittent booster dosages to supplement and reinforce initial input delivery.

Ideally, the client will begin to assimilate and integrate the content, and it may become transformed (possibly obscured) within other cognitive constructs or complex behaviors, so the counselor may not be able to evaluate learning in its originally delivered form. He/she may have to redefine it in its various idiographic and operationalized ramifications, in terms of how it is implemented by each client. Having the client periodically reflect on the original learned content, assists the counselor in determining where and how it has progressed along the way, providing greater clarity regarding its past, present, or future value.

In situations where clients resist learning, the counselor may dialogue with them to study the input style and the form in which content was delivered, as a way to evaluative input delivery. The counselor then makes changes followed by test-retest procedures, which compare input before and after changes have been imposed, to enhance the attractiveness and perceived utility and value of the content.

Inputs as Placebos

On some occasions, the counselor provides input which is intended not to have a direct effect, but keep the client in a relatively stable holding pattern, without causing trauma by relationship termination. This will rule out additional independent or intervening variables as significant factors causing client problems (e.g., neurological, intelligence, or physical disease problems); allow environmental supportive, stimulative, or consequential factors to take effect; or await positive effects of client developmental process or input unfolding (wait for previously input seed to grow).

In these cases, the counselor should determine whether the placebo is part of a planned strategy, rather than an example of ambivalence, incompetence, or ignorance; which is difficult to honestly evaluate, without external observations and assistance of a supervisor or peer evaluator. In the case of a married couple the author worked with, direct intervention to stop negative relationship process had been successful, but the couple needed time to learn to be close again, and to decide if they could have each other in the absence of a previous parent-child relationship. Input in this area was on hold, with more attention given to areas of career development and child-rearing, to allow the previous input's effects to have opportunity to blossom.

In other cases, the counselor could decide to simply provide support or altered input, to allow the client opportunity to discover personal dynamic stimulus power for change, without the counselor diminishing this by suggesting it was all part of a professional strategy all along.

Great patience is required here, to insure the client is not actively responsive to the non-input, especially if other stimuli are intended to provide a significant pay-load (since the counselor cannot avoid some communicated message or behavior). The counselor may even decide that a temporary suspension of therapeutic appointments is necessary, to allow other previously-delivered inputs to take effect. The evaluator must clearly determine the stimuli to which the client is attending and responding, so related outcome measurement rules out client response to placebos, intended to have no active effect.

Sometimes the counselor wants the client to believe he or she is changing as a result of placebo input, with the strategy of subsequently withdrawing the nonactive ingredient to allow the client to see that no change in responsiveness occurs, therefore supporting the argument that some other independent variable (within the client's social system or psyche) is responsible for any good or bad occurrences. The evaluator establishes baseline measures or perceptions of client behaviors, to substantiate that they do not change with variations in the placebo, and must help the client also learn to observe their constant occurrences. The point of withdrawal of placebo inputs must be clearly documented, so pre- and posttest observations can be compared as representing different time frames, when the occurrence of the input has been present vs. absent.

Theoretical Consistency

In many cases, the clinician will not be privileged to immediate feedback about client outcome as a result of interventive input, either because the client is resistant, developmental changes have not yet jelled, goals for treatment have not been fully formulated, or the client is not receptive to therapeutic influence, or does not possess the capability to change. In these situations, especially if the counselor has not yet made a determination that treatment will not work, much of the early intervention has to be based on hypotheses/guesses about what will be influential with a particular client, as well as on theoretical guidelines which represent synthesis and average perspectives based on practice wisdom or research findings.

Without empirical indices of client outcome thought, feeling, or behavior, the counselor makes input decisions based on assumptions about eventual outcomes, or preliminary minor client responses, which indicate approximations to eventual outcomes. The counselor may gather some data about similarities between present counselor-generated therapeutic inputs, and previous significant-other generated inputs in the client's past life; comparing previous client responses to past stimuli, to potential decisions, or responses to present stimuli. For example, the therapist can ask clients if they have ever heard feedback about their excessive anger in the past and, now that they also hear it from the counselor, how they responded before, if the feedback was effective, whether it helped them, if they changed, and why they should expect the same or a different response, now that they receive the feedback again. The counselor may, in some cases, change the input content, format, and timing, if a similar input (even from a nontherapist, as long as a special conflict was not present with the previous stimulator) was previously not effective. Unfortunately, there may still be a delay in the returns on present data about the new input, but some client progressive responses in the past can be compared to developmental progression in handling present input.

The author pursues this route with clients who admit that in the past, they have seen a large number of counselors, whom they have rejected as unknowledgeable or ineffective, by asking: "How do I know they will not also see me as ineffective and reject me? What can we do together that is different from the past, with a better chance of success in keeping a productive relationship going?" In this case, evaluatively, present input is compared to past inputs (of other counselors), with the association between observed outcomes in the past (positive or negative) and hypothetical (not yet existing) outcomes in the future (see Figure 14).

Although an actual outcome in the present has not yet occurred, the counselor gains some evaluative benchmark data (and some security in later selection of input rationale and format), by using reconstructed past data as a reflection of future phenomena. The therapist can also present incremental client responses (short of desired outcome behavior), to reflect back on the past. When this is not possible, the counselor may rely only on the degree of consistency between theoretical prescriptions for inputs (based on normative research findings, or practice experience), and actual inputs delivered. This, of course, requires comprehensive knowledge of the theory and its specific operationalized directives, which is not an easy task, since some theoretical formulas may not be substantiated by overwhelming research verification, or specifically detailed skill descriptions.

Some counselors pursue this allegiance to theory beyond reasonable degrees of practical sensibility, because they are not collecting data on client incremental approximations to desired outcomes, or behavioral goals are too general or too monumental; so minor observations become (but should never be) irrelevant. This slavishness to theory also occurs because counselors compulsively respond to personal self-reflections and to their own previous behavior, viewing it as validating successive behavior; or because they define perseverance or tenacity, as critical components of their service delivery format and style.

Counselors should rely on theoretical consistency at all times, but especially when cross-referencing data is not available. They must remember to assess intermediate feedback (verbal, behavioral), to insure the theory is correct; that the client is not converting only basic tenets of the theoretical perspective to different reality domains, so they and the counselor are really in different worlds; and that the input is, in fact, being delivered properly. By using both theoretical consistency and empirical outcomes, counselors are able to make adjustments in input, and continually evaluate the relevance of a theory they may usually accept largely on faith.

Figure 14
Input Comparisons

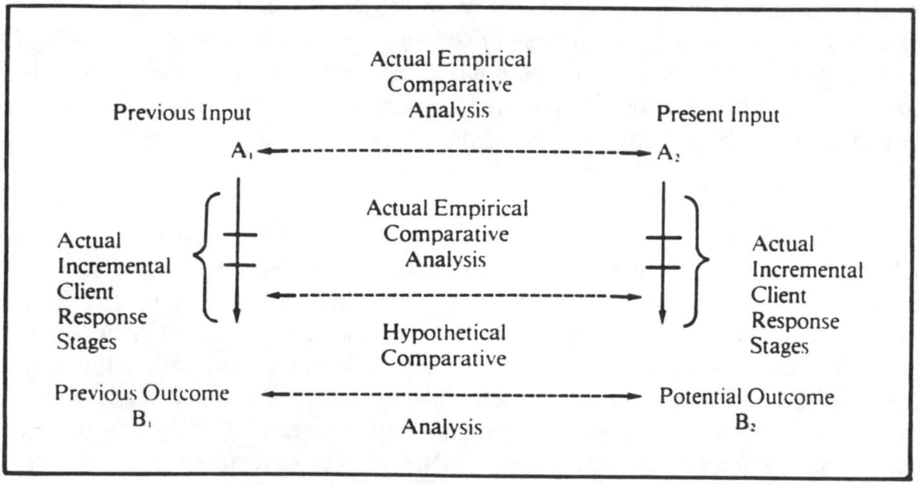

Change is Not Feasible

A very important, but often neglected form of input, relates to ways a counselor communicates to the client, that continuation of the therapeutic relationship is not possible. There are a number of reasons for this, among them that the therapist's objectives are beyond the motivation or psychosocial capabilities of the client, there is insufficient time to accomplish necessary or desired tasks, or that goals must be redefined to accurately represent the client's reality and environmental situation, or fit in with the developmental nature of the needed growth. Change in the client may cause aversive and possibly unacceptable negative reactions from the client's primary or sociocultural significant environmental groups, or the counselor may simply be unwilling or unable to work with him/her, because of personal antagonism, counter-transferential conflicts that cannot be worked out, lack of expertise in a particular problem area, or for some other reason.

The clinical evaluator dealing with any of these situations, should assess the interpretive impact this message will leave, and help clients correctly and comprehensively analyze the value placed on the information. Clients should strive to understand decisions they make about the self, the counselor, or significant phenomena relative to the communication, and project how this information will fit into their future plans and activities.

The delivery of this type of input sometimes pushes clients into deeper states of awareness of their own dynamics (especially if defensive passivity, obstructionism, or other patterns have interfered with successful pursuit of therapeutic growth) or causes a dependency, loss, or crisis, which might help the client become temporarily motivated to work with the counselor, to become a more receptive learner. If this is the case, the evaluator should help the client understand this dynamic, and in particular, how and why the client status has changed. This event can then become, in and of itself, a new form of input which counselor or client modify for repeated use in the therapeutic relationship. The client's response may be a significant component of an overall pattern, so a baseline or past crisis measurement at this point, will provide useful data longitudinally if the relationship continues.

Developmentally, clients may also make cognitive, emotional, or value changes after being advised that the relationship will not continue, so the evaluator should do long-term follow-up to determine if the client may become, at some later time, more receptive to therapeutic inputs, at which point they could be invited back into the relationship. Each input may have a delayed developmental impact, even if the input at time of delivery, seems logically not related to direct therapeutic work.

The counselor must be sensitive to possible regression or negative identity confirmation on the part of clients, when they hear they are being abandoned or rejected, and special efforts should be made to insure that the input is true, but as positive in nature as possible. Subsequent inputs may also correct negative effects of the premature termination. This should involve scheduling several counseling sessions after the client is advised he or she will not be continuing. This gives counselor and client sufficient time to work through the immediate effects of the counselor's decision.

Advising the client that change is not feasible in one area, of course, does not necessarily mean other work cannot continue. Additional planning inputs can identify or reprioritize new goals, but the client must also discuss specifically what it means to undergo this process. The client should also identify positive aspects of this directional change, so this positive foundation can then provide data for comparison to future changes in this area of goal planning. The counselor must remember that every aspect of the therapeutic process is a piece of data, and everything that occurs (even if it seems like waste product that has been trimmed away) should be recycled through the system at least one time, to see if its new status (as recently-trimmed excess) has transformed either its nature, or the client's perception of its stimulus value, into a new independent variable which produces change.

Intensity, Power, and Strength of Inputs

It is important to say a brief word about force behind the input, although this has been discussed in many different ways throughout this chapter.

Inputs cannot be conceived as having nominal or qualitative natures exclusively. Individual personality, the nature of the client's learning format and receptivity, type of problem being dealt with, and the strength of defenses, all result in differential power with which any input may be delivered, which simultaneously influences its impact on different outcomes.

The counselor must come to grips with the issue of whether or not an input delivered with differential intensity, represents the same basic action-oriented therapeutic dynamic influence; or its change in intensity transforms it into an entirely new category of input, both theoretically and in the mind of the client. When positive results do not materialize, this independent variable may be changed to another entirely different strategic maneuver when, in fact, what should have occurred is an increase or decrease in intensity or strength, without tampering with the basic nature of input.

For some clients, smaller doses over a longer time period may be preferable to one or two large doses, but many clinicians may not be acutely aware of the different volume levels they use. In these cases, counselors may use a different intensity scale than their clients, and may not properly vary this quantitative dimension of inputs, in a way that offers a more logical and reasonable opportunity to achieve success. On the other hand, it is dangerous to continue altering intensities (especially increases) in a frustrated attempt to produce change, when an entirely different input may be appropriate. The counselor should make decisions in advance about range of intensities she/he is willing to try, so planned decision points exist for changing inputs altogether (see Figure 15).

Although it is difficult and probably impossible for clinicians to measure intensity, power, or strength with specificity, the more closely counselors conceptually perceive and understand differences in these dimensions, the more accurate they become in varying them, to determine differential effects on client outcomes.

Figure 15
Input Intensity Matrix

			Type of Input						
	A			B			C		
			Delivery Frequency						
	Short (S)			Medium (M)			Long (L)		
S	M	L	S	M	L	S	M	L	
									1
			Client Outcome Indices and						2
			Counselor Decision Categories						3
									4
									5

Intensity Level

Termination of Counseling

An important issue for every clinician, is that termination represents the end of one phase of the counseling process but, more importantly, the beginning phase of the client's development through the rest of life. Baseline and outcome data are absolutely necessary at this point, so changes or continuations of behavioral or psychodynamic patterns, can be accounted for and explained relative to results of counseling, as well as sequential effects of counseling inputs and other intervening variables which occur in the client's daily living.

Any decision about therapeutic effectiveness is only tentative, and should be considered hypothetical at the time of termination, since numerous experiential, developmental, and learning dynamics materialize in the client's longitudinal life journey. Most counselors with whom the author consults do not follow clients with even superficial assessment criteria past the time of termination, and almost none check up on clients (with qualitative open-ended verbal questions, surveys, or other instruments) two or three or ten years after they formally left the counseling milieu. This is absolutely necessary for counselors to understand the impacts of their work, and also meets ethical requirements to offer assurance of the quality of one's work in the long run.

References

1.   William Eldridge, "Practitioner Approaches to Self-evaluation," (Doctoral dissertation, University of Denver, 1979).
2.   Edwin Thomas, "Research and Service in Single-case Experimentation: Conflicts and Choices," *Social Work Research and Abstracts.*
3.   Michel Hersen and David Barlow, *Single-case Experimental Designs: Strategies for Studying Behavior Change* (New York: Pergamon Press, 1976), pp. 82-83.
4.   For a discussion of systematic case management adjusted continuously to client response see, Barbara Melamed and Lawrence Siegal, "Self-directed In Vivo Treatment of an Obsessive-Compulsive Checking Ritual," *Journal of Behavior Therapy and Experimental Psychiatry,* 6:2:31-35, April, 1975.
5.   For a discussion of the many nonspecific variables in treatment, see, for example, Alan Kazdin and Linda Wilcoxon, "Systematic Desensitization and Nonspecific Treatment Effects: A Methodological Evaluation," *Psychological Bulletin,* 83:3:729-759, September, 1976; and Terrence Wilson and Ian Evans, "Adult Behavior Therapy and the Therapist-Client Relationship," *Annual Review of Behavior Therapy: Theory and Practice,* eds., C. M. Franks and G. T. Wilson (New York: Brunner/Mazel, 1976), pp. 771-793.
6.   For observations on research on treatment 'packages,' see, for example, Montrose Wolf, "Reviewers' Comments," *Journal of Applied Behavior Analysis,* 6:1:532-534, Fall, 1973.
7.   Donald Baer, Montrose, Wolf, and Todd Risley, "Some Current Dimensions of Applied Behavior Analysis," *Journal of Applied Behavior Analysis,* 1:1:95, Spring, 1965.
8.   Bernard Berelson, *Content Analysis in Communication Research* (Glencoe, IL: Free Press, 1952).
9.   University of Michigan, *School of Social Work, Practice Skill Assessment Instrument* (Ann Arbor, MI: University of Michigan, School of Social Work, Campus Publishers, 1967).
10.   William Reid, "Mapping the Knowledge Base of Social Work," *Social Work,* 26:2:124-132, March, 1981.
11.   Joseph Matarazzo, Arthur Wiens, and George Saslow, "Studies in Interview Speech Behavior," *Research in Behavior Modification: New Developments and Their Clinical Implications,* eds., L. Krasner and L. Ullman (New York: Holt, Rinehart and Winston, 1965), p. 209.
12.   Leonard Krasner and Leonard Ullman, eds., *Research in Behavior Modification: New Developments and Their Clinical Implications* (New York: Holt, Rinehart and Winston, 1965), p. 209.
13.   Albert Bandura, "Behavior Modification Through Modeling Procedures," *Research in Behavior Modification: New Developments and Their Clinical*

Implications, eds., L. Krasner and L. Ullman (New York: Holt, Rinehart and Winston, 1965), pp. 310-340.

14.   Stuart Rice, ed., *Methods in Social Science* (Chicago: University of Chicago Press, 1931), p. 561.

15.   Encyclopedia Britannica (Vol. 8; Chicago: William Benton, 1960), pp. 437-438; and see, Clayton Thomas, ed., *Taber's Cyclopedic Medical Dictionary* (Philadelphia: F. A. Davis, 1973), pp. 37-38.

16.   Leland Hinsel and Robert Campbell, *Psychiatric Dictionary* (New York: Oxford University Press, 1974), p. 267.

17.   Carl Jung, *Contributions to Analytical Psychology* (London: Kegan Paul, 1928).

18.   Norman Cameron, *Personality Development and Psychopathology* (Boston: Houghton Mifflin, 1963), pp. 152-167.

19.   William Eldridge, "Practitioner Approaches to Self-evaluation," (Doctoral dissertation, University of Denver, 1979).

20.   Bernard Berelson and Robert Carkhuff, *The Sources of Gain in Counseling and Psychotherapy* (New York: Holt, Rinehart and Winston, 1967).

21.   Robert Carkhuff, *Helping and Human Relations: A Primer for Lay and Professional Helpers* (Vol. I; New York: Holt, Rinehart and Winston, 1969).

22.   Randy Frost, Joseph Becker, and Michael Graf, "Self-devaluation and Depressed Mood," *Journal of Clinical Psychology,* 47:5:958-962, 1979.

23.   T. Beck, "The Development of Depression: A Cognitive Model," *The Psychology of Depression: Contemporary Theory and Research,* eds., R. Friedman and M. Katz (Washington, DC: V. H. Winston, 1974).

24.   Edward Velten, "A Laboratory Task for Induction of Mood States," *Behavior Research and Therapy,* 6:6:473-482, 1968.

25.   Albert Bandura, *Social Learning Theory* (Englewood Cliffs: Prentice-Hall, 1977).

26.   J. Richard Eiser and B. Elizabeth Osmon, "Linguistic Social Influence: Attitude Change Produced by Feedback Concerning Others' Use of Evaluative Language," *European Journal of Social Psychology,* 8:1:125-128, 1978.

27.   Charles Osgood, "Conservative Words and Radical Sentences in the Semantics in International Politics," *Social Psychology and Political Behavior,* eds., G. Abacarian and J. Soule (Columbus, OH: Charles E. Merrill, 1971).

28.   J. Richard Eiser and S. Pancer, "Attitudinal Effects of the Use of Evaluatively Biased Language" *European Journal of Social Psychology* (in press); and J. Richard Eiser and Moss, "Partisan Language, Immediacy, and Attitude Change," *European Journal of Social Psychology,* 7:4:477-489, May, 1976.

29.   J. Richard Eiser and Camilla White, "The Persuasiveness of Labels: Attitude Change Produced Through Definition of the Attitude Continuum," *European Journal of Social Psychology,* 4:1:89-92, 1974.

30.   Jean-Paul Codol, "On the So-called 'Superior Conformity of the Self-Behavior': Twenty Experimental Investigations," *European Journal of Social Psychology,* 5:4:457-501, 1975.

31.   William Eldridge, "Evaluation of Clinical Practice Forms of Communication by Which Counselors Receive Self-evaluative Information," *Journal of Clinical Psychology,* 37:4:211-215, October, 1981.

32.   William Eldridge, "Practitioner Approaches to Self-evaluation," (Doctoral dissertation, University of Denver, 1979).

33.   Robert Morris and Ollie Randall, "Planning and Organization of Community Services for the Elderly," *Social Work,* 1:10:96-103, January, 1965.

34.   Virginia Satir, *Conjoint Family Therapy* (Pablo Alto: Science and Behavior Books, 1964).

35.   Arthur Combs and D. Soper, "The Perceptual Organization of Effective Counselors," *Journal of Counseling Psychology,* 10:30:222, September, 1963.

36.   Bruce Biddle and Edwin Thomas, *Role Theory: Concepts and Research* (New York: John Wiley, 1966).

37.   Srinika Jayaratne, "Single-subject and Group Designs in Treatment Evaluation," *Social Work Research and Abstracts,* 13:3:35-42, Fall, 1977.

38.   Donald Kiesler, "Some Myths of Psychotherapy Research and the Search for a Paradigm," *Psychological Bulletin,* 65:2110-136, February, 1966.

39.   Wayne Duehn and Nazneen Mayadas, "Starting Where the Client Is: An Empirical Investigation," *Social Casework,* 60:2:67-74, February, 1979.

40.   Aaron Rosen, "The Treatment Relationship: A Conceptualization," *Journal of Consulting and Clinical Psychology,* 38:1:321-337, June, 1972.

41.   John Thibaut and Harold Kelley, *The Social Psychology of Groups* (New York: John Wiley, 1959).

42.   Stephen Richardson, Barbara Dohrenwend, and David Klein, *Interviewing: Its Forms and Function* (New York: Basic Books, 1965), p. 156.

43.   Henry Lennard and Arnold Bernstein, *Patterns in Human Interaction: An Introduction to Clinical Sociology* (San Francisco: Josey-Bass, 1969), p. 169.

44.   Charles Truax and Robert Carkhuff, *Toward Effective Counseling and Psychotherapy* (Chicago: Aldine, 1967); and Robert Carkhuff, *Helping and Human Relations: A Primer for Lay and Professional Helpers, Practice and Research* (New York: Holt, Rinehart and Winston, 1969).

45.   Robert Holt and L. Luborsky, *Personality Patterns of Psychiatrists* (New York: Basic Books, 1958).

46.   Charles Truax and Robert Carkhuff, *Toward Effective Counseling and Psychotherapy* (Chicago: Aldine, 1967); and Robert Carkhuff, *Helping and Human Relations: A Primer for Lay and Professional Helpers, Practice and Research* (New York: Holt, Rinehart and Winston, 1969).

47.   E. Bordin, "The Personality of the Therapist as an Influence in Psychotherapy," *Studies in Psychotherapy and Behavioral Change,* ed., M. F.
Feldman (Buffalo: University of New York Press, 1968), pp. 37-54.

48.   Michael LaCrosse, "Comparative Perceptions of Counselor Behavior: A
Replication and Extension," *Journal of Counseling Psychology,* 24:6:464-471,
June, 1977.

49.   Azy Barak and Michael LaCrosse, "Comparative Perceptions of Practicum
Counselor Behavior: A Process and Methodological Investigation," *Counselor
Education and Supervision,* 16:1:202-208, 1977.

50.   Hans Strupp, "On the Basic Ingredients of Psychotherapy," *Journal of
Consulting and Clinical Psychology,* 41:41-48, 1973; and Stanley Strong,
"Counseling: An Interpersonal Influence Process," *Journal of Counseling
Psychology,* 15:3:15-224, 1968.

51.   D. Horenstein, et al., "Clients,' Therapists,' and Judges' Evaluations of
Psychotherapy," *Journal of Counseling Psychology,* 20:5:149-153, 1973; and
Manuel Silverman, "Practicum Perception of Initial Interviews: Client-
Counselor Divergence," Counselor Education and Supervision 13:158-161,
1973.

52.   Manuel Silverman, "Perceptions of Counseling Following Differential
Practicum Experiences," *Journal of Counseling Psychology,* 19:1:11-15,
1972.

53.   Azy Barak and Michael LaCrosse, "Multidimensional Perception of Counselor Behavior," *Journal of Counseling Psychology,* 22:5:471-476, 1975.

54.   Duane Brown and Merilynn Cannaday, "Counselor, Counselee, and
Supervisor Ratings of Counselor Effectiveness," *Counselor Education and
Supervision,* 8:2:113-118, Winter, 1969.

55.   Robert Holt and L. Luborsky, *Personality Patterns of Psychiatrists* (2
Vols.; New York: Basic Books, 1958).

56.   Alan Bergin, "The Evaluation of Therapist Outcomes," *Handbook of
Psychotherapy and Behavior Change,* eds., A. Bergin and S. Garfield (New
York: John Wiley, 1971).

57.   Mary Richmond, *Social Diagnosis* (New York: Russell Sage Foundation,
1917), p. 108.

58.   Alfred Adler, *The Practice and Theory of Individual Psychology* (New
York: Humanities Press, 1951); and George Kelly, *The Psychology of
Personal Constructs* (Vol. 1; New York: Norton, 1955).

59.   Carl Jung, *Psychological Types or the Psychology of Individuation*
(London: Kegan Paul, 1938).

60.   John Thibaut and Harold Kelley, *The Social Psychology of Groups* (New
York: John Wiley, 1959).

61. Henry Lennard and Arnold Bernstein, *The Anatomy of Psychotherapy* (New York: Columbia University Press, 1960), p. 153.

62. Wayne Duehn and Enola Proctor, "Initial Clinical Interaction and Premature Discontinuance in Treatment," *American Journal of Orthopsychiatry,* 47:2:284-290, April, 1977.

63. Bert Meltzer, Walter Crockett, and Paul Rosenkrantz, "Cognitive Complexity and the Integration of Potentially Incompatible Information in Impressions of Others," *Journal of Personality and Social Psychology,* 4:3:338-343, September, 1966.

64. Allan Press, Walter Crockett, and Paul Rosenkrantz, "Cognitive Complexity and the Learning of Balanced and Unbalanced Social Structures," *Journal of Personality,* 37:2:541-553, December, 1969; George Kelly, *The Psychology of Personal Constructs* (Vols. I and II; New York, Norton, 1955).

65. Allan Press, Walter Crockett, and Paul Rosenkrantz, "Cognitive Complexity and the Learning of Balanced and Unbalanced Social Structures," *Journal of Personality,* 37:2:541-553, December, 1969; George Kelly, *The Psychology of Personal Constructs* (Vols. I and II; New York, Norton, 1955).

66. Nazneen Mayadas and Wayne Duehn, "The Effects of Training Formats and Interpersonal Discriminations in the Education of Clinical Social Work Practice," *Journal of Social Science Research,* 1:2:147-161, Winter, 1977.

67. Arnold Goldstein, *Psychotherapeutic Attraction* (New York: Pergamon Press, 1971); and Alan Gurmon and Andrew Rozin, *Effective Psychotherapy: A Handbook of Research* (New York: Pergamon Press, 1977); and Aaron Rosen and Dina Lieberman, "The Experimental Evaluation of Interview Performance of Social Workers," *Social Service Research,* 46:3:398, September, 1972.

68. Cedric Clark, "Cultural Differences in Reactions to Discrepant Communication," *Human Organization,* 27:2:125-131, Summer, 1968.

69. Leon Levy, *Psychological Interpretation* (New York: Holt, Rinehart and Winston, 1963), p. 7.

70. John Dewey, *How We Think* (Rev. ed.; New York, D. C. Heath, 1933).

71. Joseph English and G. Colmen, "Psychological Adjustment Patterns of Peace Corps Volunteers," *Psychiatric Opinion,* 3:6:29-35, December, 1966.

72. Elizabeth McBroom, "A Comparative Analysis of Social Work Interventions in Two Types of AFDC Families," (Doctoral dissertation, University of California at Berkeley, 1965).

73. Nathan Markus, "Staff Participation in Organizational Change: A Study of the Participation of Staff Members of Social Service Organizations in Activities Aimed at Influencing Changes in the Services and Functions of the Employing Agencies," (Doctoral dissertation, University of Toronto, School of Social Work, 1969); and Norman Maier, "Acceptance and Quality of

Solutions as Related to Leaders' Attitudes Toward Disagreement in Group Problem-solving," *Applied Behavioral Science,* 1:4:373-386, October-December, 1965; and R. Bor Yoref and E. Schlid, "Pressures and Defenses in Bureaucratic Roles," *American Journal of Sociology,* 71:6:665-673, May, 1966.

74.   Jack Rothmon, *Planning and Organizing for Social Change* (New York: Columbia University Press, 1974).

75.   Nathaniel Raskin, "An Objective Study of the Locus-of-evaluation Factor in Therapy," *Success in Psychotherapy,* eds., W. Wolff and J. Precker (New York: Grune and Stratton, 1952), pp. 143-163.

76.   Malcolm Klein and Neal Snyder, "The Detached Worker: Conformities and Variances in Work Style," *Social Work,* 10:4:60-68, October, 1965.

77.   Jack Rothmon, *Planning and Organizing for Social Change* (New York: Columbia University Press, 1974), p. 64.

78.   William Eldridge and Beverly Toomey, "Issues in Family Dynamics," (Interactive Radio Broadcast, WOSU Radio, The Ohio State University, Columbus, Ohio, Fall, 1984).

79.   Thomas Lyons, "Role Clarity: Need for Clarity, Satisfaction, and Withdrawal," *Organizational Behavior and Human Performance,* 6:4:99-110, January, 1971.

80.   Aaron Rosen, "The Influence of Perceived Interpersonal Power and Consensus of Expectations on Conformity of Performance of Public Assistance Workers," (Doctoral dissertation, University of Michigan, School of Social Work, 1963).

81.   Arnold Gurin and Robert Perlman, *Social Planning and Community Organization* (New York: John Wiley, 1972).

82.   George Miller, "Professionals in Bureaucracy—Alienation Among Industrial Scientists and Engineers," *American Sociological Review* 32:5:755-768, October, 1967.

83.   Harry Gottesfeld, "Professionals and Delinquents Evaluate Professional Methods with Delinquents," *Social Problems,* 13:1:45-59, Summer, 1965.

84.   Edwin Thomas, "Research and Service in Single-case Experimentation: Conflicts and Choices," *Social Work Research and Abstracts,* 14:4:20-31, Winter, 1978.

85.   Alan Kazdin, "Methodological and Assessment Considerations in Evaluating Reinforcement Programs in Applied Settings," *Journal of Applied Behavior Analysis,* 6:1:517-532, Fall, 1973; and Gordon Paul, "Behavior Modification Research: Design and Tactics," *Behavior Therapy: Appraisal and Status,* ed., C. Franks (New York: McGraw-Hill, 1969), pp. 29-63.

86.   Gerald Davison and Richard Stuart, "Behavior Therapy and Civil Liberties," *American Psychologist,* 30:5:755-763, July, 1975.

87. Edwin Thomas, "Uses of Research Methods in Interpersonal Practice," in *Social Work Research Methods for the Helping Professions,* ed., N. Palonsky (Chicago: University of Chicago Press, 1975), pp. 254-284.

88. A Jack Turner and William Goodson, "Behavioral Technology Applied to a Community Mental Health Center: A Demonstration," *Journal of Community Psychology,* 5:209-224, 1977; and Robert Liberman, Larry King, and William DeRisi, "Behavior Analysis and Therapy in Community Mental Health," *Handbook of Behavior Modification and Behavior Therapy,* ed., Leitenberg (Englewood Cliffs, NJ: Prentice-Hall, 1976), pp. 566-604.

89. Donald Campbell, "Reforms as Experiments," *American Psychologist,* 24:4:411, April, 1969.

90. Arthur Leader, "The Notion of Responsibility in Family Therapy," *Social Casework,* 69:3:131-136, March, 1979.

91. Alberta Szalita, "Psychoanalysis and Family Interviews," (Paper presented at The New York Academy Psychoanalysis, New York, December, 1976).

92. Seymour Halleck, *The Patterns of Therapy* (New York: Science House, 1971).

93. Jorge de la Forre, "Psychoanalytic Neutrality," *Bulletin of the Menninger Clinic,* 41:4:69, July, 1977; and Ivan Boszormenyi-Nagy and Geraldine Spark, *Invisible Loyalties: Reciprocity in Intergenerational Family Therapy* (New York: Harper and Row, 1973), p. 95.

94. Joan Zaro, Roland Barach, and Deborah Nedelman, *A Guide for Beginning Psychotherapists* (Cambridge, England: Cambridge University Press, 1977), p. 7.

95. Herbert Strean, *Clinical Social Work Theory and Practice* (New York: Free Press, 1978), pp. 186 and 219.

96. Herbert Strean, *Clinical Social Work Therapy and Practice* (New York: Free Press, 1978), p. 207.

97. Nathan Ackerman, "Family Healing in a Troubled World," *Social Work with Families,* ed., C. Munson (New York: Free Press, 1980), pp. 165-166.

98. Albert Ellis and Robert Harper, *A New Guide to Rational Living* (Hollywood, Wilshire, 1975).

99. Golda Edinberg, Norman Zinburg, and Wendy Kelman, *Clinical Interviewing and Counseling* (New York: Appleton-Century-Crofts, 1975), p. 23.

100. Alfred Freedman, Harold Kaplan, and Benjamin Sadock, *Modern Synopsis of Comprehensive Textbook of Psychiatry* (Baltimore: Williams and Williams, 1972), p. 500.

101. Roger MacKinnon and Robert Michaels, *The Psychiatric Interview in Clinical Practice* (Philadelphia: W. B. Saunders, 1971), pp. 11-16.

102. Golda Edinburg, Norman Zinburg and Wendy Kelman, *Clinical Interviewing and Counseling* (New York: Appleton-Century-Crofts, 1975), p. 7.

103. William Eldridge, "The Illusion of Rational and Relevant Clinical Practice," *Corrective and Social Psychiatry,* 28:4:131-136, 1982.

104. Jules Henry, *Pathways to Madness* (New York: Vintage Books, 1965), p. 107.

105. J. Wolk, "Are Social Workers Politically Active?" *Social Work,* 26:4: 287-288, September 1981.

106. Ronald Dear and Rino Patti, "Legislative Advocacy: Seven Effective Tactics," *Social Work,* 26:4:289-296, July, 1981; and Joan Hasimi, "Environmental Modification: Teaching Social Coping Skills," *Social Work* 26:4:289-296 and 323-326, July, 1981.

107. Robert Browning and Donald Stover, *Behavior Modification in Child Treatment: An Experimental and Clinical Approach* (Chicago: Aldine-Atherton, 1971), p. 9.

108. Donald Baer, Montrose Wolf, and Todd Risley, "Some Current Dimensions of Applied Behavior Analysis," *Journal of Applied Behavior Analysis,* 1:2:94, Spring, 1965; and Donald Campbell and Julian Stanley, Experimental and Ouasi-experimental Designs for Research (Chicago: Rand McNally, 1966).

109. Sidney Bijou, et al., "Methodology for Experimental Studies of Young Children in Natural Settings," *Psychological Record,* 19:1:117-220, 1969; and Donald Hartmann and Carol Atkinson, "Having Your Cake and Eating it Too: A Note on Some Apparent Contradictions Between Therapeutic Achievements and Design Requirements in N=1 Studies," *Behavior Therapy,* 4:4:589-592, July, 1973; and Michel Hersen and David Barlow, *Single-case Experimental Designs: Strategies for Studying Behavior Change* (New York: Pergamon Press, 1976), pp. 82-83.

110. Daniel O'Leary and Ronald Kent, "Behavior Modification for Social Action: Research Tactics and Problems," *Behavior Change: Methodology, Concepts, and Practice,* eds., L. Mamerlynck, L. Handy, and E. Mash (Champaign, IL: Research Press, 1973), pp. 89-97.

111. Philip Kendall, W. Robert Nay, and John Jeffers, "Timeout Duration and Contrast Effects: A Systematic Evaluation of a Successive Treatments Design," *Behavior Therapy,* 6:4:609-616, October, 1975.

112. Donald Kiesler, "Some Myths of Psychotherapy Research and the Search for a Paradigm," *Psychological Bulletin,* 65:5:110-136, 1966.

113. Arthur Combs, *Florida Studies in the Helping Professions* (Gainesville, FL: University of Florida Press, 1969).

114. Norman Harway, et al., "The Measurement of Depth of Interpretation," *Journal of Consulting Psychology,* 19:4:247-253, 1955.

115. Henry Lennard and Arnold Bernstein, *The Anatomy of Psychotherapy* (New York: Columbia University Press, 1960); and E. Murray, "A Content-

analysis Method for Studying Psychotherapy," *Psychological Monographs,* 70:13:420, 1956.

116. Marlin Blizinsky and William Reid, "Problem Focus and Change in a Brief Treatment Model," *Social Work,* 25:2:89-93, March, 1980.

117. Jay Haley, *Strategies of Psychotherapy* (New York: Grune and Stratton, 1963).

118. Paul Watzlawick, Janet Beavin, and Don Jackson, *The Pragmatics of Human Communication* (New York: Norton, 1967), p. 236.

119. Marlin Blizinsky and William Reid, "Problem Focus and Change in a Brief Treatment Model," *Social Work,* 25:2:89-93, March, 1980.

120. Donald Campbell and Julian Stanley, "Experimental and Quasi-experimental Designs for Research," *Handbook of Educational Research,* ed., N. Gage (Chicago: Rand McNally, 1963), p. 37.

121. Michael Shernoff, "Family Therapy for Lesbian and Gay Clients," *Social Work,* 29:4:393-394, July-August, 1984.

122. See, for example, Alan Gurman and David Kniskern, *Handbook of Family Therapy* (New York: Brunner/Mazel, 1981).

123. Deborah Siegal, "Defining Empirically-based Practice," *Social Work,* 29:4:325-337, July-August, 1984. The problem-solving paradigm was first postulated by John Dewey in How We Think (Boston: D. C. Heath, 1933), a volume that described the thought processes of a human being faced with a problem. Dewey maintained that to eliminate a difficulty, a person must think according to a rational, orderly procedure. Adherence to this well-defined step-by-step sequence guards against uncritical and impulsive conclusions about the nature of the problem or the solutions to the difficulty. Although Dewey omitted evaluation as the final phase of the process, contemporary writers generally opt for its inclusion.

124. Sandra Reeves, "What I Have Learned as a Result of Dr. Eldridge's Practice with Individuals Class," (Master's term paper, Ohio State University, College of Social Work, May, 1984).

125. David Kaplan, "Interventions for Disorders of Change," *Social Work,* 27:5:404-410, September, 1982.

126. Alvin Toffler, *Future Shock* (New York: Random House, 1970).

127. Clayton Sharkey and Salena Crocker, "Frustration Theory: A Source of Unifying Concepts for Generalist Practice" *Social Work,* 26:5:374-379, September, 1981.

128. Kurt Lewin, *A Dynamic Theory of Personality: Selected Papers* (New York: McGraw-Hill, 1935); and John Dollard, et al., *Frustration and Aggression* (New Haven, CN: Yale University Press, 1939), p. 7.

129. See, Larry Trexler, "Frustration Is a Fact, Not a Feeling," *Rational Living,* 11:4:19-22, Fall, 1976.

130. Sigmund Freud, "Types of Onset of Neurosis," *The Standard Edition of the Complete Psychological Works of Sigmund Freud, A General Introduction to Psychoanalysis,* trans., J. Riviere (New York: Liveright, 1935), pp. 354-355.

131. Norman Maier, *Frustration: The Study of Behavior Without a Goal* (Ann Arbor: University of Michigan Press, 1961).

132. Saul Rosenzweig, "An Outline of Frustration Theory," *Personality and Behavior Disorders,* ed. J. McV. Hunt (Vol. 1; New York: Ronald Press, 1944), pp. 381-383.

133. Robert Mager, *Goal Analysis* (Belmont, CA: Pitman Learning, 1972), p. 10.

134. Clayton Sharkey and Salena Crocker, "Frustration Theory: A Source of Unifying Concepts for Generalist Practice," *Social Work,* 26:5:374-379, September, 1981.

135. Melvin Delgado and Renise Humm-Delgado, "Natural Support Systems: Source of Strength in Hispanic Communities," *Social Work,* 27:1:83-89, January, 1982.

136. Bronislaw Malinowski, *Magic, Science, and Religion* (Garden City, NY: Anchor Books, 1943), p. 87.

137. Theodore Brameld, *The Remaking of a Culture: Life and Education in Puerto Rico* (New York: Harper and Bros., 1959), pp. 105-106; and Leo Grebler, Joan Moore, and Ralph Guzman, *The Mexican American People* (New York: Free Press, 1970), pp. 486-512; For material on Spiritists, see, Vivian Garrison, "Doctor, Espiritista or Psychiatrist? Health-seeking Behavior in a Puerto Rican Neighborhood of New York City," *Medical Anthropology,* 1:1:65-191, Spring, 1977. For material on Santeros, see, Judith Gleason, *Santeria, Bronx* (New York: Atheneum Press, 1975). For material on herbalist, see, Melvin Delgado, "Herbal Medicine in the Puerto Rican Community," *Health and Social Work,* 4:1:24-40, May, 1979. For material on santiguadores, see, Melvin Delgado, "Puerto Rican Folk Healers in the Big Cities," *Forum on Medicine,* 2:2:784-793, December, 1979.

138. Allan Kardec, *El Libro de los Espiritus* (Mexico: Editorial Diava,, m.d.), as quoted in, Cesar Garcia, "Spirits, Mediums, and Social Workers," (Master's thesis, New York School of Social Work, Columbia University, 1956), p. 8.

139. Stanley Fisch, "Botanicas and Spiritualism in Metropolis," *Milbank Memorial Fund,* 41:5:377-388, July, 1968.

140. Allan Harwood, *Rx: Spiritist As Needed—A Study of a Puerto Rican Community Mental Health Resource* (New York: John Wiley, 1977), pp. 45-46.

141. John Janzen, "Traditional Medicine Now Seen as National Resources in Zaire and Other African Countries," *Ethnomedicine,* 4:2:161-170, 1976-1977;

and Joseph Kadows, *Encyclopedia of Medicinal Herbs* (New York: Arco, 1975).

142. George Foster, "Relationship Between Spanish and Spanish-American Folk Medicine," *Journal of American Folklore,* 66:7:201-217, July, 1953.

143. Melvin Delgado, "Folk Medicine in the Puerto Rican Culture," *International Social Work,* 21:5:52-53, April, 1978.

144. Carlos Ortiz, *Esperanza: An Ethnographic Study of a Peasant Community in Puerto Rico* (Tucson: University of Arizona Press, 1973), p. 161.

145. Victor Frankel, *Man's Search for Meaning* (New York: Washington Square Press, 1963).

146. Sandra Reeves (Master's term paper, Ohio State University, College of Social Work, May, 1984); and Crabb, 1975.

147. Edwin Thomas, "Research and Service in Single-case Experimentation: Conflict and Choices," *Social Work Research and Abstracts,* 14:4:20-31, Winter, 1978.

148. J. Chassan, *Research Designs in Clinical Psychology and Psychiatry* (New York: Appleton-Century-Crofts, 1967); and Murray Sidman, *Tactics of Scientific Research: Evaluating Experimental Data in Psychology* (New York: Basic Books, 1960).

149. See, for example, Alan Kazdin and Steven Kopel, "On Resolving Ambiguities of the Multiple-baseline Design: Problems and Recommendations," *Behavior Therapy,* 6:6:601-609, October, 1975; and Beth Sulzer-Azaroff and Roy Mayer, *Applying Behavior Analysis Procedures with Children* (New York: Holt, Rinehart and Winston, 1977); Janice LeLange, "Exemplars of Single-subject Research Methodology Applied in Field Agencies by Graduate Students," (Paper presented before the Annual Meeting at the Counsel on Social Work Education, New Orleans, February, 1978).

150. Walter Miller, "Casework and the Medical Metaphor," *Social Work,* 25:4: 281-285, July, 1980.

151. Colin Turbayne, *The Myth of Metaphor* (New Haven, CN: Yale University Press, 1962).

152. This simple disease model of single pathogens may now be outmoded in medicine, see George Engle, "The Need for a New Medical Model: A Challenge for Biomedicine," *Science,* 8:8:129-135, April, 1977.

153. See, Richard Cloward and Irwin Epstein, "Private Social Welfare's Disengagement from the Poor: The Case of Family Adjustment Agencies," *Social Welfare Institutions,* ed., M. Zald (New York: John Wiley, 1965), pp. 623-644.

154.   Gordon Hearn, ed., *The General Systems Approach: Contributions Toward an Holistic Conception of Social Work* (New York: Counsel on Social Work Education, 1969); and Carel Germain and Alex Gitterman, *The Life Model of Social Work Practice* (New York: Columbia University Press, 1980).

155.   Darielle Jones, "African-American Clients: Clinical Practice Issues," *Social Work,* 24:2:112-119, March, 1979; and John Mbiti, *African Religions and Philosophy* (Garden City, NY: Doubleday, 1970), p. 161.

156.   Joyce Ladner, *Tomorrow's Tomorrow: The Black Women* (Garden City, NY: Doubleday, 1971), p. 57.

157.   Robert Hill, *The Strengths of the Black Family* (New York: Emerson Hall, 1971).

158.   Wade Nobles, "African Philosophy: Foundations for Black Psychology," *Black Psychology,* ed. R. Jones (New York: Harper and Row, 1972), p. 30.

159.   Andrew Billingsley, *Black Families in White America* (Englewood Cliffs, NJ: Prentice-Hall, 1968).

160.   K. Mitchell, J. Bozarth, and C. Krauft, "A Reappraisal of the Therapeutic Effectiveness of Accurate Empathy, Nonpossessive Warmth and Genuineness," *Effective Psychotherapy: A Handbook of Research,* eds., A Gurman and A. Razin (New York: Pergamon Press, 1977); and M. Parloff, I. Waskow, and B. Wolfe, "Research on Therapist Variables in Relation to Process and Outcome," *Handbook of Psychotherapy and Behavior Change: An Empirical Analysis,* eds., S. Garfield and A. Bergin (2nd ed.; New York: John Wiley, 1971), p. 249.

161.   R. Lorion, "Research on Psychotherapy and Behavior Change with the Disadvantaged," *Handbook of Psychotherapy and Behavior Change: An Empirical Analysis,* eds., S. Garfield and A. Bergin (2nd ed.; New York: John Wiley, 1971).

162.   Alan Kazdin, "Assessing the Clinical or Applied Importance of Behavior Change Through Social Validation," *Behavior Modification,* 1:427:452, 1977.

163.   Charles Schaefer and Michael Mills, "Self-rating of a Child Care Worker: A Comparison with Children's Ratings," *Quarterly,* 227-283, Winter, 1978; and Mary Ellen Goodman, *The Culture of Childhood: Child's Eye Views of Society and Culture* (New York: Teachers' College Press, Columbia University).

164.   William Eldridge, "Traditional Academic Programs for Human Service Professionals: Poor Experiential Training in Self-Evaluation and Accountability," *Performance and Instruction,* 21:8:26-28, October, 1982.

165.   Edwin Levy, "The Importance of the Children's Needs in Residential," *Bulletin of the Menninger Clinic,* 31:1:18-31, January, 1967.

166. William Eldridge, "Nonprofessional Areas of Performance Used by Clinical Counselors for Professional Self-evaluation" (Teaching Manuscript, The Ohio State University, 1982).

167. Joseph Schwab, "Problems, Topics and Issues," in *Education and the Structure of Knowledge,* ed. S. Elam (Chicago, Rand McNally, 1964), p. 9.

168. Sonya Rhodes, "The Personality of the Worker: An Unexpected Dimension in Treatment," *Social Casework,* 60:5:259-264, May, 1979.

169. Miriam Polster and Irvin Polster, *Gestalt Therapy Integrated* (New York: Bruner/Mazel, 1973), p. 20.

170. Meyer Williams, "Limitations, Fantasies, and Security Operations of Beginning Group Psychotherapists," *International Journal of Group Psychotherapy,* 16:2:158, April, 1966.

171. Edward Suchmah, *Evaluation Research* (New York: Russell Sage Foundation, 1967), p. 11.

172. Karen Holmes, "Services for Victims of Rape: A Dualistic Practice Model," *Social Casework,* 62:7:30-39, January, 1981; and Jeanie Peak and Peter Glonkoff, "The Female Patient as Booty," *Developments in the Field of Drug Abuse,* eds., E. Sinay, V. Shorty, and H. Alksne (Cambridge, MA: Schenkmon, 1975), pp. 509-512.

173. Robert Lifton, *Home from the War* (New York: Simon and Schuster, 1973), p. 75.

174. Victor Frankl, *Man's Search for Meaning* (New York: Washington Square Press, 1963), p. 164.

175. Marguerite Babcock and Bernadette Connor, "Sexism and Treatment of the Female Alcoholic: A Review," *Social Work,* 26:3:233-238, May, 1981.

176. Edith Gomberg, "The Female Alcoholic," *Alcoholism: Interdisciplinary Approaches to an Enduring Problem,* eds. R. Tarter and A. Sugarman (Reading, MA: Addison-Wesley, 1976), pp. 603-636.

177. John Curlee, "Alcoholic Women: Some Considerations for Further Research," *Bulletin of the Menninger Clinic,* 31:4:159, May, 1967.

178. Jeanie Peak and Peter Glonkoff, "The Female Patient as Booty," *Developments in the Field of Drug Abuse,* eds., E. Sinay, V. Shorty, and H. Alksne (Cambridge, MA: Schenkmon, 1975), p. 510.

179. Inge Boverman, et al., "Sex Role Stereotypes and Clinical Judgments of Mental Health," *Journal of Consulting and Clinical Psychology,* 34:8:1-7, February, 1970.

180. Janet Gigler, "Testimony Regarding Present and Projected Women's Programming," (Unpublished presentation, Pennsylvania Task Force on Women and Addiction, Regional Forum on Women and Youth, South Hills Health System Chemical Abuse Services, Pittsburgh, April, 1978).

181. Barbara Tower, "Communications Patterns of Women and Men in Same-sex and Mixed-sex Groups," (Unpublished presentation at training session on "Women in Treatment," Women's Training and Support Program, Harrisburg, PA, December, 1978).

182. Some works most identified with this cause have been, Joel Fischer, *Effective Casework Practice: An Eclectic Approach* (New York: McGraw-Hill, 1978); and Joel Fischer, "Does Anything Work?" *Journal of Social Service Research,* 1:1:215-243, Spring, 1978. In addition, see, Katherine Wood, "Casework Effectiveness: A New Look at the Research Evidence," *Social Work,* 23:4:737-758, November, 1978.

183. Alan Bergin and Hans Strupp, *Changing Frontiers in the Science of Psychotherapy* (Chicago: Aldine-Atherton, 1972); Jerome Frank, "The Present Status of Outcome Studies," *Journal of Consulting and Clinical Psychology,* 47:4:310-316, 1979; and M. Kovacs, "Treating Depressive Disorders," *Behavior Modification,* 3:3:496-517, October, 1979.

184. Mary Smith, Goene Glass, and Thomas Miller, *The Benefits of Psychotherapy* (Baltimore: Johns Hopkins University Press, 1980), p. 125.

185. Donald Kiesler, "Some Myths of Psychotherapy Research and the Search for a Paradigm," *Psychological Bulletin,* 65:7:110-136, February, 1966; and Gordon Paul, "Behavior Modification Research: Design and Tactics," *Behavior Therapy: Appraisal and Status,* ed., C. Frank (New York: McGraw-Hill, 1969).

186. Mary Smith, Goene Glass, and Thomas Miller, *The Benefits of Psychotherapy* (Baltimore: Johns Hopkins University Press, 1980), pp. 124-125.

187. Beverly Gomes-Schwartz, "The Modification of Schizophrenic Behavior," *Behavior Modification,* 3:4:438-439, October, 1979.

188. Alan Gurman and David Kniskern, "Research on Marital and Family Therapy: Progress, Perspective, and Prospect," *Handbook of Psychotherapy and Behavior Change: An Empirical Analysis,* eds., S. Garfield and A. Bergin (2nd ed.; New York: John Wiley, 1971), p. 883; and Alan Gurman and David Kniskern, "Family Therapy Outcome Research: Knowns and Unknowns," *Handbook of Family Therapy,* eds., A. Gurman and D. Kniskern (New York: Brunner/Mazel, 1981), pp. 749-750.

189. Neil Gilbert, "Probing Issues in Primary Prevention," *Social Work,* 27:4:293-297, July, 1982.

190. Milton Wittman, "Preventive Social Work: What? How? Where?" (Paper presented at the 11th Annual Symposium on "Issues on Social Work Education," University of Utah, Graduate School of Social Work, Salt Lake City, April 17, 1980), p. 294.

191. Robert Merton, *Social Theory and Social Structure* (New York: Free Press, 1957), pp. 421-436.

192. See, for example, Gerald Caplan, *Support Systems and Community Mental Health* (New York: Behavioral Publications, 1974).

193. Michael Roskin, "Integration of Primary Prevention into Social Work Practice," *Social Work,* 25:5:193-194, May, 1980.

194. Carl Rogers, *Carl Rogers on Encounter Groups* (New York: Harper and Row, 1970), pp. 85-105, and William Gordon, "A Natural Classification System for Social Work Literature and Knowledge," *Social Work,* 26:2:134-138, March, 1981.

195. Irwin Altman, "Choice-points in the Classification of Scientific Knowledge," *People Groups, and Organizations,* eds., B. Indik and F. Berrien (New York: Teachers' College Press, 1968), pp. 47-48.

196. Larry Pool, "Evaluation as an Opportunity to Improve Goal-directed Services," *Social Work in Education,* 2:3:62-71, 1980.

197. Iowa Department of Public Instruction, *Putting Research into Educational Practice: Teacher Evaluation* (Davenport: Iowa Dept. of Public Instruction, Area IX Instructional Materials Center, 1971), p. 21-c.

198. Jill Kogle and Charles Cowger, "Blaming the Client: Implicit Agenda in Practice Research," *Social Work,* 29:2:347-351, July-August, 1984.

199. William Ryan, *Blaming the Victim* (New York: Vintage Books, 1976).

200. Nathan Caplan and Stephen Nelson, "On Being Useful: The Nature and Consequence of Psychological Research on Social Problems," *American Psychologist,* 28:4:199-211, March, 1973.

201. William Reid and Patricia Hanrahan, "Recent Evaluations of Social Work: Grounds for Optimism," *Social Work,* 27:4:329-330, July, 1982.

202. Elliot Mishler, "Meaning in Context: Is There Any Other Kind?" *Harvard Education Review,* 49:20, February, 1979.

203. Martin Rein and Sheldon White, "Knowledge for Practice," *Social Service Review* 55:1:37, March, 1981.

204. Urie Bronfenbrenner, "Toward an Experimental Ecology of Human Development," *American Psychologist,* 32:5:513-531, July, 1977.

205. Abraham Kaplan, *The Conduct of Inquiry* (San Francisco: Chandler, 1964), p. 28.

206. Alan Gurman and David Kniskern, "Research on Marital and Family Therapy: Progress, Perspective, and Prospect," *Handbook of Psychotherapy and Behavior Change: An Empirical Analysis,* eds., S. Garfield and A. Bergin (2nd ed.; New York: John Wiley, 1971), pp. 817-901.

207. William Reid and Laura Epstein, *Task-Centered Casework* (New York: Columbia University Press, 1972), pp. 82-90; and J. Butcher and M. Koss, "Research on Brief and Crisis-oriented Psychotherapies," *Handbook of Psychotherapy and Behavior Change: An Empirical Analysis,* eds., S. Garfield and A. Bergin (2nd ed.; New York: John Wiley, 1971), p. 758.

208. William Schwartz, "The Social Worker in the Group," *The Social Welfare Forum* (New York: Columbia University Press, 1961), pp. 150-151; and Herbert Bisno, "A Theoretical Framework for Teaching Social Work Methods and Skills with Particular Reference to Undergraduate Social Welfare Education," *Journal of Educational Social Work,* 5:1:9-12, Fall, 1969.

209. William Reid, "Mapping the Knowledge Base of Social Work," *Social Work,* 26:2:124-138, March, 1981; and William Gordon, "Notes on the Nature of Knowledge," *Building Social Knowledge,* ed., A Kahn (New York: National Association of Workers, 1964).

210. Abraham Kaplan, *The Conduct of Inquiry: Methodology for Behavioral Science* (San Francisco: Chandler, 1964), p. 23.

211. Samuel Osipow, et al., "Personality Types and Vocational Choice: A Test of Holland's Theory," *Personnel and Guidance Journal,* 45:5:37-45, 1966.

212. Carl Rogers, et al., *The Therapeutic Relationship and Its Impact* (Madison: University of Wisconsin Press, 1967).

213. Charles Truax and Robert Carkuff, *Toward Effective Counseling and Psychotherapy* (Chicago: Aldine, 1967).

214. N. Maier, "The Premature Crystallization of Learning Theory," *Learning Theory, Personality Theory, and Clinical Research* (New York: John Wiley, 1954), pp. 54-65.

215. Marvin Reznikoff and Laura Toomey, *Evaluation of Changes Associated with Psychiatric Treatment* (Springfield, IL: Charles Thomas, 1959), p. 12.

216. Beulah Compton and Burt Galoway, *Social Work Processes* (Homewood, IL: Dorsey Press, 1975).

217. Benton Underwood, *Psychological Research* (New York: Appleton-Century-Crofts, 1957).

218. Joel Greenspoon, "The Reinforcing Effect of Two Spoken Sounds on the Frequency of Two Responses," *American Journal of Psychology,* 58:4:409-416, 1955.

219. Amitai Etzioni, "Shortcuts to Social Change?" *Public Interest,* 8:4:40-51, Summer, 1968.

220. James Bieri, et al., *Clinical and Social Judgment: The Discrimination of Behavioral Information* (New York: John Wiley, 1966).

221. Scott Briar and Henry Miller, *Problems and Issues in Social Casework* (New York: Columbia University Press, 1971), pp. 53-54.

222. Francis Turner, ed., *Social Work Treatment: Interlocking Approaches* (New York: Free Press, 1979), p. 1.

223. Thomas Szasz, *The Myth of Mental Illness, Foundations of a Theory of Personal Conduct* (New York: Harper, 1961).

224. S. Danish, "Human Development and Human Services: A Marriage Proposal," *Community Psychology in Transition,* eds., I. Iscoe, B. Bloom and C. Spielberger (Washington, DC: Hemisphere, 1977).

225. John Gibbs, et al., "Facilitation of Sociomoral Reasoning in Delinquents," *Journal of Consulting and Clinical Psychology,* 52:2:37-45, 1984; John Gibbs and Keith Widaman, *Social Intelligence: Measuring the Development of Sociomoral Reflection* (Englewood Cliffs: Prentice-Hall, 1982).

226. Fritz Redl and David Wineman, *Children Who Hate: The Disorganization and Breakdown of Behavior Controls* (New York: Free Press, 1951).

227. Charles Wenar, "Commentary: Progress and Problems in the Cognitive Approach to Clinical Child Psychology," *Journal of Consulting and Clinical Psychology,* 52:1:57-62, 1984; Charles Wenar, *Psychopathology from Infancy Through Adolescence: A Developmental Approach* (New York: Random House, 1982); and Robert Selman, "Troubled Children's Use of Self-reflection," *Social-Cognitive Development in Context,* ed. F. Serafica (New York: Guilford Press, 1982), pp. 62-99.

228. A comprehensive review of literature is listed under this reference, which corresponds to various aspects of Action Inputs discussed in the text. Because of the length of this list, the references are not individually noted in the text.

Erwin Ackerknecht, *A Short History of Psychiatry* (New York: Hafner, 1968);

Franz Alexander and Thomas French, *Psychoanalytic Therapy: Principles and Applications* (New York: Ronald Press, 1946);

Franz Alexander, Samuel Einstein, and Martin Grotjohn, *Psychoanalytic Pioneers* (New York: Basic Books, 1966);

James Alexander and Bruce Parsons, "Short-term Behavioral Intervention with Delinquent Families: Impact on Family Process and Recidivism," *Journal of Abnormal Psychology,* 81:3:219-225, June 1973;

APA Task Force on Health Research, "Contributions of Psychology to Health Research," *American Psychologist,* 31:4:263-274, 1976;

Hank Aponte and John Van Deusen, "Structural Family Therapy," *Handbook of Family Therapy,* eds., A. Gurman and D. Kniskern (New York: Brunner/Mazel, 1981);

John Austin, *How to Do Things With Words* (New York: Oxford University Press, 1962);

James Baldwin, *Social and Ethical Interpretations in Mental Development* (New York: Macmillan, 1902);

Michael Balint, *The Basic Fault: Therapeutic Aspects of Regression* (London: Favistock, 1969);

Albert Bandura, *Aggression: A Social Learning Analysis* (Englewood Cliffs, NJ: Prentice-Hall, 1973);

Albert Bandura, et al., "Cognitive Processes Mediating Behavior Change," *Journal of Personality and Social Psychology,* 35:5:125-139, 1977;

Albert Bandura, "The Self-system in Reciprocal Determinism," *American Psychologist,* 38:5:344-358, 1978;

Azy Barak and Michael LaCrosse, "Multidimensional Perception of Counselor Behavior," *Journal of Counseling Psychology,* 22:471-476, 1975;

G. Barrett-Lennard, "Dimensions of Therapist Response as Causal Factors in Therapeutic Change," *Psychological Monographs,* 76:43:562, 1962;

Morna Barsley, "Strategies and Techniques of Divorce Mediation," *Social Casework,* 65:2:102-107, February, 1984;

Gregory Bauer and Joseph Kobas, "Short-term Psychodynamic Psychotherapy: Reflections on the Past and Current Practice," *Psychotherapy,* 21:2:153-170, Summer, 1984;

Diana Baumrind, "Early Socialization and Adolescent Competence," *Adolescence in the Life Cycle: Psychological Change and Social Context,* eds., S. Dragastin and G. Elder (Washington, DC: Hemisphere, 1975).

Aaron Beck, et al., *Cognitive Therapy of Depression* (New York: Guilford Press, 1979);

D. Bem, "Self-perception: An Alternative Interpretation of Cognitive Dissonance Phenomena," *Psychological Review,* 74:183-200, 1967;

D. Bem, "Self-perception Theory," *Advances in Experimental Social Psychology,* ed., L. Berkowitz (Vol. 6; New York, Academic Press, 1972), pp. 1-62;

Allen Berger and Thomas Morrison, "Clinical Judgments of Easy Versus Difficult Client by Counselor Trainees," *Journal of Clinical Psychology,* 40:4:1116-1122, July, 1984;

Irving Berlin, Deane Critchley, and Paul Rossmon, "Current Concepts in Milieu Treatment of Severely Disturbed Children and Adolescents," *Psychotherapy,* 21:1:118-131, Spring, 1984;

Irving Berlin and Deane Critchley, "The Work of Play for Parents of Psychotic Children," *Child Psychiatry and Human Development,* 13:111-119, 1982;

Irving Berlin, "Developmental Issues in the Psychiatric Hospitalization of Children," *American Journal of Psychiatry,* 135:9:1044-1048, 1978;

Susan Bers and Judith Rodin, "Social-Comparison of Jealousy: A Developmental and Motivational Study," *Journal of Personality and Social Psychology,* 47:4:766-779, 1984;

Andrew Billings and Rudolph Moos, "Treatment Experiences of Adults with Unipolar Depression: The Influence of Patient and Life Context Factors," *Journal Consulting and Clinical Psychology,* 52:1:119-131, 1984;

Bernard Bloom, *Community Mental Health: A General Introduction* (Monterey: Brooks/Cole, 1977);

Sara Bonkowski, Shelley Bequette, and Sara Boomhower, "A Group Design to Help Children Adjust to Parental Divorce," *Social Casework,* 65:3: 131-137, March, 1984;

Michael Bopp and Gerald Weeks, "Dialectual Metatheory in Family Therapy," *Family Process,* 23:1:49-61, March, 1984;

Murray Bowen, *Family Therapy in Clinical Practice* (New York: Jason Aronson, 1978), p. 307;

Kenneth Bowers, "Situationism in Psychology: An Analysis and a Critique," *Psychological Review,* 80:5:307-336, September, 1973;

James Bray and Hillary Anderson, "Strategic Interventions with Single-parent Families," *Psychotherapy,* 21:1:101-109, Spring, 1984;

Gregory Browning, "An Analysis of the Effects of Therapist Prestige and Levels of Interpretation on Client Response in the Initial Phase of Psychotherapy," (Doctoral dissertation, University of Houston, 1966), *Dissertation Abstracts International,* 26, 4803 (University Microfilms No. 66-7);

John Bying-Hall, "Symptom Bearer as Marital Distance Regulator: Clinical Implications," *Family Process,* 19:4:355-365, December, 1980;

Charles Carver and Michael Scheier, *Attention and Self-regulation: A Control Theory Approach to Human Behavior* (New York: Springer-Verlag, 1981);

Aaron Cicourel, "Three Models of Discourse Analysis: The Role of Social Structure," *Discourse Processes,* 3:3:101-131, April-June, 1980;

Victor Cline, Juan Meja, et al., "The Relationship Between Therapist Behavior and Outcome for Middle and Lower-class Couples in Marital Therapy," *Journal of Clinical Psychology,* 40:3:691-704, May, 1984;

Lawrence Cohen, et al., "Positive Life Events and Social Support and the Relationship Between Life Stress and Psychological Disorder," *American Journal of Community Psychology,* 12:5:567-587, 1984;

Collie Conoley and Myron Beard, "The Effects of a Paradoxical Intervention on Therapeutic Relationship Measures," *Psychotherapy,* 21:2: 273-277, Summer, 1984;

Jeff Coulter, *The Social Construction of the Mind* (London: Macmillan, 1979);

Christine Courtois and Deborah Watts, "Counseling Adult Women Who Experienced Incest in Childhood or Adolescence," *The Personnel and Guidance Journal,* 60:14:275-278, January, 1982;

Lawrence Crabtree, Jr., "Hospitalized Adolescents Who Act Out: A Treatment Approach," *Psychiatry,* 42:2:147-158, 1982;

Deane Critchley, "One Nurse's Relationship with a Psychotic Boy," *Inpatient Care for the Psychotic Child,* eds., S. Szurek, I. Berlin, and M. Boatman (Palo Alton, CA: Science and Behavior Books, 1971);

Haim Dasberg and Meir Winokur, *Teaching and Learning Short-term Dynamic Psychotherapy* (New York: Spectrum, 1978);

Habib Davanloo, ed., *Short-term Dynamic Psychotherapy* (New York: Jason Aronson, 1980);

Paul Dell, "Beyond Homeostasis: Toward a Concept of Coherence," *Family Process,* 22:2:21-41, 1982;

Ed Diener, Randy Larson, and Randy Emmons, "Person X Situation Interactions: Choice of Situations and Congruence Response Models," *Journal of Personality and Social Psychology,* 47:3:580-592, 1984;

J. Doster and J. Nesbitt, "Psychotherapy and Self-disclosure," *Self-disclosure: Origins Patterns, and Implications of Openness in Interpersonal Relationships,* ed., G. Chelune (San Francisco: Josey-Bass, 1979), 177-224;

Windy Dryden, "Vivid RET III: The Working Through Process," *Journal of Rational Emotive Therapy,* 2:1:27-31, Spring, 1984;

Shelley Duval and Robert Wicklund, *A Theory of Objective Self-Awareness* (New York: Academic Press, 1972);

Thomas D'Zurilla and Marvin Goldfried, "Problem-solving and Behavior Modification," *Journal of Abnormal Psychology,* 78:4:107-126, August, 1971;

Albert Ellis, "Technique of Handling Anger in Marriage," *Journal of Marriage and Family Counseling,* 10:2:305-315, 1976;

Lois Erickson and Joshua Martin, "The Changing Adult: An Integrated Approach" *Social Casework,* 65:3:162-171, March, 1984;

Erik Erickson, *Childhood and Society* (New York: Norton, 1950);

Geraldine Farra and Nancy Beloglavek, "Treating Female Adult Survivors of Childhood Incest," *Social Casework,* 65:6:465-471, June, 1984;

R. Fazio and M. Zanna, "Direct Experience and Attitude-Behavior Consistency," *Advances in Experimental Social Psychology,* ed., L. Berkowitz (Vol. 14; New York: Academic Press, 1981), pp. 161-202;

Larry Feldman, "Marital Conflict and Marital Intimacy: An Integrative Psychodynamic-Behavioral-Systemic Model," *Family Process,* 18:2:69-78, March, 1979;

Allan Fenigstein, "Self-consciousness and the Overperception of Self as a Target," *Journal of Personality and Social Psychology,* 47:4:860-870, 1984;

Sandor Ferenczi, "Contraindications to the 'Active' Psychoanalytic Technique," *Further Contributions to the Theory and Technique of Psychoanalysis,* ed. and trans., J. Suttie (London: Hogarth, 1950, reprinted from International Ztschr. f. Psychoanalysis, 1926);

Leon Festinger, "A Theory of Social Comparison Processes," *Human Relations,* 7:1:117-140, 1954;

Roger Fisher and William Ury, *Getting to Yes* (Boston: Houghston Mifflin, 1981);

Steven Fox, Cynthia Strum, and H. Walters, "Perceptions of Therapist Disclosure of Previous Experience as a Client," *Journal of Clinical,* 40:2:496-498, March, 1984;

David Foy, et al., "Broad Spectrum Behavior Treatment for Chronic Alcoholics: Effects of Training Controlled Drinking Skills," *Journal of Consulting and Clinical Psychology,* 52:2:218-230, 1984;

David Foy, et al., "Social Skills Training to Improve Alcoholics' Vocational Interpersonal Competency," *Journal of Counseling Psychology,* 26:1: 128-129, 1979;

James Framo, "Rationale and Techniques of Intensive Family Therapy," *Intensive Family Therapy,* eds., I. Borzomenyi-Nagy and J. Framo (New York: Harper and Row, 1965), p. 184;

Sigmund Freud, *The Interpretation of Dreams,* ed. and trans., J. Strachey (New York: Avon Books, 1972, original work published 1900);

Myrna Friedlander and Susan Phillips, "Preventing Anchoring Errors in Clinical Judgment," *Journal of Consulting and Clinical Psychology,* 52:3:366-371, 1984;

Stuart Garfield, "Research on the Training of Professional Psychotherapists," *The Therapist's Contribution to Effective Psychotherapy: Empirical Assessment,* eds., H. Gurman and A. Razin (New York: Pergamon, 1977);

Harold Garfinkel, "Common Sense Knowledge of Social Structure: The Documentary Method of Interpretation in Lay and Professional Fact Finding," *Studies in Ethnomethodology* (Englewood Cliffs, NJ: Prentice-Hall, 1967), pp. 76-103;

Naomi Golan, *Treatment in Crisis Situations* (New York: Free Press, 1978), pp. 63-64;

Martin Gold and Elizabeth Douvan, *Adolescent Development: Readings in Research and Theory* (Boston: Allyn and Bacon, 1969);

Marvin Goldfried and Thomas D'Zurilla, "Problem-solving and Behavior Modification," *Journal of Abnormal Psychology,* 78:3:107-126, 1971;

Calvin Gordon, *The Social System of the High School: A Study in the Sociology of Adolescence* (New York: Free Press, 1957);

David Gordon and George Lakoff, "Conversational Postulates," *Syntax and Semantics,* eds., P. Cole and J. Morgan (New York: Academic Press, 1975), p. 83;

Carlton Goss, "Therapeutic Influence as a Function of Therapist Attire and the Seating Arrangement in an Initial Interview," *Journal of Clinical Psychology,* 40:1:52-57, January, 1984;

John Gottman, Howard Markham, and Carl Notaruis, "The Topography of Marital Conflict: A Sequential Analysis of Verbal and Non-verbal Behavior," *Journal of Marriage and the Family,* 39:5:461-477, April, 1977;

Roger Gould, *Transformations: Growth and Change in Adult Life* (New York: Simon and Schuster, 1978);

Fromes Haemmerlie and Robert Montgomery, "Purposefully Biased Interactions: Reducing Heterosexual Anxiety Through Self-perception Theory," *Journal of Personality and Social Psychology,* 47:4:900-908, 1984;

Lurt Hahlweg, Dirk Revenstarf, and Ludwig Schindler, "Effects of Behavioral Marital Therapy on Couples' Communication and Problem-solving Skills," *Journal of Consulting and Clinical Psychology,* 52:4:553-556, 1984;

James Hall, "Empirically-based Treatment for Parent-Adolescent Conflict," *Social Casework,* 65:6:487-495, June, 1984;

David Hamilton, Lawrence Katz, and Von Leirer, "Cognitive Representation of Personality Impressions: Organizational Processes in First Impression Formation," *Journal of Personality and Social Psychology,* 39:6:1050-1063, December, 1980;

Hamid Hekmat, Ralph Lubitz, and Ralph Deal, "Semantic Desensitization: A Paradigmatic Intervention Approach to Anxiety Disorders," *Journal of Clinical Psychology,* 40:2:463-466, March, 1984;

Marybeth Hendricks-Matthews, "The Battered Woman: Is She Ready for Help?" *Social Casework,* 63:3:131-137, March, 1982;

John Holland, *Making Vocational Choices: A Theory of Careers* (Englewood Cliffs, NJ: Prentice-Hall, 1973);

Florence Hollis, "Continuance and Discontinuance in Marital Counseling and Some Observations on Joint Interviews," *Social Casework,* 49:3:167-174, March, 1968;

Leonard Horowitz, et al., "The Prototype as a Construct in Abnormal Psychology: A Method of Deriving Prototypes," *Journal of Abnormal Psychology,* 90:6:568-574, December, 1981;

Peter Horvath, "Demand Characteristics and Inferential Processes in Psychotherapeutic Change," *Journal of Counseling and Clinical Psychology,* 52:4:616-624, 1984;

Neil Jacobson, William Fallett, et al., "Variability in Outcome and Clinical Significance of Behavioral Marital Therapy: A Reanalysis of Outcome Data," *Journal of Consulting and Clinical Psychology,* 52:4:497-504, 1984;

Neil Jacobson, "The Modification of Cognitive Processes in Behavioral Marital Therapy: Integrating Cognitive and Behavioral Intervention Strategies," *Marital Interaction: Analysis and Modification,* eds., K. Hahlweg and N. Jacobsen (New York: Guilford Press, 1984), pp. 285-308;

Neil Jacobson, "A Component Analysis of Behavioral Marital Therapy: The Relative Effectiveness of Behavior Exchange and Communication/Problem-solving Training," *Journal of Consulting and Clinical Psychology,* 52:2:295-305, 1984;

Neil Jacobson and G. Margolin, *Marital Therapy: Strategies Based on Social Learning and Behavior Exchange Principles* (New York: Brunner/Mazel, 1979);

F. Kanfer, "The Maintenance of Behavior by Self-generated Stimuli and Reinforcement," *The Psychology of Private Events: Perspectives on Covert Response Systems,* eds., A. Jacobs and L. Sachs (New York: Academic Press, 1971);

Irving Kaufman, et al., "The Family Constellation and Overt Incestuous Relations Between Father and Daughter," *American Journal of Orthopsychiatry,* 24:3:266-277, April, 1954;

Irving Kirsch, "The Placebo Effect and the Cognitive-Behavioral Revolution," *Cognitive Therapy and Research,* 2:3:255-264, September, 1978;

Donald Klein and Erick Lindemann, "Preventive Intervention in Individual and Family Crisis," *Prevention of Mental Disorders in Childhood* (New York: Basic Books, 1961);

Henriette Klein, Howard Potter, and Ruth Dyk, *Anxiety in Pregnancy and Childbirth* (New York: Paul B. Hoeber, 1950);

Melanie Klein, "A Contribution to the Psychogenesis of Manic-Depressive States," *Contributions to the Psychoanalysis* (London: Hogarth Press, 1948), pp. 282-310;

Elizabeth Kubler-Ross, *On Death and Dying* (New York: Macmillan, 1969);

Theresa Kurzman, "Communication Skills Seminar: A Non-drug Approach to Drug Education," *Contemporary Drug Problems,* 3:1:187-196, Summer, 1974;

William Labov and David Fanshal, *Therapeutic Discourse* (New York: Academic Press, 1975), pp. 23-27;

Daniel Levinson, et al., *The Seasons of a Man's Life* (New York: Alfred A. Knopf, 1978);

Erick Lindemann, "Symptomology and Management of Acute Grief," *American Journal of Psychiatry,* 101:2:144-148, September, 1944;

Jane Loevinger and Ruth Wessler, *Measuring Ego Development I: Construction and Use of a Sentence Completion Test* (San Francisco: Josey-Bass, 1970);

Jane Loevinger and Ruth Wessler, *Measuring Ego Development II: Construction and Use of a Sentence Completion Test* (San Francisco: Josey-Bass, 1970);

Jane Loevinger, *Ego Development: Conceptions and Theories* (San Francisco: Josey-Bass, 1976);

Diego Lopez and George Getzel, "Helping Gay AIDS Patients in Crisis," *Social Casework,* 65:1:387-394, September 1984;

Charles Lord, Lee Loss, and Mark Lepper, "Biased Assimilation and Attitude Polarization: The Effects of Prior Theories and Subsequently Considered Evidence," *Journal of Personality and Social Psychology,* 37:11:2098-2109, November, 1979;

Gordon Lowe, "Phenomenological Congruence in the Clinical Milieu," *Canadian Psychiatric Association Journal,* 20:50:367-372, August, 1975;

David Malan, *The Frontier of Brief Psychotherapy* (London: Tavistock, 1963);

Jorge Maldonado, "Analyst Involvement in the Psychoanalytic Impasse," *International Journal of Psychoanalysis,* 65:7:263-271, 1984;

Gayla Margolin, "Conjoint Marital Therapy to Enhance Anger Management and Reduce Spouse Abuse," *American Journal of Family Therapy,* 7:3:11-20, May, 1979;

I. Marks, "Behavioral Treatments of Phobic and Obsessive-Compulsive Disorders: A Critical Appraisal," *Progress in Behavior Modification,* eds., M. Hersen, R. Esler, and P. Miller (Vol. I; New York: Academic Press, 1975); pp. 65-158;

Hazel Harkus, "Self-schemata and Processing Information About the Self," *Journal of Personality and Social Psychology,* 33:2:63-78, February, 1977;

F. Matson, *The Broken Image: Man, Science, and Society* (New York: Braziller, 1964);

Matig Mavissakalian and David Barlow, "Phobia: An Overview," *Phobia: Psychological and Pharmacological Treatment,* eds., M. Mavissakalian and D. Barlow (New York: Guilford Press, 1981), pp. 1-33;

Patricia McCarthy and Sherry Knapp, "Helping Styles of Crisis Interveners, Psychotherapists, and Untrained Individuals," *American Journal of Community Psychology,* 12:5:623-627, 1984;

William Mischel, "The Interaction of Person and Situation," *Personality at the Crossroads: Current Issues in Interactional Psychology,* eds., D. Magnusson and N. Endler (Hilldale, NJ: Erlbaum, 1977);

J. Mizes, "Reward Presentation and Criterion-setting in Self-reinforcement: A Component Analysis and Investigation of Self-Versus External Control Factors," *Journal of Clinical Psychology,* 40:2:481-489, March, 1984;

Barbara Newman and Philip Newman, *Development Through Life: A Psychosocial Approach* (Homewood, IL: Dorsey Press, 1979);

David Nilsson, et al., "Perceptions of Counselor Self-disclosure: An Analogue Study," *Journal of Counseling Psychology,* 26:5:399-404, September, 1979;

Raymond Novaco, *Anger Control: The Development of Evaluation of an Experimental Technique* (Lexington, MA: D. C. Heath, 1975);

Mary Oliveri and David Reiss, "Family Concepts and Their Measurement; Things are Seldom What They Seem," *Family Process,* 23:1: 33-48, March, 1984;

Charles Osgood, "The Nature and Measurement of Meaning," *Psychological Bulletin,* 49:2:197-237, 1952;

Peggy Penn, "Circular Questioning," *Family Process,* 21:3:267-289, 1982;

William Piper, Elie Debbone and J. Bienvenu, "A Comparative Study of Four Forms of Psychotherapy," *Journal of Consulting and Clinical Psychology,* 52:2:268-279, 1984;

Otto Rank and Sandor Ferenczi, *The Development of Psycho-analysis,* trans., C. Newton (New York: Nervous and Mental Diseases Publishing, 1925);

David Reiss, *The Family's Construction of Reality* (Cambridge: Harvard University Press, 1981);

Joan Riviere, "Some Theoretical Conclusions Regarding the Emotional Life of the Infact," *Developments in Psychoanalysis,* ed., J. Riviere (London: Hogart Press, 1952), pp. 198-236;

Arthur Robin, "Parent-Adolescent Conflict: A Skill Training Approach," *Social Competence: Interventions for Children and Adults,* eds., D. Rathjen and J. Foreyt (New York: Pergamon, 1980);

T. Rogers, N. Kuiper, and W. Kirker, "Self-reference and the Encoding of Personal Information," *Journal of Personality and Social Psychology,* 35:9: 677-688, September, 1977;

Diane Rosenbaum, "Evaluation of Student Performance in Psychotherapy," *Journal of Clinical Psychology,* 40:4:1106-1110, July, 1984;

David Rosenthal, Barbara Putnam, and James Hansen, "Racially Different Adolescents: Self-concept and Vocational Attitudes," *Urban Education,* 13:4:453-461, January, 1979;

Lee Ross, Teresa Amabile, and Julia Steinmetz, "Social Roles, Social Control, and Biases in Social Perception Processes," *Journal of Personality and Social Psychology,* 35:7:485-494, July, 1977;

Maria Roy, *Battered Women: A Psychological Study of Domestic Violence* (New York: Van Nostrand Reinhold, 1977);

Renee Royak-Schafer and Robert Feldman, "Health Behaviors of Psychotherapists," *Journal of Clinical Psychology,* 40:3:705-710, May, 1984;

Kenneth Rubin, "Social and Social-Cognitive Developmental Characteristics of Young Isolate, Normal, and Sociable Children," *Peer Relations and Social Skills in Childhood,* eds., K. Rubin and H. Ross (New York: Springer, 1982), pp. 353-374;

Kenneth Rubin and L. Krasnor, "Social Cognitive and Social Behavioral Perspectives in Problem-solving," *Minnesota Symposium on Child Development: Social Cognition,* ed., M. Permutter (Vol. 18; Hillsdale, NJ: Erlbaum, in press);

D. Ruble, et al., "Developmental Analysis of the Role of Social and Self-evaluation," *Developmental Psychology,* 16:6:105-115, 1980;

Marilyn Rumelhart, "When Understanding the Situation is the Real Problem," *Social Casework,* 65:1:27-33, January, 1984;

J. Rychlak, ed., *Dialectic: Humanistic Rationale for Behavior and Development* (Basel: Karger, 1976);

Sebastian Santostefano, *A Biodevelopmental Approach to Clinical Child Psychology: Cognitive Controls and Cognitive Control Therapy* (New York: John Wiley, 1978);

Sebastian Santostefano and C. Rieder, "Cognitive Controls and Aggression in Children: The Concept of Cognitive-Affective Balance," *Journal of Consulting and Clinical Psychology,* 52:6:46-56, 1984;

David Satin, "Erich Lindemann as Humanist, Scientist, and Change Agent," *American Journal of Community Psychology,* 12:5:519-527, 1984;

E. Schegloff, "Notes on a Conversational Practice: Formulating Place," *Studies in Social Interaction,* ed., D. Sudnow (New York: Free Press, 1972);

Thomas Schramski, et al., "Factors that Contribute to Past Therapy Persistent of Therapeutic Change," *Journal of Clinical Psychology,* 40:1:78-85, January, 1984;

John Searle, "Indirect Speech Acts," *Syntax and Semantics,* eds., P. Cole and J. Morgan (Vol. 3; New York: Academic Press, 1975);

John Searle, *Speech Acts* (Cambridge: Cambridge University Press, 1969);

Harold Searles, "The Information Value of the Supervisor's Emotional Experience," *Collected Papers on Schizophrenia and Related Subjects* (New York: International Universities Press, 1965), pp. 157-176;

Robert Selman, *The Growth of Interpersonal Understanding: Developmental and Clinical Analysis* (New York: Academic Press, 1980);

M. Selvini-Palazzoli, et al., *Paradox and Counterparadox* (New York: Jason Aronson, 1978);

Hans Seyle, *Stress Without Distress* (New York: Lippincott, 1974);

Albert Shapiro, "A Historic and Heuristic Definition of the Placebo," *Psychiatry,* 27:3:52-58, 1964;

Peter Sifneos, "Dynamic Psychotherapy in a Clinic," *Current Psychiatric Therapies* (New York: Grune and Stratton, 1961);

Peter Sifneos, *Short-term Dynamic Psychotherapy* (New York: Plenum, 1979);

Roslyn Spector, et al., "Time Sampling in Family Therapy Sessions," *Psychotherapy,* 7:1:37-40, Spring, 1970;

M. Stanton, "Family Therapy: Systems Approaches," *Treatment of Emotional Disorders in Children and Adolescents,* eds., G. Scholevar, R. Benson, and F. Blinda (New York: Spectrum, 1980), p. 159;

Suzanne Steinmetz, "Violence Between Family Members," *Marriage and Family Review,* 1:1:1-16, March, 1978;

Suzanne Steinmetz, *The Cycle of Violence: Assertive, Aggressive, and Abusive Family Interaction* (New York: Praeger, 1977);

Jerome Steuer, et al., "Cognitive-Behavioral and Psychodynamic Group Psychotherapy in Treatment of Geriatric Depression," *Journal of Consulting and Clinical Psychology,* 52:2:180-189, 1984;

Kristyn Streever and John Wodarski, "Life Span Developmental Approach: Implications for Practice," *Social Casework,* 65:5:267 278, May, 1984;

John Taylor, "Structured Conjoint Therapy for Spouse Abuse Cases," *Social Casework,* 65:1:11-18, January, 1984;

John Taylor, "Theoretical Considerations for a Male Anxiety Crisis as a Cause of Episode Family Violence," *The Many Dimensions of Family Practice* (New York: Family Service Association of America, 1980);

Ronald Taylor, "Marital Therapy in the Treatment of Incest," *Social Casework,* 65:4:195-202, April, 1984;

Abraham Tesser, "Self-esteem Maintenance in Family Dynamics," *Journal of Personality and Social Psychology,* 39:1:77-91, 1980;

Christopher Tori and Leonard Worell, "Reduction of Human Avoidant Behavior: Comparison of Counterconditioning, Expectancy and Cognitive Information Approaches," *Journal of Consulting and Clinical Psychology,* 41:2:269-278, August, 1973;

Eliot Turiel, "Conflict and Transition in Adolescent Moral Development," *Child Development,* 45:5:14-29, June, 1974;

Roy Turner, ed., *Ethnomethodology* (Harmondsworth: Penguin, 1974), pp. 197-215;

Max Uhlemann, Geoffrey Hett, and Doug Lee, "Perception of Theoretically Derived Counseling Approaches as a Function of Preference for Counseling Orientation," *Journal of Clinical Psychology,* 40:4:1111-1115, July, 1984;

George Vaillant, *Adaptations of Life* (Boston: Little, Brown, 1977);

Judith Wallerstein and Joan Berlin Kelly, *Surviving the Breakup* (New York: Basic Books, 1980);

Gerald Weeks and Luciand L'Agate, *Paradoxical Psychotherapy: Theory and Practice with Individuals, Couples, and Families* (New York: Brunner Mazel, 1982);

Ronald Wessler, "Alternative Conceptions of Rational-Emotive Therapy; Toward a Philosophically Neutral Psychotherapy," (Paper presented at the 12th European Congress of Behavior Therapy, Rome, September 5, 1982);

Wallace Wilkins, "Psychotherapy, The Powerful Placebo," *Journal of Consulting and Clinical Psychology,* 52:4:570-573, 1984;

Lloyd Williams, Grace Dooseman and Erin Kleifield, "Comparative Effectiveness of Guided Mastery and Exposure Treatments for Intractable Phobias," *Journal of Consulting and Clinical Psychology,* 52:4:505-518, 1984;

Timothy Wilson, et al., "Effects of Analyzing Reasons of Attitude-Behavior Consistency," *Journal Personality and Social Psychology,* 47:1:5-14, July, 1984;

Meir Winokur and Heim Dasberg, "Teaching and Learning Short-term Dynamic Psychotherapy; Techniques and Resistances," *Bulletin of the Menninger Clinic,* 47:5:36-52, 1983;

Ludwig Wittgenstein, *Philosophical Investigations* (Oxford: Blackwell, 1953);

Irvin Yalom, *The Theory and Practice of Group Psychotherapy* (2nd ed.; New York: Basic Books, 1975);

Maurice Zemlick and Robert Watson, "Maternal Affairs of Acceptance and Rejection During and After Pregnancy," *American Journal of Orthopsychiatry,* 23:2:570-584, July, 1953.

Chapter Five

Clinical Outcomes

Introduction

In the recent history of clinically-oriented "social science" professions (social work, psychology, counseling, psychiatric nursing, etc.), the quest for answers about therapeutic effectiveness and cost-effective/efficient results, has been pursued by researchers and practitioners alike. In cases where the answer has been "no clear evidence of effectiveness," such as Joel Fischer's[1] surveys of research studies about social casework effectiveness, and similar work by Scott Briar[2] and others; the social sciences are left with a negative lump in the throat, and confusion about where to begin digging into this complex problem for positive experiential, as well as research, findings. In other instances, where some findings are positive or at least inconclusive,[3] a similar exploratory dilemma exists. Herein, concerned professionals seek to understand the intricacies of how and why some positive outcomes can be discovered, coupled with pressing queries regarding the proper perspective to utilize, in finding out why other aspects of clinical counseling practice do not yield positive findings.

The clinician may not always invite the researcher into the complex (often defined as "artistic") world of counseling—through inducements of systematic description, process delineation, or objective empiricism. The researcher, on the other hand, may be too microscopic in circumscribed areas of interest; or remain distant from the pragmatic concerns of clinicians, who want to know "what to say" to clients, or "how to interpret" their ideas to produce immediate or developmental change.

"As in any research effort the question to be studied must be formulated in much sharper and more concrete terms, or the researcher risks going beyond the data instead of basing conclusions on personal opinion and polemics. Furthermore, the profession can do little more than become defensive and confused in reaction to such global charges of ineffectiveness since they offer little contribution to developing and improving practice."[4]

This chapter's discussion of outcomes, demonstrates basic domains of this complex aspect of clinical practice, partly to delve deeper than the perspectives of global outcome studies producing negative or nonsignificant findings,[5] but also to identify the phenomenon of outcome as a unique "component"[6] of practice. In this context, the concept "outcome" requires analytic and descriptive refinement in the specification of its nature and developmental dynamics, to understand how it must be defined for proper evaluative questions to be asked.

Clinicians are always in a dilemma within their therapeutic milieu, in requiring overall guidelines from client group studies, to make predictions of success probabilities[7] for general case situations; yet, must sufficiently understand the unique dimensions of specific clients,[8] to determine transferable units of analysis between various single cases. Clinicians must correctly understand the components of single cases to avoid oversimplifying the analysis, and missing the dynamic nature and interactive process[9] of intricate cause-effect influences on outcomes. This understanding is greatly needed to accurately conceptualize and measure, in order to draw scientifically-accepted causal inferences, from the "process" data of dyadic and small group interactions. Determining cause/effect has been particularly problematic, because the qualitative nature of much clinical data has been avoided by some practitioners and researchers, who have prematurely decided that systematic delineation and description of outcome phenomena, may be too abstract or confusing to understand precise degrees of specificity.

Although arguments about complexity of clinical outcome phenomena may be correct,

". . . they suggest that the evaluator needs the talent of Tolstoi to be able to describe these events in ways that allow the reader to draw the appropriate inference. . . . It is important to realize that nonstatistical arguments need not be valid. Yet many researchers may be timid about attempting such inferences simply because the rules as to what constitutes a reasonably sound inference are ambiguous, relative to the rules as to what constitutes a sound statistical inference. What is needed are rules of inference that reasonable people can agree on."[10]

An assumption already revealed in the author's decision to separately question outcomes, is that this is a complex concept having multiple potential values,[11] interpretations, and interventive effects,[12] which influence decisions based on self-evaluative data. This complexity, however, does not suggest that clinicians, evaluators, or researchers cannot do a better and more comprehensive job observing and studying this puzzle, to tease out meaningful explanations of what happens as a result of counseling, and why various consequences materialize. In this regard, the first facet of outcomes to be addressed, relates to problems with their basic definition as empirical referents for states of identity, or as developmental processes within the life domains of individual clients or client units (e.g., small groups or families).

Empirical Definitions

Effective evaluation obviously necessitates that phenomena be identified and measured as part of the client's personality configuration, behavioral repertoire, or attitudinal status. This is necessary so changes over time are noted, degrees of change documented, and decisions made as to whether changes in these outcomes are satisfactory, and are directly or indirectly responsive to therapeutic inputs.

The "clinical significance"[13] of outcomes is particularly important because of the potential for all outcomes to vary randomly,[14] as a result of environmental contingencies, or the outcome phenomenon's own developmental nature. Clinical significance suggests that outcomes are critical indicators of success or failure of interventive efforts. Outcomes represent degrees, directions, timing, and meaningfulness of changes which, in and of themselves, interact holistically with the client's entire life, growth, and adaptation processes.

"Although some investigators have begun to report proportions of clients who improve, the criteria for categorizing a client as improved have been inconsistent and somewhat haphazard. Standardized criteria serve a useful function, much like the conventions adopted to infer statistically significant differences between groups. Unless decision rules are agreed upon before the fact, criteria are likely to be arbitrary and easily susceptible to post hoc biases."[15]

Jacobsen, et al., as noted above, advise that clients be described as making successful growth, if the degree of change on any measured index or observation, exceeds the probabilities of chance occurrences of that behavior.

The reliable change index (RC) is one statistic Jacobsen recommends, wherein a change exceeding a standard error (SE) of measurement of 1.96 is probably not a result of measurement error (p + .05), or chance occurrence. This process usefully assesses clients relative to some criteria of outcome change during counseling:

> "For example, a couple has improved to a clinically significant degree in their level of marital satisfaction after therapy places them outside the maritally distressed population distribution and within the non-distressed population range on the dimension of marital satisfaction. Because these population distributions usually overlap, the midpoint of the overlap would be the cutoff. At this point, the client would be equally likely to fall in either population. In order to calculate this point, norms should be available on both functional and dysfunctional populations."[16]

In regard to the above concern, the value of clear, comprehensive, measurable, and observable definitions of empirical, client-related, and clinically significant phenomena, cannot be overstressed. The clinician's and client's ability to unequivocally agree perceptually on the nature, presence, or absence of outcome factors; determine whether any thought, feeling, or behavioral matrix can be applied to diagnostic and assessment categories, which allow ultimate decisions about cost/benefit and cost/efficiency of interventive efforts.

One example of the importance of these empirical definitions is seen in goal-attainment scaling,[17] which is a methodology for enhancing the adaptive ability of clients by defining, in clear operational terms, various counseling expectations and objectives for outcome assessments. Development of descriptive categories constitutes reviewing a particular domain of reality in a systematic and consistent manner, with specific observable benchmarks to confirm client behavior, which represents various levels of psychosocial development. In brief, goal-attainment scaling involves four steps:

1. accumulating comprehensive data concerning the client, for development of scaled goals;
2. outlining thought, feeling, or behavioral categories as objectives for change;
3. making calculated predictions of outcome statuses for each category; and

4.   recording scores for outcomes, through frequency observations of empirical behaviors.

Although the nature and clinical definition of specific behaviors are critical issues, one troublesome empirical difficulty concerns how to define moods, attitudes, and relationships in a way that captures their correct basic essence; while defining special conditions representing variant changes stimulated by unusual internal or external causes. It is equally challenging to plot or scale normal variability and dynamic activity of moods or identity states, which have meaning concerning their basic nature, and their relevance (correlation) to specific behaviors causing or contributing to problems clients experience.

Even though specific behaviors may be empirically defined or measured (including decisions about positive or negative trends), the complexity of social and psychic living suggests that behaviors become incorporated holistically within intricate and complex interactive patterns. This incorporation reflects conditions or states of adjustment, defense, regressions, identity, etc., which also must be categorized and scaled within standardized, empirical, analytical frameworks.

In this light, Kazdin[18] discusses the importance of special validation, social validation, and social contextual indices of change. Specific behaviors must be empirically defined in comparison to behaviors of other individuals. This creates a checks and balances protection which insures that the feeling, identity, or relationship states of being represented by the behaviors, take on their meaning relative to other criteria which are always brought into the picture for comparison. Kazdin implies that individual clients and also representatives of normative groups, have an important role in providing interpretive feedback to counselors about the integrated meaning of thoughts, feelings, and behaviors—so the professional's subjective definitional biases do not contaminate either observation or diagnostic judgment.

These definitions, as suggested in the discussion of goal-attainment scaling, can be categorized by their observable attributes, and also according to scaled criteria of qualitative and quantitative differentiation, connected to therapeutic goals for change. Goal-attainment scaling requires repeated interpretation of definitional accuracy over short, as well as extended, periods of time. The recurrent use of subjective definitional awareness over time, improves the counselor's chances of developing more objective definitional frameworks and global assessment criteria, which serve as a normative comparison for specific conforming or deviant behaviors. Subjective evaluation methods, however, also have drawbacks, especially in identifying correct reference populations and norms for client behavioral comparison, and properly interpreting the meaning and implications of global assessments.

With this brief introduction to the overall topic of empirical definitions, this domain of practice will be broken down into subcomponents, and discussed separately to help clarify the significance of basic concerns of outcome observation, definition, and measurement.

Validity

A major validity question for the clinical evaluator, is whether or not to apply any single measure (e.g., psychological test) or a combination of measures (testing, behavioral accounting, and attitude/feeling/identity awareness), to provide a real and correct picture of the complex feeling/thought/attitude/mood/phenomena of the client's life gestalt. Although there are methodological ways of testing instrument and measurement validity and reliability, there is always uncertainty about whether any instrument accurately fathoms the intricacies of the human mind set, or relationship dynamics. There is further question about changes in the client as the very measurement process is conducted. The fact that the measurement instrument necessarily "stops action," and takes a still life perspective on any emotion, thought, or sequence of actions; also negates their fluid, mobile, and changing nature which, if viewed in process, may represent a more accurate panorama of their essence. This dynamic perspective might only be achieved with frequently recurrent and multiple measures, that include client incremental interpretation of behavioral observations, and overall identity states. Frequent measurement, however, would also be potentially disruptive to the flow of therapeutic inputs, and may seriously alter the observed outcome phenomenon. Although many clinicians and researchers define common meanings for moods or attitudes, and associated psychic and behavioral processes; clinicians may never be exactly sure whether these "norms" accurately fit clients' unique interpretations of their own moods or feelings. The test may be invalidated, if it has not been standardized on each particular client.

One way to provide some client-centered standardization, is to describe and measure categories of client self-interpretation of mood or attitude, so recurrences of skewed, non-normative perspectives, can be documented and plugged in as correction factors on standardized test scores. The evaluator could also combine self-reports with behavioral measurements. This essentially means that one set of outcomes is defined and measured, in terms of behavioral frequencies of qualitative client taxonomy within predetermined ordered sets of descriptive circumstances; while a second set of outcomes relates to the client's variations in interpreting these original outcomes, and their views of themselves doing the interpreting. A validity violation with outcomes may occur, when treatment is provided for baseline-assessed client characteristics that are defined in the here and now (at the time of the baseline measurement); but the treatment is altered in the process to address alternate behaviors, or more abstract character traits not initially measured. As a result, decisions may be made about treatment effectiveness (whether to use similar inputs, for similar phenomena in the future) based on a posttest which may in reality: represent the original baseline phenomena, one of the interim or alternate phenomena, or something entirely new.

Clients may certainly change along predetermined continua in a positive direction which is good, in and of itself, and may even report they are more satisfied. However, these reports can be conditioned responses to other relationship dynamics with the therapist, or conditioned responses to pronounced behavior change, which may not reflect attitude, decision, or self-concept change. It is difficult to attribute change to particular inputs when they are associated throughout treatment, to states of being which may have never been correctly or accurately defined. Likewise, changes in inputs, based on negative results, may be unwarranted if never clearly correlated with definable dimensions of the client's holistic and interactive self, in the first place.

Since the essential concern of science is the search of phenomenologic invariance[19] (including stable, patterned, or predictable variance, which may be construed as invariance), choices clinicians make in developing representations of phenomena, are critical. Over time, these representations and professional stereotyping may actually replace (accurately or inaccurately) the true phenomena that exist in clients. The counselor may, therefore, see clients in terms of artificial or unidimensional outcome categories, and consequently make decisions about changes relative to distorted biases, or well-intentioned scientific taxonomy. This is a particular problem when the behavioral laws or operating rules of reality are examined, suggesting that any particular state of the psychic organism, is a product of a combination of variables, some of which may be constant, while others vary. Therapeutic treatment may be planned intentionally, to change the rules by which psychosocial functions vary. In contrast, outcome measurement may narrowly encapsulate the behaviors or feelings after they have been caused, rather than observing and measuring the action-oriented formulae, which show they were caused as a function of an holistic gestalt of person-in-situation.

One law of behavior suggests that both the functional form of the psychic state (relationships between variables) and the parameters (nature, not amounts of factors), are universal constants. In this case, specific amounts of need deprivation, characteristics of home environment, amounts of nonsupport, and particular ego skill deficits, always combine in a predetermined formula to produce some degree of depression, if this is the state of being of clinical concern. The main goal of establishing validity, is to accurately measure predetermined constants. There should be less concern about whether the constants actually exist, and more concern about differentiating them from other extraneous variables, so their predictable interactive nature can be manifested and therefore validated. This is a very difficult and risky conceptualization for behavioral science at this stage of development, because of indefinite understanding of developmental causality of specific behaviors later in life; and wide variability of external and internal (self-awareness and subjective interpretation by clients) intervening variables. In this case, evaluators assume that they increase the probability of some degree of validity, by accurately noting the general outcome conditions that are present, across client histories with similar current symptoms. Counselors lose the validity-seeking struggle when they artificially control for varying client idiographic interpretations of childhood events, which are usually unreportable, or may be seriously subject to distorted recollections. These interpretations may become hazily submerged within clinical assumptions, either about specific behaviors, or specific states of identity; without recognizing the evaluative advantage of categorizing behaviors and identities in observable dynamic interaction.

In an alternate perspective about behavior, the functional form of the relationships is a universal constant, but some parameters (nature of specific factors) vary with external or internal situations, and are not part of contingent relationships that can be predicted within the formula. An example is a constant formula $(AB = C)$, where A times B always equals C, but the relationship holds together because of the numeric character of B, not because of its specific nature. In geometry, length times width always equals a mathematical area, yet the width is not necessarily consistent with the phenomena for which length is measured, for an arithmetic average to occur. It is uncertain, however, what the area represents when B changes, but the outcome is still an area of space, because the formula does not change.

In a psychosocial context, this means that specific childhood experiences combined with some amount of early adult experience, might equal "ego strength." The specific type of adult experience can vary and, therefore, threaten validity because its nature may not be discovered for each client, in addition to the amounts with which some form of potency is defined. In these cases, it is difficult to standardize across client histories. It is confusing to plan strategic inputs, since the formula varies with each client, and the specific nature of critical influential factors must be constantly, and probably incrementally, reassessed throughout the treatment experience. This is a problem for input selection as well, because the counselor may never be able to hypothesize which adult behaviors the client will define as therapeutically significant or influential. As a result, inputs may have to be almost randomly selected, to test client receptivity. Any baseline outcome may be invalid, as representational of change, until the influential inputs are selected during the course of therapy, so a baseline may be constructed.

In a third basic model of behavior, both the functional relationship and the parameters are specific, and there are no constants. This means that the natures of influences on the client are such, that they may produce different effects each time they appear (A causes B or C). One example, is when the same outcome effects are produced by different phenomena (good grades and uncle's smile, produce equal amounts of positive self-image enforcement in the child, A or B causes C). A second example is when A, B, and C are not related at all, sometimes due to the presence of other variables (client attention, client interpretation, or social system norms), but they are related at other times. The evaluation problem that results, is that it may not be possible to trace the outcome back to a logical and systematic causal event. The nature of the outcome, as the product of interactive prior relationships, is unreliable, and its essence must be interpreted irrespective of its linearity; or must be interpreted based on a comparison to some other standard outside the therapeutic arena altogether. In either case, its amorphous, fluid, and deceptive nature seriously hampers logical planning of inputs.

In order for many outcomes to be conceived as constant or relatively stable, they may have to occur in the context of a rigidly controlled and static personality organization (cognitive and behavioral structure), with few allowances for intervening variables, frequencies of variable manifestation, and variable valences (potencies)—so some degree of reliability, and maybe even validity, is gained. This may create, however, an overriding negative therapeutic environment, where there is little rationale for seeking positive measures, or assessing the entire personality configuration (which encases a specific outcome) more positively, since there are no degrees of freedom for any outcome to vary or change.

Quantitative Components of Outcome Variables

The stated goal of evaluation is to correctly and consistently define phenomena (pieces of a puzzle that represent realty, or someone's facsimile thereof), and measure the presence and degrees or amounts of those variables, so decisions can be made relative to status changes which represent different levels of socially defined adequacy, adjustment, or happiness of the clientele. As therapeutic activity occurs, success or failure is determined by these decisions, as they reflect whether an outcome (1) continues to be present (qualitative, nominal measurement); (2) appears in different prioritized order (qualitative, ordinal measurement); (3) is associated with other variables in interrelated degrees of concomitant value (correlation); (4) causes other variables to appear; or (5) appears in different degrees or amounts under varying circumstances (quantitative, interval, or ratio measurement). In all circumstances, an assumption is frequently made about validity and constancy, suggesting that varying appearances or amounts of phenomena, mean that the phenomena have remained the same in nature, but simply decreased or increased in some conception of volume, length, weight, or other form of potency.

When discussing quantity or amount, therefore, clinicians must be constantly aware of whether the quantitative conception (as frequencies or amounts change on empirical or perceptual scales) continues to refer to the original phenomena, or whether there are times when particular frequencies of events (even nominal presence vs. absence of [f = 1 or 0]), actually signify the event itself has changed, to a new definitional category. One example, is whether or not a rage-induced abusive attack on a spouse is really a quantitatively high range of the phenomenon of anger, or whether anger, as it increased, actually caused a new phenomenon to develop, like dependency. Another example, is whether battlefield heroism examplifies high levels of altruistic patriotism, or low/medium/high levels of psychotic fear and cognitive disorganization.

Because of the client's selective interpretation of every outcome (the potency may change,[20] even as a simple result of degree of attention), the notion of quantity as a shared collective ideation between counselors and clients, comes under scrutiny. This is because clients may utilize an internal perceptual quantitative index of their own attitudes or behaviors, not identified in the empirical external referent behavior, defined for measurement purposes by counselors. Clinicians should remember that idiosyncratic values and emotional agendas may be influenced by frequencies or quantities (large frequencies may cause clients to cognitively subtract amounts relative to overall self-image), and may in turn, influence how clients envision quantitative phenomena (low amounts of self-esteem may cause clients to see minimal frequencies of marital communication as quite excessive). The important point is that quantity and quality are elusive and confusing ideas, requiring precise definition, but also must be coded to accurately reflect the unique perceptual and value worlds of each client, who is the subject of the evaluation. Also, the act of choosing to recognize any particular outcome, carries a value judgment about the choosing behavior, and the freedom to choose depending on choice processes; which adds definitional category to the outcome (i.e., chosen variable, forced perceived variable, high frequency variable because it is chosen). This may significantly alter the meaning itself, as this outcome becomes a value-laden stimulus for other outcome events. Conceivably, a significant linear chain reaction may be established, which is also a prelude for defining subsequent events and outcomes. As the quantitative amount changes (e.g., increases in anxiety), although the nature of behavioral indicators may ostensibly remain constant, but change in frequency distribution; the variable itself may become something entirely different, within the client's scope of real or symbolic meaning. This transformation may necessitate commensurate change in behavioral indices of frequency, since the development of new variables may mean that old behavioral indices cannot be changed symbolically, to match the client's conversions. An example is a client who perceives high frequency counts of stressful behavior, which signifies high levels of childhood self-perception (especially when the stress should be minimal, given the actual nature of the client's milieu). The client may cognitively decide to regress to a new level of childhood self-image wherein the stressful behaviors, related to pre-regression childhood status (higher level of adaptation), may no longer be adequate commentaries on the status of the more regressed child. New behaviors may be required for measurement, which could actually provide data to signify lower actual frequencies of stress than previously noted. Yet, these lower-scaled quantities may be more negative in some ways, because they correspond to a more deeply regressed state. Within this state, however, they may be more positive than higher frequencies in the same state, or lower frequencies at a higher state of adaptation.

As an outcome variable ceases to be externally and ostensibly present (overt anxiety, for example), it may become so potent (high frequency) as to necessitate its perceptual movement (by the client's defensive system) to a more centrally protected point of within-ego location, and become another different acted out behavior.[21] It may also become unconscious, and then join with other amounts (e.g., of similar or different variables, conflicted feelings), combine, or change— to vastly increase its potency, while remaining invisible to the observing evaluative eye. This change in meaning may also occur as order of appearance and functionality change, as in moving from an insignificant outcome response to a more significant stimulus, while still remaining a consequence of antecedent causes.

An example is when a passive response to a stressful event changes to an apparently more active response or stimulus, wherein the more active stimulus is both a changed frequency of a former response (more activity on an active-passive scale), and is a stimulus in its own right; therefore needing measurement on a new stimulus-related scale, even though it is still responsive to the antecedent causal stimulus.

In defining intensity of an outcome variable, not only is development of a precision instrument extremely difficult, but the phenomenon itself (a particular feeling, for example) may not be capable of conception on an interval-type basis, on a set mathematical theoretical scale—since "experienced"[22] intensity does not necessarily correspond to an accumulation of experientially definable elementary units (asking what one unit of depression means, for example, may be impossible). It may seem easy to perceive greater or lesser amounts of depression over regulated trials of clinical observation, without ever coming fully to grips with the question of what or how much there was before, and whether the domain of depressive mood can be broken down, into any types of units of perceiving or observing.

Negative-Positive Qualitative vs. Quantitative Natures of Outcomes

Measurement of outcomes for any particular client is only relevant, if a value judgment is made about those outcome frequencies, which registers a positive or negative (or possibly neutral) nature, relative to client needs assessment and consumer satisfaction indices, associated with clinical goals and objectives. In this regard, it is essential to establish a framework to predetermine a range or continuum of negative and positive behaviors. It is also necessary to establish categories of frequencies to be observed, to register positive or negative opinions by those to whom the outcome is applied. This systematic projective evaluation is identical to the MBO (management by objective) scheme of deciding goals in advance, then measuring degree of accomplishment. It is also similar to the statistical procedure of defining critical values in significant percentage areas of a normal distribution (theoretical) model, within which the sample mean $(\bar{X})$ needs to fall to reject the null hypothesis, so degrees of confidence can be projected for various outcomes.[23] Because of the selective and changing (linear, curvilinear, random) nature of client thinking, reasoning, and assessment of outcomes; it is difficult, yet important, to understand how positive vs. negative decisions are made. This ensures that categorical judgments and their outcome possibilities are based on the nature, or changing nature, of the client's idiographic cognitive or feeling phenomena.

Delineation of past and potential categories of positive or negative decisions and projected referential behavioral outcomes, helps clinicians anchor observations in a client-centered value framework, not only to avoid counselor interpretive bias, but to assist in continually focusing the treatment plan. This helps clinicians differentiate the relative influences of treatment variables, vs. environmental circumstances, vs. client self-talk, where value-oriented outcome units can be directly linked (from study of past patterns) to either type of stimuli.

It is, of course, very difficult to decide when mood, for example, changes from negative to positive (or vice versa), and when relevant ordinal subunits of negative or positive dimensions help clarify, and lend increased specificity, to explanation and assessment of the personality. This decision can be vastly improved, however, when counselors help clients identify various domains of feelings, so they can see the differences qualitatively. The definition of quantifiable behaviors then takes on greater meaning, as they manifest within an explanatory category, developed deductively from knowledge of the client's needs and overall goals for various states of being.

In the effort to make clinically—as well as scientifically—significant decisions about single case outcomes, evaluation must, as closely as possible, verify that positive or negative changes (not just behavioral frequency differences) are the result of the therapeutic intervention, rather than some other simultaneously active influence on the client, which would have produced a positive, negative, or neutral change anyway.[24] In the case of positive changes, the external influence may have produced an even greater positive change, had the therapeutic intervention not been present. In these cases, clients may view the positive change less positively, because the presence of therapy makes them feel inadequate or less healthy. The therapeutic ingredients may actually impede or retard progress. In other cases, drastic behavioral frequencies materialize, but may be insufficient to symbolically represent a positive value for clients. A small frequency change may represent a major value alteration in the client's mind. As Baer, Wolf, and Risley note, "What is needed are demonstrations that changes in behavior are under control of a specific therapeutic procedure, that desired (positive vs. negative) behavior can be turned on and off, or up and down by manipulating the therapeutic program."[25]

The positive or negative nature of outcomes is, of course, directly related to some frequency occurrence of empirically observable or reportable behavior. These frequencies place a particular outcome in a positive-negative evaluative category, to which clients attach social value and feeling; but reciprocally interdependent judgments also help control continued manifestations of varied behavioral frequencies, and are compared more globally to overall states of being or conditions of the psyche (or relationship), which constitute a second and more abstract layer of positive-negative judgments.

This raises a question of clinical significance or therapeutic criterion.[26] The importance of behavior change relative to enhancement of client functioning and need satisfaction, which is not directly comparable to specific frequencies of occurrences of defined behavioral events; always includes client subjective opinion about the events, and the way they (the behaviors) represent positive vs. negative qualitative states of being. For many behaviors, positive or negative quality may relate more to level and intensity, rather than frequency of occurrence.

In the specific case of marital satisfaction,[27] there has been much criticism of the psychometric translation of behavioral indices into qualitative states of relationship existence, because of subjective comparisons to normative criteria for marriages. Social pressure to present a desirable dyadic image, and the increased interactive behavior, may lead to greater clarity of marital dissatisfaction and decreasing levels of satisfaction overall.[28]

It is also possible for the therapist and client to make evaluative positive-negative decisions based on abstract qualitative data or impressions, rather than indexing qualitative judgments to ranges of quantitative frequencies. In these cases, it is essential that global qualitative decisions be separated from qualitative process functions of behavior, whose cumulative end result, not mere presence or frequency, necessarily dictates the positive-negative outcome judgment. A good example is the clinician who makes a positive evaluation of the phenomenon (1)—communication of formerly unrevealed message A to spouse—without considering that a positive assessment might only be relevant, after the effects of other interpersonal dynamics of this message are outlined, studied, and analyzed in terms of treatment goals and client developmental interpretation. The therapeutic importance, is that the decision to rate the interactions as positive, is not necessarily comprehensively defined to include a variable range of results of specific behavior, and therefore, is part of an external judgmental continuum; not really correlated with, or reflective of, specific variable characteristics of the client behavioral message under consideration. In this case, the behavioral continuum of communication dynamics is comparable to an external framework of success outcomes, which are precisely and uniquely associated only to each other—communication behavior A results in nothing relative to success category (1), so when behavior A is combined with communication behaviors B and C, then and only then, does it relate to success category (2). This can also be associated with a third continuum of responses from significant others, which may demand even different combinations of communication behaviors and responses, before success can be decided (see Figure 1).

Figure 1
Specific Behavior and Outcome Continuum

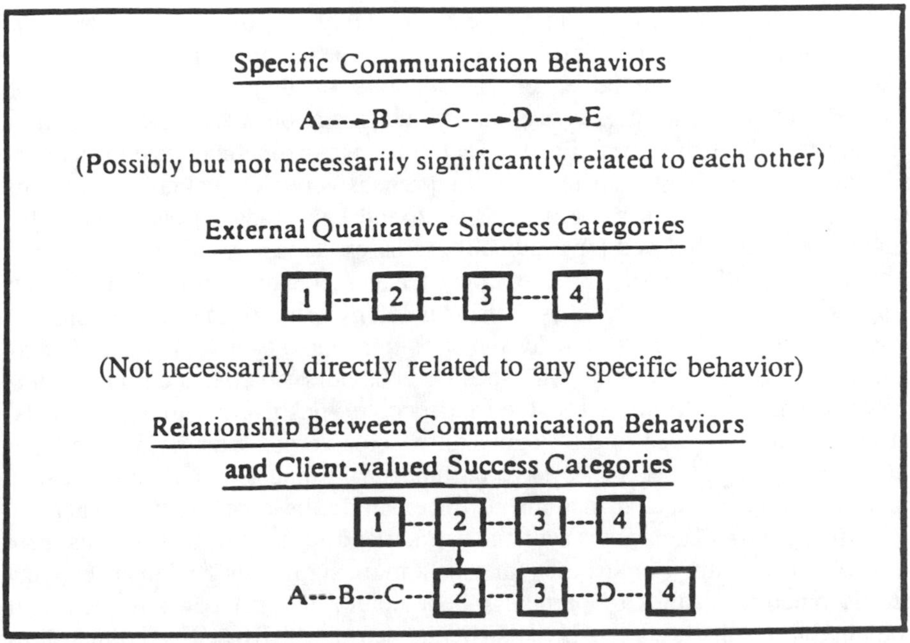

Specific Communication Behaviors

A----►B----►C----►D----►E

(Possibly but not necessarily significantly related to each other)

External Qualitative Success Categories

1 ---- 2 --- 3 --- 4

(Not necessarily directly related to any specific behavior)

Relationship Between Communication Behaviors

and Client-valued Success Categories

1 --- 2 --- 3 --- 4

A---B---C--- 2 --- 3 --D--- 4

A different continuum of positive judgments or decision-making categories, which relates only to communication behaviors A, or only to success outcome (1), would neglect to perceive the interrelationship of communication behaviors which, by nature, may only be relevant in combined sequences. This suggests that positive judgments may relate to some other phenomenon altogether, or may be associated with arbitrary categories which explain actual operational dynamics of the communicating client.

Another dimension of the natures of outcomes, is that negative or positive situational dimensions can frequently be confused with, or not differentiated from, broader functional or dysfunctional categories of identity. What may be positive behavior in one circumstance as a sign of growth, may not be positive at another time. Even more frequent, is the situation where a negative behavior (e.g., withdrawal) may be functional in some pathological relationship interchanges (although withdrawal might have formerly been defined as a negative trait, for the individual client), since the pathology in the relationship may increase due to negative results of the non-withdrawal behavior. Since positive and negative statuses can change and still be related to a single phenomenon, it is important to document circumstances involved in the change of positive-negative categories, and conceptualize these as distinct aspects of reality, having their own singular positive or negative denotation. The fact that behaviors (often the same or identical behaviors) can be either ego-adaptive or defensive, depending on environmental circumstances or the client's interpretation, means that qualitative behavior may be easily misdefined. Therefore, it is sometimes appropriate for the clinician/client therapeutic team, to comprehensively plot qualitative behaviors in advance, so the client has a map of good and bad roads; as each analyzable behavior must be observed longitudinally, to assess long-term affects—and only then be given a P-N label. Since therapy teaches clients to plot and plan their thoughts, and project ambushes by their own defensive/destructive cognitions and those of significant others, the idea of positive and negative judgments may require a more rigid definition with specific behaviors, so clients do not become torn by seemingly arbitrary (from their perspective) positive-negative judgments, at times when they need to developmentally perceive consistency in their inner and outer worlds. Clients who have problems with anger as a defense against fear of arbitrary parental abandonment, for example, become confused when the therapist suggests that anger is sometimes good and sometimes bad. Adjustment processes of reasoning, in this case, may be a more significant goal than changing specific outcome natures of particular behavior or thought content. A major problem that results however, is the difficulty setting relatively fixed dimensions or parameters of variable outcomes categories. There is no way to control client-relevant environmental circumstances, to insure that the natures of variables are not redefined; and that relevant frequency ranges which correspond to judgments about them, remain within normative parameters for individual clients, or other pertinent members of their social system. Comparison between clients is also difficult under these circumstances.

One approach to this dilemma, is to have a different framework available for variable environmental characteristics of each client-social system configuration (like changing a camera lens setting, for close vs. distant, day vs. night pictures). This becomes the judgmental standard for interpreting specific behavioral meanings. This process, however, is logistically confusing, and complicates the task of evaluating clients' total life experiences and/or transitions between divergent scenes in their social system.

Another approach has layers of lenses, so all spectra (or evaluative foci) are focused on the total environment at all times (like cameras at a sports event that cover any action that develops, and even cameras that watch the cameras). A total picture is then taken at repeated intervals, and analyzed for evaluative significance of separate, interactive, and convergent scenes. This approach is also logistically difficult, but at least it helps clinicians remember that there are multiple evaluative and judgment perspectives that give different findings, based on varying aspects of the scenarios being observed. These issues must be thought through carefully by clinicians, before positive-negative labels become part of the evaluative program.

The overall process discussed above has been called "criteria setting and appraising"[29] by one author, which refers to the establishment of value-laden categories of client performance, that correspond to selected properties of particular elements of performance. As long as the nature of the performance (identity) does not change, frequencies of behavioral manifestations can indicate particular types and dimensions of value, necessary for consumer/social service accountability.

Also, relative to concern with positive vs. negative decisions, there may be subunits not necessarily connected to an end product; not observable in the client's environment; or not yet observable, but requiring time to develop (before positive/negative values are attached). For example, some aspects of client internal psychological adjustment require positive evaluative judgments. The social outcome of these changes may retain a negative or neutral assessment, depending on overall goals of therapy, and degree to which the client and therapist have causally connected both internal and external phenomena, and the philosophical significance placed on both. Some therapists who are strong believers in powerful environmental control of individual destiny, suggest that positive-negative type criteria be considered in terms of degree of probability of positive outcome.[30] This may be seen as a ratio of internal to environmental strength, or a formula depicting positive or negative determinations, as a result of complex relationships between several related factors.

The traditional casework or individual psychology model, suggests that negative outcome awareness typically be recycled back through the individual psychic system for responsive positive readjustment, yet in many social situations, there may be a positive functional outcome for relationships between person and milieu:

A   = type and strength of previous socialization
A1 = degree of fixed and unidimensional nature of socialized facts, ideas, beliefs
B   = actual developmental level (e.g., ego skills, level of maturity, etc.)

C = strength of current social network or system

C1 = need for conformity to social system, for survival in real world circumstances

C2 = significance of client's value of social groups or environment

D = specificity of learned adaptive skills, or degree of centrality of changed perceptions to client's perceived core of his or her personality

E = client's subjectively perceived satisfaction with services rendered

F = quality of the therapeutic relationship

Even though each area requires precise operationalization, and the overall schema needs the addition of other areas, the concept gives at least some idea of how judgmental (positive or negative) model building accompanies the delivery of clinical services, for a person-in-situation relative to an outcome perspective. An example of one possible formula for decisions, resembles the one below:

$$A = (A1)^2 + B + C + \frac{D \cdot F - E}{C1 \cdot C2} = \text{Positive vs. Negative Decision}$$

As these cognitively or mathematically constructed formulae or other models are considered, the therapist must work with the client to understand (and maybe change) who is responsible for making final positive-negative judgments about sub-outcomes or outcomes, and specifically how they are made. This is important because this evaluative process may be an outcome itself, but also because it documents individual and social role requirements and adaptations. This insures the client has a significant, yet objective (as objective as possible) perspective via the use of outside feedback, planned empirical individual and social behavioral goals, spiritual and philosophical awareness, and solicitation of input from the therapist. This is particularly important when working with children, the elderly; and involuntary, psychotic, or drug abusing clients—whose lives are often intricately (not necessarily favorably) intertwined with significant others who have legal responsibility, social sanction, or other reasons for assuming decision-making power in their lives.

Positive or negative evaluations (whether made by the client, therapist, a significant other) are associated with, and may have their nature partly determined by, the values about evaluation that occur; and values about the existential relevancy of having specific decision points, about specific units of behavior, occurring at any particular time. This may be an issue of style, a cultural variant, a passive vs. active philosophy of living, or a reflection of the presence or absence of specific types of data, and the need for more or less individual and social data prior to decision-making. Some authors, in fact, debate whether processes of self-evaluation are, in fact, psychological universals. If the processes are generally the same for all individuals, positive or negative differences between individuals on outcomes, can be the only result of either different kinds of inputs into the self-evaluation and the therapeutic growth process; or differential effects of the environment, as an independent or intervening variable. If, on the other hand, observed differences in outcome (e.g., self-esteem ratings between black and white clients) are noted, this may not suggest there are necessarily different inputs (e.g., different types of therapeutic skill utilization, or specific potency of one cognitive idea). What it may suggest, is that the ways of assessing esteem and making positive-negative judgments, reflect different cultural perspectives and, more specifically, differences in "interactive instrumentalism";[31] where the self is viewed in specific, but different ways as a handler of data, an interpreter of outcomes, or a decider about how to process information.

Another dimension of the consideration of clients as "deciders" about outcome, is the cognitive set manifested by clients relative to their expectations of either positive or negative outcomes. Obviously, this phenomenon has been explained throughout the literature as a function of self-esteem, cultural deprivation, or learned access to social rewards. This cognitive process must be carefully considered by therapists as cognitive consonance (agreement between result and expectation), that may be some type of positive outcome in and of itself, which does not appear to correspond to a growth model. It may, instead, reflect the tendency of clients to be unaware of ways they interpret outcome data. In some circumstances, this means that dissonance between expected and observed outcomes, is a functional part of clients' assumed logical reasoning patterns, dealing with inner or outer reality (social acceptability of some outcomes).[32] These patterns provide intrapsychic or systemic balance (confirming a scapegoat family role), which the therapist examines to understand why positive or negative judgments are made of each outcome, and what each decision ultimately means to the clients.

Outcome Specificity

One set of complications in making empirical evaluative decisions about outcomes, is defining them, performing measurements, and making judgments about the meaning of outcomes, which precisely and specifically represent psychosocial phenomena (domains of the client's puzzle, or representation of reality). This is particularly troublesome because of concerns with significance (validity) and accuracy (reliability), over repeated trial and error episodes of association between therapeutic stimuli and client response, and vice versa. Ideally, attention to specificity should also help in diagnosing relationships between present behavioral manifestations and past developmental events, and in correlating particular therapeutic inputs with associated past or present outcomes (results), in clients' realms of thought, feeling, and activity.

In assigning particular behaviors as referents for feeling or cognitive states of being (identity or self-image), the operational boundary and unique positively valued acts are extremely difficult to pinpoint, because behaviors continuously run together, occur rapidly, have vague starting and stopping points, and lack external classificatory benchmarks for taxonomy. Defining behavior is also complicated, because frequency, variety, intensity, activity/latency characteristics, rate, amount, direction, duration, timing, juxtaposition to other behaviors, and other undiscovered dimensions; contribute to the appearance of the behavior, and also contribute to its unique meaning for each client.[33] Walking down the street, for example, can be accomplished with varying torso positions; arm, hand, and leg movements; distances and speeds; and hosts of actual and symbolic motivations for traveling. Not only is it hard to categorize any of these with unstructured observations clients often use in reporting (even if motivated to be good objective observers),[34] but the fine line between torso position that reflects depression, physical fatigue, disability, excitation, psychological happiness, etc., is often difficult to differentiate.

In working with clients who are physically demonstrative in style, the external parameters of particular behaviors may be more pronounced and obviously visible (e.g., clients who show anger), yet crisis or regressive states may keep behavioral demonstrations at the same premorbid levels, so the clinician does not become aware of serious internal changes. Conversely, crisis behaviors may become less obvious relative to normal ranges, so counselors may not notice them in this case either. Clients with normally less demonstrative style, may experience equally significant behaviors, but manifest them in smaller increments with less physiologic potency, making specific definition difficult as well.[35]

A good example noted in the literature, is the dilemma in defining, detecting, and measuring the variable "violence potential" in clients, as opposed to "overt violent action."[36] There is difference in opinion about how to specifically define violent behavioral outcomes,[37] and which behavioral indices most consistently represent various types and stages of the violent attitude, or response pattern.[38]

In addition to this definitional problem, there are numerous subcomponents of aggression or violence, for example: angry vs. instrumental aggression as a motivation issue,[39] internal inhibition vs. external instigation influences, strength of the habitual aggressive pattern, degree of perceived injury to the self (identity),[40] levels of destructiveness, and the need for social approval and environmentally available external positive evaluation.[41]

"It would appear . . . that the constructs anger, hostility, and social desirability are, in some way, associated with violence. To date, however, no theory or study has been able to identify the exact nature of the inter-action between these variables, a situation which is believed to be due in part to a lack of agreement as to what constitutes a violent act. The pur-pose of the present study was 'to ascertain the usefulness of several existing measures of hostility, anger and social desirability in the assessment of violence potential.' It was assumed, based on the available literature, that the assessment of violence is a complex problem requiring multiple assess-ment of interacting variables, and that an explicit, operational definition of the term 'violence' was essential to a meaningful outcome. Obviously, situational variables as well as other factors such as personality variables suggested by Megargee may influence violence potential. Owing to the fact that instruments or procedures for measuring these variables have yet to be adequately developed, however, their contribution to the assessment of vio-lence potential will have to be determined at a later date."[42]

In many cases, numerous behavioral themes are integrated to present composite pictures of an attitude or feeling, as in Flanagan's Critical-Incident Technique (see Reference 35). However, this does not answer the question of whether any particular behavior or collection thereof, can be precisely defined to correctly represent a personality condition under a specific set of circumstances. Many clinicians and researchers, of course, suggest that some behaviors are reflective of gross phenomenal dimensions (e.g., hitting or not hitting a child), easily seen and evaluated. Although this may assist in competent evaluation, it may neglect more subtle, incremental, and nonphysical cognitive outcome mani-festations which exist (and can be interpolated), on a continuum between the gross hit-or-not-hit outcomes. These outcomes may be closely paired with clinical inputs, for more immediate feedback about incremental approximations of desired behavior. Also, many styles of living have gradients of behavior (spanking is allowed, but abusive hitting is not O.K.). Particular dimensions, frequencies, or potencies of a pattern are considered nominally; but other dimensions of the same type of behavior, become examples of excessive, inappropriate, or deviant action, when given quantifiable dimensions.

This also occurs when two behaviors are identical (husband asking wife a question) but one ridicules, suppresses individuality, or intimidates; and the other is intended to gain information. Precise evaluation demands careful attention, not only to the idiosyncratic meaning clients give to a behavior, but also to the meaning attached to behavioral consequences in the environment, relative to social system and culture.

Another problem, is that physically observable behavior (even rapid reflex action) is reactive to antecedent cognitive-affective behaviors (thoughts, judgments about the self and others), which are even more difficult to specify. The therapist who helps clients assess and change cognitions, must systematically take small incremental steps retrogressively back from observable behavior, and help clients carefully describe their thoughts, and develop a model by which these cognitive behaviors are associated and validated with their consequent physical manifestations. These thoughts are not necessarily related to consequent physical behaviors, so must be defined and assessed as totally separate phenomena, and then considered as potential sets of interrelated actions, particularly if therapeutic inputs are directly aimed at these cognitions.

Many times the behavior of interest, in fact, is the absence of a particular behavior (especially with schizoid, dependent, passive-aggressive clients), and it is hard for the clinician to differentiate a resting state of the individual, from a functionally nonpurposive or regressive state. In one family, the wife refuses information to her husband about the children's activities, as an expression of anger (i.e., purposive refusal to communicate). It is difficult to differentiate between her non-communication as an expression of rest, and relaxation from communication. The definition of these two distinct physical behaviors appears identical, and each only has meaning if specificity is possible through intense view of eye movements, small muscle action, biofeedback functions, etc; or there is specific association of this, to other behaviors in the family (e.g., significant behavior by the children that would interest the husband, if he knew about it). Associating behaviors that do not logically or sequentially appear related, requires hypothesizing and conjectural work, and leaves more room for error than is ideal, if more precision could be attached to specific behavior of the mother.

When projective tests and standardized attitude measures define feelings or global states of being, the evaluator is faced with interesting dilemmas. On one hand, attitude and personality assessment inventories, having demonstrated validity and reliability via statistical analysis, are very useful for comprehensive premorbid and posttest assessments. On the other hand, they often are not specific enough to detect fine nuances in client behavior (physical, cognitive, affective), to be of much use incrementally, in guiding particular interventive tactics. Although they often successfully assess overall nonspecific strategies for practice, or cumulative effects of specific inputs, they give no guidance about the efficacy of any unitary aspect of therapeutic influence. This leaves considerable room for erroneous assumptions, and interpretations of cause-effect relations.

The following additional points concerning standardized measurement devices, should be kept in mind:

First, the accuracy of measures should be validated through repeated testing of norm groups, and can give general impressions of specific traits, and referent assessment of general traits.

Second, although many items on standardized tests are specific, they are typically related to attitudes or feelings ("I like dramatics"—item 126 of standard MMPI examination), leaving considerable margin for symbolic and individually selective interpretation.[43] The more closely the test item relates to a specific client problem and form of input; the more accurate, effective, and useful the measurement strategy, unless the client clearly sees herself or himself in the question, and answers defensively.

Next, general attitudinal measures are often so global that taken singularly, they could yield the same pre-posttest results, and be interpreted positively one time and negatively another; since changes in more specific, and possibly more basic areas of identity, could occur in the client in the interim.[44] This problem is partly corrected by the process of accumulative item tabulation. However, evaluation remains invalid if the client does not accumulatively build perspectives the way the norm group data suggests, if qualitative answers on global attitude outcomes are not sensitive to client interpretations of the meaning of the item, or if the items are not corroborated with behavioral counting, or other observational criteria.[45]

Another concern about testing, is that standardized items are predicated on hypothesized behaviors that the client may have experienced in the past, desires or fears for in the future, is currently engaged in, or may have repressed but unconsciously acted out. The actual roles of these behaviors and their specific empirical definitions, therefore, are unclear. Outcome results in either hypothesized behaviors or the test score, have a wide range of symbolic variability, with little opportunity for cross-validations through behavioral observation. Additionally, the list itself can be conceptualized as a dependency-related parent substitute, so a host of transferential issues obscure actual outcome definition, or the meaning of any observation.

Finally, most standardized tests are not coded or skewed to reflect specific cultural norms, values, or conceptual patterns. The behaviors alluded to in the items, may have differential outcome meaning for individual clients; and may be represented with different degrees of symbolic cultural relevance, potency, and interdependent value (when related to other culture-bound behaviors), than is the case for the norm group. Although this does not suggest that standardized tests cannot be used with clients from different cultures, it does mean that culture-specific tests are needed, and clinicians must insure that questions accurately reflect the client's unique interpretation.

Outcome Potency and Amount

Problems related to specificity of outcomes, concern how the clinician understands and determines varying degrees of external forcefulness or internal power/influence of feeling, thought, or behavioral outcomes; and how to interpret and change these valences (in conjunction with, and also separate from, repetition frequencies) within clients' psychodynamic frame of reference. Changes in potency or power of an angry outburst, for example, may have tremendous significance as an incremental index, that the client perceives in a less vulnerable status vis-à-vis a friend or spouse. Changes are hard to observe and measure systematically, even though they are part of the casework dialogue all the time (e.g., "I was much less angry today," or "I notice you seem more attentive today"). An important evaluative question for clients in these situations, relates to how they make decisions about behavioral potency (distinct from frequency of repetition or occurrence), and what categories exist conceptually, to correlate variably perceived (by clients) degree ranges of potency, with varying states of being (adequacy, vulnerability, autonomy, etc.).

The outcome cognition and feeling which occur before, during, and after the specific behavior, may not be assumed to exist at the same point on a strength of response scale, or may even be most validly measured and represented on an entirely different scale. A good illustration of this, are various potencies of behaviors and feelings seen in a report of outcome research, in an alcohol treatment program.[46] Initially, a series of interdependent behavioral outcome measures were established (e.g., amount of daily drinking, blood alcohol level, residential stability, aftercare program attendance, etc.) for clients in treatment.[47] One important finding in the analysis of data,[48] was that there were distinct positive behavioral changes during the official treatment program, but these frequencies did not have sufficient magnitude to be generalized beyond the program parameters, into the post-discharge follow-up period. One explanation, obviously, is that frequency levels can be sustained within programs due to the reinforcement of such behaviors, but do not have sufficient power bases or potencies of their own, to sustain them beyond the controlling influence of contingent reinforcers in the present time frame. In fact, data from this study also revealed that these high frequency, but low potency behaviors, actually resulted in diminished positive frequencies shortly after the program ended. Therefore, loss of the program as a reinforcer, may have produced a form of contradictory high potency negative self-image, and a higher potency behavioral effort or increase of deviant behavior, connected to the nature of the program itself.

The clinician must remember that frequency of occurrence of target behaviors, does not necessarily mean the client views the behavior as a powerful self-image reinforcer. There may be situations where high frequency behavior is cognitively associated with dependency, or low frequency behavioral occurrences are viewed by clients as powerful behaviors concerning their influence on either themselves or others.

The author has experienced this incongruency in therapy, where infrequent eye-to-eye connections with clients were more powerful, than more frequent words that came before or after. At times, a lower frequency confrontive question had more impact, than more numerous declarative sentences. One factor to be considered, however, is the relative frequency of each outcome in terms of system homeostasis, expectation, and the surprise impact of deviant outcomes on an unsuspecting listener.

In the previously mentioned alcohol study, there were also socio-psychological indices which were part of the assessment,[49] in which no major successes were noted among clients. This may show there was no change in emotional status commensurate with positive behavioral frequency, but there may have been undetected psychological potency increases, to counteract or handle any stress related to positive behavioral changes (no longer representing defensive safety nets). Undetected positive emotional potency changes singly did not appear in a short time period, or were not discovered by research evaluators. One particular finding of this study, was that dependency appeared to have a significant role, and a high potency of a dependent self-perception, was strongly associated with high frequencies of abuse, as opposed to moderate drinking.

Another example of this concern appears in the cognitive psychology literature,[50] wherein some authors suggest that traditional single case operant outcome
behavioral conceptualizations, are not appropriate to assess non-operant domains
of human outcomes relating to psychic processes, powers of self-assessment,
strength of learning, adaptation, and change.[51] Skinner[52] observes that operant
research methods create an atmosphere and condition of the environment, where
stimuli, responses, and reinforcements are connected via associated linkages.[53]
The problem with this approach, however, is that inner feeling awarenesses or
other measures of strength of cognitive impression, are not often overt in nature,
are often incremental and mobile rather than fixed, do not directly respond to
behavioral contingencies, and are difficult to measure.[54] This is confirmed by
Evans and Robinson[55] in their account of a depressed female client, whose case
study spanned 19 sessions. A diary compiled privately by the client, which
illustrated the complexity and conservative nature of cognitive change, was
studied. In the early stages of counseling, her thought patterns were general and
abstract, with little demonstration of problem-solving skills. The diary showed
progressive changes in cognitive ability and increasing concentration on specific
life events; she developed progressive, but slow, awareness of this change, as it
occurred within an interdependent cognitive-behavioral systemic field. This study
informally illustrated that the clinician may appear to produce change in
designated outcome thoughts or behaviors, while the client may not necessarily
develop independent ownership of these processes.[56]

In studying various domains of the client's psychosocial process, most
literature sources recommend that singular indicators, scales, or evaluative
perspectives have numerous shortcomings, which can be somewhat counteracted
by noting combinations of potency and frequency factors, as a measure to anchor
the evaluative data and enhance perception of more abstract inner variables. This
facilitates the discovery of "meaning," as in Argyle's studies of nonverbal behavioral quality,[57] in which descriptive statistics become increasingly important to
measure level or slope, which are data about products of action, rather than more
variously defined links between earlier stimulus and client response behavioral
frequencies.

One author[58] notes that the case record of therapeutic process, as well as
other forms of qualitative impressions by the counselor, provide research data
(which must be standardized and made as precise as possible) to ground perceptions and abstract generalizations. Clients become an important factor in
delineating and interpreting qualitative awareness or abstract feeling states, which
they often cannot operationally define in behavioral terms, but describe in
unscientific, sensory awareness language. A layperson's language must be more

vigorously used and standardized for evaluative comprehensiveness and controlled comparison.[59] The clinician must collect and document cross-validating information on qualitative outcomes (potency/amount) from as many separate, but interdependent, sources as possible. Denzen calls this the "logic of triangulation."[60]

Audiotapes, videotapes, process records, or case notes represent "continuous," rather than "interrupted" time series designs.[61] These designs provide relevant in-process data, without using artificial quantitative methods,[62] or distorting client intention.[63] As examples, Reyes Ramos found that notations of jazz music were useful in setting up parallel analytic criteria, relative to improvisation within typical human language;[64] while Richard Bandler and John Grinder employed concepts of "deep structure" within transformational grammar, in explaining some processes in delivering counseling inputs.[65]

Some social scientists contend that concepts from split-brain research point to analogical thinking, which helps the counselor understand some forms of personal and social interaction.[66] The use of paradox and poetic metaphors may be less helpful as part of traditional logic, but may be very helpful in other ways, when liberal use is made of alternate explanatory models of reality.

There is also a problem when potency is assessed for different outcomes (e.g., adaptive, and defensive behavior), since the potency of one set of variables may interact in unknown ways with the potencies of the others. Also, the potency of one outcome may not be the same phenomenon as the potency level in another, so they cannot be conceptualized even on the same or similar scales. Although a pound of feathers is the same weight as a pound of water, the concept of "pound" may have totally dissimilar connotations, when considering the two distinctly different concepts and may, in fact, create an illusion of association between them, which ultimately hinders the evaluative process. The same problem exists in assigning different potency values for anger, as distinct from delusional thought content or violent physical expression. To ignore the potencies of each of these may be as grave an evaluative error, as to compare them along similar dimensions.

Furthermore, from a psychosocial perspective, the clinician must also examine varying strength valences of different behaviors (outcomes) within the client's social milieu and cultural framework, since frequencies and potencies will be valued differently and result in different reinforcing or punishing social consequences, for each individual. Categories of socially-defined potency become benchmarks, to help interpret the specific behaviors elicited by clients.

Developmental Nature of Outcomes

One key, and possibly basic, component of outcomes, is that they are fluid in representing (actually and symbolically) different time frames (childhood, present adulthood, and future aspirations). They have a dynamic and developmental character as they change *form* with time, and *exposure* to various real and fantasized (also previously experienced) stimuli. Considerable learning therapy research, shows relationships between client behavioral outcomes at one point in time, and related, but changed, behavior subsequently.[67] This suggests (1) absence of strong learning continuity and cognitive pattern building (contradicted by our knowledge of socialization and cultural imprinting), and significant influence of associated learning stimuli; (2) some behaviors continue to demonstrate long-term responses to initial strong stimuli; (3) there is a continuum of action and reaction to sub-outcomes, with means that behavior has, to some extent, a life of its own and a cybernetic growth, change, or developmental loop which is self-reinforcing and interactive.

There is mounting research that clearly suggests outcomes have a developmental nature, but that this development is influenced by inputs from a clinical psychosocial-oriented program; which produces an adaptive, self-actualizing, and expanding payoff with passage of time, some environmental support, and successful achievement experiences.[68] In conducting single case experimental designs officially, or in applying less formal principles of standardized evaluation to cases, the idea of "data trends"[69] is very important. It helps identify stable baseline patterns, but also notes whether client outcome phenomena seem to be increasing or decreasing in any particular direction (trend or slope). It also calls attention to whether this invariability is related to significant intervening variables in the environment, or some self-contained developmental energy or dynamic influence, whereby clients learn from their own behavioral manifestations, and make adjustments vis-à-vis their phenomenologic and social conditions.

Sometimes this behavior may be constantly progressing or increasing in frequency, or regressing and moving backward toward the mean, or toward a baseline starting point. Also, the behavioral outcomes may manifest themselves in a random or multidirectional pattern, which may not be easily predicted. In any case, the important point is that behavior may be moving, active, alive, and dynamic, and has capability to forecast its own future through the developmental process of manifesting itself in the present, and then serving as its own stimulus for future interconnected outcomes.

Childhood-Related Outcomes

Most theories of development suggest there are distinct and usually measurable cognitive, affective, and behavioral types of conditions which reflect various stages of the growth process. In childhood, these behaviors are not static,[70] (although seemingly static behaviors are certainly observable), but dynamic. This means they have multiple layers of symbolic and evaluative meaning about motivation, parent-child relations, self-esteem, autonomy/dependency, etc.; which also have future action potentials as integral aspects of their nature.

The way the behavior is defined is certainly influenced by the "why?" of its occurrence, and also by intentionality, suggesting it cannot be seen in isolation, but as a consequence of, and prelude to, other connected aspects of a relationship gestalt. This is primarily supported by significant others in the child's milieu, whose adequacy and needs depend on the predictability (or assumed predictability) of the future; and the plan that expected outcomes will materialize as self-fulfilling prophecies, for maintenance of esteem and consistently growing identity. One example of a static definition of a dynamic behavioral situation, is the statement: "You can bring a horse to water, but you can't make him drink." It is certainly possible in the horse-water situation for (1) conditions to be conducive to the drinking behavior (trough availability); (2) motivation to be factored into the equation (feeding the horse salt to induce thirst); (3) level of deprivation to become a significant factor (withholding water), etc. In this example, motivation is essential in differentiating static from dynamic behavior, and suggests that even in childhood the apparently empirical behaviors which can be documented at any specified time, are in the state of motion. This motion is not always detectable (as in clock hand movement), or is detectable at stages which represent multiple behavioral units, incrementally combined or fulfilled to the point of mandating specific behavioral manifestations, which might obscure interactive catalytic influences.

Behaviors also dynamically change with time, opportunity, and stimulus; and some blossom or unfold (as in cognition) to create greater outcome opportunities and more developmental change, in a snowballing pattern. One dynamic which makes childhood behaviors complicated to understand, is that many develop and remain in existence because of the powerful and lasting nature of related behavioral-centered environmental contingencies (e.g., parental control of hysterical childhood manipulation). These are transposed conceptually by the client into adult time periods as a result of earlier trauma, developmental deficit, continued parental control, fear, or transference with the therapist. These functional dynamics[71] become one way of defining and classifying behaviors which ostensibly appear topographically different, although their past goal is to handle yesterday's regressive anxiety, and attempt to resolve conflict through childlike symbolic efforts. Understanding the dynamic functions of developmental behaviors, also helps the counselor define similar and different classes of maintaining, stimulus, or consequent behavior,[72] which are systematically related to target symptoms.

In deciding about the static versus dynamic nature of outcomes, the clinician must consider variables which make a consequence effective, the behaviors which produce the consequence, the consequence itself which maintains the antecedent behavior, and discriminative stimuli in whose presence behavior has produced this consequence. In addition to relevance and definition given to childhood behaviors regarding their stimulus and consequent conditions, the behaviors are also defined differentially, given their frequency and reason for emergence into adult cognitive constructs or behavioral repertoire, and in the process by which this entry (fixation, appearance of excess baggage) occurred. The evaluative problem for clinicians, is (1) how to identify and measure which behavioral outcomes are actually reactivated childhood outcomes, (2) how to determine what meaning the outcomes had within family of origin social systems, (3) how to classify client interpretations of outcomes' past meanings and present functions, and (4) how to also correlate specific therapeutic behaviors the client will or will not associate along any definitional continuum—with maintenance, change, or extinction of key targeted behavioral patterns.

Some therapeutic modalities specify that the client and therapist actually regress (re-parent and transfer) to earlier periods in the client's life, for redoing inadequate developmental sequences. Practitioners must also differentiate behaviors perceived by the client to be in the past, at the time of the therapeutic interventions; and when these outcomes either transfer to real present time in their unchanged state, or begin to *change* in either past or present time. Because the client is a key assessor of these meanings, and the symbolism and dynamic meaning may be unconscious, the therapist must conduct a thorough check, cross-check, and corroboration procedure to produce data convergence as frequently as possible, to assure validity and correct identification and interpretation.

Some definitional dynamic categories which counselors or caseworkers might encounter, are these:

1.   specific topographic and static manifestation of behavior, antecedents, and consequences,
2.   definition of childhood behavior by its functional stimuli,

3.   definition of childhood behavior by its functional consequences,
4.   definition of childhood behavior by its internally perceived symbolization, as a result of previous, but not current stimulus or consequent parental behavior,
5.   definition of adult behavior relative to actual/symbolic similarity to childhood behavior,
6.   definition of childhood behavior as functional within (stimulus and/or consequence) adult framework,
7.   dynamics of movement of childhood behavior between ego states and stimuli, to produce movement,
8.   definition of childhood behavior (in adult ego conditions) as adaptive within childhood expectations of inflexible significant others in the present,
9.   variations in childhood behavior to reflect differential control (including increases in negative acting out), as opposed to nonvariability to reflect helplessness,
10. specific childhood behaviors as degree of importance in reflecting states of identity and variability, as this does not represent commensurate variability of identity state.

In thinking specifically about outcomes, the therapist must continually bounce back and forth between present and past time, helping clients differentiate (1) which behaviors were appropriate, adaptive, life-saving (defensive), and functional in the past (and why they were); (2) which of these behaviors can be transferred to the present, for adaptive utility (e.g., asking questions, seeking nurturance); (3) which components of identity and self-other awareness can and cannot accompany more specific childhood behaviors into the present, and which parts of identity need to grow up and change; (4) which behaviors and identity states (usually defined as healthy superego and ego skills) observe, judge, and make decisions about past vs. present manifestations of personality and behavior, and how these external, more objective evaluative states of being sustain themselves, and exist outside more subjective states of being (here and now child and adult); and (5) which behaviors and states of identity can be mobile, and actually thrive via their processes of movement between past, present, and future conditions of the personality. This latter outcome is difficult to define and measure, because the child vs. adult existence, functionality, and relevance may not be consciously known to the client, and the client may be resistant to revelations or changes in these possible pathological, but undoubtedly stable, parts of personality organization and operation.

Stimulus-Response Relations Between Outcomes

Another feature of specific outcomes related to their developmental nature (particularly childhood growth outcomes, even if they appear in adult life or adult cognitive perceptual systems), is that they have the potential, energy, influence, and interconnected nature, to cause changes in other perceptions, events, or behaviors (other outcomes); and internally cause self-stimulated changes in their own nature. Just as children learn to walk and move farther away from parental control into a broader world, so do they commensurately redefine the self which, as self-definition improves, causes greater movement even farther into an expanding world.

The idea of internal relationships within a particular configuration of behavioral phenomena, is noted in the literature in an example related to self-concept, as one form of outcome.[73] Based on this literature's request for analyses of areas of congruence between conceptual and operational definitions of the construct self-concept,[74] a nomological network[75] was identified, where within-network studies investigated relationships among component and interactive parts of the self-concept phenomenon (e.g., physical, academic, social facets). This can be contrasted with between-network's emphasis on how the total self-concept, considered more holistically, interacts with separate variables (e.g., achievement, social adjustment). In some cases, in fact, within-network studies are considered necessary antecedents to the study of between-network phenomena.[76]

The importance of relationships between outcomes, is also seen in the literature describing persistence of therapeutic change, where specific factors are hypothesized which interactively contribute to long-term maintenance of changed status, and even to improvement in previous levels of change (usually noted relative to behavioral frequencies, attitude measures, or adaptive self and significant other reports).[77] Some variables found to be interactive with outcome indices, are pretherapy adjustment factors, socioeconomic status, marital status changes, number of therapy sessions, important life events, etc.[78]

In one study,[79] there was modest improvement in therapeutic gain in a post therapeutic (after termination) treatment period, when the independent treatment variable was withdrawn. This gain was evidenced on several predictors associated with degree of neuroticism, extroversion, locus of control, and socioeconomic status. It was noted that persistence of change was related to life event outcomes, such as relationship changes, occupational change, social support, and changes in socioeconomic status. This caused changes in targeted outcomes, beyond the patterns seen between baseline and posttest measures. This study suggests that many, if not all, outcomes possess energy for influence, change, and movement that, as variable factors themselves, must be assessed and measured for their potential for stimulating change. This is, so that predictions can be made about (1) which outcomes are most powerful among an array of possible phenomena that might be produced therapeutically; (2) which outcomes (because of their potency) should precede rather than follow other outcomes; and (3) which outcomes should be associated (and how the client must be helped to associate them) with others, so the nature of influence (types of effects produced) can work in an organized sequential cumulative fashion, to produce overall, long-term personality improvement.

An example of this, is the particular outcome thought or cognitive behavior of a client: "I might be an independent evaluator of the adequacy of my own behavior in many situations." This cognitive piece of present reality can certainly stand alone, and be judged by the clinician as one isolated example of client growth, particularly given the converse nature of previous conceptualizations which might have exited. If this thought is being perceived by a client who has transported themselves back in time to childhood conflicts about autonomy, self-control, etc.; the thought itself may have developmental stimulus potency to produce a second thought: "I have the diminished ability to disagree with my parents about their perceptions of who I should date," followed by a third self-directed, angry thought of disappointment about "how trapped I have been all these dependency-laden years." These thoughts may lead to a thought about how "I chose my current occupation to passive-aggressively rebel against my parents," and to a final thought expanding on the first thought: "I am not an independent evaluator of the adequacy of my own behavior, in most situations." These thoughts could then be followed by an angry behavior directed to the therapist, upon whom the client has been dependent in a pseudo parent-child relationship. Evaluative decisions about the first outcome and the wisdom of producing it therapeutically, or making decisions about it, are directly related to the outcome's ability to stimulate changes in itself.

The final outcome only has meaning, therefore, if analyzed and assessed in the context of its significant relation to antecedent and consequent outcomes. The clinician must conjecture about whether encouragement of the final expression of anger (via behavior) could, in reverse order, subsequently produce the cognitions representative of adult autonomy; and should compare the stimulus potential of both ends of this stimulus/response continuum.

In considering psychodynamic conflict, there are outcomes achieved as a result of therapeutic input, that relate to the client's perception and life as a fearful child within an adult body. There are also changes which occur to the adult, who has a fearful child somewhere within. It is unclear how changes in one area cause, or are associated with, changes in the other life space; and the degree to which units of outcome change in one area, can be translated meaningfully into significant changes in the other. However, the counselor must be constantly aware of the locus of intervention, or the venue (life space locality) of entry perceived by the client, and type and degree of change the client will allow and validate. After this occurs, one outcome in childhood may interact with other thoughts or feelings in the adult condition, so new outcome changes in each separate and/or new additive effect, result from outcome combinations.

This process can also occur regarding two outcomes within the child or adult, or between ego states as previously discussed. As natural contingencies[80] develop between outcomes (e.g., the frightened child begins to think that parental injunctions were/are subjective and non-absolute, and this child sees less need for their adult compulsive behavior to control anxiety, or resolve the conflict), the outcomes develop an interactive life of their own that the counselor can monitor, as changes set up chain reactions and cause reciprocal interaction changes in other outcomes. There is a critical ratio of child to adult behaviors $\left(\dfrac{C}{A}\right)$ of negative, positive, or mixed dimensions, contributing to the overall definitions of the personality, $\left(\dfrac{-C}{-A}\right)$ $\left(\dfrac{+C}{-A}\right)$ $\left(\dfrac{-C}{+A}\right)$ $\left(\dfrac{+C}{+A}\right)$ which is difficult to understand and certainly more complicated to measure.

The nature of this ratio and interactive outcome relations, is a significant determiner of client change and improvement. There is also a relationship between defensive behavior and adaptive, healthy behavior. Many clients the author has experienced, are cognitively intelligent and aware of their conflicts, but allow a relationship between their defensive awareness of the conflict, and healthy potential change. This relationship symbolizes safety or adequacy for them, which would not occur if their defensive behavior had failed. The relationship between defensive and adaptive outcomes seems in many respects, to prevent some clients from perceiving their lives as separate, changeable entities. Examples of this dilemma, are clients who play games and say they understand their conflict or fear, yet because of the degree of this understanding and the interactive balance between pro and con, decide not to make any changes in their best interests and, therefore, retain other destructive behaviors, thoughts, or feelings.

There is a consistency in this ratio relationship;[81] and the nature of this relationship between defensive, pathological, and adaptive behaviors, keeps the personality balanced, and to some degree intact, as a functioning organism at some presumed level of security and equilibrium. The adaptive character of defense, in fact, may be one outcome therapists can illustrate to clients, as a positive dimension of self-preservation/control. The illustration might, in turn, cause some changes in a childlike perception, that formerly implied to the client that the self has no protective mechanism, and is hopelessly vulnerable.

The counselor should help each client examine these outcome relationships, especially since an outcome behavior can also have its own developmental (maturational unfolding) process which, in time, causes it to become a changing outcome, thereby causing differing effects on other outcomes that are also unfolding. It is often confusing to decide which direction the influential stimulus/ response energy is going; which end of the continuum is the independent variable or the dependent variable; or whether the movement is from the center outward, in progressing or regressive directions. The counselor must hypothesize a variety of relationships, and systematically check them out with each client through observations, questions, and especially confrontations to block presumed associations, to study resistance the client elicits to keep the relationship intact. A case example of the confusing direction of stimuli and responses, is when the client behaves in a way in the present that is defined as failure, and then makes regressive redefinitional, negative decisions about previous marginal (neither failure nor success decisions have been made by the client) behaviors, which confirm a negative identity. This leads to assumptions about highly probable future failures.

In this case, influence conceivably can go in at least two directions, with questions about the number of times the stimulus-response nature of outcomes causes or allows directional changes or reversals; and then, whether the directional changes themselves influence other outcomes. Another example of this is seen in the literature that suggests a relationship between control of hostility, overt expression of deviant behavior, and capabilities of the environment to produce instigating ideas. It is unclear whether any one of these factors is part of a causal or responsive chain of events, yet they seem associated in some definable relationship.[82]

In some cases, there are also outcomes that have little stimulus energy for their own unfolding, or for influencing other outcomes (sometimes they do not have stimulus value because the client is resisting, unmotivated, or does not invest them with energy potency). These low energy outcomes must also be identified and measured. Decisions must be made about their utility to (1) fill space until outcomes with a higher potential payoff valence can be produced, or emerge naturally/developmentally; (2) enhance the therapist/client relationship, but with little insight or change function; (3) create anxiety by disrupting systemic homeostatic patterns, but only give a blocking rather than change-producing effect; (4) nurture the therapist so s/he can resolve his/her own conflict, or feel more adequate (without direct benefit to the client), but may have an indirect client benefit by facilitating sustained, reinstated positive, and energetic input on the part of the therapist (see Figure 2):

Figure 2
Developmental Outcome Claims

M = Marginal   F = Failure   S = Success   P = Probable

	Past Time	Present Time	Future Time
Actual Behaviors:	Redefinition MFSMMFFSM	F	M or S or F
Redefined Behavior:	FFMFFFFMF	F	(P) FFFMMM
Identify Definitions:	F	(P)S or (P)F	F

These issues are important because of the ultimate goal of single case experimentation, to illustrate effectiveness of the independent treatment variable, via control of behavioral processes.[83] It becomes complicated when the client's own behaviors serve as internal independent stimulus variables, that may be equally or more significant than the external control variables in the treatment situation.[84]

The literature relative to stimulus nature of outcomes,[85] notes that the nature of linkages between psychosocial variables in the client's life, is not only a function of the rules of linkage, but the nature of the variables. This means the internal state of their identity, is directly related to the transactional nature of the system, within which the variables potentially have functional relevance (even if the overall system outcome is negative, maladaptive, or pathological). Each variable (or outcome) has a value A (1-N), and this is a function (f) of the values of other variables which influence it, and a function of its internal nature. These different values might, therefore, be better coded as External Respondent Value $ERV_{(1-N)}$ and Internal Stimulus Value $ISV_{(1-N)}$, to help the clinician and client differentiate proactive vs. reactive nature of the energy within thoughts, feelings, etc. As variables combine (as in chemistry, for example) to produce new outcomes A $[ERV_{(15)}]$ + B $[ISV_{(25)}]$, the new resultant outcome could also be coded as to its new accumulated energy, or loss of energy, as the combinations occur. A hypothetical example, is that if a dependent behavior has an ERV value of 10, and this is combined with an independent thought variable with an ISV value of 5, the ISV value may reduce the ERV value by 2 and, as a result of observing its own power to control, enhance its own future ISV by 25. Although the precise measurement of these is probably impossible, given the current nature of clinical practice theory and skill, the clinician should at least consider internal vs. external potency of all outcomes, as they may represent stimuli to other outcomes, or responses to power exerted on them from outside. This illustrates the systemic[86] nature of interacting variables or outcomes, and suggests that the values of each, should be documented and used as part of the assessment and treatment plan.[87] It also suggests that outcomes, depending on their reactive or proactive energy, create changes and energy dispersions, buildups, collections, and foci in other parts of the system. Another example, is when the child receives stress energy from parents and the environment, and redefines the self as less stress tolerant or adaptable; and therefore uses this new (even though possibly temporary) identity as a stimulus for more energized defensive behavior which causes, in turn, more stress on the environment in a circular, energy-transferring pattern, as an attempt to adapt.

In thinking specifically about the response characteristics (dependent variable characteristics) of outcomes (their potential to be influenced, and typical nature of this influence), the counselor not only assesses the stimulus potentials from the client's surrounding social environment, but also the stimulus potential of other variables within the cognitive, behavioral, and affective system of the client's intrapsychic and interpersonal functioning. If, for example, the client elicits a series of thoughts (T) and behaviors (B) in a relationship sequence: T1-T2-B1-T3-T4-B2-B3; not only are each of these significant, due to the connective links (— —) between them (which have a unique type and degree of potency, as in mathematical operations of plus, minus, exponential operations, etc.); but they are also potentially responsive to each other, and to external stimuli, that might be introduced as intervening variables (external job stress, for example).

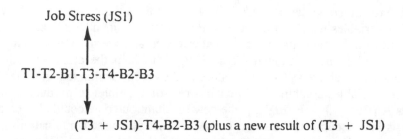

Although the clinician will want to emphasize the strength of the external stress, he or she will also need to carefully document the exact point of entry of the stressor, and determine which particular thought (possibly feeling or behavior, depending on how one interprets psychodynamics) serves as the avenue of access to infiltrate the psychic, affective, and behavioral systems. The potential to be an easy or resistive avenue of entry, is a function of the power of the stressor and response characteristics of the thought outcome (in the above example, this is thought T3). As mentioned previously, thought T3 can also have its own developmental nature which, when combined with external stressor JS, extrapolates its own stress factor in longitude, depth, or intensity, to produce an exponential equation like this:

$$T3 + JS1 = (T3) \; 6 + 2 + 1 + 8 \text{ (increases given specific periods}$$
$$\text{of developmental time)}$$

This process may produce other unknown outcomes, which become part of this complicated intrapersonal system. As noted previously, the client's perception of these stress-carrying outcomes includes childhood developmental sequences, current adult developmental sequences, or a combination of both, all of which may not be fully and continually conscious to the client.

Dubin, in *Theory Building*,[88] provides insight by noting that units of reality (called outcomes here) are symbolically and operationally represented as concepts and constructs, that can be categorized by characteristics, along the following dimensions (units):

1.   Enumerative unit or concept: The portion of reality represented, is characterized by internal defining properties present in all its conditions. This means a particular thought or behavior always exhibits its primary defining characteristics, each time it is observed. Although amounts of these characteristics vary, they must always be present in some degree.

2. Associative unit: This small piece of reality has its primary defining characteristic present in only some of its conditions (i.e., occurrences in a sequence or scenario of events, thoughts, behavior). There is, therefore, a true zero point potential, so there can sometimes be *no* amount of a particular property.

3. Relational unit: This is a property of a phenomenon or outcome characteristic, determined only by the unique and specific nature of the relationship between various properties, based on interaction and combinations of phenomena, as subgroups of a component of reality. These relational properties are derived from at least two other properties, combined in specified ways to produce a new and separate category of phenomenon.

4. Statistical unit: This property of a phenomenon summarizes the distribution of that property within the phenomenon, including its central tendencies (most common, middle, and average values), dispersion (range of values), and relative position in a distribution of other phenomena.

5. Summative unit: This unit is a global concept representing entire complex phenomena, including a wide range of specific properties (e.g., schizophrenia), as it draws them together and gives them a label. It reflects the most important aspect of complex nature, while suggesting a composite picture of other interactive causal and consequential characteristics, which are necessary to define their full nature. The concept does not specify exactly what the other properties are, and it does not indicate how and under what specific circumstances they interact. The perceiver of the reality is expected to know that a range of properties are interactively associated, and should know through definition, what many of these interactive patterns are.

To illustrate the above ideas, an outcome with enumerative characteristics might be a dependent behavior or identity representation, wherein its reactive and subordinate nature is present in all its manifestations, therefore giving the clinician some indication that the client will see all situations in terms of dependency needs, and the resources of external objects to meet these needs. An associative characteristic of an outcome might be an angry word or feeling, present in a healthy personality only under certain environmental conditions within which they function. A specific angry behavior, however, which occurs as a manifestation of an angry identity, is not associative at all, so the therapist who searches for situation determinants, may miss a larger relevant picture.

If the clinician observes relational characteristics of client thoughts, feelings, or behaviors, the client might exhibit a particular destructive self-impression, only when interacting with a spouse who exhibits a cued unique behavior, to cause the client to perceive that he/she has only one specific behavioral, cognitive, or affective option (usually this is an exact replica of parent-child behavior the client experienced previously). In this case, the client is not similarly stimulated (although this could conceivably occur, but with low probability) by other relationship dynamics. It is, of course, important to differentiate basic identity-related outcomes, from acted-out defensive manifestations of these identity conflicts. The type of responsibility of specific outcomes is related to their properties, and inherent natures. This is especially true if other aspects of the environment are not able to be changed, and the client is the only potential source for adaptation. In thinking about enumerative vs. associative vs. relational characteristics, clinicians must keep in mind the critical necessity of moving in their perspectives through various levels of defensive, symbolic, manipulative, behavior. Clinicians must rest their gaze on the bottom-line identity of the client, so they not only observe and understand enumerative, associative, and relational characteristics at their psychodynamic point of origin; but also use these categories of description to differentiate pseudo from real identity characteristics, and chronic indigenous vs. active situational phenomena which change in manifestation, but not basic nature.

In thinking about a summative unit, the therapist seeks to understand the importance of reviewing outcomes as results of subunit psychodynamic and behavioral interactions, so they do not become lost in the trees and miss the larger forest. They, conversely, identify specific subcomponents which are necessary and sufficient to produce outcome. In this context, the counselor decides which ones need to change, and how much they must change for the outcome to alter its overall nature as both stimulus and response to other phenomena in the intrapsychic, interpersonal, and sociocultural environments.

In "Baseball and Hot Sauce: A Critique of Some Attributional Treatments of Evaluation,"[89] the authors initially differentiate primary qualities of objects, secondary qualities, and human evaluations of these qualities. They agree with other philosophers,[90] that primary qualities of phenomena (bulk, shape, mass, and motion) exist independent of the human specie's perception of them. They also agree that secondary qualities (taste, odor, sound, color), have a nature and existence because of human interaction with a primary object, which is an answering perception on the part of the evaluator. They also agree that primary and secondary objects are associated, so mass and motion, for example, can be significant defining characteristics of resultant sound, which has to be perceived by a human evaluator to be culturally meaningful. Where the current authors disagree with other philosophers[91] they cite, is in their contention that characteristics of phenomena in reality are sufficiently real and potent as to have an identity of their own, apart from identity given to them by the external evaluator. Evaluation is not just a reaction to a phenomenon, but is also a potentially accurate perceptual description of its true nature. The present author would add, that within the current operating standards, patterns, and commonly shared perspectives of reality, even though each individual places a unique trademark perspective on each component of reality; they experience certain thoughts, moods, or behaviors having explicit (possibly complex and concealed) definitions (e.g., self-depreciation), which have some degree of predictability given potency and length of existence, and absence of intervening variables. This predictable responsiveness also exists irrespective of the clinician's or client's ability to react to, or perceive it.[92] However, the act of attempting to perceive any phenomenon, can potentially alter its nature and predictable pattern of manifestation.

Although it is reasonable to assume that culturally defined phenomena receive some part of their identity through repeated consensual validation; once validated perspectives exist, they have their own nature and dynamic stimulus value, and not only exist when everyone revalidates them continually, but produce changes in the social groups from which individuals view the particular perspectives, and therefore change their own nature circumferentially.

Also, the social scientist must remember that even though consensus might exist in the present tense, additional knowledge in the future (like theories of nuclear energy) might prove a distinct reality separate from consensually-validated perspectives which have unique identity, so it is acceptable for the present reality to be equally valid by consensus, and yet change and be revalidated consensually with improved data or information:

> ". . . when all parties to an action agree as to its cause, they can, in terms of their own culture's selection practices, be wrong. Believing something is true only makes it true (W. I. Thomas not withstanding) if this belief so fits with other practices for assessing fact in the society that no contrary evidence would be possible in that society."[93]

Personality/Social System
Structure for Defining Outcomes

In considering that outcomes have statistical significance relative to occurrence frequencies/intensities, rates/ratios of manifestation, and clinical importance as representations of psychosocial identity and being; the counselor must remember that evaluation necessarily counts the number of times a phenomenon occurs, but also studies and understands various ways that phenomenon is defined and validated, as representing the worldwide/intrapsychic milieu which gives life its value and meaning. Sometimes, the most important questions revolve around the concern for why certain behavioral or attitudinal outcomes are, or are not, present within conceptual or philosophical frames of reference, that give them meaning (e.g., why autonomous behavioral exploration is not seen in an adolescent, who is supposed to be exploring and testing). Other times, however, questions center on how and why a particular perceptual framework develops, and whether its nature allows behaviors which already exist to be defined in positive ways, and to have intrinsic validity without changing the frequency of their occurrence.

A third area of evaluative interest, is the middle ground between these two positions, and relates to how the individual, family, or group (whichever is the focus of therapeutic intervention) select and make decisions about the relationship between categories of meaningful reality for them, and specific behaviors which have unique function or value. These are either determiners of abstract values to support their existence, or operant manifestations of existing individual or cultural frameworks—determining values and meanings of various dimensions of existence. The following sections briefly note some of these issues as they relate to outcome assessment, evaluation, and change. The first discussion involves consideration of personality structure, as a focus of clinical evaluation.

Personality Structure

One issue the clinician/evaluator must remember, is that each outcome is defined within directly or symbolically observable categories of psychodynamic action, that is further explained within theoretical constructs of personality dynamics and organization (ego states, impulse areas, cognition, behavioral repertoire, games, etc.). This partly gives the outcome its meaning, relevance, and unique nature, as a proportionate component of specific-to-global continua of functionality.

Rablain[94] notes that many "inner space" concepts of personality organization, may have outlived their usefulness as metaphors or hypothetical structures, which are valued as weak, strong, in conflict, or related to layers of developmental "something or other,"[95] which may have little, or at least unclearly-defined, meaning. A considerable number of evaluative judgments are made about these and other categories, which may not accurately reflect either correct overall nature of the personality, or specific behavioral manifestations which serve as operational referents, to justify the existence of these valuative explanatory and often predictive categories.

An example of this is seen in the gerontological literature. One group of authors[96] noted significant difference between the personality concepts of "self-esteem" and "morale," as descriptive as well as analytic categories, to make determinations about the meaning of behavioral manifestations relative to the well-being of the entire personality. The difference in these concepts is related to:

1. inherent characteristics of stability over time,[97] susceptibility to influence from internal and external stimuli;[98]
2. multi vs. uni-faceted nature relative to mastery, physical health, social acceptability, and spirituality;
3. availability via conscious awareness[99] and report;
4. tendencies for inverse variability with nature of self-report; measurability;
5. association with mastery, and control and productivity;[100]
6. positive correlation with women's widowed status, but inverse correlation with women's divorced status;
7. inverse association with frequency of contact with children or grand-children;
8. non-association with previous marital vs. nonmarital status;
9. non-relationship to past or present sexual satisfaction; and
10. non-relationship with physical appearance.

In the above cases, it is important for the clinical evaluator to understand that specific behavior (e.g., frequency of aged person's contact with grand-children) has meaning and clinical significance, only if it can be associated with some construct to define the personality (e.g., self-esteem) and validate its existence, related to its specific frequency direction (up or down). This provides definitional refinement, not by the nature of the behavior, but through definition of the construct that allows the behavior to have meaning.

An obvious problem in integrating evaluative findings about outcomes, with components of the personality structure that give them their foundational validity, is that the more holistic[101] the definition of self, the more complicated the validity problem. Greater specificity is needed to insure that behavioral frequencies (outcomes) are assessed relative to: their probability of occurrence within any particular domain of the self; the relative value of their occurrence, as associated with other dimensions of the self which are interactive; influence the outcome has on further reinforcements or alterations of the self which, in turn, potentially redefine the behavior subsequently; and the significance of the outcome behavior and personality construct within the clinical theoretical framework, which is superimposed on the entire therapeutic process.

The clinician should keep in mind that theoretical goals of therapeutic strategy, must be translated into operational actions and behavioral categories, so accurate observation is possible, but also to insure that explanatory principles of the therapeutic process, are systematically integrated into the behavioral activities that are the instruments of change. Another example of this issue is seen in the literature, in discussions of cognitive framework of the personality for determining type and meaning of particular outcomes, and for insuring the right instruments are used to measure them. McKenna,[102] for example, discusses the importance of differentiating cognitive ability and its implied levels of performance, from cognitive style, which is more related to the manner of performance, both of which are subunits of the domain of cognitive field dependence. Decisions about which psychological test to use and the interpretive meanings extrapolated from it, are secondary to a preliminary decision of the definitional category, so interpretive values can be attached to the outcome findings, regardless of the test used.

Another example comes from trait psychology, which divides cognitive and emotional components of the personality into subsections.[103] These dimensions have predefined functional interrelationships that theoretically maintain an ideally-balanced inner equilibrium, having various degrees of deterministic[104] purpose and identity, that are related to hypotheses about coordinated and integrated psycho-emotional functioning.

Most theorists recognize the important role of the enabling and conditioning environment, and also maintain the significance of the internal life space and epigenetic ground plan, where separate parts of the personality have a propensity for linear causality. An example is the notion of basic trust, which may develop in the context of esteem-building secure relationships, or may be in existence from birth, and come to its natural developmental fruition, only when destructive defensiveness is removed. Separate aspects of the personality then interact with each other (and/or the social environment) according to preprogrammed formulae, with the resultant outcome of trust or a trusting ability. The important point for the clinician, is that this specific outcome has meaning only as a consequence of the nature of its past stimuli functions in the various personality domains, and cannot be viewed as exclusively an external state of being, without comprehensive appreciation of its component and contingent parts inside the personal cognitive structure.

The division of the personality into functional domains is good in one sense, because it provides a theoretical framework within which specific and sometimes apparently unrelated thoughts, have meaning within a wider spectrum of personality integration and adaptations. There is concern from an evaluative perspective, however, because outcomes (thoughts, feeling, behaviors) may be defined by incorrect, inappropriate, convergent, biased, discriminatory, or irrelevant constructs, only providing superficial accuracy in professional taxonomy, and not explaining how to change them. If the categories are relatively fixed lenses for taking a snapshot of behavior for diagnostic purposes, then behaviors which are thereby defined, may have limited evaluative significance as they become transitional behaviors (outcomes), in movement toward new states of defined adequacy.

A good example appears in the author's work with clients who maintain rigid defensive postures, and repeat behaviors which totter on the fence of ambivalence, but never move to new behavioral manifestations on the other (presumably healthier) side of the fence. The author is often stuck looking for smaller increments of transitional behaviors and transitional stimuli to move the fulcrum increasingly off center, so the new, more ideal behavior, eventually appears on the greener side of the fence without a major anxiety-producing leap. In this clinical case, definitional categories of personality may be insufficient to envision dynamically transitory behavioral outcomes or sub-outcomes and, therefore, force the defining of behaviors as either on the left side of the fence as deviant (D), on the right side of the fence as adaptive (A), or in the middle, conflictual and therefore deviant (CD). What may be needed are definitions of movement toward A $(\longrightarrow A)$ or relative to A, in a proportional conceptualization similar to not-yet A but part of A, and becoming more a part per time sequence $\left(\longrightarrow \dfrac{A}{A}\right)$. Even if outcome frequencies are tabulated for either deviant (D) or adaptive behaviors (A), there is a question of how one gets from one category to the other, and if there is no definable crossing bridge, the theorist must question whether or not either category is real.

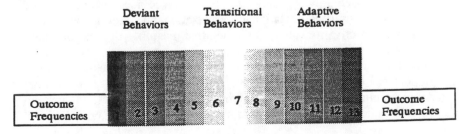

Deviant Behaviors   Transitional Behaviors   Adaptive Behaviors

Outcome Frequencies   2 3 4 5 6 7 8 9 10 11 12 13   Outcome Frequencies

The reader should also remember, that categories of personality organization may represent client self-selected areas of personal performance; areas of
adaptability necessitated by social roles and their contingencies, to maintain
systemic equilibrium and reciprocal need-meetings; or even categories into which
the client is forced to behave, as a result of therapist behaviors. These behaviors
are part of an interpersonal process, wherein attitudes of acceptance, denial,
support, neutrality,[105] and many others, not only condition (reinforce or punish)
subsequent client reactions, but more basically serve as empirical therapist-
produced evidence of presumed correct definitions of the client personality,
reflecting both client and therapist perspectives, and giving specific meaning to
any outcome that emerges.[106]

Robert Langs[107] refers to the realities of the therapeutic milieu, and notes
that concepts of transference, for example, may not be related to the resistive
domain of the personality, but are in response to errors or specific stimuli from
the counselor. In fact, some transference behaviors may be positive adaptive
messages for particular types of clients.[108]

In considering solutions to the aforementioned problems with personality
domain, several interesting perspectives emerge from the literature. One
approach to the conflict of behavioral transition (although not directly dealing
with symbolic meanings of outcomes), is Fairbanks'[109] discussion of type-token
ratio (TTR) conceptualization, which is the communicational analysis of frequency of a ratio of different words, to the total number of words. This conceptualization and technique has been used as an index of changed status, to differentiate types of patients. It might also more broadly suggest that various parts of
the personality can be compared to other parts, and to the whole, so the way they
are manifested helps the clinician reflect on the meaning they have, as an integral
and functional part of the whole.[110] This ratio might also be used to represent
changing categories of self-perceptions or identity judgments, reflecting proportionate movement of the total personality (which has been divided into fixed, but
not mobile or transitional categories) toward substantive change.

Another approach to this challenge, is the basic idea behind semantic
differential,[111] which is a combination of association and scaling procedures,
designed to give objective measures of connotative meanings of concepts, based
on factor analysis. This also serves as a commentary on the basic organizational
framework of the whole personality. In these cases, various concepts representing important life perspectives, categories of identity, or other abstractions,
are rated by the client along various dimensions of significance (e.g., potency,
activity level, evaluative value, etc.) to put measured outcome behavioral changes

in perspective, as they can be compared to various dimensional models of the client's life domain. This perspective, however, is always subject to the influence of the social environment.

Sociocultural processes (and particularly, more pronounced movements or trends) often function to transform notions of inherent traits[112] to those of learned traits,[113] particularly as changes in social norms[114] are expected to result (e.g., women's movements helped differentiate selective role socialization, from biologic hereditary predispositions and role capabilities). As social learning contingencies are identified, the meaning of any specific behavior and the messages[115] behind its various occurrence patterns and frequency distributions, can fluctuate accordingly. Evaluative conclusions can be correct or incorrect, depending on the defined stability of the personality framework used, and its capability to assume different contingent configurational images over time,[116] and in light of different learning environments. Although philosophies do not guarantee the validity of theoretical perspectives, they at least interpret portions of reality within each culture.[117] There may be alternate ways of defining the reality of the psyche or personality. Clinicians must always be sensitive to each client's potential milieu and cultural linkages in relating his or her own interpretation, to further redefine all definitions and meanings of outcomes.[118]

A final illustration points out the implication of philosophical influences on social definitions of the personality, that influence outcome interpretations relative to I.Q. testing. The I.Q. was initially viewed as genetically preconditioned and resistive to change (especially as years of living increased), as it was politically interpreted to control and question the capabilities of blacks.[119] Later, the I.Q. was defined relative to developmental learning and cognitive programming, connected to heightened responsivity to childhood sensory stimulation.[120] Later on, motivational and differential opportunity contingencies were added, to reflect new ways of socially conscious thought, which further refined the definition. The counselor must bear in mind, therefore, that the meaning of I.Q. may be clouded as a result of theoretical, rather than personal, intelligence distinctions and definitions.

A related problem for evaluation, is that if the clinician uses fixed character trait evaluative and assessment categories[121] that evolve from social custom, the freedom of specific behaviors to vary naturally, to align themselves more accurately with the real nature of psychodynamic categories, may be inhibited. For example, scratching one's ear may mean only that, rather than an obsessive ritualistic expression of autonomy/control struggles. Excessive editorial and descriptive license falls in the hands of those who define, and own the personality categories.

If specific behaviors, as noted in Schafer's[122] conceptualization of "action language," are identified through verb tenses or dynamic action characteristics, the need for more abstract categories to supply the significance-validity criteria, may not be as necessary. This is because the behaviors may survive (have meaning) independently as correct representations of components of reality, which can be defined and explained via translations of outcome observation and frequency counts.[123] In fact, specific behaviors seen separately from their determining problem-context, may be conceptualized as examples, not of acute conflict, but of more longitudinal lifelong modes of adaptation.[124] The behaviors may relate to overall personality construction, like being or becoming (having), as noted by Fromm,[125] rather than to particular subsets of experiencing various personality problems.[126]

The epistemological dilemma for the clinical practitioner, is whether knowledge can, in fact, be achieved and verified as part of the process of defining (drawing definitional lines), which may result in the assemblage of categories or segments of the personality (or any other) domain. In the psychological, social, and even medical communities, there is increasing criticism of definitional disease categories, as it may be more important to define categories related to process of *thinking* and *feeling,* rather than static and inflexible feeling states or behavioral manifestations of outcomes themselves.[127]

One approach which has been suggested, is the ecological or holistic model,[128] which stresses processes of intercommittedness rather than unitary outcomes. This model allows, according to its supporters, a more accurate perspective of personality matrices of interrelating factors. It also permits definition of movement or transitional phenomena, wherein frequencies of particular outcomes take on a unique and dynamic character, for evaluative interpretation.

"Modern medicine is guilty of what Alfred North Whitehead termed the fallacy of misplaced concreteness. Nowhere is this more true than with mental, intellectual, or behavior disorders. Contemporary psychiatry, aping the worst distortions of the rest of medicine, is going through a program of line-drawing. It is attempting to divide all human behavior into discrete categories of 'illness' decided by a consensus of its most elite practitioners and pronounced as truth by administrative fiat of their professional association. Even if there is a spectrum between black and white, one is legitimized in using those terms if, in describing a sample of colors, there are more instances of 'black' and 'white' than 'gray' or, in the language of mathematics, if there is a bimodal distribution of the observed symptoms between schizophrenia and manic-depressive psychosis, the two most important illnesses in the psychiatric nomenclature.

The obsession with categories and boundaries displayed by the designers of DSM-III may have gotten out of hand. It went so far as to the creation of a category within a boundary. It is now correct to refer to 'the borderline personality,' a designation that would make a semanticist wince. On the other hand, the scientific techniques used to elaborate the borderline condition would also make a statistician wince. Using more than a hundred variables to discriminate patients diagnosed borderline from such skewed and unrepresentative samples of the human population as those hospitalized at McLean Hospital or the Menninger Foundation addresses about as much variance as it would descriptions by the proverbial blind men clustered at the elephant's tail."[129]

A case in point is with the diagnosis of schizophrenia, often applied as a label at time of demonstration of any one set of behaviors, whose lineage and categorical connectedness are not yet clearly established. The clinician can then use the absence of that behavior and the category itself, to further define schizophrenia in remission, which further defines either presence or absence of additional behaviors.[130] Szasz,[131] in fact, labeled schizophrenic nomenclature as a sacred symbol around which inputs are defined and comparisons made, relative to success or failure (usually failure, given traditional concepts of degree of schizophrenic regression).

The counselor must remember that any particular outcome may have an integrated function, ecologically speaking, with a host of other phenomenologic occurrences and functions. Any one behavioral representation may not necessarily be directly translatable into meaningful abstractions of existence, and cannot necessarily be visualized unitarily, but must be seen collectively as part of the more complex pattern:

"In the same way, patterns of behavior result from a template, an orientation of different mechanisms and structures. It is as if gossamer threads connected memory, imagination, emotion, perception, and countless other functions of the individual nervous system into a gem-like pattern of facets, an intricate three-dimensional hologram. The gesture of a hand coordinated with an utterance of speech, the flicker of a smile attached to the shadow of a memory (the remnant of a greeting to a passing friend), the reaching out to a child tottering at the edge of a well, these and myriad other micro movements whose smooth, integrated function spell human behavior all represent the endless distillation of endlessly unfolding holograms. A mind is not damaged because one or another structure in the brain does not work. A damaged mind is a disturbance in a gossamer orientation, so that holograms are detesselated."[132]

Personality and Social Structures

Although the conceptual picture developed for each personality, is an important backdrop against which outcomes are compared and contrasted to highlight their meaning, there is a more complex problem when the evaluator joins the individual and social frameworks, and then makes evaluative decisions based on the integrated holism, rather than viewing each part separately. This has also been a keen theoretical issue in deciding treatment orientation, wherein the social scientist must come to grips with the separate and combined influences of idiographic and group influences. They decide how, where, and when to initiate a treatment approach that takes each area of influence into proper and correct perspectives, rather than assuming that each exists unilaterally, with little or no possibility of joint influence, or change.

From an evaluative standpoint, the process of forming opinions based on specific behaviors alone, without attachment to explanatory categories within the social structure as well, can provide data with little meaning within a spectrum that considers total personality integration relative to social conditions, opportunities, or blockages to adaptation. A simple example is the analysis frequently heard by sports reporters, who make unilateral evaluative judgments of team spirit, identity, feelings of winning or losing, etc., based exclusively on current point scores. They do not remember that point scores may be converted or transformed into identity-related scores or impressions, or that view of scores and view of self, are also filtered through a social situation with values, norms, expectations, opportunities, and other contingencies. Some team members have low scores, or even lose to some extent, to give meaning to winning, or to balance winning and losing relative to other external criteria. Also, scores themselves may not, in some instances, be related to identity at all. Likewise, a high-spirited, confident client with adequate esteem, may not experience even a serious setback as a loss, just as a successful situation may have no effect on an endogenously depressive characterological problem.

A series of examples noted by Strupp and Hadley[133] clarify this perspective, when they ask the questions: "Do assessments of change in self-concept, have anything in common with observations of overt behaviors, as in the treatment of snake phobia? If a client manifests an increase in assertive behavior after therapy (determined to mean decreased fear of snakes), does this overt behavior really give a valid readout on self-esteem or symbolic conflict, etc.?" This is a particularly difficult question, when one abandons the unitary disease pathology model of illness; and considers that clients may all achieve some level of adaptation in a complex world environment which, to many extents, may determine not only their adaptive potential via its socialization (positive or negative) influences, but provide here and now doorways which are either open or closed, for clients' entry into person-in-situation matrices of survival.

Unless criteria are clarified and given operational referents for individuals, systems, and cultures relative to mental health; it is irrelevant to define outcome categories or indices of success or failure relative to counseling inputs. To fully consider the complexities of the client's milieu, a three-part model is necessary, to understand the meaning of any outcome as it represents the convergent vortex of separate areas of phenomenologic life domain: society, client, and health professions.[134]

In traditional psychodynamic perspectives about client outcomes, functioning has been defined within a theory of personality structure which, according to many, circumvents the social milieu, as an equally important independent or dependent variable:

> "Structures appear as independent variables wherever individual differences in behavior, under (relatively) constant motivation and stimulation are studied: for instance in the comparative study of symptoms in various neurosis, and in the studies of individual differences in perception . . . Structures as intervening variables are commonplace in clinical observation. They account for the lack of one-to-one relationship between motivations and behavior. Defensive structures countermand motivations and replace them by derivative motivations (as for instance, in reaction formation). Controlling structures direct and channel motivations, as in delay and detour behavior and in the choice of substitute goals . . .

> It is less easy to conceive of structures as dependent variables, though they appear as such in processes of structural change, including those of learning. Insofar as psychoanalysis as therapy achieves its goals of changing existing structures, in at least some of the observations made in therapy, structures appear as dependent variables.

Any limitation on the choice of variables seems to result in a limited range of observables and observational methods, and it is the dearth of methods which is probably the major obstacle to bridging the gap between psychoanalysis and academic psychology and between the various schools of psychology."[135]

As Strupp and Hadley note, ". . . we assert that more is involved in assessments of psychotherapy outcome than changes in the person's feeling state and/or behavior. For example, it is one thing to observe that following therapy a previously anxious and shy male asks a girl for a date (overt behavior); one may also inquire whether he is now happier than he was previously (well-being); and it is quite another matter to determine the extent to which any observed behavioral and affective changes have become a part of a generalized disposition to deal differently with women or to determine the quality of the experience; for example, whether a rigid defensive structure has been replaced with a more modulated approach in interpersonal relations. Empirical studies of therapy outcomes have rarely dealt with these topics . . . however, if one is interested in a comprehensive picture of the individual, evaluations based on a single vantage point are inadequate and fail to give necessary consideration to the totality of individual functioning."[136]

There is also another evaluative dimension to the above, which relates to influences of the new behavior (asking girl for a date) on the client's social system (alienated feelings from mother, who sees rejection instead of emancipation), and also influences on the girl being approached. The model suggested by Strupp and Hadley, therefore, is a good illustration of the need for simultaneous evaluation of multifaceted aspects of the person-in-situation, since multiple values converge to give specific outcomes significant meaning for the client. Figure 3 which follows, is an illustration of eight possible combinations of positive and negative poles (represented by plus and minus signs), for the states of behavior, well-being, and structure of one's individual psychology, as they give guidance and projective input to a more comprehensive picture of social adaptation.

In considering these categories, which represent convergence of real and symbolic meaning for any particular therapy-induced or otherwise manifested outcome, the reader should keep in mind that numerous other categories may be added to this framework.

There are probably incremental gradations between the positive and negative poles that are presented, and each category can be viewed singularly as a potential therapy outcome. To illustrate how any category becomes part of the counselor's thinking and decision-making process, an example in Strupp and Hadley's own words[137] (with some paraphrasing) is represented here, to clarify the reasoning processes in using convergent perspectives relative to clinical outcomes.

(1) Outcome Category 3 (B+ W+ S-). As noted in Figure 3, a person in this category emerges from psychotherapy well-adapted to his/her social role, and feels comfortable within the self, but is judged by the mental health professional as suffering from ego defects (e.g., brittle defenses, characterological distortions, deficient impulse control). Such a person may have entered psychotherapy feeling anxious, depressed, lonely, etc. (W-). Therapeutic interventions may have boosted the individual's morale and perhaps increased self-esteem, resulting in self-report of positive outcome. Assuming, however, there were initially serious ego defects (S-), which would lead most mental health professionals to diagnose psychopathology of varying degrees, the observed change in feeling state would be seen by them as "symptomatic improvement," without significant radical or permanent change. Short-term supportive, or relationship forms of psychotherapy, perhaps administered by an inexperienced therapist, lay counselors, etc., might produce such an outcome. Similarly, participation in a sensitivity training program, encounter weekend, and the like, might give rise to changes in the person's feeling state (from W- to W+), but such changes might be short-lived. Whether changes in subjective well-being are seen as consequential or otherwise, clearly depends on the perspective of the judge. In the present instance, changes in feeling state, because they were not accompanied by positive structural modifications, would not be regarded by many mental health professionals as having great significance, although the individual might value them highly.

It is possible that prior to therapy, a patient exhibited behavioral deficits (e.g., poor job performance, academic underachievement, phobias that interfere with ability to earn a living, etc.). In this case, observations of the person's changed behavior (from B- to B+), lead to positive therapeutic outcome.

With respect to the dimension of inferred structure, one situation is that in which the person was found to have marked ego defects prior to entering therapy, (S-), and these remained unchanged during therapy. Most mental health professionals rate such lack of change, as a therapeutic failure. Their judgments of negative outcome would thus be discrepant with judgments of positive outcome made by the individual (based on a greater sense of happiness), and by society

Figure 3
Tripartite View of Therapy Outcomes 137

Category	Configuration	Mental Health Status
1	B + W + S +	Well-functioning adjusted individual, optimal "mental health."
2	B + W - S +	Basically "healthy" person; troubled by dysphoric mood, perhaps due to minor trauma affecting self-esteem, temporary reverses, discouragement, loss, grief reaction.
3	B + W + S -	May have fragile ego (borderline condition, schizoid personality, etc.) but functions as well in society and feels content. Underlying psychotic processes may be present, but defenses may be reasonably effective.
4	B + W - S -	Similar to 3, but affect may he labile or dysphoric. Has basic ego weakness, but functions adequately in society.
5	B - W + S +	Society judges person's behavior as maladaptive (e.g., unconventional lifestyle), but his sense of well-being and personality structure are sound.
6	B - W - S +	Similar to 2, except that social performance is considered maladaptive. Example: As part of a grief reaction, person may withdraw, give up job, etc.
7	B - W + S -	Person with ego defects; psychopaths, character disorders, conversion reactions (la belle indifference), individuals who have poor reality testing and poor insight.
8	B - W - S -	Clearly "mentally ill."

Note: B = adaptive behavior (society); W = sense of well-being (individual); S = personality structure (professional).

(based on more adaptive behavior). Such discrepancies may contribute to the view that therapy is esoteric. Because of inability to assess factors beyond immediately observable behavior or feelings, neither sees the usefulness of therapy beyond the attainment of these goals.

Some professionals may hold the view that behavioral adjustment and feeling states are not therapeutic ends in themselves, but reflections of the individual's underlying psychological structure. It would thus be their opinion, that any B- to B+ and/or W- to W+ changes observed in Category 3 individuals, are likely to be superficial and temporary.

In the event the patient's psychological structure had changed from positive to negative, or from mildly to strongly negative, most mental health professionals (including the present authors) would rate this outcome as having deteriorated; although, from the standpoint of society and the individual, there would be a judgment of therapeutic improvement. An illustration of this outcome is a person who entered some form of highly directive therapy aimed at modification of maladaptive behavior, such as nail biting or insomnia. As a result of therapy, the individual might learn to master the problem, and concomitantly experience a greater sense of well-being. Such a person would be rated by self and society as improved. The therapist would likewise consider the therapy a success. However, a more dynamically-oriented or otherwise broadly-trained mental health professional might judge that the patient has achieved the behavioral changes, at the cost of increased rigidity and compulsivity (S+ to S-). This, in turn, renders the patient more susceptible to exacerbations (e.g., depression) at a later period in life. Such outcomes are by no means uncommon, and may occur as a function of training programs in assertiveness, self-control, etc.

Again, the implications of such an outcome, with society judging the therapy result as positive, and the mental health profession perceiving it to be a negative effect, are considerable, particularly concerning immediate effective social functioning, as opposed to the goal of long-term psychological restructuring. Patients, by the same token, may be motivated to continue therapy only as long as they experience some psychic distress. Thus, only to the extent that therapists demonstrate the relevance of sound psychological structure, to long-lasting effective behavior and subjective well-being; will there be consensus on a definition of mental health and how it may be attained.

(2) Outcome Category 4 (B+ W- S-). Therapeutic outcomes in this category are essentially a variant of those described for Category 3, the only difference being that the patient's self-reported feeling state following therapy, is one

of unhappiness and discontent. As is true of all configurations discussed here, the patient may have entered therapy in Category 8 with negative evaluations of behavior, feeling state, and psychic structure. If so, a Category 4 outcome would be judged a therapeutic success by society (B+), although the individual has remained unhappy (W-), and his/her psychological structure remains unchanged (S-). Such an outcome is most likely when therapy is overly attentive to society's demands, and fails to deal adequately with the patient's personal needs.

It is also possible that at intake, the patient was experiencing no feelings of distress, and thus manifested a B- W+ S- (or less likely, a B- W+ S+) configuration. It is highly unlikely that a person would voluntarily enter therapy feeling positively about self (W+), although there are instances in which a behavioral deficiency is noted by society, which the individual does not perceive as a problem, so the patient may be relatively unmotivated for therapy. By contrast, society diagnosis a problem and attempts to force the individual to change against his or her will. The mental health professional may concur with society, that the individual manifests psychopathology (S-), particularly if on closer examination, it is inferred that, contrary to self-defined feeling state (W+); the individual is unhappy and suffering, on a deeper level, with self-reported contentment based on defensive operations, such as denial.

Clearly, if an individual entered therapy with a fairly sound psychological structure and sense of well-being, although a nonconformist in behavioral terms, and emerged a behavioral conformist with feelings of unhappiness and an impaired psychological structure; this outcome would be judged as negative. Further, if the person's psychological structure remained unchanged from an originally negative state, and behavioral conformity was achieved at the price of lessened subjective well-being, this would also be seen as a negative effect.

The B+ W- S- outcome is particularly likely, when behavior is modified without consideration for its adaptive function in the patient's life. If non-conforming behavior meets important defensive needs, and the patient is then deprived of those behaviors, such modifications may have an important negative effect. An example of such behavior is overeating, which meets important intra-psychic needs; or self-induced starvation, which may be manifestation of a deep-seated conflict, rather than a "bad habit." Category 4 outcomes may be brought about in such cases, by crude or coercive attempts at behavior modification. While the patient's behavior might have become more adaptive and conforming, there may be increases in feelings of negativism, and the patient may feel betrayed by the therapist, and indirectly by society. Concomitant resentment may be associated with depression, renewed or exacerbated interpersonal conflicts, and a sense of estrangement and unhappiness.

Another therapy blunder that might lead to outcomes of the B+ W- S- type, is exemplified by a therapist who encourages the patient to undertake new roles in life, for which he/she is insufficiently prepared, and which require deployment of nonexistent psychic resources or energies that must be diverted from other areas. If failure occurs, such adverse consequences for subjective well-being as guilt and depression, which have reverberations in his psychological structure, may occur. In summary, a Category 4 outcome is particularly likely when modification of behavior is the primary goal of therapy, because the psychotherapeutic enterprise should be aimed at helping the individual with W+ to W- and/or S+ to S- changes, seen as clear-cut negative effects.

One important criticism of the aforementioned structures within which outcomes are conceptualized, is that behaviors which are not categorized, can be subjectively and superficially explained; and not assessed in terms of overriding client developmental growth, defense, or adaptive process. The counselor can simultaneously be overwhelmed by the process of explaining each single behavior, rather than noting their similarities and differences, via an outside system of categories to streamline practice. The problem may be partly one of integrating major categories of personality adaptation (social, individual), so valid and useful new categories emerge, placing each client at the convergent vortex of all relevant categories, with predictable outcomes hypothesized (and tested) for each system of interconnected domains. This includes areas of motivation and conscious/unconscious defensive postures, which provide significant impact to lessen values and potencies of the other categories of need, anxiety, capability, or deficit. The power of therapeutic inputs must always be indexed relative to client probability of change.

Krill[138] speaks partly to this concern, as he discusses the necessity of diagnosing categories of "modifiability," which range from client need to endure what they perceive to be an unchangeable situation with the support of a therapist for crisis periods, to those clients desiring a complete personality overhaul from top to bottom. This idea is discussed by another author as an issue of client "will,"[139] seen as a composite of both internal organizing forces of creative self-expression and counter-balancing forces of impulses and inhibition, that represent a paradox for creative or destructive outcomes.[140] The will or ordered will, as opposed to the "disordered will" noted by Farber,[141] represents an area of personal and social commitment, involvement, feeling, and assertion; which is a categorical state of being (global criteria with socially validated operational referents, and behavioral manifestations), and has dimensions of feeling, passion, emotion, excitement. All these have a unifying, balancing, and dualistic nature and function.

These internal states, however, also have interactive dimensions in the social structure, as noted by May,[142] as in the case of love, which in some sense can only be defined as a composite of individual and social energy input. This energy also includes social goals toward which one moves,[143] and which help define status of outcomes once goals have been achieved. In addition, Assagioli[144] notes the will's connectedness to more abstract transpersonal values, which have attributes of power, focus, competence, initiative, creativity, direction, choice, and others. As one's individual will associates with the external environment, especially its nurturing and developmental characteristics to produce growth, the concept of synergy[145] becomes important as a collective phenomenon of individual and cultural self-actualization. Within a synergistic environment, need satisfaction occurs via investment of human interactive resources in social units, that acquire a separate normative and functional meaning as a result of the energy outcomes. Self-actualization represents concomitant dualistic satisfaction, of both personal and group need for security.

Rank[146] defines this dualistic framework relative to life and death fears, which are essentially conflicts over separation, autonomy, independence, creativity, and self-assertion. These fears begin in early stages of parent-child dependency, but are reaffirmed and perpetuated through social institutional and cultural patterns of living. Each act of individual creation within social reciprocal relationship contingencies, is the enactment of temporary balance between these conflicting forces.

An additional point about personal will, is that specific behaviors can be assessed, encouraged, confronted, etc. by the therapist, in terms of whether they contribute to the maintenance of this person/situation homeostasis. Clients should be encouraged to understand their acts and intentions from the perspective of these states of balance, relative to personal rewards they give themselves concerning state-specified functions; and rewards and punishments forthcoming from society, relative to specific behaviors that society defines as manifestations of synergistic functionality. Clients will probably need to devise a third compromise psychic state, which encompasses some components of both ideal personal meaning, and culturally socialized existence. Clients need to define adequacy of the self relative to degree of safety from social negative reinforcements, rewards of personal will which coincide with social expectations, and rewards to self as a result of deviance from social control. Deviance might include suffering as a positive index, in which the self is not totally lost.

One problem, is deciding which specific behavioral outcome is associated with probable states of interactive functionality, especially with evidence as reported by Bergin and Strupp,[147] that therapeutic outcomes among clients are multifactorial.

There may be lack of clarity concerning the degree to which any specific behavior is correlated with a corresponding state of the person's existence at a more abstract level of interactive relationship with society. Yet, without the abstract categories, behaviors themselves that are correlated, may have little relevance as implications for a bigger picture of the client's reality. The other problem, is that the self often differs from that of the theory or therapist, so behaviors must be explained in terms of client frameworks; so treatment goals are designed to create convergence between the theoretically-oriented clinician and client abstract categories, before any behaviors are defined, measured, or interpreted.

An example of this complexity relates specifically to deviance situations, when clients, who conceptually feel good and might be defined as healthy within an intrapsychic definitional category, actually perform negative or progressively negatively-appearing behaviors. This is because they are identity-wise, more honest about their socially deviant status, and allow it to manifest its negative dimensions as a prelude to feeling power and self-assuredness. In these cases, analysis of direct meaning of the deviant behaviors might obscure an indirect sense of conformity, because society is seen as a valued parent from whom to rebel. This orientation provides some sense of security that may be reported relative to direct meaning of comfort in one's actions, yet is viewed or reported indirectly concerning its implications for interpersonal phenomena, and directly measured as a negative behavioral index.

The counselor experiences a complicated dilemma trying to decide which perceptual focus (i.e., client, societal, small groups, etc.) to use in comparing and contrasting outcomes, but also must struggle where perceptual slopes or angles of view *overlap,* and constitute potentially new and different foundations for outcomes.

One interpretation of this matrix is provided in Figure 4. In the center of the square, the evaluator is concerned about locus of perception, which may be separate from, but also possibly a combination of, abstract categorical positions (in the outer parts of the square), that are used to define behaviors. Assuming the client or therapist makes decisions about specific behaviors consistently, by using one cognitive framework, is highly questionable. In reality, decision-making might parallel the process of taking pictures of a fountain by encircling it with a vehicle, and snapping the picture at various points on the circumference; and then taking reverse angle pictures of the vehicle, from the fountain or some-where in between.

Figure 4
Matrix of Domains of Conceptional Convergences
Related to Clinical Outcomes

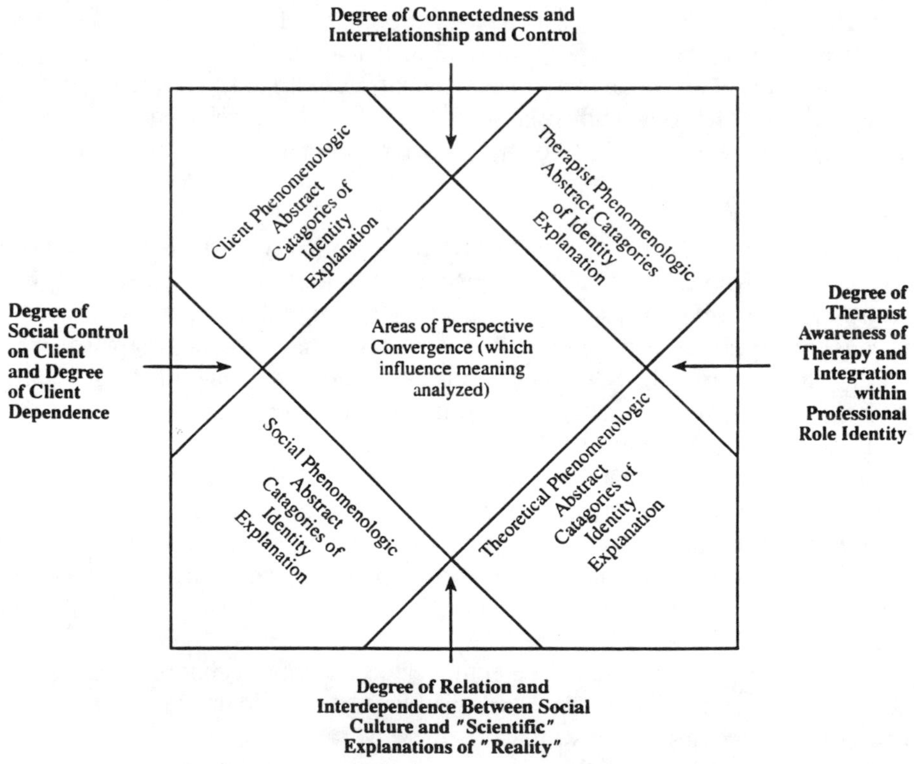

Another interpretation which relates to this area of convergence, is in the process of measuring outcomes related to self-esteem, where many authors emphasize the multifaceted nature of the construct itself, and clinical compli-cations in making valid and reliable decisions about related outcomes. Brisset,[148]

for example, stresses the complementary relationship between inner and outer influences on self-evaluation, and divides self-esteem into two social psychological processes (self-evaluation and self-worth), that materialize as part of interaction of the individual and social system. Competence (or other success indicators), therefore, is assessed in terms of goal-achievement in the "object world," but also the "symmetry" between one's conception of self, and manifestation of this self-concept through behavioral outcomes. Empirical outcome measurement within the scientific model, for example, might neglect consideration of this notion of "symmetry," and provide evaluation of only part of the relevant dimensions involved.

Leitner[149] also studied socialization and personality development, with respect to clients' abilities to make accurate evaluations of themselves and others. In studying "discriminative ability" and "self-assessment," he found that counselors with the most experience and training in self-evaluation, were more accurate in discriminating (evaluating) the helpfulness of others and themselves, as compared to counselors with either less training or experience.[150] These associations between experience, training, and self-discrimination, are extremely relevant in demonstrating the complexity and individuality of each practitioner's encounter with the challenge of self-evaluation, and perceptions of outcomes from various perceptual categorical locales.

Marolla[151] also conceptualizes self-evaluation within a network of interchanges between personality and environment, but goes farther than other authors in specifying patterns which these associations assume. He confirms that self-esteem comes from within the individual (inner), or social structure (outer), and suggests inner self-esteem is a function of self-valuated congruence between the individual's self-defined intents for action, and actual behavioral outcomes. The inability of the individual, however, to define her/his own goals for competence, stimulates more personal dependence on valuation of effectiveness from sources within the environment. He concludes that people inclined to self-validation (self-evaluation), are more motivated to achieve inner self-esteem, and have a great probability of accomplishing this goal. His data suggests that subjects who evaluate themselves on criteria other than reflected appraisals of others, not only feel more competent, but also feel better about how others see them.[152] This is particularly relevant for evaluation of clinical practice, in suggesting that self-evaluative capability goes hand in hand with the practitioner's ability to assume a creative role in defining goals for competence. Inability to develop individual relevant and meaningful goals and criteria for performance would, according to Marolla, cause the practitioner to be less responsible for self-evaluation, and more dependent on external evaluative sources. Marolla also suggests that criteria of evaluation should combine the practitioner's behavioral outcomes and self-defined intents, based on personality needs and characteristics.

This illustrates that the conceptual juxtaposition of self-evaluation and self-esteem or identity, reflect the depth and intricacy of psychological processes which underlie individual evaluation. The relevancy of these considerations is often overlooked in the evaluative literature, and often falls outside the conceptual vision of classical evaluative models:

"A major shortcoming of many measures and concepts used by researchers is that they lack a relationship to the perspective of the actors (in this case, the clients) within the studied reality. This comment does not assume that such a perspective is the only one involved in a clinical situation. In fact, theoretically there would be a variety of non-client perspectives, including the worker's, which must also be attained to have *valid* accounts in the practice situation. If you cannot hear the client's definitions of a problem, their interests will most likely not exist in your treatment of the problem. Therefore, if you measure the client's problems without their perspective, your treatment is likely to only reflect the concerns and interests of the most vocal set of non-clients."[153]

In thinking about the importance of conceptual categories to give relevance to behaviors, there are images or expectations of these behaviors and their dynamics, inherent within any definitional model itself. The model specifies through projective images, the appearance and meaning of behaviors which should appear in each category, and also forecasts whether dynamics are constant, variable, independent, dependent, etc. once behaviors are manifested.

One issue is the validity of expected categories, even though specific defined empirical behaviors seem to support the existence of the category (impulsive behavior justifies the existence of the id). A second concern, is that behaviors may be so comprehensively and completely defined, that even behaviors elicited to test the categories, are also defined within a category (a child questioning family norms is disloyal and, therefore, the norms are supported, and the process of defining behaviors and norms is also supported). This validation makes the behaviors questionable, as benchmarks from which to draw clinical conclusions.

This becomes a tricky issue if one accepts the deterministic and absolute nature of some social definitional systems, wherein the behavioral and conceptual categories are not relative, but are fixed facts of reality; and the only variance occurs with individual and social definition of conformity or deviance. Determination of motivation becomes relative to purposeful/accidental attitudes. As noted in Figure 5, there are a range of cells within which the individual can be defined,[154] but within a system of fixed definitions of conformity and deviance, as in systems of organized religion or military totalitarian cultures. The category usually defines the behavior. Some human factors, like strength of character and difficulty of social influences, are factored in, but do not have the power to move the definition from one major category to the other (they only allow movement within categories). This modifies the overall-definition, but does not substantively change it, as noted in both Good Scenario #1 and Bad Scenario #1, which retain their goodness and badness, irrespective of selective perceptions. For clients who affirm (in some defined state of non-pathological mental process) dependence and symbiotic unity, for example, as necessary components of life adaption and identity, with a broad set of life principles or organizing norms; the therapist has latitude to work on perceptions of conformity/deviance or other types of status, and on factors relating to behavioral manifestations of varying options; but has no authorization by the architect of the system (God, for example), to use client perception as a modifier of actual categories.

The author encounters this dilemma when adult clients who are members of organized religions, say they felt guilty about premarital sexual activity (which the church defines as sinful) as adolescents, but now do not feel guilt. The question is, what happens to sins already committed, which are not obliterated simply because the client "grew up" and redefined the act, self, or the church?

This issue is also expressed in a slightly different fashion, with establishment of goal categories for client outcomes, whose degree of rigidity or flexibility (including permanency in the course of therapy) becomes the criterion for judging other behaviors, seen in proximity to the focal criteria.[155] This can be seen with counselors who define an overall condition of client rigidity. In these cases, the client may philosophically or culturally feel s/he has no options for flexible and variable interpretation of concepts, and treatment goals may be defined to reduce this "defensive rigidity," while simultaneously ignoring or narrowly defining other areas of client thought, that occur within a philosophical domain that does allow more flexibility. A clear perspective on client outcome goals and feedback, helps alleviate some decision-making error on the part of the counselor/evaluator. Particular behavior patterns which develop incrementally, can always be compared to the preset goals, to focus them as value parameters in the client's life.

The clinician must insure that outcome goal objectives do not continually and arbitrarily change with client movement, since the dynamic correlation and

Figure 5
Outcome Matrix for Deviant - Conforming Behaviors

P = Power
W = Weak
SS = Social Stimuli

Perceived as Conforming		Perceived as Deviant					
By Self	**By Others**	**By Self**	**By Others**				
Hero	Hero		Victim	P	SS	Strong Character	Behavior
			Victim	W	SS	Strong Character	
			Victim	P	SS	Weak Character	
			Victim	W	SS	Weak Character	
Hero #1 Good Scenario	Hero	Good #1 Scenario	Victim	P	SS	Strong Character	Attitude
			Victim	W	SS	Strong Character	
			Victim	P	SS	Weak Character	
			Victim	W	SS	Weak Character	
Fixed Impenetratable Boundary							
	Secret Deviant	Purest Deviant	Purest Deviant	P	SS	Strong Character	Behavior
	Secret Deviant			W	SS	Strong Character	
				P	SS	Weak Character	
				W		Weak Character	
	Secret Deviant	Purest Deviant	Purest Deviant	P	SS	Strong Character	Attitude
Bad #1 Scenario	Secret Deviant	Bad #1 Scenario		W		Strong Character	
				P	SS	Weak Character	
				W	SS	Weak Character	

(Right margin: Fixed Definition of CONFORMITY; Fixed Definition of DEVIANCE)

movement may provide a mobile target, that never allows a definite decision about goal attainment success or failure. If goals are established and achieved, one aspect of the new goals may be a revised definition of the person who has just arrived, and hence; a retroflective, regressive, mirroring effort defines goal attainment. For example, police officers who have not been police officers previously, are rookies and, therefore, apprehensive police officers, insecure police officers, etc. When they attain certain behavioral goals, however, amount of new experience may mean they no longer are rookies, but have become new identities who moved beyond rookie status. Once this status is achieved, new goals can be set, which reflect expectations for a person who is not a rookie.

Setting new goals too early, means clients have not had time to reflect and learn from their new status, so they still think like rookies, despite new behavioral frequencies which indicate otherwise. Each category also defines a new status, which may not necessarily take the previous status into consideration, even if those *anticipating* behaviors are necessary as part of the goal. For example, a faculty member becomes tenured and, therefore, is not viewed as a hard, aggressive, striver, even though s/he has been previously, and may want to still be defined as such, while also having tenure. Goals may also have mandatory subgoals, which may or may not be part of a desired repertoire or agenda for clients. For example, in becoming a bona fide freshman, one first survives the hazing process. Finally, there are future goals assumed to be part of each new attained goal category. In the case of Carl Lewis, the Olympic track star, he won four Olympic gold medals and was expected to never lose a race again. He lost the first race he attempted after the Olympic success, possibly as a result of this expectation.

The important points are that, while goals are pursued, enough consistency in the goals must be retained, to provide a stable focus for studying the dynamic process involved to attain them. Sub-attainments prior to goal attainment do not modify or change the goals or the focus on them, so that no valid decisions are made about attainment. It is also important that characteristics of goals be clearly considered, so once arrival has been negotiated; a variety of options for past, present, and future thoughts, feelings, and behaviors, are also available to the client. The counselor insures that bridges from the past have not been burned, so safe return is possible, if the client discovers he or she is in undesirable territory.

Termination[156] as an outcome goal category, is another example of this issue. For the client and counselor to conclude their work together, some measurable form of perceptual convergence must occur, representing correlation of person and social levels of satisfaction, with treatment results and agreement about the outcomes. Sometimes, however, clients and counselors part company with lack of clarity about goal attainment, so the terminated condition places the client deeply within a conceptual framework similar to the one before termination, which stressed the client's feelings, for example, of never being able to terminate. This may cause the client to define previous statuses differently, and allow opportunity and time for total reconceptualization of all that went before. A client, who is now not helpless, might conceive the past period of helplessness as not having been helpless at all, but an illusion of helplessness. This suggests that time should be spent during termination to redefine past reality, and note changes in the terminated status, since each segment of the past is updated to contribute an incremental new meaning to the present. This chaining process is similar to movement of waves toward the shore, where a wave that has reached the shore begins a return trip, and influences the water mass through undercurrents returning to the mass, which defines a new wave, and in turn, wears away sand and rocks and redefines the coast line. This provides a new arena within which successive waves must be operationalized. The changing ecology of the coast and wearing away or development of land and mountains, redefine weather patterns, which redefine ocean, air, and moisture patterns, in a circular progressive spiral movement pattern.

From a psychological perspective, the more distance one moves from a previously experienced object, the more it can potentially be redefined. This may have a necessary catch-up effect, with variable rates of catching up, to assist in redefining present status. This process of redefinition then generates a series of new outcome objectives related to the redefinition process itself, and the state of being of the redefined client, with implications for future action and adaptation. Behavior of the therapist can also be seen differently, as the client continues termination, which may be addressed from a philosophical or relationship status perspective in future therapy sessions.

An example of this occurred in the author's therapy practice, where a client who had made considerable progress, began reflecting on uses of therapeutic power and manipulation, which she felt were necessary to create a transference relationship and help her change, but also became examples of relationship domination she now resented. Using the termination process to deal with this retroflective indignation, helped her further consolidate present growth, at a higher level of adequacy.

Another example is the hysterically frightened individual, slapped by a friend to *bring him/her around*. In a state of heightened adequacy, he/she may address the physical violence and domination issues, rather than the rehabilitative nature of this act. She/he may require more sessions with the worker to deal with new and previously obscured issues. It is also important for the worker or client, not to make premature decisions that a termination status has been reached, and assume incorrectly, that reworking the past does not occur or is unnecessary to evaluation. Including only present outcome or end of treatment goal categories, might also provide a platform to look back and consider a fuller range of observations. These include the client's changing perspectives on these past events, as reobserved from a new vantage point, therefore becoming a new independent variable contributing to redefinition of the present observational paradigm.

Cook and Campbell address this problem:

"Quantitative researchers in the past have used poorly framed questions to generate quantitative scores and these scores have then been applied uncritically to a variety of situations. In uncritical quantitatives research, measurement has been viewed as an essential first step in the research process, whereas in physics the routine measures are the products of past critical experiments and elegant theories, not the essential first steps. Also, the definitional operationalism of logical positivists has supported the uncritical reitification of measures and has encouraged research practitioners to overlook the measure's inevitable shortcomings and the consequences of these shortcomings."[157]

One interesting research example of these processes relates to self-esteem, need for approval, and perceptions of success on an academic examination. Prediction of low grades occurred in terms of whether the exam in question had actually been taken or not (a completed, but undefined outcome), where this seemed to dominate other findings of the power of overall self-esteem, to have a significant interactive effect on predictions.[158]

Discussions of the studies of these variables, suggest a complicated relationship between (a) baseline personal low self-esteem, which causes lower estimation of successful outcomes (on the examination),[159] (b) baseline low personal self-esteem, causing deflation of success indices after outcomes are achieved (when good test scores are produced),[160] (c) personal conservative low predictions[161] of outcome success, based on high social need for approval,[162] irrespective of actual examination outcomes,[163] (d) variation in predicted outcome, partly based on whether the actual performance task had been completed, (e) variation in predicted outcome, partly based on the completion of related tasks, but not the task of social focus, and (f) the actual nature of environmental reward/punishment contingencies, related to both task completion and overall social status.

To determine status of any client along a series of potentially interrelated outcome indicators, or measuring a single index; a sufficiently steady state of the individual must be attained to clearly differentiate changes which have occurred, and to also assess how stable variations of the observed phenomena are, since clients serve as their own control. Once termination has occurred and a steady state (without direct therapeutic input) attained, one set of evaluations of changes can certainly occur. Since this steady state, however, may represent a new status of adequacy, there is value in using this outcome condition to interact with previous outcomes and sub-outcomes in the past, as it is placed in a new perspective, and may continue long after official termination.

Interpersonal Structure and Interactional Definitions

Systems (including sociocultural) and communication theorists very correctly and comprehensively provide a solid appreciation of units of reality, which are defined and maintained by types, amounts, frequencies, natures, positions, etc. of verbal, nonverbal, and more recently psychic (transcendental) communications between individuals. From an evaluative therapeutic perspective, these are different from, yet interrelated to, individual outcomes, and have a number of significant inner space structures discussed earlier.

This increased emphasis on interactive, multi-personal domains, includes intra- and interpersonal structures of definition, within which are patterns of circular interactions,[164] and the very presence or absence of communicational messages.[165] The more refined sub-dimensions of direction, power, style, etc. become relevant outcome symbols of the nature of the collective identity between people. Some theorists recognize the value of linguistic and other communicational structures as independent variables, which influence belief systems and definitions of reality from which the messages emerge.

One pointed discussion of deficits in this area, is presented by Berlin,[166] who specifically discusses areas of social work practice. She notes that traditional theoretical frameworks, have not accurately defined outcomes which represent the unique interactional dimensions of the client within the situation. The absence of unifying procedure has led to the unsystematic and piecemeal use of theory, as a theoretical approach representing a technical eclecticism,[167] neglecting both environmental determinism and internal psychodynamics.[168]

She goes on to recommend a cognitive learning/behavioral perspective which, as noted in the following article excerpt,[169] captures the notion of reciprocal interdependency as a unique structure from which to observe and make decisions about jointly produced outcomes:

"Briefly, the cognitive-learning perspective considers that the reciprocal influence of people and environments occurs largely through information exchange. Rather than automatically shaping or extinguishing behavior by dispensing reinforcement or punishment, the environment exercises influence, as an information source and a generator of experience on how to achieve positive results. People gauge their behavior and subsequent cognition in response to their interpretations of the meaning of events. If individuals do not attend to environmental cues or if they misperceive or misinterpret them, they are unable to cope. Furthermore, this perspective recognizes that messages sent by the environment may be ambiguous, punitive, or overwhelming. Thus, the properties of a situation along with personal factors such as attention, skills, and beliefs and associated emotions determine a person's responses.[170] In addition, cognitions are seen as both the cause and effect of an experience—that is, cognitions are influenced by past and present environmental input and also shape the environment by giving it meaning and selecting actions to change it."[171]

In considering the influential nature of environment in the above interactive context, studies increasingly recognize the interactive influence of life events on individual behavioral, cognitive, and emotional processes.[172] The data, however, are still not conclusive about (1) the relative importance of positive vs. negative life event influences and life satisfaction indices, (2) interaction between positive and negative life events as balancing factors, (3) the variable influence of naturally occurring vs. induced life experiences, and (4) different individual interpretations of what, in fact, constitutes social support.[173] One study,[174] for example, finds clear indications of detrimental effects of negative life events on individual psychology, and mild support for the idea of a buffering effect of positive and negative events. This suggests that clinicians should establish situationally relevant and circumscribed procedures that begin "where the client is," by encompassing diagnostic and goal setting objectives, relative to content and process of interactive relationship dynamics.[175]

As an example, George Kelly and Arnold Lazarus developed role-indication methodologies.[176] Clinicians might also give serious consideration to Epstein's warning about "preoccupations with what is inside people's heads,"[177] which ignore "social contexts of problems." Neglect of intervention in the social context may really reflect a major technological or skill deficiency, and not a lack of perspective of any theory as applicable on a single case or caseload basis.

Because of their attention to the relationship of person and community, clinicians may need to contribute more to the analysis of treatment models, to foster comprehensive psychosocial perspectives:

1. Type and Degree of Interactive Communicational Control: One of the first problems encountered by the evaluator, regarding the interpersonal interactive system as a set of dynamics which define reality; is to understand how, when, and to what degree specific communicational signals condition, cause, are responsive to, or are in other ways associated with other responses from the communicating partner in the relationship.

   In working with couples and families, the author develops a code book for words, voice tone, visual style, etc., used by each participant which, through conditioned learning and socio-ethnical patterning and modeling, automatically cause particular (or even variable) responses from other members of the system. The clinician, in this regard, must be a communications content analyst, to temporarily put aside issues of symbolism and specific meaning, to initially understand the formula by which interactions are dependent or independent of one another.

   An interesting example of these interaction patterns comes from the behaviorist literature, which discusses the functionality of operant conditioning. In this context, behavioral reinforcement occurs by relating the progression of behaviors of one individual, to formerly unrelated behaviors of another, wherein both participants have an important reciprocal influence on each other. This process occurs in the ecological system of the client, which includes the therapist, as well as significant individuals in the client's social system.

   To understand communications between counselor and client, it is essential that interactive dynamics and behavioral patterns in relationships be defined, and systematically related to their content and process goals of counseling; although specific communicational behaviors have, in fact, become important focal points of varying degrees to which this dependence/independence operates. This occurs as communicating partners develop a cultural and normative interactive style, and patterns of relating which are a unique part of their association. Consciously or unconsciously, this style becomes habituated as a cultural relationship pattern, to maintain identity and longevity.

Some authors note, however, that particular clinicians have difficulty identifying these interactional processes, partly exemplified by use of broad or general theoretical processes and conceptualizations about cases, and difficulty connecting these abstract paradigms to specific behaviors.[178] This results in continuing questions about the relationship between theory and clinical practice, with lack of clarity about particular technical "know how" which must be "observed and described in detail, before used in a definition and category."[179]

Practitioners have been advised, therefore, to "start where the client is," without specific guidance to determine where this point is developmentally, ecologically, and communicationally; and without a framework to understand various units of movement toward or away from this point of origin, or behavioral progression. Studying the relation between stimulus-and-response and content relevance,[180] is a way to think about this task, by focusing on issues of interactional satisfaction and outcome success,[181] as a ratio of costs to rewards resulting from the interaction.

In writing about clinical interaction, Richardson, Dohrenwend, and Klein observe the following about interviewing techniques: "First, the continued use of questions which do not refer to prior responses—that is, questions with no antecedents or with interviewer antecedents—may make the interview appear to the respondent as a highly fragmented, discontinuous process in which the interviewer takes little interest in the responses."[182]

They recommend that the counselor utilize the client's antecedent responses and offer responsive support, to enhance satisfaction with the therapeutic interchange. Henry L. Lennard and Arnold Bernstein also emphasize congruent exchanges in therapy: "The therapist endeavors to maintain continuity in content and mood between the patient and himself (herself). In such an interactive configuration, the patient experiences himself (herself) as engaged in an interaction in which congruence and relevance are safeguarded by his (her) co-participant."[183] Truax and Carkhuff discovered that content specificity, was a critical component of successful results in counseling;[184] and Ivey affirmed that "verbal follow" behavior and "reflection of content," are directly correlated with positive client outcome.[185]

It is the present author's contention that, despite the symbolic nature of message content, each dyadic and systemic (including communications of some clients with deceased significant others, or ego ideals, etc.) message represents a set of stimuli and responses, whose transaction dynamics frequently maintain the patterns. This is noted when individual client cognitive conceptions start to change, but specific behaviors linger as habitual vestiges of interactively secure, even if pathological, systems. These patterns define the nature of the reality within which the counselor must work, and provide avenues through which initial and continuing efforts to change, support, confront, etc. must be shown.

The particular nature of therapeutic outcomes is frequently defined within the boundaries of communication style, which, in turn, through repetitive patterning, influence continuing definitions of symbolic or real content-oriented components of the relationship (life space),[186] and individual identity within that interactive framework. It is critical for each counselor to tactically plan communication messages at times, places, and with purposeful amounts of pressure, to use the interactive formula to have the most impact, and be most helpful for client change. For example, client patterns might be as follows:

a.   two questions from wife
b.   one defensive response from husband
c.   one defensive counter from wife which has an exponential emotional power value of 10 magnitude
d.   two questions from husband (helpless retreat)
e.   one question from husband which is genuine
f.   two questions from wife (to repeat pattern)

The counselor may have the most impact on the system by intervening at a point between 5 and 6, as opposed to a point between 1 and 2, where the husband has not yet been engaged, and therefore may not be responsive; and where his wife's anxiety may not be sufficient to provide motivational impetus for her. An analysis of the particular communication pattern of this couple, therefore, provides not only a useful guide about interdictive opportunity; but also produces data to use inductively, to build comprehensive perspectives about the overall nature of their individual and collective conceptualizations, and the general norms which bind the relationship together. In addition to communication patterns and dynamics, the counselor is also concerned about particular content of messages, as they combine style to further determine the nature of outcomes.

2. Content Power of Messages (Cognitive and Affective): In considering content relevance, as the degree to which the clinician's communication is viewed by a client as correctly corresponding to treatment issues, behaviors can be maintained by either a positive reinforcement foundation, or aversive conditioning, both of which can include either introduction or withdrawal of the reinforcing condition, with different variations of behavioral conditioning scenarios. As conditioning situations occur through communicational messages, the client may gradually change states of being or identity, as a reflection of reinforcement to deal with content domains (thought and feelings) that are reactive to the messages themselves.

There are two formats for relations between behaviors, which exemplify the connection between communicational and behavioral interactions. Changing occurs when a series of behaviors are learned in reverse order, so the final reinforcement is in development of evaluative clinical models. Their functional relationship dynamics and sequential patterns have not received widespread attention, and occur and have clinical meanings, which may not be recognized by the worker as they appear in process.

Content is the doorway for access to the client's important inner life space, and facilitates awareness of thoughts, feelings, and conflicts related to the counseling milieu,[187] and to the client's life as a whole. Inattention, therefore, to specific content issues, and particularly the psychosocial processes by which content categories and values develop, marks likely inability of the counselor to have significant impact.

> "When both members of a dyad are in agreement regarding their reciprocal obligations and returns, there is consensus or similarity of expectations, and harmony or stability occurs in their interpersonal relations . . . But when there is any degree of discrepancy or lack of consensus between participants, and their expectations are dissimilar . . . manifestations of strain appear in their interpersonal relations. If expectations are too dissimilar, the social system disintegrates unless the differences can be reconciled."[188]

In light of this issue, in fact, some clients even drop out of counseling, where content discrepancies cannot be resolved within the interpersonal client-therapist gestalt.[189] A major dilemma about content, however, is that the presenting communicational stimuli from the client, are often confusing and symbolically coded.[190] This means that counselors develop skills of awareness and analysis in order to decode confusing messages, and also form message inputs into categorical groups of content, used as evaluative criteria and an interpretive framework from which to provide feedback to clients, at a higher level of abstraction and learning potential than their original bit of communication.

Some research suggests, that clinicians must possess high levels of ability to integrate complex cognitive stimuli, and that those who do, use significantly more information units than their peers. These practitioners make fewer generalized assumptions about clients, and are reluctant to make decisions based on limited information or predetermined categories, which form preset structures for interactional processes.[191]

This implies, of course, that the quality, quantity, and explanatory frameworks for data are critical for competent interventive efforts.[192] Cognitively complex counselors also change areas of focus when clients reorient their communication,[193] and demonstrate flexibility in the creative use of information to help clients learn.[194]

Counselors who are good evaluators, therefore, need to assess their own discriminative ability, and appreciate their ability to seek and handle cognitive complexibility, so these facilitative skills can be more systematically connected to stimuli provided by clients, and to need-relevant outcomes evolving from the interaction.[195] There is always the thorny question, however, about whether counselors can be aware of their own cognitive style, and if so, whether changes can be made, once counselors have begun their professional practice careers.[196]

The specific subjects and topics which are cognitively part of interactive dynamics, are conveyor belts which must be used (they are the only alternatives from clients' perspectives, as they envision self-entrapment) to deliver incrementally changing messages. They are also necessary to move to various positions in the interactive system (as in using pontoon boats as temporary anchors, to build a bridge over water), to build new interactive options so messages can flow to previously forbidden, repressed, inoperative, or rusty parts of the client system. The types of subjects which are part of interactive relationships define the relationship itself, because the relationship generates symbols to represent its nature, and the symbols themselves have inherent power to define, when shared and supported by the communicants. An example occurred regularly in a family the author had little success working with, where the cognitive idea of responsibility was a frequently communicated message. It had, however, lost its meaning as a caring reaction to meet emotional needs, and had become feared loss of adequacy with the other partner's development of her own separate identity. It had also become a measurement criteria for normative performance, which means that (a) compliance was determined by the developer of the term, (b) adequacy was a unilateral assessment, since the term had different and almost irrelevant meaning for the deviant, irresponsible partner, (c) conforming acts of responsibility became admissions of dependency, and submission to other-directed control. The term responsibility had a series of definitional meanings which had become part of interactive structure, and as long as the term was a mandatory component of this interactive structure and a component of the vocabulary (offensive for one, defensive for the other), it had a significant role in influencing subsequent outcomes related to its use and meaning. The specific range of subjects and admissible/forbidden subjects which communicators discuss, also enhance or limit the quality of outcomes. Absence of communication is often seen in the inability of families to resolve relationship problems, where secrets of incest, extra marital affairs, drug use, etc., are not part of message content, yet their absence becomes a focal point which (like scapegoating) maintains family defensive balance, yet does not allow further growth.

There are, of course, always problems in helping dyads, triads, and large interactive units of one culture adapt to a larger, majority social scene, when some societies have little congruence or similarity in even conceptualizing the same environment. An example this author saw, was in working with American Indian populations of the Southwest, who organized self-concept and adequacy around a totally different language and cognitive structure than the white Anglo-Saxon community, which controlled economic and social resources the Native Americans needed for basic survival. It was impossible for the Indians to survive and be fulfilled in a society so heavily weighted against them, and they could not even share important perceptions or awarenesses with those who wanted to help them, because of limitations of interactive symbols, and their culture bound dimensions.

This also suggests that the range and variability of content,[197] have some relation to outcome, since the communicable content may be so limited to exclude some domains of reality for certain clients and, therefore, prohibit shared concepts and plans or growth. Content which is, on the other hand, too varied or massive, may be perceived as threatening or overwhelming to clients who resist—and restrict probabilities of certain change-oriented outcomes. This restriction can be based as much on type and volume of content, as compared to the actual meaning of that content, developmentally[198] associated to their identity maintenance and self-concept. This is particularly a problem with multiple content areas in family systems.[199]

As suggested previously, the generic vs. specific, positive vs. negative, open vs. closed, etc. nature of message and communication content, as a reflection of cognitive ideas, may lay either a helpful or detrimental foundation for change outcomes, despite the specific nature of content, or its interpreted symbolic meaning. Important factors interpersonally, are degree of interaction, forcefulness of interactive influence, and quality and accuracy of message transmittal/reception between key factors, as these relationship messages influence outcomes.[200]

The clinician should also keep in mind, that various types of content (as an interpersonal structure) contain diagnostic subunits which (even if not pathologically intended to cause pain, manipulate, attack, defend, etc.) contain predisposing outcomes of a personal or interpersonal nature, and expectations for interpersonal roles. Comments of interactive areas of communication with directives/expectations for future action/status ("You are a terminally ill patient"), judgments about past/future/present actions ("My daughter's boy crazy"), or implications for interdependency ("She is helpless in our relationship"); may create limiting conditions on a wider range of potential outcomes. They may also simply focus on such a small part of a holistic individual, that particular outcomes are already perceived, or become self-fulfilling prophesies, partly based on language shared between communicators. The clinician helps clients realize the nature and functions of content, as these messages do or do not accurately reflect the total individual (an "alcoholic" is also a father, child of god, nonalcoholic at times, accountant, etc.). The clinician can help the client determine the degree to which, once communicated publicly, this content limits the capability of all parties to the communication—to experience, perceive, and act within a different arena of reality, than that defined rigidly by the type of content. One author, in fact, suggests that since children are growing organisms, there is no such thing as childhood psychosis or schizophrenia,[201] which implies a static state of existence.

In thinking about affective content as it becomes a linking variable in interpersonal structures, the relationship between two individuals[202] certainly retains components of individual affectivity (and cognition as well);

but the bonding, mutuality, and interdependency of the association, create an affective phenomenon (self and other) as well, which becomes a focal point, influence, and evaluative guideline for particular empirical outcomes of thought, feeling, and behavior of each participating individual. This affective dimension of relationships can be measured and discussed by clients in terms of its character, intensity, and directionality (who communicates what feeling to whom), but also has a separate identity existing as a relatively substantial commodity, even though each individual exercises considerable interpretive perceptual license (see Figure 6).

Figure 6
Interactive Affective Reality and Outcomes

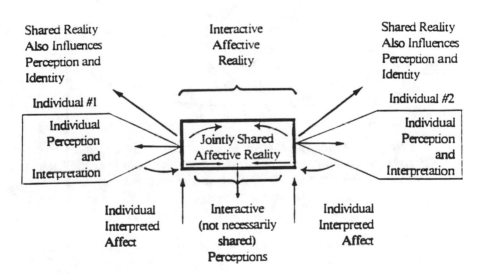

The therapist is challenged to help individuals understand how they selectively perceive the central affect as a unique reflection of their identities, but more importantly, how the shared affective reality causes retroflected self perceptions, and contributes to personal evaluative decisions about self-esteem, adequacy, life goals, etc. This can be seen when individuals are interacting and communicating together in the present, but it also helps form the theme and substance of historical memory and relationship norms, when individuals are separated. The counselor needs to help couples and families understand characteristics of individual vs. shared affect, but also their degree of dependence on both, to provide needed feelings of personal security, individual and mutual protection, and life purpose.

The author worked with one couple, on the verge of a very bitter divorce, who reported positive affective feelings about each other as long as affect was seen as a separate individual phenomenon surrounding each, with the only contact being individual perceptions (see Figure 7).

Figure 7
Individual and Shared Affect

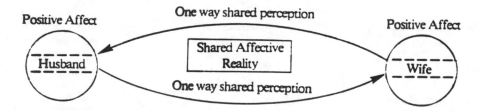

When, however, the two considered their joint and interdependent affective and cognitive reality (the dashed square), both were too frightened to enter this nebulous and fantasized uncontrollable world, and their life roles and identity scripts were too divergent to allow development of sufficient areas of shared affect, to make the relationship worthwhile.

With another couple married only four years, the author helped them develop clearer perceptions of the shared central core of their affective relationship, initially by developing acute self-awareness of cognitive and affective personality, and then exchange and mutual sharing procedures to build a jointly acceptable and satisfying shared affectivity. The counselor needs to understand the process by which this affective dimension of relationships becomes balanced, dysfunctional, denoted by one partner, or fluctuates chaotically or in a predetermined pattern of potency and directionality, because of its significant influence on the thoughts and behaviors of both partners.

In therapeutic situations, behaviors will often be confusing when seen as outcomes, in and of themselves, or even as direct products of role negotiations and patterns. They will, however, subsequently make more sense and have deeper (hopefully more correct) meaning, when explained within affective norms or structures which, in many ways, dictate or predetermine ranges of behaviors which appear as outcomes, and have attached meaning even before they occur.

Also, there are situations when one member of an interactive system elicits an outcome the counselor would view as positive (sometimes the behaving client would concur), but the outcome would not be translatable into a positive contribution to the system, even if a reciprocal positive behavioral reception were negotiated and completed, by an interactive partner. What happens, is that the influence of specific outcome behaviors (including their positive ramifications) is not powerful enough to counteract negative affective dimensions of shared reality which define the relationship, irrespective of one behavioral unit. Possibly a change could occur if numerous positive behaviors were strung together, but as each one occurs and registers negatively in the affective data bank, a positive sequence often never develops. The opposite of this occurs in relations where one or two specific behaviors which are negative, are not powerful enough to disrupt the affective reality which has been developing; by registering sufficient previous amounts of positive behavior, or being jointly perceived based on other less objective, less empirical/physical association between individuals (e.g., spiritual union, etc.).

A simple example, is that one member of a family can throw a ball and another can catch it, but the acts, although interdependent, are not really positive because ball throwing, as an affective interchange in this relationship, is defined negatively. This is frequently seen when one member of a marriage has an extramarital affair, and is never really forgiven, and the affective state of unforgiveability becomes part of the marital foundation, permanently.

Another example is a couple with a shared affective bond related to victimization, to which each secretly subscribes, but neither will own or admit to publicly. Regardless of whether either party manifests a trust/positive behavior or deceitful/negative behavior, any behavior emitted by either party, is predestined (with a high probability) to be seen negatively. This is their way of relating to each other (holding the association together), as it confirms and enables them to retain transferred relations to parents, where victimization was one way of controlling anger and maintaining some form of relationship, even though destructive. The affective dimension is one component of interpersonal relations which must be defined and, itself, measured as it influences types and meanings of possible outcomes.

3. Interactive Relationship Cycle: Patterns of behavioral, cognitive, and affective stimulus, response, correlation, and juxtaposition, etc. occur, which become part of habituated and stable security-producing norms for system equilibrium. These patterns develop initially to meet needs or defend against anxiety, but become socialized subcultural routine procedures. They contribute to definitions of what behaviors mean (as a function of where they occur), and which behaviors are allowed or expected at varying times in the cycle, as this contributes (either positively or negatively) to the functionality of the interpersonal system. Many behaviors are oriented and primarily perceived, in terms of sequences or patterns of task functionality. The demands of functional necessity cause behaviors to continue in sequence, with little opportunity or immediate utility to perceive their purpose in terms of esteem, self-actualization, identity enhancement, etc.; or any other abstract interpretive domain. The tasks involved, for example, in managing the after school activities of children (latency and adolescent aged), are issues frequently discussed by families, wherein a parent has jumped into the family taxi or shuttle bus, and begins a pick up and delivery cycle which must run its full course; without option, time, or reward, for thinking about the intrapsychic or family identity/affective meaning until the cycle is complete. At this point, self-actualizing energy or interpretive acuteness are frequently at low levels, or new cycles begin to prevent analysis of the old cycles. The linkage forces between events often are so strong, that variable directions are not possible, new outcomes cannot enter the system, or other preferred systems cannot be incorporated, or supercede the habituated sequence.

The therapist must carefully construct a model of these sequential patterns (and their parallel symbolic meanings), to help clients understand their reality, and discover the most effective points of entry into this sequence, so new seeds begin to grow and gradually transform specific components of the pattern. Hereby, new dimensions of variables, or multiple directions of sequences can emerge. Massive attacks on these entire sequences, in the author's opinion, do not work, but only create systemic anxiety and solidify the patterns even further. A more insidious, infiltration approach is suggested by many systems analysts, to gradually replace rotten wood with fresh new timber, for a stronger but continuous foundation.

In some cases, the therapist may believe the pattern has been inter-rupted, but the client continues deceptive segments; or the client has a substitute defensive game plan which makes the therapist believe the cycle is broken, but in fact it is being delayed or symbolically transformed, into acceptable client manifest behaviors (a deceptive smoke screen). Premature entry into this system of sequenced patterns by the therapist, scares the client away, or transforms the therapist into part of the pattern, so the therapist permanently loses sight of the complete pattern until s/he extracts him or herself from the system. This only occurs if the client allows the therapist to be separate, which is difficult to determine, and sometimes requires termination of treatment, so the foreign substance (therapist intru-sion) can be removed, due to its inability to produce positive changes.

With many clients, outcomes occurring at specific points or locations in sequences, have a greater probability of being perceived as positive, or actually having positive functionality. This is similar to the problem of hearing bad news, when one returns home at night after a difficult work day; while the reception might be very different, if perceived on Saturday morning after a good night's sleep. These patterns vary with situational task demands, psychological themes and profiles which are adopted, and the ebb and flow of physiology variables like sugar level, muscle tension, state of alertness, etc.

The researcher/evaluator/clinician should also remember that some points on the sequential continuum have constant vs. variable natures; different influences on subsequent variables down the line; fluctuating degrees of freedom to vary within the system; different ranges of opera-tionalized intensity; duration as symbols of intrapsychic identity, esteem, etc.; and direct, indirect, or uncorrelated directionality. The challenge, is to identify all check points along the client's sequenced journey, to find out (this means hypothesize, then systemically test) which variables or functions are related, and how this relation occurs, including its function and purpose for the sequential pattern in the system. It is important to remember that a system only ceases to operate or change, when the dependency linkages between variables take on a zero value, or new variables maintain the dependency, while being moved into place without disrupting the system's balance.

4.   Client-Therapist Joint Ownership of Outcome Goals or Symptoms: Another concern for therapeutic progress, is development of objectives as criteria against which to compare ideal (realistic) vs. actual behavior. As part of

the interaction between client and counselor, there is always concern about whether the therapist establishes sufficient therapeutic conditions within which clients select and have ownership of their own goals (self-determination) or, on the other hand, whether goals are nonexistent, or become the property and identity of the counselor. In reporting research on a wide range of case studies, Katherine Wood notes the need for "partialization," and speaks about the actual development of client-related goals:

> "Since many of the human problems are complex . . . one of the primary skills of the work must be 'partialization'—picking apart that tangled knot, assigning priority status to the pieces of the problem that can be worked with most realistically and feasibly, and then choosing interventions that are sharply focused on these problems. None of the studies began with the adolescents' own perceptions of what their problems were and what help they needed. Rather, the researchers and practitioners involved in these studies appeared to start with their own theoretical and ideological orientations, which they applied to their clients like a magic formula. They did not explore and assess the problems being experienced by individual clients; instead, the professionals assumed that they knew what ailed their young clients and what was good for them. The intervention did not grow out of a contract between helpers and helped concerning problems and goals that were meaningful to the clients.

> . . . Analysis of the problem means identifying, weighing and assessing the factors in the client's intrapersonal, interpersonal, and social systems that are contributing to the problem or that might be enlisted in resolving or ameliorating it.

> With few exceptions, many of the studies began from an implicit assumption that the problem existed only within the personality of the person who had it, confusing the problems with the people who had them. Once this assumption is made, there is a kind of quasi logic in an interventive strategy focused on changing people internally, in spite of the social circumstances that are requiring the adaptive behavior labeled as the problem. A number of studies claimed to have a 'family focus' or to have used a 'family approach,' but on close examination, all that was work with one or a few key family members around either their own particular problems or the problems of the identified client. This is totally different from a focus that uses the

great power of the natural small-group system to influence and often to direct the behavior of members. The workers must be able to show that certain specific changes in the natural-group system will create reverberations that will force the individual member to change also in response. General systems theory, organization theory, and crisis theory all make clear that for change to occur in any human system, a state of critical imbalance in its normal system processes must exist or be brought about . . . and a system must be in an unstable state before change can occur. The intervenor's role may be considered that of an 'irritant' in the system, either causing or exacerbating disequilibrium as a first step toward change in the individual or small group natural systems.

If the problem involves a natural interpersonal system, the concept of the contract must be extended to agreement among the members of that group on their perception of the problem and the changes they individually and collectively would like to see brought about. The process of change does not begin until the work has succeeded in helping the members perceive the problem as a family one, rather than the exclusive possession of the identified patient, in terms of each member's investment in changing the way the family operates."[203]

To the degree that clients do not understand the intervention, or the relationship it bears to the problem and treatment goals they would like to achieve, they may not be invested in the change effort, and will probably resist the clinician's interventions. A significant evaluative dilemma emerges, if the nature of interactive therapist-client dynamics causes the client to lose authorship and responsibility for goal selection, because subsequent attainment, although possibly positive, may represent feelings or attitudes that cannot necessarily be attributed to independent client actions. The outcome, therefore, cannot be presumed to be a positive dimension of longitudinal client-related life scripts or agendas. Behaviors can be fabricated to please the therapist, to manipulate, or defend against more fearful conflicts (e.g., independent thought and feeling). Outcomes can often be explained as a result of specific interactive dynamics of control, submission, dependency, manipulation, etc., rather than results of client self-actualization. In cases where goals are established or even achieved as a result of this interaction (especially where therapists see themselves as boosters, temporary healthy parents, etc.), this independent variable must be gradually and systematically removed, to insure that outcome goal achievement can stand alone. This is also a problem because dependent clients may sustain this reinforcement to retain the therapist's approval, long after the formalized therapeutic contract has ended, so longitudinal sustenance criteria need to be used once the maintaining influence of therapeutic direct contact, has been removed.

In some ways, termination of treatment might involve work with clients to help them understand that many goals or obtained objectives may, in fact, be transient, temporary, or artificial; suggesting they must continue to experience (assume or expect) the power of the therapist in their lives, to ultimately reject this control. They can do so, by admitting their continuing dependence after treatment ceases. Many therapists attempt to deal with this issue via graduated termination timetables, and maintenance of decreasing amounts of contact with clients years after formally leaving regular treatment encounters.

Another factor which must be explored, is the process by which treatment goals are formulated. It is often good to invite an outside co-therapeutic consultant into early appointments, to help correct the need of therapists to have goals for clients, and to note the autonomy with which clients experience the individual selection or acceptance of treatment goals. One approach uses an inductive-deductive evaluative scheme, or a devil's advocate approach, so the client can be assessed on ability to (1) question and critically assess the way goals were developed, relative to their potential for achievement, (2) resist imposition of externally generated goals from the therapist, (3) select and abandon goals, to test out their viability, (4) role-play inappropriate or questionable goal attainment scenarios, to learn more about their nature, or (5) challenge the counselor on probable attempts to impose inappropriate, incorrect, unnecessary, or insufficient goals in the therapeutic life of a client.

A sound process orientation toward interpersonal dynamics of therapy, helps with this evaluative problem, along with provocative challenging and questioning by the therapist, to be certain the client has freely accepted treatment aspirations. One possible interference in the collective decision-making about outcome goals noted by Aronson, et al.,[204] is the dilemma with interpersonal attraction and evaluation. First, evaluation tends to be positive when a significant other (client or therapist) conforms to expectations (outcome goal selection), and also manifests similar personality attributes, or those that are preferred. Santee and Jackson[205] found that attraction is predicated on expected positive evaluation, and that judgments of the attractiveness of outcome categories are made, when positive appraisal is expected from the person whose attractiveness is being judged. In these cases, selection and ownership of relevant clinical outcomes can be contaminated by the mutual attraction or evaluative expectations of the therapeutic dyad, and may not accurately reflect reasonably attainable client-centered goals; or represent a logical negotiation of the pros and cons of the outcome itself, clouded by assumptions relative to interpersonal congruence.

In the above cases, the therapist's evaluation of the client, or the client's need for assumptions about that evaluation, should be studied as to possible influence on goal selection. Measurement of therapist evaluative change, given different conditions or stages of client goal selection, may also help, along with assessment of similarity or difference between therapist and clients, with commensurate efforts to assess and control for the biased factors related to this association or disassociation. Since research is not definitive about either condition, the important point for the therapist, is that the association must be viewed as a significant variable, whose effects must regularly be checked within the process of client goal selection. This choice, although possibly stimulated by therapist agendas, should ultimately stand as dependent only on internal or external factors, related to the client's intrapsychic needs (even if goals must temporarily be sustained by the therapist, when clients are unable to develop rational cognitive process, to seek their own best interests); or their interpersonal interests within the arena of life where they survive physically, emotionally, and culturally. Degree of self-determination can only be measured, when extraneous interpersonal dynamics are sufficiently controlled to allow the client's true level of goal ownership to be manifested. In cases where there are joint client-therapist goal selections; the degree, reasons, and dynamics of mutuality must be assessed carefully. This is necessary so end results (goal outcomes) are measured in cost-effective parameters, wherein deficits of the mutuality can be measured against the gains of mutuality-condition goal achievement. Clients are likely to consider the probability of their behavior being controlled or modified by the counselor, and loss they might attribute to this process,[206] vs. gains of the relationship association.

5.   Client Ego-Splitting and Conflictual Dialogue Framework: One interacting framework which presents a considerable dilemma to the counselor, is the interactive network (with dyads as the foundation) where clients create or re-create intrapsychically. When therapeutic inputs by the counselor, or individually generated insights by the client, produce outcomes (e.g., a new perspective about the self, or a different behavioral objective), they

frequently are defined by the client as part of silent, hypothesized, or fantasized conversations between the client and one or two (typically) significant others (parents, spouse); or between two different components of the client's personality (e.g., the practical and the daring side of their conflictual ego). Very often, the counselor is not aware of moments these conversations take place, and until the client is well-known in therapy, the personalities of the key interactors are not fully known or understood. Outcomes, once interpolated into this interactive framework, are often modified, changed, eliminated, or substituted (with an impostor, to make the counselor think the real outcome is present). They are susceptible to non-control by the therapist, because the professional is not a legitimate part, invited guest (resistance), or powerful interrupter, of this inner discourse. Even when efforts identify and interdict these inner voices (not necessarily hallucinatory), the client often does not readily accept the therapist as a substitute communicator (of unproven loyalty, supportive power/normative orientation). Clients reluctantly give up their cognitive structure, fearing the child-envisioned consequences of ending up with no structure, or inner voices which become angry or vindictive.

One approach to this problem helps clients externalize these inner interpersonal relations, so they can understand them better; and for the therapist to very gradually attempt to be invited as a guest discussant for increasing periods of time, so the system does not become too quickly disrupted to seriously frighten the client. Outcomes should not be discussed at all within this plan, until the counselor has a fairly firm membership in the re-created family (nuclear, family of origin, or family of ego parts) and, therefore, can introduce controversial topics without creating partial or total shutdown of the system. Sub-outcomes can be related to communication clarity, historical origin, manifestation of actor goals, and objectives of the intrapsychic communicants, until new conclusions or premises can be interjected into the syllogisms of logic, which emerge within discussions.

These frameworks are very alive and influential for clients and have an historical entrenchment which cannot easily be disrupted, but can be gradually changed as interactions are externalized and validated; and as the client reviews the self as the discussion moderator, who can initially control the pace of the discussion, and ultimately contradict destructive content that emerges.

Generic vs. Specific (Differentiated)
Nature of Outcomes

Perhaps as a component of linguistic or psychosocial diagnostic impreci-
sion, complexity of outcome (behavioral, cognitive, affective) subcategorization,
or developmental/functional taxonomy; outcomes are so nonspecific and general
in nature, that it is difficult to understand their specific meaning for any one
individual. The precise nature of outcomes like self-esteem, adequacy, safety,
etc. (however behaviorally operationalized) is accepted by many (including
cultural norms) as a universal truth, which does not necessarily break down the
specifics, so individual life agendas can be discerned. This means that individuals
may predicate significant decisions about the self, on global ideologies and
confusingly loose interpretations; or never gain insight into the uniqueness of their
outcomes, as related to their own autonomous, inner function. The author has
worked with many families, for example, who feel they must define and agree on
jointly shared outcome plans, expectations, and goals. However, self-esteem for
an adolescent may in no way be comparable to self-esteem for an adult. Self-
esteem may necessarily require subcategorization which, in fact, makes the
species very different from the overarching genius; one might even consider that
two species may be so different, as to reflect entirely different genus categories.
One couple in particular, struggled around the issue of active vs. passive
lifestyles, and at times there was no common ground upon which these outcomes
could be compared, and some other more general or more specific category was
required to define commonalities. Another example occurred at a party, where
the author discussed with two parents, their problems in handling the stress and
manipulativeness of a gifted, highly-intelligent child. It was obvious very early
in this discussion, that the term gifted child was used as a common denominator
by parents (as one generic outcome), to define life perspectives which were very
different and mutually incompatible, since the parents' individual goals for their
gifted child were totally unrelated to the assumed common conceptualization of
this phenomenon. A massive redefinition of "giftedness" (with its associated
outcomes) to relate specifically to an 8-year-old female, and differently to 40-
year-old parents in need of a missing piece of their own life puzzle, not related
to "children's performance"; would help the clinical evaluator be more responsive
to problems experienced by either party. Also, if parents are unable to specify
their separate outcome expectations, the child must either choose her own or one
of the parents', or subdivide the self to integrate a dual outcome conceptualization.

The social pressure for commonly shared values, beliefs, and perceptions
to provide personal security, also complicates the therapeutic process. This

occurs as words (e.g., love) refer to a multitude of highly different phenomena, and cause individuals to assume there are shared beliefs, without reliable or valid ways of deciding if behavior can be correlated with thought, or if anyone ever reads from the same sheet of music.

It may be nearly impossible, in fact, to develop shared definitions of outcomes, so that interpersonal conflicts about meeting needs for nurturance, or agreeing about values; are irrational, in and of themselves. There may be no way, given limitations of spoken and written language, to discuss common themes. These may really be individual themes, that clients are conditioned to believe can actually interface with the partner's simultaneous and equally important individual selves, when in fact, there is no taxonomic system to even make this decision, given nonspecific natures of human definitions of reality (outcomes).

Arguing an alternate (not necessarily opposite) position, highly specific and individually-defined outcomes (particularly if they remain intrapsychic or intra-systemic, rather than externalized and more public) can be so functional in the private, secret, or pretend worlds of clients, that it may be impossible to externalize and explain them vis-à-vis more generic/abstract frameworks, which could provide a more useful and meaningful perspective than exists with individual definitions and views. Outcomes may, by nature, be highly specific, individual, selective, and subjective perceptions that are unable to be differentiated from their functional dimensions (what they are and what they do for the personality, are one and the same). They may constitutionally have limited degrees of freedom to vary, except as they become entirely separate functions. Therefore, they may not be variables, but large numbers of highly specific and separate constants. This makes the job of therapist very difficult, as the author notes with one client with a highly and precisely functional inner psychic reality of redefinition of the world (not overtly psychotic), making every external situation come out to be positive (including suffering, pain, loss, joy, etc.). The client may be unable to relinquish these perceptions, because there is no way of using any criteria, to discuss any particular cognitive function (e.g., "I find value in the negative aspects of every situation, because this is not an example of suffering to corroborate negative parental judgments, and maintain some degree of parental support; but is a separate phenomenon which has nothing to do with pleasure/pain relating to childhood dependency"). The client, of course, can pretend or sincerely try to describe behavior in more general and commonly accepted definitions, but continue to behave in the same inner fashion, because no external criteria fully explain the highly unique perception. Another example with this client, is the role of water in her life, via dreams and in reality, which may have nothing to do with traditional symbolic connotations of guilt removal, physical cleansing, or transportation medium. Water may have a specific defined function, earned individually in childhood, that relates to no other shared perspective on earth.

A slightly different perspective about outcomes relative to their nature, is the range of operationalization they have, as perceived by a similarly "range-defined" host individual. Most outcome behaviors, especially considering typical or average social definitions, can be categorized along various dimensions which label their nature or dynamics, and allow them to share commonalities with other outcomes, while at the same time being different from others. For example, certain outcomes can be grouped as active vs. passive, public vs. private, overt vs. symbolic, conforming vs. deviant, masculine vs. feminine. In cases where the personality is also divided into similar or at least corresponding categories, the degrees of variation of outcomes are limited more by constitutional nature of person and behavior, than possibly by a more specific definition of choice selection or individual preferential option. In cases where outcomes fit with personality, typical patterns of response (e.g., passive behaviors in a passive-dependent personality) vastly circumscribe the outcome arena within which the individual can, and will probably operate. In these cases, the counselor may find it more meaningful to scrutinize a narrower range of behaviors with a much finer differential viewpoint, so continua within that particular range, may be meaningfully discerned. In this case, clients will not learn to evaluate their current behavior and reasonable behavioral goals within too broad a categorical system, where failure would be highly probable for a wider range of activity.

There is also a range of outcomes which can be grouped as safety measures, that will not disrupt systemic or intrapsychic equilibrium. They reinforce one another, as other behaviors from this family emerge and are judged by the client, as similar and consistent with the generic or genus nature. As behaviors within a definitional or taxonomic genus appear, they can become habituated not only because one has a specialized reinforcing function for a subsequent behavior, but also because of their nature and dimensions. These fall within generic definitional parameters and, by definition, become mutually reinforcing to the defining client. Those behaviors that are defined as socially successful (e.g., hard work, honesty, participating in the Olympics, etc.), are relevant partly because of their general nature, and sometimes this generic attribute overshadows a more neutral or negative specific component.

For example, competitive behavior in world Olympic competition is, ipso factor, considered good and routine, which lessens the impact of a 3rd or 4th place finish (the athletes may be successful, simply because they were there); but also, the general category of winning often obscures the other rewards of competing, when winning is not one of the results. In other situations, athletes may compete in the Olympics for fear of failure, to compulsively and dramatically prove their diminished adequacy. Their helplessness will not be seen at all, because of generic vs. specific considerations which obscure a clear perception of either one separately.

Other outcomes defined as positive internal behaviors (having a compassionate inner feeling of sadness for someone else), may have a great deal of specific personal value, but not have a corresponding external definition of public adequacy; because there is no direct conversional, definitional transition, into public and generic arenas. One client in particular, was internally much healthier than a large portion of the author's caseload, yet had not been able to transform specific inner health to more global or macro examples of outer health. She felt deviant and unsuccessful, received social ostracism, withdrew toward the positive inner life, produced fear and confusion in others, and began to question even the adequacy of internal things. It is difficult to help this client conceptualize the gamesmanship needed to appear healthy externally, the loss to internal health by defocusing on it, the need to consider external other-directed health as legitimate, steps to integrate internal and external into a new holistic state of being, and issues of control of the self as sick or healthy. In some cases, in fact, clients are unable to escape specific functional definitions of interpersonal outcomes, to allow other people to be legitimately defined as the problem. This appears like existentialism-turned-against-the-self, as some clients are unable to extract their self as perceiver of causality, to allow an external random process to be defined, over which they have no control, but which they must recognize to unhook themselves from behaviors of others. Although it is easy for the therapist to say "Let them be responsible for their own behaviors," or "This is none of your concern," some clients correctly recognize that they can never divorce themselves as perceivers of reality, from objects the therapist suggests are separate. In fact, suggesting that clients have capability to make them separate, may accentuate a distortion of valid reality, and constitute a greater form of irresponsibility by extracting problems from the self, and projecting them onto others. In any case, the counselor should carefully consider the general and specific definition and nature of outcomes, as they partly dictate how they will be evaluated as part of clinical process.

Primary, Secondary, Tertiary Levels
of Thoughts, Feelings, and Behaviors

A major concern of single case evaluators, is to make theoretical, experiential, or personal decisions about the relative significance and value of various outcome thoughts, feelings, or physical behaviors. Some therapists suggest that all outcomes exist on an equal horizontal plane initially, where each is equally significant because of its own identity; but become prioritized relative to their effect or significance within client personalized value systems and social recognition, utility, and cultural values.

This is only significant if vertical ordering is associated with client perception of quality of life, or societal priorities for appropriate and nonconflictual norms of interpersonal behaviors; to ultimately contribute to selection of therapeutic goals. It is a relatively easy task to assign equal values to horizontal outcomes which have the same potential to move into variable and possibly changing positions of significance, at the discretion of the outcome owner (client) or monitor (society). It becomes a more difficult task, to understand different qualitative (possibly quantifiable) rating criteria which might be assigned any outcomes, and more deeply understand processes by which these valuative decisions are made, and whether the value assignments help or hurt the client. In working with clients relative to this issue, the counselor not only has to evaluate the presence of outcomes relative to their weighted values, but helps clients make decisions about overall end products, as positive and negative values are added, resulting in one overall index of happiness, success, and adequacy.

The numerous values may be the only criteria [e.g., 2 third place outcomes (3 + 3), plus 1 eighth place (8), minus 2 first place outcomes (1 + 1) may equal and grand total of (6 + 8 - 2 = 12)] to place the outcome well within a numeric and conceptual range, to be considered positive by the client (low scores based on ranking, are most positive). On the other hand, some clients personally require at least first place outcomes per time period assessed, in order to be anywhere within a self-defined adequate range, even if numbers of other ranked outcomes cumulatively suggest considerable accomplishment. The therapist not only has to be sensitive to this primary, secondary, tertiary subject valuation process, but must consider the willingness of clients to respond to various inputs, and the relative value they place on inputs, to cause change in a prioritized potential outcome. Some clients will make a multitude of lower level changes, and directly attribute this to therapeutic inputs (without overly dependent or manipulative motives), yet assume that no input is powerful enough to produce change in a #1 or #2 priority, and will make overall negative judgments about their lives, because a #1 never shows up on the behavioral ledger. This, of course, relates to level of trauma, childhood fear, etc., but some clients are able to substitute (mix and match) high and low priority successes and failures, to piece together a generally successful life scenario with which they, comfortably live. The author has not found this phenomenon directly associated with any one diagnosis or demographic characteristic, and is presently uncertain about its origin and operating principles. In cases where clients are cognitively or behaviorally very active (generate a large number of outcomes in close and repeated proximity, not in a manic type syndrome, but more related to lifestyle), it is difficult (and maybe impossible) to prioritize all outcomes, and too time-consuming to place them into prioritized categories. There may be, however, groups of these outcomes which the client does see differentially from all others. Some outcomes which have much less potency and value, can be lumped into clusters to collectively give them a different meaning. Sometimes, a dichotomous qualitative rating is helpful (Hi-Low), wherein high outcomes can be further subdivided, once the larger number of less significant, lower outcomes that are time-consuming (in terms of client's time), can be relegated to a categorical status. A problem here, may be the setting of priorities by clients; yet many outcomes occur as a result of lifestyle activities and, if eliminated, change the character of the life, more than many clients would desire or find tolerable. The multiplicity of outcomes, by sheer numbers, may create a type of significance, in and of itself (for example, when someone is "on a roll," and a larger number of small successes feed into, and reinforce one another, creating a more abstract and general level of success or massing of forces which, considered holistically, may have substantial identity-related significance but, individually, would not be amenable to more finite prioritization).

Because of character styles, social learning and opportunities, interactional situations, job natures, and culture; many clients choose, or are somewhat forced to place primary significance on, one of the three major categories of personal activity: (1) cognitive thought, (2) emotional feeling (cognitive thought + cognitive valuation + social reward + physical associated reaction), or (3) physical behavior. Given the permanency of many of these proclivities, the counselor may reorient evaluative contingencies to take into account the primary nature of one particular approach relating to the world, and then make important psychodynamic decisions about lesser evaluative priorities, given possible priority conflicts within theoretical models. Cognitive clients, for example, may demonstrate (even with years of sound therapeutic inputs) minimal frequencies of feeling outcomes or emotionality; but attain greater depth, richness, flexibility, or self-actualization in their exclusively cognitive demeanor and activity, which have significant reward value as measures of change and progress. When theory is challenged and exceptions or modifications have to be made, possible losses of some form of personality development, must be integrated into the holistic scheme. It is fruitless to maintain criteria as even referentially or evaluatively significant, when they will not become a truly significant component of the client's agenda or life space.

Another component of outcome categorical prioritization, relates to cultural ethnocentrism, allegiance, and habituation. Certain types of outcomes are either weighted as cultural necessities (at various levels of significance), or are excluded—and put clients in serious anxiety-provoking jeopardy, if introduced into their repertoire. As a prelude to this, an important evaluative and therapeutic concern is the degree to which cultural conformity or deviance are significant examples of developmental status, growth, or adequacy for the client. This partly suggests the need for culturally deviant (objective outsider) status, to even make a decision about the intra-cultural life. Assuming this obstacle can be addressed, some outcomes will never be totally acceptable or totally eliminated from cultural rule books, and it is important for the evaluator to match up degrees of adequacy in several important arenas, so common areas of competency criteria can be delineated (see Figure 8).

Figure 8
Variations in Adaptability to Different
Culture-Dependency Contingencies

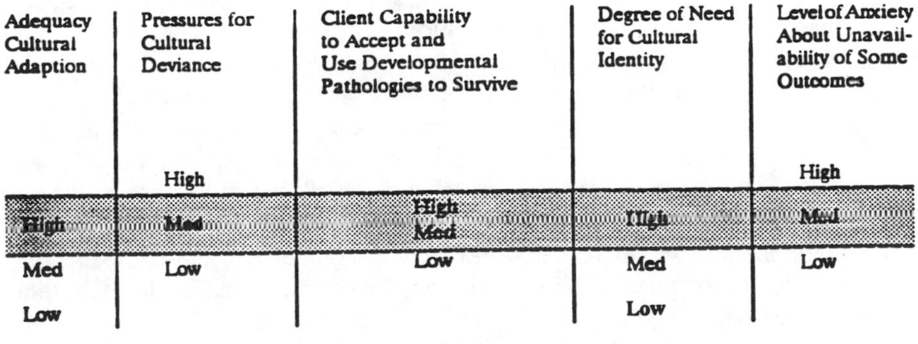

Adequacy Cultural Adaption	Pressures for Cultural Deviance	Client Capability to Accept and Use Developmental Pathologies to Survive	Degree of Need for Cultural Identity	Level of Anxiety About Unavailability of Some Outcomes
	High			High
High	Med	High Med	High	Med
Med	Low	Low	Med	Low
Low			Low	

If any other criteria do not consistently line up (for example, a high level of anxiety without the ability of this category to be adjusted to fit themes of the other category), then a particular group of outcomes which the client has been avoiding (but needs), will have to be reintroduced and prioritized into the evaluative scheme. In cases where there is a matched alignment across categories, some outcomes may be eliminated from serious consideration, as long as systemic adjustments are made throughout all relevant areas of the client's thought, value, and sociocultural life.

As a result of cultural socializations, personal need, and reference group goal setting, each client views and maintains (for security purposes) a framework for prioritizing outcomes, and also a system for adaptively or defensively dealing with other people who have differing programs of outcome prioritization. It is difficult, of course, to expect change in these priority assignments, unless the current configuration produces pain or displeasure for the client, or if the outcome priorities move into more predominate positions for trial and error learning. This is difficult for individuals who have highly prioritized outcomes related to inner spiritual, psychic, or philosophical identity and growth, which are hard to extrapolate for empirical investigation, and also tough to compare with other more public/external outcomes. Many clients in this type of situation, redefine some negative external outcomes as positive for internal growth or adequacy (including those who appear to be externally deprived, suffering, obscured, or neglected), and come to social service professionals to work on developing even richer internal high priority outcomes (with little desire or great fear, in tampering with external or lower priority empirical outcomes). They have a hard time deciding how much external change is necessary, to return internal dimensions to a state of self-defined pleasure or balance.

In evaluation of counseling with couples who have different priorities, it is important for the therapist to place attention on the partners' degrees of qualitative capability to conceptualize and understand the other partner's dynamics; their ability to convert the other partner's framework of outcome priorities into their own framework, in some qualitative or quantitative variable transformation; and ability of both partners to devise a third separate framework ("ours"), with outcome priorities upon which both agree, and which do not compromise other individual priority systems (his - his; hers - hers; his - hers) which must be retained for identity stability. In working with couples or families to become more flexible in their relationship negotiation, the counselor might also help them identify which outcomes have flexible priority assignment, to allow change with varying circumstances, and help them think through the gains or losses to the priority change assignment, with varying circumstances. They should also consider gains and losses to other priority configurations as they observe themselves manipulating as mobile priority outcomes, to more flexibly meet their needs through relationship interdependent negotiable role alignment.

This is particularly important in families where partners must deal with their differing outcome priorities, as the children grow and develop their own priorities, and also achieve interdependent ability to reprioritize parental primary, secondary, or tertiary agendas. Parents with highly prioritized outcomes related to child conformity when kids are young, may have a difficult time when their children become adolescents, because they need to reprioritize outcomes related to children, in terms of adequacy or ability for their own self-evaluation of conformity and deviance. They may also note that children may define conformity as a low priority, if they feel parents have not placed a high priority on adolescent choice; whereas parents who give high priority to adolescent change, might note that children can choose to conform, which they then assign an equally high priority. Adolescents who perform deviant outcomes may define the external behavior as negative, but the internal symbolic autonomy as positive, all of which may be directly related to parental priorities to which the adolescent is reactive. It is significant for families to discuss these issues, so the evaluator develops a scheme to document changes in priority ratings, and interpret meaning associated with multiple variations of this prioritization process. In many of these cases, clients, in order to maintain internal equilibrium, define the process (an outcome itself) of rejection of certain outcomes as positive, which the counselor/evaluator might code as a positive index of self-assertion, or a negative index of open-mindedness or fear, etc. It may not be the act of rejecting low priority outcomes which is the problem, but the process by which this decision is rationally or irrationally made.

A final area which is more controversial, relates to the author's personal perspectives about thoughts, feelings, or behaviors which are psychodynamically and developmentally of more primary therapeutic and evaluative importance than others. There is no question of bias involved in the clinician making this decision, but there also needs to be some framework used in approaching a wide range of possible outcomes the client presently manifests, and which have been significant in the past. One example, is differential priority the author places on feelings of hurt as a primary emotion, and the feeling of anger the author feels is a secondary reactive emotion, more distant from the true center of the psychodynamic issue. In thinking about evaluating therapeutic outcomes, the author places greater value on client awareness and understanding of primary feelings and associated social or intrapsychic conditions, where hurt is the outcome product. In this regard, he has found that time is lost and considerable confusion ensues, when assessments of anger cause the client to focus on a level of adaptation (defined as defensive, unless real physical fears of physical violence are present, and necessitate a fight response) which leads to relatively few definitive answers; until the client conceptualizes hurt and its relation to childhood dependency, which is transferred to present adult relationships with associated anxiety, need deprivation, punishment, and/or parental abandonment. Each clinician undoubtedly has his or her own selectively perceived priorities of thoughts, feelings, and behaviors, and needs to carefully think about how their outcomes will be measured, as compared to other outcomes the client might focus on with more intensity. The ratio of high to low priority outcomes within the clinician's theoretical model, gives some indication of success with various clients, yet does not always appear in the normal curve of client purposeful random behavior, with as much normal frequency as would support its higher level of prioritization in the therapist's mind. This is not necessarily a problem, as long as the client knows something about the priority system, so he/she can make a decision that these goals are too widely divergent to warrant attention in the present therapist- client alignment.

Outcome Stability, Transiency, and Responsiveness to Inputs

This particular issue is specifically germane to the measurement of definitive progress in treatment, as well as established subgoals and objectives. This issue becomes paramount at time of termination, although some counselors do not carefully consider the issue of permanency or stability of outcomes, when making a judgment that the client has attained success in treatment, or that the therapist has done a good job.

There are many thoughts or behaviors that clients manifest (as outcomes) and, as a result of their characteristics, have a greater sustaining power or degree of permanency, which exists to some degree, separate from other thoughts or behaviors which interact with them as sustaining or extinguishing reinforcements. One example may be the outcome behavior of cognitive inquiry, which (not considering defensive and evasive intellectual characteristics in certain individuals, and at certain times) may be a unique type of outcome extending over longer periods of time, and producing other similar behaviors; as opposed to the physical behavior of writing or preparing manuscripts, which may have less sustaining power as a result of its nature, more empirical energy expenditure, capability for refutation and external criticisms, and degree of permanency (maybe entrapment) which it presupposes. An example of this is seen in very healthy Ph.D. students in the dissertation stage of their academic program, who find greater longevity in studying various research topics, than in actually getting down to the writing process, even though it might be obvious to them and faculty supervisors that they are ready for the writing stage. Of course, there are personal conflictual issues related to dependency, assertion, self-confidence, etc., but some students sustain one process longer than the other, even when study comes after writing has begun, and where no personal pathology seems apparent.

Other examples are direction of anger inward as opposed to externalization, feeling intellectually as opposed to physically attractive, performing non-nail biting as opposed to non-overeating behavior, etc. The author agrees that these differences in the repetition frequency or sustaining characteristics are influenced by socialized values, degrees of externalization, cultural reinforcement and complexity; still, he notes that some outcomes maintain relatively differential degrees of permanency, even when other interactive contingencies are varied to try to produce change.

One client the author worked with around a serious obsessive compulsive disorder, was more capable of sustaining physical exercise activities as a process of personal nurturance, as opposed to physical relaxation exercises; since the nature of passive vs. active, overt vs. covert, work vs. rest, movement vs. non-movement, had a different characteristic not entirely related to, or able to be modified by, identical cognitive inputs which we tried to associate equally with each activity. Another example of transient outcomes might be the behavior of gentleness in men, as opposed to assertiveness, or withdrawal from others' games. One client, for example, who previously mothered her husband, continued, for a long time, refusing to mother (which we both considered positive); but experienced more in the behavior of nurturing or directing the self, although equal amounts of therapeutic energy had been directed (or intended to be directed) at each area of activity (outcome).

In planning evaluation, the therapist might benefit from considering the natures of particular outcomes which have more longitudinal stability, as opposed to those appearing very positive at the time of treatment termination, but diminishing in intensity as time passes. From a research perspective, each counselor must identify which outcomes seem to be equally responsive to the same input, and then compare them relative to their own natures; and also consider different therapeutic inputs which might increase the permanency characteristics of any particular outcome.

These hypotheses can and should be shared with clients, so they understand the nature of various behaviors (many of which, of course, are products of psychosocial learning, and philosophical preference), since this helps them piece together interdependent dynamic parts of their personalities. It also constructs a stable image and identity presentation, wherein more permanent behaviors work together to maintain equilibrium and maximize potential, at times when the personality needs or desires movement or non-movement in specific psychic or social directions.

Another example occurs in perceptions (or self-perceptions) of being a needy and emotionally deprived child, as contrasted to an angry child, because of various unfair blows dealt physically and psychologically by parents. The author considers both perspectives in adulthood to be irrational distortions of current reality, yet they have differing degrees of permanency or stability for different clients. The question here, is related to the social acceptability of being weak as opposed to being angry. This includes the depth at which each can be felt and conceptualized, and the ability to see similar reinforcing conditions (social conditions of helplessness vs. conflict) in the outer environment for reinforcement of the self; and particular physical, hormonal, or endocrinologic factors which produce one response more than the other. The enculturated view of destruction, violence, and aggressiveness which surrounded the Vietnam War, for example, may key in one set of anger-related outcomes, which have more permanency in the recovery process of conflicted veterans (of militaristic systems), as opposed to other permanent outcomes related to the current generation of children, tuned into the computer explosion, music video phenomena, etc. Therefore, angry-type outcomes may not be as predominant for them, as outcomes for people socialized during Vietnam. Children now, may experience a high preponderance of less aggressive, more artistic, escapist, or less interpersonal categories of outcomes, which have, for them, greater staying power as a result of socialized cultural learning.

References

1. Joel Fischer, "Is Casework Effective? A Review," *Social Work,* 18:1:5-20, January, 1973.
   Joel Fischer, ed., *The Effectiveness of Social Casework* (Springfield, IL: Charles C. Thomas, 1976).
2. Scott Briar, "The Current Crisis in Social Casework," in *National Conference on Social Welfare Social Work Practice* (New York: Columbia University Press, 1967), pp. 19-33.
3. Bernice Polemis, "Is the Case Closed?" in *The Effectiveness of Social Casework,* ed. Joel Fischer (Springfield, IL: Charles C. Thomas, 1976), pp. 232-261.
   Mary Gyarfas and Robert Nee, "Was It Really Casework?" *Social Work,* 18:1:3-4, July, 1973.
4. Jerome Cohen, "A Brief Comment: Evaluating the Effectiveness of an Unspecified 'Casework' Treatment in Producing Change" in *The Effectiveness of Social Casework,* ed. Joel Fischer (Springfield, IL: Charles C. Thomas, 1976), pp. 176-189.
5. Allen Bergin, "The Evaluation of Therapeutic Outcomes," *Handbook of Psychotherapy and Behavior Changes,* eds., A. E. Bergin and S. L. Garfield (New York: Wiley, 1971).
   Neil Jacobson, "A Review of Research on Marital Therapy," *Marriage and Marital Therapy: Psychoanalytic, Behavioral and Systems Theory Perspectives,* eds. T. J. Paoline and B. S. McCurdy (New York: Brunner/Mazel, 1978).
6. Stanley Witkin and Dianne Harrison, "Single Case Designs in Marital Research and Therapy," *Journal of Social Service Research,* 3:1:51-66, Fall, 1979.
7. Mary Kennedy, "Generalizing from Single Case Studies," *Evaluating Quarterly,* 3:4:661-678, November, 1979.
8. Paul Meehl, "When Shall We Use Our Heads Instead of the Formula?" *Journal of Counseling Psychology,* 4:4:268-273, Fall, 1957.
9. Alexander Bryk and Hilda Weisburg, "An Alternative Paradigm for Evaluating and Individualizing Demonstration Programs," Presented at the Annual Meeting of the American Educational Research Association, Toronto, Canada, April, 1978; and
   Edward Glaser and Thomas Backer, "A Clinical Approach to Program Evaluation," *Evaluation,* 1:1:54-55, Fall, 1972.
10. Mary Kennedy, "Generalizing From Single Case Studies," *Evaluation Quarterly,* 3:4:661-678, November, 1979.
11. M. Scriven, "Maximizing the Power of Causal Investigations: The Modus Operandi Method," in *Evaluation Studies Review Annual,* ed., G. Glass (Beverly Hills: Sage, 1976).

12.   Eugene Edgington, "Statistical Inference from N = 1 Experiments,"
Journal of Psychology, 65:195-199, March, 1967.
13.   Neil Jacobson, William Jellette, et al., "Variability in Outcome and
Clinical Significance in Behavioral Marital Therapy: A Re-analysis of Outcome Data," *Journal of Consulting and Clinical Psychology,* 52:4:497-504,
1984.
14.   Alan Kazdin and G. Terence Wilson, *Evaluation of Behavior Therapy:
Issues Evidence, and Research Strategies* (Cambridge, MA: Ballinger, 1978).
        Donald Barlow, "On the Relation of Clinical Research to Clinical Practice:
Current Issues, New Directions," *Journal of Consulting and Clinical Psychology,* 49:2:147-155, 1981.
15.   Neil Jacobsen, W. C. Follette, and D. Revenstorf "Psychotherapy Outcome Research: Methods for Reporting Variability and Evaluating Clinical
Significance," *Behavior Therapy* (in press).
16.   Neil Jacobsen, W. C. Follette, and D. Revenstorf "Psychotherapy Outcome Research: Methods for Reporting Variability and Evaluating Clinical
Significance," *Behavior Therapy* (in press).
17.   Thomas Kiresuls and Geoffrey Garwick, "Basic Goal Attainment Scaling
Procedures," Chart 1 of *Program Evaluation Project Evaluation Report* (Min-
neapolis: National Institute of Mental Health, 1969-1973).
18.   Alan Kazdin, "Methodological and Interpretive Problems of Single Case
Experimental Designs," *Journal of Consulting and Clinical Psychology,* 46:
4:629-642, 1978.
19.   Paul Herbst, *Behavioral Worlds: The Study of Single Cases* (London:
Tavistock Publications, 1970).
20.   Leon Festinger, *A Theory of Cognitive Dissonance* (Stanford, CA: Stanford University Press, 1957).
21.   Aubrey Yates, "Symptoms and Symptom Substitution," *Psychological
Review,* 65:6:371-374, November, 1958.
22.   William Russel, et al., "A Basic for the Quantitative Study of the
Structure of Behavior," *Behavior,* 6:6:154-157, 1954.
23.   Jack Levin, *Elementary Statistics in Social Research* (New York: Harper
and Row, 1977), pp. 92-118.
24.   Harold Lertenberg, "The Use of Single Case Methodology in Psychotherapy Research," *Journal of Abnormal Psychology,* 82:1:87-101, 1972.
25.   Donald Baer, et al., "Some Current Dimensions of Applied Behavior
Analysis," *Journal of Applied Behavior Analysis,* 1:1:91-97, 1968.
26.   Alan Kazdin, "Methodological and Interpretive Problems of Single Case
Experimental Designs," *Journal of Consulting and Clinical Psychology,* 46:
629-642, 1978.

27. Stanley Witkin and Dianne Harrison, "Single Case Designs in Marital Research and Therapy," *Journal of Social Science Research,* 3:1:201-205, Fall, 1979.

28. Stanley Witkin and Dianne Harrison, "Single Case Designs in Marital Research and Therapy," *Journal of Social Science Research,* 3:1:201-205, Fall, 1979.

29. Sanford Dornbusch and Richard Scott, *Evaluation and the Exercise of Authority* (San Francisco: Josey-Bass, 1977).

30. Paul Herbst, *Behavioral Worlds: The Study of Single Cases* (London: Tavistock Publications, 1970).

31. Thomas McCarthy, The Critical Therapy of Jurgen Habermas (Cambridge, MA: M.I.T. Press, 1978), p. 283.

32. Perry London, *The Modes and Morals of Psychotherapy* (New York: Holt, Rinehart and Winston, 1964).

33. Richard Walls, *Planned Short-Term Treatment* (New York: Free Press, 1982).

34. Charles Atherton and David Klemmach, *Research Methods in Social Work* (Lexington, MA: D. C. Heath and Co., 1982).

35. John Flanagan, "The Critical Incident Technique," *Psychological Bulletin,* 51:4:327-358, July, 1954.

36. Michael Selby, "Assessment of Violence Potential Using Measures of Anger, Hostility, and Social Desirability," *Journal of Personality Assessment,* 48:5:531-543, 1984.

37. Leslie Lothstein and P. Jones, "Discriminating Violent Individuals by Means of Various Psychological Tests," *Journal of Personality Assessment,* 42:2:237-243, June, 1978.

Thomas Dieker, "A Cross Validation of MMPI Scales of Aggression on Male Criminal Criterion Groups," *Journal of Consulting and Clinical Psychology,* 42:2:196-202, April, 1974.

Henry Kozol, "The Diagnosis of Dangerousness," in *Violence and Victims,* ed., S. Pasternack (New York: Spectrum, 1975).

38. Michael Selby, "Assessment of Violence Potential Using Measures of Anger, Hostility, and Social Desirability," *Journal of Personality Assessment,* 48:5:531-543, 1984.

39. Arnold Buss, *The Psychology of Aggression* (New York: Wiley, 1961).

40. Albert Bandura, *Aggression: A Social Learning Analysis* (Englewood Cliffs, NJ: Prentice-Hall, 1973).

41. Douglas Crowne and David Marlow, "A Scale of Social Desirability Independent of Pathology," *Journal of Consulting Psychology,* 24:2:349-354, August, 1960.

42.   Michael Selby, "Assessment of Violence Potential Using Measures of Anger, Hostility, and Social Desirability," *Journal of Personality Assessment,* 48:5:552-553, 1984.

43.   Martin Bloom and Joel Fischer, *Evaluating Practice: Guidelines for the Accountable Professional* (Englewood Cliffs: Prentice-Hall, 1982), pp. 133-137.

44.   Stephen Haynes and Chrisman Wilson, *Behavioral Assessment* (San Francisco: Josey-Bass, 1979), pp. 217-219.

45.   Allen Belloch and Michael Hersen, "Inventories in Behavioral Assessment," *Behavioral Assessments,* eds., J. D. Cone and R. P. Hawkins (New York: Brunner/Mazel, 1977), pp. 52-76.

46.   David Foy, Lawrence Nunn, and Robert Rychtarik, "Broad Spectrum Behavioral Treatment for Chronic Alcoholics: Effects of Training Controlled Drinking Skills," *Journal of Consulting and Clinical Psychology,* 52:2:218-230, 1984.

47.   Mark Sobell and Linda Sobell, "Second Year Treatment Outcome of Alcoholics Treated by Individualized Behavior Therapy: Results," *Behavior Research Therapy,* 14:3:195-215, 1976.

48.   Roger Kirk, *Experimental Design: Procedures for the Behavioral Sciences* (Belmone, CA: Brooks Cole, 1968).

49.   Charles Emrick, "A Review of Psychologically-Oriented Treatment of Alcoholism: I. The Use of Interrelationships of Outcome Criteria and Drinking Behavior Following Treatment," *Quarterly Journal of Studies in Alcohol,* 35:5:523-549, 1974.

        Elvin Jellinek, *The Disease Concept of Alcoholism* (New Haven, CT: College and University Press, 1960).

50.   James McCollogh, "The Need for New Single Case Design Structure in Applied Cognitive Psychology," *Psychotherapy,* 21:3:389-400, Fall, 1984.

51.   M. B. Shapiro, "A Method of Measuring Psychological Changes Specific to the Individual Psychiatric Patient," *British Journal of Medical Psychology,* 34:4:151-155, 1961.

        M. B. Shapiro, "The Measurement of Clinically Relevant Variables," *Journal of Psychosomatic Research,* 8:1:245-254, 1964.

52.   B. F. Skinner, *Contingencies of Reinforcement A Theoretical Analysis* (New York: Appleton-Century-Crofts, 1969).

53.   Murray Sidman, *Tactics of Scientific Research* (New York: Basic Books, 1960).

54.   Laren Chapman and Jean Chapman, "Genesis of Popular But Erroneous Diagnostic Observations," *Journal of Abnormal Psychology,* 72:3:193-204, June, 1967. Loren Chapman and Jean Chapman, "Illusionary Correlation as

an Obstacle to the Use of Valid Psychodiagnostic Signs," *Journal of Abnormal Psychology,* 74:4:271-280, September, 1969.

55. Ian Evans and Craig Robinson, "Behavior Therapy Observed: The Diary of A Client," *Cognitive Therapy and Research,* 2:4:335-355, December, 1978.

56. James McCullough, "The Need for New Single Case Design Structure in Applied Cognitive Psychology," *Psychotherapy,* 21:3:389-400, 1984.

57. Romano Harre and Paul Secord, *The Explanation of Social Behavior* (Oxford, Basil Blackwell, 1972), p. 132.

58. Roy Ruckdeschel and Buford Farris, "Assessing Practice: A Critical Look at the Single Case Design," *Social Casework,* 62:7:413-419, 1981.

59. Randall Collins, *Conflict Sociology: Toward an Explanatory Science* (New York: Academic Press, 1975), p. 4.

60. Norman Denzin, *The Research Act* (Chicago: Aldine, 1977).

61. Thomas Cook, and Donald Campbell, *Quasi-Experimentation: Design and Analysis Issues for Field Settings* (Boston: Houghton Mifflin, 1979).

62. Richard Daft, and John Wiginton, "Language and Organization," *Academy of Management and Review,* 4:2:179-191, April, 1979.

63. Anthony Giddens, *Central Problems in Social Therapy: Action, Structure, and Contradiction in Social Analysis* (Berkeley: University of California Press, 1979).

64. Reyes Ramos, "The Use of Improvisation and Modification in Natural Talk: An Alternative Approach to Conversational Analysis," *Studies in Symbolic Interaction:* Vol. 1; ed., Norman K. Denzin (Greenwich, CT: J.A.I. Press, 1978), pp. 319-337.

65. Richard Bandler and John Grinder, *The Structure of Magic: A Book About Language and Therapy* (Palo Alto, CA: Science and Behavior Books, 1975).

66. Paul Watzlawick, *The Language of Change: Elements of Therapeutic Communication* (New York: Basic Books, 1978).

67. Sherwood Waldron, "The Significance of Childhood Neurosis for Adult Mental Health," *American Journal of Psychiatry,* 133:532-538, May, 1976. *Learning Failure Task Panel Report,* Task Panel Reports Submitted to the President's Commission on Mental Health (Vol. 3; Washington, DC: U.S. Government Printing Office, 1978).

68. Emory Cowen, et al., *New Ways in School Mental Health: Early Detection and Prevention of School Maladaption* (New York: Human Science Press, 1975).

Christine Chandler, Roger Weissberg, Emory Cowen, and John Guare, "Long-Term Effect of a School-Based Secondary Prevention Program for Young Maladapting Children," *Journal of Consulting and Clinical Psychology,* 52:2:165-170, 1984.

69. Donald Baer, et al., "Some Current Dimensions of Applied Behavior Analysis," *Journal of Applied Behavior Analysis,* 1:2:91-97, 1968.

70. Israel Goldiamond, Jarl Dyrud, and Miles Miller, "Practice in Research Professional Psychology," *The Canadian Psychologist,* 6A:1:110-129, 1965.
   Israel Goldiamond, "Perception," *The Experimental Foundations of Clinical Psychology,* ed., A. J. Bachrach (New York: Basic Books, 1962).

71. James Holland, Burrhus Skinner, *The Analysis of Behavior* (New York: Appleton-Century-Crofts, 1975), pp. 211-215.

72. J. Brady, et al., "Experimental Analysis of Hysterical Blindness," A.M.A *Archives of General Psychiatry,* 4:4:331-339, 1961.

73. Ronald Marx and Philip Winne, "Construct Interpretations of Three Self-Concept Inventories," *American Educational Research Journal,* 15:1:99-109, 1978.

74. William Purkey, *Self-Concept and School Achievement* (Englewood Cliffs, NJ: Prentice-Hall, 1970).
   Ruth Wylie, *The Self-Concept* (Vol. 1; Lincoln, NE: University of Nebraska Press, 1974).

75. Lawrence Cronback, "Test Validation," *Educational Measurement,* ed. R. L. Thorndike (Washington, DC: American Counsel on Education, 1971).

76. Richard Shavelson, Judith Hubner, and George Stanton, "Self-Concept Validation of Construct Interpretations," *Review of Educational Research,* 46:3:407-441, Summer, 1976.

77. R. B. Sloane, et al., *Psychotherapy vs. Behavior Therapy* (Cambridge, MA: Harvard University Press, 1975).

78. Sol Garfield, *Research on Client Variables in Psychotherapy and Behavior Change,* 2nd ed.; eds., A Bergin and S. Garfield (New York: Wiley, 1978).
   Gordon Paul, "Insight Versus Desensitization in Psychotherapy Two Years After Termination," *Journal of Consulting Psychology,* 31:4:338-348, August, 1967.

79. Thomas Schramski, et al., "Factors that Contribute to Post-Therapy Persistence of Therapeutic Change," *Journal of Clinical Psychology,* 40:1:78-85, January, 1984.

80. Donald Baer, et al., "Some Current Dimensions of Applied Behavior Analysis," *Journal of Applied Behavior Analysis,* 1:2:91-97, 1968.

81. Leon Festinger, *A Theory of Cognitive Dissonance* (Stanford, CA: Stanford University Press, 1957).

82. Michael Selby, "Assessment of Violence Potential Using Measures of Anger, Hostility, and Social Desirability," *Journal of Personality Assessment,* 48:7:531-543, 1984.

83. James McCullough, "The Need for New Single Case Design Structure in Applied Cognitive Psychology," *Psychotherapy,* 21:3:389-400, Fall, 1984.

84. Don Dulany, "Awareness, Rules, and Propositional Control: A Confrontation with S-R Behavior Theory," *Verbal Behavior and General Behavior Theory,* eds., T. Dixon and D. Horton (Englewood Cliffs, NJ: Prentice-Hall, 1968).

85. Paul Herbst, *Behavioral Worlds: The Study of Single Cases* (London: Tavistock Publications, 1970).

86. Kenneth Berrien, *General and Social Systems* (New Brunswick, NJ: Rutgers University Press, 1968).

   Irma Stein, "The Systems Model and Social Systems Theory: Their Application to Social Work," in *Social Casework: Theories in Action,* ed. H. Strean (Metuchen, NJ: Scarecrow Press, 1971).

87. Harriette Johnson, "Integrating the Problem-Oriented Record with Systems Approach to Case Assessment," *Journal of Education for Social Work,* 14:3: 71-77, Fall, 1978.

88. Robert Dublin, *Theory Building* (New York: The Free Press, 1969), pp. 52-60.

89. John Sabini and Maury Silver, "Baseball and Hot Sauce: A Critique of Some Attributional Treatments of Evaluation," *Journal of Theory of Social Behavior,* 10:2:83-95, July, 1980.

90. Edward Jones and Robert Nesbitt, *The Actor and Observer: Divergent Perceptions of the Cases of Behavior* (New York: General Learning Press, 1971).

91. H. Kelley, "Attribution Theory in Social Psychology," in *Nebraska Symposium on Motivation,* ed. D. Levine (Lincoln: Nebraska Press, 1967).

92. Arthur Schutz, *Collected Papers* (The Hague: Nijhoff, 1962).

93. Erving Goffman, *Relations in Public* (New York: Harper, 1971).

94. Richard Rablain, *Inner and Outer Space* (New York: W. W. Norton, 1970), pp. 44-55.

95. Erik Erikson, "Growth and Crises of the Healthy Personality," in *Psychological Issues* (Vol. 1; New York: International Universities Press, 1959).

96. Ann Gifford and Peggy Golde, "Self-Esteem in the Aging Population," *Journal of Gerontological Social Work,* 1:1:69-81, Fall, 1978.

97. John Robinson and Philip Shaver, *Measures of a Social Psychological Attitudes* (Ann Arbor: University of Michigan, Institute of Social Research, 1970).

98. Kenneth Gergan, *The Concept of Self* (New York: Holt, Rinehart and Winston, 1971).

99. Stanley Coopersmith, *The Antecedents of Self-Esteem* (San Francisco: W. M. Freeman, 1967).

100.   Margaret Clark, "The Anthropology of Aging, A New Area for Studies of Culture and Personality," *Gerontologist,* 7:1:55-64, March, 1967.

101.   Florence Harris, et al., "Methodology for Experimental Studies of Young Children in Natural Settings," *Psychology Record,* 19:2:177-210, 1969.

102.   Frank McKenna, "Measure of Field Dependence: Cognitive Style or Cognitive Ability?" *Journal of Personality and Social Psychology,* 47:3:593-603, 1984.

103.   Harry Guntrip, *Psychoanalytic Theory, Therapy and the Self* (New York: Basic Books, 1971).

104.   Harry Guntrip, *Psychoanalytic Theory, Therapy and the Self* (New York: Basic Books, 1971).

105.   Henry Miller, "Value Dilemmas in Social Casework," *Social Casework* 13:2:127-133, June, 1968.

106.   Hans Strupp and Michael Wallack, "A Further Study of Psychiatrist Responses in Quasi Therapy Situations," *Behavioral Science,* 10:4:113-134, 1965.

107.   Robert Langs, *The Technique of Psychoanalytic Therapy* (New York: Jason Aronson, 1974), p. 149.

108.   Roy Schafer, *A New Language of Psychoanalysis* (New Haven: Yale University Press, 1976).

109.   Lynn Fairbanks and Michael McGuire, eds., *Ethnology Psychiatry: Psychopathology in the Context of Evolutionary Biology* (New York: Gaune & Stratton, 1977), pp. 125-138.

110.   Kenneth Berrien, *General and Social Systems* (New Brunswick, NJ: Rutgers University Press, 1968). Irma Stein, "The Systems Model and Social Systems Theory: Their Application to Social Work," in *Social Casework: Theories in Action,* ed. H. Strean (Metuchen, NJ: Scarecrow Press, 1971).

111.   Kathleen Berger, *The Developing Person Through the Life Span* (New York: Worth, 1983), pp. 232-242.

112.   Sigmund Freud, "The Economic Problems of Masochism," in *Collected Papers* (Vol. 2; London: Hogarth Press, 1924).

113.   Helen Deutsch, *The Psychology of Women* (New York: Grune and Stratton, 1944), pp. 239-278.

114.   Karen Horney, "The Problem of Feminine Masochism," *Psychoanalytic Review,* 12:2:241-257, 1935.

115.   Paula Johnson, "Women and Power: Toward a Theory of Effectiveness," *Journal of Social Issues,* 32:2:32-35, 1976.

116.   Matina Horner, "The Motive to Avoid Success and Changing Aspirations of College Women," *Readings on the Psychology of Women,* ed. Judith Bardwick (New York: Harper and Row, 1972).

Judith Bardwick, *Readings on the Psychology of Women* (New York: Harper and Row, 1972).

117.   Rebecca Meda, Robert Hefner, and Barbara Oleshansky, "A Model of Sex-Role Transcendence," *Journal of Social Issues,* 32:4:197-205, Summer, 1976.

118.   Andrea Dworkin, *Women Hating* (New York: E. P. Dutton and Co., 1974).

119.   Arthur Jensen, "How Much Do We Boost I.Q. and Scholastic Achievement?" *Higher Education Review,* 39:1:1-23, Winter, 1969.

120.   McViffer Hunter, "The Psychological Basis for Using Preschool Enrichment as an Antidote for Cultural Deprivation," *Merrill-Palmer Quarterly,* 10:5:209-248, July, 1964.

121.   Leon Kamin, *The Science and Politics of I.Q.* (New York: Halsted Press, 1974.

122.   Roy Schafer, *A New Language of Psychoanalysis* (New Haven: Yale University Press, 1976), pp. 134-136.

123.   Roy Schafer, *A New Language of Psychoanalysis* (New Haven: Yale University Press, 1976), p. 349.

124.   Harvey Guntrip, *Psychoanalytic Theory Therapy and the Self* (New York: Basic Books, 1971), p. 104.

125.   Erich Fromm, *To Have or To Be* (New York: Harper and Row, 1976), p. 16.

126.   Erich Fromm, *To Have or To Be* (New York: Harper and Row, 1976), p. 16.

127.   Han Selye, *Stress in Health and Disease* (Boston: Butterworths, 1976).

128.   L. Sever, "Anencephalous and Spina Bifida: An Ecological Approach," *Human Ecology,* 4:3:209-221, 1976.

129.   Matthew Dermont, "The Nonspecificity of Mental Illness," *American Journal of Orthopsychiatry,* 54:2:307, April, 1984.

130.   D. Rosehan, "On Being Sane in Insane Places," *Science,* 179:4070:250-258, 1973.

131.   Thomas Szasz, *Schizophrenia: The Sacred Symbol of Psychiatry* (New York: Basic Books, 1976).

132.   Matthew Dermont, "The NonSpecificity of Mental Illness," *American Journal of Orthopsychiatry,* 54:5:329, April, 1984.

133.   Hans Strupp and Suzanne Hadley, "A Tripartite Model of Mental Health and Therapeutic Outcomes," *American Psychologist,* 32:3:187-196, March, 1977.

134.   Morris Parloff, et al., "Comfort Effectiveness, and Self-Awareness as Criteria of Improvement in Psychotherapy," *American Journal of Psychiatry,* 3:343-351, 1954.

135.   David Rapaport, "The Structure of Psychoanalytic Theory: A Systemizing Attempt," *Psychological Issues,* 2:2:1-158, 1960.

136.   Hans Strupp and Suzanne Hadley, "A Tripartite Model of Mental Health and Therapeutic Outcomes," *American Psychologist,* 32:3:187-196, March, 1977.

137.   Hans Strupp and Suzanne Hadley, "A Tripartite Model of Mental Health and Therapeutic Outcomes," *American Psychologist,* 32:3:192-194, March, 1977.

138.   Donald Krill, "A Framework for Determining Client Modifiability," *Social Casework,* 49:5:602-611, December, 1968.

139.   Joseph Anderson, "What Will Social Workers Will," *Social Casework,* 60:11-18, January, 1979.

140.   Otto Rank, *Beyond Psychology* (New York: Dover Publishing, 1958), p. 59.

141.   Leslie Farber, *The Ways of the Will: Essays Toward a Psychology and Psychopathology of Will* (New York: Harper and Row, 1966).

142.   Rollo May, *Love and Will* (New York: Dell Publishing, 1969).

143.   Rollo May, *Love and Will* (New York: Dell Publishing, 1969).

144.   Robert Assagioli, *The Act of the Will* (New York: Viking Press, 1973).

145.   Abraham Maslow, *Religion, Values, and Peak Experiences* (Columbus: Ohio State University Press, 1964).

146.   Otto Rank, *Beyond Psychology* (New York: Dover Publishing, 1958), p. 59.

147.   Allen Bergin and Hans Strupp, *Changing Frontiers in the Science of Psychotherapy* (Chicago: Aldine-Atherton, 1972), pp. 10-11, 54.

148.   Dennis Brisset, "Toward a Clarification of Self-Esteem," *Psychiatry,* 35:5:255-263, August, 1972.

149.   Lewis Leitner, "Discrimination of Counselor Interpersonal Skills in Self and Others," *Journal of Counseling Psychology,* 19:6:509-511, November, 1972.

150.   Robert Carkhuff, *Helping and Human Relations* (New York: Rinehart, and Winston, 1969).

151.   Joseph Marolla, "A Study of Self-Esteem as a Two Dimensional Construct," (Doctoral dissertation, University of Denver, 1974).

152.   Oliver Bowman, *A Longitudinal Study of Selected Facets of Children's Self-Concepts as Related to Achievement and Intelligence* (Charleston: The Citadel, 1974).

153.   Lawrence Shulman, *The Skills of Helping Individuals and Groups* (Hasca, IL: F. E. Peacock, 1979).

154.   Richard Kolm, "Ethnicity in Social Work," *Social Thought,* 4:1:3-14, Winter, 1978.

155. Phyllis Richter, "Evaluation of Change as a Tool in Treatment," *Social Thought,* 4:11:15-26, Winter, 1978.

156. Phyllis Richter, "Evaluation of Change as a Tool in Treatment," *Social Thought,* 4:11:24-26, Winter, 1978.

157. Thomas Morrison and Randall Morrison, "Self-Esteem Need for Approval and Self-Estimates of Academic Performance," *Psychological Reports,* 43:5: 503-507, 1978.

158. Thomas Petzel, "Approval Motive and Self-Estimates of Academic Performance," *Journal of Consulting and Clinical Psychology,* 39:4:199-201, 1972.

159. K. Keefer, "Characteristics of Students Who Make Accurate and Inaccurate Self-Predictions of College Achievement," *Journal of Educational Research,* 64:4:401-404, 1971.

160. J. Schrauger, "Self-Esteem and Reactions to Being Observed by Others," *Journal of Personality and Social Psychology,* 23:2:192-200, 1972.

161. Thomas Morrison and Randall Morrison, "Self-Esteem and Self-Estimates of Academic Performance," *Journal of Counseling and Clinical Psychology,* 41:3:412-415, December, 1973.

162. Thomas Petzel, Approval Motive and Self-Estimates of Academic Performance, *Journal of Consulting and Clinical Psychology,* 39:2:199-201, 1972.

163. Paul Watzlawick, Janet Beavin, and Don Jackson, *The Pragmatics of Human Communication* (New York: W. W. Norton, 1967).

164. Paul Watzlawick, Janet Beavin, and Don Jackson, *The Pragmatics of Human Communication* (New York: W. W. Norton, 1967).

165. Jay Haley, *Strategies of Psychotherapy* (New York: Grune and Stratton, 1963).

166. Sharon Berlin, "Cognitive Behavioral Interventions for Social Work Practice," *Social Work,* 27:3:218-226, May, 1982.

167. Shrinka Jayaratne, "A Study of Clinical Eclecticism," *Social Service Review,* 52:2:621-631, December, 1978.

168. Michael J. Mahoney, "Reflections on the Cognitive Learning Trend in Psychotherapy," *American Psychologist,* 32:6:5-13, January, 1977.

169. Sharon Berlin, "Cognitive Behavioral Interventions for Social Work Practice," *Social Work,* 27:3:218-226, May, 1982.

170. Sharon Berlin, "A Cognitive Learning Perspective for Social Work," *Social Service Review,* 4:5:537-555, December, 1980.

Michael Mahoney and Diane Arnkoff, "Cognitive and Self-Control Therapies," in *Handbook of Psychotherapy and Behavior Change: An Empirical Analysis,* eds. S. Garfield and A Bergin (New York: John Wiley and Sons, 1978), pp. 689-722.

Albert Bandurs, *Social Learning Theory* (Englewood Cliffs, NJ: Prentice-Hall, 1971).

Donald Meichenbaum, *Cognitive Behavior Modification: An Integrative Approach* (New York: Plenum Press, 1980), pp. 29-33.

171.   Donald Meichenbaum and Lynda Butler, "Ego Centrism and Evidence: Making Raget Kosher," in *Psychotherapy Process: Current Issues and Future Directions* (New York: Plenum Press, 1980), pp. 29-33.

172.   Amiram Vinokur and Melvin Selzer, "Desirable Versus Undesirable Life Events: Their Relationship to Stress and Mental Distress," *Journal of Personality and Social Psychology,* 32:2:329-337, August, 1975.

B. Wilcox, "Social Support, Life Stress, and Psychological Adjustment: A Test of the Buffering Hypothesis," *American Journal of Community Psychology,* 9:2:371-386, 1981.

M. Barrera, "Social Support in the Adjustment of Pregnant Adolescents: Assessment Issues," in *Social Networks and Social Support,* ed. B. Gottlieb (Beverly Hills: Sage, 1981).

173.   Amiram Vinokur and Melvin Selzer, "Desirable Versus Undesirable Life Events: Their Relationship to Stress and Mental Distress," *Journal of Personality and Social Psychology,* 32:2:329-337, August, 1975.

174.   Lawrence Cohen, et al., "Positive Life Events and Social Support and the Relationship Between Life Stress and Psychology Disorder," *American Journal of Community Psychology,* 12:5:567-587, 1984.

175.   Aaron Rosen, et al., "Content Classification System for Sexual Counseling: Method and Applications," *Journal of Sex,* 25:2:114-117, 1973.

176.   Arnold Lazarus, *Behavior Therapy and Beyond* (New York: McGraw-Hill Book Co., 1971).

George Kelly, *The Psychology of Personal Construct* (Vols. 1 and 2; New York: W. W. Norton, 1955).

177.   Laura Epstein, *Helping People: The Task-Centered Approach* (St. Louis: The C. V. Mosby Co., 1980), p. 79.

178.   Wayne Duehn and Nazneen Mayadas, "Starting Where the Client Is: An Empirical Investigation," *Social Casework,* 60:2:67-74, February, 1979.

179.   Helen Perlman, "Social Work Method: A Review of the Past Decade," *Social Work,* 10:2:166-178, October, 1965.

180.   Aaron Rosen, "The Treatment Relationship: A Conceptualization," *Journal of Consulting and Clinical Psychology,* 38:5:321-337, June, 1972.

181.   John Thibaut and Harold Kelley, *The Social Psychology of Groups* (New York: John Wiley and Sons, 1959).

182.   Stephen Richardson, Barbara Dohrenwend, and David Klein, *Interviewing: Its Forms and Functions* (New York: Basic Books, 1965), p. 156.

183. Henry Lennard and Arnold Bernstein, *Patterns in Human Interaction: An Introduction to Clinical Sociology* (San Francisco: Josey-Bass, 1969), p. 169.

184. Charles Truax and Robert Carkhuff, *Toward Effective Counseling and Psychotherapy* (Chicago: Aldine Publishing Co., 1967).
Robert R. Carkhuff, *Helping and Human Relations: A Primer for Lay and Professional Helpers, Practice and Research* (New York: Holt, Rinehart and Winston, 1969).

185. Allen Ivey, *Microcounseling: Innovation in Interviewing Training* (Springfield, IL: Charles C. Thomas, 1971).

186. Kurt Lewin, *Field Theory in Social Science* (New York: Harper and Row, 1952).

187. John Thibaut and Harold Kelley, *The Social Psychology of Groups* (New York: John Wiley and Sons, 1959).

188. Henry Lennard and Arnold Bernstein, *The Anatomy of Psychotherapy* (New York: Columbia University Press, 1960), p. 153.

189. Wayne Duehn and Enola Proctor, "Initial Clinical Interaction and Premature Discontinuance in Treatment," *American Journal of Orthopsychiatry,* 47:8:284-290, April, 1977.

190. Bert Meltzer, Walter Crockett, and Paul Rosenkrantz, "Cognitive Complexity and the Integration of Potentially Incompatible Information in Impressions of Others," *Journal of Personality and Social Psychology,* 4:4:338-343, September, 1966.

191. Allan Press, Walter Crockett, and Paul Rosenkrantz, "Cognitive Complexity and the Learning of Balanced and Unbalanced Social Structures," *Journal of Personality,* 37:7:541-553, December, 1969.

192. Allan Press, Walter Crockett, and Paul Rosenkrantz, "Cognitive Complexity and the Learning of Balanced and Unbalanced Social Structures," *Journal of Personality,* 37:7:541-553, December, 1969.

193. Wayne Duehn and Enola Proctor, "Initial Clinical Interaction and Premature Discontinuance in Treatment," *American Journal of Orthopsychiatry,* 47:8:284-290, April, 1977.

194. Wayne Duehn and Enola Proctor, "A Study of Cognitive Complexity in the Education for Social Work Practice," *Journal of Education for Social Work,* 10:2:20-26, Spring, 1974.

195. Nazneen Mayadas and Wayne Duehn, "The Effects of Training Formats and Interpersonal Discriminations in the Education of Clinical Social Work Practice," *Journal of Social Service Research,* 1:2:147-161, Winter, 1977.

196. O. J. Harvey, David E. Hunt, and Harold M. Schroeder, *Conceptual Systems and Personality Organization* (New York: John Wiley and Sons, 1961).

197. Paul Swingle, ed., *Social Psychology in Natural Settings* (Chicago: Aldine Publishing Co., 1973), p. 261.

198.   Ed Goldstein, "The Influence of Parental Attitudes on Psychiatric Treatment Outcomes," *Social Casework,* 60:6:350-359, June, 1979.

199.   Karl Beutner and Russel Branch, "The Psychiatrist and the Patient's Relatives," *Psychiatric Quarterly,* 33:3:1-8, January, 1959.

Donald Bloch, "Family of the Psychiatric Patient," *American Handbook of Psychiatry,* 2nd ed.; Silvano Arieto (New York: Basic Books, 1974), pp. 179-201.

200.   Delores Kreisman and Virginia Joy, "Family Response to the Mental Illness of a Relative: A Review of the Literature," *Schizophrenia Bulletin,* 10:7:34-57, 132-142, Fall, 1974.

201.   David Beres, "Ego Deviation and the Concept of Schizophrenia," *The Psychoanalytic Study of the Child* (New York: International Universities Press, 1965), II, pp. 164-235.

202.   Paul Herbst, *Behavioral Worlds: The Study of Single Cases* (London: Tavistock Publications, 1970).

203.   Kathering Wood, "Casework Effectiveness: A New Look at the Research Evidence," *Social Work,* 23:6:443-456, November, 1978.

204.   E. E. Jones, L. Bell, and E. Aronson, "The Reciprocation of Attraction from Similar and Dissimilar Others," *Experimental Social Psychology,* ed. C. McClintock (New York: Holt, Rinehart and Winston, 1972).

205.   Richard Santee and Susan Jackson, "Similarity and Positivity of Self-Description as Determinants of Estimated Appraisal and Attraction," *Social Psychology,* 41:2:162-165, June, 1978.

206.   Howard Levanthal and Sidney Perloe, "A Relationship Between Self-Esteem and Persuasibility," *Journal of Abnormal and Social Psychology,* 64:5:385-388, May, 1962.

Chapter Six

Implications of Clinical Evaluation

Introduction

At this point, the reader has ideally developed a more thorough appreciation for the philosophical and operational significance and complexity of clinical evaluation. Although there are numerous dimensions of processes of psychosocial development and conflict resolution, the basic character and nature of the human condition is not unfathomable. It does, however, require a thorough and perceptive investigation by a scholarly clinician, who understands what evaluative questions to ask; how to ask questions that yield value, and relevant and true responses; and which biases influence the interpretation and utilization of evaluative data. The clinician must also realize proper ways to use information, to develop hypotheses to test new knowledge for the future, and make decisions and take actions which, themselves, become independent variables to be assessed relative to measurable or clearly-discernable outcomes for clients.

There is little question in the author's mind that the counseling and casework professions, as a whole, are not pursuing the previously-enumerated comprehensive understanding, which is absolutely necessary to move closer to a point where consumers can be confidently assured, that their selected practitioner can produce highly-probable and successful results. The clinical professions are, furthermore, a great distance from a clear delineation of specific therapeutic inputs, and a complete understanding of their degrees, types, and rates of effectiveness with each client condition. Routes to achieve clinical goals are still debated in the literature and agency hallways, and goals to improve evaluative competence are unevenly manifested, and still of questionable clarity and strength of commitment.

This particular section of the book, therefore, suggests major tasks which lie ahead, among segments of the vast professional community from which particular development thrusts must emanate. Each practice domain will be discussed separately, with general suggestions as to strategic and tactical actions which assist counseling and clinical professions; to develop a clear and common evaluative philosophy, and produce clinicians who competently use systematic conceptual and methodological frameworks, to insure delivery of quality therapeutic products.

Education

Direct Self-Evaluative Experience

Although increasing numbers of academic programs which train counselors, therapists, caseworkers, or other direct human service professionals, have developed or improved formal courses in single subject evaluation, empirical and behavioral measurement, statistics and research methodology, and program evaluation; many students have not been socialized or experientially-oriented[1] to integrate and assume adult learning and self-evaluative attitudes and role behaviors, as critical components of their academic training. Students may have cognitive information about evaluation, but lack internalized self-evaluative norms and routine behavioral experience, for subsequent sustained personal assessment in professional careers. Students who have never formally participated in their own legitimate[2] self-evaluation in academic programs, have a limited foundation to build a career of meaningful evaluation for personal and professional growth. Most students in social service programs have seldom done self-evaluation, and the subject remains externalized and separate, preventing holistic integration of theory and practice. Many undergraduate and graduate programs, although exclusively responsible for education of adults, maintain norms for childlike student dependency, and lack of personal responsibility for learning and evaluation, characterized by earlier pedagogical relationships in elementary and high schools.[3] The professional role remains dominant within the didactic lecture format, where students are expected to diligently take notes, only to be reproduced in exams or papers in their original form, as delivered by the *expert*. In this method of determining competency, establishment of criteria for proficiency and conduct of evaluative assessment (grading), remain sole responsibilities of the instructor. The student, within this process, is a relatively passive receiver of cognitive information, and certainly a nonparticipant in evaluative decision-making, which symbolically results in competency determinations through grade assignment. Since most academic programs do not conduct formalized needs assessment research on students, knowledge and skill levels are assumed to be deficient (the learner is in a "state of error"), and the degree of deviance and remedial action are officially defined by the professor.

Students rarely are invited to identify and define their own needs for learning,[4] so the academic program robs them of beginning, as well as interim and outcome phases of evaluation. This includes developing personal awareness of varying levels of competence in both knowledge and skills, and then establishing learning objectives which are subsequently measured and compared to original baselines, to determine degree of change. Taking personal responsibility for achieving competence through self-evaluation, goes along with Chickering's[5] concept of becoming autonomous, as a significant developmental task for higher education. As course work progresses, students usually have no experience evaluating their work through comparison of actual and ideal states of competency, so they only witness the evaluative process second hand, as the instructor assigns grades. When practitioners finally confront evaluative requirements or opportunities in postgraduate employment, they may be armed with limited cognitive information, without having integrated evaluative attitudes or experimental awareness and norms, by actually conducting self-evaluation in their training programs.

In thinking about goals of adult educational experiences, various educators discuss the importance of learning skills to critically assess the environment's idealistic and realistic dimensions; and making evaluative choices relative to goals and aspirations[6] within an atmosphere of conflict between alternatives, from which students must make choices and assess their value-laden and pragmatic efficacy. Education should be individualized to the extent that students establish some of their own learning objectives and needs assessments, and use experiential data to assess compliance relative to personal as well as academic criteria. They can also learn personal responsibility for growth,[7] wherein inductive and deductive logic refine perceptions,[8] and move students toward fact-based decisions about the self in interaction with the environment.

Many educators emphasize a holistic[9] perception of the student clinician, where personality as well as cognitive development are emphasized, within a total environmental context of content plus learning process.[10] Developmental needs of students include achieving competence, managing emotions, becoming autonomous, establishing identity, freeing interpersonal relationships, clarifying purpose, developing integrity,[11] and meeting the challenge of self-improvement; by developing a critical mind, self-directedness, and sound ethical decisions related to values and life goals.[12]

These educational responsibilities increasingly include involvement of students in need analysis, assessment of personality potential and personal aspirations, diagnosis of obstacles to learning within the individual's environment,[13] and development of sound appreciation of the individual need to learn, as part of experiential education.[14]

The student should experience a decrease in evaluation defensiveness related to traditional control of grades by instructors, increasingly mastering development of self-control and goal achievement;[15] where objectives, indicators, and evaluative procedures are worked out mutually between instructors and students.[16] This healthy self-questioning[17] and development of curiosity about the professional self, are part of discriminating perception, reasoning, and comparison of knowledge content for decision-making,[18] regarding probable success ratios for intended outcomes—as new information is incorporated into existing cognitive structures.

Research and Evaluation Curriculum

Another implication for the educational environment, is the dire necessity of more and better quality courses to counsel students in the specific areas of clinical research utilization, design development, and evaluative methodology. Traditional courses in group-oriented statistics and methodology, have not produced substantial numbers of practitioners using or developing scientific studies of clinical practice phenomena. Although many practitioners feel they do effectively evaluate their practice,[19] research consistently reveals that few practitioners consult or independently create research designs or studies,[20] and many feel research is a lower professional priority.[21] This suggests that practitioners have serious questions about the relevance of traditional research courses for their specific practice needs.[22] Students may be negatively socialized about research courses,[23] especially when methodology and design are emphasized, without proper emphasis on direct practice and clinical implications.[24]

The first part of the solution to this problem, is simply to increase the number of clinical and evaluative research courses in the curriculum, to enhance student perceptions of the relevancy of these courses,[25] related to the solution of practical clinical problems.[26] These courses should present a wide range of designs and methods to reflect variability in the clinical practice world, along with emphasis on survey, quasi-experimental needs assessment, and exploratory research designs, of interest and pragmatic value to students. Courses should stress the study and interpretations of existing research studies, and the more preliminary foci on instrument development and design innovation.[27]

These courses should also include discussions of negative evidence which repudiates the effectiveness of clinical practice,[28] or challenges the effectiveness of social service programs.[29] This necessitates the development of clear definitions of areas of evaluative competence, to include learning operationalization relative to performance outcomes, creating definitions of behavioral indicators, delineation of decision-making criteria, specification of relations between out-comes,[30] and definitions of input units.

To fully learn about evaluation, competency-based education[31] should include: (1) specification of a hierarchy of tasks to be learned, with emphasis on their interrelationships as part of clinical decision-making,[32] (2) characteristics of the *learner* whose cognitive orientation, motivation, and value hierarchy, are important factions to enhance learning about learning (evaluating), and (3) characteristics of the learning environment, which include degree of structure, form of feedback and reinforcement, presentation mode, and value content of the instructional presentation.[33]

One particular task which might be more strongly encouraged, is a thesis/ comprehensive examination requirement, which specifically relates to some area of clinical evaluative significance.

A second component of the solution to the problem of curriculum deficits, is partly answered through more comprehensive and thorough interpretation of the heretofore-separated content areas of clinical practice and research. The more students conceptually see the interface and consequence of research, evaluation, and clinical practice, the more highly they will value them; and the more experience they have in utilizing each area to enhance their perception of the other.[34] One way is to use one model, or paradigm, to explain, analyze, or critique the other one,[35] or use the decision-making framework of one content area, to assess information and arrive at conclusions in the alternate arena:

> "Scientific method and problem-solving through the research method are not alien to the teaching of sound practice with client systems, it is suggested that implementation of this goal might be achieved by four main educational strategies: (1) teaching from the point of view of scientific

epistemology; (2) including the findings of evaluative research; (3) integrating practice models designed by researchers; and (4) introducing issues relevant to research designs."[36]

Another approach produces a conceptual convergence of the two areas, whereby concepts and constructs from one, are used interchangeably with concepts and constructs from the other; or new concepts are developed, representing a synthesis of the two fields of awareness.

The main problem for researchers and counselors, is that both groups have erroneously assumed there are major "conceptual" differences concerning evaluation, between the two camps. In fact, these differences are assumed to be so pronounced, that curricular content within professional schools is typically separated into "research," or "evaluative" content—and "clinical" content. When this happens, practitioners do not associate scientific evaluation or research with counseling activities, and researchers may not fully understand the practical uses of their methodology in direct service functions. It may be necessary to demonstrate, through direct comparison of research and counseling concepts, the similarities between concepts and conceptual thought processes used by practitioners and researchers, with respect to evaluation.

The author's perspective, then, is to begin with basic conceptual thinking which underlines practice evaluation, as it exists in the present; and see if there are "conceptual" connections to the ideas or tools used by the research community. There may be an overemphasis in the behavioral sciences on the differences in technique between caseworkers and researchers, obscuring important similarities in the way both groups conceptualize evaluation. In comparing tools, we may have ignored common conceptual patterns, and deflated the importance of focusing on conceptual approaches to evaluation. The ways practitioners and researchers think about evaluation may, in fact, be very similar, with the major difference being the tools.

The final and maybe most basic approach to teaching and learning clinical evaluation, is to more broadly emphasize general processes of scholarly thinking, intellectual scientific productivity, exploration, epistemological conceptualization, and professional responsibility for systematic theory building and practice exploration.

Some studies report a general neglect within the academic community, of genuine and concentrated development of the personality of the student, which includes fostering a lifelong pattern of intellectual curiosity,[37] critical analytic ability, independence,[38] and thirst for truth;[39] as an attack on reality, rather than a more passive taking-in of existing facts. "Let education be the process by which we awaken in each learner the truth that he (or she) is responsible for his (or her) very desire to flee responsibility."[40]

The student, in the above context, might ask the following questions about clinical practice:

1. What is the source of my knowledge?
2. What hypotheses might I form on the basis of my knowledge?
3. How might I acquire new knowledge?
4. How might I collect and analyze data, to substantiate my hypotheses?
5. How might I design my investigation to evaluate outcome?
6. What conclusions might I draw?
7. How do my conclusions fit with existing theory?
8. How do the potentially applicable theoretical and interventive models differ from each other, and what elements do they have in common?[41]

Continuing Education

Because there are so many clinical counselors from all human service professions, either unmotivated to pursue more systematic, comprehensive evaluation of their work, or untrained to do so; the role of continuing education in social agencies, professional associations, academic institutions, and consulting organizations becomes extremely important. Baker and Northman,[42] for example, discuss responsibilities of organizations to continually update direct service employees relative to contemporary knowledge and skills areas: "It is likely that the future will see an increased emphasis on lifetime learning and the requirement that professionals continue their education throughout their careers."

These activities should not only emphasize critical topics related to accountability, but should also constitute staff training tied to competency criteria for role performance, promotion and tenure status, career upgrade, and requirements for continuing professionals' growth, which reflect personal counselor interests and goals, as well as professional agency mandates for staff development. Training activities should be taught by competent evaluators with sound credentials, and the learning should be measured by examination, as well as observation in longer-term practical demonstrations, in specific work with clients. One way to approach this, is to engage staff in a longitudinal project of adult self-observation, awareness and learning through the use of personal logs,[43] or other self-assessment or analysis techniques; that define learning goals, report on outcomes, and plan remediation of deficits perceived by self or supervisors, in any components of clinical or counseling performance.

Certification and Licensing

Improvements relative to accountability can be made also, in conjunction with current efforts to develop or improve procedures to certify or license professionals from each discipline.[44] A problem which all professional associations and certification boards have, is related to definition of professional competence, and consequent establishment of criteria to measure short- and long-term competency attitudes, behaviors, and knowledge areas. This, of course, reflects the abstract and complicated nature of psychological and social phenomena and services, but likewise suggests lack of assertiveness and politically-based reluctance to get tough in areas of evaluation and accountability. This is especially true in operationally defining various levels and categories of competent self-evaluation, and enforcing violations or failures to comply with certification standards. Norms must be established, however, to demand competence of professionals, and mandate attitudes and behaviors which are prerequisites to explore and prove competencies. This is especially necessary since many negative outcome studies in the literature, may actually reflect adequate theories of intervention and input techniques, but highlight professionals who are not competent to execute the game plan.

In the area of professional psychology, for example, some state boards and conferences have identified professional insufficiencies and the responsibilities of state, federal, and international organizations, to develop standards of a competency continuum, along with legislative action to insure professional compliance.[45] As noted by Middleman,[46] "Twentieth-century America continues to become an information-processing and service-oriented work force, that requires extended and specialized education and training, plus some means of assessing people's learning and competence. The magnitude of this work force, whose products are service and influence, demands broad-scale, uniform, systematic, and accountable means of identifying, monitoring, regulating, and credentialing vendors, so the general public is informed and safeguarded. Therefore, licensure tests administered en masse are required—not necessarily as the best means of assessing competence, but as the most expedient means."

She goes on to note that licensure[47] is the most forceful type of public regulation, where differential status can be awarded to advanced or basic levels of practitioners, related not only to knowledge of theory, but also various forms of self-evaluation activity: "Decisions by professional bodies on competence for certification in advanced or specialty areas, need not be determined by normative standards and procedures by which individuals compete for rank order with other candidates. This is true when they compete for a limited portion of the requisite knowledge/skill domain, based on a content-referenced standard; developed a priori by acknowledged experts in the profession, and judged to represent what should be known in the particular domain."[48]

Several important processes should be kept in mind. The determination of self-evaluative mastery, should be determined at various points throughout a professional's career.[49] Definitive adequacy decisions should be made at time of certification, observation, or testing, concerning (1) ability to conduct competent practice, (2) motivation, (3) capability to improve deficiencies, and (4) need for supervision or monitoring, to insure professional performance in the future.[50] Additionally, multiple means of assessment should be used to overcome biases in assessment procedures which are utilized.[51] There should be clear and complete processes of assessment feedback to professionals participating in the certification process, and communications of degrees of normative deviation and changes in status, over repeated certification examinations. Finally, special plans and techniques must monitor behavioral self-assessment skills,[52] including local peer review procedures, examination of audio and video tapes or case records, or simulation exercises,[53] to test conceptualization and evaluative abstraction capabilities.

Policy and Administration

Policies in Social Service Agencies

1. *Delineating Self-Evaluative Requirements:* The most important implication for the policy author, designer, analyst, or implementor, is to insure that the subject of individual clinical self-evaluation is definitively and clearly present in any policy statements, which outline (1) organizational philosophy or service delivery mission; (2) perceptions or definitions of client needs, specific units of service, or client characteristics; (3) organizational operating procedures; (4) funding considerations or guidelines; (5) responsibilities of administrators, supervisors, or staff members relative to specific role requirements; (6) hiring, retention, and firing contingencies and other organizational reward, benefit, or disciplinary guidelines; and (7) evaluative reports of organizational impact, service results, community outcomes, and goals.

Not only should agency policy statements reflect the philosophy and specific methodology of staff and administrator evaluative requirements, but policy guidelines should also precisely delineate the relationship and operating connective linkages between data from individual performance assessments, and broader outcomes for agency programs or overall organizational output. Of course, the more specific and powerful the evaluative policy, the greater the probability and quality of actual staff compliance. This will ultimately enhance the staff's continual revisions and modifications of evaluative procedures to meet their needs, and will contribute to production of higher quality data and decision-making about performance.

2.   *Encouraging Consumer Involvement:* Several authors suggest that a major roadblock in the conceptualization and implementation of meaningful evaluation, is neglect of client or community consumers in the planning of counseling or other social services. From a broader perspective, some writers suggest that theory and practice methodology must be predicated on a more exact knowledge of client needs, and specific (realistic and unrealistic) service expectation,[54] to arrive at precise definitions of competence.[55]

Most authors who advocate consumerism, suggest that clients be invited to assume (through policy mandates, administrative program requirements, and counseling contracts) active roles[56] in the evaluative process; to enhance the validity and relevancy of data, by defining outcomes from the client's anticipatory expectations,[57] rather than from the counselor's biased framework. The inclusion of clients as active evaluators not only enhances the valuation of their self-determination and basic respectability,[58] but insures accuracy and precision assessment in clarifying client identity behavioral meanings, outcome priorities, and perceptions of client motivation and receptivity to various forms and steps of therapeutic input.[59]

Clients might even form consultative groups to provide feedback to staff about development of instruments that collect and analyze data, participate in analysis and interpretation of overall findings for individuals as well as groups of clients, stimulate all counselors to pursue sound principles of accountability and evaluation,[60] and insure congruence in conceptual/ philosophical perspectives and value systems in the service delivery system.[61] From a political perspective, evaluators should, by policy mandate, include greater consumer participation to understand market perspectives, needs, and service purchasing profiles; so counseling services can be validly matched to needs,[62] and insure that needy clients are attracted to the services which can help them.[63]

Administrative Practices

1. *Evaluation Mandates:* Since most clinicians do not evaluate practice in any systematic, standardized, or comprehensive scientific fashion which can be understood by an external observer, some researchers comment that evaluative activity by staff, does not seem related to factors concerning their employment or qualitative status within the organizational structure.[64] However, the more frequently staff evaluate their performance, the more they report satisfaction with the evaluative process.[65]

    There is no question that the administrator must insist that each practitioner conduct some form of systematic practice assessment, and further discipline herself or himself to use individual evaluative data to make decisions about overall program effectiveness. An administrative attitude of skepticism[66] about assumed outcomes or philosophically-valued effectiveness would be helpful, along with personal assertiveness;[67] to connect staff evaluative effort, attitude, and success, with other status-related rewards within the organization. The administrator must design precise standards[68] of evaluative performance (in addition to service input performance) attached to every organization role/position, and monitor compliance on a continuous, rigorous basis. These role performance criteria should also be used to differentiate unmotivated or inexperienced clinical evaluators who apply for job positions, and should discriminate those who should not be retained in the agency system.

    Of course, training and consultative opportunities must be made readily available to older staff who have not been socialized as counselor evaluators, and pressure must be placed on feeder academic programs and professional associations, to produce graduates already skilled and philosophically-oriented to quickly assume appropriate self-cvaluative and organizational evaluative attitudes. The administrator should encourage agency-wide interaction relative to issues of evaluation (in-staff meetings, in-service training, exercises, etc.), and insure that evaluative questions and results are disseminated regularly and frequently to all levels of agency operation, especially front-line staff;[69] via written reports, personal presentations, and interactions.[70]

2. *Effective Planning:* The administrator who is an effective consumer and producer of sound evaluation, is also a capable planner who should devote substantial attention to the relationship between program goals, hypothesized outcomes for clients, systematic delivery of services, collection of information about impact, and careful analysis of data.

  First, the administrator should plan programs where results answer specific questions about program inputs, so these questions continually remain the focal points to guide the processes of collecting and analyzing data.[71] Second, the administrator must continually consider agency data in terms of its probability of use for goal attainment[72] planning; and the ease with which it can be transformed into usable forms for organizational analysis and interpretation. The administrator also must use a standardized decision-making and planning model, with clear delineation of the points at which data must be introduced for the model to be complete, functional, and coherent.

  Other activities include the design of evaluative studies dealing with concrete, highly specific, and immediate (as immediate as possible, given the developmental nature of some client outcomes, as discussed previously in other chapters) programs and individual counselor issues of efficacy, efficiency, and impact. This is necessary so data has a pragmatic and valid effect on staff behaviors, which vary and change in dynamic interplay with assessment information within realistic timetables. The administrator also should design evaluative questions regarding the input, process, and outcome of every staff and supervisor position, so an entire system of interactive and interdependent roles is involved in the assessment and consequent planning process. Finally, the administrator must plan, relative to criteria and categories of continual growth and developmental status of all staff, the use of performance criteria as a backdrop against which to interpret evaluative results;[73] and should include all staff in planning activities, so their evaluative efforts are viewed as significant and valuable within a total agency frame of reference.

3. *Streamlining Operations:* The final point to be made about the administrator's role in the improvement of evaluation, is that the excess baggage of bureaucratic procedure, administrative paperwork, complicated operating activities, superfluous staff activities, and serendipitous philosophical perspectives, often obscures an otherwise clear and fairly simple picture of evaluative needs of staff and organizations. Excessive case recording in longhand (especially insane in this computer age), excessive time spent with

clients without a justifiable rationale, attention to senseless ritualistic agency practices (e.g., exhaustive history-taking prior to client refusal of service, or referral) and other activities which take large amounts of time, only prevent staff from having energy left for evaluation.

If there is no evidence proving that an organizational process is effective, the administrator has much to gain by reducing, streamlining, or eliminating excesses, so a clearer picture of clients and staff emerges, to focus the evaluation. The less confusion there is in the process of conducting a day's business, the greater the chance of stepping back from that process, to ask critical evaluative questions about its meaning, value, and overall quality in meeting human needs.[74]

Clinical Practitioners

Assertive Identity

One of the most important challenges for the counselor, is to overcome individual and organizational resistance and inertia for qualitative evaluation. Personal commitment[75] and willingness to assume somewhat deviant roles, are necessary to competently ask skeptical and fearful questions about effectiveness, to vigorously test assumptions in a world which frequently wants to hear only the right answers; and survives on the basis of past philosophical tradition or distorted information about service input or client outcome.

The assertive counselor questions the relevancy[76] and operational process of every aspect of counseling, and transforms personal values related to adult learning and growth,[77] into specific actions that methodologically and cognitively investigate the meaning and value of their daily work.[78]

"Skill implies . . . an activity, an ability to perform (which) . . . is clearly distinguishable from knowledge. Skill might be defined then as the capacity to set in motion and control a process of change . . . (and) . . . is developed only as one turns concepts to convictions. As a group worker gets hold of these basic concepts—has them 'in his (her) muscles' . . . he (she) finds a steady and sure way to . . . make a contribution. . . ."[79]

Assertiveness among all practitioners is also necessary to confront and eliminate grossly ineffective counselors or administrators[80] plagued by personal problems such as countertransference,[81] unresolved counselor conflicts, dependency or ambivalence, ignorance or irresponsibility, or simply personal or cognitive[82] styles or idiosyncracies that cause them to be ineffective counselors and poor evaluators. This confrontation is especially needed relative to those who cannot be objective, realistic, quantitative, honest, or positive about themselves and their professional practice.[83] The continual presence of peers or associates who are unwilling or unable to scholastically and energetically pursue evaluative accountability, not only damages the delicate relationship between consumers and practitioners, but hampers efforts of capable counselors to pursue evaluation in a healthy, supportive, and rewarding environment.

Clarity of Perspective

Another implication for practitioners, is that they clearly and comprehensively understand the overall function of the therapeutic relationship, and have a sound appreciation of the theoretical and operational dynamics of psychological growth and development, and the dynamic components which facilitate client change. Counselors must understand how and when their social values are translated into therapeutic action,[84] and become criteria by which to categorically define differential levels of therapeutic competence. The counselor must understand all aspects of client bio-psychosocial development (including etiology of pathology), and various ways clinical power and influence interact with client thoughts, to reflect opportunities for change. These dynamic principles can then be empirically referenced with behavioral indices as the methodologic cornerstone of evaluation, based on logical hypotheses about causality for human change within the social environment.[85]

From a broad perspective, this involves corrective strategy and action via inductive and deductive models of clinical inference and logical reasoning,[86] precise observation of relevant phenomena and properties of events, and relationships translated clinically into probability hypotheses. This suggests that counselors be familiar with multiple paradigms of practice, as well as having specific, detailed knowledge of individual theories of intervention.

More specifically, counselors must develop and maintain a clear focus on the concept of empirical accountability,[87] and pursue forms of counseling practice which allow the greatest potential for developing objective outcome indices, within goal-directed and task-centered approaches that facilitate development and measurement of clearly-definable client behavioral objectives.[88] Counselors must be organized, goal-directed, systematic, concise, structured, and efficient in delivering inputs, so results or non-results can be defined quickly and relatively easily, as components of future case management planning activities.[89]

This necessitates that counselors more fully integrate the scientist/scholar role into their practice perspective, so knowledge-building and systematic investigative problem-solving become cores of their daily orientations and activities.[90] Counselors must truly believe in comprehensive evaluation as a practical necessity, and incorporate self-evaluation standards and morals into their specific practice activities, as well as overall life goals for self-actualization and growth.

Researchers

Emphasis on Single Case Studies

One of the most important actions researchers can take to improve the clinical evaluative state-of-the-art, is to place increased emphasis on single case rather than group-comparison research. Researchers must design models to further clarify and improve knowledge and comprehensive understanding of many aspects of therapeutic work. They must focus on client growth and development and, especially, individual causal dynamics which produce psychosocial conflicts and cognitive/behavioral processes, maintaining conditions of maladaptation. Evaluators must assess various individual conditions of motivation, and receptivity to various forms of interventive or interpersonal influence; and refine descriptions or classifications of client-counselor interactions, family or group relationships, and discoveries of various growth-oriented dynamics connected with type of personality and social situation. Too, professionals must understand the social, philosophical, and psychological backgrounds and characteristics of clients and counselors who are positively and productively disposed toward adult learning from a self- or interpersonal-evaluative viewpoint. They must also improve descriptions and classifications of specific therapeutic input skills, with comprehensive analyses of their capability to facilitate, accompany, or cause various types of cognitive, emotional, or behavioral changes.[91] Understanding the comprehensive, behavioral, cognitive and emotional classifications of client-related outcomes, and development of improved instruments to document their immediate occurrence, long-range continuity, developmental characteristics, and symbolic intrapsychic and cultural meanings for particular clients—are essential. Researchers must examine variables or variable relationships which have not been discovered or studied thoroughly, which would probably emerge with more emphasis on exploratory, descriptive case study, and key informant/expert forms of research. Further, they must study forms and causes of counselor bias, discrimination, ineffective judgment, or destructive decision-making, and ways of correcting counselor deficits or reducing their negative impact. Finally, we should examine various forms of informal or idiosyncratic self-evaluative data collection, analysis of information, or clinical decision-making which: (a) are used frequently in practice; (b) have potential for increased standardization and measurement; (c) are ineffective; (d) can assist in building new areas of knowledge, or in changing traditional theoretical assumptions; or (e) are inconsequential and have no direct positive or negative effect, except indirectly, based on counselor need.

Single subject evaluative studies must be conducted for longer periods of time, and should include client, counselor, and social milieu as separate, but interrelated, components of a potentially-therapeutic clinical influence system. This includes the need for researchers to encourage more flexibility and innovativeness in social programs; to manipulate, alter, and utilize a variety of independent variable skills or strategies, so various effects can be studied. It also implies that researchers press hard to encourage counselors to standardize and stabilize each input phenomenon or behavioral unit for a sufficient period of time, to measure outcome effects without continually introducing change stimuli which confound each case situation.

Researchers should emphasize the value of audio and video recordings of sessions, and the use of external observers and organized self-report; to learn more about counselor input, evaluative decision-making about each client and across caseloads for each counselor, and the genuine effects of therapeutic connections between people.

Researchers should emphasize specific topics of study or variables of interest within programs or overall agency strategies, so specific and highly-precise "clinical" information is not lost or obscured by the economically-, politically-, and philosophically-pressured emphasis on overall programs or large groups of clients.[92] Each of the above areas of emphasis will help, if collectively undertaken with serious resolve to bring expert emphasis on the scene; so researchers can stimulate one another with precise answers to complex questions which materialize. The present condition of scattered pockets of often-unrelated research, not only hampers the building blocks philosophy, but produces either research results which are unrelated to other equally meaningful studies, or results that are out of sequence with the logical and rational set of questions which form a coherent continuum, relating to the clinical evaluative dilemma.

Pursue Clinical Theory Building

Many authors suggest that researchers take more active and direct responsibility to build clinical theory and methodology.[93] This begins with the translation of clinical and evaluative/research languages into each arena's alternate form; or with development of a new set of conceptual units, so the helping professionals can be more unified in their perspectives and communications, about common problems related to evaluation.

This might give a higher priority to clinical research among academic institutions, agencies, or funding sources. It might also result in development of research/evaluative theory building staff positions at organizational locations, where actual clinical theory is implemented,[94] interpreted, and evaluated. Also, more opportunities must become available for dissemination of research and evaluative questions and findings to the consuming audience of counselors, administrators, board members, clients,[95] and students of human and behavioral science.

A more concentrated responsibility for theory building, might also facilitate consensus about optimum models for evaluation. It may speed the conversion of existing instruments into a usable format for widespread dissemination and trial testing in actual clinical situations, and increase the frequency and quality of the much-needed dialogue between the research/evaluation and counseling professional communities.[96] Improvement of researcher-clinician relationships helps both groups market their respective experiential, philosophical, and methodological products[97] to one another, so a team effort evolves to define and solve common evaluative dilemmas.[98]

All of the above recommendations suggest that social agencies and private practice offices or clinics, be more flexible in differentially defining objectives for their services, so rigid traditionalism does not hamper needed exploratory research. The necessary variations of experimental designs, also must increasingly become integral parts of social service organizational operation, in order to improve the quality and applicability of evaluative study and practice.

This suggests increased use of computer technology at the front lines, so evaluative data can be quickly processed and analyzed to keep the flame of research going, and to facilitate critical decision-making about programs for clients. This prevents staff members, researcher/evaluators, and administrators from becoming bored, complacent, or overwhelmed by delayed or antiquated management, and evaluative information systems.

Expand Research and Specialized Teaching Roles

Another implication of the need for improved study and practice of evaluation, is that researchers within academic institutions be selected for faculty appointments, with weighted criteria relative to expertise or interest in clinical self-evaluation. A major component of their job responsibilities should be directed toward acquisition of grant monies for substantive research projects.

Some clinical evaluation advocates even suggest that researchers within universities spend most of their time conducting clinical studies and writing about evaluation, and that their teaching be limited to areas specifically relating to assessment of clinical practice, counseling, and casework, as specific courses within newly developed clinical/evaluative curricular areas.

Students with special interest in clinical evaluation may also be recruited, so that their interactions with evaluative faculty provide greater stimulation and learning for both groups. This includes emphasis on doctoral research within counseling agencies, that centers on the most relevant evaluative issues and questions. Educational institutions could also establish internships for clinical/ evaluators which emphasize assessment of counseling or direct practice activities for the student-learner, rather than provision of counseling services directly, as the main learning objective. A variant of this, of course, is the university-based clinic where clients are brought to the researchers and are recipients of service, within more controllable environments for the measurement of inputs, process, and outcomes.

Develop Evaluation as a Distinct Profession

A final implication pertaining to the advancement of knowledge and skill in clinical (and other types) evaluation, is that evaluation can, and maybe should, become a distinct professional discipline.[99]

Becker,[100] for example, notes that a profession has the following character-istics: (1) a monopoly over an esoteric and socially valuable body of knowledge; (2) theoretical knowledge that is also concretely technical or experimental; (3) control of the quality of practitioners in the profession; and (4) an overriding ethic of altruistic and client-centered practice.[101]

Although evaluation may not fall fully within the above criteria, a body of specialized knowledge is clearly developing,[102] and evaluative experts are increas-ingly distinguishable from other professionals through their use of specialized language, theories, and methodologies. There is increasing emphasis on public responsibility for sound evaluation, not only from a professional policy stand-point,[103] but also from a consumer ethical and moral set of principles.[104]

Evaluation as an emerging profession may also be associated with newly-developed autonomy of evaluative action as a separate specialization, and with the prestige that accompanies this specialist status;[105] especially as members of the nonsocial science community begin to assume or are persuaded that counselors and clinicians are making serious efforts to prove the effectiveness and social utility of their service commodities. The professionalization of evaluation may further aid in validating evaluative expertise, and marketing the methodology and theory to clinicians, administrators, policy developers, clients, and the general public.[106] The eventual development of evaluation as a significant discipline, ultimately depends on the answers to these important questions:[107]

1. Exactly what is it that evaluators do, or should be doing?
2. Which specific questions about the social sciences or other social domains should be studied and why?
3. Who are the appropriate clients or consumers of the evaluator's service?
4. What is the specialized knowledge base of evaluation, and how/why is it different from other areas of research or practice?
5. What degree of control will evaluators have over public knowledge areas, and over members' roles, certification, accountable public obligations, and functions?

The answers to the above questions will partly determine extent to which evaluation may become a more specialized area of knowledge and expertise, thereby assisting clinical counselors in learning and growing as more competent accountable professionals.

References

1. Cyril Houle, *The Inquiring Mind: A Study of the Adult Who Continues to Learn* (Madison: University of Wisconsin Press, 1961).
2. An essential ingredient of effective and sustained evaluation is the permission, authorization, support and validation of self-evaluative thoughts, actions, and behaviors as legitimate and normal components of social service or student roles.
3. Malcolm Knowles, *The Modern Practice of Adult Education: Androgogy versus Pedagogy* (New York: Association Press, 1970).
4. Richard Bretall, ed., *A Kierkegaard Anthology* (Princeton: Princeton University Press, 1951), p. 158.
5. Arthur Chickering, *Education and Identity* (San Francisco: Josey-Bass, 1972).
6. Paul Dressel, *Handbook of Academic Evaluation* (San Francisco: Josey-Bass, 1976), p. 339.
7. Jerome Bruner, *Toward a Theory of Instruction* (Cambridge, MA: Harvard University Press, 1966).
8. Martin Trow, "Methodological Problems in the Evaluation of Innovation," in *Readings in Evaluation Research,* ed., F. Caro (New York: Russell Sage Foundation, 1971).
9. Mike Seelig, William Eldridge, Marie Schirtzinger, "A Holistic Perspective on Student Growth and Development: A Look at Academic Programs in Graduate Schools of Human Service," *International Social Work,* 25:2:26-41, 1982.
10. Theodore Miller and Judith Prince, *The Future of Student Affairs* (San Francisco: Josey-Bass, 1976), p. 2.
11. Arthur Chickering, *Experience and Learning: An Introduction to Experiential Learning* (New York: Change Magazine Press, 1977).
12. Carnegie Foundation for the Advancement of Teaching, *Missions of the College Curriculum* (San Francisco: Josey-Bass, 1977).
13. Malcolm Knowles, *The Modern Practice of Adult Education: Androgogy Versus Pedagogy* (New York: Association Press, 1970).
14. Paul Dressel and Laurence Mayhew, *General Education: Exploration in Evaluation* (Washington, DC: American Council of Education, 1964).
    James Davis, *Going to College: The Study of Students and the Student Experience* (Boulder, CO: Westview Press, 1977).
15. Alex Gitterman and Naomi Gitterman, "Social Work Student Evaluation: Format and Method," *Journal of Education for Social Work,* 15:3:103-108, Fall, 1979.
16. Karen Hess and Larry Morreau, "The Expanding Classroom: Trends and Issues in Postgraduate Medicine-Why Self-Assessment?" *Postgraduate Medicine,* 59:1:203-210, January, 1976.

17.   E. Rothkopf, "Some Theoretical and Experimental Approaches to Problems in Written Instruction," *Learning and the Educational Process,* J. Krumblatz, ed. (Chicago: Rand McNally, 1965).

18.   Gus Dalis, "The Effect of Precise Objectives Upon Student Achievement in Health Education," *Journal of Experimental Education,* 39:2:20-23, Winter, 1970.

19.   William Eldridge, "Practitioner Approaches to Self-Evaluation" (Doctoral dissertation, University of Denver, 1979).

20.   Aaron Rosenblatt, "The Practitioner's Use and Evaluation of Research," *Social Work,* 13:1:53-59, January, 1968.

       Stuart Kirk and Joel Fischer, "Do Social Workers Understand Research?" *Journal of Education for Social Work,* 12:1:63-70, Winter, 1976.

21.   Betsy-lea Casselman, "On the Practitioner's Orientation Toward Research," *Smith College Studies in Social Work,* 42:2:233, June, 1972.

22.   Charles Guzzetta, Untitled paper delivered to a meeting of the Group for the Advancement of Doctoral Education, Hunter College, 1980, p. 8.

23.   Aaron Rosenblatt, "The Practitioner's Use and Evaluation of Research," *Social Work,* 13:1:53-59, January, 1968.

24.   Joel Fischer, "Is Casework Effective? A Review," *Social Work,* 18:5-20, January, 1973.

       Martha Heineman, "The Obsolete Scientific Imperative in Social Work Research," *Social Service Review,* 55:3:373-397, September, 1981.

       Edwin Thomas, "Research and Service in Single Case Experimentation: Conflicts and Choices," *Social Work Research and Abstracts,* 14:4:20-32, Winter, 1978.

25.   Helen Reinberg and Jean Anastoa, "A Research Curriculum for Future Clinicians: A Multimodal Study," *Journal of Education for Social Work,* 19:2:35-47, Spring, 1983.

26.   Dustin Austin, "Research and Social Work: Educational Paradoxes and Possibilities," *Journal of Social Science Research,* 2:2:159-176, Winter, 1978.

27.   John Strauss and Hiaham Hafez, "Clinical Questions and Real Research," *American Journal of Psychiatry,* 138:5:1596-1599, December, 1981.

28.   William Reid and Ann Shyne, *Brief and Extended Casework* (New York: Columbia University Press, 1969).

       Joel Fischer, *The Effectiveness of Social Casework* (Springfield, IL: Charles C. Thomas, 1976).

29.   Michael Lambert, Allen Bergin, and John Collins, "Therapist-Induced Deterioration in Psychotherapy," in *Effective Psychotherapy: A Handbook of Research,* eds., A. Gurman and A. Razin (Elmaford, NY: Pergamon Press, 1977), pp. 452-481.

30.   Helen Reinherz, Molly Grob, and Barbara Berkman, "Health Agencies and a School of Social Work: Practice and Research in Partnership," *Health and Social Work,* 8:1:40-47, Winter, 1983.

31.   Frank Clark, "Characteristics of the Competency-Based Curriculum," in *Competency-Based Education for Social Work: Evaluation and Curriculum Issues,* eds., Arkava and E. C. Brennen (New York: Council on Social Work Education, 1976), pp. 29-38.

32.   John DeCecco, *The Psychology of Learning and Instruction: Educational Psychology* (Englewood Cliffs, NJ: Prentice-Hall, 1968), pp. 238-476.
     Robert Gagne, *The Conditions of Learning* (New York: Holt, Rinehart and Winston, 1970), p. 329.
     J. W. Atkinson, ed., *Motives in Fantasy, Action, and Society* (Princeton, NJ: D. Van Nostrand, 1958).

33.   David Hunt, *Matching Models in Education* (Toronto, Ontario: Institute for Studies in Education, 1970), p. 75.

34.   Rosemary Lukton, "Barriers and Pathways to Integrating Research and Practice in Social Work: Suggestions for Innovations in the MSW Curriculum," *Journal of Education for Social Work,* 16:2:20-25, Spring, 1980.
     John Shuerman, "On Research Practice Teaching in Social Work," *Sourcebook on Research Utilization,* A. Rubin and A. Rosenblatt, eds. (New York: Council on Social Work Education, 1979), p. 145.

35.   Samuel Mencher, *The Research Method in Social Work Education: Project Report of the Curriculum Study* (Vol. 9; New York: Council on Social Work Education, 1959, p. 3.

36.   Rosemary Lukton, "Barriers and Pathways to Integrating Research and Practice in Social Work: Suggestions for Innovation in the MSW Curriculum," *Journal of Education for Social Work,* 16:2:22, Spring, 1980.

37.   James Davis, *Going to College: The Study of Students and the Student Experience* (Boulder, CO: Westview Press, 1979).

38.   Paul Dressel and Irvin Lehmann, "The Impact of Higher Education on Student Attitudes, Values, and Critical Thinking Abilities," *Education Record,* 46:6:248-258, Summer, 1965.

39.   Erich Fromm, *Escape from Freedom* (New York: Holt, Rinehart and Winston, 1941).
     Van Cleve Morris, *Existentialism in Education* (New York: Harper and Row, 1966).

40.   Jean-Paul Sartre, *Being and Nothingness,* trans by Hazel Barnes (New York: Philosophical Library, 1956), p. 458.

41.   Rosemary Lukton, "Barriers and Pathways to Integrating Research and Practice in Social Work: Suggestions for Innovation in the MSW Curriculum," *Journal of Education for Social Work,* 16:2:22, Spring, 1980.

42. Frank Baker and John Northman, *Helping: Human Services for the 80's* (St. Louis: C. V. Mosley, 1981), p. 232.

J. McNamara, "Continuing Education Requirements for Psychologists in Ohio: A Proposed Model," (Paper presented to the Executive Committee of the Ohio Psychological Association, Columbus, Ohio, December 15, 1973).

43. William Eldridge, "The Use of Personal Logs to Assist Clinical Students in Understanding and Integrating Theories of Counseling Intervention," *Journal of the International Association of Pupil Personnel Workers,* 27:3:147-151, Summer, 1983.

44. "Highlights of the Vail Conference-Preliminary Report Recommendation," *The Clinical Psychologist,* 27:7:5-10, 1974.

45. National Institute of Mental Health, Continuing Education in Mental Health (DHEW Publication No. HSM-73-9126; Washington, DC: U.S. Government Printing Office, 1974).

Lillian Terris, "The National Licensing Examination," *Professional Psychology,* 4:4:386-391, November, 1963.

46. Ruth Middleman, "How Competent is Social Work's Approach to the Assessment of Competence," *Social Work,* 29:2:146-153, March-April, 1984.

47. David McClelland, "Testing for Competence Rather than for Intelligence," *American Psychologist,* 28:2:1-14, 1973.

David Hardcastle, "The Profession, Professional Organizations, Licensing and Private Practice," *Handbook of the Social Services,* eds., N. Gilbert and H. Specht (Englewood Cliffs, NJ: Prentice-Hall, 1981), pp. 666-687.

48. Ruth Middleman, "How Competent is Social Work's Approach to the Assessment of Competence," *Social Work,* 29:2:146-153, March-April, 1984.

49. James McNamara, "How Quickly Do Psychologists Become Outdated?" (Paper presented at the meeting of The Ohio Psychological Association, Cambridge, Ohio, April 12, 1974).

50. Alan Ross, "Continuing Professional Development in Psychology," *Professional Psychology,* 5:2:122-128, May, 1974.

51. Winston Manning, "Educational Research, Test Validity and Court Decisions," (Princeton, NJ: Educational Testing Service, 1977).

Elizabeth Keith, "Assessing Professional Competency: The Academy of Certified Social Workers, 1960-1980," (Report to the Competence Certification Board, Washington, DC, January, 1981).

52. John McMillan, "Peer Review and Professional Standards for Psychologists Rendering Personal Health Services," *Professional Psychology,* 5:1:51-58, February, 1974.

53. W. Harlesa, et al., "CASE: A Computer-Aided Simulation of the Clinical Encounter," *Journal of Medical Education,* 46:443-448, 1971.

54.   Harriett Bartlett, *Analyzing Social Work Practice by Fields* (New York: National Association of Social Workers, 1961), pp. 37-52.

Helen Perlman, "Generic Aspects of Specific Case-Work Settings," *Social Service Review,* 23:3:293-301, September, 1949.

55.   Henrietta Williams, et al., "Some Factors Influencing Treatment Expectations of Neurotic Outpatients," *Journal of Nervous and Mental Disease,* 14:4:208-220, September, 1967.

56.   Lorraine Luft, Kevin Smith, and Morris Kace, "Therapists' Patients, Inpatient Stages, Views of Treatment Modes and Outcomes," *Hospital and Community Psychiatry,* 29:7:505-511, August, 1978.

57.   Sidney Block, et al., "Patients Expectations of Therapeutic Improvement and Their Outcomes," *American Journal of Psychiatry,* 133:12:1457-1460, December, 1976.

58.   Janet Coye, "Assuring Exercise and Appropriate Limitation of Patients Rights," (Paper presented at The World Congress of Psychiatry, Honolulu, 1977).

59.   John Cohrsaen and Louis Kopolow, *Court Screening and Patient Advocacy: A Handbook of Principles for Community Mental Health Centers* (Rockville, MD: Alcohol, Drug Abuse and Mental Health Administration, U.S. Public Health Service, 1979), p. 15.

60.   Edward Proger and Henry Tanabra, "Self-Assessment: The Client's Perspective" *Social Work,* 25:1:29-34, January, 1980.

John Borghi, "Premature Termination of Psychotherapy and Patient-Therapist Expectations," *American Journal of Psychotherapy,* 22:3:460-473, 1968.

61.   John Evans, "Evaluating Social Action Programs," *Social Science Quarterly,* 50:5:568-569, December, 1969.

William Ryan, *Blaming the Victim* (New York: Vintage Books, 1971).

62.   Bertram Cross, "Social Systems Accounts," *Social Indicators,* R. Bauer, ed. (Cambridge, MA: M.I.T. Press, 1966), pp. 201-202.

John Wilson, Henry Beyers, and Bernard Yudowitz, "Advocacy for the Mentally Disabled," *Mental Health Advocacy: An Emerging Force in Consumers' Rights,* eds., Kopolow and H. Bloom (Rockville, MD: Alcohol, Drug Abuse, and Mental Health Administration, U.S. Public Health Service, 1977), p. 11.

63.   James George, "Research by Social Health Departments—Problems, Methods, Results," *American Journal of Public Health,* 48:2:354, March, 1958.

Lyle Saunders and Julian Samara, "A Medical Care Program in a Colorado County," in *Health, Culture, and Community,* ed., Paul (New York: Russell Sage Foundation, 1955), pp. 377-400.

Dorothy Faho Beck and Mary Ann Jones, *Progress in Family Problems: A Nationwide Study of Client's and Counselor's Views of Family Service Agencies* (New York: Family Service Association of America, 1973).

64.   Elliot Jacques, *Measurement of Responsibility* (Cambridge, MA: Harvard University Press, 1956).

65.   Sanford Darnbusch and William Scott, *Evaluation and the Exercise of Authority* (San Francisco: Josey-Bass, 1977).

66.   Roy Turner, ed., *Ethnomethodology* (Baltimore: Penguin Books, 1974).

67.   Jerry Turem, "The Call for a Management Stance," *Social Work,* 19:5: 615-623, September, 1974.

68.   Ralph Brody and Holly Krailo, "An Approach to Reviewing the Effectiveness of Programs," *Social Work,* 23:3:226-232, May, 1978.

69.   Betty Rossman, Diane Hober, and James Ciarlo, "Awareness, Use and Consequences of Evaluation Data in a Community Mental Health Center," *Community Mental Health Journal,* 15:1:7-16, 1979.

70.   Henry Goldsmith and Edgar Unger, "Social Areas: Identification Procedures Using 1970 Census Data," (Laboratory Paper No. 37, Mental Health Study Center, National Institute of Mental Health, Washington, DC, 1972).

Diane Hober, "Decision-Making in a Community Mental Health Center: A Summary of Six Studies," (Mental Health Systems Evaluation Project Report, Northwest Denver Community Mental Health Center, Denver, CO, 1976).

71.   William Berg and Richard Theado, "The Utilization of Evaluative Research in Social Welfare Programs," *Social Service Review,* 55:2:183-192, 1981.

72.   Peter Drucker, "What Results Should You Expect? A User's Guide to MBO," *Public Administration Review,* 36:6:12-36, January-February, 1976.

Thomas Kiresuk, "Goal Attainment Scaling at a County Mental Health Service," *Evaluation,* Special Monograph, 1:1:12-18, 1973.

73.   Herbert Schulberg and Frank Baker, "Program Evaluation Models and the Implementations of Research Findings," *Program Evaluation in the Health Fields,* Schulberg, Sheldon, and Baker, eds. (New York: Behavioral Publications, 1969), pp. 249-254.

74.   William Eldridge, "Streamlining Casework and Counseling," *Public Welfare,* 40:1:23-27, Winter, 1982.

75.   William Eldridge, "Social Service Professionals with an Assertive Identity: A Necessity for Practice and Its Evaluation in the 1980's," *Urban and Social Change Review,* 16:2:23-27, July, 1983.

76.   William Eldridge, "The Illusion of Rational and Relevant Clinical Practice," *Corrective and Social Psychiatry,* 28:4:131-136, 1982.

77. Hiasaura Rubenstein and Mary Block, eds., *Things that Matter: Influences on Helping Relationships* (New York: Macmillian, 1982), pp. 360-361.

78. Howard Smith and Paul Brouwer, *Performance Appraisal and Human Development* (Reading, MA: Addison-Wesley, 1977), p. 17.

79. Helen Phillips, "What is Group Work SkIll?" *Perspectives on Social Group Work Practice,* A. Alissi, ed. (New York: Free Press, 1980), pp. 192-193.

80. Mary Gottesfeld and Florence Lieberman, "The Pathological Therapist," *Social Casework,* 60:70:387-392, July, 1979.

81. Sigmund Freud, "The Future Prospects of Psychoanalytic Theory," in *The Standard Edition of the Complete Psychological Works of Sigmund Freud,* ed., J. Strachey (Vol. 11; London: Hogarth Press, 1975, pp. 139-151.

Frieda Fromm-Reichmann, *Principles of Intensive Psychotherapy* (Chicago: University of Chicago Press, 1950).

Otto Kernberg, *Borderline Conditions and Pathological Narcissism* (New York: Jason Aronson, 1975).

Heinz Kahut, *The Analysis of the Self* (New York: International Universities Press, 1971).

82. Sonja Rhodes, "The Personality of the Worker: An Unexplored Dimension in Treatment," *Social Casework,* 60:5:259-264, May, 1979.

Selma Fraiberg, "Psychoanalysis and the Education of Caseworkers," *Oriented Casework,* H. Parad, and R. Miller (New York: Family Service Association of America, 1963).

83. George Mead, *The Mind, Self, and Society* (Chicago: University of Chicago Press, 1967), pp. 155-156.

84. Kenneth Krause, "Social Work Values for the Future," *Social Work in the 1980's,* R. Washington and B. Toomey, eds. (Davis, CA: International Dialogue Press, 1982), p. 32.

Milton Rokeach, *The Nature of Human Values* (New York: Free Press, 1973), p. 5.

Henry Miller, "Value Dilemmas in Social Casework," *Social Casework,* 13:27:33, 1968.

85. Carel Germain, "Social Context of Clinical Social Work," *Social Work,* 25:6:483-488, November, 1980.

Margaret Mead, *Culture and Commitment* (New York: Natural History Press, 1970).

Carel Germain and Alex Gitterman, *The Life Model of Social Work Practice* (New York: Columbia University Press, 1980).

Willard Gaylin, et al., *Doing Good: The Limits of Benevolence* (New York: Pantheon Books, 1978).

86.   Srinika Jayanatne and Rona Levy, *Empirical Clinical Practice* (New York: Columbia University Press, 1979).

87.   Srinika Jayanatne and Rona Levy, *Empirical Clinical Practice* (New York: Columbia University Press, 1979).

88.   Francis Turner, ed., *Social Work Treatment: Interlocking Theoretical Approaches* (New York: Free Press, 1979), p. XV.

Helen Northern, *Clinical Social Work* (New York: Columbia University Press, 1982), pp. 241, 248, 255.

89.   Hilde Bruch, *Learning Psychotherapy* (Cambridge, MA: Harvard University Press, 1974), pp. 83-84, 119.

Paul Karoly and John Steffen, eds., *Improving the Long-Term Effects of Psychotherapy: Models of Durable Outcome* (New York: Gardner Press, 1980).

90.   Arnold Lazarus and Gerald Davison, "Clinical Innovation in Research and Practice," in *Handbook of Psychotherapy and Behavior Change: An Empirical Analysis,* eds., Bergin and S. Garfield (New York: John Wiley, 1971), pp. 196-214.

Allen Edwards, *Experimental Design in Psychological Research* (Third Edition; New York: Holt, Rinehart and Winston, 1968).

Wayne Holtzman, "Statistical Models for Study of Change in the Single Case," in *Problems in Measuring Change,* ed., C. Harris (Madison: University of Wisconsin Press, 1963), pp. 199-211.

91.   Leslie Alexander and Alan Siman, "Fischer's Study of Studies," *Social Work,* 18:4:104-106, July, 1973.

John Behling, *An Experimental Study to Measure the Effectiveness of Casework Service* (Columbus, OH: Franklin County Welfare Department, 1961).

92.   Michael Raskin, "Evaluation Research: Bridge Between Social Work Administrator, Practitioner, and Researcher," *International Social Work,* 22:1:27-32, 1977.

93.   J. Cohen, "Evaluating the Effectiveness of an Unspecified Casework Treatment in Producing Change," *The Effectiveness of Social Casework,* ed., J. Fischer (Springfield: Charles Thomas, 1967), pp. 176-189.

94.   Robert Dubin, *Theory Building* (New York: Free Press, 1969), pp. 231-240.

95.   See the following for a discussion of the dynamics of power and influence of specific interest and consumer groups on public services.

Martin Rein, "Social Planning: The Search for Legitimacy," *Planning for Social Welfare: Issues. Models and Tasks,* eds., Gilbert and H. Specht (Englewood Cliffs, NJ: Prentice-Hall, 1977), pp. 50-69.

96.   Alan Kazdin, "Characteristics and Trends in Applied Behavior Analysis,"
Journal of Applied Behavior Analysis, 8:8:332, 1975.
       Alan Kazdin, "Statistical Analysis for Single Case Experimental Designs,"
Single Case Experimental Designs: Strategies for Studying Behavior Change,
eds., M. Hersen and D. Barlow (New York: Pergamon Press, 1976).
       Alan Kazdin, "Methodology of Applied Behavior Analysis," *Social and
Instructional Processes: Foundations and Applications of a Behavior Analysis,*
eds., T. Brigham and A. Catania (New York: Irvington-Naiburg-Wiley,
1977).
97.   Donald Baer, et al., "Some Current Dimension of Applied Behavior
Analysis," *Journal of Applied Behavior Analysis,* 1:2:91-97, 1968.
       M. Sidman, *Tactics of Scientific Research* (New York: Basic Books,
1960).
98.   Irwin Epstein and Tony Tripodi, *Research Techniques for Program Planning, Monitoring, and Evaluation* (New York: Columbia University Press,
1977), pp. 1-2.
       Robert Washington, *Program Evaluation in the Human Services* (Lanham,
MD: University Press of America, 1980), pp. xii, 209-216.
       Tony Tripodi, *Evaluative Research for Social Workers* (Englewood Cliffs,
NJ: Prentice-Hall, 1983), pp. 10-14.
       Roger Kaufman and Susan Thomas, *Evaluation Without Fear* (New York:
New Viewpoints, 1980), pp. 4-5.
99.   Jonathan Morell and Eugene Flaherty, "The Development of Evaluation
as a Profession: Current Status and Some Predictions," *Evaluation and
Program Planning* 1:1:11-17, January, 1978.
100.   Howard Becker, "The Nature of a Profession," *Sociological Work,* ed.,
H. Becker (Chicago: Aldine, 1970), pp. 87-103.
101.   William Goode, "The Theoretical Limits of Professionalism," in *The
Semi-Professions and Their Organization,* ed., A. Etzioni (Vol. 6; New York:
Free Press, 1969), pp. 266-313.
102.   Eugene Flaherty and Jonathan Morell, "Evaluation: Manifestations a New
Field," *Evaluation and Program Planning,* 1:1:11-17, January, 1978.
103.   Peter Rossi and Walter Williams, *Evaluating Social Programs: Theory,
Practice, and Politics* (New York: Seminar Press, 1972).
104.   Clifford Attkisson, et al., *Evaluation of Human Service Programs* (New
York: Academic Press, 1977).
       Marcia Guttentag and Elmer Struening, *Handbook of Evaluation Research*
(Vol. 2; Beverly Hills, CA: Russell Sage Foundation, 1975).
105.   R. Bucher and A Strauss, "Professions in Process," *American Journal of
Sociology,* 66:6:325-334, 1961.

106.   Jonathan Morell, "The Conflict Between Research and Mental Health Services," *Administration in Mental Health*, 5:2:52-58, Spring, 1977.

107.   H. Wilensky, "The Professionalization of Everyone," *The American Journal of Sociology*, LXX:2:2:229-232, 1964.

Author's Biographical Sketch

WILLIAM D. ELDRIDGE, Ph.D.

I was born in Cincinnati, but grew up in Tucson, Arizona where my parents moved when I was five-years-old. After graduating from High School, I studied briefly to become a Carmelite Catholic priest at the University of San Diego. I later transferred to the University of Arizona, where I completed my Bachelor of Arts degree in Sociology and Psychology in 1970. My specialty cognate areas of study and employment at this time were juvenile delinquency, psychosocial deviance, and macro theory building.

I immediately pursued my Master of Social Work degree at Arizona State University in Phoenix, and concentrated on psychoanalytic, ego-psychologic and behavioral theories of mental health, and completed my studies in 1972. My internships were at the Veteran's Administration Hospital where I specialized in inpatient psychiatry and psycho-drama, and at a community mental health center, where I worked intensively in individual, family and group psychotherapy.

I then fulfilled an R.O.T.C. commitment and joined the U.S. Army Medical Service Corps, completed two duty assignments, and was discharged as a Captain in 1977. My first assignment entailed considerable individual and family counseling at the Mental Hygiene Consultation Service at Kimbrough Army Hospital, Ft. Meade, Maryland. During this time, I also received a good deal of training in psychological development and therapeutic methodology at Walter Reed Child Guidance Clinic, and various other training institutes throughout the country. My expertise at this time was Gestalt therapy, family systems analysis, and ego-psychology intervention. My second military assignment was as the Division Social Work Officer, 25th Medical Battalion, 25th Infantry Division at Schofield Barracks, Oahu, Hawaii. My work here involved emergency psychiatry, community consultation, performance evaluation and short-term crisis intervention (and lying on the beach a whole bunch!).

In 1977 I began work on my Ph.D. in Social Work at the University of Denver, where my Dissertation emphasized the theory and methodology of evaluating clinical treatment. My other area of emphasis was educational and learning orientations and development, and also social science research and theory building.

In 1979 upon graduation, I received my current faculty appointment at The Ohio State University College of Social Work, where I teach a variety of courses in our undergraduate, graduate and doctoral programs of study. My predominant areas of teaching are growth and development, clinical practice, research/statistics and evaluation, and advanced practice theory development. I teach a variety of electives and workshops however in spirituality and Zen Buddhism, cooperative social change, peace theories, psychosocial development, program evaluation, and innovative thinking for the 21st century.

For the first 10 years of my work in Columbus, I also conducted a private psychotherapy practice at Columbus Psychological Services where I specialized almost exclusively in individual and couples mental health counseling. In 1989 I terminated this practice and developed a curriculum and theory format to create The Center for Peace Studies and Community Development, which is a citizen-based community education, self-development and social action not-for-profit organization. I remain the Director of this activity and supervise various training programs in peace practice, psycho-spiritual therapy groups, a creative learning and mentorship program at Reynoldsburg High School, and various other community involvement projects. I work with some clients individually both in and outside this program, and supervise B.S.W. and M.S.W. OSU students in their field placement internships at our Center.

Currently, I describe myself as an existential theorist, a model developer for world cooperative change, a Zen psychotherapist and a strong advocate for socialistic balance and ecological/environmental holism in all aspects of life. I spend most of my time teaching, providing supervision at The Center for Peace Studies, and volunteering community lectures and presentations on social change for the century to come. I hold certification as a Licensed Independent Social Worker (L.I.S.W.) and Academy of Certified Social Workers (A.C.S.W.).

I am also about half-way through a Masters of Liberal Studies degree at OSU in spiritual development, culture, social process and religious symbolism. In whatever spare time is left, I play drums in an "oldies" rock' n roll band, play tennis and hike regularly, swim, read philosophy, and watch myself getting older.

ADDITIONAL BOOKS
BY
DR. WILLIAM D. ELDRIDGE

A. University Press of America
    4720 Boston Way
    Lanham, Maryland 20706
    (301) 459-3366

    - Some Thoughts on Social Responsibility (Revised Edition)

    - The Challenge of Maturity: A Comprehensive Guide to Understand and
      Achieve Psychological and Social Self-Actualization As We Grow Older
      (Second Edition)

B. Ginn Press: A Division of Simon & Schuster
    160 Gould Street
    Needham Heights, Massachusetts 02194
    (617) 455-7000

    - Free Your Child of the Past for Future Success

C. Greyden Press
    2020 Builders Place
    Columbus, Ohio 43204
    (614) 488-2525

    - Can You Hear the Trumpets? An Existential Interpretation of Enlighten-
      ment, Non-Alienation, Social Justice, Human Compassion, Mental
      Health . . . and You!

Dr. Eldridge's published books are usually in stock in the Social Work Textbook
Section, or can be easily ordered at:

    Student Book Exchange (SBX)
    1806 N. High Street (near Ohio State)
    Columbus, Ohio 43201
    (614) 291-9528 (Paul Watkins - Owner)